THE A-Z OF
GARDEN FLOWERS

THE A-Z OF GARDEN FLOWERS

bay books

CONTENTS

Abelia

ABELIA

FEATURES

Semi-evergreen and vigorous in mild districts, *Abelia x grandiflora* makes a dashing statement and a fine flowering hedge. From July to September, its arching shoots, clad with small, oval, pointed leaves, 4–5ft long, are sleeved with showy heads of tubular, pale pink flowers with reddish calyces. The decorative calyx persists into late fall.

"Francis Mason" is a stunning variety with golden-variegated leaves that complement a wealth of pink blossom. Other prized kinds are lilac-pink *A. chinensis* "Edward Goucher" and rosy-lilac *A. schumannii.*

CONDITIONS

ASPECT   Thriving in full sun and tolerating very light shade, abelia is best planted against a sheltered, south- or west-facing wall.

SITE   Abelia prospers in a wide range of well-drained soils, from clay-loam to sand. Enrich rapid-draining, chalky, and sandy soils with well-rotted and moisture-conserving, bulky organic materials.

GROWING METHOD

FEEDING   Topdress the root area with bone meal in spring and fall to encourage sturdy growth and profuse blooms.

Water freely after planting and mulch thickly with old manure, bark, cocoa shell, or rotted garden compost to keep roots cool and active.

PROPAGATION Take soft-tip cuttings in late spring and semi-ripe cuttings from mid- to late summer.

PROBLEMS   Shoots are brittle and easily snapped, so be careful when pruning and planting.

PRUNING

Flowers form on current-year shoots. Once mature, keep it youthful by cutting out a third of its oldest branches in spring.

ABELIA'S PRETTY PINK FLOWERS appear at the end of summer. Striking, red calyces prolong the display. An informal abelia hedge adds a little magic to a sunny and sheltered garden. Trim it lightly in spring.

AT A GLANCE	
Sporting clusters of pink or lilac flowers from late summer to fall, it needs a sheltered position. Hardy to 14˚F (zone 8).	

Month	Activity	Recommended Varieties
Jan	/	*A. chinensis*
Feb	/	"Edward Goucher"
Mar	prune	*A. x grandiflora*
Apr	plant, prune	"Francis Mason"
May	plant	*A. schumannii*
June	plant	
July	plant, flower	
Aug	plant, flower	
Sept	plant, flower	
Oct	/	
Nov	/	
Dec	/	

Abelia x grandiflora

ABELIA

FEATURES

This evergreen shrub with slightly arching canes makes an easy-care informal hedge or screen. Growing to about 6¹/₂ft high and wide, it has glossy green leaves and produces masses of pink flowers throughout summer and into early fall. Its decorative effect is prolonged by the persistent pinky-red calyces (flower bases) which remain on the bush until fall. This is a long-lived plant. There is a variegated leaf form known as "Francis Mason," which is generally less vigorous in growth.

CONDITIONS

ASPECT   Grows best in full sun but tolerates some shade for part of the day. Since it isn't fully hardy, provide a warm, protected spot. These plants are best grown in city gardens that do not get blitzed by frosts.

SITE   Needs well-drained soil, preferably enriched with organic matter, although it will grow in poorer soils.

GROWING METHOD

PROPAGATION Grow abelia from semi-hardwood cuttings taken in late summer to early fall, or from hardwood cuttings of leafless canes taken during the winter months. This is a remarkably unfussy plant.

SPACING   Set plants at about 3¹/₂ft intervals.

FEEDING   Apply complete plant food in spring and again in midsummer.

PROBLEMS No problems are known.

FLOWERING

SEASON   There is a long flowering period through summer and sometimes into fall. Afterwards, the red calyces of the flower will often remain on the shrub, giving color until the fall.

PRUNING

GENERAL   The main pruning should be done in early spring. As an informal hedge it does not need shearing, which would spoil the arching habit of the growth. *Abelia triflora* is the tallest, reaching about 10ft high. It can be rather gaunt though. The best looking hedge plant is *Abelia x grandiflora* which is slightly shorter.

AT A GLANCE		
Abelia x grandiflora is a fine evergreen shrub with dark glossy leaves and scented white flowers. Hardy to 23°F (zone 9).		
Jan	foliage	**Recommended Varieties**
Feb	foliage	*Abelia chinensis*
Mar	foliage	"Edward Goucher"
April	foliage	*A. floribunda*
May	foliage	*A. x grandiflora*
June	foliage	"Francis Mason"
July	flowering	"Goldsport"
Aug	flowering	*A. triflora*
Sept	flowering	
Oct	foliage	
Nov	foliage	
Dec	foliage	

Abutilon

FLOWERING MAPLE

FEATURES

A deciduous tender shrub that is easy to raise from seed sown in the spring, with maple-like leaves and showy, hanging, bell-shaped flowers in a wide range of colors. Plants make bushy growth, and are useful in summer bedding schemes and for courtyard containers sited in a warm spot, but they must be protected from frost. Abutilon can be kept in a conservatory or frost-free greenhouse in the winter and will flower throughout spring and summer. Plants grow to 2–3ft tall. Varieties such as *Abutilon pictum* "Thompsonii," with variegated leaves, are available from garden centers as young plants in the spring; these can be potted up, grown on, and then planted outdoors after the last frosts.

CONDITIONS

ASPECT   Grow in full sunlight in borders or on a south-facing courtyard. In southern areas, plants grown against a south-facing wall in well-drained soil will often survive mild winters outdoors without protection.

SITE   Mix plenty of rotted manure/compost into soil before planting, and use multipurpose compost in containers. Soil should be well-drained but moisture-retentive for best results.

GROWING METHOD

SOWING   In February, sow in $3^{1}/_2$in-diameter pots, cover seed with its own depth of multipurpose compost, and keep at 70°F in light. Seedlings appear over 1–2 months, so check regularly. When plants are 2in tall, pot up into $3^{1}/_2$in pots and grow on. Plant out in early June after the last frosts.

FEEDING   Apply liquid feed weekly. Mix slow-release fertilizer granules with container compost.

PROBLEMS   Use sprays containing pirimicarb for aphids, malathion for mealy bugs, and bifenthrin for red spider mite, or, on plants growing in conservatories, use natural predators.

FLOWERING

SEASON   Flowers appear all summer outdoors, and some may appear year-around on indoor plants and those grown in southerly, mild areas, especially near the coast.

CUTTING   Not suitable.

GENERAL   Plants can be potted up before frosts and kept indoors. Increase favorites by taking cuttings in spring, rooting them on a windowsill or in a heated propagator.

AT A GLANCE	
A deciduous shrub grown as a summer bedding and container plant, with bell-like flowers. Frost hardy to 23°F (zone 9).	
Jan /	**Recommended Varieties**
Feb sow	*Abutilon* hybrids
Mar pot up	"Large Flowered Mixed"
Apr pot on	"Mixed Colors"
May harden off/plant	
Jun flowering	
July flowering	
Aug flowering	
Sept flowering	
Oct /	
Nov /	
Dec /	

Abutilon megapotamicum

FLOWERING MAPLE

FEATURES

A native of Brazil, this thin-stemmed evergreen or semi-evergreen shrub is fairly hardy. However, it prefers to be grown and trained against a warm sheltered wall or fence for protection from severe weather. The bright green leaves are oval or spear-shaped but the plant is grown primarily for its exotic-looking, symmetrical red and yellow bell-shaped flowers, which are produced continuously throughout summer and into fall on arching shoots. Height and spread 6ft. This is an ideal plant for a sheltered courtyard garden or other enclosed area. The stems are trained out evenly on the support to form a permanent woody framework.

CONDITIONS

ASPECT	It should be grown in full sun against a warm sheltered wall or fence.
SITE	This shrub grows best in reasonably fertile, well-drained soil.

GROWING METHOD

PROPAGATION	Sow seeds in the spring and germinate at 59–64°F. Take softwood cuttings in the spring.
WATERING	Apply water only if the soil starts to dry out in summer.
FEEDING	Feed annually in the spring with a slow-release fertilizer such as the organic blood, fish, and bone.
PROBLEMS	Generally trouble free out of doors.

FLOWERING/FOLIAGE

FLOWERS	The flowers are produced continuously in summer and fall.
FOLIAGE	This species is evergreen or semi-evergreen but the leaves are not particularly attractive, except in the cultivar "Variegatum," which has variegated foliage.

PRUNING

REQUIREMENTS	This shrub needs annual pruning to encourage flowering and to prevent congested growth. Cut back old flowered shoots to within two or three buds of the main stems in early spring.

IIN THE RIGHT PLACE this graceful evergreen shrub is a fast grower, but it needs a good soil and plenty of sunshine and shelter. A continuous supply of red and yellow bell-like flowers is produced by this exotic climber throughout summer and into the fall.

AT A GLANCE	
This wall shrub creates an exotic effect with its masses of colorful bell-shaped flowers. Hardy to 23°F (zone 9).	

		Recommended Varieties
Jan	/	Abutilon megapotamicum
Feb	/	"Variegatum" has yellow and
Mar	planting	green variegated foliage.
Apr	planting	
May	/	
Jun	flowering	
July	flowering	
Aug	flowering	
Sep	flowering	
Oct	flowering	
Nov	/	
Dec	/	

Abutilon vitifolium

ABUTILON

FEATURES

There are few more exhilarating, summer sights than a mature shrub of *Abutilon vitifolium* festooned with white to purple-blue, saucer-shaped blooms. Studding stems clothed with three- to five-lobed, soft,gray, hairy leaves are flowers that have you looking closely at them. Making an upright "obelisk" to around 15ft, this shrub is worth a little cosseting—as are its eye-catching varieties, mauve-flowered "Veronica Tennant" and "Tennant's White".

Closely related *A. x suntense*, a fast-growing hybrid to 12ft, rewards us with pendent, white to violet-blue "saucers". Choice forms of this hybrid are purple-blue "Geoffrey Gorer," white "Gorer's White," deep mauve "Jermyns," and dark violet-blue "Violetta". Look out, too, for "Canary Bird," whose radiant lemon-yellow blooms illuminate a border.

CONDITIONS

ASPECT   Position all varieties in full sun where shoots grow stocky and are massed with bloom. Make sure abutilon is sheltered from shoot-killing, icy winds.

SITE   This shrub tolerates a wide range of well-drained soils, but for the best results enrich the planting area with plenty of crumbly organic matter.

GROWING METHOD

FEEDING   For the strongest shoots and bounteous blossom, topdress the root area with fish, blood, and bone meal or Growmore in spring and midsummer.
          Water young plants regularly and mulch them with bulky organics to keep soil cool.

In long, dry spells, take out a moat around the plant and fill it repeatedly with water. When subsoil is soaked, replace excavated soil and cover with moisture-conserving mulch.

PROPAGATION   Increase favoured varieties from semi-ripe cuttings from mid- to late summer. *A. vitifolium* produces masses of fertile seed.

PROBLEMS   Control aphids colonizing soft stems by spraying with pirmicarb, pyrethrins, or insecticidal soap. Leaves may be damaged by caterpillars and other chewing insects. If damage is slight, ignore it. If severe, control these pests biologically with *Bacillus thuringiensis*, or apply rotenone or pirimiphos-methyl.

PRUNING

Keep bushes compact and packed with flowering shoots by cutting back dead or dying stems to healthy growth in mid-spring. In early summer, shorten flowered stems to two-thirds their length.

AT A GLANCE	
Loosely branched, deciduous shrub sleeved with saucer-shaped, white, blue, or purple blooms in summer. Hardy to 32°F (zone 10)	
Jan /	**Recommended Varieties**
Feb /	*A. x suntense*
Mar /	"Geoffrey Gorer"
Apr plant, prune	"Gorer's White"
May plant	"Jermyns"
June flower, plant	"Ralph Gould"
July flower, prune	"Violetta"
Aug plant	*A. vitifolium*
Sept plant	"Tennant's White"
Oct /	"Veronica Tennant"
Nov /	
Dec /	

Acacia

WATTLE

FEATURES

Acacias are quite tender, best grown in sheltered gardens in the warm south-west, where they escape the frosts. They can be used as novel, mainly evergreen hedges about 7ft high. They provide marvellous soft delicate foliage and fluffy flowers, usually yellow, in early spring. The flowers appear on last year's wood. The best kinds for a hedge are *Acacia cultriformis*, and *A. verticillata*, known as prickly Moses. Both are natives of Australia. They need to be well pruned after flowering to promote an abundance of short stems creating a thick, bushy effect. In colder regions acacias are best grown against warm sheltered walls where they will not get blitzed by icy winds.

CONDITIONS

ASPECT   Most acacias prefer full sun for best results. Some, such as *Acacia binervia* and *A. longifolia* will tolerate exposed coastal conditions.

Site   The soil must be well drained, but need not be particularly rich. Acacias will tolerate sites with slightly acid soils.

GROWING METHOD

PROPAGATION   Grow from seed removed from ripe pods. Pour almost boiling water over the seed and allow it to soak overnight before planting. Alternatively take semi-ripe cuttings in the summer.

SPACING   Plant at $3^1/2$–5ft intervals.

FEEDING   Fertilizing is not essential. A light application of blood and bone may be given in spring.

PROBLEMS   In the open acacias are remarkably trouble-free, assuming that frosts do not get them. Under glass, however, they are prone to red spider mites.

FLOWERING

SEASON   Depends on the species chosen. Most flower in early spring. The milder the winter has been the better the flowers.

PRUNING

GENERAL   For a formal shape, pruning may be necessary two or three times during the growing season but then you may get little or no flowering.

A YELLOW WATTLE in full bloom is a magnificent sight, and many have the added advantage that they bloom in winter.

AT A GLANCE		
Acacias make a highly attractive, unusual, yellow-flowering hedge in warm-climate gardens. Hardy to 32°F (zone 10).		
Jan	foliage	**Companion Plants**
Feb	foliage	Crocus
Mar	flowering	Daffodil
April	foliage	Erythronium
May	foliage	Fritillaria
June	foliage	Iris
July	foliage	Scilla
Aug	foliage	Tulip
Sept	foliage	
Oct	foliage	
Nov	foliage	
Dec	foliage	

Acanthus mollis

BEAR'S BREECHES

FEATURES

Also known as bear's breeches, this handsome foliage plant grows from 28 to 39in high, and can make a clump close to 39in wide. The dark, glossy leaves provided the inspiration and model for the decoration on Corinthian columns. This striking feature plant is at its best when mass-planted, although one generous clump can be extremely effective in quite a small area. It enjoys full sunlight, but also tolerates shade. The stiff flower spikes of purple-and-white flowers appear among the foliage from the spring into summer. It can be quite a vigorous grower, although it dies back after flowering. It can multiply quickly once established, but is rarely troublesome.

CONDITIONS

ASPECT   It flowers best in full sun, but also grows in light shade.

SITE   Needs well-drained soil that contains plenty of organic matter to aid water retention. Give plants a deep layer of mulch with compost in the spring, and then a second application in mid-summer, if necessary.

GROWING METHOD

PROPAGATION Grows from seed sown in spring, or divide clumps in the spring or fall. Plant new divisions 12–16in apart. Young plants must be given ample water in dry weather during the spring and summer. After flowering, cut back on the watering.

FEEDING

FEEDING   Apply a complete plant food as growth starts during the spring.

PROBLEMS   Since slugs and snails can cause a lot of damage to young growth, badly disfiguring it, take precautions. No other problems are known.

FLOWERING

SEASON   The tall spikes of purple-and-white flowers appear in late spring and summer.

CUTTING   It is possible to use this as a cut flower; the dried spikes make good indoor decoration.

AFTER FLOWERING

REQUIREMENTS Protect young plants with straw over winter. Cut off the flowering stems once faded.

LITTLE FLOWERS in purple and white open along tall spikes above the foliage.

AT A GLANCE		
A. mollis is a vigorous Mediterranean perennial liking dry, stoney ground. Hardy to 5°F (zone 7), with bold, shapely foliage.		

		Recommended Varieties
Jan	/	*Acanthus mollis*
Feb	sow	"Fielding Gold"
Mar	divide	"Hollard's Gold"
Apr	transplant	"Latifolius Group"
May	flowering	**Companion Plants**
Jun	flowering	*Bergenia* x
July	/	"Ballawley"
Aug	/	Forsythia
Sept	/	Gypsophila
Oct	divide	*Syringa vulgaris*
Nov	/	
Dec	/	

Achillea

YARROW

FEATURES

Yarrow are vigorous perennials offering heights from 2in to 4ft. The species has flattish heads of white flowers and feathery foliage, but cultivars have flowers in a lovely range of shades, including yellow, pink, apricot, and crimson. Flowers are long-lasting. Yarrow is quick and easy to establish, and may need to be controlled; however, the runners are quite easy to pull out. Some of the cultivars are less invasive than the species. *A. filipendulina* has flat heads of bright yellow flowers that last all summer. Selected forms have deep or pale yellow blooms. Best planted in large drifts, yarrow is ideal for the back of borders or among annuals.

CONDITIONS

ASPECT   Needs full sunlight for the best results, but will tolerate some shade for part of the day.
SITE   Any well-drained soil is suitable.

GROWING METHOD

PROPAGATION   Grows easily if established clumps are lifted and divided in the spring. Plant the vigorous new divisions 8–12in apart, and discard the old ones. New, young plants need regular watering in prolonged dry spells, but once established achillea is remarkably drought-tolerant, and needs only an occasional deep drink.
FEEDING   Apply a complete plant food as growth commences in the spring.
PROBLEMS   No specific pest or disease problems are known to attack achillea.

FLOWERING

SEASON   The long flowering period lasts throughout the summer into early fall. Regular removal of the spent, fading flower stems will significantly prolong blooming.
CUTTING   The flowers are good for cutting because they have a reasonably long vase life. Take handfuls of cut flowers for the vase as soon as the heads are fully open. Also excellent for drying.

AFTER FLOWERING

REQUIREMENTS   Cut off any spent flower stalks that remain on the plant in late fall.

ACHILLEA IS ALSO KNOWN as soldier's woundwort, nosebleed, and sanguinary, which reflects its value in herbal medicine.

AT A GLANCE		
Mainly deciduous perennials grown for their attractive, daisy-like summer and fall flowers. Hardy to 5°F (zone 7).		
Jan	/	**Recommended Varieties**
Feb	sow	*Achillea*
Mar	sow	"Coronation Gold"
Apr	transplant	*Achillea filipendulina*
May	divide	"Cloth of Gold"
Jun	flowering	"Gold Plate"
July	flowering	*A. x lewisii*
Aug	flowering	"King Edward"
Sept	flowering	*A. millefolium*
Oct	/	"Cerise Queen"
Nov	/	"Lilac Beauty"
Dec	/	"White Queen"
		"Moonshine"
		A. tomentosa

Achimenes

HOT WATER PLANT

FEATURES

Achimenes are easy to grow and undemanding; they are raised from small rhizomes that look a little like miniature fir cones. Leaves are toothed, elongated, and slightly furry in texture, and the colorful, trumpet-shaped flowers are carried in profusion on short stems above the foliage. The plants often assume a semi-trailing habit, making them good for growing in a basket, or in a raised pot where the stems can cascade.

Flowers are available in a wide range of shades including cream, pink, red, purple, and blue; some varieties have attractively veined throats. Although individual flowers are quite short lived, they are quickly replaced by a profusion of others throughout the season. The plants grow to about 10in.

CONDITIONS

ASPECT   Bright light is necessary, but not direct sun, which may scorch the foliage and flowers.

SITE   House plant, preferring cool to moderately warm conditions without marked temperature fluctuations. Use soil-less potting compost, based on peat or peat substitute.

GROWING METHOD

PLANTING   Bury the rhizomes shallowly—about $^3/_4$in deep—in a pot of moist compost, spacing them about $^1/_2$in apart, in early spring. Keep the pot in a warm room.

FEEDING   Feed with a high potash liquid fertilizer every 10 days or so from when the flower buds appear. Keep the compost just moist when the rhizomes start to grow, increasing the watering slightly as flowers start to form, but ensure the compost is never saturated. Tepid water is preferred, hence their common name. Stop watering when the flowers have faded.

PROBLEMS   No specific problems, though aphids may attack the new growth.

FLOWERING

SEASON   Flowers profusely throughout the summer.

CUTTING   Flowers are not suitable for cutting.

AFTER FLOWERING

REQUIREMENTS Stop watering once the flowers have faded and allow the plants to dry off. Remove the dead top growth and keep the rhizomes in the pot of dry compost over winter in a frost-free place. The following spring, tip them out, pot them up carefully in fresh compost, and water to start them into growth again.

AT A GLANCE	
A colorful house and greenhouse plant, flowering throughout the summer. Minimum temperature 50°F (zone 11).	

Month		Recommended Varieties
Jan	/	"Little Beauty"
Feb	plant	"Paul Arnold"
Mar	plant	"Peach Blossom"
Apr	/	"Queen of Sheba"
May	/	
Jun	flowering	
July	flowering	
Aug	flowering	
Sept	flowering	
Oct	/	
Nov	/	
Dec	/	

Aechmea

AECHMEA SPECIES AND CULTIVARS

FEATURES

These are possibly the most widely grown and best known of all the bromeliads. Generally very easy to cultivate, they can be container grown or attached to a log "tree". Although aechmeas originate from Central and South America, most tolerate temperatures down to about 41°F making them suitable for cooler conservatories. Species vary in size from a petite 6in to over 24in, although this size would be rare in cultivation. Larger plants can become top heavy so a terracotta or earthenware pot is advisable for extra stability.

FOLIAGE

There is an amazing diversity of form and foliage color in these bromeliads. Leaves are in a rosette, forming a vase shape with an open cup in the center. They may be completely shiny green, or green above and burgundy beneath, deep burgundy on both sides or streaked, banded, or spotted with silver, or entirely silvery black. There are also variegated forms with either yellow-gold or pink variegations on a green background. Many are sharply spined along the leaf margins (needing careful handling) while others are almost smooth edged.

FLOWERS

Many aechmeas have long-lasting flowers that make them popular for indoor decoration. Although the true flowers are often quite small they are enclosed within showy bracts that come in a great range of colors. The inflorescence or flowering spike may be red, blue, yellow, purple, pink, orange, or white and lasts for months.

FRUITS

Berry-like fruits follow the flowers and often persist on the plant over a long period.

A. FASCIATA One of the most popular species is Aechmea fasciata or "Urn" plant, which has gray-silver spined leaves cross-banded in silver. The whole leaf surface is densely covered with silvery scales, giving a powdery effect. The flower spike is a large, showy pyramid of pink bracts enclosing the blue flowers, which age to red.

FOSTER'S FAVORITE An attractive dwarf variety is *A.* "Foster's Favorite," which has deep burgundy foliage and a pendulous flowering spike of deep blue flowers. These may be followed by red berries. Both these forms are tolerant of a wide range of conditions.

A. CHANTINII *A. chantinii* is variable both in size and foliage color. It is sometimes called Amazonian zebra plant because of its green to almost black foliage, which is heavily barred. The long-branched flowering spike is generally red or orange with flowers being red or yellow. Tends to be more cold sensitive than some.

OTHER SPECIES

A. fulgens discolor has attractive foliage and is commonly called the "Coral berry" aechmea. This species is hard to beat with its green strap-shaped leaves that are a deep purple beneath. A spike of purple flowers will turn into decorative coral red berries.

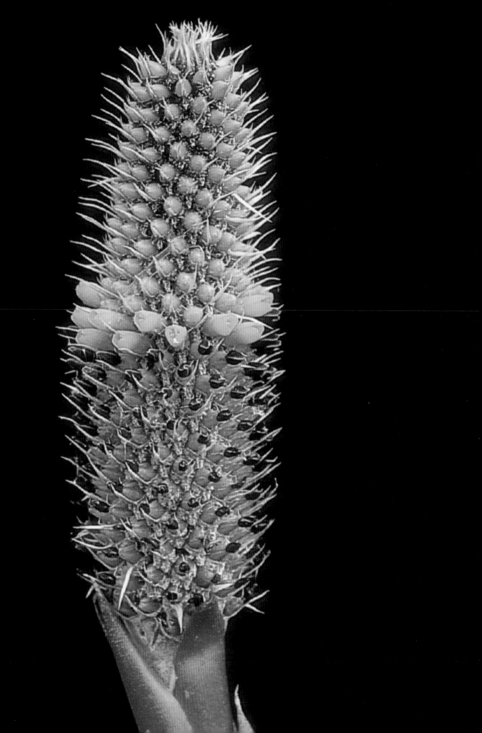

CONDITIONS

POSITION | Needs a frost-free climate. The plants do best in warm to hot, humid conditions with a cooler spell in winter. Morning sun, filtered sunlight or shade seems to suit this plant group. Most aechmeas like sheltered situations, preferably with overhead shading. Although some species have origins in harsh environments it is best to give them all some shelter in non-extreme conditions.

POTTING mix | Plants will thrive in a very coarse, open, soil-less compost. Water must be able to drain straight through. Take care not to plant too deep to avoid rotting.

GROWING METHOD

PROPAGATION | Start new plants by removing the offsets or pups from the parent plant once the offsets have reached about one-third of the size of the parent. Cut off and pot separately.

WATERING | The cup at the center of the rosette must be kept filled with water. Plants probably need watering twice weekly or more in summer and every week or two in cold weather. Be guided by the weather and feel how moist the compost is. Mounted plants need spray watering daily in summer but much less often in winter.

FEEDING | Apply slow release granules to the compost in spring. Mounted specimens may be given a foliar spray of liquid plant food at about one-third the recommended strength. Over feeding will not encourage more vigourous growth—it will scorch the leaves and roots.

PROBLEMS | There are no specific problems for this group if given reasonably good cultural and environmental conditions.

FLOWERING SEASON

Flowering times are variable but many bloom in late summer and fall, and many of them continue into winter.

LONG FLOWERING and adaptable, Aechmea makes a good choice of plant for fairly warm conditions.

AT A GLANCE		
A tolerant plant. Leaves are strap-like and vary in color. Plants produce floral bracts after three years.		
Jan	grow on, reduce watering	**Recommended Varieties**
Feb	grow on, reduce watering	A. chantinii
Mar	re-pot, feed	A. fasciata
Apr	remove and pot on offsets	A. fulgens discolor
May	remove offsets, mist foliage	
Jun	bracts, flowers, mist and water	
July	flowers, mist and water	
Aug	/	
Sept	/	
Oct	flowers, fruit; keep frost free	
Nov	flowers, reduce watering	
Dec	flowers, reduce watering	

Agapanthus

AFRICAN BLUE LILY

FEATURES

Agapanthus has dark green, strap-shaped leaves that grow to about 20in long. It produces rounded heads of blue or white flowers on top of stems 39in or more tall, but even without the flowers it makes a great foliage accent. It is hardy in moderate areas, but in colder regions needs winter protection. The Headbourne hybrids are particularly hardy. It can be grown in containers, and looks excellent in eye-catching tubs. Several attractive dwarf forms have foliage that rarely exceed 8in.

CONDITIONS

ASPECT	Tolerates some shade, but the flowering will be poor. Full sunlight is ideal.
SITE	Grows in almost any soil, but well-drained ground with organic matter is perfect. In colder yards, grow near a south-facing wall.

GROWING METHOD

PROPAGATION	Divide clumps in the spring, ensuring that each division has a crown and a good batch of healthy roots. The latter can be shortened and some outer leaves removed, if necessary. Plant approximately 10in apart. Also grows from seed sown in the spring. It needs regular watering to establish, but once settled it can cope with long, dry periods. However, for the best growth and flowering, do not let new, young plants dry out.
FEEDING	Apply complete plant food in the early spring. Potted plants will perform better with an application of slow-release granules, or a monthly liquid feed, carefully following the manufacturer's recommended rate.
PROBLEMS	There are no particular problems, but clumps will harbor groups of snails. Pick off.

FLOWERING

SEASON	Blooms appear in mid- to late summer, depending on the conditions.
CUTTING	Agapanthus can be used as a cut flower if the stems are plunged into boiling water for 15 seconds immediately after cutting.

AFTER FLOWERING

REQUIREMENTS	No pruning needed, other than cutting off spent flower stems and dead leaves. Protect crowns over winter with a thick mulch of straw or dry leaves.

AT A GLANCE		
A vigorous perennial, forming bold, eye-catching flowering clumps, from southern Africa. Many hardy to 23˚F (zone 9).		
Jan	/	Recommended Varieties
Feb	sow	*Agapanthus africanus*
Mar	sow	"Albus"
Apr	divide	*A. caulescens*
May	transplant	"Lilliput"
Jun	/	"Loch Hope"
July	flowering	"Peter Pan"
Aug	flowering	*A. praecox*
Sept	flowering	"Variegatus"
Oct	/	
Nov	/	
Dec	/	

Ageratum

FLOSS FLOWER

FEATURES

Ageratum, a half-hardy annual, has fluffy long-lived flowers in blue, pink, white and bicolors such as blue-white. Use dwarf varieties for edging, as they grow up to 6in. Tall varieties are used in borders and for cutting, growing to 2$\frac{1}{2}$ft. Use for bedding/containers. Available as young plants.

CONDITIONS

ASPECT	Needs full sun and a sheltered position.
SITE	Prefers well-drained soil enriched with rotted manure or compost well ahead of planting. In containers use multipurpose compost and ensure that there is good drainage.

GROWING METHOD

SOWING	Sow seeds in 3$\frac{1}{2}$in pots in February/March and just cover, and keep at 70°F. Seedlings appear after a week and can be moved to cell trays of multipurpose compost when two leaves are developed. Harden off and plant outside after frosts, spacing tall varieties 12–16in apart, dwarf varieties 4–6in apart.
FEEDING	Apply liquid feed fortnightly to maintain strong growth, or mix slow-release fertilizer with compost before planting up.

PROBLEMS

Ageratum can suffer from root rot so grow in well-drained containers on heavy clay soils, and avoid getting the compost too wet.

FLOWERING

SEASON	Flowers appear all summer until the first frosts. Regular dead-heading, especially after heavy rain, will prolong flowering and often encourage a second "flush" of color.
CUTTING	Tall varieties are suitable for cutting.

AFTER FLOWERING

GENERAL	Remove plants when past their best, usually after the first sharp frosts of fall.

MODERN VARIETIES of ageratum for bedding produce masses of flowers which gradually rise above the leaves as they open.

AT A GLANCE	
A half-hardy annual grown for its fluffy flowers, ideal for edging, bedding, containers, and cutting. Frost hardy to 32°F (zone 10).	
Jan /	**Recommended Varieties**
Feb sow	*Ageratum houstonianum*
Mar sow	**For bedding**
Apr grow on	"Adriatic"
May plant	"Bavaria"
Jun flowering	"Blue Champion"
July flowering	"Blue Mink"
Aug flowering	"Pink Powderpuffs"
Sept flowering	"White Blue"
Oct /	"Capri"
Nov /	"White Hawaii"
Dec /	**For cutting**
	"Blue Horizon"

Agrostemma

CORNCOCKLE

FEATURES

A very easily grown hardy annual for use in cottage gardens and borders where it self-seeds year after year. Plants are tall, growing 2–3ft tall, and carry pink, purple, or white trumpet-like blooms. The seeds are poisonous. Commonly known as corncockle.

CONDITIONS

ASPECT | Grow in full sun.
SITE | Succeeds on well-drained and even light, sandy soils that are quite "hungry" (it used to grow as a weed in cornfields). Excessive feeding may actually reduce the number of flowers.

GROWING METHOD

SOWING | Sow outdoors from March onward when the soil is warming up, in patches or drills 1/2in deep where you want the plants to flower. Thin seedlings so they are eventually 6–12in apart. Do not transplant. Can also be sown in pots in the fall, overwintered in a sheltered spot then potted up in spring for flowers in early summer.
FEEDING | Extra feeding is unnecessary, but water occasionally but thoroughly in dry spells.

PROBLEMS | Agrostemma is a floppy plant and twiggy supports can be useful.

FLOWERING

SEASON | Summer onward, but earlier flowers are produced by sowing in the fall.
CUTTING | Short-lived as a cut flower, and rather floppy.

AFTER FLOWERING

GENERAL | Dead-heading throughout summer will keep flowers coming but always leave a few to ripen and set seeds. Plants will self-sow and germinate the following spring. Alternatively, collect seedheads in paper bags and store.

GROW AGROSTEMMA in bold clumps in borders where the tall lanky, swaying plants help to give each other support.

AT A GLANCE	
A tall hardy annual grown for its pink, purple, or white flowers which are ideal for cottage borders. Frost hardy to 5°F (zone 7).	
Jan /	**Recommended Varieties**
Feb /	*Agrostemma githago*
Mar sow	"Milas"
Apr thin out	"Ocean Pearl"
May flowering	"Purple Queen"
Jun flowering	"Rose of Heaven"
July flowering	
Aug flowering	
Sept flowering	
Oct sow	
Nov /	
Dec /	

Ajuga reptans

BLUE BUGLE FLOWER

FEATURES

A lovely groundcover for shady, slightly moist sites, *Ajuga reptans* grows as a neat rosette of leaves but spreads by stolons (running stems). Leaves are shiny and may be dark green or bronzed green. The cultivars "Burgundy Lace" and "Multicolor" are mottled cream, pink, or burgundy. This long-lived plant rarely grows more than 6in high, although the deep blue flower spikes may be taller. It is an ideal groundcover under trees and is a good soil binder. It is also used as a border plant and can be grown in troughs or pots. Once the plant is established, growth is dense so that it suppresses weeds very well.

CONDITIONS

ASPECT	A woodland and hedgerow plant, *A. reptans* prefers shade or dappled sunlight.
SITE	This plant does best in well-drained, but somewhat moisture-retentive soil that has been enriched with plenty of organic matter prior to planting. It can also sometimes occur in surprisingly boggy places.

GROWING METHOD

PROPAGATION	Best grown from divisions of existing clumps, *A. reptans* roots easily from stem nodes and any small sections that are dug up will rapidly re-establish.
FEEDING	Feed with an application of blood and bone, pellets of poultry manure or any complete plant food after flowering.
PROBLEMS	*A. reptans* can be badly affected by powdery mildew if air circulation is poor

or the soil is badly drained. If the weather is not too hot, sulphur dust or spray can suppress this mildew. Otherwise use a fungicide registered for powdery mildew.

FLOWERING

SEASON	The attractive bright blue flower spikes are produced in spring, or in the early summer in cool areas. They make a lovely garden display. "Variegata" is probably the best form with its highly-decorative white edged leaves. It is not that reliable though and needs close attention. "Braunherz" has a remarkably rich bronze color.
CUTTING	The flowers of *A. reptans* are good as cut flowers.

PRUNING

GENERAL	Pruning should be restricted to the removal of the spent flower stems.

AT A GLANCE		
Ajuga reptans is a quality groundcover plant, with excellent colored forms for the late spring garden. Hardy to 5°F (zone 7).		
Jan	foliage	**Recommended Varieties**
Feb	foliage	*Ajuga reptans*
Mar	foliage	"Braunherz"
April	foliage	"Burgundy Glow"
May	flowering	"Catlin's Giant"
June	flowering	"Multicolor"
July	foliage	"Tricolor"
Aug	foliage	"Variegata"
Sept	foliage	
Oct	foliage	
Nov	foliage	
Dec	foliage	

Akebia quinata

CHOCOLATE VINE

FEATURES

The fascinating and unusual purple-brown flowers of the Chocolate vine, a native of China, Japan and Korea, have a light but distinctive smell of chocolate. The foliage is also decorative, and therefore this climber looks good even when not in flower. It is a long-lived twining semi-evergreen climber capable of growing up to 30ft, although it may be less in some gardens. Growth is fairly vigorous once the plant is established but it is rather open in habit and never ends up looking heavy. This climber is seen to best advantage when grown over a trellis screen, pergola or arch, and is also a suitable subject for growing into a large tree.

CONDITIONS

ASPECT   *Akebia* will grow equally well in full sun or partial shade.

SITE   The soil must be well-drained, moisture-retentive, and reasonably fertile.

GROWING METHOD

PROPAGATION Sow seeds in fall and place in a cold frame. Take semi-ripe cuttings in summer. Carry out serpentine layering in the spring.

WATERING   Make sure the soil does not dry in the summer.

FEEDING   This is necessary only once a year in spring. Apply a slow-release organic fertilizer such as blood, fish, and bone.

PROBLEMS   Not troubled by pests or diseases.

FLOWERING/FOLIAGE

FLOWERS   The scented flowers are produced throughout spring and followed by long fleshy fruits. Warm conditions throughout spring and summer are necessary for fruit to be produced.

FOLIAGE   The foliage consists of five deep green leaflets. Leaves may become flushed with an attractive purple color in the winter.

PRUNING

REQUIREMENTS If necessary trim the plant after flowering to keep it within bounds. It may eventually need some of the oldest stems thinned out, or renovation pruning.

THE CHOCOLATE VINE is not over-vigorous but this particular vine is producing a great show of flowers. It is hard to describe their color but it is a dark pinkish or purplish brown, and they have an unusual chocolate smell. Leaves consist of five deep green leaflets.

AT A GLANCE		
One of the earliest climbers to flower, with unusual chocolate-scented blooms. Hardy to 5˚F (zone 7).		
Jan	/	**Companion Plants**
Feb	planting	Strong-growing summer-flowering
Mar	flowering	clematis or climbing roses will take
Apr	flowering	over from the spring display.
May	flowering	
Jun	/	
July	/	
Aug	/	
Sep	/	
Oct	/	
Nov	/	
Dec	/	

Alcea

HOLLYHOCK

FEATURES

Alcea is also known as althaea, and is the familiar "hollyhock" found in cottage borders. Flowers are single or double in a range of colors, and carried on stems which can be up to 8ft tall depending on variety. Tall varieties are best at the back of borders. *Alcea* is grown as an annual sown in spring, or as a biennial sown in summer. Spring-sown plants suffer less with rust disease. Fully hardy.

CONDITIONS

ASPECT	Needs full sun.
SITE	Plants can often be found growing in cracks between paving slabs and in walls but the tallest spikes are produced by adding generous amounts of rotted manure or compost to the soil before planting. Soil must have good drainage. In windy spots stake tall varieties.

GROWING METHOD

SOWING	To grow as an annual sow seed in 3^1/$_2$in pots of multipurpose compost in February. Just cover the seeds and keep at 68°F. Seedlings appear in about two weeks and can be transplanted to individual 3^1/$_2$in pots of compost. Grow on and plant in May after hardening off. Seeds can also be sown outdoors in April. To grow as biennials, sow seed in midsummer but germinate outdoors in a shaded spot. Plant in September.

FEEDING / PROBLEMS

FEEDING	A monthly liquid feed encourages growth.
PROBLEMS	Rust disease spoils the look of and weakens growth and is worse in wet summers. Control is difficult but for a few plants pick off leaves and try a spray containing mancozeb.

FLOWERING

SEASON	Early spring-sown plants grow rapidly and flower from early summer. Those planted in fall will overwinter in the ground and flower in early summer the following season.
CUTTING	Striking as cut flowers—take them when there are plenty of flowerbuds still to open.

AFTER FLOWERING

GENERAL	Leave a few spikes to set self-sown seeds, but remove dead plants to reduce rust problems.

AT A GLANCE	
A hardy biennial grown as an annual or biennial for its tall spikes of flowers suited to cottage gardens. Frost hardy to 5°F (zone 7).	
Jan /	**Recommended Varieties**
Feb sow	*Alcea rosea*
Mar grow on	**Single flowered**
Apr sow outdoors	"Nigra"
May plant	"Single Mixed"
Jun flowers/sow	**Double flowered**
July flowering	"Chater's Double Mixed"
Aug flowering	"Majorette Mixed"
Sept flowers/plant	"Peaches 'n' Dreams"
Oct /	"Powder Puffs Mixed"
Nov /	"Summer Carnival Mixed"
Dec /	

Alchemilla

ALCHEMILLA VULGARIS

FEATURES

Alchemilla vulgaris (*A. xanthochlora*), the wild lady's mantle, is a hardy perennial native to the mountains of Europe, Asia, and America. It grows to 9–18in and has rounded pale green leaves, with lobed and toothed edges that collect the dew or raindrops. The water thus collected once was reputed to have healing and magical powers. Feathery heads of yellow-green flowers are produced in early summer and can continue into fall. More popular, and very widely grown as a garden plant, is *Alchemilla mollis* which is very similar in both appearance and properties. The alpine lady's mantle, *Alchemilla alpina*, a smaller plant growing to 6in, is also said to have similar, but more effective, properties.

CONDITIONS

ASPECT   Lady's mantle will grow in sun or moderate shade.

SITE   It is tolerant of most soils except waterlogged conditions.

GROWING METHOD

SOWING   Lady's mantle self-seeds freely and removing self-sown seedlings is an easy way to get new plants. Seed can be sown in early spring or fall. Germination takes about two or three weeks but can be erratic.

PLANTING   Fall-sown seedlings will need to be overwintered under glass. Plant them out in spring 18in apart. Established plants can be propagated by division either in spring or fall.

FEEDING   The lady's mantles are tolerant plants, but be careful to avoid overwatering. Mulch alchemillas lightly in the spring and the fall and apply a balanced general fertilizer in spring.

PROBLEMS   None.

PRUNING   Cut back flowerheads as they start to fade to prevent self-seeding. Cut back dead foliage in late fall.

HARVESTING

PICKING   Young leaves can be picked as required throughout the summer, after the morning dew has dried.

STORAGE   Leaves can be dried and stored in airtight dark glass jars.

FREEZING   Not suitable for freezing.

USES

CULINARY   Young leaves can be added to salads in small amounts. They have a mild, but somewhat bitter taste.

MEDICINAL   In medieval times the lady's mantle was dedicated to the Virgin Mary, and was

AT A GLANCE		
A pretty perennial with rounded leaves and feathery flowerheads, it was traditionally a woman's herb. Hardy to 4°F (zone 7).		
Jan	/	**Parts used**
Feb	/	Leaves
Mar	plant	Flowers
Apr	plant	**Uses**
May	plant harvest	Culinary
Jun	harvest	Medicinal
July	harvest	Cosmetic
Aug	harvest	Gardening
Sept	plant harvest	
Oct	/	
Nov	/	
Dec	/	

considered to be particularly a woman's herb, as it was used to treat a wide range of womens' problems, including menstrual problems, menopause, breastfeeding, and inflammations. It was also used as a wound healer for external use, and to make a mouth rinse for use after tooth extraction.

COSMETIC Lady's mantle can be used to make a soothing and healing rinse that is good for skin complaints.

GARDENING *Alchemilla* is widely used as an edging plant as well as being grown in flower borders, and the attractive feathery heads of yellow-green flowers are particularly popular with flower arrangers.

THE "LADY" to whom the name lady's mantle refers, was the Virgin Mary, to whom the herb was dedicated during medieval times.

Alchemilla mollis

LADY'S MANTLE

FEATURES

This is a quick-growing herbaceous perennial mostly used as a border plant to edge paths and beds. An abundant self-seeder, it is good for suppressing weeds, filling any free spaces, often popping up in cracks in paths. Growing anywhere between 8 and 16in high, one plant may spread to 11–16in. The rounded, slightly hairy leaves overlap one another, and the plant produces trusses of bright lime-green flowers through summer. It provides a lovely contrast with other, stronger colors. The leaves tend to trap raindrops or dew, adding to the effect.

CONDITIONS

ASPECT Thrives in full sun, although it tolerates a degree of light shade.

SITE Needs well-drained soil that has a high organic content.

GROWING METHOD

PROPAGATION Self-sown seedlings can be easily transplanted to other positions. Clumps can be divided in the spring or fall with the divisions spaced 8–10in apart. Newly planted specimens may need watering, but mature plants tolerate dry periods. Justifiably known as a great survivor and spreader.

FEEDING Apply a complete plant food as the new growth begins.

PROBLEMS No specific problems are known.

FLOWERING

SEASON Masses of lime-green flowers appear from late spring through the summer.

CUTTING A great favorite with flower arrangements.

AFTER FLOWERING

REQUIREMENTS If you do not want plants to self-seed, trim spent flowers as soon as they fade. Once flowering has finished and growth begins to die down, the plants can be cut back hard with shears, or even a trimmer if you want to be ruthless.

LIME-GREEN FLOWERS light up Alchemilla mollis. Although it is not a particularly bright color, it lifts the whole area.

AT A GLANCE	
A. mollis is a hardy perennial grown for its prolific self-seeding and attractive lime-green foliage. Hardy to 5°F (zone 7).	
Jan /	**Companion Plants**
Feb sow	Delphinium
Mar sow	Dicentra
Apr transplant	Eremurus
May transplant	Eucomis
Jun flowering	Euonymus
July flowering	Geranium
Aug flowering	Gladiolus
Sept flowering	Lupin
Oct divide	Rose
Nov /	
Dec /	

Allium

ORNAMENTAL ONION

FEATURES

There are a large number of *Allium* species, including edible onions, garlic, and chives as well as many ornamental plants. Typically, they produce rounded heads of flowers, often in rosy purple shades, but there are also yellow- and white-flowered species. Some are small-growing and suitable for the rock garden, while others make excellent plants for the middle or back of borders. *A. giganteum* produces its eye-catching heads of mauve-pink, starry flowers on stems 3ft or more high, while *A. moly* grows to only 8in and has loose clusters of golden yellow blooms. Many alliums make excellent cut flowers. They are usually long lasting in water, and the dried inflorescence that remains after the blooms have fallen can be used successfully in dried arrangements, too.

CONDITIONS

ASPECT | Best in full sun but will tolerate light shade.

SITE | Alliums in borders should be positioned where other plants will help to hide their often untidy foliage. Smaller species are suitable for rock gardens. The soil must be well-drained and should contain plenty of well-decayed manure or compost. Add a dressing of lime to acid soils before planting.

GROWING METHOD

PLANTING | Plant in fall. Planting depth varies according to the size of the bulb: cover bulbs with soil to three times their height.

FEEDING | Apply a high potash liquid fertilizer as buds form. Water during dry spells, but never allow the soil to become sodden. After flowering, stop watering altogether.

PROBLEMS | Plants may suffer from the fungal disease rust, causing orange pustules on the foliage: destroy affected specimens. Feeding with high potash fertilizer may increase resistance to attacks.

FLOWERING

SEASON | Flowers in late spring and summer.

CUTTING | Cut alliums when about half the flowers are fully open.

AFTER FLOWERING

REQUIREMENTS | Foliage starts to die down before blooming is complete. Cut off the spent flower stems if required. Overcrowded clumps can be divided in fall, replanting immediately.

AT A GLANCE		
Versatile and varied bulbs with usually rounded heads of starry flowers in spring and early summer.		
Jan	/	**Recommended species**
Feb	/	*Allium albopilosum*
Mar	/	*A. beesianum*
Apr	flowering	*A. caeruleum*
May	flowering	*A. giganteum*
Jun	flowering	*A. karataviense*
July	flowering	*A. moly*
Aug	/	"Jeannine"
Sept	plant	*A. neopolitanum*
Oct	plant	*A. oreophilum*
Nov	/	*A. schubertii*
Dec	/	*A. siculum*

Alstroemeria

PERUVIAN LILY

FEATURES

The Peruvian lily is grown commercially on a large scale, since the flowers are long lasting when cut. In the garden it is a herbaceous perennial with flower spikes growing mostly 12–24in high, although there are dwarf forms and very tall ones. The flowers are beautifully marked with streaks and spots of color, contrasting with a wide range of base colors of cream, yellow, orange, pink, and red. If conditions are suitable, these plants spread by means of fleshy rhizomes (roots) to form large clumps. Also excellent when grown in pots.

CONDITIONS

ASPECT Needs full sunlight and shelter to thrive, especially in colder areas. Also requires shelter from strong wind. Makes an excellent potted greenhouse plant.

SITE Must have very free-draining soil containing plenty of decayed organic matter.

GROWING METHOD

PROPAGATION Many grow readily from seed sown in the spring, but division of established clumps is easiest; spring is generally considered the best time. Bare-root plants can be hard to establish; pot-grown plants, available in the summer, are better. Plant the roots 2in deep and about 6in apart. In a prolonged dry period, water the bedded plants regularly in the spring and summer, but restrict watering after flowering.

FEEDING Apply slow-release granular fertilizer in spring.

PROBLEMS No specific problems are known.

FLOWERING

SEASON Most species and their cultivars flower from the spring into summer, some into fall.

CUTTING This is a first-class cut flower.

AFTER FLOWERING

REQUIREMENTS Cut off spent flower stems at ground level. Protect crowns with straw during cold winters.

THE FLOWERS OF ALSTROEMERIA are very delicately marked when viewed close-up, and have an almost orchid-like appearance.

AT A GLANCE		
A hardy perennial surviving 14˚F (zone 8). Grown for their excellent showy flowers—many make unbeatable cut flowers.		
Jan	/	**Recommended Varieties**
Feb	/	*Alstroemeria ligtu* hybrids
Mar	/	"Orange Gem"
Apr	sow	"Orange Glory"
May	/	"Princess Mira" (and all
Jun	transplant	"Princess" varieties)
July	flowering	"Solent Crest"
Aug	flowering	"Solent Rose"
Sept	flowering	"Stamoli"
Oct	divide	"Strapripur"
Nov	/	"Staroko"
Dec	/	"Stasilva"

Amaranthus

LOVE-LIES-BLEEDING

FEATURES

Amaranthus is grown for its colorful, exotic-looking foliage and its spiky, erect or drooping tassels of blood-red, green, golden-brown, purple, or multi-colored flowers up to 18in long. Leaves can be red, bronze, yellow, brown, or green, depending on the variety grown. Size ranges from 15in to 4ft tall. Use plants as potted plants, in courtyard containers, and as dramatic centerpieces in summer bedding displays. Superb when used cut for fresh or dried flower arrangements indoors.

CONDITIONS

ASPECT   Full sun and shelter is essential for success.

SITE   Soil should be well-drained, with plenty of rotted compost or manure added. Varieties of *Amaranthus caudatus* will also succeed on thin, dry soils. Use multipurpose compost in containers and pots. In northern areas grow in 8–10in diameter pots in the greenhouse or conservatory. Tall-growing varieties may need staking.

GROWING METHOD

SOWING   Sow seeds in March at 70°F in 3^1/2in-diameter pots of multipurpose compost, just covering the seed. Seeds germinate in 7–14 days or sooner, and should be transplanted into cell trays or 3^1/2in-diameter pots of multipurpose compost. Plant outside after the last frosts in late May/early June, 1–3ft apart, and water.

FEEDING   Feed weekly from early summer onward with general-purpose liquid feed. In containers, mix slow-release fertilizer with compost before planting, and also feed every two weeks with half-strength liquid feed.

PROBLEMS   Aphids can feed on the colorful leaves and build up into large colonies, unless caught early. Use a spray containing permethrin.

FLOWERING

SEASON   Foliage is colorful from early summer onward, and is joined by flowerheads and then colorful seedheads later on.

CUTTING   Varieties grown for their flowers can be cut and used fresh, while seedheads can be left to develop, then cut and dried for indoor use.

AFTER FLOWERING

GENERAL   Remove plants when past their best.

AT A GLANCE		
A half-hardy annual grown for its leaves and flowers for bedding, containers, and for drying. Frost hardy to 32°F (zone 10).		
Jan	/	**Recommended Varieties**
Feb	/	*Amaranthus caudatus*
Mar	sow	"Green Thumb"
Apr	transplant	"Viridis"
May	transplant	*Amaranthus cruentus*
Jun	flowering	"Golden Giant"
July	flowering	"Split Personality"
Aug	flowering	"Ruby Slippers"
Sept	flowering	*Amaranthus hybridus*
Oct	flowering	"Intense Purple"
Nov	/	*Amaranthus tricolor*
Dec	/	"Aurora Yellow"
		"Joseph's Coat"

Amaryllis belladonna

BELLADONNA LILY

FEATURES

This beautiful South African bulb produces its multiple and sweetly perfumed blooms on sturdy purple-green stems 24in or more high. The funnel-shaped flowers may be various shades of pink or white and the flowering stem appears before the leaves, giving the plant its alternative common name of naked lady. This bulb is a great asset in the garden as the flowering period is fall, while the glossy strap-like leaves look good throughout winter and early spring. It makes an excellent cut flower. Best flowering comes from clumps that are left undisturbed for several years.

CONDITIONS

ASPECT   Prefers a warm, sheltered spot in full sun—the bulbs need a good summer baking to produce the best flowers.

SITE   A good plant for a flower bed under a south-facing wall. *Amaryllis belladonna* can also be grown in containers, planting the large bulbs singly in 8in pots. Well-drained soil is required: poor soil is tolerated but best results are achieved by digging in decayed organic matter a month or more before planting.

GROWING METHOD

PLANTING   Plant bulbs with their necks just at ground level and 8–12in apart in early to mid-summer.

FEEDING   Apply a balanced fertilizer after flowering, as the leaves appear. Water in dry periods while the plant is in growth.

PROBLEMS   It is rarely troubled by any problems.

FLOWERING

SEASON   Flowers in very late summer and fall.

CUTTING   A good cut flower for large arrangements.

AFTER FLOWERING

REQUIREMENTS Remove spent flower stems. Protect the crowns with a mulch of peat over winter. Leave bulbs undisturbed for several years. If lifting and dividing, do so in early summer.

BRIGHT PINK BELLADONNA LILIES brighten the late summer and fall garden. The foliage here is from a clump of daylilies.

AT A GLANCE	
A tall plant producing its stems of fragrant, funnel-shaped flowers in fall. Needs a warm, sheltered, sunny position.	
Jan /	**Recommended Varieties**
Feb /	"Johannesburg"
Mar /	"Kimberley"
Apr /	"Major"
May /	
Jun plant	
July plant	
Aug /	
Sept flowering	
Oct flowering	
Nov /	
Dec /	

Ananas

ANANAS SPECIES

FEATURES

Pineapple, *Ananas comosus,* is one of several species that make up this terrestrial bromeliad genus. All originate in tropical America. They have a rosette of very stiff, spiny leaves and produce purple-blue flowers with red bracts on a stem rising from the center of the plant. After the flowers fade the fruit is formed. *A. bracteatus* is grown for its showy flowers, which are followed by bright red mini pineapples. The variety striatus has leaves edged and striped cream to white. Unfortunately, to produce pineapples *A. comosus* must be grown in the right conditions. The form with cream striped leaves is the most popular. In bright light variegations may turn pinkish. Take care when siting these plants as the foliage spines are sharp.

CONDITIONS

POSITION
Needs a frost-free climate with a winter temperature above 50˚F. Needs full sun or very bright light to flower and fruit. Very bright light also brings out the best color of variegated forms.

POTTING MIX
All growing media must be well drained. Use coarse bark or peat-based mix and a heavy pot for additional stability.

GROWING METHOD

PROPAGATION
Grows from suckers or offsets from the base of the plant or from the tuft of leaves on top of the fruit. Peel off the lower basal leaves to reveal a stub and leave the stub in a dry, airy place to dry before planting it sometime from spring to fall.

WATERING
In summer water two or three times a week. In winter check before watering, which may be needed only every week or two.

FEEDING
Give slow release fertilizer in spring and early summer if desired.

PROBLEMS
No specific problems are known for home growers but base and stem will rot if plants are too wet.

FLOWERING SEASON

FLOWERS
Appear from late spring to summer, depending on the season.

FRUIT
Fruit may take two years or more to mature, especially in cooler conditions, but the foliage makes up for this.

AT A GLANCE		
To produce pineapples grow in a hot conservatory. Flowers are purple-blue with red bracts; fruit forms after flowers.		
Jan	reduce water, move to 50˚F	**Recommended Varieties**
Feb	water every two weeks	*A. comosus*
Mar	remove and pot on offsets	*A. comosus striatus*
Apr	remove and pot on offsets	
May	feed and light	
Jun	flowering, water three times weekly	
July	flowering	
Aug	water three times weekly	
Sept	water every two weeks	
Oct	water every two weeks, keep frost free	
Nov	water every two weeks	
Dec	water every two weeks	

Anemone

WINDFLOWER

FEATURES

Anemones are a large genus with lots of excellent woodland plants like *Anemone ranunculoides*. It is a spreading perennial growing about 4in high, and 18in wide, with yellow flowers in spring. Other good woodland-type anemones include the white *A. nemorosa*, slightly shorter and it does not spread quite as far. Most of the other anemones are more strikingly obvious, like the dark pink *A. hupehensis* which grows 2ft high or more. The Japanese anemone, *A. hupehensis japonica*, has striking white flowers. It lasts well into the fall.

CONDITIONS

ASPECT	*Anemone ranunculoides* needs a rather shady position, as if growing in an open woodland. Some shade during the day is necessary.
SITE	The soil should be dampish, and definitely not hot, dry, and free-draining. Adding well-rotted organic matter should aid moisture retention, and improve and feed the soil.

GROWING METHOD

PROPAGATION	Divide the rhizomes in the spring, or in the fall when the leaves have dropped. One mature plant should yield plenty of new vigorous plants.

FEEDING	Apply a slow-release fertilizer in the spring. This should ensure a spectacular flower display through the season.
PROBLEMS	The most typical problem comes from hungry slugs. They can ruin the foliage and new shoots. Spreading sharp sand or gravel round the plants keeps slugs away.

FLOWERING

SEASON	*A. ranunculoides* flowers in the spring.
CUTTING	It makes good cut flowers.

PRUNING

GENERAL	No pruning is necessary.

ANEMONES COME IN just about all the colors of the rainbow, with various shades of red, pink, mauve, blue, and yellow. There are species, such as Anemone ranunculoides, that enjoy a partially shaded position and are therefore perfect for woodland areas of the garden.

AT A GLANCE	
Anemone ranunculoides is a spring-flowering woodland plant with a good spread. There is a double form. Hardy to 5°F (zone 7).	

		Recommended Varieties
Jan	/	*Anemone blanda*
Feb	/	"Radar"
Mar	/	"White Star"
April	foliage	*A. hupehensis*
May	flowering	"Hadspen Abundance"
June	foliage	"Bressingham Glow"
July	foliage	*A. x hybrida*
Aug	foliage	"Honorine Jobert"
Sept	foliage	*A. ranunculoides*
Oct	/	
Nov	/	
Dec	/	

Anemone x hybrida

WINDFLOWER (ANEMONE X HYBRIDA, SYN. A. HUPEHENSIS VAR. JAPONICA)

FEATURES

Also known as the Japanese windflower, this herbaceous perennial is one of the great joys of the fall garden. The leaves are three-lobed, somewhat maple-like, and the single or double flowers are carried on stems up to 39in high. Flowers may be single or double-colored white, pale, or deep pink. Once established, they spread into large clumps quite rapidly, traveling by underground stems, and also self-seeding. Some consider them invasive, but plants can be easily dug out and a mass-planting in full bloom is a real delight. Grow where they can remain undisturbed for some years. Site at the back of a shady bed or in dappled sunlight under trees.

CONDITIONS

ASPECT	Prefers shade or semi-shade with shelter from strong winds.
SITE	Grows best in well-drained soil that contains plenty of organic matter.

GROWING METHOD

PROPAGATION	Increase from root cuttings in the winter, or divide established clumps in early spring, ensuring that each division has a thick set of roots. This vigorous plant can sometimes be tricky to divide and transplant. Replant the new, vigorous younger growths from the outside of the clump, generally about 12in apart.

New young plants require ample watering in prolonged dry spells during the growing season.

FEEDING	Fertilizing is not essential, but a complete plant food can be applied in the spring.
PROBLEMS	No specific problems are known.

FLOWERING

SEASON	Flowers appear prolifically from late summer through the fall months.
CUTTING	Though they seem perfect for cut-flower displays, the flowers do not last that well.

AFTER FLOWERING

REQUIREMENTS	Cut back spent flower stems to ground level once they begin to fade, and cut the plant right back to the ground in late fall.

RELIABLE IN BLOOM year after year, the Japanese anemone is an attractive garden addition that softens stiff, geometric schemes.

AT A GLANCE	
This is a free-flowering, quick-spreading herbaceous perennial with lovely, pale pink flowers. Hardy to 5°F (zone 7).	

Jan	/	**Recommended Varieties**
Feb	/	*Anemone x hybrida*
Mar	divide	"Honorine Jobert"
Apr	transplant	"Konigin Charlotte"
May	/	"Luise Uhink"
Jun	/	"Margarete"
July	/	"Pamina"
Aug	flowering	"Richard Ahrends"
Sept	flowering	
Oct	sow	
Nov	/	
Dec	/	

Anguloa

TULIP ORCHID

FEATURES

This fascinating orchid—known as the tulip orchid due to its tulip-shaped flower—has another common name, cradle orchid. This names describes the lip inside the cup-shaped flower which rocks back and forth when the bloom is tipped. The genus *Anguloa* is closely related to the *lycastes* with which they can interbreed, making an *Angulocaste*. The species originate from Colombia, Venezuela, and Peru and are mainly terrestrial plants. Large, broad leaves are produced in the summer months from the new growth, but in the fall these die off as the plant goes into its deciduous rest for winter. Its dark green pseudobulbs will then lie dormant until the following spring. Another feature of this genus is that the long-lasting flowers are strongly scented, often similar to a liniment fragrance.

CONDITIONS

CLIMATE	The anguloas need cool conditions with a winter minimum of 50°F, and summer maximum of 86°F.
ASPECT	Due to the soft, annual leaves, shade is required in the summer.
POTTING MIX	A medium grade bark is ideal with some finer grade bark or peat mixed in.

GROWING METHOD

PROPAGATION	It is quite a slow growing orchid, often making just one pseudobulb a year, so will not increase in size enough to divide easily. Back bulbs will sometimes re-grow if removed and potted up separately.

WATERING	While the plant is in its winter rest, and is leafless, the compost should be kept dry. Watering can be resumed at the start of the new growth in spring. While it has leaves the plant should not dry out. In the fall the new pseudobulb will have been completed and the leaves will turn brown and drop off. Stop watering the plant at this point.
FEEDING	Plants will benefit from regular feeding while in growth so that the new pseudobulb can develop in the short growing season.
PROBLEMS	As long as the compost is kept dry during winter then no problems should occur. Avoid water collecting inside new growth.

FLOWERING SEASON

Late spring to early summer.

AT A GLANCE	
Better for the experienced grower. The flowers last a long time and are hightly scented. Will reach 24in.	
Jan rest	**Recommended Varieties**
Feb rest	*A. cliftonii* (yellow with
Mar water and feed	red markings)
Apr water and feed	*A. clowesii*
May flowering, water	*A. uniflora* (white)
and feed	*A. virginalis*
Jun flowering, water	
and feed	
July water and feed	
Aug water and feed	
Sept water and feed	
Oct rest	
Nov rest	
Dec rest	

Anise Hyssop

AGASTACHE FOENICULUM

FEATURES

Anise hyssop, or agastache, is a perennial herb, similar to mint in appearance, but with a somewhat neater, clump-forming habit, and growing to about 2–3ft. The mid-green, nettle-shaped leaves have an aniseed scent. Long spikes of purple flowers, attractive to bees and butterflies, are produced from mid summer onward. A native of North America, it is not quite as hardy as the better known European members of the mint family. Although perennial, it tends to be short-lived and is best propagated every year, or at least every three years.

CONDITIONS

ASPECT   Anise hyssop needs full sun (although it may tolerate a little light shade in mild areas) and shelter from cold winds. It may need winter protection if the temperature drops below about 23°F.

SITE   It grows best in a rich, moisture-retentive soil, although it will grow in most garden soils if given a sunny position.

GROWING METHOD

SOWING   Anise hyssop can easily be propagated by division in spring and also by seed and cuttings. The seeds need warmth to germinate and are best sown under glass in spring. Germination takes approximately 10–20 days.

PLANTING   Prick out the seedlings when they are large enough to handle and plant out in mid spring at about 18in apart. Seed can also be sown outdoors in fall when the soil is warm, but the young plants will need winter protection. Cuttings can be taken in mid to late summer, and the rooted cuttings can be overwintered in a greenhouse or cold frame and then planted out in spring.

FEEDING   Do not allow to dry out. Keep well watered in summer. Mulch lightly in spring and fall and apply a balanced general fertilizer in spring.

PROBLEMS   Anise hyssop rarely suffers from pests or disease, except that seedlings may damp off and the plants may suffer from mildew in hot summers.

PRUNING   Cut back old flowerheads and woody growth in fall to keep plants compact and to prevent them becoming straggly.

HARVESTING

PICKING   Pick the young leaves just before the plant flowers. Cut flowers just as they are beginning to open.

STORAGE   Dry leaves in a cool, airy space and store in dark, airtight, glass jars.

FREEZING   Freeze leaves for up to 6 months.

AT A GLANCE		
A perennial herb, very similar to mint in appearance, and with a refreshing aniseed flavour. Hardy to 14°F (zones 8-9).		
Jan	/	Parts used
Feb	/	Leaves
Mar	plant	Flowers
Apr	plant	**Uses**
May	plant harvest	Culinary
Jun	harvest	Craft
July	plant harvest	Gardening
Aug	plant harvest	
Sept	plant	
Oct	/	
Nov	/	
Dec	/	

USES

CULINARY
The leaves can be used to make a refreshing aniseed-flavoured tea. They can also be used, like borage, in summer fruit cups, and can be added to salads and used as a seasoning, particularly in savoury pork and rice dishes. The flowers will add color to salads and fruit cups.

CRAFT
The scented leaves of anise hyssop can be used in pot-pourri.

GARDENING
Anise hyssop is an excellent bee herb. Attractive white-flowered varieties, "Alabaster" and "Alba," are also available.

Anomatheca

SYN. LAPEIROUSIA LAXA

FEATURES

Occasionally known as scarlet freesia, this pretty little plant is trouble-free and most rewarding in the garden. It multiplies readily from seed sown in spring. The trumpet-shaped flowers are pale scarlet with darker markings. They appear in mid-summer and are followed by seed pods which split open to expose red seeds. The slightly stiff, ribbed, sword-shaped leaves grow about 6–8in high while the flowers are held on spikes which extend well above the foliage. There is a pure white cultivar, "Alba," but this is not nearly as vigorous as the species. *Anomatheca viridis* has unusual green flowers and is normally grown as an indoor plant, flowering in early spring.

CONDITIONS

ASPECT   Grows happily in full sun or partial shade.
SITE   This bulb is very useful for the front of borders, or for growing in pots for the patio or in the house or conservatory. Ideally, soil should be well drained but it need not be rich.

GROWING METHOD

PLANTING   Plant corms about 2in deep and 4in apart in spring.
FEEDING   Supplementary feeding is generally not needed, but on poor soils a balanced fertilizer can be applied after planting. Plants in containers should be given a liquid feed every 14 days throughout the growing season.

In very dry springs, water occasionally once plants have started into growth.
PROBLEMS   No specific pest or disease problems are known for this plant.

FLOWERING

SEASON   Flowers generally appear in mid-summer.
CUTTING   This is not a good choice as a cut flower.

AFTER FLOWERING

REQUIREMENTS   Cut off faded flower stems immediately after flowering if you do not want seed to set. In warm gardens the corms can be left in the ground, but in cooler areas they are better lifted in the fall and stored for replanting next spring.

THE OPEN-FACED, trumpet-shaped flowers resemble those of freesias, and are carried on slender spikes above the foliage.

AT A GLANCE	
A graceful, pretty bulb with sprays of trumpet-shaped flowers. Reasonably hardy in most areas.	
Jan /	**Recommended Varieties**
Feb /	*Anomatheca laxa*
Mar /	"Alba"
Apr plant	"Joan Evans"
May /	*Anomatheca viridis*
Jun /	
July flowering	
Aug flowering	
Sept flowering	
Oct /	
Nov /	
Dec /	

Anthemis tinctoria

OX-EYE CHAMOMILE

FEATURES

With ferny foliage and bright yellow daisy flowers, Anthemis tinctoria makes a striking and easy-care groundcover. The plant may grow up to 3ft high and spread by the same amount. The floral display is long lasting: it should be around through late spring and summer. There are a number of named cultivars available. This is a vigorous plant that may sometimes need restraining, although it never gets totally out of hand. Ox-eye chamomile plants need renewing every two or three years but they are easy to propagate. An alternative common name for this plant is dyer's chamomile, because the flowers yield a distinctive yellow dye.

CONDITIONS

ASPECT   Must have full sun all day for best flowering. Keep it well out of the shade.

SITE   Soil should be well drained but need not be rich. A. tinctoria will tolerate quite poor soil.

GROWING CONDITIONS

PROPAGATION   The one big problem with A. tinctoria is that it has quite a short shelf-life. Either prune (see below) or regularly grow new young plants from divisions. Divide plants in the spring or the fall, making sure each section has good roots. You can also increase your stock by taking cuttings in the spring.

FEEDING   Fertilize lightly with blood and bone, poultry manure or complete plant food in early spring.

PROBLEMS   No specific problems are known.

FLOWERING

SEASON   Flowering right through the summer.

CUTTING   Flowers can be picked for posies.

PRUNING

GENERAL   Prune flowers as they fade to prolong blooming. This also forces plants to develop new strong growths which prolong their lifespan. Also note that plants can be cut back at any time during the growing season if they need restricting.

THE LONG FLOWERING PERIOD, pretty foliage and ease of maintenance make A. tinctoria *a good choice for busy gardeners.*

AT A GLANCE		
Anthemis tinctoria gives both decent cover and a fine array of yellow flowers at the height of summer. Hardy to 0°F (zone 7).		
Jan	/	**Recommended Varieties**
Feb	/	*Anthemis*
Mar	/	"Grallagh Gold"
April	/	*A. punctata cupaniana*
May	foliage	*A. tinctoria*
June	flowering	"Alba"
July	flowering	"E. C. Buxton"
Aug	flowering	"Kelwayi"
Sept	foliage	"Sauce Hollandaise"
Oct	foliage	"Wargrave Variety"
Nov	/	
Dec	/	

Antirrhinum

SNAPDRAGON

FEATURES

Antirrhinums fall into three groups: tall varieties up to 4ft for cutting; intermediates for bedding, 18in; dwarf varieties for edging/containers, 12in. Color range is wide, and includes bicolors and doubles. Flowers of older varieties open when squeezed at the sides, hence the name "snapdragon." Grow as a half-hardy annual. Available as young plants.

CONDITIONS

ASPECT	Must be in full sunlight all day.
SITE	Soil must be very well-drained but have plenty of rotted compost or manure dug in before planting. In containers, use multipurpose compost and ensure good, free drainage.

GROWING METHOD

SOWING	Sow in February/March and barely cover the very fine seed. Use $3^1/2$in pots of multipurpose compost and keep in light at 64˚F. Seedlings appear after a week and can be transplanted to cell trays when two young leaves have developed. Plant outside after hardening off, following the last frosts, 6–18in apart, depending upon the variety. Those grown for bedding purposes should have the growing tip pinched out when 6in tall to encourage bushy growth.
FEEDING	Liquid-feed plants in beds with a handheld feeder fortnightly. Mix slow-release fertilizer with container compost before planting up.

PROBLEMS

Seedlings are prone to "damping off," so water the pots with a copper-based fungicide. Plants suffer with rust disease. Grow a resistant variety such as "Monarch Mixed" or use a spray containing penconazole at regular intervals.

FLOWERING

SEASON	Flowers appear all summer and should be removed as they fade to keep buds coming.
CUTTING	Tall varieties are excellent as cut spikes.

AFTER FLOWERING

GENERAL	Pull plants up when they are over.

DWARF VARIETIES reaching just 6in are colorful for bed edges and have bushy growth without the need for pinching out.

AT A GLANCE	
A half-hardy annual grown for tubular flowers, used for containers, bedding displays, and cutting. Frost hardy to 32˚F (zone 10).	
Jan /	**Recommended Varieties**
Feb sow	*Antirrhinum majus*
Mar sow	**For containers**
Apr grow on	"Lipstick Silver"
May plant	"Magic Carpet Mixed"
Jun flowering	"Tom Thumb Mixed"
July flowering	**For bedding**
Aug flowering	"Brighton Rock Mixed"
Sept flowering	"Corona Mixed"
Oct /	"Sonnet Mixed"
Nov /	**For cutting**
Dec /	"Liberty Mixed"

Aporocactus

RAT'S TAIL CACTUS

FEATURES

A good group of cacti with its botanical name in dispute; this is now classified as *Aporocactus*. These lovely, epiphytic plants are native to rainforests or damp mountainous areas of tropical and subtropical regions of the Americas where they grow from the branches of trees. Their stems are mainly jointed and flattened, tending to be long and narrow with few if any spines. They are pendulous and branching, bearing scarlet or pink flowers on the tips of the branches in late spring or early summer. These plants are delightful when grown in pots or hanging baskets which can be used for indoor decoration while the cactus is in flower. Where temperatures fall below 50°F they should be grown in a glasshouse.

VARIETIES

The two most commonly found plants are *Aporocactus flagelliformis* and *A. martianus*. The latter has larger flowers than the former. Appearing in early summer, they are vivid red on gray-green stems. The plant only grows to 5in high, but can spread up to 3ft. *A. flagelliformis* is easier to grow. Its hanging growth may reach 5ft. Its purple-red blooms appear in spring when it makes a terrific sight with its snake-like stems topped by the colorful flowers.

CONDITIONS

ASPECT   Being epiphytic, the plants need to be grown with some degree of shade during the day. It is particularly important during the hottest, brightest part of the day. A morning of sun, and afternoon of shade is fine.

SITE   Grow in special epiphytic compost. Make sure that it is extremely free-draining.

GROWING METHOD

PROPAGATION   Plants can be grown from seed sown in spring, but are easier to grow from stem cuttings taken in spring or summer.

FEEDING   From late spring until late summer, provide a high potash or tomato feed once a month. Exceeding this dose is counter productive.

PROBLEMS   Will not thrive in full sun or if overwatered.

FLOWERING

SEASON   Rat's tail cactuses will flower either in late spring or early summer.

FRUITS   Flowers are followed by papery fruits.

APOROCACTUS FLAGELLI IS ONE of the most common types to be found and is quite easy to grow, it's colorful purple-red blooms adding a touch of vibrant color.

AT A GLANCE	
Dramatic cactuses for a hanging basket, with long trailing stems and bright showy flowers. 43°F min (zone 11).	
Jan /	**Recommended Varieties**
Feb /	*Aporocactus flagelliformis*
Mar transplant	*A. martianus*
Apr repotting	**Companion Plants**
May flowering	Epiphyllum
Jun flowering	Hatiora
July /	Schlumbergera
Aug /	Selenicereus
Sept /	
Oct /	
Nov sow	
Dec /	

Aquilegia

COLUMBINE

FEATURES

These old-fashioned favorites, also called granny's bonnets, give a fine display in the garden and make decorative cut flowers. The foliage is often blue-green, and the flowers come in single colors—white, pink, crimson, yellow, and blue—and combinations of pastel and brighter shades. There are also excellent black and whites ("Magpie"). The older forms have short-spurred flowers that resemble old-fashioned bonnets, especially "Nora Barlow," a good double which is a mix of red, pink, and green. Modern hybrids are long spurred, and available in many single colors and bicolors. Plants may be 16–28in high. Columbines are not long lived but are easily seed grown. Ideal for the dappled garden, grow them under deciduous trees and in borders.

CONDITIONS

ASPECT   Prefers semi-shade, and thrives in woodland gardens, but full sun is not a problem.

SITE   Needs well-drained soil that contains plenty of organic matter.

GROWING METHOD

PROPAGATION   Clumps are actually quite hard to divide, but it can be done, the fall being the best time. Columbine also grows from seed sown in early spring, or in the fall. Self-sown plants are hardy, but note that they may not always be true to type. Space plants about 12in apart. New young plants must not be allowed to dry out in prolonged dry spells in the spring and summer months. Keep a careful watch.

FEEDING   Apply complete plant food in the spring as the new growth begins to emerge.

PROBLEMS   No particular pest or disease problems are known for this plant.

FLOWERING

SEASON   There is a long flowering period from mid-spring to mid-summer.

CUTTING   Flower stems can be cut for the vase, and they make an attractive display, but the garden show lasts considerably longer.

AFTER FLOWERING

REQUIREMENTS   Spent flower stems can either be removed or left on the plants enabling the seeds to mature. Cut back the old growth to ground level as it dies off.

AN OPEN WOODLAND SETTING is ideal for columbines, letting them freely self-seed forming, bold, distinctive groups.

AT A GLANCE		
A clump-forming perennial, happy in semi-shade, perfect for the cottage garden where it freely self-seeds. Hardy to 5°F (zone 7).		
Jan	/	Recommended Varieties
Feb	/	*Aquilegia bertolonii*
Mar	sow	*A. canadensis*
Apr	transplant	*A. flabellata*
May	flowering	*A. f. var. pumila*
Jun	flowering	*A. f. var. f. alba*
July	/	"Henson Harebell"
Aug	/	"Magpie"
Sept	divide	Music series
Oct	sow	*A. vulgaris*
Nov	/	"Nora Barlow"
Dec	/	

Arabis caucasica

ROCK CRESS

FEATURES

Of the many species of rock cress, this is probably the most commonly grown. It spreads to form mats of leafy rosettes and will grow to around 6in high. This vigorous plant may spread to 1ft. It can be grown in rockeries, between paving stones or as a border plant. Flowers are produced over a long season from late winter into summer. They are white in the species but there is a pink form and also a double white variety, "Flore Pleno." There are a number of other named cultivars. *Arabis caucasica* is related to stock as is obvious from the flowers, and it has the fragrance associated with stocks.

CONDITIONS

ASPECT	Needs full sun.
SITE	Soil must be very well drained but need not be rich. Add lime or dolomite to very acid soils before planting. Heavy soils must be broken up with sharp grit and sand.

GROWING METHOD

PROPAGATION	Make divisions of an existing clump in the fall or spring. Generally, though, it is often easier to leave plants where they are and then to propagate from cuttings taken in the summer.
FEEDING	Apply a light dressing of complete plant food in spring.

PROBLEMS

Avoid overwatering and make sure these plants are situated where air circulation is good. Plants can collapse in warm, moist conditions but this is extremely unlikely to occur in our climate.

FLOWERING

SEASON	The brief but eyecatching display happens in spring with the warm weather.
CUTTING	Flowers can be picked for posies if the stems are long enough.

PRUNING

GENERAL	Can be cut back hard once after blooming.

THIS DOUBLE WHITE FORM of rock cress closely resembles its relative, the stock. The light fragrance is reminiscent of stock too.

AT A GLANCE	
Arabis caucasica is a white-flowering evergreen perennial best grown in walls. It can be quite invasive. Hardy to 0°F (zone 7).	
Jan foliage	**Recommended Varieties**
Feb foliage	*Arabis* x *arendsii*
Mar foliage	"Rosabella"
April foliage	*A. blepharophylla*
May flowering	"Fruhlingszauber"
June foliage	*A. bryoides*
July foliage	*A. caucasica*
Aug foliage	"Flore Pleno"
Sept foliage	"Variegata"
Oct foliage	"Variegata"
Nov foliage	
Dec foliage	

Arctotis

AFRICAN DAISY

FEATURES

African daisy is a perennial grown as a half-hardy annual for its flowers in shades of pink, red, yellow, gold, white, and even blue, often with darker center. Plants reach 18in in height and have attractive silvery leaves. Use in bedding or as a container plant. Flowers are good for cutting.

CONDITIONS

ASPECT Must have full sun all day long for the flowers to stay open and give the best display, so choose a south-facing border, patio or bank.

SITE Soil must be well-drained but moisture-retentive, so work in rotted compost before planting. In containers use multipurpose compost and ensure drainage by adding a 2in layer of gravel or polystyrene chunks.

GROWING METHOD

SOWING Sow in February/March in small pots of multipurpose compost, just covering the seed, and keep at 64°F. Seedlings appear in 2–3 weeks and are transplanted individually into 3^{1}/2in pots. Grow on, harden off at the end of May before planting after frosts, spacing plants 12–18in apart.

FEEDING Extra feeding is rarely necessary but container-grown plants benefit from liquid feed every two weeks. Avoid getting the compost too wet, especially in cooler, wet spells.

PROBLEMS Grows poorly on heavy, badly drained soils. Plants in containers must receive full sun.

FLOWERING

SEASON Flowers from early summer onwards.

CUTTING A useful but short-lived cut flower.

AFTER FLOWERING

GENERAL Pot up before frosts and keep dry and frost-free over winter. Take and root cuttings in spring.

AFRICAN DAISIES should be pinched out when they are 5in tall to encourage branching and masses of summer flowers.

AT A GLANCE	
A half-hardy annual grown for its flowers, used in bedding, containers and as a cut flower. Frost hardy to 32°F (zone 10) .	
Jan /	**Recommended Varieties**
Feb sow	*Arctotis hybrida*
Mar sow	"Harlequin"
Apr transplant	"Special Hybrids Mixed"
May transplant	"Treasure Chest"
Jun flowering	"T&M Hybrids"
July flowering	*Arctotis hirsuta*
Aug flowering	*Arctotis venusta*
Sept flowering	
Oct /	
Nov /	
Dec /	

Aristolochia
DUTCHMAN'S PIPE

FEATURES

Aristolochia macrophylla is a deciduous climber from the south-east USA. It has very unusual pipe- or siphon-shaped flowers in summer. These are green, strikingly marked with brown, purple and yellow. The foliage is also very attractive so the plant looks good all through spring and summer. It is a strong grower and in good conditions can reach a height of 30ft, but in some gardens it may be considerably less. Another aristolochia is *A. littoralis*, which can only be grown in a warm greenhouse or conservatory. You will need plenty of space to grow Dutchman's pipe, such as a high wall or fence.

CONDITIONS

ASPECT   This climber will grow well in full sun or partial shade.
SITE   The soil should be well-drained and reasonably rich. Even a dryish soil is suitable.

GROWING METHOD

PROPAGATION Sow seeds in spring and germinate at 61°F. Take softwood cuttings in summer.
WATERING   Only apply water if the soil is drying out in the summer. It likes to be on the dry side throughout the winter.
FEEDING   Do not over-feed, as this is a naturally vigorous climber. A slow-release organic fertilizer applied each spring will be sufficient.

PROBLEMS   Not usually troubled by pests or diseases.

FLOWERING/FOLIAGE

FLOWERS   Grown mainly for its flowers but unfortunately they are inclined to be obscured from view by the plant's lush foliage.
FOLIAGE   The large, heart shaped, deep green leaves are very attractive.

PRUNING

REQUIREMENTS This climber can either be spur pruned in early spring, or simply trimmed in spring to keep it within bounds, but eventually it will need thinning or renovation pruning.

ARISTOLOCHIA FLOWERS are strangely beautiful and intriguing objects. They might need to be encouraged from under the dense foliage.

AT A GLANCE	
An exotic-looking climber with bizarre flowers and attractive heart-shaped leaves. Hardy to 23°F (zone 9).	
Jan /	**Companion Plants**
Feb /	It needs an equally vigorous
Mar /	companion. For a long period of
Apr planting	interest, try it with wisteria, which
May planting	flowers before aristolochia, in spring.
Jun flowering	
July flowering	
Aug flowering	
Sep /	
Oct /	
Nov /	
Dec /	

Armeria maritima

SEA THRIFT

FEATURES

Also known as sea thrift, this evergreen perennial grows in little grassy mounds 2–5in high. It occurs naturally in northern Europe and around the Mediterranean, often in very exposed situations, including cliff tops. The rounded flowerheads are carried above the foliage on stems 6–12in high. Flowers vary in color in the species and may be white, pink, or almost red, and there are a number of named cultivars available. Thrift can be used as a groundcover or edging plant, or can be planted in rockeries, on dry walls, or in poor soil where few other plants will survive. It also makes a good container plant.

CONDITIONS

ASPECT   Needs full sun all day. Thrift tolerates dry, windy conditions and salt spray, and is an excellent choice for coastal gardens.

SITE   Grows in any kind of soil so long as it is very well drained. Adding sharp sand will improve the drainage.

GROWING METHOD

PROPAGATION   Divide established clumps in the spring and replant about 6–8in apart. The species can be grown from seed sown in the spring, or from semi-ripe cuttings taken in the summer

FEEDING   Give a light dressing of complete fertilizer in early spring.

PROBLEMS

PROBLEMS   Thrift has a tendency to rot if soils are in any way too heavy, poorly drained, or overwatered. In humid weather and in sheltered positions it may also be susceptible to the fungal disease which is called rust. Use a fungicide to attack the problem.

FLOWERING

SEASON   Thrift has a long flowering period through spring and summer, provided the plants are deadheaded regularly.

CUTTING   Makes a good cut flower.

AFTER FLOWERING

REQUIREMENTS   Regularly remove spent flower stems to give a prolonged flowering period.

ARMERIA MARITIMA is known as "sea pink" in its natural habitat where it forms dense mounds on exposed sea cliffs.

AT A GLANCE	
A. maritima is an attractive evergreen, clump-forming perennial which colonizes inhospitable areas. Hardy to 0°F (zone 7).	
Jan /	**Recommended Varieties**
Feb /	*Armeria maritima*
Mar division	"Alba"
Apr /	"Corsica"
May transplant	"Launcheana"
Jun flowering	"Ruby Glow"
July flowering	"Splendens"
Aug flowering	"Vindictive"
Sept /	
Oct /	
Nov /	
Dec /	

Aspasia

ASPASIA SPECIES

FEATURES

This is a compact and flowering orchid perfect for the beginner. Aspasias are a small group of orchids, the genus containing only about ten different species. These originate from the tropical Americas, and are found growing from Nicaragua to Brazil over quite a widespread area. Although not a common orchid, it is actually quite easy to grow, increasing freely in size and producing flowers regularly and easily. Its habit is fairly compact, the height of the soft-leafed pseudobulbs reaching only around 6in, making it ideal for a small collection. Due to its naturally epiphytic nature, the plant has a creeping habit with an elongated rhizome connecting the pseudobulbs. This means that it quickly outgrows pots and is in need of annual re-potting. However, with orchids that have a tendency to do this, the plant is often happier out of the pot than in it.

CONDITIONS

CLIMATE	Slightly cold sensitive so prefers a minimum temperature of 54°F in winter, up to 86°F in summer.
ASPECT	Has pale, soft leaves so a little shade in summer will prevent paling or scorching.
POTTING MIX	A medium grade general bark potting mix.

GROWING METHOD

PROPAGATION	This orchid readily produces new growths and so multiplies quite quickly. Therefore, the plant can be divided every few years if required but will do well to be left alone to grow into a specimen plant, which will produce many flowers at once.

WATERING	The plant does not always follow a strict seasonal pattern so keep it simple by watering more frequently only when in active growth and reducing this to a minimum when not.
FEEDING	Use a higher nitrogen feed when applying in the growing season, a weak solution every two to three waterings.
PROBLEMS	If cultural conditions are suitable then it should have no specific problems.

FLOWERING SEASON

Varies but mostly spring and summer. Flower buds emerge from the base of the new growth and stay around plant's base.

AT A GLANCE		
Easy to grow. Compact, attractive plant up to 5in high. Flowers, often in succession, $1\frac{1}{4}$in across.		
Jan	rest	**Recommended Varieties**
Feb	rest	A. epidendroides (brown
Mar	flowering, water and feed	petals with a purple and white lip)
Apr	flowering, water and feed	A. lunata
May	flowering, water and feed	
Jun	flowering, water and feed	
July	flowering, water and feed	
Aug	flowering, water and feed	
Sept	water and feed	
Oct	rest	
Nov	rest	
Dec	rest	

Aster

MICHAELMAS DAISY

FEATURES

There is a wide variety of asters, and all of them flower in late summer and the fall. The most commonly grown is *A. novi-belgii*, which has a range of cultivars from dwarf forms 10in high to tall varieties reaching 39in. Flowers are blue, violet, pink, red, or white, and all are good for cutting. *A. ericoides* has very small leaves and produces stems of white flowers up to 39in high. *A.* x *frikartii* grows about 30in tall and has violet-blue flowers. All of these plants are extremely easy to grow and tolerate a wide range of conditions. They multiply readily. Taller varieties need staking.

CONDITIONS

ASPECT   Grows best in full sun. Tolerates light shade, but blooming may not be so prolific and growth will be less compact.

SITE   Add well-rotted organic matter to the soil. Feed and water well to counter disease.

GROWING METHOD

PROPAGATION   Divide clumps in late winter. These plants are prolific growers—one plant will multiply itself tenfold in a season. Replant divisions 8in apart. The best results are from regular watering during the spring and summer, especially in long, dry periods.

FEEDING   Apply complete plant food in early spring.

PROBLEMS

PROBLEMS   Powdery mildew can be a major problem, especially with varieties of *A. novi-belgii*. Mildew-resistant varieties include *A.* x *frikartii* and varieties of *A. amellus*.

FLOWERING

SEASON   The long flowering display lasts from late summer into the fall.

CUTTING   Cut flowers last very well if given a frequent change of water.

AFTER FLOWERING

REQUIREMENTS   Cut off spent flower stems close to ground level after blooming. Plants will gradually die back, but should not need more close attention until new growth appears in the next spring.

ASTERS MAKE A GREAT SHOW even though their season isn't very long. Don't plant them in the same bed two years running.

AT A GLANCE		
Hardy perennials creating large clumps, giving strong fall color in most situations. Hardy to 5°F (zone 7).		
Jan	/	**Recommended Varieties**
Feb	sow	*Aster alpinus*
Mar	sow	*A. amellus*
Apr	divide	"Framfieldii"
May	transplant	"Jacqueline Genebrier"
Jun	/	"Coombe Fishacre"
July	flowering	*A. ericoides*
Aug	flowering	"Golden Spray"
Sept	flowering	*A.* x *frikartii*
Oct	divide	"Monch"
Nov	/	*A. novae-angliae*
Dec	/	*A. novi-belgii*
		"Audrey"

Astilbe hybrids

ASTILBE

FEATURES

These perennial hybrids revel in moist soil and light shade, although they can be grown in an open, sunny position if well watered. The shiny, compound leaves are quite attractive, with astilbe also bearing tall plumes of soft flowers 20in or more tall, in shades of pink, red, mauve, or white. They look best when mass-planted, and are ideal for surrounding ponds, or naturalizing in a wild garden. They can be used as cut flowers, but they are probably best left in the yard where their big, theatrical effect can be enjoyed for much longer. They can quickly flag in a heat wave; water at the first sign of wilting.

CONDITIONS

ASPECT These are versatile plants, performing equally well in bright sunlight and dappled shade.

SITE The ideal soil is rich in organic matter and retains plenty of moisture. Regular, heavy applications of mulch are essential.

GROWING METHOD

PROPAGATION Divide clumps in late fall, ensuring that each division has a crown and a decent set of roots. Plant at 8–10in spacings. New, young plants need plenty of water in prolonged dry spells in the spring and summer months. Do not let them dry out.

FEEDING Apply a general fertilizer as growth starts in the spring, and repeat 6–8 weeks later.

PROBLEMS No specific problems are known.

FLOWERING

SEASON Flowers from late spring through the summer. The flower display is longer lasting in a cooler summer.

CUTTING Flowers can be cut for indoor decoration.

AFTER FLOWERING

REQUIREMENTS Spent flowerheads will turn a pleasant rich brown color, and are quite attractive through the winter months. They add considerable interest to the yard. Do not cut back spent flower stems to ground level until the following spring.

SOFT AND FEATHERY, the pale pink plumes on this astilbe will provide a long display of bright flowers and fern-like foliage.

AT A GLANCE		
A rhizomatous perennial that enjoys damp soil. Striking, tall flowerheads can reach 4ft tall. Hardy to 5°F (zone 7).		
Jan	/	**Recommended Varieties**
Feb	sow	*Astilbe* x *arendsii*
Mar	divide	"Brautschleier"
Apr	transplant	"Bronce Elegans"
May	flowering	"Fanal"
Jun	flowering	"Irrlicht"
July	flowering	"Snowdrift"
Aug	flowering	*A.* x *crispa*
Sept	flowering	"Perkeo"
Oct	/	"Rheinland"
Nov	divide	*A. simplicifolia*
Dec	/	"Sprite"

Astrantia major

MASTERWORT

FEATURES

Also known as masterwort, *Astrantia major* is a "must-have" for the "cottage garden," a clump-forming perennial that produces delightful sprays of green or pink, sometimes reddish flowers, surrounded by green-veined white bracts. A native of central Europe, it grows about 24in tall, forming clumps 18in wide. Flowering in early and mid-summer, it can be left to colonize areas of dappled shade, though it also enjoys full sunlight. There are some excellent cultivars, including the new "Hadspen Blood," a striking blood red, "Shaggy" with long bracts, and "Sunningdale Variegated," with pale pink bracts and yellow/ cream leaves. Best in large clumps.

CONDITIONS

ASPECT
Thrives in either dappled shade or a more open, sunny position.

SOIL
Likes compost-rich, moist, fertile soil, though it will tolerate drier conditions. Woodland gardens and streamsides are ideal.

GROWING METHOD

PROPAGATION
Can either be grown from seed sown in late summer, once ripe, or by division in the spring. Plant out at least 18in apart, or closer for an immediate covering. Do not let young plants begin to dry out in a prolonged dry spring or summer spell. The variants do not require such moist conditions, and will tolerate drier soil.

FEEDING
Lay a mulch around the plants in the spring. This has two advantages: it enriches the soil and also prevents moisture loss.

PROBLEMS
Slugs can be a major problem, attacking the stems and foliage. Pick off when seen. Powdery mildew can also strike; spray against attacks.

FLOWERING

SEASON
The one flowering spell is in early and mid-summer.

CUTTING
Makes good cut flowers, which can be used to soften a stiff, structural arrangement, or as part of a more flowery display.

AFTER FLOWERING

REQUIREMENTS Cut down the spent flower stems, and tidy up the foliage.

AT A GLANCE	
A. major is a clump-forming perennial grown for its abundant, attractive flowers. Excellent cultivars. Hardy to 0°F (zones 6–7).	
Jan /	**Recommended Varieties**
Feb /	*Astrantia major alba*
Mar divide	"Claret"
Apr divide	"Hadspen Blood"
May transplant	*A. m. involucrata*
Jun flowering	"Shaggy"
July flowering	*A. m. rosea*
Aug sowing	*A. m. rubra*
Sept /	"Sunningdale Variegated"
Oct /	
Nov /	
Dec /	

Astrophytum

BISHOP'S CAP

FEATURES

This very small genus originates in Texas and Mexico. The two most sought-after species are virtually spineless and covered in white scales instead. The bishop's cap or bishop's mitre, *Astrophytum myriostigma*, has an unusual dull purple, bluish, or green body that is speckled all over with white scales. In the wild it may be 2ft high and 8in across, but in cultivation it is unlikely to reach melon size—and then only after many years. Its flowers are bright yellow, with the outer petals black tipped. A. asterias, known as the sea urchin or sand dollar cactus, is gray-green, slow growing and rarely more than 2–3in high, eventually growing to a width of about 4in. It has spectacular bright yellow flowers with deep red centers.

VARIETIES

A. ornatum has pronounced spines on its very well-defined ribs. It is a cylindrical shape and it grows to about 1ft. During the summer it produces yellow flower. There are many different varieties and hybrids of these popular and attractive species. If you are just starting a collection of astrophytum, it is well worth growing *A. capricorne*, known as the goat's horn cactus. It is quite a small cactus, reaching a height of only about 8in. Its common name was inspired by the bizarre form of its twisted spines which wrap themselves around the cactus instead of sticking up vertically in the usual way. This makes handling the plant quite a problem as its spines tend to get snapped off very easily.

CONDITIONS

ASPECT	Plants grow best in full sun, but may need a little shading if grown under glass.
SITE	Soil must be very free draining and should contain very little organic matter.

GROWING METHOD

PROPAGATION	Easy to raise from seed sown in spring.
FEEDING	Give low-nitrogen liquid plant food in spring and mid-summer or use slow-release granules.
PROBLEMS	Overwatering causes them to rot and die.

FLOWERING

SEASON	Warm spring or summer flowering.
FRUITS	Flowers followed by fleshy, ovoid green or red berries with long seeds within.

FASTEST GROWING of all species of bishop's cap, Astrophytum ornatum *bears many yellow flowers annually after about five years.*

AT A GLANCE		
There are four species of these slow growing, attractive roundish cactuses that like arid conditions. 50°F min (zone 11).		
Jan	/	**Recommended Varieties**
Feb	/	*Astrophytum asterias*
Mar	/	*A. capricorne*
Apr	sow	*A. myriostigma*
May	transplant	*A. ornatum*
Jun	flowering	**Companion Plants**
July	flowering	Echinocactus
Aug	flowering	Epostoa
Sept	/	Gymnocalycium
Oct	/	Mammillaria
Nov	/	Rebutia
Dec	/	

ASTROPHYTUM

Aurinia saxatilis

GOLDEN DUST

FEATURES

This is a little, rounded, evergreen perennial that can grow from 4 to 12in high, forming a mound up to 16–20in across. In the species the flowers are a clear yellow, but the various cultivars produce flowers in white, cream, lemon, or rich gold. Since its natural habitat is rocky, mountainous country, it is ideal for a rock garden, for dry, sloping ground, or for edging garden beds, provided the drainage is excellent. It is also ideally suited to troughs and the edges of large pots, perhaps containing a shrub. Although golden dust is a perennial, some gardeners grow it as part of an annual spring display.

CONDITIONS

ASPECT	Needs an open position in full sunlight.
SITE	Soil must contain plenty of chalk, sand, or grit, and be free-draining but not rich.

GROWING METHOD

PROPAGATION	Grows readily from seed sown in the fall. Cultivars can be grown from tip cuttings taken in late spring and early summer. Space the plants about 4in apart, giving them plenty of growing room. Aurinia is sold among the alpines at garden centers.
FEEDING	Small amounts only of complete plant food may be given in early spring as a boost, but feeding is not essential.

PROBLEMS

No specific problems are known besides poor drainage. Overwatering pot-grown specimens can quickly rot and kill the plants.

FLOWERING

SEASON	Flowers appear from mid- to late spring, the flowers completely covering the plant and hiding the foliage.
CUTTING	The flowers are not suitable for picking.

AFTER FLOWERING

REQUIREMENTS	It is probably easiest to shear radically over the whole plant with clippers, unless you are waiting for the seed to ripen. Shearing the plants also helps to keep a compact, neatly rounded shape.

A SHARP, ATTRACTIVE CONTRAST, with the bright yellow flowers of golden dust against clusters of green, spoon-shape foliage.

AT A GLANCE	
	*A. saxatilis* is an evergreen, hardy perennial that forms thick clumps topped by yellow flowers. Hardy to 0˚ F (zone 6–7).

Jan	/	**Recommended Varieties**
Feb	/	*Aurinia saxatilis*
Mar	transplant	"Citrina"
Apr	/	"Compacta"
May	flowering	"Dudley Nevill"
Jun	flowering	"Goldkugel"
July	/	"Silver Queen"
Aug	/	**Companion Plants**
Sept	/	*Aurinia corymbosa*
Oct	sow	Aubrieta
Nov	/	
Dec	/	

Azalea

RHODODENDRON

FEATURES

Enchanting us from April to June, deciduous and evergreen azaleas come in a kaleidoscope of colors and range in height, 2–8ft. They are derived from various species of rhododendron and are among the world's most widely hybridized plants. Long-lived, azaleas mature within 3–5 years and flower from the first year of planting. Grouped in mixed shrub borders, taller varieties make a stunning backcloth for annuals or small perennials. It is best to buy plants in flower so that you can be sure of getting exactly what you want. Azaleas are often planted with acid-soil-loving camellias and purple- and green-leaved Japanese maples, where the foliage tempers the more vibrant-hued varieties.

DECIDUOUS GROUPS: Cherished for their May to June performance of clustered, trumpet blooms in glowing pastel and strident hues and vivid fall leaf tints, there are four deciduous types:

MOLLIS HYBRIDS: Making stocky bushes to about 6ft high, their large heads of scentless, bright yellow, orange, red, cream, and salmon blooms open before leaves appear. Choice among them are orange-scarlet "Spek's Brilliant" and "Koster's Brilliant Red."

KNAPHILL AND EXBURY HYBRIDS: Also unperfumed, their May blooms can be as large as a hardy hybrid rhododendron's. Dramatic varieties are: light yellow "Showers"; salmon-pink "Coronation Lady"; and deep carmine "Homebush."

GHENT HYBRIDS: Making neat, twiggy bushes clothed in long-tubed, sweet-smelling, honeysuckle-like flowers with showy stamens, blossoms peak in late May and June. Fine forms are soft yellow "Narcissiflorum" and rose-pink "Norma".

OCCIDENTALIS HYBRIDS: Flowering from mid- to late May, they reward us with trusses of sumptuous, fragrant, pastel-hued blooms. Pure white and yellow-eyed "Bridesmaid" is a good example.

EVERGREEN AND SEMI-EVERGREEN GROUPS: There are four widely grown divisions. Largest flowering are the prolific Vuyk and Glendale hybrids, whose blooms can be 3in in diameter. The Kaempferi hybrids, such as violet "Blue Danube," have slightly smaller flowers. Smallest of all are the very popular and bounteous-performing Kurume hybrids. These have slightly greater tolerance to low temperatures than other evergreen varieties and blooms are single or hose-in-hose—when one flower appears inside another.

CONDITIONS

ASPECT   Most azaleas prefer semi-shade and shelter from strong winds and hot afternoon sunshine. A new race of "sun-loving" varieties is being bred for more open situations.

SITE   The soil should be acid, well-drained, and humus-rich and fortified with plenty of well-decayed organic matter several weeks before planting. In even slightly alkaline conditions, when the pH hovers just above 7.0, azaleas will suffer from

AT A GLANCE	
A form of deciduous or evergreen rhododendron bearing trumpet blooms. Hardy to 4°F (zone 7).	
Jan /	Recommended Varieties
Feb /	Deciduous
Mar plant, prune	"Bridesmaid"
Apr flower, prune	"Coronation Lady"
May flower, prune	"Firefly"
Jun flower, prune	"Gibraltar"
July plant	"Koster's Brilliant Red"
Aug plant	Evergreen
Sept plant	"Addy Wery"
Oct plant	"Blue Danube"
Nov plant	"Driven Snow"
Dec /	"Hinode-giri"

iron deficiency and creamy-green, chlorophyll-deficient leaves will die. Keep plants perky in hot spells by mulching with a thick layer of organic material, such as well-rotted manure, leaf mould, compost, or decayed grass clippings.

GROWING METHOD

FEEDING Nourish plants by applying an acidifying fertilizer in spring and summer and watering it in if the soil is dry.
Water new plants regularly in droughty periods to help them establish quickly. In prolonged dry weather, gently dig a moat around a bush and fill it with water. Refill it several times when the water has soaked away. Finish by replacing the soil.

PROPAGATION Azaleas are easily increased from soft-tip cuttings taken from mid-spring to early summer; semi-ripe cuttings from mid- to late summer; and layers pegged down from mid-spring to late summer.

PROBLEMS

Unfortunately azaleas suffer from a number of pests and diseases.

POWDERY MILDEW: Causing yellow patches to blemish upper leaf surfaces it can, occasionally, trouble heavily shaded plants in areas of high rainfall. It can also be aggravated by sluggish air flow, so remove crowded plants and set them elsewhere. Pick off and burn badly affected leaves and avoid wetting the foliage. Do not grow Rhododendron cinnabarinum or its hybrids, which are prone to this fungus. Control the disease chemically by spraying with bupirimate with triforine or mancozeb the moment symptoms appear.

AZALEA GALL: Blame the fungus Exobasidium vaccinii, which causes leaves to become swollen, fleshy, and pinkish red. Later, ripe, white spores powder the surface. In the fall, galls wither and turn brown.

Fortunately, the plant does not appear to suffer from its presence. Some varieties are more susceptible than others to azalea gall. Remove and destroy affected leaves. There are no chemical controls.

RHODODENDRON LACE BUG damages azalea and rhododendron leaves in spring, summer and into the fall in mild seasons. Affected foliage is heavily mottled grayish white. Black or brown, shiny spots, the insect's excreta, are seen on the underside of leaves. When damage first appears, it may be possible to reduce the outbreak by hosing up under the foliage; otherwise, spray with horticultural soap, pyrethrins, pirimiphos-methyl, or permethrin as soon as the symptoms are seen.

THRIPS—brownish black and $1/8$in long—suck sap from the leaves. The damage is similar to that of lace bug but the leaves may have a more silvery appearance. Control these pests by spraying with pirimiphos-methyl, malathion, or dimethoate. If the infestation is severe, in dry, warm weather when thrips multiply rapidly, you may need to repeat the dosage every three weeks.

TWO-SPOTTED MITE, commonly known as red spider mite, also sucks sap from the underside of leaves. Using a magnifying glass, it is possible to see the mites. Almost colorless, with two black spots on their backs, they are usually carrying clear, round eggs. An attack is first noticed when leaves turn bronzy, tiny webs can be seen and minute creatures, with the aid of a hand lens, can be seen on the backs of leaves. Mites are more prevalent in hot, dry weather and more inclined to infest plants in sheltered spots, such as under eaves, than in open, airy situations. If the plants are not in flower when red spider mite invades, direct a hose up into the bush every couple of days to help reduce their numbers. Alternatively, spray with bifenthrin or horticultural soap.

PRUNING

Cutting flowers for a vase is usually all the pruning these plants need. But deadhead, too, to channel energy into new growth, by nipping out faded blooms when petals fall. Rejuvenate overgrown deciduous varieties by cutting back branches to within 2ft of the ground in March, before buds burst. Try and keep cuts

moist to keep alive invisible buds around the stump edge. An easy way to achieve this, apart from splashing them with water, is to coat them with Christmas tree needle spray, which covers them with a plastic film that seals in moisture. If the buzsh is very old, prune back half the branches in the first year and the remainder the following year. Wayward stems may be cut back at any time.

Ballota

BALLOTA

FEATURES

Ballota pseudodictamnus is a mound-forming evergreen sub-shrub, growing about 18in high, and spreading to about 2ft. It has an abundance of rounded leaves covered with silvery gray wool. It needs very little care beyond a spring prune, and its whitish flowers appear from spring into early summer. It thrives best in full sun and, like the other ballotas commonly available, is not quite fully hardy. *B. acetabulosa* is slightly bushier and taller, making a more dominant plant. Neither belong to the first division of shrubs, but they are good at covering bare patches of soil. They can be pruned giving a shorter height, emphasizing the spread.

CONDITIONS

ASPECT
Full sun or sun for most of the day is the key to success with these plants. Keep them away from the shade.

SITE
Completely avoid any soil that has been enriched. Ballotas will flourish in soils other plants would consider poor. It should also be quite light and free draining.

GROWING METHOD

PROPAGATION
The best and cheapest method for propagation is to take dozens of cuttings in the early part of summer. They quickly take but do need protection through the cold winter months. Plant out the following spring when they are well hardened off.

FEEDING
This is one occasion when feeding of any description is really not necessary.

PROBLEMS
Ballotas are remarkably trouble free. The plants take care of themselves.

FLOWERING

SEASON
The small white flowers with a pink tinge appear through late spring, and the first part of summer. In the case of *B. acetabulosa* they appear in the middle and end part of summer.

PRUNING

GENERAL
A spring prune produces plenty of fresh new growth and keeps it in good shape.

THE PLEASANT SCALLOPED FOLIAGE of Ballota pseudodictamnus *creates a variegated effect as the lighter-colored undersides of the leaves curls up and catch the sunlight. The downy texture of these plants also provides an attractive contrast of texture with glossier, darker green foliage.*

AT A GLANCE		
Ballota pseudodictamnus has all-year woolly leaves, and white flowers with a pink tinge. Hardy to 23°F (zone 7).		
Jan	foliage	**Recommended Varieties**
Feb	foliage	*Ballota*
Mar	foliage	"All Hallows Green"
April	flowering	*B. nigra*
May	flowering	"Archer's Variegated"
June	flowering	*B. acetabulosa*
July	foliage	*B. pseudodictamnus*
Aug	foliage	
Sept	foliage	
Oct	foliage	
Nov	foliage	
Dec	foliage	

Barberry

BERBERIS THUNBERGII

FEATURES

A huge, easy family of evergreen and deciduous species and varieties, berberis will grow almost anywhere. Small bushes enhance a rock garden; larger kinds light up a border or form a burglar-proof hedge. The most popular leaf-shedding kind is Berberis thunbergii. A dense, rounded shrub to about 5ft high and across, it is armed with long, sharp spines. Long-lived, with small, bright yellow flowers that sleeve slender, whippy stems and cheer spring, its leaves turn scarlet in fall. Bright red berries are a winter feature. Reddish-purple-leaved *B. thunbergii* "Atropurpurea" becomes a firebrand in October. Other choice varieties of *B. thunbergii* ideal for small gardens are golden-leaved "Aurea," purple-blackish-leaved "Dart's Red Lady" and "Harlequin". Fetching, evergreen kinds are *B. x stenophylla* and *B. candidula.*

CONDITIONS

ASPECT   Very hardy. Deciduous kinds especially resist icy winds. Berberis needs full sun to flower and fruit freely, but will tolerate light shade.

SITE   Berberis prospers on a wide range of soils, from sand to heavy, often waterlogged clay.

GROWING METHOD

FEEDING   Work bone meal into the root area in the fall.
             Water copiously and regularly in the first year after planting, to encourage good growth. Thereafter, little watering is necessary.

PROPAGATION Layer shoots from spring to fall, or take semi-ripe cuttings from early to mid-fall.

PROBLEMS   Control rust disease by spraying with a proprietary spray.

PRUNING

BUSHES: Apart from cutting back frost-damaged shoots in May, no regular pruning is needed. Renew old gaunt bushes by cutting back a third of the older stems to near ground level in April.

HEDGES: Trim when blooms fade in spring.

AT A GLANCE	
Undemanding shrubs—many have fiery fall leaf tints—bearing yellow or orange spring flowers. Hardy to -13˚F (zone 5).	
Jan /	Recommended Varieties
Feb /	Deciduous
Mar plant	*B. thunbergii*
Apr flower, prune	"Atropurpurea"
May flower, plant	"Dart's Red Lady"
June plant	"Aurea"
July plant	"Harlequin"
Aug plant	Evergreen
Sept plant	*B. candidula*
Oct plant	*B. x stenophylla*
Nov plant	
Dec /	

Begonia
BEGONIA

FEATURES

Excellent for bedding and containers, begonias have fleshy green or bronze leaves and flowers in many colors, and are grown as half-hardy annuals. "Fibrous" rooted varieties of *Begonia semperflorens* grow up to 8in, have many small flowers and do well in shaded spots. "Tuberous" rooted types reach 10in tall with fewer but larger flowers up to 4in across. Trailing varieties are also available for hanging baskets, reaching 1–2ft. Flowers are in mixed or single colors. A wide range of all types are available as young plants.

CONDITIONS

ASPECT   Will succeed best in partial shade with at least some protection from direct hot sun.

SITE   Soil should be very well prepared with plenty of rotted manure or compost mixed in. Begonias produce masses of fine feeding roots. Plants do not like very heavy clay soils that stay wet for long periods, so grow in containers if necessary, using multipurpose compost when potting up in spring.

GROWING METHOD

SOWING   Sow January/February. Seed is as fine as dust, so mix with a little dry silver sand and sow on the surface of $3^{1}/_{2}$in pots of seed compost based on peat or coir. Stand the pot in tepid water until the compost looks moist. Keep at 70°F in a heated propagator in a light spot, and carefully transplant seedlings to cell trays when they have produced several tiny leaves. Seed raising is a challenge so consider growing from young plants. Plant outdoors after the last frosts in early June, 6–8in apart depending on variety.

FEEDING   Water regularly in dry spells and liquid feed bedding displays every 2–3 weeks, or mix slow-release fertilizer with compost first.

PROBLEMS   Overwatering causes root rot and death. Remove faded flowers, especially in wet spells.

FLOWERING

SEASON   Flowers from early summer until frost.

CUTTING   Not suitable as a cut flower.

AFTER FLOWERING

GENERAL   Varieties that form round tubers can be potted up in the fall, dried off and then grown again the following spring.

AT A GLANCE		
A half-hardy annual grown for its flowers and green/bronze foliage, useful for bedding/containers. Frost hardy to 32°F (zone 10).		
Jan	sow	**Recommended Varieties**
Feb	sow	*Begonia semperflorens*
Mar	transplant	"Ambassador Mixed"
Apr	grow on	"Cocktail Mixed"
May	harden off	"Pink Sundae"
Jun	flowering	**Tuberous varieties**
July	flowering	"Non-Stop Mixed"
Aug	flowering	"Non-Stop Appleblossom"
Sept	flowering	"Pin-Up"
Oct	/	**Trailing varieties**
Nov	/	"Illumination Mixed"
Dec	/	"Show Angels Mixed"

Bellis

DAISY

FEATURES

All varieties of bellis are related to garden daisies, and are perennials grown as hardy biennials. Use in spring bedding and containers, with bulbs like tulips. Plants are spreading, 4–8in high, with white, pink, red, or bicolored double or "eyed" flowers. Petals can be tubular, or fine and needle-like. Available as young plants.

CONDITIONS

ASPECT — Needs a sunny, warm spot to encourage early flowers when grown for spring displays.

SITE — Most soils are suitable, but adding well-rotted manure or compost before planting increases plant vigor and flower size. In containers, use multipurpose compost and make sure the container is very free-draining.

GROWING METHOD

SOWING — Sow seed outdoors in May/June in fine soil in drills $1/2$in deep. Keep well-watered and when plants are large enough, space small clumps out in rows, 4–6in apart. Alternatively, pot up into $3^1/2$in pots. Grow on during the summer, then water, lift carefully, and plant out in beds or containers in the fall, spacing 6–8in apart.

FEEDING — Liquid feed can be given every 2–3 weeks in the spring when growth starts, but avoid feeding in winter, and take special care not to overwater containers or plants will rot off.

PROBLEMS — Bellis is trouble-free.

FLOWERING

SEASON — Flowers appear from early spring into the summer. Removal of faded flowers helps prolong flowering and reduces self-seeding.

CUTTING — Can be used in small spring posies.

AFTER FLOWERING

Plants are removed to make way for summer bedding and can either be discarded or replanted and left to grow as perennials.

VARIETIES OF BELLIS differ greatly. Some have small flowers with yellow centers, or the whole flower is a mass of fine petals. After the spring show is over bellis can be replanted on rock gardens where it will grow as a perennial in spreading clumps.

AT A GLANCE	
A perennial grown as a biennial for spring bedding displays and used with bulbs in yard containers. Frost hardy to 5°F (zone 7).	

		Recommended Varieties
Jan	/	*Bellis perennis*
Feb	flowering	**Small flowers**
Mar	flowering	"Carpet Mixed"
Apr	flowering	"Medici Mixed"
May	flowers/sow	"Pomponette Mixed"
Jun	sow	"Pomponette Pink"
July	grow on	**Large flowers**
Aug	grow on	"Blush"
Sept	grow on	"Giant Flowered Mixed"
Oct	plant	"Goliath Mixed"
Nov	/	"Habanera Mixed"
Dec	/	

Berberidopsis corallina

CORAL VINE

FEATURES

A spectacular evergreen climber from Chile, valued for its exotic-looking pendulous red flowers, and ideal for a shady wall or fence. It can be especially recommended for a shady courtyard that is well protected from cold winds, but it also looks at home in a woodland garden, with suitable perennials and shrubs, as it grows in woodland in the wild. The Coral vine can also be grown through large shrubs or up mature trees. It can reach a height of up to 15ft. A severe winter may kill back the stems but it may still go on to produce new shoots from the base in the spring.

CONDITIONS

ASPECT
: The Coral vine needs a position in shade or partial shade, with shelter from cold winds.

SITE
: The soil must be acid or neutral, contain plenty of humus, and be able to retain moisture yet well drained. A deep organic mulch applied in fall will protect the roots from severe frosts. Coral vine grows best on wire or trellis but will also scramble over fences, tree stumps, and other objects.

GROWING METHOD

PROPAGATION
: Sow seeds in spring and germinate in a cold frame. Carry out serpentine layering in spring. Take semi-ripe cuttings toward the end of summer.

WATERING
: Do not allow the plant to dry out at any time. Keep the soil steadily moist.

FEEDING / PROBLEMS

FEEDING
: Once a year in spring, using a slow-release fertilizer, but avoid alkaline types.

PROBLEMS
: Neither pests nor diseases are a problem.

FLOWERING/FOLIAGE

FLOWERS
: Long-stalked pendulous flowers are carried in rows on the shoots.

FOLIAGE
: Elliptical deep green leaves have spiny edges and gray-green undersides.

PRUNING

REQUIREMENTS
: Minimal pruning is needed for this climber. It is best not to prune unless it is considered essential. The Coral vine certainly does not like hard cutting back. Spring is the best time for pruning, removing dead growth and any very weak stems. Eventually, as the plant matures, some judicious thinning may be necessary.

THE INTENSE SCARLET of these Berberidopsis corallina *flowers makes up for their small size.*

AT A GLANCE	
Pendulous red flowers and deep green spiny foliage. Hardy to temperatures of 23°F (zone 9).	
Jan / Feb / Mar / Apr planting May planting Jun flowering July flowering Aug flowering Sep flowering Oct / Nov / Dec /	**Companion Plants** Looks good with x *Fatshedera lizei*, which will also take shade. Also woodland-garden shrubs and perennials, including ferns.

Berberis thunbergii

BARBERRY

FEATURES

Growing about 3ft high and wide, this is a very spiny plant that makes a useful hedge where a real barrier is wanted. Although it is deciduous, growth is very dense. In the species, leaves are deep green but there are cultivars with foliage that is burgundy or burgundy splashed with pink. This shrub gives year-round value, producing small, bright yellow flowers in spring, followed in fall by bright red berries that persist through winter. The foliage colors well before falling.

CONDITIONS

ASPECT | Prefers full sun all day, though many happily tolerate part shade, or shade for some of the day.
SITE | Although barberry is tolerant of a range of soil types, this shrub will give its best growth in well-drained soils that contain plenty of organic matter.

GROWING METHOD

PROPAGATION | The species can be grown from seed that is taken from ripe berries, cleaned and planted. Cultivars are best grown from semi-ripe cuttings taken in the summer.
SPACING | Barberry needs planting at about 20in intervals for hedging.
FEEDING | Apply complete plant food as soon as growth begins in spring. A thick spring layer of well-rotted organic matter will act as a mulch, keeping in moisture and feeding the soil.

PROBLEMS

PROBLEMS | Barberry is sometimes attacked by scale insects, which are readily controlled by spraying with insecticidal soap. In general though, these plants suffer from few problems, and they tend to look after themselves.

FLOWERING

SEASON | Bright yellow flowers appear in spring.
BERRIES | Flowers are followed by berries that ripen to bright red by fall. They may persist during the early winter months.

PRUNING

GENERAL | The main pruning should be done in late winter but tip pruning can be done at almost any time. Thin each year by removing some growth down near the base.

AN UNPRUNED BARBERRY has a loose, open habit. Full sun is needed to maintain the color of the burgundy and pink forms.

AT A GLANCE	
Deciduous *Berberis thunbergii* has good fall orange-red colors, and makes an ornamental hedge. Hardy to 0°F (zone 7).	
Jan /	**Recommended Varieties**
Feb /	*Berberis darwinii*
Mar /	"Flame"
Apr flowering	*B. dictyophylla*
May flowering	"Goldilocks"
Jun foliage	"Red Jewel"
July foliage	*B. x stenophylla*
Aug foliage	*B. thunbergii atropurpurea*
Sep foliage	*B. wilsoniae*
Oct foliage	
Nov /	
Dec /	

Bergamot

MONARDA DIDYMA

FEATURES

A member of the mint family with a pungent citrus-like flavour, bergamot can reach 2–3ft in height. The wild bergamot, *Monarda didyma*, also known as bee balm, is a hardy herbaceous perennial, but there are annual, biennial, and perennial varieties with brilliant scarlet red, purple, pink, or white flowers in summer. Bergamot is semi-dormant during winter, sending up squarish stems in spring bearing dark green, ovate leaves with toothed margins. The flowers attract bees.

CONDITIONS

ASPECT | Prefers a sunny location; tolerates partial shade.
SITE | An excellent border plant for moist soil. Grow in a humus-rich soil containing a lot of organic matter. Mulch well with leaves, straw, or compost to retain moisture and keep down weeds around this shallow-rooting herb.

GROWING METHOD

SOWING | Can be grown from seed, but seeds are very fine and often unreliable—this herb is easily cross-pollinated and plants may not be true to the parent in color or form. Sow seeds in spring in trays of seed compost, covering the tray with glass. Seeds germinate within 2 weeks.
PLANTING | Transplant seedlings to the garden when they are 3in high. More reliable is root division in spring: take sections of runners or sucker shoots from the outside of the clump, which will have roots throughout the bed. Discard the center of the clump and pot the other sections. Plant out in the garden when they are growing strongly, 32in apart.
FEEDING | Water well—like all members of the mint family, bergamot requires water at all times.
Add general fertilizer to the backfill when planting. Give another application of fertilizer each spring.
PROBLEMS | Powdery mildew and rust can affect bergamot. Cut back and remove diseased parts.
PRUNING | In late fall prune the plant back close to ground level. It will regenerate in spring. To increase the strength of the plant, cut flowerheads before they bloom in the first year. After flowering, the plant may be cut back to within $1\frac{1}{4}$in of the soil surface as this can promote a second flowering in fall.

AT A GLANCE	
Attractive perennial border plant, with aromatic leaves that can be used to make a refreshing tea. Hardy to 4˚F (zone 6).	

Month		Parts used
Jan	/	Leaves
Feb	/	Flowers
Mar	plant	**Uses**
Apr	plant	
May	plant harvest	Culinary
Jun	plant harvest	Medicinal
July	harvest	Craft
Aug	harvest	Gardening
Sept	plant harvest	
Oct	plant	
Nov	/	
Dec	/	

HARVESTING

PICKING
Leaves for making tea are stripped from stems both just before and just after flowering. The colorful flower petals can also be harvested.

STORAGE
Leaves can be part dried in a shady place for 2 or 3 days and then drying can be completed in a very low oven. Flowers do not store well and so should only be picked as required.

FREEZING
Put sprigs in a freezer bag. They can be frozen for up to 6 months.

USES

CULINARY
Fresh leaves can be used in summer fruit drinks or punches, and fresh flower petals are good for decorating salads. Leaves are also used for making tea.

MEDICINAL
The herb tea can be used to relieve nausea, flatulence, vomiting, colds, etc.

CRAFT
Dried leaves can be used in pot-pourris. The oil is used in perfumery, to scent candles etc.

GARDEN
The colorful flowers attract bees and this herb is therefore a good companion for plants that need insect pollination.

Bergenia ciliata

ELEPHANT'S EARS

FEATURES

Bergenias make excellent evergreen groundcover plants. They are also known as elephant's ears because of the large, rounded leaves about 8–12in long. They are often leathery and glossy, generally green, many turning reddish in the fall. The flowers are held on short stems from mid-spring to early summer. Bergenia ciliata has pink flowers and tends to lose its foliage in cold winters. It should survive most winters but in very bad freezing spells it may succumb, and should be protected. It grows about 1ft high, and 18in wide. Like all bergenias it is generally long living and easy to propagate. It is a useful plant, able to colonize areas other plants can't reach, such as beneath trees. It can also be used at the front of a border, or even to line the edge of paths.

CONDITIONS

ASPECT   It grows in either full sun or shady areas, but avoid extremes of the latter.

SITE   Likes well composted, moist soil with good drainage. It will tolerate much poorer conditions that bring out a richer leaf color in winter.

GROWING METHOD

PROPAGATION   Grow from seeds sown in the spring to produce hybrids, or divide in the spring or fall every five years or so. This will rejuvenate a declining plant. Place up to 2ft apart, depending on the variety, or closer for immediate coverage.

FEEDING   Feed generously in early spring with a complete plant food, especially on poorer

ground, and give a generous layer of mulch both in the spring, and again in the fall.

PROBLEMS   Slugs and snails can be a major problem to the young foliage, ruining its shapely appearance. Pick off, or attack with chemicals. Spray with a fungicide if leaf spot occurs.

FLOWERING

SEASON   The flowers appear from late winter or early spring, depending on variety, for a few weeks.

CUTTING   Though the flowers are useful in cut flower arrangements, the foliage, especially when red in winter, makes a particularly attractive foil.

PRUNING

GENERAL   Remove the spent flower stem and foliage.

AT A GLANCE		
Bergenia ciliata is a large-leaved, pink flowering perennial that thrives in a wide range of conditions. Hardy to 5°F (zone 7).		
Jan	/	Recommended Varieties
Feb	/	Bergenia
Mar	flowering	"Adenglut"
April	flowering	"Baby Doll"
May	foliage	"Bressingham Salmon"
June	foliage	"Bressingham White"
July	foliage	B. ciliata
Aug	foliage	B. cordifolia
Sept	foliage	"Purpurea"
Oct	/	"Morgenrote"
Nov	/	B. purpurascens
Dec	/	"Silberlicht"

Bifrenaria

BIFRENARIA SPECIES

FEATURES

The charming and popular bifrenarias were once classified as cymbidiums, and show a resemblance to them in their flower shape. These orchids, however, mostly come from Brazil but can also be found widely distributed throughout Panama, Trinidad, northern South America, and Peru. Bifrenaria has always been a popular orchid for beginners and proves easy to grow and flower in the amateur's cool mixed collection. It is a compact growing plant with long-lasting, heavily textured flowers sitting around the base of the plant. As a bonus the flowers are sweetly scented. They are epiphytic orchids in nature, growing on the higher branches of trees in the South American rain forests. It is possible to grow these orchids quite successfully in a cool to intermediate greenhouse, conservatory, or even on a windowsill with other companion plants. If in a greenhouse, the plants could be grown in a hanging basket near the light coming through the roof.

CONDITIONS

CLIMATE   A temperature range of 50–77°F, with ventilation in the summer months.
ASPECT   Good light all the year round but provide some shade in the hottest months.
POTTING MIX A general medium grade bark compost is ideal with good drainage qualities.

GROWING METHOD

PROPAGATION This orchid is a fairly slow grower so it could be a few years before it is ready to be divided. Best to leave as a specimen plant for as long as possible. May propagate from back bulbs that are removed and are potted up separately at potting time.
WATERING   Keep compost on the dry side during the winter months when the plant is not growing. With the onset of the new growth in the spring resume watering to get the new pseudobulb plumped up by the fall.
FEEDING   The plant responds to a light feeding during the growing season. Use a higher nitrogen plant food every two or three waterings.
PROBLEMS   No specific problems known if the cultural conditions are suitable.

FLOWERING SEASON

Long-lasting through spring and summer.

AT A GLANCE		
Dark green broad foliage reaches 8in from pseudobulb. Single flowers with bearded lip low at base.		
Jan	rest	Recommended Varieties
Feb	rest	*Bifrenaria atropurpurea*
Mar	flowering	(dark purple-brown)
Apr	flowering, water and feed	*B. harrisoniae*
May	flowering, water and feed	*B. tyrianthina*
Jun	water and feed	
July	water and feed	
Aug	water and feed	
Sept	rest	
Oct	rest	
Nov	rest	
Dec	rest	

Billbergia

BILLBERGIA SPECIES

FEATURES

One of the most easily grown of all bromeliads, billbergias are widely grown as house plants and are suitable for colder rooms in the house. They adapt to a wide variety of conditions, making them a good choice for the beginner. Leaves are rather stiff and form tall, tubular rosettes. Foliage is spiny and may be mottled, banded or variegated in colors from mid-green to blue-, or gray-green. Flower spikes often arch or droop. Flowers are generally not long lasting but some species flower on and off all year. Bracts are often pink or red with green or blue flower petals. Queen's tears, *Billbergia nutans*, is probably the most common. It has narrow, gray-green leaves to 12in with blue and green flowers and pink bracts. It has been widely used in hybridizing.

OTHER SPECIES

B. x windii is a much larger leaved species producing 18in flower spikes over the gray-green leaves. Also, look out for *B. zebrina* and *B. pyramidalis*—both larger, more exotic species.

CONDITIONS

POSITION   Needs frost-free conditions with a minimum temperature above 41˚F. Most species do best in fully sunny locations but need shade from the hottest summer sun, which tends to scorch leaf tips.

POTTING MIX   Any open, free-draining mix is suitable. Many experienced growers consider this plant does best without enriched soil conditions.

GROWING METHOD

PROPAGATION   Grows fairly easily from divisions or offsets of older plants taken during the winter months.

WATERING   Don't water too frequently but keep the cup filled with water. Spray misting to maintain a humid atmosphere around the plant is an ideal way to maintain good growth.

FEEDING   Some growers advocate regular liquid feeding through the growing season, others prefer not to give supplementary feeding.

PROBLEMS   There are generally no problems.

FLOWERING SEASON

Flowering times vary according to species and growing conditions.

AT A GLANCE	
Suitable for mounting on a log or in a pot. Flowers on and off all year but not long lasting. Pink bracts are spectacular.	
Jan flowering, water	**Recommended Varieties**
Feb water	*B. decora*
Mar /	*B. nutans*
Apr feed	*B. nutans*
May flowering, mist, repot	"Variegata"
Jun water and mist	*B. pyramidalis*
July water and mist	*B. x windii*
Aug buy plant	
Sept water	
Oct /	
Nov remove offsets	
Dec flowering	

Bletilla

CHINESE GROUND ORCHID

FEATURES

Bletilla is one of a small group of terrestrial orchids from China, Japan, and Taiwan. This is a very easy orchid to cultivate. It is deciduous, dying back to ground level in the fall or early winter. It grows from a pseudobulb that looks like a corm, each producing about three bright green pleated or folded leaves up to 16in long. Flowers are slightly bell shaped, cerise-purple to magenta, and carried on one slender stem—there may be 10-12 blooms on a stem. The lip of the flower is beautifully patterned in white and cerise. There is a white form, "Alba," but it is not as vigorous. The blooms usually last a few weeks if conditions are good.

CONDITIONS

CLIMATE   This is a very cool growing orchid and will thrive in a greenhouse if it is kept frost-free, at a minimum temperature of 41°F. Can be placed outside in summer and even planted in the ground in frost-free areas.

ASPECT   This orchid needs to be planted in a sheltered spot with dappled shade. It must have protection from hot sun in the middle of the day.

POTTING MIX   Needs well-drained mix or soil with plenty of humus so that it can retain moisture during dry periods.

GROWING METHOD

PROPAGATION   Congested clumps of plants can be divided in late winter to early spring.

Replant the pseudobulbs at the same depth as they were previously and remove dead leaves.

WATERING   Needs plenty of regular watering during hot weather through spring and summer. When the leaves begin to yellow off, decrease watering and then stop as the plant dies down.

FEEDING   Apply slow release fertilizer in spring or give liquid plant food at half strength every two or three weeks during the growing season to help increase growth.

PROBLEMS   No specific problems are known. Foliage burns if exposed to too much hot sun in summer and plants will rot in a poorly drained medium. Keep the plant dry when not in leaf.

FLOWERING SEASON

Flowers between late winter and spring.

AT A GLANCE	
A tolerant plant. Leaves are strap-like and vary in color. Plants produce floral bracts after three years.	
Jan flowering, rest	**Recommended Varieties**
Feb flowering, rest, re-pot	*B. striata*
Mar flowering, water and feed, re-pot	
Apr flowering, water and feed, re-pot	
May water and feed	
Jun water and feed	
July water and feed	
Aug water and feed	
Sept water and feed	
Oct rest	
Nov rest	
Dec rest	

Borage
BORAGO OFFICINALIS

FEATURES

A fast-growing annual or biennial growing 2–3ft tall, borage bears star-shaped flowers with protruding black anthers in summer. They are usually bright sky-blue, although they can sometimes be pink or white. The bush bears many sprawling, leafy branches with hollow stems, which can be quite fragile. The stems are covered with stiff white hairs and the grayish-green leaves are also hairy.

CONDITIONS

ASPECT   Prefers sunny locations but grows in most positions, including partial shade. It needs plenty of space. The brittle stems may need staking to prevent wind damage.

SITE   Grows well in most soils that are aerated, moist and mulched to keep weeds down.

GROWING METHOD

SOWING   Sow seed directly into the garden and thin out the seedlings later, leaving 24in between plants. Seedlings do not transplant well once established. Successive sowings every 3 to 4 weeks will extend the harvesting period. It self-sows readily and its spread may need to be controlled.

FEEDING   During spells of hot, dry weather borage plants should be kept well watered. Apply a balanced general fertilizer once each spring or use controlled-release granules.

PROBLEMS   Blackfly can be a problem. Treat with liquid horticultural soap. Mildew may also be a problem late in the year. If so, plants are best dug up and removed.

HARVESTING

PICKING   Pick the leaves as required while they are fresh and young. Caution: handling fresh leaves may cause contact dermatitis. Use gloves. Harvest the open flowers during the summer months.

STORAGE   The leaves must be used fresh; they cannot be dried and stored. The flowers can be crystallized and then stored in airtight jars.

FREEZING   The leaves cannot be frozen. The flowers may be frozen in ice cubes.

USES

CULINARY   Borage has a faintly cucumberish taste and leaves can be added to salads, and drinks such as Pimms. Flowers may be frozen in ice cubes for cold drinks, used raw on salads, or to decorate cakes and desserts if crystallised. Caution: it may be a danger to health. It is now under study because of the presence of alkaloids.

AT A GLANCE	
A tall, fast-growing annual with bristly leaves and small bright blue star-shaped flowers. Hardy to 4°F (zone 6).	

		Parts used
Jan	/	Flowers
Feb	/	Leaves
Mar	plant	**Uses**
Apr	plant	Culinary
May	plant harvest	Medicinal
Jun	plant harvest	Cosmetic
July	harvest	Craft
Aug	harvest	Gardening
Sept	harvest	
Oct	/	
Nov	/	
Dec	/	

MEDICINAL	Borage tea was used for colds and flu. The leaves and flowers are rich in potassium and calcium. Borage has been found to contain gamma linoleic acid (GLA) and is now being more widely grown as a commercial crop.

COSMETIC	The leaves can be used to make a cleansing facial steam.
CRAFT	The flowers can be added to pot-pourri.
GARDENING	Borage is regarded as an excellent companion plant in the garden, especially when it is planted near strawberries.

Bottlebrush

CALLISTEMON

FEATURES

Commonly called bottlebrush because its flower—principally stamens—reminds you of a bottle cleaner, the blooms enclasp slender stems clad with narrow, deep green leaves. There are several choice kinds. Hardiest is reckoned to be *Callistemon sieberi*, whose spikes of creamy-yellow flowers appear from late spring to summer. Also appealing are willow-leaved *C. salignus*, a species that glows with red, pink, or mauve flowers; *C. rigidus*, another hardyish, red-flowered kind for "borderline" gardens; and rich matt-red *C. linearis*, the narrow-leaved bottlebrush. Lemon-scented *C. citrinus* "Splendens" treats us to a memorable display of soft, pinkish-red, new shoots and vivid crimson flowers. All grow to around 7ft. Create a focus by underplanting a wall-trained shrub with white petunias.

CONDITIONS

ASPECT   Callistemon flowers best if fan-trained against a sheltered, sunny wall that is never shaded. This showy Australian is not for chilly gardens whipped by icy winds. If in doubt, consign it to a conservatory.

SOIL   Preferring organically rich, light, loamy soil that drains freely, it thrives in clay if you add grit and bulky organics to improve aeration.

GROWING METHOD

FEEDING   Callistemon copes reasonably well without added fertilizer but performs better if fed with fish, blood, and bone meal in spring and midsummer.

Water new plantings regularly to encourage robust growth and rapid establishment. Mature plants tolerate long, dry periods but flower more profusely if the soil is moist.

PROPAGATION   The species are easily grown from seed, but named varieties must be raised from semi-ripe cuttings, ideally with a heel of wood, in late summer.

PROBLEMS   Avoid alkaline soils in which leaves may turn pale yellow and die, and north- or east-facing sites, where cold winds may shrivel new shoots.

PRUNING

Trimming is not normally required, but occasional cutting back when blooms fade helps to keep growth compact and branches furnished with fresh green shoots. Old shrubs can be rejuvenated if you prune them back quite hard in spring, but remove only a third of the bush in any one year. Keep stumps moist to encourage new growth.

AT A GLANCE	
An evergreen, frost-tender shrub with scarlet or creamy-yellow, bottlebrush flowers in June and July. Hardy to 23°F (zone 9).	

Jan	/	Recommended Varieties
Feb	/	*Callistemon citrinus*
Mar	/	"Splendens"
Apr	plant, prune	*C. linearis*
May	plant	*C. rigidus*
Jun	flower, plant	*C. salignus*
July	flower, prune	*C. sieberi*
Aug	plant	
Sept	plant	
Oct	/	
Nov	/	
Dec	/	

Box

BUXUS

FEATURES

Both common box (*Buxus sempervirens*), to around 15ft, and lower-growing, small-leaved (Japanese) box (*B. microphylla japonica*) are favored for planting in tubs and large pots and clipping into drumsticks, spirals, balls, pyramids, and other forms of topiary. *B. sempervirens* "Suffruticosa" makes the best low hedge. Box is long-lived and slow growing. If unclipped, it attains little more than 3ft within 4–5 years.

Common box has darker, more pointed foliage than the Japanese form, where leaves are shinier and lighter green. In spring, tiny, starry, and delicately perfumed, yellowish-green flowers appear in leaf axils.

CONDITIONS

ASPECT	Plants are more compact in full sun than shade, in which the foliage has less appeal. Creamy-mottled forms must be grown in good light or the variegation will fade to green.
SOIL	Box thrives on chalk but also prospers on a wide range of other soils. Good drainage is vital. Enrich impoverished areas with bulky organic manure several weeks before planting.

GROWING METHOD

FEEDING	Encourage lusterous leaves by fortifying planting holes with fish, blood and bone meal or Growmore, and topdressing the root area with bone meal in spring and

fall. These plants are not heavy feeders and normally flourish if you do forget to fertilize them. Established box tolerate fairly dry conditions.

PROPAGATION	Box species can be grown from seed but varieties must be increased from semi-ripe cuttings from early to mid-fall. Plants may also be divided in mid-spring.
PROBLEMS	If not fed regularly, box is rather slow to establish on poor, sandy soil.

PRUNING

After planting, use hedging shears to shorten shoots by a third to encourage a bushy habit. Trim hedges and topiary from April to August. If a bush is old and gaunt and needs revitalizing, cut it hard back in April or May. Keep stumps moist to help them sprout. Cut out any all-green shoots on variegated plants.

DROUGHT-RESISTING common box makes a tight, neat plant in full sun. Tiny, yellow flowers stud shoots in spring.

AT A GLANCE		
A hardy evergreen for topiary or low hedges. Variegated forms must be positioned in full sun. Hardy to -13°F (zone 5).		
Jan	/	**Recommended Varieties**
Feb	/	*B. microphylla*
Mar	/	"Winter Gem"
Apr	flower, prune	"Faulkner"
May	plant, prune	*B. sempervirens*
June	flower, plant	"Handsworthensis"
July	plant, prune	"Suffruticosa"
Aug	plant, prune	"Elegantissima"
Sept	plant	
Oct	/	
Nov	/	
Dec	/	

Brachyscome

SWAN RIVER DAISY

FEATURES

Brachyscome is covered in mounds of daisy flowers, and is good in beds and in hanging baskets and courtyard containers. It makes an effective edging plant, where it can develop unhindered without being crowded out by more vigorous plants. Leaves are light green and feathery, with a delicate appearance. Plants grow 9in tall with a similar spread. Choose single colors or mixtures. Brachyscome can be planted in May before the last frosts, and will tolerate short dry spells. A half-hardy annual, also seen as "brachycome."

CONDITIONS

ASPECT | Choose a south-facing position in full sunlight.
SITE | Choose a warm, sheltered spot away from wind. Brachyscome likes rich, well-drained soil, with plenty of rotted compost or manure added. Use multipurpose potting compost in containers.

GROWING METHOD

SOWING | Sow in March and April in 3^1/$_2$in diameter pots, just covering the seeds, and germinate at 64°F. Seedlings emerge within three weeks. Transplant into cell trays of multipurpose compost, and plant out in beds, 9–12in apart.
FEEDING | Liquid-feed each week outdoors. Add slow-release fertilizer granules to container compost, and also liquid-feed every two weeks in the summer. Avoid overwatering, especially in dull, wet spells, or plants may rot off.

PROBLEMS | Support floppy plants with small twigs. Avoid planting among large, vigorous container plants that will swamp low growers and cast them in shade at the height of summer. Control slugs with pellets or set slug traps in bedding displays.

FLOWERING

SEASON | Flowers appear all summer and are faintly scented—this is best appreciated by growing them at nose height in hanging baskets, flower bags, and windowboxes.
CUTTING | Not suitable.

AFTER FLOWERING

GENERAL | Remove when flowers are over and add to the compost heap or bin.

SWAN RIVER DAISIES produce mounds of small, daisy-like flowers in profusion throughout the summer months.

AT A GLANCE	
A half-hardy annual grown for its daisy-like flowers, useful for bedding, baskets, and containers. Frost hardy to 32°F (zone 10)	
Jan /	**Recommended Varieties**
Feb /	*Brachyscome iberidifolia*
Mar sow	"Blue Star"
Apr sow/transplant	"Bravo Mixed"
May plant outdoors	"Mixed"
Jun flowering	"Purple Splendor"
July flowering	"White Splendor"
Aug flowering	
Sept flowering	
Oct /	
Nov /	
Dec /	

Brassia

SPIDER ORCHID

FEATURES

This group of epiphytic orchids are extremely popular. The attractive leafy plants are easy to keep and flower well when given plenty of light. They are known for their spidery flowers, which give them their common name. The blooms are long lasting, staying on the plant for many weeks and giving off a very pleasant fragrance. There have been many hybrids developed between the species, giving extra size and quality to the flowers, for example *B. Edvah Loo*. Brassias have also been used to make hybrids with other genera such as *miltonias* and *odontoglossums*, to produce *miltassias* and *odontobrassias*, which inherit the star-shaped flowers and showy appearance of the parent. Grow the brassias in hanging baskets near the light to achieve maximum flowering potential. In this environment they also produce prolific aerial root growth.

CONDITIONS

CLIMATE	They thrive in a cool or intermediate temperature; 50–54˚F at night in winter to 68–77˚F in summer.
ASPECT	Brassias need light to encourage flowering, so place in a south facing aspect with a little shade from the brightest sun.
POTTING MIX	Medium or coarse mixture of bark chippings.

GROWING METHOD

PROPAGATION	The plant should produce several growths from one pseudobulb when it reaches a mature size, which will increase the size of the plant quickly. It can then be divided. Make sure divisions are not too small otherwise they will not flower well. Keep a minimum of four to six pseudobulbs.
WATERING	Keep the compost moist all the year round. Watering can be reduced in winter months to prevent compost waterlogging. Regular watering while in growth and spraying of leaves and aerial roots will benefit the plant.
FEEDING	Only apply fertilizer when the plant is in growth. Use a water-soluble feed and pour through the compost as well as adding it to the water used for misting leaves and roots.
PROBLEMS	Brassias may not flower well if not enough light is provided, especially in winter.

FLOWERING SEASON

Generally late spring and summer.

AT A GLANCE		
Easy to grow. Fragant flowers on long spike, up to 20in. Compact plant, 6–8in high.		
Jan	rest	**Recommended Varieties**
Feb	rest	*B. giroudiana*
Mar	rest	*B. maculata*
Apr	rest	*B. verrucosa*
May	flowering, water and feed	*B. Edvah Loo*
		B. "New Start"
Jun	flowering, water and feed	*B. Rex* (all green/yellow)
July	flowering, water and feed	
Aug	flowering, water and feed	
Sept	rest	
Oct	rest	
Nov	rest	
Dec	rest	

Brassica

ORNAMENTAL CABBAGE AND KALE

FEATURES

Ornamental cabbages and kales are grown for colorful fall and winter foliage, growing 12–18in tall and wide. Use for bedding or large pots. Leaf color is pink, rose, or white, and improves with temperatures below 50°F. Damage is caused by severe frost. Available as young plants.

CONDITIONS

ASPECT	Needs full sunlight to develop good color.
SITE	Enrich soil with rotted compost or manure ahead of planting. Adding lime will improve results in acid soils. Avoid places exposed to driving winter winds. Plant up containers using multipurpose compost, making sure pots and tubs are free-draining.

GROWING METHOD

SOWING	Seed is sown in June/July in 3^1/2in pots of multipurpose compost and kept out of the sun. Large seedlings appear after a week and are transplanted to individual 3^1/2in pots. Grow these on outdoors, watering frequently, and then plant out in beds or in containers in the early fall where the display is required.
FEEDING	Give a high-potash liquid feed fortnightly throughout the summer months. Tomato food is suitable and encourages leaf color.

PROBLEMS

Cabbage caterpillars will also attack ornamental varieties and kales. Pick off by hand or use a spray containing permethrin.

FLOWERING

SEASON	Plants are at their best in the fall and early winter. Any surviving the winter will produce tall clusters of yellow flowers during spring.
CUTTING	Whole heads makes a striking, unusual element in winter flower arrangements.

AFTER FLOWERING

General Remove in the spring or if killed by frosts.

ORNAMENTAL KALES help pack a punch in the yard during the fall, with their bright leaves that deepen in color when the temperature falls below 50°F. Plants grown in containers should be kept in a sheltered spot during spells of severe winter weather.

AT A GLANCE		
A hardy annual grown for its brightly colored leaves that last from the fall until spring. Frost hardy to 5°F (zone 7).		
Jan	leaves	**Recommended Varieties**
Feb	leaves	**Cabbages**
Mar	leaves	"Delight Mixed"
Apr	leaves	"Northern Lights"
May	leaves	"Ornamental Mixed"
Jun	sow	"Tokyo Mixed"
July	sow	**Kales**
Aug	grow-on	"Nagoya Mixed"
Sept	plant	"Red & White Peacock"
Oct	leaves	"Red Chidori"
Nov	leaves	
Dec	leaves	

Broom

CYTISUS

FEATURES

Treating us to whippy stemmed and thickly clustered cascades of fragrant, pea flowers, deciduous and butter-yellow-flowered *Cytisus scoparius* and its kaleidoscope-hued hybrids make May and June special. Plant them singly to punctuate a border, or group several of one color or in harmonizing shades to create an unforgettable statement. Its fetching, leaf-shedding relation Moroccan (pineapple) broom (*C. battandieri*) is famed for its June display of pineapple-scented cones of bright yellow blooms amid silvery, tri-lobed leaves. It has a lax, floppy habit so train it to embrace a sunny wall or frame a patio door. Alternatively, plant it to entwine a tall, metal obelisk in a border or at the end of a path. When in flower, a warm, breezy day wafts crushed pineapple scent around the garden.

CONDITIONS

ASPECT	*C. scoparius* and its varieties are hardier than *C. battandieri*, which needs to be sheltered from cold winds. Both flower at their best in full sun.
SITE	Encourage robust growth by setting plants in free-draining and well-manured, neutral, or acid, sandy soil. Lime tends to cause weak, pale green leaves.
FEEDING	After adding balanced fertilizer to planting holes, encourage sturdy growth by topdressing the root area with fish, blood, and bone meal in spring and again in midsummer. If your soil is chalky and hybrids are suffering from iron deficiency, help them recover by applying a soil-acidifying fertilizer.

PROPAGATION	Increase *C. scoparius* and *C. battandieri* from semi-ripe cuttings taken from mid- to late summer.
PROBLEMS	When *C. scoparius* and its hybrids become woody and flower less—after ten or so years—they cannot be refurbished by hard pruning, so it is best to replace them with young, potted plants.
	Occasionally, in summer, leaf buds develop into cauliflower-like growths covered with silvery hairs. Gall mites cause them. There is no chemical control, so remove affected plants and replace them with healthy stock.

PRUNING

Keep *C. scoparius* and its hybrids youthful and ablaze with flowers in spring by shearing flowered stems to just above older growth when pods form. *C. battandieri* isn't normally pruned, but cut out badly placed and weak stems after flowering If you are growing it against a wall, tie in new shoots then.

AT A GLANCE	
Massed, tiny, pea blooms or chunky, golden flower cones brighten borders from late spring to early summer. Hardy to 14°F (zone 8).	
Jan	/	**Recommended Varieties**
Feb	/	*C. battandieri*
Mar	plant	*C. scoparius*
Apr	plant	"Andreanus"
May	flower, plant	"Burkwoodii"
June	flower, prune	"Goldfinch"
July	plant	"Killeney Red"
Aug	plant	"Killeney Salmon"
Sept	plant	"Lena"
Oct	plant	"Zeelandia"
Nov	/	
Dec	/	

Browallia

BUSH VIOLET

FEATURES

Browallia takes its common name from its violet-blue flowers, which have a pale "eye." White flowered varieties and mixtures are available. Plants grow up to 12in and are suitable for containers and baskets, and in warmer areas, bedding. Varieties of *Browallia speciosa* are grown as half-hardy annuals and can also be used as indoor potted plants.

CONDITIONS

ASPECT SITE	Needs a warm, sheltered spot in sunlight. Browallia does not tolerate poor drainage, and on heavy soils should only be grown as a container plant, using multipurpose compost. Otherwise, mix in well-rotted compost or manure several weeks before planting out.

GROWING METHOD

SOWING	For summer bedding, sow the seed on the surface of 3$^{1}/_{2}$in pots of multipurpose compost in February/March. Keep at 64°F and do not let the surface dry out. Seedlings appear in 2–3 weeks and should be transplanted to individual cell trays or 3in pots. Harden off at the end of May and plant in early June. For flowering potted plants, seed can be sown in the same way until June.
FEEDING	Give plants a liquid feed fortnightly or, in containers and windowboxes, mix slow-release fertilizer with the compost first.

PROBLEMS

Aphids sometimes attack the soft leaves, so use a spray containing permethrin if they appear.

FLOWERING

SEASON	Flowers appear from early summer onward and continue until the first frosts. Take off faded flowers regularly to encourage buds.
CUTTING	Not suitable as a cut flower.

AFTER FLOWERING

GENERAL	Plants die when frosts arrive. Potted plants indoors can be kept alive indefinitely.

BROWALLIA FLOWERS have an almost crystalline texture when lit by the sun. They appear in masses on rounded plants, and at the height of summer can almost completely hide the leaves. Seen here are the varieties "Blue Troll" and "White Troll."

AT A GLANCE		
A half-hardy annual grown for its blue, white, or pink flowers, useful for bedding/container planting. Frost hardy to 32°F (zone 10).		
Jan	/	Recommended Varieties
Feb	sow	*Browallia speciosa*
Mar	sow	BLUE FLOWERS
Apr	grow on	"Blue Troll"
May	plant	"Blue Bells"
Jun	flowering	"Starlight Blue"
July	flowering	White flowers
Aug	flowering	"White Troll"
Sept	flowering	Blue/pink/white flowers
Oct	/	"Jingle Bells"
Nov	/	
Dec	/	

Bulbophyllum

BULBOPHYLLUM SPECIES AND HYBRIDS

FEATURES

The genus *Bulbophyllum* is one of the largest in the orchid family and includes some of the most extraordinary looking flowers in the orchid kingdom. It is closely related to, and often classified with, the genus *Cirrhopetalum.* They are extremely widespread, being found in South East Asia, Africa, Australia, and the tropical Americas. The habit and appearance of the plants and flowers are as variable as their place of origin. Some have tiny flowers that you need a magnifying glass to see; others have large, unusually shaped, showy blooms. A characteristic of many of these orchids is a curiously rocking lip, which attracts certain pollinating insects to the flowers. Some are also fragrant, however this is not always pleasant. The orchids try to attract carrion flies, so they send out the scent of rotting meat. They make good specimen plants, growing well in, and over the edge of, hanging baskets, in which they can stay for years.

CONDITIONS

CLIMATE   Due to the widespread nature of these orchids, there are both cool and warm growing species available, so check with your supplier when making a purchase. Most of the Asian types are cool, whereas the African species tend to be warmer.

ASPECT   They can take a lot of light so grow well in a hanging basket near the greenhouse roof.

POTTING MIX Need an open medium or coarse grade bark with even some perlite or larger perlag mixed in to make it free draining.

GROWING METHOD

PROPAGATION Most will grow quickly into large clumps with multiple growths so can be divided after only a few years. Alternatively leave growing in a basket for many years until the orchid completely envelops the basket.

WATERING   Let bulbophyllums dry out in between waterings and take care not to overwater them when in growth. If the pseudobulbs start to shrivel then they are too dry.

FEEDING   Give feed only when in growth, and apply this as a foliar feed by spraying it on the leaves as well as pouring through the compost. A weak dilution every two or three waterings is ideal.

PROBLEMS   No specific problems are known if the cultural conditions are suitable.

FLOWERING SEASON

Depends on the species or hybrid grown.

AT A GLANCE		
Strange appearance, with a variety of shapes and sizes, from $1\frac{1}{4}$–12in high. Flowers $\frac{1}{8}$–3in across.		
Jan	rest	**Recommended Varieties**
Feb	rest	*B. careyanum*
Mar	rest, re-pot	"Fir Cone Orchid"
Apr	rest, re-pot	*B. graveolans* (cluster of
May	water and feed, re-pot	green and red flowers at the base)
Jun	water and feed	*B. lobbii*
July	water and feed	*B. macranthum* (purple)
Aug	water and feed	*B. purpureorachis* (brown
Sept	water and feed	flowers creeping up a
Oct	rest	spiral stem)
Nov	rest	*B. vitiense* (small pink)
Dec	rest	

Butia capitata

JELLY PALM

FEATURES

A native of the cooler parts of South America, this plant is popularly known as the Jelly palm because of its edible but rather tough fruits, which can be boiled to make a jelly. The distinctive gray-green arching fronds consisting of numerous leaflets contrast well with many other palms. This species makes a sturdy trunk from 18–20ft in height and the fronds spread to 10–15ft. It is a very long-lived palm but slow growing and ideally suited to cultivation in a container. Suitable for a cool conservatory or glasshouse, it also makes a good houseplant.

CONDITIONS

ASPECT   Although the Jelly palm needs very bright light it should not be subjected to direct sun or the fronds may become scorched. Provide moderate humidity. If placed outdoors ensure it is sheltered from cold winds to prevent frond damage.

SITE   In containers grow in soil-based potting compost.

GROWING METHOD

PROPAGATION   Raise from seeds sown as soon as available and germinate at 77–82°F.

WATERING   Moderate watering in growing season from late spring to late summer, then for the rest of the year water sparingly.

FEEDING   Apply a balanced liquid fertilizer monthly during the growing season from late spring to late summer.

PROBLEMS   Under glass this palm is prone to attacks by red spider mites and scale insects.

FOLIAGE/FLOWERING

FOLIAGE   Looks good all the year round but at its best in the growing season—spring and summer.

FLOWERS   Trusses of yellow flowers in summer are followed by purple fruits.

GENERAL CARE

REQUIREMENTS   Remove dead fronds when necessary by cutting them off close to the trunk.

THE SPECTACULAR Butia capitata is a highly effective feature palm, with its gently arching branches and sprays of spiny gray-green fronds creating a stunning display. This plant is suitable for growth in a container, but indoor specimens are unlikely to achieve these proportions.

AT A GLANCE		
A slow growing half-hardy palm with gray-green feathery foliage. Provide a minimum temperature of 41–50°F (zone 11).		
Jan	/	**Companion Plants**
Feb	/	Because of the distinctive
Mar	planting	color of its fronds, *Butia*
Apr	planting foliage	*capitata* contrasts well with
May	foliage	many other palms.
Jun	flowering	
July	flowering	
Aug	flowering	
Sep	/	
Oct	/	
Nov	/	
Dec	/	

Butterfly bush

BUDDLEJA DAVIDII

FEATURES

There are three distinctive, hardy species: deciduous *Buddleja davidii*, whose cone-shaped flowers are dark purple, purplish red, pink, white, or blue; *B. alternifolia*, yielding a waterfall of shoots sleeved with soft purple flowers; and evergreen *B. globosa*, with its clusters of small orange balls.

CONDITIONS

ASPECT   These plants perform best in full sun, but tolerate slight shade; *B. davidii* resists chilly winds.

SITE   Thriving in most soils, they prefer a well-drained position enriched with organic matter.

GROWING METHOD

FEEDING   Boost growth by sprinkling bone meal around the shrub in April and October and hoeing it in. Take care not to damage roots. Water new plants regularly in spring and summer to encourage robust growth and bounteous blossom. Mulching helps to retain soil moisture in droughty spells.

PROPAGATION All kinds are easily increased from soft-tip cuttings in early summer and hardwood cuttings in the fall.

PROBLEMS   Control leaf-crippling aphids with pirimicarb, rotenone, permethrin, or pyrethrins. *B. alternifolia*, grown as a standard, needs staking throughout its life.

PRUNING

B. DAVIDII Cut back the previous year's flowering shoots to within 2in of the base in March.

B. ALTERNIFOLIA and *GLOBOSA*: Unlike *B. davidii*, which flowers on its current-year shoots, both *B. alternifolia* and *B. globosa* bloom on wood produced the previous year. Keep them youthful and flowering freely by shortening to the base a third of the oldest stems when the flowers fade.

IRRESISTIBLE TO BUTTERFLIES that cluster on its nectar-rich flowers, varieties of Buddleja davidii *make summer special. Spectacular blooms, large handsome leaves and an ability to grow almost anywhere sunny, buddleja is a good choice for beginners.*

AT A GLANCE	
Hardy, deciduous, and evergreen or semi-evergreen shrubs. Cones or globes of blossom light up summer. Hardy to 14°F (zone 8).	
Jan /	**Recommended Varieties**
Feb /	*B. alternifolia*
Mar plant, prune	*B. davidii*
Apr plant	"Black Knight"
May plant	"Dartmoor"
June flower, plant	"Empire Blue"
July flower, plant	"Peace"
Aug flower, plant	"Pink Delight"
Sept plant	"Santana"
Oct plant	*B. fallowiana*
Nov plant	"Alba"
Dec /	*B. globosa*
	B. x *weyeriana*

C

Calceolaria

SLIPPER FLOWER

FEATURES

Only a few varieties of calceolaria are suitable for outdoors; these are different to the indoor pot type. By nature shrubs, they are grown from seed each year as hardy annuals and are useful for bedding and containers. None grow more than 16in tall and wide.

CONDITIONS

ASPECT   Needs full sun or part shade.
SITE   Slipper flowers thrive in moist soil where their roots stay as cool as possible. Mix in well-rotted compost or manure before planting and use a peat- or coir-based multipurpose compost for filling containers.

GROWING METHOD

SOWING   The fine seed can be sown on the surface of peat- or coir-based multipurpose compost in a 3^1/2in pot, January–March, at a temperature of 64˚F. Keep in a bright place. Seedlings appear in 2–3 weeks and can be transplanted to cell trays, then hardened off and planted after frosts, 6–12in apart, or used with other plants in containers.
FEEDING   Liquid feed every 3–4 weeks or mix slow-release fertilizer with compost before planting.

PROBLEMS

PROBLEMS   Slugs will eat the leaves of young plants in wet spells during early summer. Protect plants with a barrier of grit or eggshell or scatter slug pellets sparingly around plants.

FLOWERING

SEASON   Plants will flower from early summer until frosts. Take off dead flowers weekly.
CUTTING   A few stems can be taken but avoid damaging the overall shape and appearance of the plant.

AFTER FLOWERING

GENERAL Remove plants in fall when finished.

THE HOT COLORS OF THE "SUNSET" strain of calceolaria excel outdoors and combine well with marigolds.

AT A GLANCE	
A half-hardy annual, calceolaria is used for bedding and containers, with bright flowers. Frost hardy to 32˚F (zone 10).	
Jan sow	**Recommended Varieties**
Feb sow	Calceolaria hybrids
Mar transplant	"Little Sweeties Mixed"
Apr grow on	"Midas"
May harden off	"Sunshine"
Jun flowering	"Sunset Mixed"
July flowering	
Aug flowering	
Sept flowering	
Oct /	
Nov /	
Dec /	

Calendula

POT MARIGOLD

FEATURES

Also known as English marigold, calendula is a fast-growing, hardy annual with daisy-type flowers in shades of yellow, orange, red, pinkish, and even green. Flowers can be fully double, while others have a distinct darker "eye." The edible petals can be used in salads. Perfect for a "cottage garden" bed or border, and very easy to grow, the large curled seeds are sown straight into the soil outdoors. Plant size ranges from 12 to 28in tall and wide.

CONDITIONS

ASPECT — Needs full sunlight to succeed.

SITE — Does well even in poor soil, which can increase the number of flowers. Add rotted organic matter to the soil ahead of planting time to improve results. Calendula does not do well on heavy, badly drained soils, so grow in containers under these conditions.

GROWING METHOD

SOWING — March to May or August/September are the sowing periods. Sow the seeds direct into finely raked moist soil where you want plants to flower, in drills $^1/_2$in deep, and cover. Thin out as seedlings grow so that plants are eventually spaced 10–12in apart. Fall-sown plants flower earlier the following year. If flowers for cutting are required, sow seed thinly in long rows.

FEEDING — Liquid feed once a month to encourage larger blooms. Use a feed high in potash to encourage flowers rather than leafy growth—tomato fertilizers are a good choice.

PROBLEMS — The leaves are prone to attack by aphids, causing twisting and damage. Use a spray containing permethrin, but avoid eating flowers. Powdery mildew can affect leaves in late summer, but is not worth treating—pick off the worst affected leaves and compost them.

FLOWERING

SEASON — Flowers appear in late spring on plants sown the previous fall, and from early summer on spring-sown plants. Removal of faded blooms will keep up a succession of flowers.

CUTTING — Good as a cut flower—cutting helps to keep flowers coming. Cut when flowers are well formed but before petals open too far.

AFTER FLOWERING

GENERAL — Pull up after flowering. Will self-seed if heads are left to ripen and shed seeds.

AT A GLANCE		
A hardy annual for growing in beds and borders and a useful cut flower in many shades. Frost hardy to 5°F (zone 7).		
Jan	/	Recommended Varieties
Feb	/	*Calendula officinalis*
Mar	sow	"Art Shades Mixed"
Apr	sow	"Fiesta Gitana Mixed"
May	thin out	"Greenheart Orange"
Jun	flowering	"Kablouna Lemon Cream"
July	flowering	"Kablouna Mixed"
Aug	flowers/sow	"Orange King"
Sept	flowers/sow	"Pacific Beauty"
Oct	/	"Pink Surprise"
Nov	/	"Princess Mixed"
Dec	/	"Touch of Red Mixed"

Californian Lilac

CEANOTHUS

FEATURES

Prized for their massed clusters of principally pale blue to deep violet-blue, powderpuff blooms, there are evergreen and deciduous varieties. They range from carpeters to imposing bushes of around 15ft high.

Most evergreens, such as "Blue Mound" and *Ceanothus thyrsiflorus* "Edinensis," bloom from May to June. Two exceptions, "Fallal Blue" and "Burkwoodii," perform from July to September. The best of the deciduous group—pink "Marie Simon" and blue "Gloire de Versailles"—flower from July to October.

CONDITIONS

ASPECT All kinds, especially evergreen varieties which are best grown against a south-facing wall, need a sunny, sheltered spot where air circulates freely.

SITE Ceanothus prospers on well-drained clay loam, sandy or humus-rich, gravelly soils. It will not thrive on heavy clay that waterlogs in winter, where roots are liable to rot.

GROWING METHOD

FEEDING Keep plants lustrous and flowering freely by applying bone meal in spring and fall. Breaking down slowly, it is rich in phosphates, which encourage robust root growth.

In its native habitat, this plant receives rain only in winter and has adapted to very dry summers.

PROPAGATION Most varieties are grown from semi-ripe cuttings taken from mid- to late summer.

PROBLEMS *Ceanothus* is susceptible to root rot, caused by wet soil. It is seldom troubled by pests.

PRUNING

EVERGREEN Trim spring-flowering kinds when blooms fade in early summer, and cut late summer performers in April.

DECIDUOUS In early spring, shorten the previous varieties year's flowered shoots to within 2–3in of the older wood.

THERE ARE FEW more riveting, spring- and early summer-flowering shrubs—ideal for light soils that dry out quickly—than evergreen members of the Californian lilac family.

AT A GLANCE		
Evergreen or deciduous shrubs with blue or pink blooms from spring to early fall. Hardy to 14°F (zone 8).		
Jan	/	**Recommended Varieties**
Feb	/	**Evergreen**
Mar	plant, prune	"Blue Mound"
Apr	plant, prune	"Cascade"
May	flower, plant	"Concha"
Jun	flower, plant	"Puget Blue"
July	flower, plant	*C. thyrsiflorus*
Aug	flower, plant	"Repens"
Sept	flower, plant	"Zanzibar" (variegated)
Oct	flower, plant	**Deciduous**
Nov	/	"Gloire de Versailles"
Dec	/	"Marie Simon"
		"Perle Rose"

Callistephus
CHINA ASTER

FEATURES

China asters are half-hardy annuals and are not to be confused with the perennial asters or Michaelmas daisies. Grow as bedding, as cut flowers, and in large pots. Flowers come in a wide range, from narrow, quill-like petals to bicolors, and also single shades. Size ranges from 8 to 36in tall, depending on the variety. Available as young plants.

CONDITIONS

ASPECT	Must have a warm spot in full sunlight all day.
SITE	Plants need well-drained soil with added organic matter, such as rotted manure or compost, dug in before planting. If grown in containers, use multipurpose compost mixed with slow-release fertilizer granules.

GROWING METHOD

SOWING	Sow in March/April in 3^1/2in pots of compost and keep at 61°F. Seedlings appear after a week and can be transplanted to cell trays and grown on. Planted in late May, plants are not damaged by the last frosts. Seed can also be sown direct into the ground in late April and May. Plant 8–24in apart.
FEEDING	Water regularly and give plants in containers a general liquid feed every two weeks. In beds, feed when you water with a handheld feeder.
PROBLEMS	Aphids cause the leaves to distort, which can affect flowering. Use a spray

containing dimethoate. If plants suddenly collapse and die, they are suffering from aster wilt and should be removed with the soil around their roots and put in the trashcan. Avoid growing asters in that spot and try "resistant" varieties.

FLOWERING

SEASON	Early summer to early fall.
CUTTING	An excellent and long-lasting cut flower.

AFTER FLOWERING

GENERAL	Remove plants after flowering and compost any that do not show signs of wilt disease.

CHINA ASTERS, with their large, showy, and often double flowers, can be used as summer bedding plants for massed displays. As a cut flower, callistephus is unrivalled for producing long-lasting blooms in late summer when other flowers are past their best.

AT A GLANCE		
A half-hardy annual grown for its flowers, used in bedding, containers and as a cut flower. Frost hardy to 32°F (zone 10).		
Jan	/	**Recommended Varieties**
Feb	/	*Callistephus chinensis*
Mar	sow	"Apricot Giant"
Apr	sow	"Dwarf Comet Mixed"
May	plant	"Matsumoto Mixed"
Jun	flowering	"Moraketa"
July	flowering	"Milady Mixed"
Aug	flowering	"Ostrich Plume Mixed"
Sept	flowering	"Red Ribbon"
Oct	flowering	"Teisa Stars Mixed"
Nov	/	
Dec	/	

Calluna vulgaris

HEATHER

FEATURES

The heathers are evergreen shrubs that demand acid soil. There is just one species with scores of excellent cultivars. The best way to choose between them is to visit special heather gardens and nurseries, buying forms that make a fun "patchwork quilt." Many have colored foliage with red, purple, bronze, gray, and gold, and many green-leaved ones change color come the fall. The key difference between heathers and ericas is that the latter include varieties that flower in late winter/spring, while heathers peak from midsummer to fall. Most heathers spread about 18in. Some have flowers that contrast with and stand out against the foliage. One such is the cultivar "Firefly," with magenta flowers and beige leaves.

CONDITIONS

ASPECT   Full bright sun is vital. The sun also emphasizes the color of the foliage, its chief virtue in the winter garden.

SITE   These plants will only flourish in acid soil that is free draining. It should also be rich in well-rotted organic matter.

GROWING METHOD

PROPAGATION Increase your number of plants by taking semi-ripe cuttings in the first part of summer. They root quickly.

FEEDING   Make sure that the soil has plenty of organic matter added to keep it rich and fertile.

PROBLEMS   Only in extremely persistent humid conditions might heathers develop gray mold or disease. Otherwise, once planted, these are remarkably problem free.

FLOWERING

SEASON   The flowers appear after midsummer, and continue their display right through into the fall. There is a wide range of colors with dark red "Allegro," white "Beoley Gold," mauve "Blazeaway," pink "Elsie Purnell," and purple-pink "Johnson's Variety." The white "Mair's Variety" makes good cut flowers.

PRUNING

GENERAL   Give the plants a light prune in the spring if required, or for shape. Other than these cases, pruning is not necessary.

HEATHER CAN BE A SPECTACULAR display plant, as this group demonstrates. The variety of colors creates a stunning patchwork effect.

AT A GLANCE		
Heathers are vital components of the winter garden, valued for their range of colored foliage. Hardy to 0°F (zone 7).		
Jan	foliage	**Recommended Varieties**
Feb	foliage	*Calluna vulgaris*
Mar	foliage	"Allegro"
April	foliage	"Beoley Gold"
May	foliage	"Blazeaway"
June	foliage	"Elsie Purnell"
July	flowering	"Firefly"
Aug	flowering	"Johnson's Variety"
Sept	flowering	"Mair's Variety"
Oct	foliage	"Peter Sparkes"
Nov	foliage	"Wickwar Flame"
Dec	foliage	

Camassia

QUAMASH

FEATURES

The botanical name of this plant is derived from that given to it by Native Americans, who grew the bulbs for food. It is relatively unusual among bulbous plants in preferring moist, heavy soils. The tall, graceful flower stems carry dense spires of starry blue flowers. *Camassia leichtlinii* is very reliable, with 3ft flowering stems: *C. quamash* (*C. esculenta*) is a little shorter and has flowers varying from white, through pale blue to deep purple. C. cusickii produces its 4ft pale lavender flower spikes in late spring.

CONDITIONS

ASPECT	Full sun or light, dappled shade will suit these bulbs.
SITE	Camassias make excellent border plants, valuable for early summer color. A moisture-retentive, fertile soil is preferred, though they will also grow adequately in free-draining conditions.

GROWING METHOD

PLANTING	Plant the bulbs in early to mid-fall, 3–4in deep. Space them about 6in apart.
FEEDING	Feeding is not usually necessary, but an application of a balanced, granular fertilizer can be made in spring, especially on poor soils. Water thoroughly in dry conditions and on free-draining soil.
PROBLEMS	Camassias are usually trouble free.

FLOWERING

SEASON	Flowers from late spring through early summer.
CUTTING	Stems can be cut as the lowest buds on the spike begin to open.

AFTER FLOWERING

REQUIREMENTS	Cut down the flowering spikes when the flowers have faded. Do not disturb the bulbs until they become overcrowded, when they can be lifted and divided in fall.

THE INTENSE BLUE flower spikes of Camassia leichtlinii make a striking group among other border plants. A moisture-retentive soil is needed for best results— regular watering is likely to be necessary if the weather is dry. Camassias can cope with heavier soil conditions than many other bulbs.

AT A GLANCE		
Tall, stately spikes of blue, starry flowers provide valuable color in the perennial border in early summer.		
Jan	/	**Recommended Varieties**
Feb	/	*Camassia cusickii*
Mar	/	*C. leichtlinii*
Apr	/	"Electra"
May	flowering	"Blue Danube"
Jun	flowering	"Semiplena"
July	flowering	*C. quamash*
Aug	flowering	
Sept	plant	
Oct	plant	
Nov	/	
Dec	/	

Camellia
CAMELLIA

FEATURES

Glossy-leaved and showered with blossom, evergreen camellias are a great asset. Some species and varieties flower successively from late fall through to spring. Blooms are white, pink, deep rose, or crimson, and suffusions of these colors. Ranging in size from 4–15ft, most varieties flower when 2–3 years old and mature within ten years. They grow to a great age. Plant them to form a statement in a lawn or mixed shrub border, or set them in a large pot or tub and clip them to form a loose obelisk, pyramid or drumstick. They also make a dashing flowering hedge.

SELECTION

Most camellias species come from China and Japan; some from *N. India* and the Himalayas. They have now been extensively hybridised to yield a wide range of varieties. Specialist camellia nurseries and garden centers display flowering plants in spring. Choose a variety suited to the position you have in mind.

TYPES

There are four main types of camellia.
Camellia japonica. Large and glossy leaved, hardier varieties will prosper in sheltered spots. Its varieties brighten fall to spring.
C. sasanqua. Fall-flowered, from October to December, it thrives outdoors in the south. In cooler areas, varieties are better planted in pots, displayed outdoors for summer and transferred to a cool conservatory, porch or greenhouse for flowering in fall.
C. reticulata. Flowering from February to April, varieties can be grown outside in warm, sheltered, gardens. Elsewhere, display them under glass.

C. x williamsii. Producing tough, weather-resistant foliage, and flowering from November to April, its varieties bloom freely despite low light intensity. Each group is discussed in more detail on pages 348–349.

CONDITIONS

ASPECT Camellias grow best in sheltered, dappled shade. In cooler climates, set them in full sun or very light shade to ensure that blossom buds develop from July to October. Protect them from hot, drying, or frosty winds.

Ideally, position plants where early morning sunlight does not heat up frosted blossom buds and cause frozen tissues to rupture.

Sasanqua varieties tolerate more sun than most other camellias and reticulatas need full sun for part of the day. Some varieties of *Camellia japonica,* such as "The Czar" and "Emperor of Russia," happily take full sun.

AT A GLANCE	
Evergreen, frost-tender, or hardy shrub with single, semi-double, or fully double blooms. Hardiness according to species.	

Jan	flower	**Recommended Varieties**
Feb	flower	*C. japonica*
Mar	flower	"Adolphe Audusson"
Apr	plant	"Berenice Boddy"
May	plant, prune	"Captain Rawes"
June	plant, prune	"Fuji-No-Mine"
July	plant	"Nodami-Ushiro"
Aug	plant	*C. x williamsii*
Sept	plant	"Donation"
Oct	flower	"Jury's Yellow"
Nov	flower	
Dec	flower	

SITE   They need very acid, well-drained soil rich in decomposed organic matter. Heavy, badly drained soils cause root rot and plants often die. Fortify thin, sandy soils with well-rotted leaf mould or bulky manure, before planting.

GROWING METHOD

FEEDING   Encourage lustrous leaves and a wealth of blossom by applying a balanced ericaceous fertilizer in April and July. It is vital that border soil or container compost is always moist, so water daily, if necessary, during prolonged hot spells. Mulch with crumbly, bulky organic manure to conserve moisture, but keep it well away from the stem, lest it causes bark to rot.

PROPAGATION   Increase plants from semi-ripe cuttings in late summer, removing a thin strip of bark from the base to reveal wood and stimulate rooting. Leaf-bud cuttings, 1in or so long, again "wounding" the base of the shoot, are also taken then. Alternatively, layer low, flexible shoots from mid-spring to late summer. Some varieties, which are very hard to grow from cuttings, are grafted on to understocks of *C. sasanqua.*

PROBLEMS   You may encounter the following:
BUD DROP: This can be caused by overwet or overdry soils, root rot, or root disturbance. Some very late-flowering varieties may have buds literally pushed off the stem by new spring growth.
BROWN PETALS AND BALLED BLOOMS: This usually occurs when buds or flowers are lit by early morning sunshine while still wet with dew. Petals may be scorched and some buds "ball" and fail to open.

Some varieties with clusters of big buds are prone to this. Gently breaking off some of the buds when they first form helps to reduce balling.
OEDEMA: If plants are overwet and conditions overcast, small, brown, corky swellings may develop on leaves. Reduce watering and try to improve air circulation.
SCALE INSECTS: These may be found on the upper or lower leaf surface. Limpet-like scales suck sap and debilitate plants. Spraying with malathion controls them, but spray only in cool or cloudy weather so that it does not scorch leaves.
LEAF GALL: This causes abnormal thickening and discoloration of new growth. It occurs in spring and is caused by a fungus. Pick off and destroy affected leaves before spores disperse.
VIRUSES: May be responsible for variable, bright yellow patterns on leaves, or ring spot. Rings develop on leaves. As the leaf ages it becomes yellowish; the center of the ring becomes bright green. There is no cure for viruses, but plants rarely lose much vigor or have their blooming affected. Pick off the worst-looking leaves if they are spoiling your plant's appearance.

PRUNING

Little pruning is needed. Cutting blooms for the vase is usually enough to keep plants compact. However, any thin, spindly, unproductive growth should be removed from the center of the shrub after flowering.

Ageing, overgrown camellias can be rejuvenated by quite heavy pruning, provided cuts are made directly above a leaf bud. If severe pruning is necessary, do it in stages, over two years, to avoid stressing the plant.

Camellia sasanqua

CAMELLIA

FEATURES

Although other species of camellia can be grown as screening plants, *C. sasanqua* is the most suitable for use as hedges, whether formal or informal. Like all camellias, it is long lived. The growth habit of the cultivars varies and for hedging it is best to choose an upright grower such as "Narumigata," "Navajo," and "Nodami-ushiro." You can choose the height of your hedge but camellias are usually topped off somewhere between 6^{1}/$_{2}$–10ft. Blooming in mid- to late fall, the flowers may be single or double, and they come in a color range of white, pale pink, rose, cerise and red.

CONDITIONS

ASPECT These camellias tolerate sun or shade but are probably best in shade for part of the day. They only withstand wall-to-wall sun when fully established, and even then their roots must be kept on the cool side. As a general rule, keep them sheltered from harsh cold winds which can quickly send them into a major sulk.

SITE Needs well-drained, slightly acid soil that has been heavily enriched with organic matter. Plants also need mulching with decayed manure or compost.

GROWING METHOD

PROPAGATION From semi-ripe cuttings taken in late summer.

SPACING Plant at about 20in intervals.

FEEDING Apply blood and bone fertilizer, or camellia and azalea food, when growth starts in spring and again in midsummer.

PROBLEMS

Root rot caused by overwatering or poorly drained soil will kill these plants, but otherwise they are fairly trouble free. In some years a fungal leaf gall has been known to occur on selected varieties, causing abnormal thickening and discoloration of new growth. Pick off and destroy any leaves that are affected by this pest.

FLOWERING

SEASON There is a late flowering period which begins in the fall.

CUTTING Flowers dismantle easily and so are not suitable for picking.

PRUNING

GENERAL The main pruning should be done in late winter just before new growth begins. Trimming can be done at any time of the year.

AT A GLANCE		
Camellia sasanqua is a terrific late-season flowering hedge, but is not suitable for the cold north. Hardy to 5˚F (zone 7).		
Jan	foliage	**Recommended Varieties**
Feb	foliage	*Camellia japonica*
Mar	foliage	"Bob Hope"
April	foliage	"Guilio Nuccio"
May	foliage	"Kumasaka"
June	foliage	"Miss Universe"
July	foliage	"Leonard Messel"
Aug	foliage	*C. sasanqua*
Sept	foliage	"Narumigata"
Oct	flowering	"Navajo"
Nov	flowering	"Nodami-ushiro"
Dec	foliage	*C.* x *williamsii*
		"Elsie Jury"

Campanula

BELLFLOWER

FEATURES

Also known as the bellflower, campanula contains about 300 species of annuals, biennials, and perennials. Generally easy to grow in either full sunlight or dappled shade, on walls, banks, and in borders, it has a wide range of flowers, from the tubular to the saucer-shaped. They also vary considerably in height, from the low, 3in-high spreaders, like *C. betulifolia*, to the 5ft-tall *C. lactiflora*. The former are excellent at the front of a border, the latter need staking at the rear. There are many excellent forms: *C. glomerata* "Superba" is a vigorous grower, reaching 24 x 24in, while *C. burghaltii* produces pale lavender tubular bells around the same time.

CONDITIONS

ASPECT   Campanula thrive in both sunny yards and those with dappled shade.
SITE   There are three broad types of campanula, each requiring different conditions: well-drained, fertile soil for border plants; moist, fast-draining ground for the rock garden species; and a gritty scree bed for the alpines that dislike being wet over winter.

GROWING METHOD

PROPAGATION Grow the species from seed in spring in a cold frame, or from cuttings, and sow alpines in a frame in the fall. Varieties must be propagated by spring cuttings, or spring or fall division if they are to grow true to the parent.

FEEDING   Apply a complete plant food in the spring, especially on poorer soils, or plenty of dug-in, organic material.
PROBLEMS   Slugs and snails are the major problem, and if not kept under control they can ruin a border display. In some areas *C. persicifolia* is prone to rust.

FLOWERING

SEASON   The long-lasting flowers appear from midwinter to the spring.
CUTTING   Makes an excellent display of cut flowers, especially the taller plants.

AFTER FLOWERING

REQUIREMENTS Cut back to the ground in late fall.

ON ITS OWN or among other plants, the bellflower is undemanding and gives the gardener great rewards. It is a pretty plant that never fails to delight.

AT A GLANCE		
A near 300-strong genus, thriving in a wide variety of conditions, grown for their abundant flowers. Hardy to 5°F (zone 7).		
Jan	/	Recommended Varieties
Feb	/	Campanula arvatica
Mar	sow	C. carpatica
Apr	transplant	C. garganica
May	flowering	C. latiloba
Jun	flowering	C. medium
July	flowering	C. persicifolia
Aug	flowering	C. thyrsoides
Sept	flowering	C. trachelium
Oct	divide	
Nov	/	
Dec	/	

Canna

INDIAN SHOT

FEATURES

Canna is an exotic-looking plant with bold, brilliantly colored flowers carried on tall stems, up to 4ft, above large, paddle-shaped leaves. The large blooms form an impressive spike; colors available are mainly shades of yellow, orange, and red. Sometimes the flowers are bi-colored, or spotted, streaked, or splashed with a contrasting shade. The foliage is also attractive, and in some varieties is tinged with bronze or purple. There are a number of varieties with attractively variegated foliage, which has yellow or pink veins.

Cannas are not hardy and must be protected from frost. *Canna indica* is the best known species, but most varieties generally available are hybrids, often sold as Canna hybrida. A wide range of named varieties is available from specialist suppliers.

CONDITIONS

ASPECT   These plants must have an open but sheltered position in full sun.
SITE   Cannas make an impressive focal point in a bedding display, in mixed or herbaceous borders, or grow well in tubs and large containers. Soil should be free draining but rich in organic matter. In cold areas, the plants are best grown in a greenhouse or conservatory.

GROWING METHOD

PLANTING   Set the rhizomes about 3in deep in fertile soil in late spring, once the risk of frosts is over. Better plants will be obtained by starting the rhizomes off in pots in a frost-free greenhouse in April, and planting them outide in early summer, once all risk of frost is over and the weather is suitably warm.
FEEDING   Give an occasional high potash liquid feed as the flower buds develop. Keep the soil moist at all times but make sure that it is never waterlogged.
PROBLEMS   No specific problems are generally experienced.

FLOWERING

SEASON   Flowers in mid to late summer, until the first frosts.
CUTTING   Flowers are not suitable for cutting— they are best enjoyed on the plants.

AFTER FLOWERING

REQUIREMENTS Lift and dry the rhizomes in early fall, before the first frosts. Store them in a cool, frost-free place in just-moist peat or sand through the winter. If kept bone dry, the rhizomes will shrivel.

AT A GLANCE		
An impressive, exotic-looking plant with tall stems of brightly colored flowers and lush, attractive foliage.		
Jan	/	Recommended Varieties
Feb	/	"Durban"
Mar	plant (indoors)	"Lucifer"
Apr	plant (indoors)	"Oiseau de Feu" ("Firebird")
May	plant (outdoors)	"Picasso"
Jun	plant (outdoors)	"Wyoming"
July	flowering	
Aug	flowering	
Sept	flowering	
Oct	/	
Nov	/	
Dec	/	

Cape Leadwort

PLUMBAGO

FEATURES

Usually grown to color a conservatory, greenhouse, or windowsill with a mist of starry, sky-blue flowers from midsummer to fall, *Plumbago auriculata* is a rambling, evergreen climber. Ideally, grow it in a large pot or tub to allow you to move it on to a patio when frosts finish in late May or early June. Growing to 15ft or so, in cultivation it is best pruned regularly to keep it neat, compact, and floriferous. In very sheltered, frost-free gardens, create a sensation in summer by training it over an arch, arbour, obelisk or trellis.

CONDITIONS

ASPECT   Though plumbago flowers best in full sun, it tolerates very light shade.

SITE   Set this shrub in a large, well-drained pot or small tub of multi-purpose compost.

GROWING METHOD

FEEDING   Insert clusters of slow-release fertilizer granules into the compost in spring. From late spring to summer, apply a high-potash tomato feed.
            When potting plants, add moisture-storage granules to help keep the compost damp during long, dry spells. In late summer, when nights turn cold, return plumbago to a frost-free spot in good light. Keep the compost dryish from fall to spring.

PROPAGATION Take semi-ripe cuttings from early to midsummer.

PROBLEMS   Under glass, fluffy, waxy, white mealy bugs may colonize leaf joints and cripple growth. Control them biologically with *Aphidius colemani*, a parasitic wasp, or spray with horticultural soap.

PRUNING

Shorten the previous year's flowering shoots to within 2in of the older wood in February.

COMMONLY CALLED CAPE LEADWORT, plumbago rewards us with a succession of silvery-blue flowers from mid- to late summer. Encourage it to flower bounteously every year by shortening the previous year's flowered stems in February.

AT A GLANCE	
Scrambling, frost-tender climber studded with pale blue flowers from midsummer to early fall. Hardy to 46°F (zone 11).	
Jan /	**Recommended Varieties**
Feb prune	*P. auriculata*
Mar /	*P. auriculata alba*
Apr plant	"Royal Cape"
May plant	
June plant	
July flower	
Aug flower	
Sept flower	
Oct flower	
Nov /	
Dec /	

Carpinus betulus

HORNBEAM

FEATURES

The common hornbeam, *Carpinus betulus*, grows wild in many areas. An extremely strong wood, it is used for butchers' chopping blocks. If left to grow it can form a massive tree, 60ft high. But it is also the mainstay of wild hedges, withstanding severe pruning, and is grown for its spring catkins and fall color when the leaves turn yellowish-orange. It is particularly useful on heavy ground, and is worth using if you have thick clay soil. It also makes a quick growing, traditional formal hedge, and is a good alternative to hawthorn, beech, holly, privet, laurel and yew. The form "Aspleniifolia" has more shapely, toothed leaves. For a long hedge, seek a specialist supplier who sells inexpensive young plants in bulk.

CONDITIONS

ASPECT | Hornbeam thrives in full sun and partial shade. The lighter the position the more quickly and densely it grows.

SITE | Gardeners on heavy clay soil need not worry too much. Extreme cases should be lightened, but it is not necessary to spend hours trying to provide impeccable drainage by adding copious amounts of horticultural sand and grit.

GROWING METHOD

PROPAGATION | Take fresh cuttings in early summer.

SPACING | Set plants about 3ft apart, depending on the density required.

FEEDING | Hornbeam does not require over-rich, well-worked soil. Moderate fertility is quite acceptable. On planting add plenty of well-rotted organic matter, and mulch to keep in moisture. It should get off to a very good start.

PROBLEMS | Highly robust trees that take care of themselves. Need little fussing.

FLOWERING

SEASON | The big decorative feature is a massed display of catkins (yellow when male, and greenish when female) in the spring. Useful in cut-flower displays.

PRUNING

GENERAL | One of the principle advantages of growing hornbeam is that you can cut it back quite severely and it will always re-shoot, putting on plenty of new growth.

LINES OF DIFFERENT COLOR help this Carpinus betulus *to look quite at home, as well as creating a graceful corridor effect. Although it does produce flowers in the spring, the vibrant leaves make a wonderfully lush display of their own.*

AT A GLANCE	
Ever-reliable deciduous hedging plant, looks best in a cottage garden. Hardy to 0°F (zone 7).	
Jan /	**Companion Plants**
Feb /	Bluebell
Mar /	Crocus
April foliage	Cyclamen
May foliage	Erythronium
June foliage	Fritillaria
July foliage	Poppy
Aug foliage	Primrose
Sept foliage	Rose
Oct foliage	
Nov /	
Dec /	

Catharanthus

MADAGASCAR PERIWINKLE

FEATURES

Varieties of *Catharanthus roseus* have pink/rose, mauve, or white flowers, often with a deeper center. These plants quickly spread, growing to 10–16in, and are suitable for massed bedding displays or pots indoors. Grow as a half-hardy annual.

CONDITIONS

ASPECT	Needs full sunlight to succeed outdoors.
SITE	Needs good drainage, but enrich the soil with well-rotted manure or compost before planting. For containers, use multipurpose compost mixed with extra slow-release fertilizer before planting up.

GROWING METHOD

SOWING	Sow seed in March/April in 3^1/$_2$in pots of multipurpose compost and lightly cover. Keep at 64°F in a light spot and transplant seedlings when they are 1in tall, into cell trays. Keep in a warm greenhouse or warm spot indoors and do not get the compost too wet. Harden off in late May and plant 8–12in apart in their final positions or use in containers.
FEEDING	In bedding displays, apply a liquid plant food monthly to keep plants growing vigorously throughout the summer months.

PROBLEMS

Overwatering and wet soil/compost can lead to rotting. If red spider mite attacks the leaves, use a spray containing bifenthrin.

FLOWERING

SEASON	Flowers appear throughout the summer.
CUTTING	Not suitable for cutting.

AFTER FLOWERING

GENERAL	Remove plants after the first fall frosts and use for composting.

THE FAMILIAR FLOWERS of catharanthus look similar to those of its close relative, the hardy vinca. For bedding displays, catharanthus is available in mixed colors that often contain flowers with darker "eyes," as seen here.

AT A GLANCE	
A half-hardy annual grown for its bright flowers and ideal for use in containers on a warm sunny yard. Frost hardy to 32°F (zone 10).	

		Recommended Varieties
Jan	/	*Catharanthus roseus*
Feb	/	"Apricot Delight"
Mar	sow	"Pacifica Red"
Apr	transplant	"Peppermint Cooler"
May	harden off/plant	"Pretty In… Mixed"
Jun	flowering	"Tropicana Mixed"
July	flowering	"Terrace Vermillion"
Aug	flowering	
Sept	flowering	
Oct	/	
Nov	/	
Dec	/	

Catmint

NEPETA CATARIA

FEATURES

Nepeta cataria, catmint or catnip, is a perennial, native to Europe and Asia. There are several varieties of catmint grown in gardens, all with slightly different growing habits, including *N. mussinii* and *N. x faassenii*, which have similar properties. In general they are low-growing perennials reaching 1–3ft in height. Fine white hairs cover both the stem, which is square as in all members of the mint family, and the gray-green leaves. These are coarse-toothed and ovate, although the base leaves are heart-shaped. The tubular summer flowers are massed in spikes or whorls. White, pale pink, or purplish blue in color, they produce very fine seeds. Cats find some catmints very attractive.

CONDITIONS

ASPECT	Prefers an open, sunny position but tolerates partial shade. Most fragrant in good sunlight.
SITE	Catmint does best in fertile sandy loams.

GROWING METHOD

SOWING	Catmint self-sows readily by seeding, once it is established, and can also be grown from cuttings taken in spring. To do this, cut a 4in piece from the parent plant, remove the tip and lower leaves, and place the cutting in a moist soil medium. Cuttings take root in 2 to 3 weeks. Divide mature plants into three or four clumps in spring or fall.

FEEDING	As members of the mint family have a high water requirement, keep this plant moist at all times. Do not stand pots in water, however, as this can drown the plant. Mulch lightly in spring and fall, and give a balanced general fertilizer in spring. Feed with nitrogen-rich fertilizer such as poultry manure in spring for more leaf growth.
PROBLEMS	Catmint is basically pest free.
PRUNING	Prune back each year to keep bushes in shape.

HARVESTING

PICKING	Pick fresh leaves as required. Cut leafy stems in late summer when the plant is in bloom. Hang them to dry in a cool, shady place.
STORAGE	Strip leaves and flowers from dried stems and store in airtight jars.
FREEZING	Leaves can be put in a freezer bag and frozen for up to 6 months.

AT A GLANCE

Sporting clusters of pink or lilac flowers from late summer to fall, it needs a sheltered position. Hardy to 14°F (zone 8).

			Parts used	
Jan	/		Leaves	
Feb	/		Flowers	
Mar	plant		**Uses**	
Apr	plant		Culinary	
May	plant	harvest	Medicinal	
Jun	plant	harvest	Craft	
July	harvest		Gardening	
Aug	harvest			
Sept	plant	harvest		
Oct	plant			
Nov	/			
Dec	/			

USES

CULINARY   Fresh young leaves were once a popular salad ingredient and were used for herbal teas, although they are less popular now.

MEDICINAL   Catmint was once used as a cold remedy. (The leaves have a high vitamin C content.)

CRAFT   Dried flowers and leaves are used in pot-pourri mixtures, and in toys for cats.

GARDENING   Plant it near vegetables to deter flea beetles. The scent is also said to deter rats.

THE POWDER BLUE FLOWERS and softly aromatic leaves of catmint are most attractive to human eyes and noses.

Celosia
PRINCE OF WALES' FEATHERS

FEATURES

Also known as Prince of Wales' feathers, celosia, or cockscomb has plume-like or crested flowers (shown left) ranging in color from deep crimson to scarlet, orange, and yellow. Tall forms grow to 30in, the dwarf forms to 10–12in. Grow it as a half-hardy annual and use in bedding or as a striking plant for containers. Good for cutting.

CONDITIONS

ASPECT   Must have a sunny, warm spot to do well.
SITE   Needs well-drained soil that has been enriched with well-rotted manure or compost. Good soil preparation is essential to ensure strong plants and large flowerheads. Plant up containers using multipurpose compost

GROWING METHOD

SOWING   Celosias dislike having their roots disturbed so sow 2–3 seeds per cell in a multi-cell tray using multipurpose compost, in February/March. Keep at 64°F and when the seedlings appear after 2–3 weeks, remove all but the strongest. Carefully pot the young plants on into 3$^{1}/_{2}$in pots, then harden off for two weeks before planting after the last frosts. Plant without damaging the roots, 6–12in apart, and water.
FEEDING   Feed bedding monthly with liquid feed. Mix slow-release fertilizer with the compost before planting up containers.

PROBLEMS   Wet, cold soil/compost can cause rotting of the roots, so avoid heavy soils and grow in pots.

FLOWERING

SEASON   Flowers appear throughout summer.
CUTTING   May be used as a cut flower for unusual indoor decoration. Cut some plumes and hang them upside down in a dry, airy place for later use in dried flower arrangements.

AFTER FLOWERING

GENERAL   Remove plants after the first frosts of fall.

THE FEATHERY FLOWERS of celosia are made up of masses of smaller flowers, and have a distinctive, plume-like shape. The brilliant plumes always look good in patio pots and containers when planted together in groups of 4–6 plants.

AT A GLANCE	
A half-hardy annual grown for its feathery, plume-like flowerheads in a range of colors. Frost hardy to 32°F (zone 10).	
Jan /	**Recommended Varieties**
Feb sow	**Plumed**
Mar sow	*Celosia argentea*
Apr pot on	"Kimono Mixed"
May harden off/plant	"Dwarf Geisha"
Jun flowering	"Century Mixed"
July flowering	"New Look"
Aug flowering	*C. spicata*
Sept flowering	"Flamingo Feather"
Oct /	**Crested**
Nov /	*C. cristata*
Dec /	"Jewel Box Mixed"

Centaurea

CORNFLOWER

FEATURES

Cornflower, *Centaurea cyanus*, is one of the easiest hardy annuals to grow and can be used in bedding, containers, and for cut flowers. Other than blue, there are mixtures available and single colors such as the "Florence" types in red, pink, and white, reaching 14in tall. Taller varieties like "Blue Diadem" are best for cutting. Regular removal of dead flowers is essential to prolong flowering and to stop plants from becoming shabby.

CONDITIONS

ASPECT   Needs full sunlight all day.

SITE   Must have very well-drained soil, but no special soil preparation is necessary. Staking is necessary when grown in windy situations, but the plants are self-supporting when they are planted in groups. For container growing, use multipurpose compost.

GROWING METHOD

SOWING   Sow seed in the spring where plants are to flower in short rows ½in deep and approximately 12in apart. Thin out so the plants are finally 3–6in apart. This can also be done in late September for stronger plants and earlier flowers, but leave thinning out until the following spring. Can also be sown in pots and transplanted to cell trays for plants to use in courtyard containers.

FEEDING

FEEDING   Extra feeding is usually unnecessary.

PROBLEMS   White mildew affects leaves but is not serious.

FLOWERING

SEASON   Summer until early fall.

CUTTING   Cut before the petals open too far.

AFTER FLOWERING

GENERAL   Remove plants once flowering is finished. Plants self-seed if they are left in the ground.

CORNFLOWERS should have pale, fading flowers removed regularly. For indoor use, cut the stems when the buds are still closed. Grown in groups like this, cornflowers will support each other quite naturally. In windy spots, push twigs in between plants.

AT A GLANCE	
A hardy annual grown for its "cottage garden"-style flowers in various colors, useful for cutting. Frost hardy to 5°F (zone 7).	

Jan	/	Recommended Varieties
Feb	/	*Centaurea cyanus*
Mar	sow	Short varieties
Apr	thin out	"Florence Blue"
May	flowering	"Florence Mixed"
Jun	flowering	"Florence Pink"
July	flowering	"Florence Red"
Aug	flowering	"Florence White"
Sept	flowers/sow	"Midget Mixed"
Oct	/	Tall varieties
Nov	/	"Blue Diadem"
Dec	/	"Black Ball"

Centranthus ruber

RED VALERIAN

FEATURES

This evergreen perennial is very easy to grow, but it often exceeds its allotted space by self-seeding (seedlings are easy to pull out). It has a long flowering period and can survive in poor, dry soil. It generally reaches 16in tall, but in good soil tops 28in. Flowers are a deep pink to red, and there is a white form, too. Ideal for a low-maintenance yard, it is often planted in mixed borders for its long display. It is also grown in large rock gardens and on dry, fast-draining slopes. Self-sown plants can be found in almost no soil on rocky outcrops, and thrive in chalky ground.

CONDITIONS

ASPECT   Likes full sunlight all day.
SOIL   Needs very well-drained soil, but it need not be particularly rich.

GROWING METHOD

PROPAGATION Grows readily from tip cuttings taken in late spring and summer, or from seed sown in the spring. Space the plants 8in apart.
FEEDING   Fertilizer is generally not necessary, but you may give a little complete plant food in the spring, as new growth begins. Needs regular watering to establish, after which plants are extremely drought-tolerant.
PROBLEMS   No specific problems are known.

FLOWERING

SEASON   The very long flowering period extends from the spring until early fall, especially if plants are cut back after each flowering flush to encourage plenty of new buds.
CUTTING   Does not make a good cut flower.

AFTER FLOWERING

REQUIREMENTS No attention is needed, beyond removing the spent flower stems. This has a double advantage: it keeps the plant looking neat, and prevents abundant self-seeding.

TRUSSES OF RICH CRIMSON and softer pink valerian provide months of bright color in the yard, rivalling the display of annuals.

AT A GLANCE	
C. ruber is a hardy, herbaceous perennial, a favorite in "cottage gardens" with tall, red summer flowers. Hardy to 10°F (zones 7–8).	
Jan /	**Companion Plants**
Feb sow	*Argyranthemum foeniculaceum*
Mar sow	*A. frutescens*
Apr transplant	*Cytisus*
May transplant	*Geranium robertianum*
Jun flowering	*Hedera colchica*
July flowering	"Dentata Variegata"
Aug flowering	*Helleborus orientalis*
Sept flowering	*Stipa*
Oct /	*Yucca*
Nov /	
Dec /	

Cerastium tomentosum

SNOW-IN-SUMMER

FEATURES

Cerastium tomentosum is an attractive plant with small, silver-gray leaves and sprays of white flowers that appear in late spring and summer. The silvery foliage provides a good color contrast with brighter colors in the garden. It has a low, creeping habit with stems that root down as they travel along. Ideal for sunny rockeries and dry areas, it is quite quick growing and long lived in the right conditions. Position the plants at about 1ft intervals for quick cover. Once it is established, *C. tomentosum* suppresses weeds well but it may also invade areas where it is not wanted. It is, however, a simple matter to dig out any offending sections.

CONDITIONS

ASPECT	This plant must be grown in full sun to achieve its potential.
SITE	Soil must be well drained.

GROWING METHOD

PROPAGATION	The easiest method of propagation is by division of a rooted clump, but tip cuttings may be taken in late spring and summer. Given the rate at which it spreads, it is unlikely you will need more plants.
FEEDING	Apply complete plant food or pelleted poultry manure in early spring. However, feeding is unnecessary, and snow-in-summer is almost as vigorous on quite poor soil.

PROBLEMS

This plant has no specific pest or disease problems, but overwatering or poorly drained soil will cause plants to rot and die.

FLOWERING

SEASON	Pretty white flowers are produced through spring and into early summer in cool areas.

PRUNING

GENERAL	No pruning is needed beyond shearing off spent flower stems or trimming growth to control its spread. You can be as ruthless as you want. *C. tomentosum* is quite tough, and keeps coming back even when you thought you'd pruned it excessively hard.

THE FLOWER STEMS of snow-in-summer rise high above the silvery foliage. This plant likes dry conditions and flourishes on a steep slope.

AT A GLANCE		
Cerastium tomentosum is a sun-loving, white-flowering spreader, excellent on any spare piece of ground. Hardy to 5°F (zone 7).		
Jan	/	**Companion Plants**
Feb	/	Berberis
Mar	flowering	Cotoneaster
April	flowering	Elaeagnus
May	flowering	Ilex
June	flowering	Prunus
July	foliage	Pyracantha
Aug	foliage	Rosa
Sept	foliage	Viburnum
Oct	/	
Nov	/	
Dec	/	

Cereus
COLUMN CACTUS

FEATURES

With a diverse range of origins from the West Indies to eastern South America, many of these cactuses are almost tree-like, while most form upright sturdy columns. The best-known species, *Cereus uruguayanus* (syn. *C. peruvianus*), is tree-like and can grow to 10ft or more with a stout, blue-green body notched where spines emerge. The "Monstrose" form makes a jumble of oddly shaped, blue-gray stems. Another tree-like species, *C. validus*, can also reach about 10ft high. Once established, it has pink-tinged white flowers in summer. *C. chalybaeus* is a column cactus, often tinged blue or purple, with well-defined ribs bearing spines that mature to black. Its flowers are also white with the outer petals magenta or red.

CONDITIONS

ASPECT   These cactuses prefer to be grown in an open situation in full sun. Keep them well away from even the lightest shade.

SITE   The soil must be free draining, but need not be rich. Column cactuses come from areas with poor rocky soil. Although the size and proportion of these plants make them easiest to accommodate in a desert garden, column cactuses can also be grown in containers, which may need some extra weight such as stones or gravel in the base to stop them tipping over. Note however that some, such as the columnar *C. validus* and *C. hildmannianus monstrose*, have the potential to reach 20ft and 15ft. Of the two, the latter makes the most interesting shape with a contorted vertical stem.

GROWING METHOD

PROPAGATION   Grow plants from seed sown in spring or from cuttings of side branches.

FEEDING   Feed container-grown plants low-nitrogen liquid fertilizer monthly in summer. Ground-grown plants do not need feeding.

PROBLEMS   No pest or disease problems are known.

FLOWERING

SEASON   The large and lovely nocturnal flowers appear during spring and summer. The flowers usually appear after dark and fade before dawn.

FRUITS   Flowers are followed by round or oval fleshy fruits that ripen to yellow or red or purple.

AT A GLANCE		
A good choice if you like tall, quick growing vertical cacti, many with night-opening flowers. 45°F min (zone 11).		
Jan	/	**Recommended Varieties**
Feb	/	*Cereus aethiops*
Mar	sow	*C. chalybaeus*
Apr	transplant	*C. hildmannianus*
May	repotting	*C. uruguayanus*
Jun	flowering	*C. validus*
July	flowering	**Companion Plants**
Aug	/	Astrophytum
Sept	flowering	Echinocactus
Oct	/	Gymnocalycium
Nov	/	Mammillaria
Dec	/	

Chaenomeles speciosa

FLOWERING QUINCE

FEATURES

This deciduous spiny shrub, a native of China, is very amenable to training flat against a wall or fence. The spines and thick growth of this plant make it a practical barrier shrub—and it can also be trained as a hedge. It flowers only from young shoots, so build up a system of permanent stems, tying them in to their support, and the flowers will be produced on the previous year's side shoots. The rich red blooms appear in spring, often very early in the season. Although of vigorous habit, growing up to 8ft high with a spread of 15ft, it is ideally suited to growing on a wall of the house, or on a fence of normal height, as it can be kept smaller if desired by pruning.

CONDITIONS

ASPECT	The Flowering quince should be grown in full sun or partial shade. However, flowering is most prolific in sun.
SITE	This shrub will thrive in any well-drained soil that is reasonably fertile.

GROWING METHOD

PROPAGATION	Sow seeds in fall and stratify them over winter. Take semi-ripe cuttings in summer.
WATERING	Watering is only needed if the soil starts to dry out excessively in the summer.
FEEDING	In the spring apply a slow-release organic fertilizer such as blood, fish and bone.
PROBLEMS	The plant may be attacked by pests including aphids and scale insects.

FLOWERING/FOLIAGE

FLOWERS	Bowl-shaped flowers, which are usually red with yellow anthers, are produced in the spring. They are followed by fragrant, apple-shaped, greenish yellow edible fruits, which can be used to make jelly.
FOLIAGE	The oval leaves are shiny and deep green.

PRUNING

REQUIREMENTS	Build up a permanent framework of stems and then spur prune annually after flowering—cut back the old flowered shoots to within two to four buds of the framework.

DENSE, TWIGGY GROWTH and ease of cultivation make japonica a practical and secure choice for boundary planting. The delicate appearance of the flowers belies the tough nature of japonica. Flowers can be apricot, white, pink or crimson.

AT A GLANCE		
A spiny shrub with cup-shaped flowers, often on bare stems, in the spring. Hardy to 5˚F (zone 7).		
Jan	/	**Recommended Varieties**
Feb	planting	"Geisha Girl" (double, deep apricot)
Mar	planting	"Moerloosei" (white and pink)
Apr	flowering	"Nivalis" (white)
May	flowering	"Simonii" (double, deep red)
Jun	/	
July	/	
Aug	/	
Sep	/	
Oct	/	
Nov	/	
Dec	/	

Chamaedorea elegans

PARLOUR PALM

FEATURES

A native of Mexico and Guatemala, it is called the Parlour palm because of its widespread popularity as a houseplant. Hailing from a jungle environment, they are quite happy in poorly lit rooms. A smallish palm, it produces a clump of slender stems topped with deep green pinnate fronds about 2ft in length. Eventually it reaches a height of 6–10ft, with a spread 3–6ft. The Parlour palm flowers more freely than many other palms, even indoors, but does not usually set fruits when grown as a houseplant and in any case male and female plants would be needed. A long-lived palm, it is ideal for growing in containers and is a suitable subject for a warm conservatory or glasshouse.

CONDITIONS

ASPECT   Grow the Parlour palm in bright light but do not subject it to direct sun that may scorch the foliage. Provide high humidity. Outdoors avoid windy situations that may result in damage to the fronds.

SITE   In containers grow this palm in soil-less potting compost.

GROWING METHOD

PROPAGATION   Sow seeds as soon as available and germinate at a minimum temperature of 77°F.

WATERING   Plenty of water in growing season from late spring to late summer, then for the rest of the year water sparingly.

FEEDING   Apply a balanced liquid fertilizer monthly during the growing season from late spring to late summer.

PROBLEMS

Under glass the Parlour palm is liable to be attacked by scale insects, red spider mites, and thrips.

FOLIAGE/FLOWERING

FOLIAGE   Being evergreen the foliage looks good all the year round. At its best in spring and summer.

FLOWERS   Yellow flowers are produced from spring to fall and are followed by tiny black fruits.

GENERAL CARE

REQUIREMENTS Remove dead fronds when necessary by cutting them off close to the trunk.

NEAT FOLIAGE and tolerance of low light levels make the parlour palm most useful. This one shows an immature flower stem.

AT A GLANCE		
A smallish palm producing thin stems with rich green feathery fronds. Provide a minimum temperature of 61°F (zone 11).		
Jan	/	Recommended Varieties
Feb	/	The variety "Bella" is more
Mar	planting	compact in habit and
Apr	planting flowering	flowers more freely than
May	flowering	the species.
Jun	flowering	
July	flowering	
Aug	flowering	
Sep	flowering	
Oct	/	
Nov	/	
Dec	/	

Chamaerops humilis

DWARF FAN PALM

FEATURES

A native of the Mediterranean region, this is a moderate sized, very bushy, suckering palm with somewhat variable, fan-shaped, pinnate, gray-green or blue-green leaves, up to 39in in length. These leaves have a very feathery appearance and are highly attractive. The Dwarf fan palm eventually reaches a height of 6–10ft, with a spread of 3–6ft. It has a moderate rate of growth (it is fully grown after 10 years) and is long lived, making it ideal for growing in containers. This palm rarely grows a full trunk—except in perfect conditions. Suitable for a cool conservatory or greenhouse, it is ideal, too, for growing as a houseplant and it fares especially well outside in the summer.

CONDITIONS

ASPECT Grow the Dwarf fan palm in bright light but do not subject it to direct sun that may scorch the foliage. Provide moderate humidity. Outdoors place in a sheltered position.

SITE In containers grow this palm in soil-based potting compost.

GROWING METHOD

PROPAGATION Sow seeds as soon as available and germinate them in a minimum temperature of 72°F. Remove rooted suckers in spring and pot up individually.

WATERING Moderate watering in growing season from late spring to late summer, then for the rest of the year water sparingly.

FEEDING Apply a balanced liquid fertilizer monthly during the growing season from late spring to late summer.

PROBLEMS Under glass this palm may be attacked by red spider mites.

FOLIAGE/FLOWERING

FOLIAGE This evergreen palm looks good all year round but is especially useful for summer displays.

FLOWERS Yellow flowers are produced in spring and summer followed by brown to yellow fruits.

GENERAL CARE

REQUIREMENTS Remove dead fronds when necessary by cutting them off close to the trunk.

THE EXPLOSIVE DISPLAY of Chamaerops humilis fronds, reminiscent of a fireworks display, makes it a useful feature plant. The ronds radiate outward from the stem. These serve to direct much-needed water to the base of the plant.

AT A GLANCE	
A bushy suckering palm with fan-shaped, very feathery leaves. Half-hardy, it can take temperatures down to 32°F (zone 10).	
Jan /	Companion Plants
Feb /	Looks good with other
Mar planting	cool-growing palms and
Apr planting flowering	is an ideal subject for
May flowering	combining with brightly
Jun flowering	colored summer bedding
July flowering	plants outdoors. Under
Aug flowering	glass could combine with
Sep /	bougainvilleas.
Oct /	
Nov /	
Dec /	

Cheiranthus
WALLFLOWER

FEATURES

Wallflowers have fragrant flowers of yellow, brown, cream, red, and orange and are grown for their sweet spring scent. These hardy biennials grow between 8 and 18in, depending on the variety, and are available as mixed or single colors. Plants are used for bedding but may also be used in courtyard containers, where they can be moved near doors and windows when in bloom. Ready-grown plants can be bought in early fall.

CONDITIONS

ASPECT	Grow in full sunlight for the best scent.
SITE	Must have very well-drained soil. Add lime before planting to reduce the effect of clubroot disease. Use multipurpose compost in containers and windowboxes. Avoid places exposed to winter winds and move containers to shelter during severe winter weather.

GROWING METHOD

SOWING	Sow May/June outdoors in rows 12in apart and $^1/_2$in deep. As plants grow, thin them to 12in apart, and pinch when 3in tall to make growth bushy. Can also be sown in pots and transplanted into $3^1/_2$in pots. Plant in October in beds or containers. When lifting plants, keep as much soil on the roots as possible.

FEEDING	Give a liquid feed monthly during summer.
PROBLEMS	Avoid growing in soil known to be infected with clubroot disease, or raise plants in pots using multipurpose compost.

FLOWERING

SEASON	Late winter through to the spring.
CUTTING	Cut stems last well in water.

AFTER FLOWERING

GENERAL	Remove plants in late spring after flowering.

THE INTENSE COLORS of wallflowers are only matched by their strong, lingering scent that is best on warm, still days.

AT A GLANCE		
With its bright flowers and strong scent, this biennial is useful for spring bedding and for containers. Frost hardy to 5°F (zone 7).		
Jan	/	**Recommended Varieties**
Feb	flowering	*Cheiranthus cheiri*
Mar	flowering	**Tall**
Apr	flowering	"Blood Red"
May	sow	"Cloth of Gold"
Jun	sow	"Harlequin"
July	thin out	**Medium**
Aug	grow on	"My Fair Lady Mixed"
Sept	grow on	"Vulcan Improved"
Oct	plant	**Dwarf**
Nov	/	"Prince Mixed"
Dec	/	"Tom Thumb Mixed"

Chicory

CICHORIUM INTYBUS

FEATURES

This is a large perennial plant, often grown as an annual. It reaches 3–5ft or more in height. The intense sky-blue, fine-petalled flowers, borne in summer, open in the morning but close up in the hot midday sun. The broad, oblong leaves with ragged edges, reminiscent of dandelions, form a rosette around the bottom of the tall, straggly stems. The upper leaves are much smaller, giving a bare look to the top of the plant. Some varieties can be cultivated by forcing and blanching, when the lettuce-like heart of the chicory plant turns into chicons.

CONDITIONS

ASPECT	Prefers full sun. May need support.
SITE	These plants require deep, rich, friable soil for best growth.

GROWING METHOD

SOWING	Sow seeds in spring, into drills or trenches 1.25in deep, and thin the seedlings to 12in apart when they are established. Seeds may also be germinated in seed trays and seedlings transplanted into the garden during the months of spring.
FEEDING	Keep chicory well watered during spells of hot weather. Add compost to the garden bed in mid summer, but do not provide too much nitrogen or the leaves will grow rapidly at the expense of root growth.
PROBLEMS	No particular pests or diseases affect this plant.

HARVESTING

PICKING	Pick young green leaves of chicory when they are required. Pick newly opened flowers in summer. Dig up roots in fall.
STORAGE	The leaves cannot be stored either fresh or dried. The root can be dried and then rendered into a powder.
FREEZING	Not suitable for freezing.
FORCING	Lift roots in fall or winter, trim off the leaves to about 1inch from the root, and keep in the dark in a bucket of dry sand to force sweet, new growth which can be harvested in a few weeks.

USES

CULINARY	Use young leaves as soon as they are picked, either in salads or in cooking, and forced leaves as winter salad. The flavour is similar to dandelion. Flowers can be crystallised and used to decorate cakes and puddings. Roasted chicory root is widely used as a coffee substitute.

AT A GLANCE		
A tall, straggly perennial with intense bright blue flowers, often grown as annual for forcing. Hardy to 4°F (zone 6).		
Jan	/	Parts used
Feb	/	Leaves
Mar	plant	Flowers
Apr	plant	Roots
May	plant harvest	Shoots
Jun	plant harvest	Uses
July	plant harvest	Culinary
Aug	harvest	Medicinal
Sept	harvest	
Oct	force	
Nov	force	
Dec	force	

| MEDICINAL | A bitter tonic and digestive can be made from the leaves, and a laxative from the roots. |
| CAUTION | Excessive continued use may cause eye problems. |

CHICORY IS THOUGHT to have been one of the "bitter herbs" the Israelites ate with the Passover lamb. Christians thought it was an aphrodisiac.

Chionodoxa

GLORY OF THE SNOW

FEATURES

This dainty little bulb is ideal for rock gardens or raised beds, with its mass of open, star-shaped blue flowers with white centers. They are carried on short spikes of up to a dozen or so flowers per spike. The strap-shaped leaves form loose, rather untidy rosettes.

Chionodoxa luciliae (*C. gigantea*) grows to 4in tall with clear blue, white-eyed flowers some 1½in or more across. *Chionodoxa siehei*, which used to be known as *C. luciliae*, and is sometimes listed as *C. forbesii*, reaches 4–10in, with slightly smaller flowers that are available in pale blue, white, or purplish-pink forms. The flowers have a distinct white eye and a central boss of stamens, tipped with gold. *C. sardensis* has flowers of a striking gentian blue with a tiny white center that is almost unnoticeable.

CONDITIONS

ASPECT   Full sun or dappled shade is suitable, though they grow best in an open, sunny position.

SITE   *Chionodoxa* is suitable for window boxes, rock gardens, raised beds, the front of borders, or naturalized in grass. Soil should be free- draining, but otherwise these bulbs are not fussy about their growing conditions.

GROWING METHOD

PLANTING   Plant the bulbs in groups about 3in deep and 3in apart in early fall.

FEEDING   A balanced granular fertilizer can be sprinkled over the soil surface in spring, but plants usually grow well without supplementary feeding, except in very poor, thin soils. Watering is necessary only in very dry conditions.

PROBLEMS   Apart from occasional slug damage, plants are generally trouble-free.

FLOWERING

SEASON   *Chionodoxa* flowers in early spring, sometimes appearing as the snow is thawing to live up to its common name.

CUTTING   Flowers can be cut when they begin to open. They are valuable for cutting when few other flowers are available in the garden.

AFTER FLOWERING

REQUIREMENTS Lift and divide overcrowded plants when the foliage dies down in early summer after flowering, otherwise little attention is needed.

AT A GLANCE		
A low-growing bulb producing plenty of bright blue flowers in early spring.		
Jan	/	**Recommended Varieties**
Feb	flowering	*Chionodoxa siehei*
Mar	flowering	"Alba"
Apr	flowering	"Pink Giant"
May	/	"Rosea"
Jun	/	
July	/	
Aug	/	
Sept	plant	
Oct	/	
Nov	/	
Dec	/	

Chives

ALLIUM SCHOENOPRASUM, A. TUBEROSUM

FEATURES

Chives are perennial herbs that make an attractive edging for a herb garden or bed of mixed annuals and perennials. They grow in clumps from very small bulbs that send up 12in tall grass-like, hollow, tubular, green leaves, tapering to a point at the top. The plants produce flower stems in summer. The flowers of the common chive, *A. schoenoprasum*, take the form of a dense, globular head of pinkish to pale purple blossoms. Chinese or garlic chives (*A. tuberosum*) have a flowerhead composed of star-like, white flowers and flat, narrow, light to dark green leaves. Chives can be grown successfully in small containers and clumps can even be potted up and brought indoors to keep in the kitchen.

CONDITIONS

ASPECT   Chives tolerate a wide range of conditions but grow best in a sunny position.

SITE   Chives do best in rich, moist, but well-drained soil, but will tolerate a wide range of conditions.

GROWING METHOD

SOWING   The simplest way to propagate chives is by division. Lift a clump in spring, separate into smaller clumps and replant into fertile ground. Chives can also be grown easily from seed, but need warm conditions to germinate, so are best sown indoors in early spring, with bottom heat. Alternatively, wait until late spring or summer to sow outdoors. Plant clumps 8in apart, in rows 1–2ft apart.

FEEDING   Water chives well, especially during hot months. At planting time dig in compost or well-rotted manure and a balanced general fertilizer.

PROBLEMS   Chives can suffer from rust. Cut back and burn diseased growth, or, if bad, remove the plant completely. Mildew may also be a problem, and greenfly may attack pot-grown plants.

HARVESTING

PICKING   Pick leaves as available. Do not snip off the tips or the chive will become tough and fibrous. Clip the leaves or blades close to the ground, leaving about 2in still intact. Harvest chives regularly to keep the crop growing. Pick flowers when fully open, but before the color fades.

STORAGE   Chives do not store very well.

FREEZING   Leaves can be frozen for about 6 months. Chop them, put them in a freezer bag, and freeze them for use when needed at a later date.

AT A GLANCE		
This hardy perennial herb is highly valued for its tasty green leaves. Ideal for salads. Hardy to 4°F (zone 6).		
Jan	/	**Parts used**
Feb	/	Leaves
Mar	plant	Flowers
Apr	plant harvest	Buds
May	plant harvest	**Uses**
Jun	plant harvest	Culinary
July	plant harvest	Medicinal
Aug	harvest	Gardening
Sept	harvest	
Oct	harvest	
Nov	/	
Dec	/	

USES

CULINARY Leaves of the chive, *A. schoenoprasum*, have a delicate, mild onion flavour and are added to soups or casseroles during the last moments of cooking. Chopped leaves are also used in salads, in herb butter, as a garnish over other vegetables and in the French fines herbes. The flowers can be eaten fresh, tossed in salads, or made into spectacular herb vinegars or butters. All parts of the Chinese chive, *A. tuberosum*, have a mild garlic flavour and the unopened flower bud has a special place in Asian cuisines.

MEDICINAL The leaves are mildly antiseptic and also promote digestion.

GARDENING Chives are recommended companions for roses, carrots, grapes, tomatoes, and fruit trees. They are said to prevent scab on apples and blackspot on roses.

Christmas box

SARCOCOCCA

FEATURES

An easy, suckering, lance- or oval-leaved evergreen, sarcococca is a delight in February when tufted flowers of white or creamy male petals and smaller female blooms sleeve stems and release rich vanilla fragrance.

On a warm, breezy day, scent is detectable many yards from the bush. If you plant a group of it beneath a living-room window, the perfume will waft indoors. Cut blooms will scent a room.

Carpeting thickly and suppressing weeds, *Sarcococca hookeriana* forms a 12in high thicket, 3ft across. *Digyna*, a form of *S. hookeriana*, has purple-tinged leaves and thrusts to 4ft. Its flowers are followed by black berries. Resembling privet, *S. confusa* is a neater version, to 2.5ft. Appealingly different, *S. ruscifolia* forms a rugged bush of broader leaves, to 3ft high and across, and blooms are followed by red berries.

CONDITIONS

ASPECT Ideal for clothing dappled shady areas beneath trees or borders on the north side of a wall or fence and between houses, it prospers in full sun, too. Avoid deeply shaded sites where growth is less compact and flowering inhibited.

SITE Sarcococca favours deep, humus- and nutrient-rich, acid or alkaline soils that drain freely. Improve poor, sandy patches by working in bulky organic manure. Lighten and aerate heavy clay by digging in some grit or pea shingle.

Plant it in a large tub or pot to perfume a patio or terrace in mild spells during winter. Alternatively, set it to flank a path or driveway where you will brush against it and enjoy its "clean," rich scent.

GROWING METHOD

FEEDING Encourage robust growth by working bone meal into the planting hole and pricking it into the root area in spring and fall. Help young plants establish quickly by watering copiously after planting and in dry spells in their first year.

PROPAGATION Increase your stock by using a spade to slice off rooted suckers in spring or take semi-ripe cuttings of new shoots in midsummer.

PROBLEMS Small, young plants may take several months to settle down and grow enthusiastically. Encourage them to develop quickly by liquid feeding fortnightly with a high-nitrogen fertilizer in spring and summer.

PRUNING

No regular cutting back is necessary. Remove dead or damaged shoots in spring.

AT A GLANCE	
White-flowered and sweetly scented, bushy or carpeting evergreen for sunny or lightly shaded places. Hardy to 4°F (zone 7).	
Jan /	**Recommended Varieties**
Feb flower	*S. confusa*
Mar plant	*S. hookeriana digyna*
Apr plant, prune	*S. hookeriana humilis*
May plant	*S. ruscifolia*
Jun /	
July /	
Aug plant	
Sept plant	
Oct /	
Nov /	
Dec /	

Chrysanthemum hybrids
DENDRANTHEMA

FEATURES

Chrysanthemums probably originated in China, but were introduced into Japan a very long time ago. A big favorite in garden and florists' displays, they are the highlight of the late summer and fall border. They are also widely used as a long-lasting cut flower. Chrysanthemums have been renamed and moved to the genus *Dendranthema*, though the name has yet to catch on. Four kinds to look out for include: the Korean (e.g. "Yellow Starlet"), which give a long flowering performance but dislike excessive winter wet (store inside in severe conditions); the thigh-high, dwarf, bushy pompons ("Mei Kyo") with a sea of rounded flowers; the clump-forming rubellums (named hybrids of *C. rubellum*) which are hardiest, have a woody base, but again dislike extreme damp; and the sprays ("Pennine") which are grown both for the border and cutting.

COLOR

The color range is wide, covering white, cream, yellow, many shades of pink and lilac, burgundy, pale apricot, and deep mahogany.

TYPES

There are many forms of chrysanthemums, and they have been classified by specialist societies and nurseries according to floral type. Some of the types are decorative, anemone centered, spider, pompon, single, exhibition, and Korean spray. There is virtually a shape for every taste.

STAKING

Many of the taller varieties need staking, which needs to be carefully thought out if the display is to avoid looking too structured. One reliable, traditional method is to insert bamboo canes at intervals around and through the planting, and thread twine from cane to cane in a criss-cross fashion, perhaps 20–24in above the ground.

CONDITIONS

ASPECT   Grows best in full sun with protection from strong winds.

SITE   Needs well-drained soil that has been heavily enriched with organic matter before planting. Plants should also be mulched with decayed compost or manure.

AT A GLANCE		
Chrysanthemums are the colorful mainstay of the the end-of-season border. The hardy forms will tolerate 5˚F (zone 7).		
Jan	/	Recommended Varieties
Feb	sow	"Anna Marie"
Mar	sow	"Bronze Elegance"
Apr	divide	"Cappa"
May	transplant	"Faust"
Jun	/	"Lord Butler"
July	/	"Mrs Jessie Cooper"
Aug	flowering	"Poppet"
Sept	flowering	"Salmon Fairie"
Oct	/	
Nov	/	
Dec	/	

GROWING METHOD

PROPAGATION In spring lift and divide the new suckering growth so that each new plant has its own roots and shoots. Cuttings of the new growth can be taken. Space plants 16in apart.

FEEDING Once the plants are well established you can fertilize them every four to six weeks with a soluble liquid fertilizer.

PROBLEMS You can spot chrysanthemum leaf miners by the wavy white or brown lines in the foliage. Furthermore, hold up the leaf to the light and you might see the pupa or grub. Control by immediately removing the affected leaves and crushing the grubs, or better still by regular spraying with a systemic insecticide. Chrysanthemum eelworm is evident by browning, drying leaves. Immediately destroy all infected plants. There is no available remedy.

A number of fungal diseases can attack these plants, including leaf spot, powdery mildew, rust, and white rust. Avoid overhead watering or watering late in the day, and ensure that residue from previous plantings is cleared away. You may need to spray with a registered fungicide. White rust is a particularly serious disease, and affected plants are probably best removed and destroyed. Watch for aphids clustering on new growth. Pick them off by hand, wash them off, or use an insecticidal spray.

FLOWERING

SEASON Flowering time is mid to late fall. The exciting new race of Yoder or cushion chrysanthemums from America are dwarf, hardy, free-flowering (starting in late summer), and perfect for the front of the border. Those to look out for include "Lynn," "Robin," and "Radiant Lynn."

CUTTING Cut flowers will last two to three weeks with frequent water changes, as long as the foliage is removed from the parts of the stems that are under water.

AFTER FLOWERING

REQUIREMENTS Once flowering has finished, cut off plants 5–6in above the ground.

CASCADING OVER the fence onto the massed erigeron below, this wonderful garden chrysanthemum gives a prolific display. They are justifiably highly popular in the cut flower trade, and are available for most of the year.

Clematis

CLEMATIS SPECIES AND CULTIVARS

FEATURES

There are at least 200 species, deciduous and evergreen, and countless cultivars and hybrids of clematis, the most popular of all climbers. They are native mostly to the northern hemisphere. *Clematis vitalba* (Traveller's joy, Old man's beard), sprawls over hedgerows and produces greeny white flowers in summer followed by silky seed heads. This is not generally grown in gardens as it is not sufficiently decorative. The many other species, cultivars and hybrids are more preferable.

The deciduous spring-flowering *C. montana* and its cultivars are especially popular, with flowers in white or in shades of pink. *C. armandii* and its cultivar "Apple Blossom" are vigorous spring-flowering evergreens, with white and pink-tinged flowers respectively.

The large-flowered hybrids are the most popular of all, flowering in the summer. They have some of the most spectacular flowers imaginable. All are deciduous and of modest growth. They come in a range of colors, including white, blue, purple, mauve, and red shades, and some are bicolored. Perhaps the best known is "Jackmanii" with deep purple flowers.

Tall clematis such as *C. montana* are often allowed to climb into mature trees where their flowers tumble out over the canopy. Less-vigorous clematis, such as the large-flowered hybrids, are excellent for walls, fences, pergolas, arches, arbors, obelisks, and tubs. Thin stemmed, light and airy clematis, such as the Viticella Group, are ideal for growing over large shrubs or for use as ground cover. They are also good for containers.

CONDITIONS

ASPECT Clematis like to have their top growth in full sun but their roots in the shade. Roots can be shaded with plantings of groundcover plants or with other low-growing subjects, with paving slabs or with even a deep mulch of organic matter.

SITE Clematis grow well in any well-drained, reasonably rich soil containing plenty of humus. They are particularly suitable for chalky soils. Keep the plants permanently mulched with organic matter.

GROWING METHOD

PROPAGATION Sow seeds as soon as collected in the fall and stratify them over winter. They should then go on to germinate in the spring. Take softwood or semi-ripe leaf-bud cuttings in spring or summer. Carry out serpentine layering in the spring.

AT A GLANCE	
Very variable climbers, suitable for many situations. Flat, bell-shaped or cup-shaped flowers. Most are hardy to 5°F (zone 7).	
Jan /	**Recommended Varieties**
Feb planting	*Clematis alpina* (blue flowers, spring)
Mar planting	*C. cirrhosa* var. *balearica* (cream,
Apr flowering	winter/spring)
May flowering	*C. macropetala* (blue, spring)
Jun flowering	*C. orientalis* (yellow, summer)
July flowering	*C. tangutica* (yellow, summer/fall)
Aug flowering	
Sep flowering	
Oct flowering	
Nov /	
Dec /	

WATERING   Clematis should not be allowed to suffer from lack of moisture, so water plants well during rainless periods if the soil starts to dry out.

FEEDING   An annual application of slow-release organic fertilizer, such as blood, fish, and bone, should be applied in the spring.

PROBLEMS   Clematis wilt is the biggest problem. To help overcome this disease, plant clematis deeply, covering the top of the rootball with 3in of soil. This also ensures that new stems grow from below ground. Aphids may infest plants in the summer.

FLOWERING/FOLIAGE

FLOWERS   Clematis flower mainly in the spring, summer and fall, according to type. A few species bloom in the winter. Flowers come in all colors and they may be flat, bell-shaped, or cup-shaped.

FOLIAGE   This may be deciduous or evergreen, according to the individual species. Generally the leaves have twining stalks.

PRUNING

REQUIREMENTS   Pruning varies according to the group that clematis are in.

GROUP 1 contains clematis that flower early in the year on previous year's shoots, including *C. montana* and cultivars, *C. alpina*, *C. cirrhosa* var. *balearica*, *C. macropetala*, and *C. armandii*. The only pruning these plants need is thinning when they become congested. This is done after flowering. If renovation pruning is needed, cut down the complete plant to within 12in of the ground after flowering.

GROUP 2 contains large-flowered hybrids that produce a flush of flowers in early summer on last-year's shoots, and then another flush of blooms in late summer and fall on current year's shoots. These are pruned in late winter or early spring. Established plants can get by with very little pruning. The simplest technique is to cut them to within about 12in of the ground, every three to four years. After pruning you will lose the early summer flowers but they will bloom in late summer.

GROUP 3 contains clematis that flower in late summer and early fall on current season's shoots. This growth comes from the base of the plant. Included in this group are *C. viticella* and its cultivars and hybrids, *C. orientalis*, and "Jackmanii." Plants are pruned annually in late winter or early spring down to within 12in of the ground.

Cleome
SPIDER FLOWER

FEATURES

The spider-like flowers of *Cleome spinosa*, in pink, white, or rose, have narrow petals with long stamens. They appear all summer up and down the length of the stem. These large half-hardy annuals grow to 5ft tall with a single stem, and with lobed leaves. Plant at the back of borders or use them as central "dot" plants in large tubs for an "exotic" feel. Look out for the thorny stems and pungent leaves.

CONDITIONS

ASPECT Needs full sunlight and a sheltered position to achieve maximum height during the summer.

SITE Needs good drainage but tolerates a wide range of soils. For best results, improve soil by digging in rotted manure or compost, and use multipurpose compost with slow-release fertilizer added when planting containers. Stems are generally strong enough that they can be grow without extra support.

GROWING METHOD

SOWING Sow seeds in 3^1/$_2$in pots of multipurpose compost in February/March and keep at 64°F. Seedlings appear after two weeks and are transplanted to 3^1/$_2$in pots, grown on in a warm greenhouse or conservatory. Pot on into 5in containers in early May, and harden off before planting after the last frosts.

FEEDING Feed plants in beds fortnightly with liquid feed from a handheld applicator. Don't allow the compost in containers to become over-wet.

PROBLEMS Aphids attack young plants and cause twisted growth. Check under the leaves regularly and use a spray with permethrin if necessary, making sure the spray gets under the leaves.

FLOWERING

SEASON The long flowering period extends throughout summer and well into mild falls. The long thin seed pods give it a real "spidery" look.

CUTTING Useful as a cut flower, but watch the spines.

AFTER FLOWERING

GENERAL Remove plants after flowering, but wear gloves for protection, since the stems are spiny.

AT A GLANCE	
A half-hardy annual grown for its exotic flowers and ideal as a centerpiece for bedding/containers. Frost hardy to 32°F (zone 10).	

		Recommended Varieties
Jan	/	
Feb	sow	*Cleome spinosa*
Mar	sow	**Mixed colors**
Apr	grow on	"Color Fountain Mixed"
May	harden off/plant	**Single colors**
Jun	flowering	"Cherry Queen"
July	flowering	"Helen Campbell"
Aug	flowering	"Pink Queen"
Sept	flowering	"Violet Queen"
Oct	/	
Nov	/	
Dec	/	

Clianthus puniceus

GLORY PEA

FEATURES

This flamboyant semi-evergreen or evergreen climber will provide a touch of the southern hemisphere, as it is a native of the north island of New Zealand. Flowering in spring and early summer, it produces clusters of unusual, scarlet, claw-like flowers, another of its popular names being Lobster claw. These flowers are the plant's principal attraction. It will grow up to 12ft tall and needs to be grown against a warm sheltered wall. When grown unsupported it tends to spread horizontally. The Glory pea is an ideal subject for a small courtyard or other enclosed area. In parts of the country that are subject to hard frosts, it would be better to grow this climber in a frost-free conservatory or glasshouse.

CONDITIONS

ASPECT   It must have a position in full sun and be well sheltered from cold winds.

SITE   The soil should be very well drained. This climber will thrive in quite poor soils. A deep permanent mulch of organic matter is recommended to protect roots from frost.

GROWING METHOD

PROPAGATION   Take softwood or semi-ripe cuttings in spring or summer. Sow seeds in spring, first soaking them in water or abrading them (see pages 690–691). Germinate at 64°F.

WATERING   Fairly drought tolerant but apply water if the soil dries out excessively in the summer.

FEEDING   Give an annual spring application of a general purpose slow-release organic fertilizer, such as blood, fish, and bone.

PROBLEMS   There are no problems from pests or diseases.

FLOWERING/FOLIAGE

FLOWERS   Valued for its early, exotic-looking flowers.
FOLIAGE   The shiny pinnate leaves are attractive.

PRUNING

REQUIREMENTS   Very little needed. This climber will not survive severe pruning. Cut out any weak or dead shoots as necessary. Stems may be killed back by hard frosts, but the plant may produce new shoots from the base in spring. Cut back dead growth to live tissue.

AS WELL AS its eyecatching red blooms in spring, C. puniceus is grown for the all-year interest of its attractive pinnate leaves. In areas subject to hard frosts in winter, grow it in a cool conservatory or greenhouse.

AT A GLANCE	
Scarlet claw-like flowers and handsome pinnate foliage. Hardy to temperatures of 23°F (zone 9).	
Jan /	**Recommended Varieties**
Feb /	"Albus" (white flowers)
Mar /	"Roseus" (deep rose-pink flowers)
Apr planting	
May flowering	
Jun flowering	
July /	
Aug /	
Sep /	
Oct /	
Nov /	
Dec /	

Clivia miniata

KAFFIR LILY

FEATURES

This evergreen forms a striking house or conservatory plant, with long, deep green, strap-shaped leaves that overlap at the base rather like a leek. In spring or summer, a stout stem pushes between the leaf bases and grows to about 18in, carrying a head of 20 or so bright orange, bell-shaped flowers. These are marked with yellow in the throat and have prominent golden anthers.

Selected hybrids have larger flowers in various rich orange shades: a beautiful yellow-flowered variety, *C. miniata citrina*, has been developed but to date these plants are scarce and expensive, as are cultivars with cream-striped foliage.

CONDITIONS

ASPECT   Clivia prefers a reasonably bright position in the home, but not one in direct sun, which will scorch the foliage. Provide shading in a greenhouse or conservatory.

SITE   Grow as a room plant while it is flowering; during the summer the container can be placed in a sheltered position outdoors. Use a loam-based or soil-less potting compost.

GROWING METHOD

PLANTING   Clivias are usually bought as house plants in growth.

FEEDING   Give a high potash liquid feed every two or three weeks from early spring through the summer. Keep the compost thoroughly moist from spring to fall, then keep the plant cool and water it very sparingly in winter.

PROBLEMS   Mealy bugs can appear as fluffy white blobs between the leaf bases; use a systemic insecticide to control them.

FLOWERING

SEASON   Flowers may be carried any time between late winter and early summer.

CUTTING   Not suitable for cutting.

AFTER FLOWERING

REQUIREMENTS   Remove spent flower stalks. Repot only when essential; crowded plants tend to flower more reliably.

CLIVIAS MAKE SHOWY and colorful house plants, and will bloom for many years if they are given a winter rest.

AT A GLANCE		
A striking house plant with large heads of orange, bell-shaped flowers on stout stems. Minimum temperature 50°F (zone 11).		
Jan	/	**Recommended Varieties**
Feb	flowering	*Clivia miniata citrina*
Mar	flowering	"Striata"
Apr	flowering	
May	transplant	
Jun	/	
July	/	
Aug	/	
Sept	/	
Oct	/	
Nov	/	
Dec	/	

Colchicum autumnale

FALL CROCUS, MEADOW SAFFRON

FEATURES

This is another beautiful plant to brighten and lift the garden in fall. It is unusual in that the 6–9in-high flowers emerge directly from the neck of the corm, the leaves not appearing until months later, in spring. Although the flowers look similar to crocuses, the plants are not related. Up to a dozen rose pink to pale lilac, goblet-shaped flowers emerge from each corm. There is a pure white form, "Alba," and a glorious double form known as "Waterlily," that has a profusion of rose-lilac petals. Always plant in quite large groups for the best effect.

This easy-care bulb gives great rewards. It has a long history of use in herbal medicine but all parts of the plant are poisonous.

CONDITIONS

ASPECT Colchicum grows in full sun or very light shade.
SITE Suitable for rock gardens, borders, or for naturalizing in grassed areas or in light shade under trees. For best results grow this plant in well-drained soil to which organic matter has been added.

GROWING METHOD

PLANTING Corms should be planted in late summer, 3in deep and 4–6in apart, in groups. Established clumps are best divided at this time, too.
FEEDING Apply a generous mulch of decayed organic matter in winter. Further feeding is not usually necessary. Water in dry spells when the leaves appear in spring, and throughout their growing period.

PROBLEMS No specific pest or disease problems are common for this plant.

FLOWERING

SEASON Flowers spring out of the ground in fall.
CUTTING Cut flowers for the vase when the goblet shape is fully formed but before it opens out. Flowers last about a week in the vase.

AFTER FLOWERING

REQUIREMENTS Spent flowers may be cut off or left on the ground. Dead foliage may need tidying up at the end of the season.

THE DELICATE COLOR and form of meadow saffron flowers are particularly prominent, as they appear long before the leaves. They are very welcome as they appear in fall when the yard is often looking rather untidy and faded after its summer exuberance.

AT A GLANCE		
A crocus-like plant valuable for its fall flowers held on delicate stems.		
Jan	/	Recommended Varieties
Feb	/	"Alboplenum"
Mar	/	"Album"
Apr	/	"Pleniflorum"
May	/	"The Giant"
Jun	/	"Waterlily"
July	plant	
Aug	plant	
Sept	flowering	
Oct	flowering	
Nov	flowering	
Dec	/	

Comfrey
SYMPHYTUM OFFICINALE

FEATURES

This large, coarse, hairy perennial grows to 39in or more high. It has dark green, lanceolate leaves, which reach 10–12in long, and clusters of bell-shaped flowers in pink-purple or white in summer. The sticky qualities of its rhizome, which is black outside and has juicy white flesh within, gave rise to its nickname of slippery root; its other name, knit-bone, comes from its use in healing. The plant dies down over winter but makes a strong recovery in spring and can be quite invasive in the garden. Confine it to distant parts of the garden where it forms a backdrop.

CONDITIONS

ASPECT   Prefers sun or semi-shade, but tolerates most conditions.

SITE   Prefers moist, rich soils. Prepare beds with plenty of compost and farmyard manures.

GROWING METHOD

SOWING   Comfrey can be propagated from spring plantings of seed, by root cuttings at any stage of its life cycle or by root division in fall.

FEEDING   Comfrey requires a great deal of water. For best growth mulch in spring and fall and apply a balanced general fertilizer in spring.

PROBLEMS   May suffer from rust or powdery mildew from late summer. Destroy affected parts.

PRUNING   Cutting flowers encourages more leaf growth.

HARVESTING

PICKING   Leaves can be picked from early summer to the fall. Up to 4 cuttings a year can be taken. Dig up roots in fall.

STORAGE   The leaves can be dried and then stored in airtight containers.

FREEZING   Can be frozen for 6 months.

USES

CULINARY   Not recommended as controversy surrounds the use of young leaves in salads. Dried leaves are sometimes used to make a herbal tea.

MEDICINAL   The plant contains high concentrations of vitamin B12 but a great deal would need to be eaten daily to have any beneficial effect, and some studies suggest that certain alkaloids in the plant can cause chronic liver problems. Roots and leaves are used as a poultice for inflammations.

COSMETIC   An infusion of leaves makes a cosmetic wash.

AT A GLANCE		
A coarse, hairy, spreading perennial, which can be used to make an excellent organic fertilizer. Hardy to 4°F (zone 6).		
Jan	/	**Parts used**
Feb	/	Leaves
Mar	plant	Roots
Apr	plant	**Uses**
May	plant harvest	(Culinary)
Jun	plant harvest	Medicinal
July	plant harvest	Cosmetic
Aug	plant harvest	Gardening
Sept	plant harvest	
Oct	plant harvest	
Nov	/	
Dec	/	

GARDENING Comfrey is best used as a liquid manure: steep fresh leaves in water for several weeks. Leaves can also be used to promote decomposition in the compost heap, and so plant it close by.

ATTRACTIVE IN GROWTH and in foliage, comfrey makes an unusual tall groundcover. Other species have blue or white flowers.

Consolida

LARKSPUR

FEATURES

Consolida ajacis, larkspur, is related to delphinium but is not as tall and is grown as a hardy annual. Ideal for a "cottage garden" border, larkspur grows up to 3ft tall and has spikes of pink, white, red, blue, and violet single or double flowers, with finely cut leaves. Good for cutting. Seeds are poisonous.

CONDITIONS

ASPECT	Grow in a sunny, open spot.
SITE	Soil can be enriched with manure or compost well ahead of planting, but it must be well- drained. Plants will also grow well on thin and hungry soils. Plants should support each other as they grow and not need artificial support. Use taller varieties at the rear of borders.

GROWING METHOD

SOWING	Sow direct where the plants are to grow for best results, in short rows $^{1}/_2$in deep, in either March or September. Expect seedlings to appear in 2–3 weeks. Thin plants out as they grow so they are eventually 3–6in apart, depending on the variety.
FEEDING	Extra feeding is not necessary.
PROBLEMS	Slugs eat young seedlings so scatter slug pellets around plants or protect them with a 2in wide barrier of sharp grit.

FLOWERING

SEASON	Flowers appear from spring onward on fall-sown plants, June onward from spring sowings. Removing faded flower spikes will encourage more flowers.
CUTTING	An excellent cut flower. Cut long stems and scald ends before soaking in cool water.

AFTER FLOWERING

GENERAL	Leave a few plants to die down naturally and self-seed into the soil, otherwise pull up when finished and use for composting.

LARKSPUR IS DOUBLY useful as a cut flower, because the spikes can be dried and used for dried flower arrangements.

AT A GLANCE		
A hardy annual grown for its spikes of bright flowers that are useful for borders and cutting. Frost hardy to 5°F (zone 7).		
Jan	/	Recommended Varieties
Feb	/	*Consolida ajacis*
Mar	sow	**Tall, for cutting**
Apr	thin out	"Earl Grey"
May	thin/flowers	"Frosted Skies"
Jun	flowering	"Giant Imperial Mixed"
July	flowering	"Hyacinth FloweredMixed"
Aug	flowering	**Short, for bedding**
Sept	flowers/sow	"Dwarf Hyacinth Flowered Mixed"
Oct	/	"Dwarf Rocket Mixed"
Nov	/	
Dec	/	

Convallaria

LILY-OF-THE-VALLEY

FEATURES

Lily-of-the-valley is a one-species (sometimes considered three) genus, featuring the bell-shaped, fragrant *Convallaria majalis*. A native of Europe, it grows in woods and meadows, and produces 8in-tall stems of nodding white flowers shortly after the foliage has unfurled. Given the correct conditions—specifically, a cool, moist area—it can spread extremely quickly by means of underground shoots, but it is easily controlled. There are several attractive forms, "Albostriata" having cream striped foliage, and "Fortin's Giant" has flowers up to ¹⁄₂in across. Lily-of-the-valley is essential in a woodland area, or in a damp shady spot where little else of note will grow.

CONDITIONS

ASPECT   Shade is essential.
SITE   The soil must be damp, rich, and leafy. For an impressive, vigorous display, apply a thick mulch of leaf mold around the clumps of plants every fall.

GROWING METHOD

PROPAGATION   When the seed is ripe, remove the fleshy covering, and raise in a cold frame. Alternatively, divide the rhizomes in the fall. A 6in piece will provide approximately six new plants. The success rate is generally high. Make sure that young plants are not allowed to dry out. Mulch them to guarantee against moisture loss.
FEEDING   Every other year, apply a scattering of complete fertilizer in the spring.
PROBLEMS   Botrytis can be a problem, but is rarely anything to worry about.

FLOWERING

SEASON   One brief display in late spring.
CUTTING   Lily-of-the-valley makes excellent cut flowers, providing a striking spring display, while emitting a gentle sweet scent. They can also be lifted and grown indoors in a pot to flower the following spring. When finished, replace in the garden.

AFTER FLOWERING

REQUIREMENTS   Remove the spent flower stems, but leave the foliage intact to provide the energy for next year's display.

LILY-OF-THE-VALLEY makes a vivid display because of the strong contrast between the shapely oval leaves and the small, bright white flowers. It can be left to naturalize in woodland conditions, or allowed to spread through a shady border. Though invasive, it is quite easily controlled.

AT A GLANCE		
Basically a one-species genus with wonderful, waxy, scented spring flowers. Hardy to 5°F (zone 7). Good cultivars available.		
Jan	/	**Companion Plants**
Feb	/	Bergenia
Mar	/	*Euphorbia robbiae*
Apr	transplant	Galanthus
May	flowering	Primula
Jun	/	Pulmonaria
July	/	Rodgersia
Aug	sow	
Sept	division	
Oct	division	
Nov	/	
Dec	/	

Convallaria majalis

LILY-OF-THE-VALLEY

FEATURES

This is a tough little plant with a dainty appearance that belies its ease of growth. It is ideal for naturalizing in shady spots in the yard and also under trees where it can grow undisturbed. The dainty little white bell flowers are borne in spring; they are delightfully scented and last well in the vase. Flower stems may be 8–10in high, just topping the broadish, furled leaves that clasp the flower stems in pairs. There are several named cultivars but the straight species is by far the most popular. Previously used in folk medicine, the plant is now known to contain several poisonous substances although research continues on its potential medical use. The fleshy rhizomes with their growth shoots are known as "pips."

CONDITIONS

ASPECT   Prefers to grow in partial shade; ideal under deciduous trees.

SITE   A good ground cover plant; also suitable for mixed beds and borders. Soil should be free- draining but moisture-retentive, containing large amounts of decayed organic matter.

GROWING METHOD

PLANTING   The pips are planted in late fall about 1in deep and 4in apart. Congested clumps can be divided in fall or winter.

FEEDING   In early winter apply a generous mulch of decayed manure or compost, or pile on the decaying leaves of deciduous trees. Keep soil moist throughout the growing season, giving a thorough soaking when necessary.

PROBLEMS   Few problems are encountered but poor drainage may rot the root system.

FLOWERING

SEASON   Flowers appear from mid-spring.
CUTTING   This lovely cut flower perfumes a whole room. Pull the stems from the plant. It is traditional to use the foliage to wrap around the bunch.

AFTER FLOWERING

REQUIREMENTS   If possible, leave the plants undisturbed for several years. If clumps are extremely dense and flowering poor, lift and divide sections during fall or early winter.

LONG A FAVORITE with spring brides, fragrant lily-of-the-valley is an easy and rewarding bulb to grow. Ideal for edging a shady garden, these beautiful plants are also completely reliable, increasing, and flowering every year.

AT A GLANCE	
A low-growing plant with very fragrant, dainty white bells on arching stems in late spring. Ideal for light shade.	
Jan /	**Recommended Varieties**
Feb /	"Albostriata"
Mar /	"Fortin's Giant"
Apr flowering	"Flore Pleno"
May flowering	"Prolificans"
Jun /	*Convallaria majalis rosea*
July /	
Aug /	
Sept /	
Oct plant	
Nov plant	
Dec plant	

Coral Berry

ARDISIA CRENATA

FEATURES

Frost-sensitive, this evergreen shrub, clothed with attractive, rounded, toothed, and glossy, leathery leaves, has much to commend it. Coveted for its sprays of small, white, summer flowers, followed by a fetching and long-lasting display of bright red berries, it is easy to manage. Seldom more than 3ft high and across, it is normally grown in a large pot and confined to a frost-free conservatory in which temperatures are at least 20°F above freezing. In early summer when frosts finish, ardisia can be moved to highlight a lightly shaded patio.

CONDITIONS

ASPECT   Outdoors, ardisia prefers a shaded to semi-shaded position sheltered from strong winds. Indoors, from early fall to late spring, display it in a lightly shaded conservatory.

SITE   Help it excel by setting it in a large pot of John Innes potting compost No. 3. Based on moisture-retentive loam, it reduces the need for watering and encourages robust growth.

GROWING METHOD

FEEDING   Encourage lustrous leaves and bounteous flowers and fruits by feeding weekly with a high-potash liquid fertilizer from spring to late summer. Alternatively, add a slow-release fertilizer to the compost in spring and replace it a year later. Water regularly from spring to fall to keep the compost nicely moist, but ease up from fall to winter when growth is slower. Cease feeding too.

PROPAGATION   Take soft-tip cuttings in spring or summer.

PROBLEMS   Plants are occasionally attacked by sap-sucking scale insects, which cling like limpets to stems and leaves. Control them by spraying with malathion. Well-grown plants are seldom troubled by pests.

PRUNING

Ardisia is neat and symmetrical and cutting back is not normally necessary. If it grows too large, shorten stems to side shoots in spring.

FETCHING WHEN ENHANCING a patio in summer, or conservatory in winter, ardisia is famed for its large clusters of scarlet berries. A choice, compact evergreen, ardisia's panoply of white flowers in summer prelude a bounteous display of fruits.

AT A GLANCE	
Sculptural evergreen with glossy leaves. White, summer flowers are followed by bright scarlet berries. Hardy to 50°F (zone 11).	
Jan /	Recommended Varieties
Feb /	A. crenata
Mar /	
Apr plant, prune	
May plant	
Jun plant	
July flower	
Aug flower	
Sept flower	
Oct /	
Nov /	
Dec /	

Coreopsis
COREOPSIS

FEATURES

Perennial coreopsis carries a profusion of bright yellow daisy-like flowers over a long period, generally through summer into the fall, though some do flower in spring. Regular deadheading will ensure a long display. *C. lanceolata*, known as calliopsis, has become naturalized in many parts of the world. The strong-growing *C. grandiflora* may grow 24–36in high, with *C.verticillata* about 8in shorter. There are several species worth trying, some with dwarf form or flowers displaying a dark eye. The foliage is variable too. The plants are easy to grow. Plant in bold clumps in a mixed border.

CONDITIONS

ASPECT   Prefers an open, sunny position right through the day, with little shade.

SITE   Performs best in well-drained soil enriched with organic matter, but it will grow in poor soils too. Over-rich soil may produce a profusion of foliage with poor flowering.

GROWING METHOD

PROPAGATION   Grows most easily from divisions of existing clumps lifted in the spring. Space new plants at about 12in intervals. Species can be grown from seed sown in mid-spring. Since cultivars of *C. grandiflora* can be ephemeral, sow seed for continuity.

FEEDING   Apply complete plant food as growth begins in the spring. However, no further feeding should be needed.

PROBLEMS   No pest or disease problems are known.

FLOWERING

SEASON   The long flowering period extends through summer and the fall. *C.* "Early Sunrise," *C.lanceolata*, and "Sunray" flower in their first year from an early sowing.

CUTTING   Flowers can be cut for indoor decoration.

AFTER FLOWERING

REQUIREMENTS   Cut off spent flower stems and tidy up the foliage as it dies back. In mild, frost-free winters, coreopsis may not totally die back.

COREOPSIS ARE wonderful plants which can quickly colonize a space, say between shrubs, producing striking, bright yellow flowers.

AT A GLANCE		
A genus with well over 100 species that make a big contribution to the summer and early fall display. Hardy to 5°F (zone 7).		
Jan	/	Recommended Varieties
Feb	/	*Coreopsis auriculata*
Mar	/	"Schnittgold"
Apr	sow	"Goldfink"
May	divide	*C. grandiflora*
Jun	flowering	"Early Sunrise"
July	flowering	"Mayfield Giant"
Aug	flowering	"Sunray"
Sept	flowering	*C. verticillata*
Oct	/	"Grandiflora"
Nov	/	"Zagreb"
Dec	/	

Corydalis
CORYDALIS

FEATURES

Pretty, fern-like foliage and tubular, spurred flowers are characteristic of the 300 or so species of corydalis. Only a small number of species are grown in cultivation, and they mainly flower in shades of yellow or blue, but there are some in pink or crimson. Some of the brilliant blues make a distinctive feature, and a recent cultivar with electric blue flowers, known as *C. flexuosa* "China Blue," is now available. It mixes well with *C. solida* "George Baker," salmon-pink, and *C. ochroleuca*, white. Heights vary from 6 to 24in. Many corydalis are excellent rock garden plants, while others are suitable for mixed borders or planting under deciduous trees.

CONDITIONS

ASPECT   The preferred aspect varies with the species. Some tolerate an open, sunny position, while others need degrees of dappled sunlight. Species grown in "hot spots" should be given plenty of shade.

SITE   Needs very well-drained soil that is able to retain some moisture in the summer.

GROWING METHOD

PROPAGATION   Grows from seed sown as soon as it is ripe, in the fall. The seed is ripe when the small elongated capsules, which form after the flowers have fallen, turn brown and dry. Some species can be divided, while others produce tubers from which offsets can be taken. Plant at 4–6in intervals. New young plants need regular watering in prolonged, dry weather during the spring and summer months.

FEEDING   Apply a sprinkling of slow-release fertilizer when growth commences in the spring.

PROBLEMS   There are no specific pest or disease problems.

FLOWERING

SEASON   Most species flower in the spring, or from spring into summer. *C. flexuosa* dies down in the summer.

CUTTING   The flowers are unsuitable for cutting.

AFTER FLOWERING

REQUIREMENTS   Remove spent flower stems, unless you are waiting for seed to set. Tidy up the foliage as it dies back.

THE FOLIAGE and flowers of corydalis are dainty and highly decorative. It looks good in walls and ornamental pots.

AT A GLANCE		
A large group of annuals, biennials, and perennials, growing in a wide range of moist and dry conditions. Hardy to 5°F (zone 7).		
Jan	/	**Recommended Varieties**
Feb	/	*Corydalis cashmeriana*
Mar	/	*C. cava*
Apr	divide	*C. cheilanthifolia*
May	transplant	*C. elata*
Jun	flowering	*C. lutea*
July	flowering	*C. sempervirens*
Aug	flowering	*C. solida*
Sept	divide	"Beth Evans"
Oct	sow	*C. transsylvanica*
Nov	/	"George Baker"
Dec	/	

Cosmos
COSMOS

FEATURES

Cosmos, with their finely cut, feathery foliage and large daisy-type flowers grow up to 5ft tall, but shorter varieties are available and can be used in containers. Varieties of Cosmos bipinnatus have red, pink, purple, or white flowers, while yellow, orange, and scarlet are available in varieties of *Cosmos sulphureus*. Cosmos is grown as either a hardy or a half-hardy annual, and is an excellent choice for a cottage yard-style border. "Seashells" has tubular "fluted" petals, and the taller varieties such as "Sensation Mixed" are good for cutting.

CONDITIONS

ASPECT   Needs full sunlight to flourish.
SITE   Well-drained soil is essential for success, and good results are guaranteed on light and slightly hungry soils. Pea sticks or twiggy shoots may be needed for support in exposed spots. Any multipurpose compost will give good results in courtyard pots and containers.

GROWING METHOD

SOWING   Raise plants by sowing in March at 61°F. Sow the long thin seeds in 3^1/$_2$in pots of multipurpose compost, then transplant to cell trays and grow on. Harden off at the end of May before planting after frosts, or sow in April/May directly into the ground where the plants are to grow. Final spacing between plants should be 6–18in, depending on the variety grown.

FEEDING   Generally not necessary.
PROBLEMS   Slugs will eat young seedlings outdoors, so protect with slug pellets.

FLOWERING

SEASON   Flowers appear from the early summer onward.
CUTTING   The taller varieties are ideal as cut flowers. Ensure regular removal of faded flowers.

AFTER FLOWERING

GENERAL   Pull up plants when frosted, but leaving a few to die off will ensure some self-sown seedlings.

DURING THE SUMMER, varieties of cosmos grown in borders form masses of feathery leaves topped by flowers.

AT A GLANCE		
A hardy or half-hardy annual grown for its large daisy-like flowers. For borders, pots, and cutting. Frost hardy to 32°F (zone 10).		
Jan	/	**Recommended Varieties**
Feb	/	*Cosmos bipinnatus*
Mar	sow	"Daydream"
Apr	sow/transplant	"Gazebo"
May	sow/plant	"Picotee"
Jun	flowering	"Seashells/Sea Shells"
July	flowering	"Sensation Mixed"
Aug	flowering	"Sonata Mixed"
Sept	flowering	*Cosmos favorureus*
Oct	/	"Ladybird Mixed"
Nov	/	"Ladybird Scarlet"
Dec	/	"Sunny Red"

Cotoneaster
COTONEASTER

FEATURES

This versatile, evergreen, semi-evergreen, or deciduous family ranges in height from carpeters of 12in to towering bushes more than 10ft high. Choice kinds are dense and weed-suppressing, evergreen "Coral Beauty," whose glowing orange berries light up fall; semi-evergreen *Cotoneaster horizontalis*, ideal for clothing a bank or wall beneath a ground floor window; and semi-evergreen "Cornubia," an imposing, arching bush to 10ft. Evergreen *C. lacteus* and semi-evergreen *C. simonsii* make splendid, low, flowering, and berrying hedges.

Sprays of small, white spring flowers are followed by a glowing fall to winter display of red or yellow fruits. Cotoneasters take 5–10 years to mature, depending on species and conditions, and are long-lived. Fruits are nutritious food for garden birds and winter migrants.

CONDITIONS

ASPECT All kinds grow best and flower and fruit more freely in full sun. They will tolerate partial shade, but shoots are looser and berries sparse.

SITE Cotoneasters prefer well-drained, medium to heavyish loam, but any reasonably fertile soil encourages stocky growth. Improve thin, sandy, or gravelly areas by digging in bulky, humus-forming, well-rotted manure, decayed garden compost, or leaf mould.

GROWING METHOD

FEEDING Not essential, but an application of Growmore or fish, blood, and bone meal, carefully pricked into the root area in spring and midsummer, encourages lustrous leaves.

If you are growing a small-leafed, bushy variety such as *C. simonsii* as a close-planted hedge, apply fertilizer in spring and summer.

Water newly planted cotoneasters regularly in spring and summer to help them grow away quickly. Once established, they will tolerate long periods without supplementary watering.

PROPAGATION Take semi-ripe cuttings from mid- to late summer; layer shoots from spring to summer.

PROBLEMS Fireblight: Causing flowers to wilt and wither—they appear scorched—it is controlled by cutting back affected shoots to healthy, white wood. Burn prunings.

PRUNING

Keep plants flowering and fruiting well by removing one stem in three. Tackle evergreens in mid-spring and deciduous kinds in mid-fall.

AT A GLANCE		
Deciduous, semi- or fully evergreen shrub; white blossom heralds an fall display of vibrant fruits. Hardy to -13°F (zone 5).		
Jan	/	Recommended Varieties
Feb	/	Ground covering to 12in
Mar	plant	"Coral Beauty"
Apr	plant	"Oakwood"
May	flower, prune	"Skogholm"
June	flower	Small bushes (12–32in)
July	plant	*C. conspicuus*
Aug	plant	"Decorus"
Sept	plant	*C. horizontalis*
Oct	plant, prune	Taller kinds
Nov	plant, prune	"Cornubia"
Dec	/	

Cotoneaster simonsii

COTONEASTER

FEATURES

Cotoneasters are highly underrated. Few people think past *Cotoneaster horizontalis* but there are about 320 kinds that you can buy from specialist nurseries. They range from tight, hard mounds as big as a large pumpkin, to giants. *C. simonsii* is an award-winning semi-evergreen (in warm areas) or deciduous shrub, upright in growth. The leaves redden in the fall, and the berries are bright orange-red. It can get quite big, about 6ft high and wide, but can be pruned and kept shorter. As a hedge it is definitely for the wilder part of the garden. Like most cotoneasters, the big selling point is the major show of bright berries, some hanging on well in winter.

CONDITIONS

ASPECT Provide full sun, though partial shade is acceptable. The more sun, the more growth, the more berries.

SITE Cotoneasters tolerate most soils, except for the extremes of dry and wet. As a general rule though, do not overfeed, and make sure that there is good drainage.

GROWING METHOD

PROPAGATION The easiest method is by seed. Sow fresh seed and cover the soil surface with grit. Keep warm indoors, and then put in the refrigerator for six weeks, followed by more warmth. Or take cuttings in mid- and late summer.

SPACING Set *C. simonsii* about 3ft apart.

FEEDING Unless the soil was remarkably poor in quality to begin with, extra feeding will not be necessary. If feeding is needed, a slow-release spring fertilizer, such as blood, fish and bone mixture, will then suffice.

PROBLEMS One drawback of these plants is that they can be afflicted by a wide range of problems. Look out for the cotoneaster webber moth which makes the foliage darken and dry up, and for signs of silk webbing. Cut away affected areas and spray with permethrin.

PRUNING

GENERAL Most tolerate regular pruning. They also survive hard pruning, but it takes several years for the shrub to perform well again.

THE INTENSE COLORS of cotoneaster berries make these useful plants true stars of the garden in the fall and early winter. The thick, twisting habit of cotoneasters provides a dense mass of foliage and stem, making for an effective barrier.

AT A GLANCE		
Cotoneaster simonsii is a high-performance shrub with white summer flowers and orange-red berries. Hardy to 0˚F (zone 7).		
Jan	/	**Recommended Varieties**
Feb	/	*Cotoneaster acutifolius*
Mar	/	*C. conspicuus*
April	/	*C. franchetii*
May	/	*C.* "Herbstfeuer"
June	foliage	*C. hupehensis*
July	flowering	*C. marquandi*
Aug	foliage	*C. nitidus*
Sept	foliage	*C. simonsii*
Oct	foliage	*C. splendens*
Nov	/	*C. divaricatus*
Dec	/	"Valkenburg"

Cotton lavender

SANTOLINA

FEATURES

Mound forming, evergreen and ideal for making a low hedge to divide a lawn from a path or to segregate open-plan gardens, cotton lavender is prized for its aromatic, feathery, silvery-white, or gray foliage. There is also a green-leaved form. If cotton lavender is left to mature, a wealth of button-like, yellow flowers appear from June to August. Flowers, however, tend to spoil its symmetry and give it a ragged look. If you prefer foliage to blooms, prune bushes hard each year.

It is a tough shrub and unaffected by salty winds, so makes a good seaside plant. It also has few enemies.

Widely planted *Santolina chamecyparissus*, grows to around 18in high and 30in across and is favoured for hedging or punctuating a border. Its dwarf form, nana, just 12in high, is fetching for edging a border or highlighting a rock garden.

Even whiter and more feathery is *S. pinnata neopolitana*, to 32in high.

Equally decorative but with thread-like, green leaves, *S. rosmarinifolia* (*virens*) is massed with long-stemmed, yellow flowers in summer.

CONDITIONS

ASPECT   Santolina is very hardy and braves low temperatures. Provided you set plants in full sun, where silvery-white-leaved varieties develop full radiance, they will excel for you. The green-leaved species tolerates light shade.

SITE   This shrub performs zestfully on sandy loam but abhors heavy clay, which becomes soggy and airless in winter. If you are stuck with heavy clay, drain it by working in grit and channelling a gravel-lined drainage trench to a soakaway.

GROWING METHOD

FEEDING   There is little need to be diligent with feeding, for cotton lavender prospers on thin and nutrient-sparse soils. However, lush growth will please you if in spring and fall you work a dressing of bone meal into the root area.

PROPAGATION   Increase your favorites from semi-ripe cuttings taken from early to mid-fall and rooted in a garden frame or multiply plants from hardwood cuttings in late fall.

PROBLEMS   Normally trouble free.

PRUNING

Shear off faded blooms in late August. Periodically—every 3 years or so when lower shoots are becoming woody—shorten stems to 6in from the base to stimulate new basal growth.

AT A GLANCE	
Evergreen bush with ferny or thread-like leaves and yellow, "button" flowers from June to August. Hardy to 14°F (zone 8).	
Jan /	**Recommended Varieties**
Feb /	*S. chamaecyparissus*
Mar /	*S. chamaecyparissus nana*
Apr plant, prune	*S. pinnata neopolitana*
May plant, prune	*S. virens*
Jun flower, plant	
July flower, plant	
Aug flower, plant	
Sept flower, plant	
Oct /	
Nov /	
Dec /	

Crassula
LONDON PRIDE

FEATURES

In warm climates, this semi-prostrate plant is a very vigorous grower, but it can be useful and decorative as a groundcover or as a filler plant in a rockery. In any event, crassula is very easy to control if it ever exceeds its allotted space. It can be upright or somewhat sprawling in habit, and when sprawling it roots itself into the ground as it spreads. It can alternatively be grown in pots or hanging baskets. Plants grow about 6–10in high, but can be taller. In warm, humid areas, one plant may spread 20in or more in a season. The fleshy leaves may be rounded, oblong, or spoon shaped, and the small pink and white starry flowers are carried on slender stems high above the foliage.

CONDITIONS

ASPECT   Crassula is suited to growing in sun or partial shade. Growth is more compact when the plant is situated in full sun. It benefits from being stood outside over summer, or it could be planted out in a special raised bed with excellent drainage.

SITE   Almost any kind of well-drained soil will suit this plant. Plants in containers prefer a mix that drains well, but also contains plenty of organic matter.

GROWING METHOD

PROPAGATION   This plant is very easily grown from stem cuttings taken any time during the warmer seasons. Tiny plantlets emerging from bulbils may sometimes form on the tips of flowered stems. These plantlets may be pegged down on a pot of coarse sandy mix to grow on and form roots.

FEEDING   Potted plants may need some slow-release fertilizer applied in spring. Plants grown in beds rarely need supplementary feeding.

PROBLEMS   Crassula is generally an easily-grown, tough, trouble-free plant. The only problems occur in the glasshouse over summer, when you should keep an eye out for mealybugs and aphids and spray accordingly.

FLOWERING

SEASON   Small pink and white starry flowers appear in spring. These are sometimes followed by bulbils, which grow into new plants.

ADAPTABLE AND TROUBLE-FREE, London pride can survive among rocks in tiny amounts of soil.

AT A GLANCE	
Superb succulents with fleshy leaves ranging from the tiny to 15ft high in the wild. (41°F min (zone 11).	
Jan flowering	**Recommended Varieties**
Feb /	*Crassula falcata*
Mar sow	*C. galanthea*
Apr transplant	*C. helmsii*
May flowering	*C. milfordiae*
Jun flowering	*C. ovata*
July flowering	*C. rupestris*
Aug /	*C. sarcocaulis*
Sept flowering	*C. schmidtii*
Oct /	
Nov /	
Dec flowering	

Crassula arborescens

SILVER JADE PLANT

FEATURES

Growing to over 8¹/₂ft in its native South Africa, this plant is more often seen at about 5ft when container-grown, or somewhat taller in the ground. It blends well with a range of plant types, including evergreens that enjoy the same conditions, and can be used most successfully to add height to a desert garden or a succulent display. It develops a sturdy trunk and numerous branches which carry leathery, gray-green oblong leaves with a fine red margin, sometimes dotted with tiny red spots. Plants sold as Crassula ovata are probably the same as or very similar to this species.

CONDITIONS

ASPECT Full sun is preferred, but this plant will tolerate shade for part of the day if necessary. However, the more light it receives the better it does.

SITE This plant can be grown in any type of well-drained soil. Container-grown plants will benefit from annual repotting, or from having the top third of the compost replaced.

GROWING METHOD

PROPAGATION This plant is most easily grown from leaf cuttings, which must be removed with the stem attached. It can also be grown from stem cuttings or seed. All methods of propagation are best carried out in warm weather.

FEEDING Fertilizing is generally unnecessary, but a small amount of slow-release fertilizer can be given to container-grown plants in spring.

PROBLEMS This is a tough, trouble-free plant that is quite easily grown. The only possible irritation is that the plant may repeatedly get too big for its container. Eventually, the best solution is to replace the oversize plant with a vigorous cutting. This will mean that you can start all over again with a small pot.

FLOWERING

SEASON Flowering is profuse. Masses of small, pink, starry flowers adorn the shrub in late fall to winter.

RUSTY RED-BROWN CALYCES remain on the bush long after the pale starry flowers have fallen.

AT A GLANCE		
C. arborescens is a highly attractive South African succulent with pink fall flowers and thick waxy leaves. 41°F min (zone 11).		
Jan	/	Recommended Varieties
Feb	/	*Crassula arborescens*
Mar	/	*C. falcata*
Apr	sow	*C. galanthea*
May	/	*C. helmsii*
Jun	transplant	*C. milfordiae*
July	/	*C. ovata*
Aug	/	*C. rupestris*
Sept	/	*C. sarcocaulis*
Oct	flowering	*C. schmidtii*
Nov	flowering	
Dec	flowering	

Crinum
SWAMP LILY

FEATURES

There are more than 100 species of crinum, but *C.* x *powellii* and the more tender *C. moorei* are the two most commonly grown. Both bear large, scented, lily-like flowers in pale pink or white on stems up to 3ft high; plants have long, strap-shaped, light-green leaves. The flowers appear from middle to late summer and sometimes into fall. The bulbs can grow very large indeed, up to 6in or more across, and can be very weighty. In time very large clumps are formed and they require considerable physical effort to lift and divide. Crinums need a sheltered position to do well. In cool areas they can also be grown quite successfully in containers that can be moved under cover in fall.

CONDITIONS

ASPECT   Grow crinum in a sunny, south-facing, sheltered position. *C. moorei* is best grown in a pot in a conservatory.

SITE   Suitable for borders or as a specimen plant in a container on a patio or similar. Soil must be free-draining but moisture-retentive.

GROWING METHOD

PLANTING   Plant in spring, which is also the best time to divide existing clumps. *C.* x *powellii* should have the neck of the bulb above soil level, while *C. moorei* should be planted with the nose of the bulb at the level of the soil.

FEEDING   Balanced fertilizer may be applied as new growth starts in spring. Keep the soil moist while the plants are in growth. Water plants in containers regularly.

PROBLEMS   Not generally susceptible to disease or pests but snails love to eat the foliage and flowers.

FLOWERING

SEASON   Flowers appear during summer and into the fall months.

CUTTING   It is possible to cut blooms for the house but they last longer on the plant.

AFTER FLOWERING

REQUIREMENTS   Cut off the flowering stalk when the flowers are over. Protect the crowns with a mulch of peat over winter, or move plants under cover. Disturb established plants as little as possible.

LIGHT PERFUME is an added reason to grow these pretty pink crinums. They are a good choice for a sheltered border.

AT A GLANCE		
Large, scented, lily-like flowers in late summer and fall. This plant needs a sheltered, sunny position to thrive.		
Jan	/	**Recommended Varieties**
Feb	/	*Crinum* x *powellii*
Mar	/	"Album"
Apr	plant	"Roseum"
May	plant	*Crinum moorei*
Jun	/	*Crinum bulbispermum*
July	/	"Album"
Aug	flowering	
Sept	flowering	
Oct	/	
Nov	/	
Dec	/	

Crocosmia
MONTBRETIA

FEATURES

Also known as montbretia, some types of crocosmia are extremely vigorous and can become invasive in warm areas. It will often survive in old, neglected yards where virtually everything else has disappeared. The foliage is slender, sword-shaped, and upright or slightly arching. The flowers are carried on double-sided spikes that also arch gracefully, reaching some 2–3ft tall. Most types have eye-catching bright reddish-orange flowers that open progressively from the base of the spike. In cold areas, plants should be protected with a mulch of dry leaves over winter, and should be planted in a reasonably sheltered position.

CONDITIONS

ASPECT   Grows best in a fully open, sunny position.
SITE   Good in beds or borders in well-drained soil.

GROWING METHOD

PLANTING   Plant corms in spring, 3in deep and about 6in apart. Pot-grown specimens can be planted throughout the spring and summer, even when in flower. It usually becomes necessary to thin out clumps every few years.
FEEDING   A balanced fertilizer can be applied in early summer, but feeding is not generally necessary.
PROBLEMS   There are no pests or diseases that commonly attack crocosmia.

FLOWERING

SEASON   There is a long flowering period all through summer. Congested clumps often seem to produce more blooms.
CUTTING   Flowers are not suitable for cutting and are better appreciated in the garden.

AFTER FLOWERING

REQUIREMENTS Cut off spent flower stems as soon as the blooms have faded to avoid seed setting and plants spreading. When the leaves have died down, protect the corms with a mulch of straw or dry leaves in all but very warm, sheltered yards.

THE VIBRANT COLOR of crocosmia flowers gives great decorative value but is matched by vigorous growth that may need to be controlled.

AT A GLANCE		
A vigorous plant with sword-shaped leaves and brightly colored spikes of flowers through the summer.		
Jan	/	**Recommended Varieties**
Feb	/	"Bressingham Blaze"
Mar	plant	"Canary Bird"
Apr	plant	"Citronella"
May	/	"Emily McKenzie"
Jun	/	"Jackanapes"
July	flowering	"Lucifer"
Aug	flowering	"Solfaterre"
Sept	flowering	
Oct	/	
Nov	/	
Dec	/	

Crocus
CROCUS

FEATURES

There are more than 80 species of crocus, mainly late winter and spring flowering, but there are some fall bloomers, too. Crocus are among the earliest flowers to appear in spring, often pushing their flowers up through the snow. In some species flowers appear some weeks before the leaves. Crocus are mostly native to the countries around the Mediterranean Sea where they usually grow at high altitudes. They do, however, extend as far east as Afghanistan.

APPEARANCE

Crocus foliage is short, rather sparse, and looks like a broad-leaf grass. The gorgeous little goblet-shaped flowers are borne on short stems 2–5in high. Most are blue, violet, white, yellow, or cream but some species have pink flowers. Many have deeper colored stripes or feathering on the petals.

USES

Although unsuitable for cutting, these little bulbous plants are one of the greatest delights of the yard. They are often mass-planted in garden beds, especially at the front of borders. They can be naturalized in lawns or grouped together under deciduous trees. Crocuses are excellent plants for rock gardens and they make good container plants, being especially suitable for winter and early spring window- boxes. The floral display of some individual species in the yard can be short, but by growing a selection of species you can enjoy these charming flowers over an extended period, from early fall right through to late spring.

POPULAR SPECIES

SPRING   Some of the most popular spring-flowering species are *C. biflorus*, *C. chrysanthus*, *C. flavus*, *C. minimus*, *C. tommasinianus* and *C. vernus*. Cultivars of a number of these species are available, with the many and varied cultivars of *C. chrysanthus* being especially popular, although each of these species have their admirers. *C. ancyrensis* is particularly early flowering, appearing in January and February.

AUTUMN   Fall-flowering species include *C. kotschyanus*, *C. niveus*, *C. laevigatus*, *C. longiflorus*, *C. nudiflorus*, *C. sativus* (the saffron crocus), *C. serotinus* (also known as *C. salzmannii*) and *C. speciosus*. *Crocus sativus* is well known as the source of the costliest of all herbs and spices. Native to temperate Eurasia and

AT A GLANCE		
Low-growing bulbs valuable for their early spring flowers in a range of colors. Good for containers.		
Jan	flowering*	**Recommended Varieties**
Feb	flowering*	*Crocus chrysanthus*
Mar	flowering*	"Cream Beauty"
Apr	flowering*	"Ladykiller"
May	/	"Snow Bunting"
Jun	/	*C. tommasinianus*
July	plant**	"Ruby Giant"
Aug	plant**	*C. vernus*
Sept	**/ *	"Little Dorrit"
Oct	**/ *	"Queen of the Blues"
Nov	**/ *	"Vanguard"
Dec	flowering**	

* spring flowering species   ** fall flowering species

widely grown in Mediterranean regions, saffron crocus needs a very specific climate to flourish and is an extremely labor-intensive crop to harvest. Saffron comes only from the stigmas of the flowers and 75,000 flowers are needed to make up a pound of pure saffron.

CONDITIONS

ASPECT   Prefers an open, sunny position but may be grown in light shade.

SITE   Good for rock gardens, raised beds, the fronts of borders or naturalized in grass. Soil must be well-drained, preferably containing plenty of well-rotted organic matter.

GROWING METHOD

PLANTING   Plant new corms about 2in deep and 2–4in apart. Spring-flowering varieties should be planted in fall, from September to November, while fall-flowering species should be planted in July and August. The corms of some species become quite large over time; lift and plant them further apart as it becomes necessary.

FEEDING   Apply a light dressing of balanced fertilizer after flowering, particularly in poor soil conditions. Watering is necessary only if conditions are very dry: however, fall-flowering types are likely to need watering after planting in summer.

PROBLEMS   Few problems are encountered when crocuses are grown in the right aspect and soil. However, birds can sometimes damage flowers. Some birds, particularly sparrows, seem to be attracted by the shape or color of flowers and can peck them to pieces. If this occurs you will have to place a frame covered in wire netting over the plants.

FLOWERING

SEASON   Flowering depends on the species; some varieties begin flowering in late winter to very early spring, others slightly later in spring. Fall-flowering species flower between September and early December, and may overlap with the earliest of the winter-flowering species growing against a warm wall.

CUTTING   Crocuses are not good cut flowers although they may last a few days in the vase.

AFTER FLOWERING

REQUIREMENTS   It is essential not to remove crocus leaves before they have yellowed as they are important in building up the corms and, therefore, next season's flowering potential. Plantings may need lifting and dividing every 3–4 years, but they can be left until corms start to push their way to the surface.

Cyclamen
CYCLAMEN

FEATURES

Cyclamen form an enchanting group of plants admired for their attractive, mostly marbled foliage and distinctive flowers with swept back, slightly twisted petals. Some, such as the florists' cyclamen, have large showy flowers, while many of the species have small flowers growing only 3–4in high. Some cyclamen flower in fall or winter, while others flower in late winter and spring. Native to parts of Europe and countries around the Mediterranean, all share a similar need to be kept rather dry during their dormant period. Plants growing in good conditions can remain undisturbed for many years. The original tubers will increase greatly in size and many new plants will come from self-sown seed.

USES

The smaller varieties make a great show when planted in masses or drifts. The floral display is quite long-lasting and even out of flower the marbled leaves make a good groundcover for many months of the year. Cyclamen can be grown in light shade under trees, in rock gardens, and in containers.

Potted plants of *C. persicum* hybrids in bloom make excellent house plants and are available from late summer right through the winter. The flowers may be delicately scented. In warm rooms in the home it can be difficult to keep these plants in good condition, and they are sometimes best considered as short-term floral decoration.

TYPES

FLORISTS
Florists' cyclamen (*C. persicum*) is usually seen as a flowering potted plant for indoor use, and many hybrids are available, including very fragrant miniature types. The beautifully marbled foliage and spectacular flowers make this a very showy plant. The flowers with their swept back petals come in every shade of pink and red, purple, cerise, white, and bicolors, and there are some fancy frilled or ruffled kinds. This species came originally from the eastern Mediterranean but many of the modern hybrids grown bear little resemblance to the original species.

GARDEN
The most easily-grown garden cyclamen is the Neapolitan cyclamen (*C. hederifolium*) which flowers during fall. It can be grown more successfully in warmer areas than most of the other species. *C. hederifolium* has beautifully marbled foliage about 3–4in high, with the small, clear pink flowers held above

GORGEOUS UPSWEPT PETALS and a range of glorious colors ensure the lasting popularity of florist's cyclamen as house plants.

AT A GLANCE		
Characteristic, upswept petals on a mound-forming plant with attractive marbled foliage. Suitable for outdoors or as pot plants.		
Jan	flowering	**Recommended Varieties**
Feb	flowering	*Cyclamen cilicium album*
Mar	flowering	*C. coum album*
Apr	flowering	*C. hederifolium*
May	/	"Bowles' Apollo"
Jun	/	"Silver Cloud"
July	plant	*C. libanoticum*
Aug	plant	*C. pseudibericum*
Sept	flowering	*C. purpurascens*
Oct	flowering	*C. repandum*
Nov	flowering	*C. persicum* (many hybrids available)
Dec	flowering	

the leaves. There is also a pure white form of this species. *C. coum* flowers from late winter into spring and has larger, very deep pink flowers on short stems. Again, there is a white form of this species available. *C. repandum*, another spring bloomer, has probably the largest flowers of all the species cyclamens but none of these have flowers that are the size of the florists' cyclamen. The foliage on *C. repandum* is noted for its reddish undersides.

CONDITIONS

ASPECT	The ideal situation for hardy cyclamen is beneath deciduous trees where there is some winter sun but dappled sunlight for the rest of the year. In the home, florists' cyclamen need a cool, bright position.
SITE	Hardy cyclamen can be grown on rock gardens, under trees and shrubs, and in borders. The soil must be well-drained with a high organic content. Indoors, choose a bright, cool windowsill or a conservatory.

GROWING METHOD

PLANTING	The flattened tubers (often wrongly referred to as corms) should be planted with their tops just below the soil surface. Plant in late summer and early fall at about 6in intervals. Pot-grown seedlings are easier to establish than dry tubers, and can be obtained from garden centers and specialist nurseries.

FEEDING	If soil is poor, a sprinkling of balanced fertilizer can be given when growth begins and again after flowering. Florists' cyclamen should be given high potash liquid fertilizer every 14 days from when the flower buds appear until flowering is over. Water carefully from the base to avoid splashing the top of the tuber; never leave the pots standing in water.
PROBLEMS	Florists' cyclamen grown indoors often succumb to overwatering, drying out, and a dry, overwarm atmosphere. Vine weevils are attracted to the tubers and may cause the sudden collapse of the plant: use a soil insecticide if they are caught in time.

FLOWERING

SEASON	*C. persicum* flowers through winter into spring. *C. hederifolium* has a long flowering period in fall, while *C. coum* and *C. repandum* flower betwen late winter and spring.
CUTTING	Pull flowers from the plant with a rolling motion and cut off the thin base of the stalk.

AFTER FLOWERING

REQUIREMENTS	Outdoors, leave spent flowering stems to set seed and do not disturb tubers. After flowering, allow pot plants to die down and keep dry over summer. Start into growth again in August.

Cymbidium

CYMBIDIUM SPECIES AND HYBRIDS

FEATURES

Cymbidiums are probably the most widely cultivated of all orchids. They originate in temperate or tropical parts of north-western India, China, Japan, through south-east Asia, and Australia. There are now thousands of cultivated varieties. These hybrids have flowers classed as standard size (4–6in across), miniature (about 2in across) or intermediate. The leaves are strap-like, upright, or pendulous, and 20in or more in length in standard growers. The foliage of the miniature plants is narrower and shorter, in keeping with the overall dimensions of the plant. Cymbidiums have a wide appeal as the flowers are decorative and long lasting.

FLOWERS

The range of flower colors covers every shade and tone of white and cream, yellow and orange, pink and red, brown and green, all with patterned or contrasting colors on the lip. Flowers are carried on quite sturdy stems standing well clear of the foliage. As many are in bloom in winter they can give a special lift to the season. Many have flowers that will last six to eight weeks.

CHOOSING

Choose plants both by flower color and time of blooming. With careful selection you can have a Cymbidium in bloom every month from early fall through to late spring. Selecting plants in flower will tell you exactly what you are getting. Some orchid nurseries sell tissue cultured mericlones of these orchids as young plants: these are much cheaper but you will have to wait three to four years for them to reach flowering size. Backbulbs, if available, are also an option although these too take up to four years to flower. Buying seedlings is also cheaper and you will have the thrill of their first flowering, not knowing in advance what the flowers will be like. The parent plants may be displayed or the nursery should be able to give you an idea of the likely color range, which extends through the spectrum.

CONDITIONS

CLIMATE Ideal conditions are humid year round, with winter temperatures not reaching much below 46–50°F and summer temperatures that are generally below 86°F. It is advisable to place the plants outside in summer. To initiate flowering many, but not all, require a distinct drop between their day and night temperatures.

ASPECT These plants will not flower if they do not get sufficient light. They will grow in the open with dappled shade from trees or with only morning sun in summer, but they can actually take full sun almost all day during the winter. A shadehouse with 50 per cent shade is suitable in summer.

AT A GLANCE	
Popular and widely grown. Flowers vary from 1½–4in. Easy to grow in light, cool conditions.	
Jan rest, flowering	**Recommended Varieties**
Feb rest, flowering, repot	C. erythrostylum (white)
Mar flowering, water	C. lowianum (green)
and feed, re-pot	C. traceyanum (brown)
Apr flowering, water	C. Amesbury (green)
and feed, re-pot	C. Bouley Bay (yellow)
May water and feed	C. Gymer (yellow/red)
Jun water and feed	C. Ivy Fung (red)
July water and feed	C. Pontac (burgundy)
Aug water and feed	
Sept rest, flowering,	
water and feed	
Oct rest, flowering	
Nov rest, flowering	
Dec rest, flowering	

If you can see that your plants have very dark green leaves then they aren't getting enough light and are very unlikely to flower. These plants need good ventilation and protection from strong winds and rain when placed outside. In winter, place them in the lightest position available within a cool greenhouse, conservatory, or in an unheated, light room.

POTTING MIX Mix or soil must be free draining. Many species in their habitat grow in hollow branches of trees, in decayed bark and leaf litter. Hybrids can be grown in aged, medium-grade pine bark, or in pine bark plus coir peat, bracken fibre, charcoal, or even pieces of foam. Plants need to be anchored and supported but must have free drainage and good aeration around the roots. Prepared, special orchid composts are satisfactory, especially if you only have a few plants. Cymbidiums must always be potted with the base of the pseudobulb either at, or preferably just above, the level of the compost.

CONTAINERS Make sure that there are enough drain holes in the container and, if not, punch in more. Cymbidiums are quite vigorous growers and if placed in 8in pots they will probably need potting and maybe dividing every two or three years. It is best to pot plants into containers that will just comfortably accommodate their roots. They can then be potted on into the next size when necessary. Plants that have filled their containers and need dividing are best left until spring, and then divided into sections with no fewer than three pseudobulbs per division. If divided soon after flowering in spring the plants will then have a full six months growing season ahead of them to settle into their new pot.

GROWING METHOD

PROPAGATION Grow new plants from backbulbs (older, leafless bulbs). These may look dead but will regrow if they are detached from the younger growths when you are dividing plants after flowering. Clean old leaf bases and trim off any old roots. Plant the bulbs into small individual or large communal pots, about one-third of their depth into a mixture of coir peat and bark. Keep damp but not wet. Once good leaf and root growth are evident, pot up into normal mix. Plants grown this way generally flower after about three years.

WATERING Frequency of watering is determined by the time of year. The mix should be moist but not wet. Always give enough at one watering for water to pour through the mix. Plants may need watering daily in summer or only every few days if conditions are wet. Water about once every one to two weeks in winter.

FEEDING Feeding can be as easy or as complicated as you like. You can simply give slow release granular fertilizers during the growing season. Or, alternatively, you can use soluble liquid feeds regularly through spring and summer. Some growers like to use high nitrogen fertilizers during spring, switching to special orchid foods or complete fertilizers that are high in phosphorus and potassium in summer. Some of these are applied monthly, others in half strength more often. It is important to follow label recommendations and not to overdo it.

PROBLEMS Unfortunately cymbidiums are prone to some diseases, quite apart from the normal range of pests. Virus disease can be a problem and so maintain strict

hygiene by disinfecting hands and tools to avoid it spreading. Bulb rots can also be a problem if potting mixes contain too much fine material, which impedes drainage. Fungal leaf spots can occur in crowded or very wet conditions. Keep an eye out for snails, slugs and aphids as your plants come into bud because they can quickly ruin your long-awaited flowers. They will attack both buds and long spikes.

SUPPORT   Light cane or metal stakes should be used to support the flower spikes as they develop. Carefully insert the support beside the developing spike and use plastic coated tie-wire or string to tie the spike as often as needed to train it into position.

FLOWERING SEASON

In bloom through fall, winter and spring with just a few summer varieties. Plants in flower can be brought into the house for decoration. Moving a plant in bud from a cool greenhouse to a warm room can make the buds drop so wait until the flowers are open and set until you move it. The cooler the plant is kept, the longer the flowers last, which is on average six to eight weeks.

CUT FLOWERS   Professional growers cut the flower spikes a week after all flowers on the spike are open to prevent any check in the plant's growth.

Cynara cardunculus

CARDOON

FEATURES

A close relative of the globe artichoke, the cardoon is generally grown for its arching, 39in-long, silver-gray foliage. Growing up to 78in tall and almost 78in wide, it is a terrific accent plant for the back of a border, or it can be combined with low-growing green plants in an open position. Both the color and form stand out against most other plants. The purple, thistle-like flowers develop in the summer, and the dried heads left on the plant make a decorative fall feature. Cardoon is edible, being grown for the tasty, fleshy base of each leaf. It is difficult to place in a small yard, since you need room to stand back and appreciate its startling form.

CONDITIONS

ASPECT	Needs full sun all day for best results. Also requires shelter from strong, leaf-tearing winds.
SOIL	Needs rich, well-drained soil. Before planting, dig in large amounts of manure or compost.

GROWING METHOD

PROPAGATION	Propagate in late spring, or grow from seed. Position plants at least 4ft apart. Seed-grown plants vary in quality, and do not normally reach maturity in their first year. During the growing season, regular, deep watering is essential for new, young plants in prolonged dry spells.
FEEDING	Apply a complete plant food as growth commences in the spring, and repeat in mid-summer. When cardoon is grown as a vegetable it is given a weekly liquid feed.

PROBLEMS

Beware of the sharp points on the flowerheads.

FLOWERING

SEASON	The purple, thistle-like flowers appear during summer on stems $6^{1}/_{2}$–10ft high.
CUTTING	If the flowers are allowed to dry on the plant, they can be cut and used as part of a big, bold indoor decoration.

AFTER FLOWERING

REQUIREMENTS	Once the flowers have lost their decorative value, cut off the whole stem low down. As the plant starts to die off and look untidy, cut it back just above the ground.

CARDOON LOOKS similar to a Scotch thistle. Its purple flowers can be left to dry, and then used for a striking indoor arrangement.

AT A GLANCE	
C. cardunculus is a clump-forming perennial grown for its long, striking foliage and purple flowers. Hardy to 0°F (zones 6–7).	

		Companion Plants
Jan	/	Brugmansia
Feb	/	Centranthus
Mar	sow	Echinops
Apr	divide	Geranium
May	transplant	Miscanthus
Jun	flowering	Rose
July	flowering	Salvia
Aug	flowering	Yucca
Sept	flowering	
Oct	/	
Nov	/	
Dec	/	

Cyrtanthus elatus

VALLOTA, SCARBOROUGH LILY

FEATURES

Still more commonly known under its earlier botanical name of *Vallota*, this old favorite should be more widely grown. Four or more brilliant scarlet, open trumpet-shaped blooms are held on a sturdy stem some 18in tall among dark green, strappy leaves. The plant originates from South Africa, and unfortunately, is not hardy enough to try outdoors except in the most favored, warmest areas of the country. However, it makes a good pot plant for a cool greenhouse or conservatory, or it can be grown indoors on a sunny windowsill. During the summer, the pots can be taken outside to decorate the patio. The Scarborough lily is not difficult to cultivate, and deserves to be more popular.

CONDITIONS

ASPECT   Grows best in a bright, sunny position.
SITE   Must be grown as a house or greenhouse plant in all but the very warmest areas of the country.

GROWING METHOD

PLANTING Plant bulbs in summer with the tip of the bulb just at or above soil level. Set one bulb in a 5in pot.
FEEDING   Apply liquid fertilizer every 14 days as soon as growth appears. Keep the plant well-watered throughout the spring and summer, but reduce watering after flowering.
PROBLEMS No specific pest or disease problems are known for this plant.

FLOWERING

SEASON   Flowers usually appear in midsummer.
CUTTING   Flowers will last well when cut but probably give better decorative value if they are left on the plant.

AFTER FLOWERING

REQUIREMENTS Cut off the spent flower stems. Reduce watering and allow the compost to dry out completely between late winter and mid-spring. Do not repot for several years as the plants flower best when the pot is crowded. Offsets are produced freely, and some of these may be removed to pot up and grow on to flowering size in two or three years.

IN WARM AREAS Scarborough lily can be grown outdoors, but it is more reliable as a pot plant for the conservatory or greenhouse.

AT A GLANCE		
A tender bulb with large, trumpet-shaped flowers in summer—an excellent house or greenhouse plant. Min 45°F (zone 11).		
Jan	/	Recommended Varieties
Feb	/	"Pink Diamond"
Mar	/	
Apr	/	
May	/	
Jun	plant	
July	flowering	
Aug	flowering	
Sept	flowering	
Oct	/	
Nov	/	
Dec	/	

D

Dahlia

BEDDING DAHLIA

FEATURES

Seed-raised bedding dahlias are close cousins of the "border" dahlia grown from tubers. A wide range is available, the dwarfer types growing only 12in tall. Flower color is varied and some, like "Redskin," also have bronze leaves. Grow as half-hardy annuals, and use for bedding displays, courtyard containers, and even windowboxes. Choose from single, double, or decorative "collarette" flowers. Widely available as young plants.

CONDITIONS

ASPECT	Bedding dahlias need full sunlight all day.
SITE	Dig in large amounts of decayed manure or compost at least two or three weeks before planting. Soil must be well-drained but moisture-retentive. For containers, use multipurpose compost with added slow-release fertilizer granules to keep growth strong through the summer months.

GROWING METHOD

SOWING	Sow seed February/March in 3$\frac{1}{2}$in pots and just cover. Water and keep at 61°F in a light spot. Transplant seedlings when large enough to handle into individual 3$\frac{1}{2}$in pots and grow on. Harden off at the end of May and plant in early June, when all frosts are over, spacing plants 6–12in apart.
FEEDING	Water and liquid-feed once a week, depending on the soil and weather conditions. Continue watering regularly throughout the season.

PROBLEMS

Dahlia leaves are eaten by slugs, so protect them with slug pellets. Flowers may be chewed by earwigs—to catch them, fill upturned pots with straw and support these on canes among the flowers. Powdery mildew can affect leaves in the late summer but is not serious.

FLOWERING

SEASON	The main show is from midsummer onward, lasting well into fall until the first frosts.
CUTTING	Taller varieties of bedding dahlias make useful and long-lived cut flowers.

AFTER FLOWERING

GENERAL	Remove plants when the leaves turn black and collapse. Fleshy tubers of favorite plants can be stored dry and frost-free over the winter.

AT A GLANCE		
A half-hardy annual grown for its pretty flowers and an ideal summer bedding or container plant. Frost hardy to 32°F (zone 10).		
Jan	/	Recommended Varieties
Feb	sow	Dahlia hybrids:
Mar	sow	Taller varieties
Apr	transplant/grow	"Collarette Dandy"
May	harden off/plant	"Coltness Hybrids Mixed"
Jun	flowering	"Pompon Mixed"
July	flowering	Shorter varieties
Aug	flowering	"Diablo Mixed"
Sept	flowering	"Dwarf Double Delight"
Oct	flowering	"Dwarf Amore"
Nov	/	"Figaro Mixed"
Dec	/	"Redskin"

Dandelion

TARAXACUM OFFICINALE

FEATURES

A perennial flower often seen as a weed in lawns or neglected places, dandelion produces a flat rosette of deeply lobed, bright green leaves from a big, fleshy taproot. Bright yellow flowers are produced in spring and summer on hollow, leafless stems and develop into puffy, spherical seedheads—Dandelion clocks—the individual seeds of which float away on the breeze when ripe. Dandelion has a milky sap and its hollow flower stems differentiate it from other similar weeds, such as hieraciums.

CONDITIONS

ASPECT   Grows best in full sun.
SITE   Not fussy as to soil but you will get the biggest and best roots and less bitter leaves by growing it in good quality, friable soil.

GROWING METHOD

SOWING   Considered a weed in most yards, the problem is usually restricting or removing it rather than growing it. Remove flowerheads before it sets seed. It is difficult to dig out as any bit of root left will regrow. It is best grown in a bottomless container to confine the roots. Although it is perennial, for the best crops dig out the mature plants each spring or two and replant from small pieces of root.

FEEDING   Keep the soil evenly moist. Avoid excessive fertilizing. If the bed had well-rotted manure dug into it, no further fertilizing is required. For container growth, incorporate controlled-release fertilizer into the potting mix at planting time and feed the growing plants monthly with liquid fertilizer.
PROBLEMS   No particular problems.
PRUNING   Remove flower stems as they rise or, if the pretty flowers are wanted, deadhead as they fade to stop unwanted seed formation. If seedheads are allowed to ripen, dandelion becomes an invasive weed.

HARVESTING

PICKING   Fresh spring leaves can be picked while small and sweet. Bigger, older leaves are very bitter. Bitterness can be reduced by blanching, that is, excluding light. Do this by covering the plant with an upturned tin or flower pot, being sure that all holes

AT A GLANCE		
This familiar "weed" with its yellow flowers and "dandelion clock" seedheads has many herbal uses. Hardy to 4°F (zone 6).		
Jan	/	**Parts used**
Feb	/	Leaves
Mar	plant	Flowers
Apr	plant harvest	Roots
May	plant harvest	**Uses**
Jun	harvest	Culinary
July	harvest	Medicinal
Aug	harvest	Cosmetic
Sept	plant harvest	Craft
Oct	harvest	
Nov	/	
Dec	/	

are covered. The leaves are ready for picking when they have lost all or most of their green color. Harvest roots only in late fall or winter or they will lack flavour and body. Pick flowers as they open for use fresh.

STORAGE
: Leaves and flowers must be used fresh but roots are stored by first roasting and grinding them and storing in an airtight jar.

FREEZING
: Roasted, ground roots will stay fresher and more flavoursome if stored in the freezer.

USES

CULINARY
: Young, sweet leaves are highly nutritious and can be used in salads, stir frys, or to make teas. The ground roots are used as a coffee substitute. The flowers are used to make wine.

MEDICINAL
: The sticky, white sap of the dandelion is used to treat warts and verrucas. Dandelion coffee is sleep inducing and a detoxicant said to be good for the kidneys and liver. The leaves are a powerful diuretic.

COSMETIC
: Eating the leaves is said to be good for the skin.

CRAFT
: A yellow-brown dye is made from the roots.

Daphne

DAPHNE

FEATURES

Grown primarily for their sweetly fragrant blooms, daphnes are best planted close to a living room where, on a warm day with a window open, scent wafts indoors. Alternatively, set bushes in pots or tubs beside a garden seat.

Herald spring with deciduous *Daphne mezereum*, to 3ft, with upright stems sleeved with starry, purplish-red flowers. Slightly taller but spreading and evergreen *D. odora* "Aureomarginata," with its cream-edged, green leaves that complement clusters of pinkish-white blooms, also flowers then.

From May to June, evergreen *D. burkwoodii* "Somerset," wondrous when filling a large pedestal urn and forming a focal point, exudes vanilla perfume from pale pink blooms.

CONDITIONS

ASPECT
: Daphne prospers in full sun or very light shade. Shelter it from strong, drying winds.

SITE
: It must have perfectly drained soil with a high organic content. Keep roots cool by mulching plants with well-decayed manure.

GROWING METHOD

FEEDING
: Sustain strong flowering shoots by feeding with bone meal in spring and fall. Encourage newly planted shrubs by liquid feeding with a high-potash fertilizer at weekly intervals from spring to summer. Deep, regular watering is necessary for young plants in long, dry spells. Make sure the soil does not become soggy, for roots may rot.

PROPAGATION
: Multiply plants by layering shoots from mid-spring to late summer or by taking semi-ripe cuttings from mid- to late summer.

PROBLEMS
: Sudden death is usually caused by root rot triggered by bad drainage. Daphne may also be attacked by blackening, leaf-spot fungi that speckle foliage. Control leaf spot by spraying with carbendazim or mancozeb. Viruses are also liable to attack daphne. Characterised by twisted and puckered leaves, there is no control, so dig up and burn affected plants.

PRUNING

No regular cutting back needed, apart from shortening young, straggly stems in spring to keep bushes tidy. Do not prune into older, black-barked wood, for stumps may not regenerate.

LIME-TOLERANT DAPHNES have an unfounded reputation for being difficult. Find them a cool, moist and sunny spot.

AT A GLANCE	
Deciduous or evergreen shrubs with purple-red to pink flowers from late winter to early summer. Hardy to 19°F (zone 8).	

		Recommended Varieties
Jan	/	*D. bholua*
Feb	flower	*D. burkwoodii* "Somerset"
Mar	flower, plant	*D. cneorum*
Apr	flower, plant	*D. mezereum*
May	flower, prune	*D. odora* "Aureomarginata"
June	flower, prune	*D. retusa*
July	plant	
Aug	plant	
Sept	plant	
Oct	plant	
Nov	plant	
Dec	/	

Decumaria barbara

DECUMARIA

FEATURES

This deciduous climber from the south-east USA has stems that produce aerial roots, so eventually it is self-supporting. Decumaria is grown for its flat heads of fragrant, cream flowers that are produced in early summer. Attaining a height of 30ft, it is ideal for growing up a tall mature tree or high wall. Be wary about growing this climber on a house wall, as it will be impossible to remove it for house maintenance without damaging the stems. There is also the risk of damaging the wall itself. This plant makes good and unusual groundcover in a woodland garden or shrub border. It will also enjoy the partial or dappled shade of these situations.

CONDITIONS

ASPECT   Grows well in full sun or partial shade. Provide shelter from cold drying winds as this climber is not fully hardy and may therefore be damaged in an exposed situation.
SITE   Any well-drained fertile soil will be suitable for this climber.

GROWING METHOD

PROPAGATION Take semi-ripe cuttings in late summer. When grown as ground cover it will self-layer, so simply remove rooted portions of stem, complete with buds or young shoots, if new plants are required.
WATERING   If the soil starts to dry out in summer water the plant well. It dislikes drying out.

FEEDING   An annual spring application of slow-release fertilizer, such as the organic blood, fish, and bone, will be sufficient.
PROBLEMS   Not troubled by pests or diseases.

FLOWERING/FOLIAGE

FLOWERS   The cream flowers, which are produced in early summer, smell of honey.
FOLIAGE   The large deep green leaves are attractive and make a good background for the flowers.

PRUNING

REQUIREMENTS No regular pruning needed. If necessary trim after flowering to keep within allotted space.

APPEARING IN EARLY SUMMER, the delightful puffs of cream-colored sweetly-scented flowers are the main attraction of Decumaria barbara. This plants is a sturdy climber and can easily scale and cover large walls and substantial trees.

AT A GLANCE		
A self-clinging climber with flat heads of cream flowers and handsome glossy foliage. Hardy to 23°F (zone 9).		
Jan	/	Companion Plants
Feb	/	Looks good with climbing
Mar	planting	roses, which should flower
Apr	planting	at the same time.
May	/	
Jun	flowering	
July	/	
Aug	/	
Sep	/	
Oct	/	
Nov	/	
Dec	/	

Delphinium

DELPHINIUM

FEATURES

Tall, handsome, and stately, delphiniums make an outstanding feature in perennial borders. Growing 39–78in high, the long-lasting spires of blooms, originally were in a rich blue only, but now offer shades of pink, lavender, white, and red. Delphiniums should be mass-planted at the back of a border for the best effect, but they can also be placed as accent plants at intervals across a border. They mix well with climbers like clematis. Tall-growing varieties may need staking unless they are in a very sheltered spot. Colors can be mixed, but the best effect comes from massing plants of the same color.

CONDITIONS

ASPECT   Needs full sun and shelter from strong winds, and staking if it is not well sheltered.
SOIL   Needs well-drained soil enriched with copious amounts of decayed manure or compost before planting. Water regularly and mulch.

GROWING METHOD

PROPAGATION Divide established clumps in the fall, ensuring each division has a crown and its own roots. Place them about 12in apart. Grows from seed sown in the spring, but the results are variable. Take 3in basal cuttings in mid-spring.
FEEDING   Apply complete plant food once growth begins in the spring, and each month until flowering.

PROBLEMS

PROBLEMS   Watch for aphids on new growth, and hose off or spray with pyrethrum or insecticidal soap. In humid conditions a bad attack of powdery mildew may need to be tackled by spraying with a fungicide. Beware of slugs.

FLOWERING

SEASON   Blooms for a long season through early and late summer.
CUTTING   Flowers make a good display, and can be dried.

AFTER FLOWERING

REQUIREMENTS Remove the flower stems when the main blooms fade and small spikes may flower in late summer and early fall.

DOZENS OF INDIVIDUAL flowers make up the striking spires of the delphinium. Blue shades, from pale to purple, predominate.

AT A GLANCE		
A hardy annual, biennial, and perennial, it is grown for its striking, vertical spires, thick with flowers. Hardy to 5°F (zone 7).		
Jan	/	Recommended Varieties
Feb	sow	*Delphinium* "Bruce"
Mar	sow	"Cassius"
Apr	transplant	"Emily Hawkins"
May	transplant	"Lord Butler"
Jun	flowering	"Our Deb"
July	flowering	"Rosemary Brock"
Aug	flowering	"Sandpiper"
Sept	/	"Sungleam"
Oct	divide	"Walton Gemstone"
Nov	/	
Dec	/	

Dendrobium

DENDROBIUM SPECIES AND HYBRIDS (ASIAN)

FEATURES

By far the largest number of *Dendrobium* species come from sub-tropical and warm regions of Burma, the Himalayas, Thailand, China, and Malaysia. Some of the most commonly cultivated are the varieties of species such as *D. nobile*. These are known as soft-cane dendrobiums. Many Asian species have long, cane-like growth which can grow up to $3^1/4$ft tall, although many others are within the 12–18in range. Some are very upright while others have pendulous growth so they must be grown in hanging baskets. The species described here can be grown in a cool glasshouse where night temperatures do not fall much below 50°F.

TYPES

Some species of *Dendrobium* are evergreen while others are deciduous. The latter lose their leaves during their dormant period, which coincides with their dry season. Both types are epiphytic and are found growing on branches of trees or sometimes on mossy rocks in their habitat. The plants will easily grow into large clumps over years, producing a very spectacular show.

FLOWERS

A few dendrobium varieties produce single flowers but most produce large, showy sprays containing numerous flowers. The color range is vast. White, cream, yellow, pale green, pink, red, maroon, purple, and magenta are all represented in this colorful group. Some have flowers of one single tone while many have contrasting blotches of color in the throat or on the lip of the flower. Many are strongly fragrant.

D. NOBILE is a soft-cane stemmed type that can grow from 12–30in high. The species is pink with deeper cerise tips on the petals and a dark maroon blotch on the lip. The numerous cultivars of this species include many with similar tonings of lavender, purple, and red, but some have pure white petals with yellow or dark red markings on the lip.

D. CHRYSANTHUM is an evergreen orchid with canes that often grow over $3^1/4$ft long. It has a pendulous habit and so is best grown where its stems can hang naturally. Simulating its natural growth this way seems to promote more consistent flowering. Flowers are deep golden yellow with deep red blotches in the lip on a graceful, arching stem.

D. APHYLLUM (syn. *D. pierardii*) is a deciduous species that prefers to grow in a hanging basket. Its canes can grow to over $3^1/4$ft and its delicate, pale flowers can best be enjoyed at eye height. The flowers are pale mauve to pink with the palest creamy yellow lip.

D. FIMBRIATUM is another yellow-flowered species of *Dendrobium* that grows with tall, upright canes

AT A GLANCE		
Popular as houseplants and flowers as cut blooms. Hybrid varieties good for beginners. Various sizes and types.		
Jan	rest	**Recommended Varieties**
Feb	rest, flowering	*D. aphyllum* (pink/cream)
Mar	water and feed, flowering	*D. chrysanthum* (yellow)
		D. densiflorum (golden)
Apr	water and feed, flowering	*D. fimbriatum* (yellow, dark center)
May	water and feed	*D. nobile* (dark pink)
Jun	water and feed	*D. "Christmas Chimes"*
July	water and feed	(white, dark center)
Sept	water and feed	*D. "Red Comet"* (dark pink)
Oct	rest	*D. "Stardust"* (pink/white)
Nov	rest	
Dec	rest	

sometimes reaching over $3^1/_4$ft. It is evergreen and the flowers are produced on the tops of canes one year or more old. Flowers may appear even on older canes that no longer bear leaves. This flower is golden yellow and the lip is delicately fringed. The variety oculatum is a richer, deeper gold with a deep maroon blotch in the center of the lip. These dendrobiums can be grown either in heavy pots that have pebbles added in the base to balance the top weight of the canes, or in a hanging basket.

CONDITIONS

CLIMATE	The preferred conditions depend on the species. Cool types grow in glasshouses or conservatories, whereas warm types will live on a windowsill indoors.
ASPECT	These dendrobiums tolerate partial shade to full sun depending on the species. Those with red, bright pink, and yellow flowers tolerate much more sun than those with white or pale green flowers.
POTTING MIX	Free-draining mixes must always be used. These may contain coarse bark, tree-fern fibre, sphagnum moss, perlite, and even pebbles if extra weight is needed to stabilise the containers. These plants should never be overpotted. Use a container that will comfortably hold the plant roots with a little room to spare.

GROWING METHOD

PROPAGATION	All grow from divisions of the existing plants once they have filled their pots.

Divide after flowering. Some species produce offsets or aerial growths which can be removed from the parent plant once roots are well developed. Older stems of deciduous species containing dormant buds can be laid on damp sphagnum moss and kept moist until roots develop. This may take several months.

WATERING	During active growth in warm weather mist or water regularly, two or three times a week. Give only occasional watering in winter; keep those from monsoonal areas dry at this time.
FEEDING	Feed only during the growing season and not during fall or winter. Use regular applications of soluble orchid fertilizer.
PRUNING	Restrict pruning to removal of spent flowering stems. Do not cut out old canes of species such as *D. fimbriatum* which flower on older stems unless they have shrivelled, turned brown or died off.
PROBLEMS	Chewing and grazing insects, such as snails, slugs, caterpillars, and weevils, can all damage these plants but they are a particular nuisance on the flowers. Plants grown in glasshouses may be troubled by mealybugs and mites, as well as fungal diseases if there is poor ventilation.

FLOWERING SEASON

Most flower in spring but the range may be from late winter to early summer depending on growing conditions and the species.

A DARK BLOTCH OF COLOR in the throat is a feature of many types of dendrobium, including this Dendrobium nobile.

Deutzia

DEUTZIA

FEATURES

Profusely blooming, deciduous, upright or rounded deutzias are easy to grow and best displayed in a mixed border. All, apart from late-flowering *Deutzia monbeigii* with its small leaves, appealingly white beneath and complementing dense clusters of starry, white flowers from July to August, perform from May to July. An elegant, upright shrub, deutzia varies in height from deep carmine-pink-flowered *D.* x *rosea*, 32in by 24in, to *D. scabra* "Pride of Rochester," a handsome leviathan that soars to 7ft. From June to July, its double, white blooms smother pleasingly, peeling-barked branches.

CONDITIONS

ASPECT   *Deutzia* prefers full sun but will tolerate light shade. Plants should be sheltered from strong, northerly or easterly winds.

SITE   This shrub flourishes on most well-drained soils, especially if fortified with organic matter.

GROWING METHOD

FEEDING   Undemanding, deutzia does not need regular feeding. If growth is poor, topdress the root area with Growmore or fish, blood, and bone meal in spring and summer.

PROPAGATION   Multiply deutzia from hardwood cuttings from mid-fall to early winter.

PROBLEMS   Late spring frosts may damage blossom buds of May-flowering varieties, so position plants carefully if you garden in a frost pocket.

PRUNING

Encourage a wealth of blossom by cutting back to near ground level a third of the older branches when flowers fade. If stems bearing flower buds are killed by frost, shorten them to healthy wood.

FLOWERING FROM SPRING to early summer, single, white-flowered Deutzia gracilis *makes a charming background to these late yellow primroses.*

AT A GLANCE	
Deciduous shrub with shoots clothed in single or double, pink or white blooms in spring and summer. Hardy to -13˚F (zone 5).	
Jan /	**Recommended Varieties**
Feb /	*D.* x *elegantissima*
Mar plant	"Rosealind"
Apr plant	*D.* x *hybrida* "Magician"
May flower, plant	"Montrose"
June flower	*D. monbeigii*
July flower, prune	*D.* x *rosea* "Campanulata"
Aug plant, prune	*D. scabra* "Pride of Rochester"
Sept plant	
Oct plant	
Nov plant	
Dec plant	

Dianthus barbatus

SWEET WILLIAM

FEATURES

Sweet Williams are varieties of *Dianthus barbatus* and have flowers in pink, white, red, burgundy, and bicolors, on large rounded heads. Individual flowers often have darker central "eyes." Plants have clumping growth up to 18in, while dwarf forms grow to just 6in. The flowers appear from the spring into early summer and are scented and ideal for cutting. They are easily grown from seed as a hardy biennial, and useful for bedding schemes and as blocks of spring color in mixed borders. Some less common varieties, like "Sooty," have dark, almost black flowers.

CONDITIONS

ASPECT Grow Sweet Williams in full sunlight.
SITE Needs well-drained soil that has been limed before planting, and has had plenty of rotted compost mixed in several weeks before.

GROWING METHOD

SOWING Sow the fine seed in rows outdoors, $1/2$in deep and just cover, in May/June. Transplant the seedlings so they are in rows 6in apart and pinch out the growing tips to make them bushy. Water regularly throughout the summer months, and then lift and plant into their flowering positions in October, keeping the roots intact. For cut flowers only, the plants can be left growing in rows.

FEEDING Liquid-feed monthly during the summer.
PROBLEMS Poor drainage during winter can kill plants. If leaves are attacked by rust disease, try a spray containing the fungicide penconazole.

FLOWERING

SEASON Flowers appear from late spring to early summer, and it is possible to get a second "flush" if all the stalks are cut hard back after the first flowers have faded.
CUTTING An excellent cut flower, and ideal for making into a small, rounded bouquet.

AFTER FLOWERING

GENERAL Pull plants up when they are past their best, or leave some to develop into bigger clumps.

AT A GLANCE		
A summer-sown biennial grown for its large heads of scented flowers in spring and early summer. Frost hardy to 5°F (zone 7).		
Jan	/	Recommended Varieties
Feb	/	*Dianthus barbatus*.
Mar	/	Tall varieties
Apr	flowering	"Auricula-Eyed Mixed"
May	flowers/sow	"Forerunner Mixed"
Jun	flowers/sow	"Gemstones"
July	flowering	"Harlequin"
Aug	grow on	"Monarch Mixed"
Sept	grow on	**Dwarf varieties**
Oct	plant	"Dwarf Mixed"
Nov	/	"Indian Carpet Mixed"
Dec	/	

Dianthus carypohyllus

WILD CARNATION

FEATURES

Carnations are very popular, both as cut flowers and as a garden subject. Flowers are carried singly or in groups on stems 12–20in high, although florists' carnations may be taller. *Dianthus caryophyllus* from the Mediterranean, a woody perennial with elegant stiff stems, bears richly scented, purple-pink flowers that grow taller than the average, reaching 32in under perfect conditions. It has given rise to several excellent series. The Floristan Series comes in a wide color range, and makes good cut flowers, the Knight Series is shorter and bushier, and includes yellow, white, and orange blooms, and the Lilliput Series, shorter still at 8in, includes a rich scarlet.

CONDITIONS

ASPECT   Needs full sunlight all day. Protect from very strong winds.

SOIL   Needs very well-drained soil, with plenty of additional, well-decayed organic matter. Unless the soil is alkaline, apply a light dressing of lime before each planting.

GROWING METHOD

PROPAGATION   Grows easily from cuttings taken at almost any time. Use leafy side shoots and strip off all but the top leaves. Roots form in 3–5 weeks. Set newly rooted plants 8in apart. Water regularly to establish, then occasionally in dry weather. Carnations tolerate dry conditions well.

FEEDING   Little fertilizer is needed if the soil contains plenty of organic matter, but you may give a complete feed twice, in the spring and again in mid-summer.

PROBLEMS   Carnation rust, a fungal disease, is common in warm, humid conditions. Grayish spots appear on leaves or stems, and the foliage may curl and yellow. Take prompt action by immediately spraying with a fungicide. Remove caterpillars when seen.

FLOWERING

SEASON   The crop of flowers appears in the summer, but it can be forced for other times. Remove any excess buds to produce good-sized, main blooms.

CUTTING   An excellent cut flower. Recut stems between nodes (joints) to aid water uptake.

AT A GLANCE		
D. caryophyllus is a colorful woody perennial, part of the large dianthus family of over 300 species. Hardy to 5°F (zone 7).		
Jan	/	**Companion Plants**
Feb	/	Campanula
Mar	sow	Cistus
Apr	/	Crepis
May	transplant	Eryngium
Jun	flowering	Helianthemum
July	flowering	Portulaca
Aug	flowering	Sedum
Sept	/	Tulip
Oct	/	
Nov	/	
Dec	sow	

Dianthus chinensis

CHINESE PINK

FEATURES

Growing 8–12in high, varieties of *Dianthus chinensis* are suitable for massed planting, edging garden beds, or for use in troughs or pots. Chinese pink is grown as a half-hardy annual, although it is fully hardy outdoors. Flower are red, pink, or white, with only slight scent. Available as young plants.

CONDITIONS

ASPECT   Needs full sunlight to flower at its best.
SITE   Needs well-drained soil, but dig in plenty of well-rotted manure or compost when preparing beds. Lime can be added to the soil before planting and raked in. Containers must have very good drainage.

GROWING METHOD

SOWING   Sow seeds in 3^1/$_2$in pots of multipurpose compost in March, just cover, and keep at 60°F in a light place. When seedlings are 1in tall, transplant to cell trays and grow on with some protection (a cold frame is suitable). Harden off at the end of May and plant out in beds or containers.
FEEDING   Do not overwater—a good weekly watering should be sufficient—and add liquid feed every 2–3 weeks. Plants in containers need no extra feeding if slow-release fertilizer is added.

PROBLEMS   Overwatering will cause yellowing of the leaves and rotting off at soil/compost level.

FLOWERING

SEASON   Plants come into flower from early summer onward and will continue until the fall if dead flowerheads are removed regularly.
CUTTING   Taller varieties can be used as cut flowers, but choose a variety known for its scent such as "Double Gaiety Mixed."

AFTER FLOWERING

GENERAL   Remove plants when finished and compost.

AS CONTAINER PLANTS, Chinese pinks are perfect as tidy edging plants, all growing to the same height. They are also valuable as colorful fillers and effectively bridge the gap between taller plants in the center of large tubs and trailing plants falling over the edges.

AT A GLANCE	
A hardy annual grown for its small brightly colored pink-type flowers, used in bedding/pots. Frost hardy to 5°F (zone 7).	
Jan /	**Recommended Varieties**
Feb /	*Dianthus chinensis:*
Mar sow	"Baby Doll Mixed"
Apr transplant	"Black & White Minstrels"
May harden off/plant	"Double Gaiety Mixed"
Jun flowering	"Princess Mixed"
July flowering	"Raspberry Parfait"
Aug flowering	"Snowfire"
Sept flowering	"Strawberry Parfait"
Oct /	"T&M Frosty Mixed"
Nov /	
Dec /	

Dianthus cultivars

PINKS

FEATURES

Pinks are crosses of *D. caryophyllus* (wild carnation) and *D. plumarius* (cottage pink). Allwood Brothers nursery in West Sussex, England, has bred an enormous range of cultivars that are free-flowering, given the correct conditions. The gray-green foliage grows in a tufted mat and flowering stems are 4–12in tall. Most flowers are heavily scented and may be single or bicolored, some with a clear margin of contrasting color. Most are white, pink, red, deep crimson, or salmon, with cultivars ideally suited for the rock garden.

CONDITIONS

ASPECT   Needs full sunlight all day, and protection from strong winds.

SITE   Needs very free-draining soil, enriched with additional decayed organic matter, well ahead of planting. Use a soil-testing kit to determine whether your soil is acid—if so, add quantities of lime according to the manufacturer's instructions. Beware of exceeding the recommended rate—it will simply do more harm than good.

GROWING METHOD

PROPAGATION   Grows easily from cuttings taken in late summer and the fall. Start fresh plants every three or four years to keep vigorous, compact growth. Space the plant approximately 6–12in apart, depending on the variety. Water until the plants are well established.

FEEDING   Apply complete plant food in the early spring, when active spring growth begins.

PROBLEMS   Aphids and slugs are the two major problems. The former can be tackled by a regular spraying program with, for example, malathion. The latter can be seen late at night or early in the morning. Either treat chemically, or pick off by hand and drown.

FLOWERING

SEASON   Some pinks only flower during the spring, others have a long flowering period from the spring to early fall.

CUTTING   Pinks make excellent cut flowers, providing indoor decoration and scent.

AFTER FLOWERING

REQUIREMENTS   Cut off any spent flower stems to the ground as they fade. No other pruning action is necessary.

AT A GLANCE	
The cultivars include perennials in a wide color range, many richly scented. Generally hardy to 5°F (zone 7).	
Jan /	**Recommended Varieties**
Feb /	*Dianthus alpinus*
Mar sow	"Bovey Belle"
Apr transplant	"Devon Glow"
May transplant	*D. deltoides*
Jun flowering	"La Bourboule"
July flowering	"Monica Wyatt"
Aug flowering	"Sam Barlow"
Sept /	"Whitehill"
Oct sow	"Widecombe Fair"
Nov /	
Dec /	

Dianthus deltoides

MAIDEN PINK

FEATURES

There are about 300 species of dianthus, including annual and perennial growers, and several of the alpine dianthus make low mounded growth suitable for groundcover. This species, *Dianthus deltoides*, makes a delightful groundcover with its thick, spreading mat-like growth. Foliage height rarely reaches more than 4³/₄in, while the pretty, fringed flowers stand about 8in high. Flowers in the species, which appear in the summer, are deep rose pink but there are cultivars with flowers in various colors, including white, red, and other shades of pink. In good conditions one plant can spread to 18in.

CONDITIONS

ASPECT   Prefers full sun all day. Keep away from anywhere remotely shady.

SITE   Soil must be well drained, and decayed organic matter added well ahead of planting time is beneficial. Very acid soils should be dressed with lime. Heavy clay soils need to be thoroughly broken up before planting with plenty of sand and horticultural grit.

GROWING METHOD

PROPAGATION   Grow from division of rooted sections of an existing plant, or from cuttings taken in late summer. Make sure that the cutting is a non-flowering one.

FEEDING   Give complete plant food in spring.

PROBLEMS

PROBLEMS   No specific problems are known, but keep an eye out for aphids and slugs. Tackle the latter either with slug pellets or, if you don't want to use chemicals, instigate a nightly patrol, picking them off when seen.

FLOWERING

SEASON   Flowers appear in the summer.

CUTTING   The flowers may be cut for posies but the stems are rather short.

PRUNING

GENERAL   Shear off flowers once they have faded. No other pruning is needed.

SPILLING OVER A GRAVEL PATH, this pink dianthus revels in the full sun and sharp drainage afforded by the small stones.

AT A GLANCE	
Dianthus deltoides is a low spreading perennial producing white, pink, or red summer flowers. Hardy to 5˚F (zone 7).	
Jan foliage	**Recommended Varieties**
Feb foliage	*Dianthus armeria*
Mar foliage	"Doris"
April foliage	*D. erinaceus*
May foliage	*D.* "Haytor White"
June flowering	*D.* "Joe Vernon"
July flowering	*D.* "Mrs Sinkins"
Aug flowering	*D. pavonius*
Sept foliage	*D. scardicus*
Oct foliage	*D. superbus*
Nov foliage	
Dec foliage	

Diascia

TWINSPUR

FEATURES

Twinspur has an extremely long flowering season, lasting from the spring until the first frosts. Though lthere is a large number of forms available, ranging from "Lilac Mist" to "Salmon Supreme," the color range is quite limited, essentially only including shades of pink. *Diascia* requires moist, rich soil, but over-feeding results in fewer flowers. The height ranges from 6 to 12in, which means the taller plants can be given free reign lto burst through their neighbors, adding to the display. "Salmon Supreme" is an attractive low-spreader, being 6in high. *D. vigilis* is twice as tall, hardier, and even more free-flowering.

CONDITIONS

ASPECT   Enjoys full sun; though it tolerates some shade, it will not flower as long or as prolifically.

SOIL   Moisture-retentive, well-drained ground.

GROWING METHOD

PROPAGATION   This is essential, since diascias are short-lived, but propagation is easily managed. Success rates are high by all methods, though cuttings are particularly easy. Either sow the seed when ripe or in the following spring, take cuttings during the growing season, or divide in the spring. Since young plants might die in severe winters, keep indoor cuttings as possible replacements.

FEEDING   Mulch well in the spring to enrich the soil.

PROBLEMS   Slugs and snails are the main enemies. Pick them off or use a chemical treatment.

FLOWERING

SEASON   An unusually long season from the spring, beyond the end of summer, to the first frosts.

CUTTING   Diascias cut well, and although they do not last particularly long in water, replacements are quickly available from the parent plant.

AFTER FLOWERING

REQUIREMENTS   Cut ruthlessly to the ground after flowering to promote a second flush of flowers.

ONE OF THE MOST USEFUL garden plants, twinspur produces flowers throughout the growing season, from the spring to fall, and at 12in tall, it makes the perfect front-of-border filler, tolerating a sunny position, and one with a degree of shade. Despite a short lifespan, it is easily propagated.

AT A GLANCE		
A near 50-strong genus of annuals and perennials, with a pink color and a long flowering season. Hardy to 23˚F (zone 9).		
Jan	/	**Recommended Varieties**
Feb	sow	*Diascia barberae* "Ruby Field"
Mar	divide	*D.* "Dark Eyes"
Apr	transplant	*D.* "Hector's Hardy"
May	flowering	*D. integerrima*
Jun	flowering	*D.* "Lilac Mist"
July	flowering	*D.* "Rupert Lambert"
Aug	flowering	*D. vigilis*
Sept	flowering	
Oct	/	
Nov	/	
Dec	/	

Dicentra spectabilis

BLEEDING HEART

FEATURES

With fern-like foliage and curving stems bearing pretty pink-and-white, heart-shaped flowers, bleeding heart is an all-time favorite perennial. It appeals to children and adults alike. There is a cultivar, "Alba," which has pure white flowers. Another species less commonly grown is *D. formosa*, which has very ferny foliage, but its flowers are not so completely heart-shaped. Bleeding heart can be grown in a mixed border or in the filtered shade of trees. Plants may reach 16–24in tall in good conditions, and form a clump approximately 20in wide.

CONDITIONS

ASPECT   *Dicentra* grows best in filtered sunlight. Strong, hot, drying winds make it shrivel up. A sheltered position protects against late frosts.

SITE   Needs well-drained soil rich in organic matter. Dig in copious quantities of decayed manure or compost several weeks before planting.

GROWING METHOD

PROPAGATION   Divide large established clumps in the fall, and plant divisions 10–12in apart. Also grows from seed sown in the spring or fall. Needs regular, deep watering during dry periods in the spring and summer.

FEEDING   Apply a sprinkling of a complete plant food whenever growth begins in the spring.

PROBLEMS   There are no specific pest or disease problems known for this plant.

FLOWERING

SEASON   Blooms for several weeks during late spring and early summer.

CUTTING   Flowers are not suitable for cutting.

AFTER FLOWERING

REQUIREMENTS   Cut out spent flower stems. As the foliage yellows and dies off, cut it off just above the ground.

THE ARCHING STEMS of this bleeding heart carry masses of bright pink, heart-shaped flowers resembling tiny lockets.

AT A GLANCE	
Dicentra spectabilis is a clump-forming perennial, with arching stems and decorative deep pink flowers. Hardy to 0°F (zones 6–7).	
Jan /	**Recommended Varieties**
Feb /	*D.* "Adrian Bloom"
Mar sow	"Bountiful"
Apr transplant	*D. cucularia*
May transplant	*D. f. alba*
Jun flowering	"Langtrees"
July flowering	"Ruby Slippers"
Aug /	*D. macrantha*
Sept /	*D. spectabilis*
Oct division	*D. s.* "Alba"
Nov sow	"Stuart Boothman"
Dec /	

Dierama pulcherrimum

FAIRY FISHING RODS, WANDFLOWER

FEATURES

The slender, arching stems of this highly desirable South African plant carry numerous bell-shaped, pendulous flowers and rise out of stiff, evergreen, sword-shaped leaves. Flowers are a rich silvery-pink in the species but there are a number of named cultivars in shades of pink, lilac, and even white.

Dense clumps of established plants produce many flowering stems, which sway in the slightest breeze to give a delightful effect. A mass planting creates a striking feature in the garden and it is often placed near water where the reflections increase its impact. Foliage grows 20in or so high but the flowering stems may be almost 6ft long in the right conditions.

CONDITIONS

ASPECT   Needs full sun all day.
SITE   *Dierama* fits well in the herbaceous border. This plant needs well-drained but moisture-retentive, fertile soil containing plenty of well-rotted organic matter such as garden compost or animal manure.

GROWING METHOD

PLANTING   Plant in mid to late fall, 3in deep and 12in apart.
FEEDING   A balanced fertilizer can be applied annually in early spring or after flowering. Water during late spring and summer if conditions are dry; the soil should remain moist throughout the growing season.
PROBLEMS   There are no specific pest or disease problems normally experienced with this plant.

FLOWERING

SEASON   Dierama bears its flowers from mid to late summer.
CUTTING Not suitable for cutting.

AFTER FLOWERING

REQUIREMENTS When spent, flower stems can be cut off at ground level, although they can be left to set seed if required. Dierama resents root disturbance, so corms should not be lifted unless it is essential. Self-sown seedlings can often be transplanted successfully to increase your stock of this plant.

SILKY FLOWERS in two shades of pink are suspended from the fine stems of this lovely South African plant. An established clump of fairy fishing rods produces many flowering stems. It is easy to see how the plant gained its common name.

AT A GLANCE		
A perennial with graceful, slender, arching stems carrying dainty pink blooms in summer. Needs moist soil to thrive.		
Jan	/	**Recommended Varieties**
Feb	/	"Blackbird"
Mar	/	"Peregrine"
Apr	/	"Slieve Donard Hybrids"
May	/	
Jun	/	
July	flowering	
Aug	flowering	
Sept	flowering	
Oct	plant	
Nov	plant	
Dec	/	

Digitalis
FOXGLOVE

FEATURES

Foxgloves are essentials for the "cottage garden," self-seeding in unexpected places, with their tall spires of often richly colored flowers. They grow in most soils and situations, from the shady to the sunny, and dryish to damp, although performance is variable at these extremes. They also make a large group of biennials and perennials ranging in height from 24in to 6^{1}/$_{2}$ft. The common foxglove (*D. purpurea*) can be grown as a perennial, but its lifespan is short, and the biennial is generally the preferred option. The color range includes red, yellow, white, and pink with the early summer Fox Hybrids. *D. grandiflora* has the largest flowers.

CONDITIONS

ASPECT   Dappled shade for part of the day is ideal, but it is not absolutely essential. Foxgloves are undemanding plants, and will grow in a wide range of yards.

SITE   The soil conditions can vary, but humus-rich ground gives the best results.

GROWING METHOD

PROPAGATION   Sow seed of new varieties in containers within a cold frame during the late spring. Space seedlings up to 18in apart. If you already have some plants, seeding is not necessary, since the foxglove is a prolific self-seeder. Dig up a new plant and transplant to where it is required. Water in well, and do not let it dry out.

FEEDING   Provide a complete feed in the spring. In particularly dry soil, provide a protective spring mulch.

PROBLEMS   Leaf spot and powdery mildew can strike. Spraying is the best treatment.

FLOWERING

SEASON   Flowers appear in early and mid-summer.

CUTTING   While they make good cut flowers, handle with extreme caution. The foliage can irritate the skin, and all parts are poisonous.

AFTER FLOWERING

REQUIREMENTS   Leave just a few stems to seed where the foxgloves look good, mixing well with other plants, otherwise deadhead to avoid masses of invasive seedlings.

FOXGLOVES are perfect for cottage-style borders and make good companions for poppies and lavatera.

AT A GLANCE		
Foxgloves are grown for their tall spires of attractive, tubular flowers, usually in soft hues. Hardy to 5˚F (zone 7).		
Jan	/	Recommended Varieties
Feb	/	*Digitalis ferruginea*
Mar	sow	*D. grandiflora*
Apr	transplant	*D. lanata*
May	transplant	*D. parviflora*
Jun	flowering	*D. purpurea*
July	flowering	*D. p.* "Excelsior Group"
Aug	/	
Sept	/	
Oct	/	
Nov	/	
Dec	/	

Dill

ANETHUM GRAVEOLENS

FEATURES

A hardy annual herb growing to 2–3ft, dill looks very like fennel, with its threadlike, feathery, aromatic, blue-green leaves. It has a single, thin taproot rising above the ground to form a long, hollow stalk. This stalk branches at the top to support a 6in wide mass of small, yellow flowers, appearing in clusters, in summer. Flat, oval seeds, brown in color, are produced quickly and in great quantities.

CONDITIONS

ASPECT   Prefers full sun. May need support and protection from strong winds.
SITE   Light, free-draining but fertile soils. Will not do well in cold, wet conditions.

GROWING METHOD

SOWING   Sow seed from spring to fall. Successive planting every fortnight is recommended to ensure that there is continuous cropping. Sow the seeds in shallow furrows, with at least 2ft between the rows, and then thin the seedlings out to 1ft apart when they have reached approximately 2in in height. Dill will quite often self-sow, so choose a permanent position for the initial plantings.
FEEDING   Keep well watered, especially in hot weather. Mulch well throughout spring and summer with well-rotted organic matter such as compost or farmyard manure.
PROBLEMS   No particular problems.

HARVESTING

PICKING   Dill leaves can be picked within 2 months of planting. Clip close to the stem in the cooler parts of the day. Several weeks after the plant blossoms, pick the flowerheads and place them in a paper bag—store in a cool, dry place until seeds ripen—or stems can be cut and hung upside down until seeds ripen and fall.
STORAGE   Leaves and stems do not keep for more than a couple of days in the refrigerator before drooping and losing flavor. Dry leaves by spreading them thinly over a firm, non-metallic surface in a warm, dark place. After drying, place them in an airtight container. Seeds are dried in a similar manner.
FREEZING   Leaves and stems can be frozen for up to six months, and pieces broken off as required.

AT A GLANCE	
A hardy annual with feathery blue-green leaves. Leaves and seeds are popular in cooking. Fairly hardy to about 14°F (zone 8).	
Jan / Feb / Mar plant Apr plant May plant harvest Jun plant harvest July plant harvest Aug plant harvest Sept plant harvest Oct harvest Nov / Dec /	**Parts used** Leaves Seeds Stems **Uses** Culinary Medicinal Gardening

USES

CULINARY

Dill has a pronounced tang which is stronger in seed than leaf. Fresh leaves are used in many dishes, and as a garnish. The seeds are used ground or whole in cooked dishes, as well as in the making of vinegars, pickles, and herb butters. Dried leaves are often added to soups or sauces. Dill is a great favorite in fish dishes. Tea can be made from the seeds.

MEDICINAL

Dill was traditionally an important medicinal herb for coughs, headaches, digestive problems etc, and dill water or "gripe water" is still used.

GARDENING

Dill is considered an ideal companion plant for lettuce, cabbage, and onions.

Disa

DISA SPECIES AND HYBRIDS

FEATURES

Only one species of *Disa* is common in cultivation: *D. uniflora*, which has generally bright scarlet flowers. Flowers are mainly scarlet with red and gold venation but some golden yellow ones are found in their natural habitat. This terrestrial genus can be difficult to cultivate successfully as many species come from habitats that have soil that is permanently damp but never waterlogged. These conditions are not very easy for the orchid grower to duplicate. Disas produce a rosette of basal leaves from which a flowering stem over 24in high will emerge. Flowers are large, 3–5in across and borne in groups of mostly three or more blooms.

ORIGIN

This group of orchids is mainly native to tropical and southern Africa and is also found in Madagascar.

CONDITIONS

CLIMATE	Disa needs a frost-free climate. Most are cool growers and tolerate temperatures down to about 41˚F; 77˚F is the preferred upper limit.
ASPECT	Grows best in partial shade with some sun early in the morning. In total shade plants will grow but not flower.
POTTING MIX	The mix or soil should be moisture retentive but never soggy. A suitable mix might contain perlite, coconut fiber peat, chopped sphagnum moss, and medium-fine bark.

GROWING METHOD

PROPAGATION	Divide plants when re-potting. This should be about every two years after flowering, never more than three years apart.
WATERING	Avoid watering the foliage if possible. Allow water to soak up from below by standing pots in a container of water. Never allow the pots to dry out but greatly decrease water in cool weather.
FEEDING	Apply soluble liquid fertilizer, at a quarter to half the recommended dilution rate, while plants are actively growing.
PROBLEMS	No specific problems are known if cultural conditions are met.

FLOWERING SEASON

Generally from early summer to fall, but this can vary.

AT A GLANCE		
Unusual and challenging orchid preferring moist conditions. Bright flowers are 2–3in across.		
Jan	water	**Recommended Varieties**
Feb	water	*D. uniflora*
Mar	water	D. "Inca Princess"
Apr	flowering, water	
May	flowering, water	
Jun	flowering, water and feed	
July	flowering, water and feed	
Aug	flowering, water and feed	
Sept	water	
Oct	water	
Nov	water	
Dec	water	

Dorotheanthus
MESEMBRYANTHEMUM OR LIVINGSTONE DAISY

FEATURES

Mesembryanthemum, also known as Livingstone daisy, is ideal for planting on dry, sunny banks, on rock gardens, and in pots of free-draining compost. It has a spreading habit, but is only 6in tall at most. The fleshy leaves have a crystalline texture with bright, daisy-like flowers in many shades. Grow as a half-hardy annual. All varieties of *Dorotheanthus bellidiformis* have the habit of closing their flowers in dull and wet spells of weather, opening again in bright sunshine.

CONDITIONS

ASPECT   Needs full direct sun all day and will perform even better on a south-facing sloping bank.

SITE   Needs very well drained soil, with no special soil preparation necessary, since plants grow better on light, sandy, and hungry soils. If grown in containers, used soil-based compost and mix with fifty percent grit for good drainage.

GROWING METHOD

SOWING   Sow seed in a 3½in pot of soil-based seed compost in March and barely cover. Keep at 64°F in a light place. When seedlings are large enough, transplant to cell trays of soil-based potting compost and grow on. Harden off at the end of May for two weeks and plant after the last frosts 6in apart.

FEEDING   Extra feeding is unnecessary and produces leaves at the expense of flowers. Take care not to overwater in beds or pots, else plants will rot.

PROBLEMS   Slugs will attack the fleshy young leaves so scatter slug pellets after planting out.

FLOWERING

SEASON   Flowers appear from midsummer onward. Remove faded flowers to encourage more.

CUTTING   Not suitable for cutting.

AFTER FLOWERING

GENERAL   Pull up and compost when finished.

LIVINGSTONE DAISIES set beds alight with color on bright sunny days when the flowers open fully. Planted 6in apart they soon knit together to create a tapestry of color, and look especially at home when creeping among pieces of stone on a sunny rock garden.

AT A GLANCE	
A half-hardy, spreading annual grown for its daisy-like flowers that open fully in sunshine. Frost hardy to 32°F (zone 10).	
Jan /	**Recommended Varieties**
Feb /	*Dorotheanthus bellidiformis*
Mar sow	"Gelato Pink"
Apr sow/transplant	"Harlequin Mixed"
May plant/harden off	"Lunette" ("Yellow Ice")
Jun flowering	"Magic Carpet Mixed"
July flowering	"Sparkles"
Aug flowering	
Sept flowering	
Oct /	
Nov /	
Dec /	

E

Echinacea purpurea

PURPLE CONEFLOWER

FEATURES

Native to the prairie States of America, the coneflower is a hardy, drought-resistant plant. Its dark, cone-shaped center is surrounded by rich pink ray petals, and there are cultivars available in shades of pink-purple and white. They make excellent cut flowers. Coneflowers often grow over 39in tall, and are a great addition to a perennial border because they bloom over a long period, from mid-summer into the fall, when many other plants have finished. *Echinacea* should be mass-planted to get the best effect. Excellent varieties include *E. purpurea* Bressingham Hybrids, "Magnus," and "White Swan."

CONDITIONS

ASPECT   Prefers full sunlight all day. Although it is tolerant of windy conditions, the blooms will have a better appearance if the plants are sheltered from strong winds.

SITE   Needs well-drained, rich soil. Poor or sandy soils can be improved by digging in large quantities of compost or manure before planting.

GROWING METHOD

PROPAGATION   Divide existing clumps in the early spring or fall, and replant divisions 8–10in apart. It can be grown from seeds sown in early spring, which may produce color variations. *Echinacea* needs regular watering to establish itself in prolonged dry spells, but occasional deep soakings in dry weather are enough, as it tolerates dry conditions well.

FEEDING   Apply complete plant food in early spring and again in mid-summer.

PROBLEMS   No specific problems are known.

FLOWERING

SEASON   There is a long flowering period from late summer into the fall.

CUTTING   Cut flowers for the vase when they are fully open, but before the petals separate.

AFTER FLOWERING

REQUIREMENTS   Remove spent flower stems. The whole plant can be cut back to ground level in winter.

BOLDER THAN MANY perennials, coneflowers are sometimes slow to appear in the spring but they are definitely worth the wait.

AT A GLANCE	
E. purpurea is an attractive, daisy-like perennial with purple flowers, ideal for naturalizing or borders. Hardy to 5˚F (zone 7).	
Jan /	**Companion Plants**
Feb sow	Allium
Mar sow	Delphinium
Apr transplant	Geranium
May transplant	Gladiolus
Jun /	Iris
July flowering	Lavandula
Aug flowering	Rosemary
Sept flowering	Yucca
Oct divide	Delphinium
Nov /	Rose
Dec /	

Echinocereus

HEDGEHOG CACTUS

FEATURES

Hailing from the south-west of North America, all 47 species in this group are in cultivation. It is a very variable genus: some types are globular, while others form short columns, some of which are pencil thin. The group is also split when it comes to their spines. Some species are heavily spined, while others are relatively smooth. Most are clump-forming or clustering, and in ideal conditions clumps of up to 3ft wide are found. Some species have edible fruits reputed to taste like strawberries. The best known of these are *Echinocereus pectinatus*, *E. engelmannii*, *E. reichenbachii*, and *E. subinermis*. The range of flower color in this group extends from white to yellow, orange, bright red, pale pink, magenta, and violet.

VARIETIES

E. knippelianus is a striking cactus, with a dark green, almost smooth body, few spines, and pink to purple spring flowers. *E. subinermis* is one of the few yellow-flowered species, while *E. triglochidiatus* has brilliant scarlet flowers and a great range of forms. The "must have" hedgehog cactus for any collector is *E. reichenbachii* with purple-pink flowers; it makes a tidy smallish shape being 1ft high and 8in wide.

CONDITIONS

ASPECT   Prefers full sun with good air circulation.
SITE   Use a well-drained standard cactus mix. If being planted outside over summer, dig plenty of grit into the soil.

GROWING METHOD

PROPAGATION   Can be grown from seed sown in spring or from offsets taken in spring or summer.
FEEDING   Apply slow-release granules in spring or use weak liquid plant food in the growing season.
PROBLEMS   Outdoors, few problems are encountered. If plants are grown under glasss, mealybugs or scales may be troublesome.

FLOWERING

SEASON   Flowers appear some time during spring or summer. The flower buds form inside the plant body and then burst through the skin near the stem tips, often leaving scars.
FRUITS   Flowers are followed by fleshy fruits, most of which ripen to red although some fruits are green or purple.

AT A GLANCE	
Dramatic small cactuses, with flowers bursting through the skin. Many attractive species. 50°F min (zone 11).	
Jan /	**Recommended Varieties**
Feb /	*Echinocereus chloranthus*
Mar sow	*E. cinerascens*
Apr transplant	*E. engelmannii*
May flowering	*E. knippelianus*
Jun flowering	*E. pectinatus*
July /	*E. reichenbachii*
Aug /	*E. scheeri*
Sept /	*E. subinermis*
Oct /	*E. triglochidiatus*
Nov /	
Dec /	

Echinops
GLOBE THISTLE

FEATURES

This plant's very distinctive appearance makes a good accent in a mixed planting. Taller species need to be placed at the rear of a border, but others can be planted in bold groups through the bed. Most have foliage that is stiff, prickly, and finely divided, with silvery stems growing from 12in to 6^1/2ft tall. Some of the species have foliage that has fine white hairs on the underside. The flowerheads are usually white or metallic blue, and are highly prized for their decorative value when cut and dried. The most commonly grown is *E. ritro* and its cultivars, some of which have deep blue flowers. *E. sphaerocephalus* has pale gray-to-silvery flowers.

CONDITIONS

ASPECT   Prefers full sunlight all day.
SITE   Soil must be very well drained but
           need not be rich. The globe thistle
           can be grown in poor, gravel-like,
           or sandy soils.

GROWING METHOD

PROPAGATION It can either be grown from seed, from
             division of existing clumps, or from root
             cuttings. All propagation is done from
             the fall to winter. Plant out about 16in
             apart and water regularly to establish.
             Although drought-tolerant, this plant
             benefits from occasional deep watering
             during prolonged dry spring and summer
             periods.
FEEDING   Apply a complete plant food or poultry
             manure in early spring.

PROBLEMS   There are no known pest or disease
             problems, but plants will rot on sticky
             clay or poorly drained soil.

FLOWERING

SEASON   Each species or variety will flower for
             approximately two months.
CUTTING   Flowerheads required for drying should
             be cut before the blooms are fully open.

AFTER FLOWERING

REQUIREMENTS Cut off any remaining spent flowerheads,
             unless you want the seed to ripen. As
             the plant dies down, clean away dead
             foliage, wearing gloves to protect yourself
             against the foliage.

EARLY MORNING LIGHT accentuates the rounded, slightly spiky heads of these globe thistle flowers, planted here in a bold drift in a countryside yard.

AT A GLANCE		
A group of annuals, biennials, and perennials grown for their geometric shapes and blue flowers. Hardy to 23–50°F (zones 9–11).		
Jan	divide	**Recommended Varieties**
Feb	divide	*Echinops bannaticus*
Mar	sow	"Blue Globe"
Apr	/	"Taplow Blue"
May	transplant	*E. ritro ruthenicus*
Jun	/	"Veitch's Blue"
July	flowering	**Companion Plants**
Aug	flowering	Buddleja
Sept	flowering	Kniphofia
Oct	divide	Perovskia
Nov	divide	
Dec	divide	

Elaeagnus pungens

ELAEAGNUS

FEATURES

For a foolproof, hardy, evergreen hedge, with a decent show of berries, elaeagnus comes in the very top league. *Elaeagnus pungens* grows about 6ft high and wide, and has small, white, sweetly scented fall flowers hidden amongst the foliage, followed by fruit that quickly reddens. The shrub only requires minimal pruning to keep it in shape. There are other excellent forms. "Dicksonii" is less vigorous but more upright, and has bright yellow-edged leaves, and "Maculata" is a quick-growing, branching plant that has a big yellow patch in each leaf center. The sunnier and hotter the summer, the better the show of berries. If you need an even bigger, denser hedge of elaeagnus, try *E. macrophylla*. The fall flowers have a strong, sweet scent.

CONDITIONS

ASPECT   Though elaeagnus will grow in shade, they then tend to produce a disappointing show of fall berries. The sunnier and hotter the conditions, the better.

SITE   Not particularly fussy, any well-tended ground, avoiding extremes, is fine. Provide rich soil and good drainage.

GROWING METHOD

PROPAGATION   Take semi-ripe cuttings in the summer. They quickly take. It is quite possible to raise elaeagnus from seed, but is hardly worth the bother given how relatively quick and successful are the cuttings.

SPACING   Set plants about 2$^{1}/_{2}$ft apart.

FEEDING   It is tempting with reliable performers like elaeagnus to plant them and leave them alone, but a regular spring mulch of well-rotted manure, or a feed of slow-release fertilizer, will ensure that the bold leaved variegated forms really develop well and stand out.

PROBLEMS   None of any note.

FLOWERING

SEASON   Though *E. pungens* does flower in the fall, the display is not anything to get excited about. The eyecatching variegated foliage scores more points.

GENERAL

PRUNING   Prune to maintain shape in the spring.

THE PLANT THAT HAS IT ALL. Elaeagnus pungens *provides year-round variegated foliage, sweetly scented fall flowers and berries.*

AT A GLANCE		
Elaeagnus pungens makes a terrific all-purpose hedge, offering shelter, color and berries. Hardy to 0°F (zone 7).		
Jan	foliage	**Recommended Varieties**
Feb	foliage	*Elaeagnus pungens*
Mar	foliage	"Dicksonii"
April	foliage	"Frederici"
May	foliage	"Goldrim"
June	foliage	"Maculata"
July	foliage	"Variegata"
Aug	foliage	
Sept	foliage	
Oct	flowering	
Nov	flowering	
Dec	foliage	

Elder

SAMBUCUS NIGRA

FEATURES

A deciduous shrub or small tree, elder or elderberry grows up to 20–28ft tall and has rough, corky bark and compound leaves composed of five or so toothed, dark green leaflets. Heads of creamy white, scented flowers appear in summer leading to shiny, blue-black berries in fall. The flowers attract bees while the berries are eaten by birds.

CONDITIONS

ASPECT   A sunny position is best although the plant will tolerate bright, dappled shade or a few hours of full shade each day.

SITE   Friable, fertile soil that drains well yet stays moist is best, but elder accepts a wide range of soil types. Grows well on chalky soils.

GROWING METHOD

SOWING   Plants can be grown from seed sown in spring, or suckers, with their own roots, can be dug and detached from the parent plant. This can be done at any time but spring is best. Elders can also be propagated by cuttings. Take hardwood cuttings in late summer or tip cuttings in spring. Root in containers of very sandy potting mix. Pot up and overwinter under glass before planting out into their permanent position. If you are planting a group or row, leave at least 10ft between plants to allow room for the suckers to develop.

FEEDING   Elders like moisture at their roots at all times, especially in hot, dry weather in summer. If rainfall is reliable and reasonably regular, mature plants usually need little extra water. In average garden soils no special fertilizing is required, especially if you mulch beneath the plants with well-rotted organic matter. If soil is not particularly fertile, a ration of a complete plant food once in early spring is sufficient.

PROBLEMS   No particular problems.

PRUNING   Elder grows rapidly and in smaller gardens may need to be cut hard back in late fall or early spring to prevent it growing too large.

HARVESTING

PICKING   Flowerheads are picked in the morning but only when all the flowers on each head have bloomed. Dry spread out on a fine net in a cool, dark, airy place. Berries are picked when ripe.

AT A GLANCE	
Deciduous tree with aromatic white flowers and purple berries, with many different uses. Hardy to 4°F (zone 6).	
Jan /	**Parts used**
Feb /	Flowers
Mar /	Berries
Apr plant	Leaves
May plant harvest	**Uses**
Jun harvest	Culinary
July /	Medicinal
Aug /	Cosmetic
Sept plant harvest	Gardening
Oct plant harvest	
Nov /	
Dec /	

STORAGE — Dried flowers can be removed from their stems and stored in airtight containers. Ripe berries can also be dried and similarly stored.

FREEZING — Berries that have been cooked for a few minutes may be frozen for later use.

USES

CULINARY — Fresh flowers are made into elderflower wine and cordials, and jams and jellies. The berries can also be made into jams or jellies and the juice can be fermented into elderberry wine. Berries should not be eaten raw.

COSMETIC — Cold elderflower tea splashed onto the face daily tones and soothes the skin and is good for the complexion generally. Leaves can also be used to make a soothing, healing wash.

MEDICINAL — An infusion of flowers is a remedy for respiratory problems, fevers, colds, and sore throats and has a mild laxative effect. Berries are a mild laxative and are also used to treat coughs, colds, bronchitis, etc.

GARDENING — Elderberries, with their dense growth and suckering habit, make a good privacy screen and reasonable windbreak.

Encyclia
ENCYCLIA SPECIES

FEATURES

Another very easy and popular group of orchids. The genus of Encyclia was originally classified with the epidendrums so are closely related and require very similar growing conditions. Most of the encyclias are found in Central and South America, but some inhabit Florida and the West Indies, as in the case of *E. cochleata.* This orchid was the first tropical epiphytic orchid to flower in the United Kingdom. Originally discovered in the Americas, it was brought back by the plant hunters to the Royal Botanic Gardens at Kew in London. It has the common name of cockleshell orchid, due to the shape of its upturned, almost black, lip, and is the national flower of the Central American country of Belize. The orchid will flower for months on large specimen plants. Most of the Encyclia species are green in color but *E. vitellina* is bright orange. Many of the green-flowered species are also sweetly scented.

CONDITIONS

CLIMATE   The most popular are cool growing needing a temperature range of 50–77°F.

ASPECT   A light position is required, out of direct sunshine in summer to avoid scorching. Grow well in hanging baskets in a shaded greenhouse, or as windowsill plants.

POTTING MIX An open and free-draining bark mix is good; aerial roots are often made outside the pot.

GROWING METHOD

PROPAGATION Can be divided and propagated after growing into a large plant over a number of years. To ensure flowering the next year, do not make individual plants too small.

WATERING   Frequently water during summer— its main growing season. When not in growth it should be partially rested; just a little water is required to keep the pseudobulbs plump.

FEEDING   Feed only when the plant is in active growth when it can gain full benefit from the added nutrients. Apply both in the water poured into the pot and also in the spray given to the leaves and aerial roots.

PROBLEMS   No specific problems are known if cultural conditions are suitable.

FLOWERING SEASON

Can vary but mainly the summer months.

AT A GLANCE	
Sporting clusters of pink or lilac flowers from late summer to fall, it needs a sheltered position. Hardy to 14°F (zone 8).	
Jan rest	**Recommended Varieties**
Feb rest	*E. cochleata*
Mar rest	*E. lancifolia* (cream)
Apr flowering, water and feed	*E. mariae* (green/white)
May flowering, water and feed	*E. pentotis* (cream/green)
	E. radiata (pale green)
Jun flowering, water and feed	*E. vitellina* (orange)
July flowering, water and feed	
Aug flowering, water and feed	
Sept water and feed	
Oct rest	
Nov rest	
Dec rest	

Epidendrum
CRUCIFIX ORCHID

FEATURES

This genus and its species is a large and varied group that originated in tropical America. Growth can be rampant and needs thinning out every couple of years. Plants in pots may need support. This orchid will grow without almost any attention but rewards good culture. The species *E. ibaguense* flower is orange and yellow but there are many cultivars with flowers in shades of red, pink, mauve, yellow, or white. Individual flowers are fairly small but they are carried in groups on top of reedy canes that can be $6^1/2$ft or more tall. The fleshy leaves are leathery in texture and yellowish green, especially in full sun. *E. ibaguense* is one of the most familiar of the *Epidendrum* species, also known as
  E. radicans or its common name of crucifix orchid, so called because of the cross shape of the lip, when turned upside down.

HABIT   The crucifix orchid has a tall, reed-like habit of growth so requires some space to grow to its full potential.

CONDITIONS

CLIMATE   Grows best in an intermediate greenhouse, with a minimum of 54°F in winter.

ASPECT   Tolerates full sun to dappled shade. Where this orchid is grown in more tropical climates, as a bedding plant in garden borders, it is very tolerant of changing conditions and rough treatment.

POTTING MIX   The mix or soil must be able to drain rapidly but any mixture of coarse bark, crushed rock, gravel, compost, or commercial potting mix is suitable.

GROWING METHOD

PROPAGATION   Is very easy to propagate as it produces plantlets with aerial roots on the older canes. Detach them and pot up when they are sufficiently developed during the warmer months. Large clumps can also be divided.

WATERING   Thrives if given regular watering during the warm months of the year and less frequent waterings in winter.

FEEDING   Give soluble liquid fertilizer every three or four weeks during warm weather or dress the roots with aged cow manure. In warm conditions feed year round.

PROBLEMS   Trouble-free but fungal leaf diseases can occur if the weather is too cool and wet. Succulent new leaves are often eaten by slugs.

FLOWERING SEASON

Can flower almost all the year round.

AT A GLANCE		
Easy to grow. Repeat flowers all year round. Can reach 5ft in height but flowers are only $1^1/4$ in across.		
Jan	rest, little water	**Recommended Varieties**
Feb	rest, little water	*E. cristatum* (brown spotted)
Mar	increase water, re-pot	*E. ibaguense* (red/yellow)
		E. ilense (pale cream)
Apr	water and feed	*E. pseudepidendrum*
May	water and feed	(green/orange)
Jun	water and feed	*E. wallissii* (lilac/brown)
July	water and feed	"Pink Cascade" (pink)
Aug	water and feed	"Plastic Doll" (green/
Sept	water and feed	yellow)
Oct	reduce water	
Nov	reduce water	
Dec	rest, little water	

OTHER EPIDENDRUMS TO GROW

This is a very large group of orchids with many varied species and hybrids available. They are easy to keep and are very rewarding. The plants have long flowering seasons, and some are sequential flowerers, producing more and more buds time after time throughout the year. All need similar cultural requirements to those of the crucifix orchid.

E. ILENSE This is a very tall growing species from the Tropical Americas, reaching up to 6¹/₂ft in height. The leafy cane-like pseudobulbs are semi-deciduous, losing their leaves after a year or so. The curious flowers come in bunches from the top of the newest and oldest pseudobulb, the old ones reflowe ing for many years. The blooms are creamy yellow and around ³/₄in across; the lip, which hangs down, is strangely frilled into lots of tiny threads giving a bearded effect. Flowers can appear on very young plants only 6in high.

E. PSEUDEPIDENDRUM Perhaps a confusing name but this is yet another different Epidendrum. This species will grow with a similar habit to the *E. ilense* and they grow well when positioned together. This one has a very hard, waxy flower with bright green petals and sepals, swept back from the brilliant orange lip, making a striking combination.

E. PLASTIC DOLL This is a primary hybrid between the two species mentioned previously and it inherits qualities from both. It flowers on very young plants, and has a waxy yellow flower with a frilled lip. When larger, the plant should re-flower continually to give a perpetual show. The plant can grow tall in time as well but generally it is a very easy and rewarding orchid to keep.

E. PINK CASCADE Another primary hybrid of *E. ilense* but this time it has been crossed with another species, *E. revolutum*. The Pink Cascade orchid tends to hold more flowers on the stem at one time. As the name suggests, its flowers are bright pink in color. Do not cut the flower stems on this orchid, as they will flower again and again from the top of the leafy cane.

Epimedium

BARRENWORT / BISHOP'S MITER

FEATURES

This low-growing perennial is grown more for its attractive foliage than its flowers, although the blooms are quite attractive. The shape resembles a bishop's miter, giving rise to its common name. Many species have small, starry flowers in white, cream, or yellow, although there are pale and rose-pink varieties, too. This is a woodland plant that makes a good groundcover or filler for shady parts of the yard. Some die down completely in winter, while others remain evergreen. Plants are rarely more than 12in tall. Combine it with plants such as Solomon's seal, primrose, or lenten rose, which enjoy similar woodland-type conditions.

CONDITIONS

ASPECT   *Epimedium* needs dappled shade and protection from strong winds.
SITE   Requires well-drained soil, heavily enriched with organic matter. Regular mulching is beneficial to retain moisture.

GROWING METHOD

PROPAGATION   Clumps can be divided in the fall, although with some varieties this is not easy. Pull apart or cut away sections of plant, keeping both roots and a bud or shoot on each piece. Plant 6–8in apart. Some species seed readily. Keep young plants well watered until they are well established.
FEEDING   Apply a slow-release fertilizer in the spring.

PROBLEMS   Snails may attack soft new growth when it appears, so take precautions.

FLOWERING

SEASON   The small flowers appear in spring, along with the leaves. But shear off the foliage of all varieties in winter, even when green (except *E. perralderianum*), to prevent the flowers being obscured. Fresh leaves will quickly follow.
CUTTING   Flowers can be cut for the vase and last quite well in water.

AFTER FLOWERING

REQUIREMENTS   Spent flower stems can be clipped off. Old, dead foliage should be tidied up and removed by the end of the fall.

NEW GROWTH on the bishop's miter bears attractive bronze or pink shadings, but the older foliage is plain green.

AT A GLANCE		
An evergreen, deciduous perennial making excellent groundcover in shady situations. Small flowers. Hardy to 5˚F (zone 7).		
Jan	/	**Recommended Varieties**
Feb	sow	*Epimedium cantabrigiense*
Mar	/	*E. grandiflorum*
Apr	transplant	"Nanum"
May	flowering	"Rose Queen"
Jun	/	*E. perralderianum*
July	/	*E. pinnatum colchicum*
Aug	/	*E. x rubrum*
Sept	sow	*E. x versicolor*
Oct	divide	"Sulphureum"
Nov	/	
Dec	/	

Epiphyllum
ORCHID CACTUS

FEATURES

This group of epiphytic tropical American cactuses is known as orchid cactus because of the gorgeous, large flowers. Few of the true species are available, but the many spectacular named varieties have huge flowers 4–8in across, in shades of cream, yellow, salmon, various pinks, and reds. Some of these cultivars have a tendency to change color according to light levels and temperatures. Stems of the orchid cactus are almost spineless, broad, flattened, and leaf-like with flowers emerging from buds that are formed on the edges of these stems. These cactuses are natural epiphytes growing in tree canopies in tropical forests. As a result, they do well growing in hanging baskets or against a wall or tree that they can use for support as they scramble up.

VARIETIES

Some of the large-flowered types are slow to produce their first blooms and must be very mature before they flower regularly. However, the lovely species *Epiphyllum oxypetalum*, known as "Belle de Nuit," is nocturnal with huge white, scented flowers unfolding on warm nights to close again by daybreak. If you only have room for one small orchid, E. laui is an excellent choice. It grows 1ft high by 1½ft wide, and produces scented white flowers about 6in long.

CONDITIONS

ASPECT Unlike many cactuses, they prefer dappled, filtered shade out of direct sunlight.

SITE The soil mix must be relatively fertile, but above all open and free draining.

GROWING METHOD

PROPAGATION Can be grown from seed sown in spring, but hybrids must be increased from stem cuttings taken during summer to early fall.

FEEDING Apply granular slow-release fertilizer in spring or regular liquid feeds in the growing season.

PROBLEMS Usually trouble free in the right conditions.

FLOWERING

SEASON Flowers are produced on mature plants from late spring through summer. Some flowers are quite long lasting. The original species are mostly night blooming, but the majority of those available today are day flowering.

FRUITS Red fruits may form on some plants.

AT A GLANCE		
Stunning, beautiful, often scented flowers on cactuses that look highly impressive in hanging baskets. 50°F min (zone 11).		
Jan	/	Recommended Varieties
Feb	/	*Epiphyllum crenatum*
Mar	sow	"Fantasy"
Apr	transplant	"Hollywood"
May	flowering	"Jennifer Anne"
Jun	flowering	*E. oxypetalum*
July	flowering	*E. pumilum*
Aug	/	"Reward"
Sept	/	
Oct	/	
Nov	/	
Dec	/	

Eranthis

WINTER ACONITE

FEATURES

The glossy yellow flowers of this tuber are a welcome sight in early spring. They are backed by a bract that forms a green leafy ruff, giving the flowers a Jack-in-the-green appearance. The true winter aconite is Eranthis hyemalis, with divided, pale green leaves and buttercup-yellow blooms: it seeds itself freely and soon spreads to form a carpet. *Eranthis* x *tubergenii* is a more vigorous hybrid, with larger, slightly later flowers. Both types grow to about 4in. Another type is sometimes sold as the Cilicica form of *E. hyemalis*, sometimes as a separate species, *E. cilicica*. It has deep yellow flowers, carried in March, backed by bronzy green, very finely cut foliage, and it grows to 2–3in tall.

CONDITIONS

ASPECT Full sun or light shade are acceptable.
SITE Winter aconites are perfect for rock gardens, the fronts of borders, or beneath deciduous trees, which allow sufficient light to the plants during their spring growing period. They prefer a free-draining but moisture-retentive soil.

GROWING METHOD

PLANTING Plant the tubers in September, as soon as they are obtained—if they dry out before planting they are difficult to establish. They should be planted 1–2in deep and 3–4in apart. Eranthis are also available freshly lifted, like snowdrops, in spring, when they establish more readily.
FEEDING Ensure the soil is kept moist during the spring, especially where the plants are growing under trees or shrubs.

Supplementary feeding is not normally necessary.
PROBLEMS Plants can become invasive where conditions suit them as they seed freely; otherwise no specific problems are generally experienced.

FLOWERING

SEASON Flowers from early February to mid-March or into April.
CUTTING Flowers can be cut just as the buds are opening.

AFTER FLOWERING

REQUIREMENTS Divide crowded clumps after flowering, replanting the tubers immediately.

THE GLOSSY, GOLDEN BUTTERCUPS of winter aconites, backed by their green leafy ruffs, give a welcome show of color in early spring.

AT A GLANCE		
A low-growing plant, welcome for its bright golden-yellow flowers in late winter and early spring.		
Jan	/	**Recommended Varieties**
Feb	flowering	"Guinea Gold"
Mar	flowering	
Apr	plant flowering	
May	/	
Jun	/	
July	/	
Aug	/	
Sept	plant (tubers)	
Oct	/	
Nov	/	
Dec	/	

Eremurus

FOXTAIL LILY

FEATURES

These stately plants produce tall spires of numerous, star-shaped flowers, giving a very impressive display and making good focal points in the garden. Their foliage is pale green and strap shaped; the flowering spikes tower above the leaves, reaching as much as 10ft or more in some species.

Eremurus robustus is among the tallest, with 8–10ft spikes of salmon-pink blooms: *E. stenophyllus* (*E. bungei*) grows to about 4ft with orange-yellow flowers. Probably most popular are some of the hybrid varieties at about 6ft, which bear flowers in a range of yellow, orange, and pink shades. Because of their height, plants need a position sheltered from wind.

CONDITIONS

ASPECT *Eremurus* are reasonably hardy but demand a sheltered position in full sun.

SITE These are excellent plants for a place at the back of a border, or plant a foxtail lily at the end of a path for a dramatic focal point. Taller varieties usually need staking. Soil must be rich and fertile but free-draining; dig some sharp sand into the site at planting time to improve drainage if necessary.

GROWING METHOD

PLANTING In early to mid-fall, set the roots 4–6in deep and 2–3ft apart.

FEEDING Keep the soil moist at all times. A dressing of balanced granular fertilizer can be made over the site in early spring, or high potash liquid feed can be given occasionally during the growing season.

PROBLEMS Usually, no problems are experienced. The young foliage is vulnerable to frost damage and may need protection in early spring when shoots first appear through the soil.

FLOWERING

SEASON Flowers in early to mid summer.

CUTTING Flower spikes may be cut as the first flowers are opening. They last well in water.

AFTER FLOWERING

REQUIREMENTS Cut down flower stems when the flowers fade. Protect the crowns from frost with a mulch of sand or dry leaves over winter. When overcrowded, divide the clumps in fall.

AT A GLANCE		
Tall, stately plants with large, showy flower spikes made up of masses of individual starry flowers.		
Jan	/	**Recommended Varieties**
Feb	/	"Shelford Hybrids"
Mar	/	"Ruiter Hybrids"
Apr	/	"Moneymaker"
May	/	
Jun	flowering	
July	flowering	
Aug	/	
Sept	plant	
Oct	plant	
Nov	/	
Dec	/	

Eria

ERIA SPECIES

FEATURES

This is quite a large genus, containing about 500 species, but not many species are grown in cultivation or in amateur collections. They are quite variable in Itheir plant size and habit, but the flowers tend to be of a similar size and shape. *E. sessiflora* is quite a large growing species with a very tall spike of many creamy white flowers; *E. coronaria* in contrast has a short habit with a short swollen stem in place of a pseudobulb but has very similar cream blooms. Many of the erias are scented as well. The family of erias are originally found growing as epiphytes on the trees in the rain forests of the Malaysian Peninsula, the islands of New Guinea and Polynesia as well as some parts of Australia. The plants often have to undergo a wet and dry season in the high altitude monsoon areas so their regime of watering and resting follows this pattern.

CONDITIONS

CLIMATE   These plants enjoy a cool to intermediate temperature range of 54–83°F from winter to summer.

ASPECT   Protect the plants from the bright sun with some shading during summer to prevent the foliage from getting too red or even burnt.

POTTING MIX   A medium grade of bark will be adequate and you may want to mix in some general potting compost to help keep them moist during the main growing season.

GROWING METHOD

PROPAGATION   These orchids are not easily propagated by division as they grow and multiply slowly.

WATERING   Take care not to over water during the winter when the plant is at rest. Give water once a week during the growing season, keeping the compost moist at all times.

FEEDING   The plant will respond to added fertilizer during the growing season. Use a soluble fertilizer every two weeks, spraying on the leaves and pouring into the pot.

PROBLEMS   No specific problems are known if cultural conditions are suitable.

FLOWERING SEASON

Quite short-lived. Blooms for three to four weeks in mainly winter and spring seasons.

AT A GLANCE	
An unusal genus and mostly for the more experienced grower. Charming, small flowers and variable plant size.	
Jan flowering, rest	**Recommended Varieties**
Feb flowering, rest	*E. coronaria* (cream)
Mar flowering, rest	*E. javanica* (yellow)
Apr flowering, rest	*E. pubescens* (yellow with
May flowering, water	hairy stems)
and feed	*E. rosea* (pink flush)
Jun water and feed	*E. sessiflora* (white)
July water and feed	
Aug water and feed	
Sept water and feed	
Oct rest	
Nov flowering, rest	
Dec flowering, rest	

Erica carnea

ERICA

FEATURES

Otherwise known as winter or alpine heath, this is a small evergreen shrub growing about 10in high at most, and spreading twice that distance. At its best on acid soil it will, however, tolerate some lime. The great virtue of ericas is that they provide indispensable winter foliage color. *Erica carnea* has dark green leaves and dark pink flowers that last from winter well into early spring. Other excellent forms of erica include "Adrienne Duncan" with bronze tinged foliage, "Ann Sparkes" with lime green leaves, and "Challenger" with rich red flowers. "Golden Starlet" has white flowers and pale green foliage, and "Vivellii" bronze leaves with pink flowers. The best way to grow ericas is in "patchwork quilts," with great sheets of merging and contrasting colors.

CONDITIONS

ASPECT   Ericas need as much sun as they can get. They not only thrive in it, but you can really appreciate the full range of hues and tones. In darker parts of the garden their virtues will not stand out.

SITE   Moist, acid soil is the key. Erica carnea is unusual because it can tolerate slightly more alkaline conditions.

GROWING METHOD

PROPAGATION The simplest method involves taking semi-ripe cuttings during the first part of summer.

FEEDING   This is not necessary. You can scatter ericaceous compost round new plants to give them a head start.

PROBLEMS   They can suffer from fungal attacks in very humid conditions, but this is extremely unlikely. Otherwise, quite indestructible.

FLOWERING

SEASON   *E. carnea* and its various excellent forms flower from around Christmas well into spring. There is a wide range of colors, many showing up well against the foliage which ranges from yellow lime green to bronze.

PRUNING

GENERAL   This certainly is not necessary to keep plants in check since growth is very slow. You can prune to shape though, and this is best done after flowering in the spring before new growth appears.

AT A GLANCE		
Erica carnea is a fine shrub with a wide range of excellent forms. A "must" on acid soil. Hardy to 0°F (zone 7).		
Jan	flowering	**Recommended varieties**
Feb	flowering	*Erica carnea*
Mar	flowering	"Adrienne Duncan"
April	flowering	"Ann Sparkes"
May	foliage	"Challenger"
June	foliage	"December Red"
July	foliage	"King George"
Aug	foliage	"March Seedling"
Sept	foliage	"Myretoun Ruby"
Oct	foliage	"Springwood White"
Nov	foliage	"Vivellii"
Dec	foliage	

Eryngium

SEA HOLLY

FEATURES

Sea holly is a 230-species strong genus, with annuals, biennials, and perennials. Although they are related to cow parsley, they bear no resemblance, being grown for their marvellous, attractive, spiky appearance, blue flowers (though some are white or green), and ability to thrive in poor, rocky, sunny ground. Heights can vary considerably, from *E. alpinum*, 28in tall, which as its name suggests grows in the Alps, to *E. eburneum* from South America, which can reach 5ft, and *E. pandanifolium*, which is much taller at 10ft. One of the most attractive is the Moroccan *E. variifolium*, which has rounded, white-veined foliage setting off the pale blue flowers. It is also more manageable at 14in high— good for the front of a border.

CONDITIONS

ASPECT   Grow in full sunlight, well out of the shade.
SITE   There are two types of sea holly, with different growing needs. Most prefer fast-draining, fertile ground (e.g. *E. alpinum* and *E. bourgatii*), and some (e.g. *E. eburneum*) poor stony ground, out of the winter wet.

GROWING METHOD

PROPAGATION   Sow the seed when ripe; alternatively, take root cuttings in late winter, or divide in the spring.
FEEDING   Only for the first kind of sea holly, which benefits from a spring feed and some well-rotted manure. Good drainage is important.

PROBLEMS

Slugs and snails are the main problem when sea holly is grown in the border, damaging the new, young leaves. Promptly remove when seen, or use a chemical treatment.

FLOWERING

SEASON   The earliest sea hollies begin flowering in early summer, while others last from mid- to early or mid-fall in dry weather.
CUTTING   Sea holly makes an invaluable cut flower. They also make exceptional dried arrangements, combining with other architectural plants and softer, flowery ones.

AFTER FLOWERING

REQUIREMENTS Cut back the spent flowering stems to the ground.

AT A GLANCE		
Annuals, and deciduous/evergreen perennials grown for their shape. Hardiness varies from 13°F (zone 8) to 0°F (zones 6–7).		
Jan	/	Recommended Varieties
Feb	sow	*Eryngium alpinum*
Mar	division	"Blue Star"
Apr	transplant	*E. bourgatii*
May	transplant	"Oxford Blue"
Jun	flowering	*E. giganteum*
July	flowering	*E.* x *oliverianum*
Aug	flowering	*E.* x *tripartitum*
Sept	flowering	
Oct	sow	
Nov	/	
Dec	/	

Erythronium

DOG'S TOOTH VIOLET

FEATURES

Plants of the dappled shade of woodlands, erythroniums have attractive spring flowers, star-shaped and generally nodding, with swept-back petals.

The dog's tooth violet (named after the shape of its tuber) is *E. dens-canis*, with pinkish- purple flowers carried about 6in above the attractively mottled leaves. Slightly taller is *Erythronium californicum*, with lush, mid-green, lightly mottled leaves and creamy flowers with bronze backs to the petals. *Erythronium revolutum* grows to 12in, with white, pink, or purple mottled flowers, and has given rise to the popular hybrid "Pagoda," with 6–10 pendent, graceful yellow flowers on a slender, 16in flower stalk.

CONDITIONS

ASPECT   As a woodland plant, erythronium thrives in cool conditions and light shade.
SITE   Excellent under trees or among shrubs in beds and borders or on rock gardens. Fertile, moisture-retentive soil with plenty of organic matter will ensure good growth.

GROWING METHOD

PLANTING   Plant the tubers in groups, 3–6in deep and 4–6in apart in late summer or early fall. Do not let the tubers dry out before planting or you will find it difficult to get the plants established: plant them as soon as possible after purchase.

FEEDING   Feeding is not usually necessary. Moist soil is essential during the growing season, but the tubers must never become waterlogged. Water carefully during dry spells.
PROBLEMS   No specific pest or disease problems are usually experienced with this plant. Plants resent disturbance and may be difficult to re-establish if lifted and replanted.

FLOWERING

SEASON   Flowers in mid-spring.
CUTTING   The taller species can be cut successfully when the buds have opened.

AFTER FLOWERING

REQUIREMENTS Disturb the roots as little as possible. If clumps become so overcrowded that flowering is adversely affected, they can be lifted and divided in late summer, replanting the tubers immediately.

AT A GLANCE	
Spring-flowering tubers with appealing, pendulous flowers in a range of heights and colors. Many also have attractive foliage.	
Jan /	Recommended Varieties
Feb /	"Pagoda"
Mar /	"Citronella"
Apr flowering	*Erythronium californicum*
May flowering	"White Beauty"
Jun /	*Erythronium dens-canis*
July /	"Lilac Wonder"
Aug plant	"Rose Queen"
Sept plant	
Oct /	
Nov /	
Dec /	

Escallonia
ESCALLONIA

FEATURES

Escallonia is evergreen in mild districts but semi-evergreen elsewhere. Its arching shoots, festooned with sprays of clustered, tubular, white, pink, or red flowers amid small, glossy leaves, highlight the summer months.

Long-lived, it makes a stunning sentinel to around 6ft and as a flowering hedge.

The hardiest species—ideal for windswept, seaside gardens—Escallonia rubra macrantha delights us with many rose-crimson flowers.

Other choice kinds are rich pink "Donard Radiance," rose-pink "Donard Star" and golden-leaved and rosy-red-flowered "Gold Brian."

CONDITIONS

ASPECT Though escallonia needs full sun to flower best, it does not object to light shade. Most hybrids tolerate buffeting wind. In chilly or northern gardens, it should be planted against a sheltered, south-facing wall.

SITE This splendid shrub thrives in any well-drained soil. Aerate heavy clay by working in grit or gravel; fortify light and nutrient-starved, sandy soils by working in plenty of bulky, moisture-conserving organic materials.

GROWING METHOD

FEEDING Ensure a steady release of plant foods by applying bone meal in spring and fall. After planting, water freely and regularly in dry spells to encourage strong new growth. Keep roots cool and questing freely by mulching with shredded bark, cocoa shell, crumbly manure, or rotted garden compost.

PROPAGATION Multiply choice varieties from semi-ripe cuttings from the middle of summer to the middle of fall.

PROBLEMS Cut darkly stained shoots infected with silver leaf back to healthy, white wood 6in beyond the point of infection.

PRUNING

Shorten a third of the oldest stems to near ground level when blooms fade. In cold gardens, cut back frost-damaged growth to strong, new shoots in late spring.

Semi-evergreen and summer-blossoming escallonia can be trained to form a fetching, flowering hedge in mild districts.

AT A GLANCE	
Evergreen or semi-evergreen, its arching shoots are sleeved with white, pink or red flowers in summer. Hardy to 14°F (zone 8).	
Jan /	**Recommended Varieties**
Feb /	"Donard Radiance"
Mar /	"Donard Seedling"
Apr plant, prune	"Glory of Donard"
May plant, prune	"Gold Brian"
June flower, plant	"Iveyi"
July flower, plant	*E. rubra macrantha*
Aug flower, plant	"Slieve Donard"
Sept flower, plant	
Oct /	
Nov /	
Dec /	

Escallonia "Edinensis"

ESCALLONIA

FEATURES

Escallonia are underrated evergreen shrubs, with glossy leaves that in hot weather give off a gentle, sweet smell. The best kind to use for a hedge are the bushy ones that can be well clipped. "Peach Blossom," growing 6ft high with pink flowers, and *Escallonia rubra* "Crimson Spire" which is slightly taller with red flowers, are both impressive. The latter is traditionally grown in seaside gardens as a hedge windbreak, since the plants can withstand both wind and salt. "Edinensis," with pinkish-red flowers in the first half of summer, grows about 6ft high. New flowering shoots keep appearing up until the fall. Other forms of escallonia, like the white-flowering "Iveyi," can be slightly more tender, and may need to be grown against warm sheltering walls in cold regions.

CONDITIONS

ASPECT | Keep out of the shade and give as much wall-to-wall sun as you can.
SITE | Good drainage and decent, fertile soil are the key requirements. A well-tended garden, without extremes of soil type, will be fine.

GROWING METHOD

PROPAGATION | The best method of propagation is to take cuttings during the summer. You can also do this over winter, but you will get quicker results with the former.
SPACING | *Escallonia* "Edinensis" can eventually grow to about 8ft wide, but with pruning allow for a gap of 3ft.
FEEDING | It is useful to keep up the soil fertility. Either mulch in the spring with well-rotted manure, or add spring helpings of slow-release fertilizer such as blood and bone.

PROBLEMS | Remarkably free of pests and diseases.

FLOWERING

SEASON | The main flowering burst lasts from late spring to midsummer, but extra flowers usually keep appearing through late summer and into the start of the fall.

PRUNING

GENERAL | Either prune after the main burst of flowering in midsummer, or if you want extra flowers leave it until the following spring. Overgrown, misshapen, tangled shrubs can be cut back hard without inflicting serious damage.

Bursting into bloom in late spring, Escallonia "Edinensis" will keep producing interest through the summer and into the fall.

AT A GLANCE		
Escallonia "Edinensis" is a versatile shrub for a windbreak and gives a good show of flowers. Hardy to 5°F (zone 7).		
Jan	foliage	**Recommended Varieties**
Feb	foliage	*Escallonia*
Mar	foliage	"Edinensis"
April	foliage	"Peach Blossom"
May	flowering	*E. rubra*
June	flowering	"Crimson Spire"
July	flowering	**Companion Plants**
Aug	flowering	Bluebell
Sept	flowering	Daffodil
Oct	foliage	Fritillaria
Nov	foliage	Hyacinth
Dec	foliage	Tulip

Eschscholzia

CALIFORNIA POPPY

FEATURES

The bright flowers and finely divided blue-green foliage of the California poppy are best in large drifts, although it grows well even in cracks in paving slabs and in gravel, and thrives on dry soils in full sun. Varieties of *Eschscholzia californica* have flowers in yellow, cream, pink/beige, apricot, and scarlet. They grow 12in tall and wide. Grow as a hardy annual, sowing where plants are to flower. Very easy to grow and quickly self-seeds.

CONDITIONS

ASPECT   *Eschscholzia* thrives in hot, sun-baked spots where other annuals struggle to grow. Must have full sunlight and likes it hot.

SITE   Poor, light soil often gives the best results, so long as drainage is good. No special soil preparation is necessary, and avoid adding compost or manure, which encourages leafy growth at the expense of flowers.

GROWING METHOD

SOWING   Sow in March or September outdoors where the plants are to flower, since it dislikes being transplanted. Spread seed thinly in short drills 1/2in deep and cover. Thin out the seedlings as they grow to allow 3–6in between plants. Water thoroughly after thinning to settle plants back in.

FEEDING   Except in spells of drought, watering is not necessary, and extra feed is not required.

PROBLEMS   No particular problems.

FLOWERING

SEASON   Long flowering period through the spring and summer months if faded flowers are removed.

CUTTING   Use as a cut flower, although flowers close at night. Cut long stems and place in water immediately to just below the flower buds.

AFTER FLOWERING

GENERAL   Often self-seeds, so seedlings can be expected the following season. These will appear in cracks in the sidewalk, along paths and drives, and in gravel, where they are perfectly at home in dry, poor soil conditions.

DRY, HOT, SUN-BAKED banks are perfect for California poppies, where conditions are very like those of their native State.

AT A GLANCE		
A hardy annual grown for its bright poppy-like flowers and ideal for light, dry soils and along paths. Frost hardy to 5°F (zone 7).		
Jan	/	**Recommended Varieties**
Feb	/	*Eschscholzia californica*
Mar	sow	"Apricot Bush"
Apr	thin out	"Apricot Chiffon"
May	thin out	"Apricot Flambeau"
Jun	flowering	"Dalli"
July	flowering	"Mission Bells Mixed"
Aug	flowering	"Prima Ballerina"
Sept	flowers/sow	"Rose Bush"
Oct	/	"Thai Silk Mixed"
Nov	/	*Eschscholzia lobbii*
Dec	/	"Moonlight"

Eucomis comosa

PINEAPPLE LILY

FEATURES

This South African plant gets its common name from the pineapple-like flower spike with its topknot of tufted leaves. The greenish-white or white flowers, sometimes tinged with pink, are scented and packed tightly onto the spike; their weight can sometimes cause the stem to flop over. The broad, sword-shaped leaves are light green and attractively spotted with purple on the underside. This flower is always of interest, whether in the yard or as a potted plant: blooms are extremely long-lasting when cut. Another species in cultivation is *E. bicolor*, with attractive green and purple flowers. Both species grow to about 24in. Pineapple lily grows from a fleshy bulbous rootstock and is dormant in winter.

CONDITIONS

ASPECT   Prefers full sun but tolerates light shade. Grows best in warm, sheltered areas, but can also be grown in colder gardens if the rootstock is protected or lifted for winter.

SITE   *Eucomis* is good for the middle or back of the flower border. Needs well-drained soil enriched with decayed organic matter before planting time.

GROWING METHOD

PLANTING   Plant in spring, 2–4in deep and 8–12in apart.

FEEDING   Apply complete plant food as new growth begins. Mulch around plants in summer with well-decayed compost or manure. Keep the soil moist while the plant is actively growing.

PROBLEMS   No specific problems are known.

FLOWERING

SEASON   Flowers during midsummer.

CUTTING   The pineapple lily is usually enjoyed as a specimen garden plant, but if there are enough blooms, or if the stems are broken by wind, the cut flowers may last for several weeks if the vase water is changed regularly.

AFTER FLOWERING

REQUIREMENTS Cut down the flowering stem when the flowers have passed their best. Either dig up the bulb and overwinter in a frost-free place, or in mild districts, mulch the planting area with peat or dry leaves to protect the bulb over winter.

THE TUFT on top of the flower spike does resemble a pineapple, but the pretty individual flowers below give a softer impression.

AT A GLANCE		
A tall, striking bulb with a pineapple-like flower stem. A sunny, sheltered spot is required.		
Jan	/	**Recommended Varieties**
Feb	/	*Eucomis bicolor*
Mar	plant	"Alba"
Apr	plant	*E. comosa*
May	/	*E. pole-evansii*
Jun	/	*E. zambesiaca*
July	flowering	
Aug	flowering	
Sept	/	
Oct	/	
Nov	/	
Dec	/	

Euonymus fortunei

SPINDLE TREE

FEATURES

The species most usually grown as a hedge is *Euonymus japonicus*, but *E. fortunei* provides plenty of extra possibilities. It is usually regarded as semi-prostrate, but it is quite capable of bulking and mounding up, creating a substantial evergreen division. It is a slow grower, but eventually will look hugely impressive. It can be pruned and smartened up. Many gardeners grow it against walls or fences, where it actually starts to climb. "Silver Queen" is the best known form, and it develops distinctive green leaves with a flashy white margin; in the cold it has a pinkish tinge. Other good forms include "Emerald Gaiety" and the eyecatching "Emerald'n'Gold," which turns reddish in winter. The more the shrub does mound up, the better it flowers and fruits, the latter being white.

CONDITIONS

ASPECT Full sun gives the best results. Light shade is acceptable, but otherwise keep away from the dark. Some wind protection helps. Cold and exposed positions do not often work well.

SITE Average fertile soil is fine, with good drainage. A thick mulch of well-rotted organic matter in the spring, especially in hot dry sites, will work wonders.

GROWING METHOD

PROPAGATION Take semi-ripe cuttings in the summer.

SPACING Reckon on 3ft apart or more, but it depends what size shrubs you buy. If small, remember that they grow quite slowly. These shrubs do not sprint away.

FEEDING Over-rich soil is not necessary. Average garden fertility is fine. A spring slow-release fertilizer is quite adequate.

PROBLEMS In general, euonymus is remarkably trouble free. In some locations powdery mildew may strike. Take appropriate chemical action and improve the growing conditions.

FLOWERING

SEASON A hot spring will produce greater flower growth, but you should get 10 days in May when it is thick with whiteish blossom.

PRUNING

GENERAL Gently prune in the spring, taking care not to try and create too formal a shape.

AT A GLANCE	
Euonymus fortunei makes a fine division in large borders, or a sprawling divider. Exceptional foliage. Hardy to 5˚F (zone 7).	
Jan foliage	**Companion Plants**
Feb foliage	*Euonymus alatus*
Mar foliage	*E. cornutus* var. *quinquecornutus*
April foliage	*E. europaeus*
May flowering	"Red Cascade"
June foliage	*E. japonicus*
July foliage	*E. latifolius*
Aug foliage	*E. lucidus*
Sept foliage	*E. planipes*
Oct foliage	
Nov foliage	
Dec /	

Euonymus japonicus

SPINDLE BUSH

FEATURES

An evergreen shrub growing 10–13ft high and 6$\frac{1}{2}$ft or more wide in very old age, Euonymus japonicus can be hedged at any height over 3ft. The species has glossy green leaves, but the many variegated cultivars with margins or splashes of cream or yellow are more common. A neat plant, *E. japonicus* is a moderate grower and long lived. It is a low-maintenance and adaptable shrub.

CONDITIONS

ASPECT   Needs full sun for good, compact growth. Avoid the shade at all costs.

SITE   Soil should be well drained and preferably enriched with organic matter.

GROWING METHOD

PROPAGATION The species can be raised from cleaned seed extracted from berries in fall and stored in the refrigerator to be sown in spring. Alternatively, cultivars can be grown from semi-ripe cuttings taken in the summer.

SPACING   Plant at about 3ft, depending on how quickly you want the hedge to be established.

FEEDING   Apply complete plant food in spring.

PROBLEMS   There are no known problems.

FLOWERING

SEASON   Greenish white flowers are produced in late spring but they are not a key feature of this plant in terms of its appearance.

BERRIES   Deep red berries follow the flowers in fall. They score more points than the flowers.

PRUNING

GENERAL   Prune in the spring. The plant can also be trimmed at other times of the year to control any wayward growth. *E. japonicus* does not generally need a great deal of pruning. As with *E. fortunei*, make sure that you take care not to ruin the attractive leaves, one of the main reasons for growing this plant, especially the variegated forms like "Ovatus Aureus". It is therefore best to use pruning shears.

THE DENSE GROWTH and neat, rounded leaves of Euonymus japonicus make for a compact habit that is ideal for hedging.

AT A GLANCE	
A good choice for a more traditional, well-shaped hedge with berries and bright leaves. Hardy to 23˚F (zone 9).	
Jan foliage	**Recommended Varieties**
Feb foliage	*Euonymus japonicus*
Mar foliage	"Albomarginatus"
April foliage	"Aureus"
May flowering	"Macrophyllus"
June foliage	"Macrophyllus Aureovariegatus"
July foliage	"Ovatus Aureus"
Aug foliage	
Sept foliage	
Oct foliage	
Nov foliage	
Dec foliage	

Euphorbia

SPURGE

FEATURES

A large group of important shrubs, annuals, biennials, perennials, and subshrubs, ranging from tree-like succulents to structural clumps for the border. The latter spurges, evergreen and deciduous, grow in a wide range of conditions, from shade to sun, and tend to be quite sturdy, many leaning at 45˚ if not standing upright. Many of the evergreens benefit from being cut back to produce vigorous new spring growth. For example *E. characias* yields stems covered in small, stiff, outward-pointing leaves and yellow-green flowers. A big clump makes a bold, striking feature. *E. griffithii* "Fireglow," deciduous, is about half as high and produces early summer orange-red terminal bracts. It spreads to form a large colony. And *E. schillingii*, a recent find in Nepal by plant hunter Tony Schilling, flowers in late summer and has yellow bracts.

CONDITIONS

ASPECT   Depending on your choice of plant, spurges like full sunlight or light shade.
SOIL   This can vary from light, fast-draining soil to damp, moist ground, rich with leaf mold.

GROWING METHOD

PROPAGATION Sow the seed when ripe, or the following spring. Alternatively, divide perennials in the spring, or take spring cuttings.
FEEDING   Spurges that require rich soil can be given a scattering of complete plant food and mulched in the spring. Those that require fast-draining ground need only be fed.

PROBLEMS   Aphids can be a problem in a bad year; spray at the first sign of an attack.

FLOWERING

SEASON   Flowers appear in the spring or summer.
CUTTING   While the stem structure of most spurges makes them theoretically good as cut flowers, note that the milky sap can badly irritate the skin; if any part of the plant is ingested, severe discomfort results. Wear gloves and goggles.

AFTER FLOWERING

REQUIREMENTS Cut back the brownish or lackluster stems in the fall to promote fresh new growth.

THE HIGHLY VERSATILE SPURGE tolerates a wide range of conditions. One of its chief attractions is its striking bracts.

AT A GLANCE	
A genus of some 2,000 species. The border kind tend to be grown for their structure. Frost-tender to hardy 0˚F (zones 6–7).	
Jan /	Recommended Varieties
Feb /	*Euphorbia amygdaloides*
Mar divide	var. *robbiae*
Apr transplant	*E. characias*
May flowering	*E. characias wulfenii*
Jun flowering	*E. griffithii*
July flowering	"Dixter"
Aug flowering	*E. myrsinites*
Sept flowering	*E. palustris*
Oct sow	*E. polychroma*
Nov /	
Dec /	

Euphorbia caput-medusae

MEDUSA'S HEAD

FEATURES

Although growing only 1ft high, this multi-branched succulent makes an impact. The rounded, thickened stem may grow partly underground, but from this stout stem a mass of gray-green knobbly branches emerge. A well-grown plant may have a diameter of up to 3ft. Small green leaves sprout from the tips of the warty branches. Ideal as a feature for a desert or succulent garden, this plant can also be container grown. Like all the plants in this group, the milky latex in the stems is caustic and may cause severe skin problems; wear gloves and protect eyes when handling it.

CONDITIONS

ASPECT   These plants should be grown in full sun with good air circulation around them.
SITE   The soil must be well drained, but does not need to be rich. Whether growing in pots, or in the open ground over summer, make sure that plenty of grit is added to the compost or soil.

GROWING METHOD

PROPAGATION Medusa's head can be grown from stem cuttings taken during the warmer months, or from seed sown in spring.
FEEDING   Plants grown in containers can be given a small amount of slow-release fertilizer in spring. Plants grown in the garden should not need supplementary feeding.

If the soil is particularly poor though, a regular liquid feed will give the plant a decent boost.

PROBLEMS   Medusa's head is generally not prone to problems unless overwatered.

FLOWERING

SEASON   The cream or green flowers of this plant appear in spring or summer. The true flower is small, but it is fringed with attractive creamy white, bract-like surrounds. In a poor summer it may be best to move it back under glass where it will flower better in the higher temperatures.

CORONETS OF SMALL FLOWERS on the mature stems of Medusa's head lighten the appearance of the heavy stems. Medusa's head can be planted out over summer in a gap between paving, producing a dramatic eye-catching effect.

AT A GLANCE	
E. caput-medusae is a fine architectural South African plant with branching stems and whitish flowers. 55°F min (zone 11).	
Jan /	Recommended Varieties
Feb /	*Euphorbia amygdaloides* var.
Mar sow	*robbiae*
Apr transplant	*E. charracias* subsp. *characias*
May flowering	*E. c.* subsp. *wulfenii*
Jun flowering	*E. griffithii*
July flowering	"Dixter"
Aug /	*E. x martinii*
Sept /	*E. myrsinites*
Oct /	*E. palustris*
Nov /	*E. polychroma*
Dec /	*E. schillingii*

Euphorbia milii

CROWN OF THORNS

FEATURES

This extremely spiny, semi-succulent plant sprawls over the ground. In warm-climate gardens it provides groundcover for places where people or animals are to be excluded, over walls or under windows, and is virtually maintenance-free. Heights vary from 3–4¹/₂ft the latter in ideal conditions. It is valued for its almost year-round display of bright red bracts which surround the insignificant flowers. In a big pot it makes a very striking feature. The leaves are a soft mid-green and can be plentiful or sparse depending on conditions, warm and wet is best.

CONDITIONS

ASPECT   This has to be grown in a pot or border in the conservatory. Sun or light shade is fine. Note that the more you adhere to its ideal conditions, also keeping it warm and wet, the taller and bushier it grows, and the more frequently the flowers appear on new growth. In its native Madagascar it makes a highly effective hedging plant which keeps out all intruders. With limited room it may be best to keep it healthy without encouraging too much spiny growth.

SITE   Grow in any type of soil that is free draining.

GROWING METHOD

PROPAGATION   Propagate from stem cuttings taken in late spring or early summer. This is also a good time to prune the plant if you need to control its spread, and the prunings can be then used as a batch of cuttings.

FEEDING   Slow-release fertilizer can be applied in spring, but this is unnecessary unless the soil is extremely poor.

PROBLEMS   This plant is generally quite trouble-free.

FLOWERING

SEASON   The long flowering period of this plant is technically from spring through to late summer. However, there are likely to be some flowers on it at almost any time of year in very warm conditions.

THE FLORAL DISPLAY of crown of thorns lasts many months but is more prolific in spring and summer.

AT A GLANCE		
An excellent if spiny plant, with good bright colors, demanding a warm, humid conservatory. 54°F min (zone 11).		
Jan	/	**Recommended Varieties**
Feb	/	*Euophorbia characias*
Mar	repotting	subsp. *wulfenii*
Apr	sow	*E. dulcis*
May	flowering	"Chameleon"
Jun	transplant	*E. griffithii*
July	flowering	"Dixter"
Aug	/	"Fireglow"
Sept	/	*E.* x *martinii*
Oct	/	*E. myrsinites*
Nov	/	*E. polychroma*
Dec	/	*E. schillingii*

Fallopia baldschuanica

RUSSIAN VINE

FEATURES

The other popular name for this deciduous climber, Mile-a-minute plant, sums up its habit of growth. It is extremely vigorous, even rampant, and grows up to 40ft tall. Grow this plant only if you have plenty of room for it to take off, otherwise you will be forever cutting it back to keep it in check. It is best suited to informal or wild gardens where it can be left to "run free." Its rampant nature also makes it ideal for filling a space or even hiding an unsightly structure in the garden. The Russian vine is originally a native of eastern Europe and Iran. From late summer and into fall it is covered in a froth of small white, pink-flushed flowers that hang in decorative swags. It is ideal for quickly covering large outbuildings, or for growing up very high walls or large mature trees.

CONDITIONS

ASPECT   Suitable for full sun or partial shade.
SITE   Any soil, even poor conditions. However, the soil should be moisture retentive yet well drained.

GROWING METHOD

PROPAGATION Take softwood or semi-ripe cuttings in spring and summer, or hardwood cuttings in late fall or winter. Hardwood cuttings are easier to root than other types and should be rooted in a frost-free glasshouse.
WATERING   If the soil starts to dry out excessively in summer, water heavily.

FEEDING   It does not need much encouragement to grow, but can be given a slow-release organic fertilizer in spring.
PROBLEMS   Not usually troubled by pests or diseases.

FLOWERING/FOLIAGE

FLOWERS   The plant flowers very freely and looks its best when covered in a froth of white blossom.
FOLIAGE   The deep green leaves are heart shaped.

PRUNING

REQUIREMENTS It can be allowed to grow without pruning as it forms a tangled mass of stems. If you need to restrict growth, prune back stems by one-third, using shears. If the plant needs renovating, cut it down to within 3ft of the ground. This will result in vigorous new growth. The time to prune is late winter or early spring.

AT A GLANCE		
One of the fastest-growing climbers available, it has luxuriant growth and a froth of white flowers. Hardy to 5°F (zone7).		
Jan	/	Companion Plants
Feb	planting	As it is such a large vigorous
Mar	planting	plant, this climber is best
Apr	planting	grown alone.
May	/	
Jun	/	
July	/	
Aug	flowering	
Sep	flowering	
Oct	flowering	
Nov	/	
Dec	/	

Feverfew

TANACETUM PARTHENIUM, SYN. CHRYSANTHEMUM PARTHENIUM

FEATURES

A perennial flower, feverfew has aromatic, finely cut leaves and clusters of long-lasting small, white daisy-like flowers in summer. The plant is densely foliaged and grows about 2ft tall. Leaves are usually a fresh, light green but a golden foliaged form, "Aureum," is also sold. Pretty double-flowered forms are also available.

CONDITIONS

ASPECT Prefers full sun or light shade. Plants may grow lax and flower poorly in areas that are too shady. The golden form may scorch in full sun.

SITE Average, well-drained garden soil is all that is needed. In over-rich soils plants produce too much soft, leafy growth.

GROWING METHOD

SOWING Easily grown from seed sown in early spring. Press seeds just beneath the surface where the plants are to grow. Established plants can be dug up in fall and divided into several new plants. Each division should have its own roots and the divisions should be replanted immediately. Soft-tip cuttings taken in early summer will also root easily. Make cuttings about 3in long and insert them into small pots of very sandy potting mix. Place in a warm but shady and sheltered spot and keep them moist. Roots should form in about 3 weeks.

FEEDING Do not overwater. Feverfew does not thrive on neglect but does not need frequent watering. Overwet conditions will cause the plant to rot.
Mulch lightly in spring and fall and apply a balanced general fertilizer in spring.

PROBLEMS No major problems.

PRUNING Can be cut back after flowering to keep a compact shape and to minimise self-seeding.

HARVESTING

PICKING All the upper parts of the plant are useful medicinally and whole plants may be harvested any time they are in full bloom. Fresh, young leaves can be harvested any time, but are best before the plant flowers. Do remember that plants need their leaves to live and you should grow enough plants so that picking is not concentrated on just one or two. Pick flowers just as they open.

AT A GLANCE		
Perennial herb with aromatic leaves and daisy-like flowers that has a reputation for treating migraines. Hardy to 4˚F (zone 6).		
Jan	/	**Parts used**
Feb	/	Flowers
Mar	plant	Leaves
Apr	plant	Stems
May	plant harvest	**Uses**
Jun	plant harvest	Medicinal
July	harvest	Cosmetic
Aug	harvest	Craft
Sept	plant harvest	Gardening
Oct	/	
Nov	/	
Dec	/	

| STORAGE | Dry upper parts, including leaves, stems, and flowers, in a cool, dark, airy place. (Hang flowers upside down to dry.) When dry, coarsely chop and store in an airtight jar. |
| FREEZING | Freshly picked leaves can be wrapped in foil and frozen, for up to 6 months, for later use. |

USES

MEDICINAL	Tea made from the dried upper parts is drunk to relieve indigestion and period pain. It has gained a reputation for the treatment of migraines. Eating one or two fresh leaves every day may help prevent the onset of migraines in sufferers but in some people this causes mouth ulcers.
COSMETIC CRAFT	Feverfew makes a useful moisturiser. Flower stems placed in linen closets will discourage moths. An infusion of the leaves makes a mild disinfectant.
GARDENING	Feverfew is attractive and gives a good display when plants are massed together or used to border paths. It is attractive to bees and is often planted near fruit trees to assist pollination.

Fig-leaved Palm

FATSIA JAPONICA

FEATURES

Stunningly architectural, the large, glossy, palmate leaves of *Fatsia japonica* have an appealing leathery texture. In fall, it delights us with an exotic candelabrum of golf-ball-sized, white flower heads. Each comprises many tiny, five-petalled flowers. Large, handsome, black berries follow them. A native of South Korea and Japan, it has a spreading, suckering habit and makes a dome to 6ft high and 8ft across. Plant it to enhance a large patio tub. It tolerates air pollution, so is a good shrub for towns or cities. It resists salty sea breezes, too. Dramatise a sunny border by grouping it with golden-leaved yuccas.

If you plant fatsia in a border, create a striking feature by embracing it with tussock-forming and ground-covering Liriope muscari, whose spikes of bell-shaped, violet flowers complement the fatsia's white bobbles.

CONDITIONS

ASPECT   Ideal for brightening sheltered and lightly shaded spots, it objects to hot sunshine, which may scorch its leaves. Protect from icy winds, which also brown its foliage.

SITE   It is not fussy about soil but prefers deep, rich loam, which encourages the largest, most sculpturally appealing leaves. Add grit or gravel to soggy clay to improve drainage. Apply an acidifying fertilizer, such as sequestered iron, to chalky soil to reduce risk of chlorosis. When iron is "locked up" by calcium, roots cannot absorb it and leaves turn yellow and die.

GROWING METHOD

FEEDING   Boost lustrous foliage by topdressing the root area in spring, and again in summer, with fish, blood, and bone meal, which enriches the soil's humus content and encourages beneficial micro-organisms. Alternatively, use quick-acting but short-lived Growmore to accelerate shoot development.

Water freely after planting to settle soil around roots. Follow with a 2in mulch of old manure, bark, or cocoa shell.

PROPAGATION   Take semi-ripe cuttings in summer and strike them in a closed cold frame or on a sunny windowsill.

PROBLEMS   Control aphids, which colonize and cripple shoot tips, by spraying with a systemic insecticide.

PRUNING

Apart from maintaining its symmetry by shortening long branches or frost-damaged shoots in spring, cutting to a joint or lower shoot, no regular attention is necessary.

AT A GLANCE	
Dashing focal point for a lightly shaded spot. Intriguing bobbles of white blossom appear in fall. Hardy to 4˚F (zone 7).	
Jan /	Recommended Varieties
Feb /	"Variegata"
Mar /	
Apr prune, plant	
May plant	
June plant	
July plant	
Aug plant	
Sept plant, flower	
Oct flower	
Nov flower	
Dec /	

Firethorn

PYRACANTHA

FEATURES

Planted mainly for screening, hedging, and training as an espalier, evergreen and hardy firethorn's spiky stems are clad with small, glossy green leaves. In early summer, showy clusters of white flowers, appearing early in the plant's life, are followed by a dramatic cloak of bright orange, yellow, or red berries from fall to winter. Garden birds feast on them. There are many long-lived varieties. Choice kinds include a trio of recently bred fireblight-resistant forms: orange-berried "Saphyr Orange"; red-berried "Saphyr Red"; and yellow-berried "Saphyr Yellow". These shrubs grow 6–10ft high, which they reach after 5–10 years.

CONDITIONS

ASPECT	Needing full sun for healthy, compact growth, firethorn flowers less and is more loosely branched in light shade. It tolerates strong gusts and is often grown as a windbreak.
SITE	Tolerating a wide range of soil types including chalk, it prefers well-drained loam or clay-loam enriched with organic matter. It also prospers on humus-rich, gravelly patches.

GROWING METHOD

FEEDING	Keep firethorn lustrous and flowering and berrying freely by working bone meal into the root area in spring and fall. Help newly planted shrubs establish quickly by watering copiously in dry spells during their first spring and summer. Mulch thickly.
PROPAGATION	Take semi-ripe cuttings from mid- to late summer.
PROBLEMS	Disfiguring leaves and berries with patches, pyracantha scab is a debilitating disease. Control it by pruning out and burning infected shoots and spraying fortnightly with carbendazim from March to July. Grow orange-red berried "Mohave," which is resistant to it.

PRUNING

FREE-STANDING SHRUBS:	Cut back overgrown plants in April to keep them flowering and berrying profusely.
WALL-TRAINED ESPALIERS:	In spring, shorten non-blossoming side shoots to 4in from the base. In midsummer, reduce current-year shoots to three leaves.

AT A GLANCE		
An evergreen shrub coveted for its white flowers and display of red, orange, or yellow berries. Hardy to -13˚F (zone 5).		
Jan	/	**Recommended Varieties**
Feb	/	"Alexander Pendula"
Mar	/	"Dart's Red"
Apr	plant, prune	"Golden Charmer"
May	plant	*P. rogersiana*
June	flower, plant	"Saphyr Orange"
July	plant	"Saphyr Red"
Aug	plant	"Saphyr Yellow"
Sept	plant	
Oct	/	
Nov	/	
Dec	/	

Flowering currant

RIBES

FEATURES

A deciduous family that heralds spring, the most popular kind—*Ribes sanguineum* "Pulborough Scarlet"—is very hardy. Growing to around 8ft high and 6ft across, its upright shoots are thickly sleeved with pendent clusters of deep red, tubular flowers. "White Icicle," another choice form of *R. sanguineum*, has drooping, creamy-white candelabra blooms, dramatic when embraced with purple-red *Bergenia* "Evening Glow." *Ribes sanguineum* "Brocklebankii," to 4ft, is illuminatingly different, rewarding us with a heartening display of golden leaves and pink flowers. All varieties of *R. sanguineum* can be planted to form a stocky, flowering boundary hedge. Starry, yellow-flowered *R. odoratum*, to 6ft, has leaves that assume purple tints in fall, and less hardy *R. speciosum*, prized for its scarlet flowers on spiny shoots and best grown against a warm wall, are also generous performers.

CONDITIONS

ASPECT   Ribes is ideal for brightening a lightly shaded spot, but *R.* "Brocklebankii" must be shielded from hot sunlight otherwise its leaves will scorch. All, apart from slightly tender *R. speciosum*, prosper in exposed gardens. Make a statement by espalier training *R. speciosum* against a warm, sunny wall or set it to cascade from a pedestal pot.

SITE   Undemanding ribes thrives almost anywhere. Fortify sandy spots, which parch in summer, with bulky, moisture-conserving organics. If you plant this shrub on heavy clay, add gravel to improve drainage. Chalky soils can cause leaves to become chlorotic (yellowish green). Avoid this by adding acidifying fertilizer to lower the pH level.

GROWING METHOD

FEEDING   Provided the soil is reasonably fertile, a single application of bone meal in the fall is all that is necessary. After planting, no matter how damp the ground, water well to settle soil around the roots.

PROPAGATION Take hardwood cuttings in late fall.

PROBLEMS   This genus is prone to coral spot fungus. Causing a rash of coral-pink or orange pustules that kills shoots, it should be controlled by cutting out and burning infected plant tissue. Remove crowded shoots to improve air flow.

PRUNING

Keep ribes youthful, shapely and flowering freely by shortening a third of older shoots to new growth or near ground level when blooms fade. Remove crowding branches and cut back diseased stems to healthy wood in spring.

AT A GLANCE	
Deciduous bush festooned with clusters of flowers from late March to mid-May. Hardiness rating according to species.	
Jan /	**Recommended Varieties**
Feb /	*R. odoratum*
Mar flower, plant	*R. sanguineum* "Brocklebankii"
Apr flower, plant	*R. sanguineum* "Icicle"
May flower, plant	*R. sanguineum* "Porky Pink"
Jun plant, prune	*R. sanguineum* "Pulborough Scarlet"
July plant	*R. speciosum*
Aug plant	
Sept plant	
Oct /	
Nov /	
Dec /	

Flowering Dogwood

CORNUS

FEATURES

Suddenly, in late winter—from February to March—sulfur-yellow, powderpuff blooms light up bare, slender stems. *Cornus* mas has few rivals. In spring, when flowers fade, oval, pointed, vivid green leaves unfold. Small, edible, cherry-shaped, red fruits, good for jam, form in fall when leaves assume reddish-purple tints before falling. A coveted, leaf-shedding native of Europe and Western Asia, it slowly forms a handsome globe to around 15ft high and across. It can also be planted to create a stocky, dense flowering hedge.

Dramatically different, the Pacific dogwood (*C. nuttallii*) bears a plethora of saucer-shaped white, pink-tinged bracts (flowers), which light up late spring. When its flowers fade, they are fetchingly replaced by orbs of multi-seeded fruits.

CONDITIONS

ASPECT — Though performing better in full sun, both species are good contenders for lightly shaded spots. In deep shade, they form a looser, less symmetrical branching system. They are not harmed by cold winds.

SITE — *C. mas* thrives on virtually any soil, from light sand to heavy clay and chalk, provided it is not waterlogged. *C nuttallii* needs acid, fertile conditions. Enrich impoverished sand and chalk with bulky organic manure or well-rotted garden compost.

GROWING METHOD

PROPAGATION — *C. mas.* Take semi-ripe cuttings of maturing side shoots—ready when the bark at the base of the stem turns brown and firms up—in late summer. *C. nuttallii.* Best increased from soft-tip cuttings from early to midsummer.

FEEDING — Boost growth by topdressing the root area with a granular form of complete plant food, or fish, blood, and bone meal in spring and midsummer. Water in if the soil is dry. In droughty spells, keep shoots vigorous by soaking the root area or digging a moat around the shrub and repeatedly filling it with water. Follow by mulching thickly with moisture-retaining, well-rotted garden compost, bark, or cocoa shell.

PROBLEMS — *C. mas* and *C. nuttallii* have a rugged constitution and are seldom troubled by pests and diseases.

PRUNING

Pruning is not needed, apart from removing awkwardly placed shoots after flowering. Use pruning shears and cut to just above a shoot.

AT A GLANCE
Cornus mas has sulfur-yellow flowers in February; C. nuttallii bears whitish-pink blooms in June. Hardy to 4˚F (zone 7).

		Recommended Varieties	
Jan	/		
Feb	flower	*C. mas* "Aurea"	
Mar	flower, prune	*C. mas* "Aureoelegantissima"	
Apr	plant	*C. mas* "Hillier's Upright"	
May	flower, plant	*C. mas* "Variegata"	
June	flower, plant	*C. nuttallii* "Colrigo Giant"	
July	plant		
Aug	plant		
Sept	plant		
Oct	plant		
Nov	plant		
Dec	/		

Freesia

FREESIA SPECIES AND HYBRIDS

FEATURES

Freesias are loved for their strong perfume as well as their appearance. The wild species have yellow or white flowers and may grow about 12in high: modern hybrids grow 18in or more high and are available in a wide range of colors which includes blue, mauve, pink, red, and purple. However, some of these large-flowered hybrids have no scent. The white-flowered *F. alba* (*F. refracta*) is generally considered to have the best perfume.

For growing outdoors, buy specially prepared freesias and plant them in a sheltered position; they will flower in summer. Other freesias should be planted in containers that are brought into the house and greenhouse in fall for winter flowering.

CONDITIONS

ASPECT   Freesias prefer full sun but tolerate very light shade for part of the day.

SITE   Grow outdoors in a sheltered border. For winter flowers, plant in pots in summer, standing the pots in a sheltered position outside until fall, then bring them into a cool greenhouse or conservatory to flower. Use free-draining, John Innes, or soiless potting compost.

GROWING METHOD

PLANTING   Outdoors, plant 2in deep and the same distance apart in mid-spring. For pot culture, plant 2in deep, six to a 5in pot in July.

FEEDING   Apply a high potash liquid fertilizer every 14 days through the growing season. Keep the compost just moist at all times.

PROBLEMS   Aphids may attack the flower stems. Control with a contact insecticide when necessary.

FLOWERING

SEASON   From middle to late winter through to mid-spring indoors, late summer outside.

CUTTING   Cut when the lowest flower on the spike is fully open and other buds are well-developed.

AFTER FLOWERING

REQUIREMENTS Remove spent flower stems. When the foliage dies down, lift corms and store them in dry peat until it is time for replanting.

AT A GLANCE	
Fragrant, tubular flowers in a wide range of colors are held on delicate spikes. Grow indoors or outside in a sheltered position.	
Jan flowering**	Recommended Varieties
Feb flowering**	"Diana"
Mar flowering**	"Fantasy"
Apr plant *	"Oberon"
May /	"Romany"
Jun /	"White Swan"
July plant **	"Yellow River"
Aug plant **/flowering*	
Sept flowering*	
Oct flowering*	
Nov /	
Dec /	

** indoors   *outdoors

Fremontodendron

FLANNEL BUSH

FEATURES

This large evergreen shrub, the full name of which is *Fremontodendron californicum*, is spectacular when laden with its large bowl-shaped bright yellow flowers in summer and fall. It grows up to 20ft tall and so needs a reasonable amount of headroom. It is a native of the USA, especially California. Unfortunately the Flannel bush can be quite a short-lived plant so it is best to propagate it to ensure you have some young replacement plants should it suddenly expire. It is a great choice for a house or other high wall and relishes a sheltered courtyard garden or other secluded area. It looks good growing with a blue-flowered ceanothus.

CONDITIONS

ASPECT   Grow against a warm sunny wall. Needs to be well sheltered from wind.

SITE   Can be grown in a wide range of well-drained soils, from dry to moist, but prefers alkaline or neutral conditions. Ideally suited to poor soils.

GROWING METHOD

PROPAGATION   Sow seeds in spring and germinate at 59–68˚F. Take semi-ripe cuttings in late summer and root in a heated propagating case. Hardwood cuttings in late fall or winter are easier. Root them in a cool glasshouse.

WATERING   This plant takes quite dry conditions, so it is not necessary to water unless the soil becomes excessively dry.

FEEDING   Give an annual application of slow-release organic fertilizer in the spring.

PROBLEMS   Not generally troubled by pests or diseases.

FLOWERING/FOLIAGE

FLOWERS   It is grown for its flamboyant yellow flowers produced over a very long period.

FOLIAGE   Dark green lobed leaves. Shoots hairy and covered in scales.

PRUNING

REQUIREMENTS Minimal pruning in midsummer after the first flowers. Wear goggles: the mealy coating on the shoots and leaves can irritate the eyes.

AT A GLANCE	
A large vigorous shrub with shallow bowl-shaped yellow flowers over a very long period. Hardy to 23˚F (zone 9).	
Jan /	**Recommended Varieties**
Feb /	*Fremontodendron* "California Glory,"
Mar /	deep yellow flowers.
Apr planting	
May planting	
Jun flowering	
July flowering	
Aug flowering	
Sep flowering	
Oct flowering	
Nov /	
Dec /	

Fritillaria

CROWN IMPERIAL, SNAKE'S HEAD FRITILLARY

FEATURES

The name fritillary comes from the Latin word *fritillus*, meaning "dice-box," as the checkered patterns on the flowers of some of the species resemble the checkerboards associated with many games played with dice. There are about 100 species of this striking bulbous plant, which is related to the lilies, but only a relatively small number are in general cultivation. The form and color of the flowers varies considerably from one species to another, and some are fascinating rather than beautiful. The flowers are generally pendent and bell-shaped, carried on leafy stems; their height varies considerably, from low-growing rock garden plants such as the 4–6in *Fritillaria michailovskyi*, to the stately and imposing crown imperials (*F. imperialis*), which can reach well over 3ft tall. Many fritillaries, especially crown imperial, have a strong "foxy" scent to them which some people find unpleasant. All parts of the plant, including the bulbs, possess this scent, which can be quite penetrating.

USES

These plants, especially crown imperial, deserve a prominent place in the spring garden. They are sometimes seen taking pride of place in a bulb garden but are more often included in a mixed border planting with other bulbs and perennials. To show them to their best advantage, plant several of the same type together as individual plants will not have the same impact. Those that multiply readily, such as the snake's head fritillary, can be naturalized in dappled shade. All species can be grown in containers but most are easier to grow in the open ground.

AVAILABILITY

Crown imperials and snake's head fritillaries are readily available from garden centers, but some of the other species may have to be obtained from mail order bulb specialists.

TYPES

F. IMPERIALIS The best known fritillary is the majestic crown imperial, *F. imperialis*, which has a cluster of orange, yellow, or red bell-shaped flowers hanging below a crown of green leaves on a stem 20–39in high.

F. MELEAGRIS The snake's head fritillary or checkered lily, *F. meleagris*, occurs in the wild in meadows throughout Europe and is one of the easiest to cultivate. The checkered flowers occur in shades of green, purple, magenta, or white.

OTHERS Among the many other species worth growing are *F. acmopetala*, with bell-shaped green and brown flowers; *F. biflora* "Martha Roderick," with brown-streaked cream flowers, *F. camschatcensis*, with very

AT A GLANCE		
Unusual bulbs in a wide range of sizes and flower forms, with striking, pendent, bell-shaped blooms.		
Jan	/	Recommended Varieties
Feb	/	*Fritillaria biflora*
Mar	/	"Martha Roderick"
Apr	flowering	*Fritillaria imperialis*
May	flowering	"Lutea"
Jun	/	"Rubra Maxima"
July	/	"Prolifera"
Aug	/	"The Premier"
Sept	plant	*Fritillaria persica*
Oct	plant	"Adiyaman"
Nov	plant	
Dec	/	

deep purple, almost black flowers; *F. michailovskyi*, with yellow-tipped purple bells, *F. pallidiflora*, with soft yellow flowers veined lime-green or burgundy; *F. persica* with deep purple flowers; *F. pontica* with greenish bells; and *F. pyrenaica*, a deep burgundy purple, spotted green outside while the inside is purple-checked green.

CONDITIONS

ASPECT   Fritillary grows best in light shade or with morning sun and afternoon shade. Some species take full sun. All are best with protection from strong wind.

SITE   Fritillaries can be grown in beds and borders, on rockeries, or in containers, according to species. *F. meleagris* can be naturalized in grass. Soil for fritillaries must be well-drained but should contain plenty of well-rotted compost or manure. The area around the plants should be well-mulched, too. *F. meleagris* prefers a more moisture-retentive soil than some of the other species.

GROWING METHOD

PLANTING   The lily-like bulbs can dry out quickly and should be planted as soon as they are available. Planting depth varies between 2–8in depending on species. Plant the large bulbs of crown imperials on their sides on a layer of sand so that water does not collect in the hollow center.

FEEDING   Apply a general fertilizer after flowering or a high potash fertilizer in early spring as growth starts. Water in dry spells during the growing season, especially before flowering.

PROBLEMS   Bulbs may rot in badly drained soil.

FLOWERING

SEASON   Flowers appear from mid-spring to early summer.

CUTTING   Despite being quite long-lasting as a cut flower, blooms are rarely used this way because of the unpleasant smell of some flowers. Unfortunately crown imperial is one of these. However, they are so striking in the garden that they are best enjoyed there.

AFTER FLOWERING

REQUIREMENTS   When flowers have faded, flowering stems can be cut down, but leave the flowerheads on snake's head fritillaries to set seed. Bulbs are best left undisturbed, but if necessary clumps can be divided in summer and replanted immediately.

Galanthus

SNOWDROP

FEATURES

The snowdrop (*G. nivalis*) is well-loved for flowering in late winter while conditions are still very bleak. Most of the dozen or so species flower in late winter to early spring although there is one fall-flowering species (*G. reginae-olgae*). *G. elwesii* and *G. caucasicus* are also very early bloomers. There are named varieties of several species available. *G. nivalis* grows only 4–5in high, but taller varieties such as *G. elwesii* can grow up to 10in. The nodding flowers have three long, pure white petals and three shorter ones marked with a bright green horseshoe shape. The dark green foliage may be matt or glossy but is usually shorter than the flowers.

CONDITIONS

ASPECT   Grows best in shade or dappled sunlight.
SITE   Ideal for rockeries, the fronts of beds, and borders or naturalizing under deciduous trees. Soil must contain plenty of decayed organic matter to prevent excessive drying out in summer. Mulching in fall with old manure, compost, or leafmold is beneficial.

GROWING METHOD

PLANTING   Plant bulbs in fall 3–4in deep (deeper in light soils) and about the same apart. Do not allow the bulbs to dry out before planting. Snowdrops are much more reliable when transplanted while in growth, after flowering—known as planting "in the green." Plants are available from specialist suppliers in late winter or early spring.

FEEDING   Mulch during fall with decayed organic matter. Watering is not usually necessary.
PROBLEMS   No specific problems are known.

FLOWERING

SEASON   Flowering is from winter through to spring, depending on species.
CUTTING   Flowers can be cut for indoor decoration.

AFTER FLOWERING

REQUIREMENTS Existing clumps can be lifted, divided, and replanted as soon as the flowers have faded. Do not leave the plants out of the soil any longer than necessary.

TRUE HARBINGERS of spring, snowdrops are among the first bulbs to appear in late winter, often pushing up through the snow.

AT A GLANCE		
A small, dainty bulb popular for its late winter and early spring flowers. Very hardy.		
Jan	flowering	**Recommended Varieties**
Feb	flowering	"Atkinsii"
Mar	flowering/ plant "in the green"	"Cordelia"
		"Sam Arnott"
Apr	/	*Galanthus lutescens*
May	/	"Magnet"
Jun	/	*Galanthus nivalis*
July	/	"Flore Pleno"
Aug	/	"Lady Elphinstone"
Sept	plant	"Lutescens"
Oct	plant	"Pusey Green Tip"
Nov	/	"Scharlockii"
Dec	flowering	"Viridapicis"

Gazania

GAZANIA

FEATURES

Gazanias come in an amazing range of brilliant colors, from pastel pinks to cream, strong reds, and mahogany. All have contrasting "eyes" to their flowers. Gazanias are grown as half-hardy annuals from spring-sown seeds and used in beds and courtyard pots. Flowers tend to close up in dull weather, but newer varieties like "Daybreak Bright Orange" stay open for longer. They grow up to 12in tall and wide and thrive in coastal yards.

CONDITIONS

ASPECT	For the flowers to open reliably, gazanias must be grown where they get roasting sun all day.
SITE	Needs well-drained soil that is not too rich or leafy growth is the result. Light sandy soils give the best results. If growing in courtyard containers, choose clay pots or troughs and use a soil-based compost with extra sharp grit mixed in to ensure good drainage at all times.

GROWING METHOD

SOWING	Seed is sown in March at 68˚F in a heated propagator, in 3^1/$_2$in pots. Just cover the seeds and keep in a light place. Seedlings appear in 1–2 weeks and can be transplanted into cell trays, when large enough. Grow on in a greenhouse or conservatory, then harden off and plant in late May, spacing plants 12in apart. In mixed containers, make sure they are not shaded out by other plants growing nearby.

FEEDING	Only water gazanias when the soil or compost is dry, and stand courtyard pots undercover during prolonged spells of summer rain.
PROBLEMS	No real problems, but slugs may attack leaves in wet weather, so protect with slug pellets.

FLOWERING

SEASON	The flowering period lasts throughout summer if dead flowers and their stalks are removed.
CUTTING	Flowers are not suitable for cutting.

AFTER FLOWERING

GENERAL	Favorite plants can be lifted, potted up, and kept dry in a frost-free greenhouse over winter. Cuttings can be taken in the spring and new plants grown on for planting out.

AT A GLANCE	
A half-hardy annual grown for its bright flowers that open fully in sun. Use in beds and containers. Frost hardy to 23˚F (zone 9).	

		Recommended Varieties
Jan	/	*Gazania rigens*
Feb	/	"Chansonette"
Mar	sow	"Chansonette Pink Shades"
Apr	transplant	"Daybreak Bright Orange"
May	harden off/plant	"Daybreak Red Stripe"
Jun	flowering	"Harlequin Hybrids"
July	flowering	"Mini Star Mixed"
Aug	flowering	"Sundance Mixed"
Sept	flowering	"Talent"
Oct	/	
Nov	/	
Dec	/	

Genista

GENISTA

FEATURES

Small or rushy leaved and wiry stemmed, this accommodating deciduous family, related to broom, embraces showy, prostrate carpeters and small or large bushes to several yards high. All sport pea-like flowers in various shades of yellow.

From May to June, cushion-like Spanish gorse (*Genista hispanica*), hummocky and cascading *G. lydia* and dazzling, carpeting *G. pilosa* "Vancouver Gold" treat us to a display so radiant that it deceives you into thinking it is sunny when it is not.

Come July and August, the spring brigade is eclipsed by bushy *G. tinctoria* "Royal Gold" and the imposing and fragrant Mount Etna broom (*G. aetnensis*), with its pendulous, rush-like shoots that shower from branches 9ft high.

CONDITIONS

ASPECT   Hardy and tolerating exposed positions, all genistas perform best in full sun. Drought resisting, they are ideal for hot spots that cannot easily be watered.

SITE   Happiest in humus-rich and light, free-draining sand and loam, they also prosper in clay if you work in gravel and crumbly organic materials to improve drainage. Usefully, *G. tinctoria* excels in chalky soil.

GROWING METHOD

FEEDING   Encourage robust growth by topdressing the root area with a slow-release organic fertilizer, such as bone meal, in spring and fall. Water freely in droughty periods and keep roots cool and active by mulching with old manure, well-rotted garden compost, or bark.

PROPAGATION   Increase genista from semi-ripe cuttings of side shoots from mid- to late summer. Root them in pots on a bright windowsill or in a lightly shaded cold frame.

PROBLEMS   Normally trouble free.

PRUNING

Avoid cutting back *G. aetnensis*, *G. lydia*, and *G. tinctoria*, whose stumps may not regrow. You can, however, rejuvenate ageing *G. hispanica* by shortening old woody stems by two-thirds their length in spring. Keep large stumps moist in dry, windy weather to help them regenerate.

THE VERY FRAGRANT flowers of Genista monosperma *appear on bare stems in early spring.*

AT A GLANCE		
Deciduous spring- or summer-flowering bushes, they need full sunshine to flower bounteously. Hardy to 14°F (zone 8).		
Jan	/	**Recommended Varieties**
Feb	/	*G. aetnensis*
Mar	plant	*G. hispanica*
Apr	plant, prune	*G. pilosa* "Vancouver Gold"
May	flower, prune	*G. tinctoria* "Flore Pleno"
June	flower, plant	*G. tinctoria* "Royal Gold"
July	flower, plant	
Aug	flower, plant	
Sept	plant	
Oct	plant	
Nov	plant	
Dec	/	

Geranium

CRANESBILL

FEATURES

There are a great many perennial species of the true, hardy geranium, and many are reliable, long-flowering plants. Most cranesbill geraniums (not to be confused with tender, pot-plant pelargoniums) are easy to grow and are ideal in perennial borders, as edging plants, or as an infill between shrubs. Some species self-sow freely, but unwanted seedlings are easily removed. Cranesbills range from about 6 to 39in tall. Most have attractive, deeply divided leaves, and the flowers cover a range of shades, mostly in violet, blue, pink, rose, and cerise. Species worth seeking out include *G. endressii* and its cultivars, especially "Wargrave Pink," *G. pratense*, *G. psilostemon*, *G. himalayense*, and *G. sanguineum*. A variety of *G. sanguineum*, "Lancastriense," is a dwarf-growing type that can be used as groundcover.

CONDITIONS

ASPECT	Most like sunlight; others prefer shade.
SITE	Needs open, well-drained soil, but it need not be rich. Very acid ground should be limed before planting; use a soil-testing kit to ascertain the quantity required.

GROWING METHOD

PROPAGATION	Most cranesbills are easily grown from seed sown in the fall, but note that the results will be variable. They can also be grown from cuttings taken in the growing season. Established clumps can be lifted and divided in the spring. The exact spacing depends on the variety, but it is usually within the range of 8–16in. Established plants tolerate dry conditions

and rarely need watering, except in prolonged droughts.

FEEDING	Apply a little complete plant food when growth starts in the spring.
PROBLEMS	No specific pest or disease problems are known for these plants.

FLOWERING

SEASON	Cranesbills flower through the spring, into late summer.
CUTTING	Flowers do not cut well.

AFTER FLOWERING

REQUIREMENTS	Remove spent flower stems, unless you want the plants to seed. Some pruning may be needed through the growing season if growth becomes too rampant. Prune to maintain shape.

THE ROUNDED FORMS of geraniums' flowers are set off perfectly by the intricate shapes of this sun-loving plant's leaves.

AT A GLANCE		
A genus of some 300 annuals, biennials, and perennials grown for their big flowering clumps. Most are hardy to 5°F (zone 7).		
Jan	/	Recommended Varieties
Feb	sow	*Geranium himalayense*
Mar	sow	"Gravetye"
Apr	divide	"Johnson's Blue"
May	transplant	*G. x oxonianum*
Jun	flowering	"Wargrave Pink"
July	flowering	*G. palmatum*
Aug	flowering	*G. pratense*
Sept	flowering	"Mrs Kendall Clark"
Oct	sow	*G. psilostemon*
Nov	/	
Dec	/	

Geum chiloense

AVENS

FEATURES

Although there are many species of geum, the two most commonly grown are cultivars. "Lady Stratheden" has double yellow flowers, and "Mrs J Bradshaw" bright scarlet double flowers. Flowers appear on stems 12–20in tall high that emerge from large rosettes of slightly hairy, lobed compound leaves. Foliage is generally evergreen, but may be herbaceous in some areas. Geums can be planted as accent plants, preferably in groups, in the wild garden or near the front of a mixed border. While flowers are not very suitable for cutting, they give a long, vibrant display in the yard if they are regularly deadheaded.

CONDITIONS

ASPECT   Prefers full sunlight, but it can also be grown successfully in dappled shade.

SITE   Needs well-drained soil. Plants will benefit from the addition of plenty of decayed manure or compost before planting.

GROWING METHOD

PROPAGATION   Clumps can be divided in the spring or fall. Cut back foliage to reduce moisture loss while divisions re-establish. It also grows from seed sown in spring, but plants may not be true to type. Plant about 10–12in apart. Since most popular varieties tend to be short-lived, propagate often for a regular supply.

FEEDING   Apply complete plant food in early spring and again in mid-summer.

PROBLEMS   No particular problems are known.

FLOWERING

SEASON   There is a long flowering display, through late spring and mid-summer. Young vigorous plants will keep going to the fall.

CUTTING   Regular cutting (or deadheading) is essential to prolong the display.

AFTER FLOWERING

REQUIREMENTS   None, apart from the removal of spent flower stems and any dead foliage that may accumulate under the rosette.

THE BRIGHT RED double geum "Mrs J Bradshaw," a justifiably popular perennial.

AT A GLANCE	
A brightly colored perennial, essential for the spring border, with plenty of attractive cultivars. All hardy to 0˚F (zones 6–7).	
Jan /	**Recommended Varieties**
Feb sow	"Borisii"
Mar divide	"Fire Opal"
Apr transplant	"Lady Stratheden"
May flowering	*G. montanum*
Jun flowering	"Mrs J Bradshaw"
July /	*G. rivale*
Aug /	*G. urbanum*
Sept /	
Oct divide	
Nov /	
Dec /	

Gladiolus callianthus

ACIDANTHERA

FEATURES

Although this plant is now classified as a species of gladiolus, many gardeners still know it better under its previous botanical name of *Acidanthera murielae*. The pure white, slightly drooping blooms have a dark purple central blotch, and are sweetly scented; their similarity to a gladiolus flower is obvious, but they are more delicate and graceful. The leaves are erect and sword shaped, growing to about 2ft. The flowers—up to a dozen per corm—are held on slender stems above the tips of the leaves, and appear in late summer.

This is not a plant for cold, exposed yards, requiring a warm, sunny position to do well. In cold regions it can be grown successfully as a conservatory or cool greenhouse plant.

CONDITIONS

ASPECT   These plants require full sun.
SITE   Acidantheras can be grown in a sheltered, sunny spot outside in mild areas: otherwise grow the corms in pots in a greenhouse or conservatory, moving the pots onto a sheltered patio or similar position in midsummer. Light, free-draining soil is required. In pots, use soilless or John Innes potting compost.

GROWING METHOD

PLANTING   Plant in late spring, 4in deep and 8–10in apart.
FEEDING   Give an occasional application of high potash liquid fertilizer (such as rose or tomato feed) during the growing season.

Pot-grown plants should be fed every 10–14 days. Watering is not necessary for plants in the open ground except in very dry conditions; water pot-grown plants sufficiently to keep the compost just moist.

PROBLEMS   Plants may fail to flower in cold, exposed yards. Corms may rot in heavy, clay soils.

FLOWERING

SEASON   Flowers in late summer; mid-August through September.
CUTTING   Pick the stems when the buds are showing white at their tips.

AFTER FLOWERING

REQUIREMENTS Allow the foliage to die down, then lift the corms before the first frosts. Allow them to dry, brush off soil and store in dry, cool, frost-free conditions until the following spring.

AT A GLANCE		
A late summer flowering plant with attractive, white, scented blooms. Suitable for growing outdoors in mild areas only.		
Jan	/	Recommended Varieties
Feb	/	"Murieliae"
Mar	plant (indoors)	
Apr	plant (outdoors)	
May	/	
Jun	/	
July	/	
Aug	flowering	
Sept	flowering	
Oct	/	
Nov	/	
Dec	/	

Gladiolus hybrids

GLADIOLUS, SWORD LILY

FEATURES

The gladiolus with which we are most familiar comes from South Africa as do many other species, but other species originated in the Mediterranean regions and western Asia. There are about 300 species of gladiolus, many of them well worth seeking out for your garden, but the modern garden gladiolus is a hybrid. The stiff, sword-shaped leaves surround a flower spike that appears in spring and may be 39in or more high, but there are dwarf forms less than half this height. Flower spikes carry numerous individual blooms, usually densely packed on the stem and of a characteristic, irregular trumpet shape. The color range is extensive, including various shades of pink, red, yellow, orange, mauve, maroon, white, and green: flowers are often bicolored.

SPECIAL TYPES

A great range of species and cultivars is now available to add to the familiar hybrids. Baby gladiolus or painted ladies, *G.* x *colvillei*, (sometimes wrongly known as *G. nanus*) grows 12–16in high and comes in a range of colors, including many with contrasting markings. Green and white "The Bride" is perhaps the best known. Other species worth seeking out include *G. tristis*, with pale creamy yellow flowers; *G. dalenii* (syn. *G. natalensis*) with red to yellow flowers; *G. carneus*, with pink flowers; *G. cardinalis*, with rich red flowers marked in white; and *G. communis byzantinus*, hardy in warmer parts of the country and producing spikes of purple-pink flowers in early summer.

USES

Gladiolus makes a great garden display and cut flower. Dwarf forms make good pot plants.

CONDITIONS

ASPECT	Grows best in full sun with some shelter from strong wind.
SITE	Gladiolus can be difficult to place, as their stiff, upright form, which usually requires staking, is very formal. They are often grown in the vegetable garden and used as cut flowers, but with care they can be grown in beds and borders. Soil should be well-drained with a high organic content. Dig in well-rotted manure or compost a month or more before planting.

GROWING METHOD

PLANTING	Corms should be planted 3–4in deep and about 6in apart. Plant hybrid varieties in spring; stagger planting between March and May to give a succession of blooms. Spring-flowering species should be planted in fall; in colder areas of the

AT A GLANCE		
Popular hybrid varieties have tall, stiff spikes, packed with large, colorful flowers; more delicate species flower in spring.		
Jan	/	**Recommended Varieties**
Feb	/	**Hybrids**
Mar	plant	"Amsterdam"
Apr	plant	"Christabel"
May	flowering */plant	"Esta Bonita"
Jun	flowering *	"Green Woodpecker"
July	flowering	"Hunting Song"
Aug	flowering	"Lady Godiva"
Sept	flowering plant *	"Victor Borge"
Oct	/	*G.* x *colvillei*
Nov	/	"Amanda Mahy"
Dec	/	"The Bride"

*fall planted species

country they are best overwintered in a cool greenhouse.

FEEDING In soils enriched with organic matter supplementary feeding should not be necessary. In poor soils apply a balanced fertilizer to the soil before planting. In dry weather, water regularly throughout the growing season.

PROBLEMS Thrips, which rasp and suck sap from foliage and flowers, are a perennial problem in some areas. Deep colored flowers, such as reds and maroons, show their damage more readily than paler ones, with light-colored flecks spoiling their appearance. The summer months are the worst time for attacks, but the pest may overwinter on corms in store. Dust the corms with a suitable insecticide before storing and again before planting. At planting time, discard corms with dark or soft spots, which may be infected with various fungal rots.

FLOWERING

SEASON Hybrids planted in spring will produce flowers through summer into early fall. Fall-planted species will flower in early summer.

CUTTING Cut spikes for indoor decoration when the second flower on the spike is opening. Cut the flower stem without removing the leaves if that is possible. Change the water in the vase daily and remove lower blooms from the spike as they fade.

AFTER FLOWERING

REQUIREMENTS Lift corms carefully as soon as foliage begins to yellow. Cut off old leaves close to the corm. Dry corms in a warm, airy place for 2–3 weeks and clean them by removing old roots and the outer sheath of corm. To increase your stock of gladiolus, remove the small cormlets from the parent bulb and store them separately. These cormlets should produce full flowering size corms in the second year. If you have had problems with thrips in previous seasons, treat corms with insecticide dust before storing.

LARGE-FLOWERED HYBRIDS of Gladiolus have a huge color range. Bright scarlet and a bi-colored purple and white are just two of them.

Gloriosa

GLORY LILY

FEATURES

This climber is always sure to attract attention. It grows from elongated, finger-like tubers, and needs greenhouse or conservatory conditions. A plant will grow up to 8ft in the right conditions, its long, slender stems twining their way through netting or wooden trellis supports by means of tendrils at the tips of the lance-shaped leaves. The unusual lily-like flowers are crimson and yellow, with their wavy-edged petals strongly recurved to show the prominent, curving stamens.

Gloriosa has a long flowering period through summer and fall and usually gives a spectacular display. It is worth growing in a prominent position where it can be admired, but it is not hardy enough to grow outdoors.

CONDITIONS

ASPECT   Grow in a greenhouse or conservatory, in bright light but shaded from direct summer sun.

SITE   Use either soilless or John Innes potting compost.

GROWING METHOD

PLANTING   The tubers are planted out in late winter or early spring about 2in deep, placing one tuber in a 6in pot of moist compost. Take care not to injure the tips of the tubers.

FEEDING   Apply high potash liquid fertilizer every 14 days during the growing season. Water sparingly until growth commences, more freely during active growth but never allow the soil to become waterlogged.

PROBLEMS   Slugs may attack the tubers, and poor drainage or overwatering will rot them.

FLOWERING

SEASON   Flowers throughout the summer.

CUTTING   Flowers last well when picked.

AFTER FLOWERING

REQUIREMENTS Snap off flowers as they fade. Reduce watering when flowering has finished and allow the tubers to dry out for the winter. Store them dry in their pots or in dry peat in a minimum temperature of 50°F and replant in spring.

FLUTED RECURVED PETALS give these flowers an airy, floating effect. Plants grow rapidly in warm, humid conditions.

AT A GLANCE		
A greenhouse climber with spectacular summer flowers. Minimum temperature 50°F (zone 11).		
Jan	plant	**Recommended Varieties**
Feb	plant	*Gloriosa superba*
Mar	plant	"Rothschildiana"
Apr	/	"Lutea"
May	/	
Jun	/	
July	flowering	
Aug	flowering	
Sept	flowering	
Oct	/	
Nov	/	
Dec	/	

Godetia

GODETIA

FEATURES

Godetia is available in a wide range of varieties and many colors. This hardy annual can be spring- or fall-sown, the latter giving earlier flowers on bigger plants. Size ranges from 8 to 36in; the taller varieties are ideal for cutting. Don't labor over godetia—the best flowers are produced on slightly hungry, dry soils.

CONDITIONS

ASPECT   Needs an open position in full sunlight.
SITE   Needs perfect drainage, but not rich soil.

GROWING METHOD

SOWING   Sow where plants are to grow, just covering the seeds in shallow drills 6in apart during March/April, or during September. Thin out seedlings until they are 6–12in apart, depending on the variety. Do not thin fall-sown plants until the following spring, to allow for winter losses.
FEEDING   Not needed, or excessive leafy growth results.
PROBLEMS   Overwatering quickly causes root rot, followed by collapse and death of plants.

FLOWERING

SEASON   Flowers appear from May onward on plants sown the previous fall. Spring-sown plants start flowering from June.
CUTTING   An excellent cut flower, especially if the taller varieties such as "Schamini Carmine" and "Grace Mixed" are grown in rows.

AFTER FLOWERING

GENERAL   Remove plants when flowering is over. A few can be left to self-seed onto the soil.

FOR A RAINBOW of summer color, sow a mixed variety of godetia that includes shades of rose, pink, and white flowers. At its peak, godetia is smothered in masses of bright flowers with large petals that have a texture similar to crepe paper.

AT A GLANCE	
Grown for its bright single or double flowers, this hardy annual can be spring- or fall-sown. Frost hardy to 5°F (zone 7).	
Jan /	Recommended Varieties
Feb /	*Godetia hybrids*
Mar sow	Tall varieties
Apr sow	"Duke of York"
May thin out	"Grace Mixed"
Jun flowering	"Schamini Carmine"
July flowering	"Sybil Sherwood"
Aug flowering	Dwarf varieties
Sept flowers/sow	"Charivari"
Oct /	"Lilac Pixie"
Nov /	"Precious Gems"
Dec /	"Salmon Princess"

Golden Bell Bush

FORSYTHIA

FEATURES

Heartening indeed is the spring sight of a bush thickly laden with starry, sulfur-yellow, or deep golden blooms. Flowers open naturally from March to April. Enjoy an earlier show by cutting fat-budded stems in February and forcing them into bloom in a warm room.

There are two principal kinds: border forsythia (*Forsythia* x *intermedia*), which makes a rounded shrub to 8ft high and across, and *F. suspensa*, a snaking, weeping, or trailing form, enchanting when cascading over a wall or over the lower branches of pink, weeping cherry. Border forsythia can be also grown as a flowering hedge or trained to frame a window or doorway. Neat and compact "Golden Curls," just 2ft high and 3ft across, is ideal for a small yard.

CONDITIONS

ASPECT A sunny position is vital. In shade a multitude of shoots form but many will refuse to flower. Growth also becomes loose and weak. Forsythia braves cold wind.

SITE This plant grows strongly in most well-drained soils, from heavy clay to light sand and chalk. Fortify impoverished borders, especially where roots from nearby trees invade, with humus-forming, old, crumbly, or proprietary composted manure, well-rotted garden compost, shredded bark, or leaf mould.

GROWING METHOD

FEEDING If the soil was initially enriched with plant foods, forsythia seldom needs further feeding. If growth is slow, boost it by topdressing with a balanced granular fertilizer. Alternatively, liquid feed weekly with a high-nitrogen fertilizer from spring to midsummer. Water newly planted shrubs copiously and frequently to help them recover quickly.

PROPAGATION Layer low flexible shoots from spring to late summer or take hardwood cuttings in the fall.

PROBLEMS Occasionally—the cause is not known—warty galls distort stems. Overcome them by cutting back affected shoots to healthy wood and burning them.

PRUNING

Once established, keep plants youthful and flowering freely by removing from the base a third of the oldest shoots when flowers fade. Clip hedges at the same time of year, so that flower buds form for the following year.

AT A GLANCE		
Deciduous, bush and trailing/weeping varieties have flowers clothing year-old shoots in spring. Hardy to -13°F (zone 5).		
Jan	/	**Recommended Varieties**
Feb	/	"Fiesta"
Mar	flower, plant	"Gold Cluster"
Apr	flower, plant	"Golden Curls"
May	plant, prune	"Gold Tide"
June	plant	"Lynwood"
July	plant	"Spring Glory"
Aug	plant	"Suspensa"
Sept	plant	"Weekend"
Oct	plant	
Nov	plant	
Dec	plant	

Gomphrena

GLOBE AMARANTH

FEATURES

Also commonly known as bachelor's buttons, gomphrena is a half-hardy annual growing 12–30in tall, depending on the variety. Its rounded heads of purple, pink, white, red, and mauve flowers are used in bedding displays and for cutting and drying. "Strawberry Fields" has bright red flowers.

CONDITIONS

ASPECT   Must have a sunny spot.
SITE   Needs well-drained soil enriched with rotted manure or compost.

GROWING METHOD

SOWING   Sow in March in 3¹/₂in pots of multipurpose compost, just covering the seeds (soaking for a few days before helps germination). Keep at 64°F in a warm, dark place such as an airing cupboard and check regularly—seedlings appear in approximately two weeks. Transplant into cell trays, grow on under cover, harden off in late May, and plant out after frosts, 10–12in apart.
FEEDING Give an all-purpose liquid feed monthly.
PROBLEMS No special problems affect gomphrena.

FLOWERING

SEASON   Flowers appear from midsummer to fall.
CUTTING Used fresh as a cut flower, but can also be dried in late summer by hanging upside-down in a warm, dry, airy place.

AFTER FLOWERING

GENERAL Pull up in the fall and use for composting.

GLOBE AMARANTH makes a good edging for paths— choose one of the lower-growing varieties such as "Gemini Mixed" at 2ft. "STRAWBERRY FIELDS" is a large-growing variety of gomphrena with red flowers 2in across, on stems 30in tall.

AT A GLANCE	
A half-hardy annual grown for its clover-like flowerheads, used in bedding and for cutting. Frost hardy to 32°F (zone 10).	
Jan /	**Recommended Varieties**
Feb /	*Gomphrena globosa*
Mar sow	"Buddy"
Apr transplant	"Full Series"
May harden off/plant	"Gemini Mixed"
Jun flowering	"Globe Amaranth"
July flowering	"Qis Mixed"
Aug flowering	*Gomphrena hybrid*
Sept flowering	"Strawberry Fields"
Oct /	
Nov /	
Dec /	

Gongora

GONGORA SPECIES

FEATURES

This fascinating and simple to grow group of orchids originate from the American tropics. They are epiphytic, growing into large clumps over the years. The distinctive ridged pseudobulbs produce pendant flower spikes of varying lengths. The flowers that are held along the length of the thin stem are curiously shaped; the column is elongated and the sepals swept back from it almost like the wings of an insect. This is designed to attract a particular flying insect for pollination. Gongoras are relatively easy to grow in the mixed collection as well as being free flowering and usually scented. Although flowers only last a few weeks, a mature plant will often produce many flower spikes in succession over the summer months. These orchids are best grown in a basket or net pot.

CONDITIONS

CLIMATE   The gongoras are cool growing, needing a drop to 50°F in winter. Around 60°F in summer is acceptable.

ASPECT   These orchids have broad, soft green leaves so can easily burn in the sun. Good light in winter and dappled shade in summer.

Potting Mix Needs an open free-draining potting material such as plain bark chippings.

GROWING METHOD

PROPAGATION Once grown into a substantial specimen can be divided up into smaller plants. Only three pseudobulbs are needed for re-flowering.

WATERING   As the plants grow in open baskets, they will dry out quickly so regular watering is necessary. Immerse the whole plant in water if need be, particularly in summer.

FEEDING   Only feed when the plant is in active growth, during spring or summer. You can put fertilizer into the water that the plant is being dunked into and leave it for several minutes to let the plant benefit.

PROBLEMS   No specific problems are known if cultural conditions are suitable.

FLOWERING SEASON

Usually summertime—very free flowering.

THE GONGORA'S PENDANT SPIKES of curious shaped flowers are a constant source of amazement. These are easy orchids to grow and are an ideal addition to any cool collection.

AT A GLANCE	
Ideal for beginners and growing indoors. Plants are 4–8in in height and flower spikes reach 1ft 4in.	
Jan rest	**Recommended Varieties**
Feb rest	*G. bufonia* (cream/red)
Mar water and feed	*G. galeata* (orange/ brown)
Apr water and feed	*G. maculata* (yellow/red)
May flowering, water and feed	*G. quinquinervis* (brown/cream)
Jun flowering, water and feed	*G. truncata* (pink/cream)
July flowering, water and feed	
Aug water and feed	
Sept water and feed	
Oct rest	
Nov rest	
Dec rest	

Gunnera manicata

GUNNERA

FEATURES

This is not a plant for small yards. Growing to 8^1/$_2$ft high, clumps grow 10–13ft wide. The huge rhubarb-like leaves can be well over 42in in diameter, and are supported by long, stout, hairy stems. This is a magnificent feature plant from Africa, Australasia, and South America. It needs a damp or wet yard area, beside a pond or stream, or to the edge of a lawn. In summer it produces a dramatic tall spike of greenish flowers, often completely concealed by the foliage, but this plant is grown for the impact of its giant, architectural foliage. It is herbaceous, dying right back to the ground in winter. This is not a difficult plant to grow in the correct conditions, but it must be carefully sited. It needs space to grow, and gardeners need space to stand back and admire it.

CONDITIONS

ASPECT   Grows both in semi-shade and sunlight in cool, damp areas.
SITE   Likes a rich, moist soil. Dig plenty of organic matter into the ground before planting, and mulch crowns heavily with decayed compost or manure for protection.

GROWING METHOD

PROPAGATION   Divide small clumps in the spring, replanting them no less than 6^1/$_2$ft apart. Cuttings can be taken from new growth, too. Pot them up and nurture them until they are well rooted. Plants can be raised from seed, but this is slow and difficult. Keep moist throughout the spring and summer.

FEEDING   Apply pelleted poultry manure as new growth commences in the early spring to give the plant a boost. Add a fresh mulch of rotted manure at the same time.
PROBLEMS   No specific pest or disease problems are known for gunnera.

FLOWERING

SEASON   Heavy spikes of greenish flowers are produced in early summer.
FRUITS   The inflorescence is followed by fleshy red-green fruits, which can be ornamental.

AFTER FLOWERING

REQUIREMENTS As the weather becomes cold in the fall and leaves begin to brown, cut off the foliage and cover the crown of the plant with a thick layer of straw. Use a large leaf as a hat to keep it dry.

AT A GLANCE	
One of the largest, most spectacular perennials, it produces huge, often lobed, leaves. Spectacular flower spike. Hardy to 5˚F (zone 7).	
Jan /	Recommended Varieties
Feb /	Gunnera arenaria
Mar /	G. flavida (groundcover)
Apr transplant	G. hamiltonii
May transplant	G. magellanica (groundcover)
Jun /	G. manicata
July flowering	G. prorepens
Aug /	G. tinctoria
Sept sow	
Oct /	
Nov /	
Dec /	

Guzmania

GUZMANIA SPECIES

FEATURES

This is a large group of mainly epiphytic bromeliads with a few terrestrial species. They are grown for their lovely spreading rosettes of satiny, smooth-edged foliage, as well as for their striking flowering stems. They have been widely hybridized with vrieseas to produce stunning cultivars. Mature plants may be from up to 3¹/₄ft wide when fully mature. *Guzmania lingulata* is a handsome species with shiny, mid-green leaves, and a rich, bright red inflorescence. Leaves can be up to 18in long. *G. lingulata minor*, the scarlet star, is much smaller with leaves just 5in long. Named varieties include "Exodus," "Empire," "Cherry" and "Gran Prix."

LEAVES

Leaves may be plain glossy green, cross-banded in contrasting colors or finely patterned with stripes. At flowering time the central leaves may color, adding to the brilliant color display.

CONDITIONS

POSITION   Grows happily in a warm, frost-free greenhouse or conservatory or on a bright windowsill in the home. Prefers bright filtered light away from draughts.

POTTING MIX   Needs a free-draining mix able to retain some moisture or use ready-made orchid compost. Use a pot that is just slightly larger than the root ball. Terracotta pots will give larger plants more stability.

GROWING METHOD

PROPAGATION   Grows from offsets or suckers that develop around the stem of the parent plant. Plant out from spring to fall.

WATERING   Mist daily in summer. Keep water in the cup at all times and water the potting Imix twice weekly in summer and just occasionally in winter as necessary.

FEEDING   Use weak liquid plant foods during periods of rapid growth. Do not feed too early in spring as it can scorch the leaves and roots.

PROBLEMS   No specific problems provided suitable cultural conditions are given.

FLOWERING SEASON

The showy flowers are long lasting on the plant—perhaps up to two months. Most species and varieties flower during summer and last well into fall.

AT A GLANCE	
Sporting clusters of pink or lilac flowers from late summer to fall, it needs a sheltered position. Hardy to 14°F (zone 8).	
Jan water	**Recommended Varieties**
Feb keep warm	*G. dissitiflora*
Mar keep warm	*G. lindenii*
Apr repot	*G. lingulata*
May remove suckers	*G. monostachya*
and offsets	*G.* "Amaranth"
Jun flowering, mist, feed	*G.* "Cherry"
July flowering, mist, water	*G. lingulata* "Empire"
Aug mist	*G.* "Exodus"
Sept reduce misting	*G.* "Gran Prix"
Oct keep frost free	
Nov keep frost free	
Dec keep frost free	

Gypsophila
BABY'S BREATH

FEATURES

Hardy annual varieties of *Gypsophila elegans* grow up to 2ft tall and wide, with many-divided stems bearing small, dainty pink, white, or rose flowers. It is widely used in flower arranging and as a "foil" for other plants in summer bedding schemes. The dwarf- growing *Gypsophila muralis* "Garden Bride," at 6in, is ideal for baskets and containers.

CONDITIONS

ASPECT	Grow gypsophila in full sunlight.
SITE	Rotted compost or manure should be dug in before planting, for strong plants and better flowers, but the soil must also be well-drained. Varieties grown in baskets and containers will succeed in any multipurpose compost.

GROWING METHOD

SOWING	Seeds can go directly into the ground, where plants will grow and flower. Sow in short drills $^1/_2$in deep in April, then thin to finally leave plants 4–6in apart to give each other support and allow room to grow. September sowing produces stronger plants with earlier flowers the following spring—do not thin out until after winter.
FEEDING	Feeding is not generally necessary if the soil has been well prepared beforehand. In dry spells, give the soil a thorough soaking, and do not let containers dry out.

PROBLEMS

PROBLEMS Gypsophila is trouble-free, but young plants are prone to rotting off in heavy soils.

FLOWERING

SEASON	Flowers appear from June onward on spring-sown plants, several weeks earlier on those sown the previous fall.
CUTTING	Excellent when cut and an ideal "filler" to marry together other flowers in a wide range of floral arrangements.

AFTER FLOWERING

GENERAL Pull up plants and use for composting.

CLOUDS OF SMALL FLOWERS are produced on annual gypsophila all summer if a few seeds are sown at two-week intervals from April until early June. For cut flowers, grow plants in a spare corner because they look bare once you begin to regularly remove stems.

AT A GLANCE		
Gypsophila is a hardy annual grown for tall, much-branching stems of flowers, for beds/cutting. Frost hardy to 5˚F (zone 7).		
Jan	/	Recommended Varieties
Feb	/	*Gypsophila elegans*
Mar	/	"Bright Rose"
Apr	sow	"Color Blend"
May	thin out	"Covent Garden"
Jun	flowering	"Kermesina"
July	flowering	"Monarch White"
Aug	flowering	"Rosea"
Sept	flowers/sow	"Snow Fountain"
Oct	/	"White Elephant"
Nov	/	*Gypsophila muralis*
Dec	/	"Garden Bride"

Gypsophila paniculata

BABY'S BREATH

FEATURES

Baby's breath is an eye-catching border perennial that grows to 4ft high, and produces a summer flower display that looks like a puffy aerial cloud. The flowers appear in mid- and late summer, and are white on the species, though there are gently colored cultivars. "Compacta Plena" is soft pink, "Flamingo" is lilac-pink, and "Rosenschleier" pale pink. The latter is also quite short, at 1ft tall, and is worth repeat-planting in a long border. "Bristol Fairy" has the advantage of large, white flowers, $^1/_2$in across, but it is not as vigorous as the rest and is relatively short-lived, needing to be propagated every few years. G. paniculata mixes well with contrasting, vertical plants.

CONDITIONS

ASPECT Full sunlight is required for it to thrive.
SITE Free-draining soil is essential, since the plant's native habitat is sandy steppes and stony sites in eastern Europe, Central Asia, and China.

GROWING METHOD

PROPAGATION Sow seed in a cold frame in spring, or in pots in a gently heated greenhouse in winter. Species can be propagated by root cuttings, again in late winter. Though adult plants tolerate some dryness, the young plants must not be allowed to dry out. Water regularly in the growing season. Plant out in its final position, since it dislikes disturbance.

FEEDING A scattering of complete plant food in the spring.
PROBLEMS Generally problem-free.

FLOWERING

SEASON The one flowering period is mid- and late summer; an unmissable sight.
CUTTING Makes excellent cut flowers—the light sprays of white-to-pink flowers add considerably to any arrangement, formal or flowery.

AFTER FLOWERING

REQUIREMENTS Cut back to ground level in the fall.

THE RIPPLING, AIRY MOUND of flowers justifiably led to its common name, baby's breath. It makes a stunning sight in its native habitats, spreading across the sandy steppes of the Far East and eastern Europe.

AT A GLANCE		
A striking, tallish herbaceous perennial that gives an impactful, flowery mid-summer display. Hardy to 0°F (zones 6–7).		
Jan	/	Companion Plants
Feb	/	Agapanthus africanus
Mar	sow	Geranium himalayense
Apr	transplant	Iris "Magic Man"
May	/	Osteospermum "Whirligig"
Jun	/	Salvia cacaliifolia
July	flowering	Silene coeli-rosa
Aug	flowering	Solanum crispum
Sept	/	
Oct	/	
Nov	/	
Dec	/	

Hatiora salicornioides

DRUNKARD'S DREAM

FEATURES

These plants bear no apparent likeness to the spiny plants so readily recognised as cactuses. They tend to be upright in early stages, but become pendulous under their own weight and so are ideal for hanging baskets. A large potted plant may need heavy stones in the container base to counterbalance the cactus's weight. The stem segments are mid-green to bronze and are topped by small, yellow to orange tubular, or funnel-shaped flowers in spring. This Brazilian group of plants includes ground growers and epiphytes and it is easy to imagine them growing from the fork or branch of a tree. *Hatiora salicornioides* is called drunkard's dream because the dense growth of tiny jointed stems resembles hundreds of tiny bottles. In Australia it is also called dancing bones.

CONDITIONS

ASPECT   Drunkard's dream grows best in filtered sunlight or in a position that has morning sun and afternoon shade.

SITE   The epiphytic kind need some shade to replicate their natural growing conditions, just under the tree canopy. Either provide filtered sunlight, or a position with morning sun and reasonable afternoon shade. Spray regularly to provide high levels of humidity, especially on hot days, when in full growth from spring to fall.

GROWING METHOD

PROPAGATION   These plants can be grown from seed sown in spring, but it is much easier to strike cuttings from the jointed stems in spring through to early fall.

FEEDING   Apply a low-level nitrogen liquid feed once a month during the growing season.

PROBLEMS   This is generally a very easy plant to grow and it has no specific pest or disease problems.

FLOWERING

SEASON   Small, orange to yellow tubular flowers appear from the lower half of the plant in spring. Although the flowers are not spectacular, they give the impression of tiny lights on the ends of the stems. The most impressive thing about most of these plants, is their distinctive, unusual, non-cactus like dangling growth. From a distance *H. salicornioides* looks a bit like the jangled stems of a mistletoe.

FRUITS   The flowers of drunkard's dream are followed by tiny white fruits.

UNOPENED BUDS FORMING on the tips of each slender segment of this plant are like small, glowing torches.

AT A GLANCE	
Genus with many excellent species, well worth including in any collection of first-rate cactuses. 50°F min (zone 11).	
Jan /	**Recommended Varieties**
Feb /	*Hatiora ephiphylloides*
Mar sow	*H. gaertneri*
Apr transplant	*H. rosea*
May flowering	*H. salicornioides*
Jun flowering	**Companion Plants**
July /	Astrophyllum
Aug /	Epiphyllum
Sept /	Rebutia
Oct /	Schlumbergera
Nov /	Selenicereus
Dec /	

Hawthorn

CRATAEGUS

FEATURES

Architectural, deciduous hawthorns—ideal for focal points or screening—can be shrubby or grow into small trees to 15ft. Clad with lobed or toothed leaves, suffused with fiery scarlet tints in fall, blossom mantles shoots in May and June. Bright orange or red berries—birds adore them—persist into winter. Stems are lusually spiny and native may or quickthorn (*Crataegus monogyna*) makes a formidable barrier. Others, such as glossy-leaved

C. x *lavallei*, whose large clusters of white blossom are followed by orange berries coupled with richly autumn-hued leaves, and deep red-flowered C. *laevigata* "Paul's Scarlet," make fetching sentinels.

CONDITIONS

ASPECT Stalwarts for exposed upland gardens raked by wind, or those fringing the sea, where leaves are powdered with salt, hawthorn flowers best in full sun. In light shade, bushes have a more open habit and fewer blooms.

SITE Though hawthorn prefers deep and heavyish but well-drained soils, it will tolerate light, sandy, or gravelly ground. Improve thin soils by working in plenty of bulky organic matter.

GROWING METHOD

FEEDING Work bone meal into the soil in spring and fall to ensure a continuous supply of root-promoting phosphates. Water copiously in the first year after planting. Thereafter, when hawthorn is established, it is seldom stressed by drought.

PROPAGATION Raise species from seed, from berries mixed with damp sand and placed in a flower pot. Break dormancy by positioning the pot in the coldest part of the garden. In spring, remove seeds and sow them in an outdoor seed bed. Seedlings quickly appear.

PROBLEMS Powdery mildew can whiten leaves. Control it by spraying with carbendazim, mancozeb, or triforine with bupirimate.

PRUNING

BUSHES Encourage a profusion of blossom by shortening the previous year's shoots by two-thirds in late winter.

HEDGES Clip in mid-July and in winter.

*'PAUL'S SCARLET', a cultivar of C*rataegus laevigata, *flowers in mid to late sprint.*

AT A GLANCE	
Large, deciduous bushes or small trees, their summer blossom is followed by orange or scarlet fruits. Hardy to -13°F (zone 5).	
Jan /	**Recommended Varieties**
Feb prune	"Crimson Cloud"
Mar plant	C. x *grignonensis*
Apr plant	C. x *lavallei*
May flower, plant	"Paul's Scarlet"
June flower	"Rosea Flore Pleno"
July prune	
Aug prune	
Sept /	
Oct plant	
Nov plant, prune	
Dec prune	

Heath

ERICA

FEATURES

A large, vibrant-flowered group of bushy and carpeting, evergreen shrubs, 9in–5ft high, their thickly clustered, tubular or bell-shaped blooms in white and a confection of pink, purple, coral, and crimson hues illuminate the year. Color winter with varieties of *Erica* x *darleyensis* and *E. carnea*, cheer spring by grouping *E. arborea*, and *E. erigena*, glorify summer and fall with *E. cinerea*, *E. tetralix*, and *E. vagans*.

Use them to brighten borders and rock gardens and suppress weeds. Ideally, associate them with dwarf conifers.

Create a tapestry of blossom by combining ericas with closely related varieties of ling (*Calluna vulgaris*), which flower from July to November, and Irish heath (*Daboecia cantabrica*). Some callunas, such as "Beoley Gold," yield radiant golden foliage.

CONDITIONS

ASPECT	Most are very hardy, tolerate chilly winds and are ideal for exposed, upland gardens. Heathers must have full sun and good air circulation. Do not crowd plants.
SITE	While all varieties prefer acid soil, winter-flowering *Erica carnea* tolerates slightly alkaline conditions. Good drainage is vital. Mulch plants annually, in spring, with leaf mould or well-rotted garden compost.

GROWING METHOD

FEEDING	Established plants need little or no fertilizer. If the soil is very poor, fortify the root area with a balanced, acidifying fertilizer in spring.
PROPAGATION	Take semi-ripe heeled cuttings from early to late summer; layer shoots in mid-spring.
PROBLEMS	Heathers quickly succumb to root rot in heavy or overwet soils.

PRUNING

Lightly shear flowered shoots when blooms fade. Never cut back into older wood. Tackle fall- and winter-flowering varieties when new shoots appear in spring.

PERFORMING FROM NOVEMBER to May, Erica carnea is prized for its white, pink, red, lavender, or mauve display.

AT A GLANCE	
Carpeting evergreens whose succession of blossom or foliage enchants us every month of the year. Hardy to 4°F (zone 7).	

Month		Recommended Varieties
Jan	flower	**Recommended Varieties**
Feb	flower	**Spring flowering**
Mar	flower	"Albert's Gold"
Apr	plant, prune	"Viking"
May	flower, plant	**Summer flowering**
June	flower, prune	"C.D. Eason"
July	flower, prune	"Pink Ice"
Aug	flower, plant	**Fall flowering**
Sept	flower, plant	"Andrew Proudley"
Oct	flower	"Stefanie"
Nov	flower	**Winter flowering**
Dec	flower	"Ann Sparkes"

Hebe hulkeana

NEW ZEALAND LILAC

FEATURES

This is an evergreen shrub from New Zealand, with a slender, loose, sprawling habit of growth. It is best grown by training it to a warm sunny wall, where it will benefit from the protection afforded, as it is not one of the hardiest subjects. The New Zealand lilac is a beautiful shrub, though, and well worth growing for its spring and summer display of lavender-blue flowers. As a free-standing shrub it grows to about 3ft high, but will grow taller against a wall, up to 6ft. For those who live in areas subject to very hard winters, this hebe can be grown in a cool conservatory. It will particularly enjoy and thrive in mild seaside gardens. The Hebe genus as a whole is valued by gardeners for its versatility, fine flowers and neat foliage.

CONDITIONS

ASPECT   Will grow in sun or partial shade, but needs to be well protected from cold drying winds.

SITE   This plant requires well-drained yet moisture-retentive soil, ranging from alkaline to neutral and low to moderate fertility.

GROWING METHOD

PROPAGATION   Take softwood cuttings in spring or early summer, or semi-ripe cuttings in summer. It is best to have some young plants in reserve to replace the main plant if it is killed off by hard frosts.

WATERING   Do not let the plant dry out. Water if the soil starts to become dry in summer.

FEEDING   Once a year, in spring, apply a slow-release organic fertilizer, such as blood, fish, and bone.

PROBLEMS   These plants may be attacked by aphids in spring or summer.

FLOWERING/FOLIAGE

FLOWERS   This shrub is grown primarily for its flowers, which are produced in decorative trusses on the ends of the shoots.

FOLIAGE   The shiny evergreen elliptic leaves with red edges are attractive.

PRUNING

REQUIREMENTS No regular pruning needed. Spread out and train young stems to their supports. Cut back any frost-damaged or dead growth in spring. Remove dead flower heads.

AT A GLANCE	
A loose, slender evergreen shrub with heads of lavender-blue flowers. Hardy to 23˚F (zone 9).	
Jan /	**Companion Plants**
Feb /	Associates well with early-flowering
Mar /	climbing roses with pink or red
Apr planting	flowers.
May flowering	
Jun flowering	
July /	
Aug /	
Sep /	
Oct /	
Nov /	
Dec /	

Hedera helix

COMMON IVY

FEATURES

Hedera helix is generally thought of as a climbing plant but it can also make an excellent, low-maintenance groundcover, with a dense mass of foliage. It is especially good in shady areas under trees and will readily climb up them, but keep ivy away from ornamental trees or they will quickly be obscured. *H. helix* may also be used in place of a lawn in formal areas where it is kept well clipped, and it is also suitable for planting where it can spill over a wall or bank. The straight species has very dark green, lobed leaves, but there are many dozens of cultivars with leaves edged, spotted, or streaked with cream or gold, as well as great variation in leaf shape and size.

CONDITIONS

ASPECT   Tolerates full sun but is at its best in dappled sunlight or shade. A wonderfully adaptable plant for which a place can generally be found in the garden.

SITE   Grows in poor soil, but best in moisture-retentive soil enriched with organic matter.

GROWING METHOD

PROPAGATION   It is easy to strike from semi-ripe tip cuttings taken through summer and early fall. It roots easily from layers, too. You can even take spring cuttings and stick them straight back in the soil.

FEEDING   Apply complete plant food in early spring.Unless the soil is in a very poor state though, ivy can be left to get on with it.

PROBLEMS   No special problems are known.

FLOWERING

SEASON   Tiny, inconspicuous flowers are produced only on very mature, adult foliage and are never seen on plants that are kept clipped.

BERRIES   Blue-black berries follow the flowers.

PRUNING

GENERAL   Restrict pruning to cutting off wayward stems or keeping the plant within bounds. Trim in any season, but severe cutting is best in late winter, just before new growth.

THE RICH GREEN leaves of ivy can be trimmed and trained into a variety of shapes, and makes a striking edging for pathways.

AT A GLANCE	
Hedera helix is a first-rate climber that also can be used as groundcover, and to romp over sheds. Hardy to 0°F (zone 7).	
Jan foliage	**Recommended Varieties**
Feb foliage	*Hedera helix*
Mar foliage	*H. h.* "Angularis Aurea"
April foliage	*H. h.* "Atropurpurea"
May foliage	*H. h.* "Buttercup"
June foliage	*H. h.* "Glacier"
July foliage	*H. h.* "Ivalace"
Aug foliage	*H. h.* "Pedita"
Sept foliage	*H. h.* "Shamrock"
Oct flowering	*H. h.* "Spetchley"
Nov foliage	
Dec foliage	

Hedychium

GINGER LILY

FEATURES

There are over 40 species of ginger lily although not many species are in cultivation. These plants are strong growers, mostly to about 6ft, their growth originating from sturdy rhizomes. They can be bedded out in borders for the summer, or grown in tubs as a patio or greenhouse and conservatory plant. Mid-green leaves are lance shaped.

The tall, showy heads of flowers are carried in late summer. White ginger or garland flower, *H. coronarium*, has white and yellow, very fragrant flowers while scarlet or red ginger lily, *H. coccineum*, has faintly scented but most attractive blooms in various shades of red, pink, or salmon. Also heavily scented is kahili ginger, *H. gardnerianum*, with large, clear yellow flowers and prominent red stamens.

CONDITIONS

ASPECT   Needs a bright, sunny spot.
SITE   In cold areas, grow in a greenhouse or conservatory; otherwise grow in a sheltered border outside. Rich, moisture-retentive soil is necessary; add well-rotted organic matter before planting time.

GROWING METHOD

PLANTING   Plant in spring, with the tip of the rhizome just buried below the soil surface. Space rhizomes about 24in apart.
FEEDING   A balanced fertilizer can be applied as growth begins in spring. Keep the soil moist throughout the growing season.

PROBLEMS   There are generally no particular problems experienced.

FLOWERING

SEASON   Flowers in mid to late summer and early fall.
CUTTING   Flowers can be cut for indoor decoration but they will last very much longer on the plant.

AFTER FLOWERING

REQUIREMENTS Cut flower stems down to the ground when the flowers have faded. Lift the rhizomes when the foliage has died down and overwinter in dry peat in a frost-free place, replanting the following spring. Pot plants can be left in their pots over winter. Rhizomes may be divided in spring to increase your stock.

THIS GINGER LILY needs room to spread out and show off its strong lines. It is a useful landscaping plant.

AT A GLANCE		
Large, showy leaves are topped by striking heads of many flowers, often scented. Needs a minimum temperature of 45°F (zone 11).		
Jan	/	Recommended Varieties
Feb	/	*Hedychium coccineum*
Mar	plant	"aurantiacum"
Apr	plant	*Hedychium coccineum*
May	/	"Tara"
Jun	/	*H. coronarium*
July	flowering	*H. densiflorum*
Aug	flowering	"Assam Orange"
Sept	flowering	*H. gardnerianum*
Oct	/	
Nov	/	
Dec	/	

Helenium autumnale

SNEEZEWEED

FEATURES

As its Latin name suggests, this herbaceous perennial flowers from late summer to mid- fall. The straight species has bright golden, daisy-like flowers with dark centers, but many of the most popular cultivars have flowers in rich tones of orange-red or copper-red. "Butterpat," "Moerheim Beauty," and "Waldtraut," are among the most popular varieties. Sneezeweed can grow 39–60in or more high, eventually forming large clumps over 20in across. Flowers cut well, but the plant is probably more valuable for its contribution to the fall garden. Place at the back of a perennial border or among shrubs. Easy to grow.

CONDITIONS

ASPECT — Needs to be grown in full sun right through the day. Avoid shade.

SITE — Needs a moisture-retentive soil heavily enriched with organic matter. It will not thrive in dry soil. Mulch around clumps to help keep soil moist.

GROWING METHOD

PROPAGATION — Established clumps can be lifted and divided about every three years. Discard the oldest central sections and replant the divisions about 12in apart in spring or fall. Give new young plants a regular watering right through the growing season.

FEEDING — Apply complete plant food as new growth commences in spring.

PROBLEMS — Sneezeweed is generally free from problems, although slugs and snails can damage newly emerging growth in damp weather.

FLOWERING

SEASON — The flowering season starts in mid-summer and continues into the fall.

CUTTING — Flowers cut well for indoor decoration.

AFTER FLOWERING

REQUIREMENTS — Spent flower stems should be removed. As the plant dies down, cut off and remove dead foliage. It can be chopped and left on the ground as a mulch. With flowers blooming into the fall, the foliage remains in good condition until attacked by frost.

ORANGE AND TAWNY COLORS are a feature of sneeze-weed, a reliable perennial that brightens the fall garden.

AT A GLANCE	
A group of annuals, biennials and perennials. Grown for their prolific, bright flowering display. Hardy to 5°F (zone 7).	
Jan /	**Recommended Varieties**
Feb sow	"Butterpat"
Mar sow	"Chipperfield Orange"
Apr transplant	"Crimson Beauty"
May transplant	"Moerheim Beauty"
Jun /	"Rotgold"
July flowering	"The Bishop"
Aug flowering	
Sept flowering	
Oct /	
Nov /	
Dec /	

Helianthus

SUNFLOWER

FEATURES

Sunflowers range in height from 18in up to 15ft depending on the variety grown. They can be used in bedding, in patio containers, as cut flowers, or can be grown as traditional "giants" to several feet tall. Plants produce single or multi-flowered heads and the color range is enormous. "Teddy Bear" has furry, double flowers. Annual sunflowers are fully hardy and flower from mid-summer onward. Certain varieties such as "Prado Sun & Fire" have been bred to be pollen-free and these are ideal for use as indoor cut flowers. Seedheads left in the yard in the fall provide food for birds.

CONDITIONS

ASPECT	Must have an open position in full sun.
SITE	Tolerates most soil conditions but soil enriched with plenty of manure or compost makes growth both rapid and vigorous, producing the largest flowerheads. Plants grown in groups in borders tend to support each other, but in exposed spots tie tall varieties to a cane. Use multipurpose compost mixed with slow-release fertilizer for planting up patio containers and windowboxes.

GROWING METHOD

SOWING	Seeds are large and easy to handle— sow three seeds outdoors where plants are to grow in March, removing all but the strongest when 6in tall. Can also be sown three seeds to a 3½in pot of compost and treated in the same way. Pot-grown plants can be kept outdoors

and planted when the roots fill the pot. Spacing depends on the variety grown.

FEEDING	Extra feeding is not usually needed but keep plants watered in long dry spells.
PROBLEMS	Slugs and snails can attack young plants cutting them off at ground level, so protect with slug pellets or a barrier of sharp grit.

FLOWERING

SEASON	Throughout summer and early fall.
CUTTING	A very good cut flower but use a heavy vase or add some weight to the bottom of it to prevent it toppling over. Pollen-free varieties should be grown if allergies are a known problem.

AFTER FLOWERING

GENERAL	Leave the seedheads as bird food during fall and winter, and then dig out the roots. Sunflower roots can help break-up and loosen heavy, compacted soils.

AT A GLANCE		
A hardy annual grown for its large flowers on both dwarf and tall plants; some are ideal for cutting. Frost hardy to 5°F (zone 7).		
Jan	/	Recommended Varieties
Feb	/	*Helianthus annuus*
Mar	sow	Tall varieties
Apr	thin out	"Italian White"
May	support	"Pastiche"
Jun	flowering	"Velvet Queen"
July	flowering	For containers
Aug	flowering	"Big Smile"
Sept	flowering	"Pacino"
Oct	/	Double flowers
Nov	/	"Orange Sun"
Dec	/	"Sungold Double"

Helichrysum

STRAWFLOWER

FEATURES

Varieties of strawflower come from *Helichrysum bracteatum*, with plants growing 6–24in tall. They are among the easiest annuals to grow for dried flowers, with double blooms in many colors, and petals that feel straw-like. Dwarf varieties make long-lasting container plants. A half-hardy annual.

CONDITIONS

ASPECT Must have a warm spot in full sun.
SITE Needs very well-drained soil that has been enriched with rotted compost or manure. If growing in containers use multipurpose compost and add slow-release fertilizer. Tall varieties will need staking as they develop.

GROWING METHOD

SOWING Sow seeds in March in $3^{1}/_{2}$in pots of multipurpose compost and germinate at 64°F. Transplant seedlings to cell trays when large enough and grow on, then harden off at the end of May, and plant 6–24in apart depending on the variety. Seed can also be sown direct into short drills in the soil during May and the young plants gradually thinned to the planting distances above. In containers pack 2–3 plants together in groups to get a good block of flower color.

FEEDING

FEEDING *Helichrysum* grows well without extra feeding, but water container-grown plants regularly.
PROBLEMS By late summer the leaves are often attacked by mildew, but it is not worth treating.

FLOWERING

SEASON Flowers appear from early to midsummer.
CUTTING Pick the flowers when the petals are still incurved. Hang the bunches upside down in a dry, airy place to dry out. Long-lasting.

AFTER FLOWERING

GENERAL Cut what you want and then pull up.

HELICHRYSUM PETIOLARE *'Limelight' has pale lime green felty leaves. It is good for lighting up a shaded corner of the garden.*

AT A GLANCE	
A half-hardy annual grown for its long-lasting dried flowers, and also used in bedding and containers. Frost hardy to 32°F (zone10).	
Jan /	**Recommended Varieties**
Feb /	*Helichrysum bracteatum*
Mar sow	**Tall varieties**
Apr transplant/grow	"Drakkar Pastel Mixed"
May harden off/plant	"Monstrosum Double Mixed"
Jun flowering	"Pastel Mixed"
July flowering	"Swiss Giants"
Aug flowering	**Dwarf varieties**
Sept flowers/cutting	"Bright Bikini"
Oct flowers/cutting	"Chico Mixed"
Nov /	"Hot Bikini"
Dec /	

Heliotrope

HELIOTROPIUM

FEATURES

Heliotropium arborescens, also known as cherry pie, is a half-hardy, soft-stemmed, evergreen Peruvian shrub. Growing to 4ft high and across, it is usually bedded out for summer and overwintered in a frost-free greenhouse. A succession of vanilla-fragrant, mauve to purple flowers are borne from summer to the middle of fall, or even longer under glass.

Plant it to spill from a border and on to paving, waterfall from a raised bed or beautify a patio tub. "Lord Roberts," with very dark purple-green leaves and deep violet flowers, is probably the most popular variety.

CONDITIONS

ASPECT Outdoors: Heliotrope needs a warm position sheltered from chilly winds. It flowers best in full sunshine. Under glass: Provide full sun but reduce risk of leaf scorch by shading plants when the temperature rises above 75°F.

SITE Outdoors: The soil should be crumbly and well drained. Enrich thin, sandy patches with humus-forming, well-decayed manure.

GROWING METHOD

FEEDING Outdoors and under glass: liquid feed weekly with a high-potash fertilizer from spring to late summer.

In late summer or early fall, lift and pot up plants bedded out in borders and patio tub plants. Move them to a frost-free greenhouse or conservatory and keep the compost dry until late winter or early spring.

PROPAGATION Heliotrope is easily increased from soft-tip cuttings taken in spring, and semi-ripe cuttings struck in late summer.

PROBLEMS Being half-hardy, this shrub must not be moved outdoors until frosts have finished in late May or early June.

PRUNING

Encourage new flowering stems by shortening a third of older, woody branches by half their length in early spring.

OLD-FASHIONED HELIOTROPE or cherry pie is festooned with spicy-perfumed blooms from early summer until the fall, when chilly nights halt the display.

AT A GLANCE	
Frost-sensitive evergreen with richly fragrant, pink, purple, violet, or white flowers, bedded out for summer. Hardy to 40°F (zone 10).	

		Recommended Varieties
Jan	/	"Dame Alice de Hales"
Feb	/	"Chatsworth"
Mar	/	"Lord Roberts"
Apr	plant, prune	"White Lady"
May	plant, prune	"Netherhall White"
June	flower, plant	"Princess Marina"
July	flower	
Aug	flower	
Sept	flower	
Oct	flower	
Nov	flower	
Dec	/	

Helipterum

EVERLASTING DAISY

FEATURES

The papery flowers of everlasting daisies come mainly in pinks and white. They grow 12–18in tall, and can be used in bedding or cut for dried flower arrangements. In catalogs they are also found listed under acrolinium and rhodanthe. Hardy annual.

CONDITIONS

ASPECT   These Australian natives need full sun.
SITE   *Helipterum* must have perfectly drained soil and does not require special preparation—the best results are obtained on thin and hungry soils that mimic the plant's natural growing conditions. Sheltered hot-spots are best.

GROWING METHOD

SOWING   Sow seeds direct into the soil in short drills ½in deep and 6in apart in April and May. Thin the seedlings as they grow, so plants are eventually 6–12in apart by early summer. Water only during long dry spells, but this is not necessary when flower buds begin to appear.
FEEDING   Do not feed.
PROBLEMS   Plants fail on heavy, wet soils that are slow to warm up in spring, so try growing them in raised beds which have better drainage.

FLOWERING

SEASON   Although the plants flower for only a brief spell the effect is long-lasting because of their "everlasting" nature.
CUTTING   Ideal as cut, dried flower. For the best results cut off whole plants when most of the flowers are still just opening out, and hang upside down in a dry, airy place.

AFTER FLOWERING

GENERAL   Plants sometimes self-seed. Any plants not lifted for drying are pulled up in fall and added to the compost heap.

WHEN PLANTS REACH this stage of growth the entire plant can be harvested and hung up to dry. Individual stems are then cut off.

AT A GLANCE	
A half-hardy annual grown for its pinkish, "papery" flowers that are good for cutting and drying. Frost hardy to 32°F (zone 10).	
Jan /	**Recommended Varieties**
Feb /	*Helipterum* hybrids
Mar /	"Bonny"
Apr sow	"Double Mixed"
May sow/thin	"Goliath"
Jun flowering	"Pierrot"
July flowering	"Special Mixed"
Aug flowers/cutting	
Sept flowers/cutting	
Oct /	
Nov /	
Dec /	

Helleborus

LENTEN ROSE

FEATURES

Various species of hellebores are known as the Christmas or Lenten rose because of their flowering times—mid-winter or early spring. *H. niger*, which has pure white flowers with green centers, can be difficult to grow to perfection; *H. argutifolius* (syn. *H. corsicus*) and *H. orientalis* are more resilient. *H. argutifolius* has lovely lime-green flowers and spiny-toothed leaf margins, while *H. orientalis* is more variable and may have white, green, pink, or mottled flowers. Cultivars include a deep crimson variety. These perennials are mostly evergreen and are best planted under deciduous trees, where they can remain undisturbed. Some are fairly short-lived, but they tend to self-seed freely so that numbers readily increase, creating an impressive sight.

CONDITIONS

ASPECT   Prefers dappled sunlight under trees, or in other partially shaded spots.

SITE   Soil must be well enriched with organic matter, and able to retain moisture. Excellent in winter containers.

GROWING METHOD

PROPAGATION Divide clumps in the spring or summer, directly after flowering, replanting the divisions about 8–12in apart. Seed can be sown when ripe, but seedlings will take about three years to flower. Seedlings often produce interesting shades. Recently planted hellebores need plenty of water in prolonged, dry spells in the spring and summer.

FEEDING   Apply a little complete plant food in the spring. Mulch each spring with manure or compost to aid moisture retention.

PROBLEMS   Leaf blotch can disfigure and weaken plants. Spray with a fungicide. Beware aphids, particularly after flowering. Slugs attack the flowers and foliage.

FLOWERING

SEASON   From mid-winter to early spring.
CUTTING   Lenten roses provide attractive cut flowers at the time of year when supply is short.

AFTER FLOWERING

REQUIREMENTS Prune off the dead flower stems and any dead leaves. Do not disturb.

PRETTY SHADINGS of color are shown on the Lenten rose. Seedlings often produce unexpected colors, which can be maintained if the plants are then propagated by division.

AT A GLANCE	
A free-spreading, attractively flowering perennial in a wide range of colors. Excellent in woodland. Hardy to 23–59°F (zones 9–11).	

		Recommended Varieties
Jan	flowering	*Helleborus argutifolius*
Feb	flowering	(syn. *H. corsicus*)
Mar	flowering	*H. foetidus*
Apr	divide	*H. lividus*
May	transplant	*H. niger*
Jun	/	*H.* x *nigercors*
July	/	*H. orientalis* "Cultivars"
Aug	/	*H.* x *sternii* "Blackthorn Group"
Sept	/	*H. viridis*
Oct	/	
Nov	/	
Dec	/	

Hemerocallis

DAYLILY

FEATURES

Easily grown in a wide range of conditions, the daylily is a trouble-free plant with single or double flowers. As its name suggests, individual flowers last only one day, but they are produced over a long period. They come in a wide range of colors, the main ones being shades of yellow, orange, red, magenta, and purple. There is an enormous number of exciting, attractive hybrids available from specialist growers. The clumps of grassy foliage may be from 10–39in high; some are evergreen while others die down in winter.

While straight species are not as readily available as the hybrids, they are important in hybridizing new varieties and several species are worth seeking out. They include *H. altissima* from China, which has pale yellow fragrant flowers on stems 5ft or so high, and *H. lilio-asphodelus*, which has pale yellow fragrant flowers above leaves 22in high.

CATEGORIES

Daylilies have been divided into five categories which list them according to flower type. The divisions are circular, double, spider-shaped, star-shaped, and triangular. Most are single; hot weather can produce extra petals and stamens.

DWARF FORMS

The number of dwarf forms available is steadily increasing and they may be better suited to today's smaller gardens. Those with a reliable reflowering habit can also be successfully grown in pots. Use a good quality potting mix and crowd three plants into a 8in pot for good effect. "Little Grapette," "Little Gypsy Vagabond," "Penny's Worth," and "Stella d'Oro" are good ones to try, all growing about 12 x 18in.

USES

Mass plantings of dwarf or tall forms create the best effect. Daylilies are not plants that should be dotted about in the garden. Use large numbers of either the one variety or use varieties of similar color; it is clearly preferable to planting a mixture of types or colors. In a mixed border they give a very pleasing effect as the foliage is very full.

CONDITIONS

ASPECT	Grows best in full sun but tolerates semi-shade. Can be mass planted on banks or sloping ground as the roots are very efficient soil binders.
SITE	Grows in any type of soil, wet or dry, but to get maximum growth from the newer hybrids the soil should be enriched with manure or compost before planting.

AT A GLANCE		
A genus of semi-, evergreen, and herbaceous perennials; 30,000 cultivars that give a long summer show. Hardy to 5°F (zone 7).		
Jan	/	Recommended Varieties
Feb	sow	"Burning Daylight"
Mar	sow	"Cartwheels"
Apr	transplant	"Golden Chimes"
May	transplant	"Neyron Rose"
Jun	flowering	"Pink Damask"
July	flowering	"Red Precious"
Aug	flowering	"Stafford"
Sept	flowering	"Whichford"
Oct	divide	"Zara"
Nov	/	
Dec	/	

GROWING METHOD

PROPAGATION Divide established clumps in spring or fall. Cut back foliage before or straight after division. Spacing may be from 6–12in, depending on variety.
New plants need regular watering to establish. Once established, plants are very drought tolerant, but better sized blooms can be expected if deep waterings are given every week or two.

FEEDING Grows without supplementary fertilizer, but an application of complete plant food in early spring encourages stronger, more vigorous growth.

PROBLEMS Daylilies growing in very soggy ground tend to survive quite well but produce few flowers. Otherwise no problems.

FLOWERING

SEASON Depending on variety, plants may be in bloom any time from late spring until the fall. Most flowers only last one day.

CUTTING Single flowers can be cut for the vase. Attractive and well worth using.

AFTER FLOWERING

REQUIREMENTS Cut off any spent flower stems. Herbaceous types that die down in the fall can have their foliage cut back too.

Herb Robert

GERANIUM ROBERTIANUM

FEATURES

A biennial herb, often grown as an annual, Herb Robert may reach a height of 12–18in. It has deeply lobed, toothed leaves which sometimes develop a reddish cast. Pinkish flowers appear in spring in airy clusters. In the wild, the plant is widely distributed in temperate parts of the northern hemisphere. Explosive seed capsules make the plant potentially invasive where the conditions suit it.

CONDITIONS

ASPECT   Full sun or part shade are equally suitable.

SITE   Not particularly fussy about soil types as long as they drain freely. Average garden soil is quite satisfactory.

GROWING METHOD

SOWING   Herb Robert can be grown from seed saved from last year and sown shallowly in spring or from cuttings of basal shoots taken in middle to late spring. Make cuttings about 3in long and insert them into small pots of very sandy potting mix. Keep lightly moist in a warm, bright, but shaded place. Roots should form within a month and the new plants can either be placed in the garden or potted up to grow bigger. Herb Robert will self-seed freely and is considered to be a weed by many gardeners.

FEEDING   Herb Robert does not need a lot of water and in places where summers are mild regular rainfall can be sufficient. If watering is necessary, water deeply once a week rather than giving more frequent light sprinklings. In garden beds that are mulched regularly with well-rotted organic matter, no further fertilizer is needed.

PROBLEMS   The fungus disease rust, which attacks all plants of the *Geranium* and *Pelargonium* genera, can disfigure the foliage and weaken the plant. It appears as yellow spots on the upper surface of the leaf with raised lumps of "rust" underneath. Rust occurs mainly during warm, humid weather. To control it, either pick off affected leaves at the first sign of infection or spray the plant with a fungicide suitable for the condition (the label will tell you). Don't drop or compost any of the affected leaves. They should be burnt or placed into the rubbish bin.

AT A GLANCE	
Traditionally used as a medicinal herb, herb Robert is now often considered a weed. Hardy to 4°F (zone 6).	
Jan /	**Parts used**
Feb plant	Leaves
Mar plant	**Uses**
Apr plant	Medicinal
May plant harvest	Gardening
Jun harvest	
July harvest	
Aug harvest	
Sept harvest	
Oct /	
Nov /	
Dec /	

HARVESTING

PICKING   Leaves are used fresh and may be
picked at any time as required.

STORAGE   Not usually stored.

FREEZING   Not suitable for freezing.

USES

MEDICINAL   Traditionally, herb Robert has been used
to treat a range of complaints as varied
as toothache and conjunctivitis. Caution:
do not use without expert supervision.

GARDENING   Herb Robert plant is pretty enough in its
own right and makes a good addition to
a wild garden.

Heuchera sanguinea

CORAL FLOWER

FEATURES

This perennial forms a low rosette of lobed leaves that make a neat plant for edging, or for mass-planting at the front of the border. The foliage is evergreen. Established plantings produce a striking display of blooms. The flower stems, which stand above the foliage, are from 12 to 18in tall. The species has red flowers; cultivars are available with pink, white, or deeper crimson blooms. Note the superb foliage varieties ("Palace Purple"—chocolate-colored; "Pewter Moon"—gray; and "Snow Storm"—white flecked). New American varieties include "Pewter Veil."

CONDITIONS

ASPECT   Prefers full sun but tolerates light shade.
SITE   Needs very well-drained, open-textured soil. Permanently wet soil will kill this plant.

GROWING METHOD

PROPAGATION Clumps can be divided in the spring or in the fall, but ensure that each division has its own set of healthy roots. It can also be grown from seed sown in the spring; cuttings will also root quite freely. Plant at approximately 8–10in intervals for a good effect.
FEEDING   Apply a complete plant food when growth commences in the spring.
PROBLEMS Vine weevil grubs may devour roots and stems. Destroy the infected clump, and use severed shoots as cuttings.

FLOWERING

SEASON   It flowers well through most of the summer, with a few spikes hanging on until the early fall.
CUTTING   Flowers do not last well as cut blooms.

AFTER FLOWERING

REQUIREMENTS Promptly remove any spent flower stems once they begin to look untidy. Apart from the removal of any dead leaves, this is all that is necessary.

DAINTY LITTLE PINK FLOWERS are massed above the attractive foliage, making the North American coral flower an excellent choice for the front of a border or a garden bed. Here they are planted to provide an excellent foil for the abundant blooms of white roses behind.

AT A GLANCE		
H. sanguinea is a red-flowering, summer perennial forming low, wide clumps, 6 x 12in. Hardy to 5°F (zone 7).		
Jan	/	**Recommended Plants**
Feb	sow	*Heuchera americana*
Mar	sow	"Chocolate Ruffles"
Apr	divide	*H. cylindrica*
May	transplant	"Green Ivory"
Jun	flowering	"Helen Dillon"
July	flowering	"Persian Carpet"
Aug	flowering	"Pewter Moon"
Sept	/	"Rachel"
Oct	divide	"Red Spangles"
Nov	/	"Scintillation"
Dec	/	

Hibiscus

HIBISCUS

FEATURES

Also known as shrubby mallow, this deciduous, late summer statement is festooned with saucer-shaped blooms from July to September. Flowers are single or double and range in color from white, pink and blue, to purple. Several are bicolored. Most popular varieties are violet-blue and white-eyed "Blue Bird," white and crimson-eyed "Hamabo" and rose-pink and dark-centerd "Woodbridge."

Long-lived, it makes an upright bush to 8ft high and across and flowers early in its life. It is very hardy.

CONDITIONS

ASPECT	Hibiscus grows best and flowers prolifically in full sun. Shield it from icy winds. Avoid even light shade, for shoots will not ripen well and so flowering is impaired.
SITE	This shrub thrives on well-drained, fertile, sandy loam but tolerates poorer soils. Enjoy good results by enriching the planting area with plenty of well-rotted organic matter.

GROWING METHOD

FEEDING	Apply all-purpose plant food, such as fish, blood, and bone meal, or Growmore, in spring and again in midsummer.

Water regularly in spring and summer to help newly planted hibiscus recover quickly.

PROPAGATION	Layer whippy shoots from mid-spring to late summer, and take semi-ripe heeled cuttings from late summer to early fall.
PROBLEMS	Control aphids with pirimicarb, horticultural soap, or natural pyrethrins.

PRUNING

Rejuvenate ageing shrubs by shortening them to half their height in spring. This is also the best time to cut back frost-damaged shoots.

HEALTHY AND SELDOM ATTRACTING pests and diseases, hibiscus is best planted in a sunny position so shoots ripen and flower well. A late-summer bonus of exotic, single, or double, saucer-shaped blooms are your reward.

AT A GLANCE		
Deciduous and slow growing, large, saucer-shaped, pink, blue, or white blooms appear in late summer. Hardy to 4°F (zone 7).		
Jan	/	Recommended Varieties
Feb	/	"Blue Bird"
Mar	plant	"Bredon Springs"
Apr	plant, prune	"Hamabo"
May	plant	"Lady Stanley"
June	plant	"Lenny"
July	flower, plant	"Meehanii"
Aug	flower, plant	"Woodbridge"
Sept	flower, plant	"William R. Smith"
Oct	plant	
Nov	plant	
Dec	/	

Hippeastrum

HIPPEASTRUM, AMARYLLIS

FEATURES

There are many species of hippeastrum but the most familiar plants, with their very large, trumpet-shaped flowers, are cultivars or hybrids of a number of species. They are popular winter-flowering house plants; between two and six large flowers are carried on thick stems that are generally over 20in high. Blooms appear all the more spectacular because they appear ahead of the leaves or just as the leaves are emerging. There are many cultivars available but most flowers are in various shades of red, pink, or white, separately or in combination. Because of the very large size of the bulb it is normal to use only one bulb per 7in pot. The bulbs should be allowed to rest during summer if they are to be brought into bloom again.

CONDITIONS

ASPECT   Needs full sun and bright conditions.
SITE   Grow as a pot plant in the home or greenhouse. Use soiless potting compost.

GROWING METHOD

PLANTING   Plant with about half to one-third of the bulb above soil level in a pot just large enough to hold the bulb comfortably. Bulbs can be planted any time between October and March. Use "prepared" bulbs for Christmas and early winter flowers.
FEEDING   Apply a high potash liquid feed every 10–14 days when the bulb starts into growth. Water sparingly until the bud appears, then more freely until the foliage begins to die down.

PROBLEMS   No problems usually, but overwatering can cause the bulb to rot.

FLOWERING

SEASON   Showy flowers appear in about eight weeks after planting, between late December and late spring.
CUTTING   With frequent water changes flowers can last well, but are usually best left on the plant.

AFTER FLOWERING

REQUIREMENTS Remove spent flower stems, continue to water and feed until foliage starts to yellow and die down. Allow the bulbs to dry off in a cool place, repot in fresh compost and resume watering in fall to start them into growth.

BIG, SHOWY TRUMPET FLOWERS on stout stems are a feature of hippeastrums.

AT A GLANCE		
A windowsill plant with very showy, large, trumpet-shaped flowers on tall stems in winter and spring. Minimum 56°F (zone 11).		
Jan	flowering	Recommended Varieties
Feb	flowering	"Apple Blossom"
Mar	flowering	"Bouquet"
Apr	flowering	"Lady Jane"
May	/	"Lucky Strike"
Jun	/	"Mont Blanc"
July	/	"Flower Record"
Aug	/	"Oscar"
Sept	/	"Picotee"
Oct	plant	"Star of Holland"
Nov	plant	
Dec	plant	

Holboellia latifolia

HOLBOELLIA

FEATURES

This unusual spring-flowering evergreen climber is originally a native of Asia, and is particularly at home in the foothills of the Himalaya mountain range. It is not one of the hardiest climbers but it will thrive in gardens in the milder parts of the country if it is provided with a warm and sheltered situation. *Holboellia* is grown just as much for its attractive foliage as for its decorative purple female flowers. When situated in suitable conditions it is a vigorous climber, growing up to 15ft tall. It is suitable for growing on a pergola, arbor or arch, or for growing up a mature tree. A high wall makes another suitable support, as does a trellis screen.

CONDITIONS

ASPECT   Grows in full sun or partial shade. Must provide shelter from wind, which could result in damage to the plant.

SITE   Any well-drained yet moisture-retentive soil that contains plenty of humus.

GROWING METHOD

PROPAGATION   Sow seeds in the spring and germinate in a temperature of 61˚F. Take semi-ripe cuttings in late summer. Layer stems in spring.

WATERING   If the soil starts to become excessively dry in summer, water the plant well.

FEEDING   In the spring each year apply a slow-release organic fertilizer, such as blood, fish, and bone.

PROBLEMS   Not troubled by pests or diseases.

FLOWERING/FOLIAGE

FLOWERS   Male flowers are green-white, female flowers are purple. Both are borne on the same plant. Long red or purple fruits may follow, but cannot be guaranteed.

FOLIAGE   Deep green, consisting of elliptical leaflets.

PRUNING

REQUIREMENTS Needs no regular pruning but you can, if desired, shorten side shoots to six buds in summer, as these tend to be vigorous and spread outward. Or just trim the plant in summer to fit allotted space.

THE GLOSSY EYE-SHAPED leaves of Holboellia latifolia *are a principal attraction of this appealing climber. Hanging in gentle cascades from a house wall,* H. latifolia *creates a verdure of pleasant sun-catching foliage.*

AT A GLANCE	
Spring-flowering evergreen climber with purple flowers and handsome deep green foliage. Hardy to 23˚F (zone 9).	
Jan foliage	**Companion Plants**
Feb foliage	Makes a good partner for
Mar planting	spring-flowering clematis.
Apr flowering	
May flowering	
Jun foliage	
July foliage	
Aug foliage	
Sep foliage	
Oct foliage	
Nov foliage	
Dec foliage	

Honeysuckle

LONICERA

FEATURES

A trio of sweetly scented, bushy honeysuckles worth cultivating are: *Lonicera fragrantissima*, with its vanilla-perfumed, creamy-white, bell-shaped blooms, which are freely borne on twiggy shoots to 6ft from January to March; slightly smaller *L.* x *purpusii*, which treats us to a similar display from November to March; and *L. syringantha*, with its profusion of clustered, lilac flowers on 3ft stems from late spring to early summer.

Twining varieties, trained to frame a door or clothe a wall, fence, arbour, pergola, or arch or to scramble through a tree, enhance a garden.

Color spring by planting yellow and red *L. periclymenum* "Belgica" and continue the show—from June to October—with white and red *L. p.* "Serotina."

CONDITIONS

ASPECT   Plant lonicera in full or lightly dappled shade to grow strongly and flower freely.

SITE   These shrubs and climbers prefer well-drained and humus-rich, sandy loam, or clay loam but also tolerate chalky soil. Improve light soils, which dry out quickly, by working in bulky organic materials well before planting.

GROWING METHOD

FEEDING   Speed robust growth and a panoply of blossom by enriching the root area with bone meal in spring and fall. Water liberally to encourage young plants to establish quickly. Once growing strongly, all varieties are unstressed by droughty periods. In spring, mulch thickly with humus-forming organics to keep roots cool and questing and encourage a fine display of blossom.

PROPAGATION   Shrubs: Take hardwood cuttings in late fall or early winter, or layer whippy stems from mid-spring to late summer. Climbers: Take semi-ripe cuttings from early to midsummer.

PROBLEMS   Blackfly are attracted to new shoots, which they quickly smother. Control them with pirimicarb, natural pyrethrins, bifenthrin, or horticultural soap.

PRUNING

Keep winter-flowering *L. fragrantissima* and *L.* x *purpusii* shapely and full of young shoots, which flower freely, by removing one stem in three in mid-spring. Help spring- and early summer-blooming *L. syringantha* prosper by cutting back flowered shoots to new growth when blooms fade. Prune *L. periclymenum* varieties and *L. japonica* "Halliana" by shortening flowered stems to new shoots when blooms fade.

AT A GLANCE		
Semi-evergreen bushes and deciduous and evergreen climbers light up spring, summer and winter. Hardy to -13°F (zone 5).		
Jan	flower	Recommended Varieties
Feb	flower	Bushes
Mar	plant	*L. fragrantissima*
Apr	flower, prune	*L.* x *purpusii*
May	flower, prune	*L. syringantha*
June	flower, prune	*L. tartarica*
July	flower, plant	Climbers
Aug	flower, prune	"Belgica"
Sept	flower, prune	*L. heckrottii*
Oct	plant	"Goldflame"
Nov	plant	"Serotina"
Dec	/	*L. japonica*
		"Halliana"
		L. tragophylla

Hosta
PLANTAIN LILY

FEATURES

Also known as the plantain lily, this herbaceous perennial is grown for its attractive, decorative foliage. It is long-lived, and foliage may be tiny or up to 18in wide and 36in high. There are hundreds of cultivars with leaves that may be light or dark green, chartreuse or yellow, gray-green or blue. Many are variegated. Leaf texture also varies: it can be smooth or shiny, matt or powdery, puckered or corrugated. Hostas are excellent at forming big, bold clumps that keep down the weeds, but until they emerge in late spring some weeding will be necessary; they also benefit from heavy mulching. Hostas look best mass-planted near water features, or when allowed to multiply in shady areas under trees.

VARIEGATIONS

Cultivars with cream, white, or yellow variegations will brighten a shady part of the yard, and so long as the tree or shrub canopy is high enough to let sufficient light reach the hostas, they will maintain their variegation. Likewise, plants with sharp chartreuse or acid-lime-colored foliage can be used to give a lift to shady areas. Types can be mixed to create a wealth of different effects.

FLOWERS

The bell-shape flowers, mostly in mauve shades, appear in the summer and are held high above the foliage.

Some species, such as *H. plantaginea* and its cultivar "Grandiflora," produce pure white, lightly fragrant flowers. However, few gardeners plant hostas just for the flowers; the leaves alone are good enough.

COMPANIONS

Since hostas do not come into leaf early in the spring, the early-flowering bulbs, such as snowdrops and snowflakes, or early perennials, such as corydalis, can be planted among them. They make a bright, successful show.

CONDITIONS

ASPECT   Most hostas grow in full sunlight if well watered. They thrive in shade or dappled light. Blue-leaved forms can be the hardest of all to place because they turn green with either too much sun or too heavy shade. Yellow or gold forms are best with direct sunlight in the early morning or late in the afternoon.

AT A GLANCE		
A mainly clump-forming perennial from the Far East. Grow in pots or the garden for the foliage. Hardy to 0°F (zones 6–7).		
Jan	/	Recommended Varieties
Feb	/	"Aureomarginata"
Mar	sow	"Blue Angel"
Apr	divide	"Francee"
May	transplant	"Frances Williams"
Jun	flowering	"Golden Tiara"
July	flowering	"Love Pat"
Aug	divide	*H. lancifolia*
Sept	flowering	"Shade Fanfare"
Oct	/	"Wide Brim"
Nov	/	
Dec	/	

SITE Needs rich, moisture-retentive soil. Large amounts of decayed manure or compost should be dug into the ground before planting. Mulch plants after planting. Superb in tubs, getting bigger and better each year.

GROWING METHOD

PROPAGATION Divide the fleshy underground rhizomes in early spring. Most hostas are best divided every four to five years. Plant the dwarf cultivars 6in apart, the larger ones at intervals of 36in. Several species can be raised from seed, though they may not be true to type.

FEEDING Apply pelletted poultry manure in the spring.

PROBLEMS Slugs and snails can be a major problem. Pick off snails, and avoid watering in the evening. Place slug pellets or sharp sand around the leaves.

FLOWERING

SEASON Flowers are produced in the summer. The color range varies from white to purple.

CUTTING Hosta provides cut flowers; the foliage is also attractive.

AFTER FLOWERING

REQUIREMENTS Cut off any spent flower stems in the spring. Continue watering the plants until the foliage begins to die down, and then tidy up the clumps, which can look unsightly. Mulch the area with supplies of compost or manure. Some hostas (sieboldiana) produce good fall tints. The seedheads can be left on for winter decoration.

Hosta "Francee"

PLANTAIN LILY

FEATURES

Every garden has room for a hosta. They are grown for their marvelous, decorative foliage which provides shade for the frogs and keeps down the weeds. "Francee" stands out with its white margined leaves. Grow it with different colored hostas like the bluish-leaved "Hadspen Blue," which makes a neat, dense clump. "Frances Williams" is blue-green with a yellowish margin. And "Patriot" is another excellent white-edged hosta if you cannot get hold of "Francee." They can also be mass planted near water features, or just allowed to multiply in the shade under trees. With room for one only, try growing it in a pot, topping the soil with pebbles to set it off.

CONDITIONS

ASPECT   Most hostas grow in full sun if well watered. They also thrive in shade or dappled light. The blue-leaved kind are the hardest to place because they turn green with too much or too little shade. The yellow forms are best with direct sun either early or late in the day.

SITE   Provide rich, moisture-retentive soil. Add well-decayed manure to the ground before planting, and mulch afterwards. Avoid dry, free-draining, infertile ground.

GROWING METHOD

PROPAGATION Divide the fleshy rhizomes in early spring. Most hostas perform best if they are divided every four to five years.

FEEDING   Apply scatterings of pelleted poultry manure in the spring.

PROBLEMS   The chief enemies of these plants are slugs and snails which can devastate the incredibly attractive foliage. Spread sharp sand around the plants to deter intruders and use traps or bait.

FLOWERING

SEASON   The white or pale violet flower spikes are interesting and usually appear in the summer, but the chief attraction has to be the foliage.

PRUNING

GENERAL   Not necessary.

THE MAIN ATTRACTION of the hostas in general are their variegated foliage, especially this H. "Francee" with its white edges.

AT A GLANCE	
Hosta "Francee" is a vigorous, clump-forming perennial that provides marvellous groundcover. Hardy to 0˚F (zone 7).	

		Recommended Varieties
Jan	/	*Hosta*
Feb	/	
Mar	/	"Aureomarginata"
April	foliage	H. "Blue Angel"
May	foliage	H. "Francee"
June	foliage	H. "Frances Williams"
July	flowering	H. "Golden Tiara"
Aug	foliage	H. "Love Pat"
Sept	foliage	H. "Patriot"
Oct	foliage	H. "Shade Fanfare"
Nov	/	H. "Wide Brim"
Dec	/	

Houttuynia cordata

HOUTTUYNIA

FEATURES

This is a groundcover plant for marshy, damp, cool parts of the garden, and can even grow in shallow water. In the right conditions the species makes a decent spreader, and can in fact become quite invasive. Its two most distinguishing features are that it has marvelously scented leaves, with the aroma of citrus fruit, and these turn reddish in the fall. There are two good forms, slightly less invasive than the species, "Chameleon" and "Flore Pleno." The first has fantastically eyecatching foliage. It has four colors, bronze, red, yellow, and dark green. The second, which is much harder to find, has white cones of petals. A highly useful plant.

CONDITIONS

ASPECT   *Houttuynia* grows in both full sun and light shade. "Chameleon" gets better colored leaves in the sun, where its colors look much more marked. Do not waste it in the shade.

SITE   The soil needs to be on the damp side, and rich with plenty of· well-rotted organic matter.

GROWING METHOD

PROPAGATION It is unlikely that you will ever need to propagate *H. cordata*, given how well it spreads, but you can easily make extra plants. Divide the plant in the spring, or take cuttings at the same time of year. The new growth quickly takes.

FEEDING   It is unlikely to need extra nutrients if grown in the right conditions.

PROBLEMS   Apart from being attacked by slugs and snails, the only problem you might encounter is when trying to grow it in a basket in the water. It will need regular potting up to stop it bursting out of the container.

FLOWERING

SEASON   The flowers appear in the spring, and show up well against the foliage.

PRUNING

GENERAL   This is rarely necessary. Use a spade to slice off any unwanted, excess spread.

DECORATIVE VARIEGATED LEAVES splashed with cream and brilliant red are the most striking feature of the cultivar "Chameleon".

AT A GLANCE	
Houttuynia cordata is an excellent stream-side plant that spreads well and provides fresh white spring flowers.	
Jan /	**Companion Plants**
Feb /	Camassia
Mar /	Euphorbia
April foliage	Francoa
May flowering	Gentiana
June foliage	Gunnera
July foliage	Heuchera
Aug foliage	Hosta
Sept foliage	Iris
Oct foliage	Ligularia
Nov foliage	Lychnis
Dec /	

Howea forsteriana

KENTIA PALM, THATCH LEAF PALM

FEATURES

A native of Australia—Lord Howe Island—this is a particularly graceful palm with feathery, gently arching leaves. The slender trunk supports pinnate mid- to deep green leaves that are carried on long stalks and reach 6–10ft in length. This palm will eventually attain a height of up to 60ft, with a spread of 20ft. However, it is fairly slow growing and is therefore good for a container. Potting on or repotting is needed only infrequently. It is suited to a warm greenhouse or conservatory and small specimens are suitable for use as houseplants.

CONDITIONS

ASPECT — Provide bright light, but direct sun may scorch the foliage. Provide moderate humidity. Outdoors place in a sheltered position.

SITE — In containers grow in soil-based potting compost with leafmould and shredded bark.

GROWING METHOD

PROPAGATION — Sow seeds as soon as available and germinate them at a temperature of 79°F.

WATERING — Moderate watering in growing season from late spring to late summer, for the rest of the year water sparingly.

FEEDING — Apply a balanced liquid fertilizer monthly during the growing season.

PROBLEMS — Under glass may be attacked by red spider mites and scale insects.

FOLIAGE/FLOWERING

FOLIAGE — This evergreen palm looks good all year but is especially attractive in spring and summer.

FLOWERS — Clusters of star-shaped flowers are produced in summer, the females green, the males light brown, followed by orange-red fruits.

GENERAL CARE

REQUIREMENTS Remove dead fronds when necessary by cutting them off close to the trunk.

THE SLOW GROWTH of Howea forsteriana *makes it a suitable candidate for indoor cultivation. It makes an elegant feature. The fine lines running along the length of* H. forsteriana's *leaves contribute to the general appearance of this graceful palm.*

AT A GLANCE	
A very slender stem supports almost horizontal feathery leaves. Provide a minimum temperature of 59°F (zone 11).	
Jan /	Companion Plants
Feb /	Under glass it associates
Mar planting	well with other palms
Apr planting foliage	requiring the same
May foliage	conditions. Also try
Jun flowering	combining this palm with
July flowering	tropical foliage plants such
Aug flowering	as philodendrons and
Sep /	*Monstera deliciosa.*
Oct /	
Nov /	
Dec /	

Hyacinthoides

BLUEBELL

FEATURES

This is the ideal bulb for naturalizing under deciduous trees or for planting in large drifts in the yard. The delicately scented blue flowers are a great foil for many spring-flowering shrubs which have pink or white flowers: there is a white and a pink form but the blue is undoubtedly the most popular. The botanical names of these plants have undergone several changes in recent years, and they are sometimes listed under endymion and scilla as well as hyacinthoides. The Spanish bluebell (*H. hispanica*) is a little larger, up to 12in high, and more upright in growth than the English bluebell (*H. non-scripta*). Bluebells multiply rapidly and can be very invasive. They can also be grown in containers.

CONDITIONS

ASPECT   These woodland plants prefer dappled sunlight or places where they receive some morning sun with shade later in the day.

SITE   Perfect when naturalized under deciduous trees; bluebells also grow well in borders but don't let them smother delicate plants. A moisture-retentive soil with plenty of organic matter suits them best.

GROWING METHOD

PLANTING   Plant bulbs 2in deep and about 3–4in apart in late summer or early fall. The white bulbs are fleshy and brittle; take care not to damage them when planting.

FEEDING   Not usually required.

PROBLEMS   No specific problems are usually experienced.

FLOWERING

SEASON   Flowers from middle to late spring, with a long display in cool seasons. Flowers do not last as well if sudden high spring temperatures are experienced.

CUTTING   Not suitable for cutting.

AFTER FLOWERING

REQUIREMENTS Remove spent flower stems unless you require plants to seed themselves. Keep the soil moist until the foliage dies down. The bulbs are best left undisturbed, but overcrowded clumps can be lifted and divided in late summer and replanted immediately.

AN ALL-TIME FAVORITE, clear sky-blue bluebells don't need a lot of attention to produce a beautiful display year after year.

AT A GLANCE		
Well-known and loved blue flowers in mid to late spring, ideal for naturalizing under deciduous trees.		
Jan	/	Recommended Varieties
Feb	/	*Hyacinthoides hispanica*
Mar	/	"Danube"
Apr	flowering	"Queen of the Pinks"
May	flowering	"White City"
Jun	/	*Hyacinthoides non-scripta*
July	/	"Pink Form"
Aug	plant	"White Form"
Sept	plant	
Oct	plant	
Nov	/	
Dec	/	

Hyacinthus orientalis

HYACINTH

FEATURES

Sweet-scented hyacinths are favorites in the garden or as potted plants. In the garden they look their best mass-planted in blocks of one color. They are widely grown commercially both for cut flowers and as potted flowering plants. Flower stems may be from 6–12in high and the color range includes various shades of blue, pink, and rose, and white, cream and yellow. Individual flowers are densely crowded onto the stem, making a solid-looking flowerhead. Bulbs usually flower best in their first year, the second and subsequent years producing fewer, looser blooms. Some people with sensitive skin can get a reaction from handling hyacinth bulbs, so wear gloves if you think you may be affected.

TYPES

The most popular hyacinths are the so-called Dutch hybrids; many varieties are available from garden centers and mail order bulb suppliers. Blues range from deep violet to pale china blue: the rose range includes deep rosy red, salmon, and light pink. As well as white varieties, there are those with cream and clear yellow flowers. Some varieties have flowers with a lighter eye or a deeper colored stripe on the petals, giving a two-tone effect.
Roman hyacinths—*H. orientalis albulus*—have smaller flowers loosely arranged on the stems: Multiflora varieties have been treated so that they produce several loosely packed flower spikes from each bulb, and have a delicate appearance that makes them ideal for growing in pots. *Cynthella hyacinths* are miniatures growing to about 6in, usually sold in color mixtures.

CONDITIONS

ASPECT	Does well in sun or partial shade but does not like heavy shade.
SITE	Grow hyacinths in pots and bowls indoors; pots and tubs outside and in flower borders. Soil must be well-drained.

GROWING METHOD

PLANTING	Plant bulbs 6in deep and 8in apart in early to mid-fall. Apply compost or rotted manure as a mulch after planting.
FEEDING	Apply a balanced general fertilizer after flowering. Watering is not usually necessary in beds and borders, but bulbs in containers must be kept just moist during the growing season.
PROBLEMS	Hyacinths are not generally susceptible to pest and disease problems, though bulbs will rot if soil conditions are too wet. Forced bulbs indoors often fail to flower if they have not had the correct cold, dark period after planting.

AT A GLANCE

Sweetly scented, densely packed flower spikes, ideal for growing indoors or outside. Frost hardy.

		Recommended Varieties
Jan	flowering	"Amsterdam"
Feb	flowering	"Anna Marie"
Mar	flowering	"Blue Giant"
Apr	flowering	"City of Haarlem"
May	/	"Delft Blue"
Jun	/	"Gipsy Queen"
July	/	"Jan Bos"
Aug	/	"L'Innocence"
Sept	plant	"Lord Balfour"
Oct	plant	"Mont Blanc"
Nov	/	"Queen of the Pinks"
Dec	flowering	

FLOWERING

SEASON Flowers appear from late winter to mid-spring. "Prepared" bulbs should be used for Christmas flowering, and must be planted in September.

CUTTING Blooms may be cut for the vase where they will last about a week if the water is changed daily.

AFTER FLOWERING

REQUIREMENTS Remove spent flower stems and continue to water and feed the plants until the foliage starts to yellow and die down.

POTTED HYACINTHS

FEATURES Potted hyacinths in bloom make a lovely cut flower substitute and are ideal as gifts. They can be grown to flower in midwinter when their color and fragrance are most welcome.

OUTDOORS If growing hyacinths outdoors choose a container at least 6in deep so that you can place a layer of potting compost in the base of the pot before planting. Bury the bulbs 4in below the surface of the compost. Water to moisten the compost thoroughly after planting and place the pot where it will receive sun for at least half a day. Don't water again until the compost is feeling dry or until the shoots appear. When the flower buds are showing color, move the pots indoors. When blooms have faded, cut off spent stems and water as needed until the foliage dies down.

INDOORS If growing hyacinths indoors, choose a container 4–6in deep but plant the bulbs just below the surface of the compost. (In pots without drainage holes, bulb fiber can be used intead of compost.) Water after planting, allow to drain and then transfer the pot to a cool, dark position. The pots can be placed inside a black plastic bag and put into a shed, cold frame or similar place with a temperature of about 40°F. Check from time to time to see if shoots have emerged. When shoots emerge (this usually takes about 10–12 weeks) and reach 1–2in in height, bring the pot into the light, gradually increasing the amount of light as the shoots green up. As buds appear, give them as much sunlight as possible.

IN GLASS Hyacinths can also be grown in a glass or ceramic container that has a narrow neck. Sometimes you can buy a purpose-built container, usually plastic, that has the top cut into segments so that the bulb sits neatly on it. Fill the container with water to just below the rim. Choose a good-sized bulb, then rest it on top of the rim of the container so that the base of the bulb is in water. Place the container in a cool, dark place and leave it there until large numbers of roots have formed and the flower bud is starting to emerge, when they can be brought into the light. These bulbs are unlikely to regrow and may be discarded after flowering.

Hydrangea

HYDRANGEA

FEATURES

Brightly studded with large, globular, mushroom-headed, or broadly conical flowers, hydrangeas richly color borders from July to September. Blooms come in white and shades of pink, blue, or red. Long-lived, this deciduous shrub grows 20in–8ft high and across.

Most widely grown are aptly named mophead and lacecap varieties of *Hydrangea macrophylla*. Yielding pink, mauve, or red blooms on alkaline soils and blue heads in acid conditions, they thrive in fertile ground. Characteristically, lacecaps have an outer ring of large, sterile flowers enclosing tiny, pink, or blue, fertile ones. Other choice kinds are white, football-headed *H. arborescens* "Annabelle" and light pink, cone-flowered *H. paniculata* "Pink Diamond."

H. quercifolia has oak-leaved foliage which complement trusses of rich creamy flowers and *H. villosa* is a gem with porcelain-blue mushrooms poised above stems clad with huge, velvety leaves.

A self-clinging climber, white, disc-flowered *H. petiolaris* beautifully transforms a cold, north-facing wall.

CONDITIONS

ASPECT	Dappled sunlight or morning sun and afternoon shade suit hydrangeas. Make sure they are sheltered from frosty winds, which will damage embryo blossoms. *H. macrophylla* varieties are reliable seaside plants for relatively frost-free areas.
SITE	These shrubs need damp soil high in organic matter, so improve poor areas by digging in plenty of well-decayed manure or compost a few months ahead of planting. Also mulch plants with well-rotted organic matter.

GROWING METHOD

FEEDING	Apply acidifying fertilizer like sulphate of ammonia in spring and midsummer to ensure a steady release of plant foods and encourage blue flowers.
PROPAGATION	Multiply favoured varieties by layering flexible shoots from mid-spring to late summer. Take soft-tip cuttings from late spring to early summer and semi-ripe cuttings from mid- to late summer.
PROBLEMS	Excessive lime prevents chlorophyll from forming and causes leaves to yellow and die. Overcome it by applying iron chelates.

PRUNING

H. macrophylla: Cut off spent flowers in spring and remove crowding shoots.

H. paniculata: Prune stems to within two buds of the base in late March.

H. petiolaris: Cut out unwanted shoots when flowers fade.

H. villosa: Remove a third of older stems in spring.

AT A GLANCE		
Deciduous shrubs bearing large heads of white, pink, red, or blue flowers from mid- to late summer. Hardy to 4°F (zone 7).		
Jan	/	**Recommended Varieties**
Feb	/	**Mopheads**
Mar	plant, prune	"Hamburgh"
Apr	plant, prune	"Madame E. Moullière"
May	plant	**Lacecaps**
June	plant	"Blue Wave"
July	flower, plant	"White Wave"
Aug	flower, plant	*H. arborescens* "Annabelle"
Sept	flower, plant	*H. paniculata* "Kyushu"
Oct	plant	*H. quercifolia*
Nov	plant	*H. villosa*
Dec	/	

Hymenocallis

SPIDER LILY, PERUVIAN DAFFODIL

FEATURES

Spider lilies are native to various parts of North and South America. They produce broad, strap-shaped, deep green leaves and fascinating, lightly fragrant flowers that are carried on a stout stem. The flower has a trumpet-shaped central cup with long, narrow, petal-like segments surrounding it; flowers are usually white but can be yellow or cream.

Hymenocallis can be grown in a sheltered, sunny position outside, but is often treated as a greenhouse or conservatory plant. All spider lilies can be container grown. *H. x festalis*, *H. narcissiflora* and the cultivar "Sulfur Queen" are the deciduous varieties most often grown, while the more difficult to find *H. littoralis* and *H. speciosa* are the most popular of the evergreen species. *Hymenocallis* is sometimes also listed as ismene.

CONDITIONS

ASPECT   Grows in full sun or light shade with shelter from strong wind.

SITE   In sheltered yards hymenocallis can be grown outside in beds and borders or containers. In cold areas, it is best grown as a greenhouse or conservatory plant. Soil must be free-draining. Use soil-less potting compost for pots.

GROWING METHOD

PLANTING   For growing in containers, plant bulbs in spring with the neck of the bulb just below the soil surface, using one of the large bulbs per 6in pot. Outdoors, plant in May, burying the bulbs 5in deep.

FEEDING   High potash liquid fertilizer can be applied as buds form. Mulching around plants with well-rotted organic matter also supplies nutrients. Water sparingly until the shoots show, then water regularly through the growing season.

PROBLEMS   No specific problems are usually experienced.

FLOWERING

SEASON   The fragrant spider lilies are produced in early summer indoors, mid to late summer outside.

CUTTING   Makes a delightful and unusual cut flower.

AFTER FLOWERING

REQUIREMENTS   Allow the foliage to die down after flowering; lift outdoor bulbs and store in dry peat in a frost-free place over winter. Leave potted plants dry in their containers over winter and repot the following spring.

AT A GLANCE	
A rather tender bulb bearing unusual fragrant blooms like exotic daffodils. Can also be grown as a conservatory plant.	
Jan /	**Recommended Varieties**
Feb /	"Advance"
Mar plant (indoors)	"Sulfur Queen"
Apr /	*Hymenocallis* x *festalis*
May (outdoors)/flowering	"Zwanenburg"
Jun flowering	
July /	
Aug flowering	
Sept /	
Oct /	
Nov /	
Dec /	

Hyssop
HYSSOPUS OFFICINALIS

FEATURES

A semi-evergreen sub-shrub growing 24–32in tall, hyssop has many erect stems clothed in narrow, lanceolate, sage green leaves. Spikes of small flowers appear on top of each stem in summer. Usually these flowers are blue-violet but they may also be pink or white. The whole plant exudes a pungent aroma and the leaves have a bitter taste.

CONDITIONS

ASPECT   Full sun produces compact growth and the strongest flavour but hyssop tolerates shade for part of the day.

SITE   Likes light, fertile, well-drained soils but will grow in any reasonably fertile soil as long as it drains freely.

GROWING METHOD

SOWING   Hyssop can be grown from seed, softwood cuttings or division of the roots. Sow seeds in spring in trays of seed compost. Cover lightly, keep moist, and when seedlings are big enough to handle, prick out into small, individual pots to grow on. Plant out about 12in apart when plants are about 8in tall. Take 3in cuttings in early summer and insert into pots of sandy potting mix. Keep moist and in bright, sheltered shade and roots will form within a month. To divide, lift an established plant in late fall or early spring. Cut the root mass into several smaller sections, each with its own roots. Replant immediately.

FEEDING   Keep soil moist, especially during the warmer months but do not overwater. Hyssop is a resilient plant that can often get by on rain. A ration of balanced general fertilizer in spring when new growth appears is enough.

PROBLEMS   No particular problems.

PRUNING   When new growth begins in spring, pinching out the tips of young stems will encourage the plant to become more bushy and thus produce more flowers. Trim after flowering to maintain shape.

HARVESTING

PICKING   Flowers for using fresh or for drying are picked when in full bloom and individual stems can be harvested as needed.

STORAGE   Cut bunches of flowering stems, tie them together and hang them upside down in a dim, airy place. When they are dry, crumble them into airtight jars.

FREEZING   Not suitable for freezing.

AT A GLANCE		
A decorative semi-evergreen shrub with narrow green leaves and spikes of blue flowers. Hardy to 4°F (zone 6).		
Jan	/	**Parts used**
Feb	/	Leaves
Mar	plant	Stems
Apr	plant	Flowers
May	plant harvest	**Uses**
Jun	plant harvest	Culinary
July	harvest	Medicinal
Aug	harvest	Cosmetic
Sept	plant harvest	Gardening
Oct	plant	
Nov	/	
Dec	/	

USES

CULINARY One or two fresh leaves, finely chopped and added late, give an appealing piquancy to soups and casseroles while fresh flowers can be used to add flavour and color to salads.

MEDICINAL Tea, made by infusing the dried stems, leaves, and flowers in boiling water, is taken to relieve the symptoms of colds; hyssop leaves are often a component in mixed herbal tonics and teas. Caution: do not use during pregnancy or for nervous people. Avoid strong doses and do not use continuously for long periods.

COSMETIC Oil distilled from hyssop is used in perfumes and other commercial cosmetics. At home, it may be added to bath water, and cooled hyssop leaf tea is a cleansing, refreshing facial rinse.

GARDENING Hyssop is a decorative plant and very attractive to bees and butterflies. Use it in a border of mixed flowers or grow it as an edging to paths.

I

Iberis

CANDYTUFT

FEATURES

Very decorative plants that grow no more than 12in tall, varieties of *Iberis umbellata*, a hardy annual, have sweet-scented flowers in white, pink, mauve, red, and purple. They produce good results even in poor soils and quickly self-seed so you get new plants springing up every year, which are at home growing in-between paving and in gravel drives.

CONDITIONS

ASPECT   Iberis prefers an open spot in full sun.

SITE   Although happy in poor soil, adding rotted manure or compost before planting will help keep moisture in and reduce the need for extra watering during summer.

GROWING METHOD

SOWING   Seed is sown outdoors in March/April where the plants are to flower. Mark out circular patches of ground with sand and make short parallel drills $^{1}/_{2}$in deep inside the circle, spaced 6in apart. Sow seeds thinly in these drills and cover with raked soil. Seedlings appear in 2–3 weeks and should be thinned out so they are 3–6in apart by early summer. Can also be sown in September for earlier flowers.

FEEDING   Extra feeding is not necessary. Watering in early summer will stop plants flowering before they achieve a good size.

PROBLEMS   Being relatives of brassicas like cabbage, they can suffer from clubroot disease. Treatment is not worthwhile, but to continue to enjoy candytuft where clubroot is present, sow a pinch of seed in $3^{1}/_{2}$in pots of multi-purpose compost in early spring and plant out clumps in early summer. Disease-free roots will support the plants and let them flower.

FLOWERING

SEASON   Flowers will appear from early summer.

CUTTING   Good cut flower. Flowers that are well-formed but not over-mature should last well if picked early in the day and immediately plunged into water to soak before arranging.

AFTER FLOWERING

GENERAL   Plants can be cut down after flowering, given a good soak with liquid feed, and they will usually produce a second "flush" of flowerheads several weeks later. Candytuft self-seeds very easily so leave a few plants to die away naturally and scatter their seeds. Seed can also be collected for sowing the following spring.

AT A GLANCE	
Iberis is a hardy annual grown for its heads of bright, scented flowers which are used in bedding. Frost hardy to 5°F (zone 7).	
Jan /	**Recommended Varieties**
Feb /	*Iberis umbellata*
Mar sow	"Dwarf Fairy Mixed"
Apr sow	"Fantasia Mixed"
May thin out	"Flash Mixed"
Jun flowering	"Spangles"
July flowering	
Aug flowering	
Sept sow	
Oct /	
Nov /	
Dec /	

Ilex aquifolium

HOLLY

FEATURES

Evergreen holly makes a hardy, long-lived hedge. The glossy green leaves are spiny in most varieties and there are many cultivars available, some with cream or gold variegated foliage. Male and female flowers are usually borne on separate plants, and a brilliant display of scarlet or orange berries follows on the female plants. Left unpruned, holly grows into a fairly large tree but it is often hedged at about 10ft high or less. It makes an extremely good windbreak hedge, and also tolerates air pollution.

CONDITIONS

ASPECT	Prefers a sunny spot. Variegated kinds look best in sun, where the colors really stand out.
SITE	These plants will need well-drained soil enriched with plenty of organic matter. Heavy clay soil must be broken up and lightened with horticultural sand and grit.

GROWING METHOD

PROPAGATION	To grow large numbers of plants, clean and sow the ripened berries, but to maintain the purity of cultivars grow them from semi-ripe cuttings taken in the summer. Use a hormone rooting powder to increase the success rate.
SPACING	Plant at 3ft intervals for hedging.
FEEDING	Apply complete plant food in early spring.
PROBLEMS	Holly has few problems but keep an eye out for aphids which can attack young shoots.

FLOWERING

SEASON	The small, creamy flowers are borne in late spring and early summer.
BERRIES	The flowers are followed by berries which ripen through fall, hanging on through winter. Note that the form called "Silver Queen" and "Golden Queen" are actually male, and that the otherwise excellent, self-pollinating "J. C. van Tol" does not actually make the best hedge.

PRUNING

GENERAL	Main pruning is done in late winter but wayward growth can be trimmed off at other times as well. To make a formal holly hedge you may need to prune two or three times during the growing season, depending on the vigor of the growth.

AT A GLANCE		
Ilex aquifolium has many excellent forms making marvellous, dense, free-berrying hedges. Hardy to 0°F (zone 7).		
Jan	foliage	**Recommended Varieties**
Feb	foliage	*Ilex aquifolium*
Mar	foliage	"Argentea Marginata"
April	foliage	"Ferox"
May	flowering	"Golden Queen"
June	flowering	"Handsworth New Silver"
July	foliage	"Silver Queen"
Aug	foliage	*I. cornuta*
Sept	foliage	"Burfordii"
Oct	foliage	*I. crenata*
Nov	foliage	
Dec	foliage	

Impatiens

BUSY LIZZIE

FEATURES

Impatiens perform well in sun or shade and a huge range is available. Use in bedding, tubs, windowboxes, hanging baskets, and flower bags. As well as busy lizzies, there are also the larger "New Guinea" types (12in), and the "balsams," with bushy growth (10in). Busy lizzies grow from 6–12in tall and wide depending on variety. All impatiens are half-hardy annuals, and raising from seed requires some care. Widely available as young plants by mail order, they can also be bought ready-grown in spring. Flowers can be single or double in mixed or various colors.

CONDITIONS

ASPECT   Will succeed in full sun or moderate shade.

SITE   Soil should have rotted manure or compost mixed in before planting, and should be well-drained. Avoid planting in windy spots. In containers and baskets use multipurpose compost with slow-release fertilizer added.

GROWING METHOD

SOWING   In late February/March sow seeds onto a fine layer of vermiculite in $3^1/2$in pots of seed compost. Tap to settle but do not cover. Seal in a clear plastic bag or put in a heated propagator, in a bright place at 70–75°F. Seedlings appear in 2–3 weeks and are transplanted to cell trays when 1in tall. Grow on, then harden off and plant out after frosts, 6–12in apart.

FEEDING   Apply liquid feed weekly to beds or containers using a hand-held feeder.

PROBLEMS   Damping off disease attacks seedlings. Use clean pots, fresh compost, and treat with a copper-based fungicide if seedlings collapse.

FLOWERING

SEASON   Flowers appear on young plants before planting and then throughout summer. Take off dead flowers to keep new ones coming.

CUTTING   Not suitable as a cut flower.

AFTER FLOWERING

GENERAL   Remove when plants are past their best.

AT A GLANCE		
A half-hardy annual grown for its flowers for bedding, containers, and hanging planters. Frost hardy to 32°F (zone 10).		
Jan	/	**Recommended Varieties**
Feb	sow	Busy lizzies
Mar	sow	"Accent Mixed"
Apr	grow on	"Bruno"
May	harden/plant	"Mosaic Rose"
Jun	flowering	"Super Elfin Mixed"
July	flowering	New Guinea impatiens
Aug	flowering	"Firelake Mixed"
Sept	flowering	"Spectra"
Oct	flowering	"Tango"
Nov	/	*Impatiens balsamifera*
Dec	/	"Tom Thumb Mixed"

Ipheion uniflorum

SPRING STAR FLOWER

FEATURES

This low-growing plant makes an ideal edging but should be planted in large drifts wherever it is grown to produce its best effect. Tolerant of rather tough growing conditions, it is most suitable for filling pockets in a rockery or growing toward the front of a herbaceous border. It also makes a good container plant. It has grey-green, narrow, strappy leaves that smell strongly of onions when crushed; the pale blue, starry, lightly scented flowers are carried on stems 6in or so high. There are several varieties available with flowers ranging in color from white to deep violet-blue.

CONDITIONS

ASPECT	Grows best in full sun but tolerates light shade for part of the day.
SITE	Good for a rockery, border, or container. Ipheion needs well-drained soil. It will grow on quite poor soils but growth will be better on soils enriched with organic matter.

GROWING METHOD

PLANTING	Plant bulbs 2in deep and the same distance apart in fall.
FEEDING	Apply some balanced fertilizer after flowers have finished. Water regularly during dry spells while plants are in leaf and bloom.
PROBLEMS	No specific problems are usually experienced with this bulb.

FLOWERING

SEASON	The starry flowers appear from early spring to mid-spring.
CUTTING	Flowers are too short to cut for all but a miniature vase but they may last a few days in water.

AFTER FLOWERING

REQUIREMENTS	Shear off spent flower stems and remove the old foliage when it has died down. If clumps become overcrowded and fail to flower well, they can be lifted in fall, divided, and replanted immediately.

SPRING STAR FLOWER is an ideal edging plant for a sunny yard and it can be left undisturbed for several years. The soft lilac of the flowers makes spring star flower very versatile as it blends into most garden color schemes.

AT A GLANCE	
A low-growing bulb with a profusion of starry blue or white flowers in spring.	

		Recommended Varieties
Jan	/	"Album"
Feb	/	"Alberto Castello"
Mar	flowering	"Froyle Mill"
Apr	flowering	"Rolf Fiedler"
May	flowering	"Wisley Blue"
Jun	/	
July	/	
Aug	/	
Sept	plant	
Oct	plant	
Nov	/	
Dec	/	

Ipomoea
MORNING GLORY

FEATURES

Look under ipomoea or morning glory in seed catalogs to find varieties of this stunning climber. Most familiar is sky-blue flowered "Heavenly Blue," others are red, pink, white, mauve, chocolate, one is striped, and "Murasaki Jishi" is double-flowered. Average height is 10–12ft. Plants will climb fences and other plants. For patios grow 3–4 plants in a 12in pot up a wigwam of 5ft canes. A half-hardy annual with flowers mostly 3in across. Seeds are poisonous.

CONDITIONS

ASPECT	Must have full sun all day.
SITE	Mix rotted compost with soil before planting. In containers use multipurpose compost with slow-release fertilizer added. All ipomoeas must have shelter from wind, and must have support for their twining stems.

GROWING METHOD

SOWING	Soak the seeds in warm water the night before sowing, then sow one to a 3^1/$_2$in pot, 1in deep, in April. Keep in a temperature of at least 70°F and put in bright light when the big pink seedlings come up 1–2 weeks later. Keep warm and grow on, potting on into 5in pots when the roots fill the pot. Support shoots with short stakes. Gradually harden-off in late May, planting out or into containers in early June.
FEEDING	Feed monthly with a high-potash tomato food.
PROBLEMS	Seedlings will turn yellow if they are kept too cold in the early stages. Red spider mite feeds on leaves—use a spray containing bifenthrin.

FLOWERING

SEASON	Summer.
CUTTING	Unsuitable for cutting.

AFTER FLOWERING

General	Use for composting when finished.

THE LARGE WHITE BLOOMS of morning glory have fluted petals and a delicious scent

AT A GLANCE	
A half-hardy annual climber grown for its trumpet-shaped flowers that open in the morning. Frost hardy to 32°F (zone 10).	
Jan /	**Recommended Varieties**
Feb /	Ipomoea hybrids
Mar /	"Cardinal"
Apr sow	"Chocolate"
May grow on	"Early Call Mixed"
Jun plant	"Flying Saucers"
July flowering	"Grandpa Otts"
Aug flowering	"Heavenly Blue"
Sept flowering	"Mini Sky-Blue"
Oct /	"Murasaki Jishi"
Nov /	"Platycodon Flowered White"
Dec /	

Iris unguicularis

WINTER IRIS, ALGERIAN IRIS

FEATURES

This beardless, rhizomatous iris is different to all others in its group because it flowers throughout the winter. The beautiful little fragrant flowers rarely exceed 8in in height and may be hidden by the stiff, grassy foliage. They are ideal for cutting and taking indoors, where their sweet scent may be almost overpowering at times. The flowers of the species are deep lavender with creamy yellow centers deeply veined in violet. There are some cultivars available, including a white form, one or two varieties in particularly deep shades of blue, one in a pale silvery lilac, and a dwarf form. A large single clump of this iris is effective but in the right position it could be mass-planted to good effect.

CONDITIONS

ASPECT   Needs a reasonably sheltered position because of its flowering time. The rhizomes must be exposed to a summer baking if plants are to flower well, so a position in full sun is essential.

SITE   Grow in beds or borders where it will be able to spread—plants can be invasive. Soil must be well-drained. If it is very poor, dig in quantities of well-decayed manure or compost ahead of planting time.

GROWING METHOD

PLANTING   Plant rhizomes in spring with the top at or just below soil level. Container-grown plants in growth can also be bought and planted virtually year-round in suitable weather.

FEEDING   Supplementary feeding is generally unnecessary. Water the plants in spring and fall if conditions are dry, but do not water in summer.

PROBLEMS   Slugs and snails will often attack the flowers. Use slug pellets if necessary.

FLOWERING

SEASON   Flowers are produced any time from late fall through winter.

CUTTING   The flowers make a lovely indoor decoration.

AFTER FLOWERING

REQUIREMENTS Cut off spent flowers and tidy up foliage when necessary. Little other attention is required. Crowded plants can be divided in spring.

AT A GLANCE	
A low-growing iris valuable for its sweetly scented flowers which appear throughout the winter.	
Jan flowering	**Recommended Varieties**
Feb flowering	"Abington Purple"
Mar plant	"Alba"
Apr /	"Bob Thompson"
May /	"Mary Barnard"
Jun /	"Oxford Dwarf"
July /	"Walter Butt"
Aug /	
Sept /	
Oct /	
Nov flowering	
Dec flowering	

Iris—bulbous types

IRISES

FEATURES

There are many species of these irises, which have true bulbs as storage organs, unlike the creeping rhizomes of their larger cousins. The leaves are not arranged in the typical fan of sword shapes like rhizomatous irises, but are usually narrow and lance shaped, or rolled.

The flowers have the typical iris form with six petals, three inner ones (standards), and three outer ones (falls). The falls are often brightly marked or veined. Many species and varieties are blue with yellow markings on the falls; some types are yellow with brown or green speckling on the falls and others are white with yellow markings. The blue varieties come in many shades, from deep violet and purple through to pale China blue.

Many bulbous irises are early-flowering dwarf forms suitable for growing on rockeries or at the front of beds: they are also excellent for shallow pots ("pans") in the greenhouse or alpine house. Other types are taller and flower in summer; they are valuable for herbaceous and mixed borders, and are particularly good for cutting for flower arrangements. There are also some spring-flowering irises that are far less commonly grown than the other groups.

POPULAR SPECIES

Bulbous irises can be split into three main groups: Reticulata irises, Xiphium irises and Juno irises.

RETICULATA These irises have bulbs with a netted tunic around them which gives them their group name. They are dwarf, growing to about 6in high, and the flowers appear early in the year, usually in February and March. I. danfordiae has lightly fragrant flowers whose yellow petals are speckled with greenish brown. I. reticulata also has fragrant flowers: the petals are thinner than those of I. danfordiae and are blue or purple with yellow markings. Several different cultivars are available. The flowers of I. histriodes and its cultivars are larger and have short stems; they are deep to light blue, with dark blue, white, and yellow markings. The flowers open before the leaves reach their full height.

XIPHIUM This group of summer-flowering irises is popular and easily grown. It consists of Dutch irises, flowering in early summer, in white, yellow, or blue with contrasting markings; English irises, flowering in early to mid-summer in shades of white, blue, or purple; and Spanish irises, flowering in midsummer in various shades of white, blue, purple, and yellow.

AT A GLANCE		
A varied group of plants with colorful flowers in early spring or in summer. Good for a range of situations.		
Jan	flowering	**Recommended Varieties**
Feb	flowering	Reticulata group
Mar	flowering	I. danfordiae
Apr	flowering	I. reticulata
May	flowering	"Katharine Hodgkin"
Jun	flowering	I. histrioides
July	flowering	"Major"
Aug	/	Xiphium group
Sept	plant	"Bronze Queen"
Oct	plant	"Excelsior"
Nov	/	"Ideal"
Dec	/	Juno group
		I. bucharica
		I. graeberiana

JUNO
The Juno irises are not as well-known as the other bulbous types, probably because they are more difficult to grow well. The group includes *I. bucharica*, bearing yellow or white flowers with yellow falls, and *I. graeberiana*, which has lavender flowers with a white crest on the falls. These two are among the easiest Juno irises to grow: others include *I. fosteriana*, *I. magnifica*, and *I. rosenbachiana*, which do best in an alpine house.

CONDITIONS

ASPECT
All bulbous irises like open, sunny, positions.

SITE
Reticulatas are good for rock gardens, raised beds, or containers; Xiphiums and Junos for sunny, sheltered borders. Soil needs to be well-drained; Juno irises require a soil containing plenty of well-rotted organic matter.

GROWING METHOD

PLANTING
Plant Reticulatas 3in deep and 4in apart. Xiphiums are planted 4-6in deep and 6in apart, and Juno irises are planted 2in deep and 8in apart, taking care not to damage the brittle, fleshy roots. They are all planted in fall, in September or October.

FEEDING
Supplementary feeding is not usually necessary.

PROBLEMS
Bulbs may rot in overwet soil. Bulbous irises in warmer areas of the country may be affected by iris ink disease, causing black streaks on the bulb and yellow blotches on the leaves. Destroy affected bulbs.

FLOWERING

SEASON
Reticulata irises flower in February and March, Junos in April and May, and Xiphiums in June and July.

CUTTING
The Xiphiums make excellent, long-lasting cut flowers.

AFTER FLOWERING

REQUIREMENTS
Remove faded flowers. Most bulbous irises are best left undisturbed for as long as possible; they can be increased by lifting and dividing the bulbs after flowering when necessary. Juno irises should not be divided until the foliage has died down, and must be handled very carefully. Spanish irises of the Xiphium group benefit from being lifted when the foliage has died down and replanted in September; this helps the bulbs to ripen.

Iris—rhizomatous types

IRIS

FEATURES

Irises comprise a very large plant group of more than 200 species. Some grow from bulbs (see the previous two pages): those covered here grow from rhizomes. They have stiff, sword-shaped leaves and carry their colorful flowers on tall, stiff stems in spring and early summer. Iris flowers have six petals; three inner, vertical ones, (standards), and three outer ones, which curve outward (falls). The color range is very varied, covering blue, purple, lavender, yellow, rose, and white; many of the flowers are bicolored, and attractively marked.

Rhizomatous irises contain several different groups, the most popular of which are bearded, Japanese and Siberian irises. Bearded irises have large, very showy flowers with a short, bristly "beard" on the falls; dwarf cultivars are also available. Japanese irises have unusual flat-faced flowers, and Siberian irises have delicate flowers with finer petals.

CONDITIONS

ASPECT Rhizomatous irises like a position in full sun, but with protection from strong winds.

SITE Excellent plants for the middle to back of a mixed or herbaceous border. Bearded irises like a slightly alkaline, well-drained soil: Japanese and Siberian irises need moisture-retentive, humus-rich loam.

GROWING METHOD

PLANTING Usually sold as container-grown plants in growth. Plant shallowly, with the rhizome barely covered, in late summer.

FEEDING Supplementary feeding is rarely necessary. Ensure moisture-loving types are never allowed to dry out during the growing season.

PROBLEMS Slugs and snails can be troublesome. Use covered slug bait where necessary, or hand pick the pests after dark.

FLOWERING

SEASON Flowers are carried in early summer.

CUTTING Make beautiful cut flowers.

AFTER FLOWERING

REQUIREMENTS Cut off spent flower stems. Every few years, lift the rhizomes after flowering, cut them into sections each containing a strong, healthy fan of leaves, and replant, discarding the old, woody, worn out portions of rhizome.

AT A GLANCE		
A low-growing iris valuable for its sweetly scented flowers which appear throughout the winter.		
Jan	flowering	**Recommended Varieties**
Feb	flowering	"Abington Purple"
Mar	plant	"Alba"
Apr	/	"Bob Thompson"
May	/	"Mary Barnard"
Jun	/	"Oxford Dwarf"
July	/	"Walter Butt"
Aug	/	
Sept	/	
Oct	/	
Nov	flowering	
Dec	flowering	

Ixia

CORN LILY

FEATURES

This plant produces starry flowers in a stunning range of colors including white, cream, yellow, orange, red, cerise, and magenta. Hybrid varieties are the most popular, but the sought-after I. viridiflora has duck-egg blue flowers with a dark center. The narrow, grass-like foliage may be 12–20in high while the wiry-stemmed flower spikes stand clear of the leaves. Corn lilies are a great addition to the garden. Being quite tall they should be planted toward the back of a bed or among other bulbs and perennials. Although colors can be mixed, a better effect is obtained by planting blocks of one color.

CONDITIONS

ASPECT	Prefers full sun all day but with shelter from strong wind.
SITE	A good border plant in reasonably mild districts. In colder areas it can be grown in containers on a sheltered patio or in a conservatory. Needs well-drained soil.

GROWING METHOD

PLANTING	Plant corms in the open garden in spring, about 2in deep and 3–4in apart. Plant in pots for the conservatory in fall.
FERTILIZING	Apply balanced liquid fertilizer in early spring to increase the size of the blooms.

In dry conditions, water if necessary in spring when the shoots are growing strong.

PROBLEMS	No specific pest or disease problems are usually experienced, though corms may rot in overwet soil.

FLOWERING

SEASON	Flowers from late spring to mid-summer.
CUTTING	Flowers can be cut for the vase but will probably give better value in the garden.

AFTER FLOWERING

REQUIREMENTS	In all but the mildest gardens, lift the corms when the foliage has died down and store them in a dry place for replanting in spring.

EACH TALL SPIKE of corn lily produces dozens of flowers. These are still producing blooms despite the many fading and falling ones.

AT A GLANCE		
A rather tender plant with masses of colorful, starry flowers on slender stems.		
Jan	/	Recommended Varieties
Feb	/	"Blue Bird"
Mar	plant	"Mabel"
Apr	plant	"Rose Emperor"
May	flowering	"Venus"
Jun	flowering	
July	flowering	
Aug	/	
Sept	/	
Oct	plant (indoors)	
Nov	/	
Dec	/	

Japonica
CHAENOMELES

FEATURES

Also known as japonica or flowering quince, this spiny, deciduous shrub makes a colorful bush to 7ft high or, if espalier-trained against a wall or fence, a striking drape to 9ft. Long-lived, it flowers early in life and reaches maturity in 3–5 years. It is valued for its thickly clustered blooms that transform bare branches from mid-winter to early spring. Flowers are followed by small, fragrant, quince-like fruits that ripen to bright yellow. Fruits are edible and make delicious jams and preserves.

Showy varieties include apricot "Geisha Girl," pink "Moerloesii," white "Nivalis," and large, bright crimson "Rowallane". In borders, it makes a showy, rounded background plant for smaller shrubs, perennials, bulbs, and annuals.

CONDITIONS

ASPECT   Usefully adaptable, chaenomeles thrives in full sun or light shade, does not mind cold winds and colors cold, north- or east-facing walls.
SITE   Though it prefers well-drained soil, it tolerates heavy, waterlogged clay. Help sandy soils stay cool and moist by working in plenty of bulky manure or well-rotted garden compost.

GROWING METHOD

FEEDING   Unlike many other shrubs, chaenomeles thrives in poorish soil. For best results, build fertility by topdressing the root area with pelleted chicken manure, fish, blood, and bone meal, or Growmore in spring and midsummer.
            Water plants regularly in their first year.
PROPAGATION Take semi-ripe cuttings in late summer or detach and replant rooted suckers in fall.
PROBLEMS   If coral spot appears—shoots are pimpled with coral-pink or orange pustules—cut back to healthy, white wood and burn prunings. Paint stumps with fungicidal pruning compound.

PRUNING

BUSHES   Apart from removing crowded shoots when flowers fade in spring, no regular cutting back is required.
WALL TRAINED Young plants: Tie espaliered shoots to a wire frame. In July, cut back to five leaves shoots growing away from the wall. Reduce to two buds further growth from shortened shoots.
ESTABLISHED Shorten the previous year's side shoots
PLANTS   to two or three leaves when flowers fade in spring.

AT A GLANCE	
A hardy deciduous shrub, its clusters of white, pink, or red, saucer-shaped flowers brighten spring. Hardy to -13°F (zone 5).	
Jan /	Recommended Varieties
Feb /	For walls
Mar flower, plant	"Geisha Girl"
Apr flower, prune	"Moerloesii"
May flower, prune	"Nivalis"
June plant	"Simonii"
July prune	For bushes
Aug plant	"Lemon and Lime"
Sept plant	"Pink Lady"
Oct plant	"Knaphill Scarlet"
Nov plant	"Rowallane"
Dec /	

Jasmine

JASMINUM

FEATURES

There are two forms of jasmine—climbing and bushy—both of which flower generously. Choice and reliable twining climbers—ideal for screening—are *Jasminum affine*, to 25ft, whose pink buds open to sweetly scented, white flowers from July to September; and *J. x stephanense*, to 15ft, which from early to midsummer pleases with a profusion of perfumed, pale pink blooms amid colorful, cream-flushed, green leaves.

Among bushy kinds, the popular, yellow-flowered winter jasmine (*J. nudiflorum*) is usually trained to transform a wall or fence from November to late February. After establishing a main framework, leave it to flower freely on cascading shoots. Aspiring to half that height, semi-evergreen *J. humile* "Revolutum" is dashingly clad with larger, fragrant, yellow blossoms from late spring to fall. Even smaller is yellow-flowered, mound forming *J. parkeri*, which when planted on a rock garden brightens it in early summer.

CONDITIONS

ASPECT   While climbing kinds need a sheltered spot and full sunshine for most of the day, the most popular bushy member—G. nudiflorum—thrives on a shaded, north wall lashed by frosty winds.

SITE   Undemanding, all flourish on most well-drained soils. Enrich and improve the water retention of thin, sandy areas by digging in bulky organics several months before planting. Help clay drain better by forking in grit.

GROWING METHOD

FEEDING   Give young plants a good start by consigning them to generous planting holes fortified with bone meal or Growmore fertilizer. Soak the soil after planting to settle it around roots and remove air pockets. Encourage robust growth by working bone meal into the root area in spring and the fall.

PROPAGATION Layer whippy shoots from spring to late summer or take semi-ripe cuttings from mid- to late summer.

PROBLEMS   Gray mold, a fungus covering leaves with a grayish, furry patina, may occur if shoots are crowded. Control it by removing affected parts and spraying with carbendazim.

PRUNING

Climbing kinds are not normally cut back. If they outgrow their situation, shorten shoots after flowering. Keep J. nudiflorum youthful and massed with bloom by removing a third of the older flowered stems when flowers fade in early spring.

AT A GLANCE	
Semi-evergreen or deciduous, twining or bush forms color walls and fences in winter and summer. Hardy to 4˚F (zone 7).	

		Recommended Varieties
Jan	flower	*J. affine*
Feb	flower	*J. humile* "Revolutum"
Mar	prune	*J. nudiflorum*
Apr	plant	*J. parkeri*
May	flower, plant	*J. x stephanense*
Jun	flower, plant	
July	flower, plant	
Aug	flower, prune	
Sept	flower, plant	
Oct	plant	
Nov	plant	
Dec	/	

Jasminum

JASMINE

FEATURES

These deciduous and evergreen climbers are among the most popular of all, many being valued for their sweetly fragrant flowers. Due to their informal habit they are great favorites for cottage and country gardens, where they combine well with old-fashioned flowers. Try grouping them with old-fashioned roses, for instance, and shrubs such as philadelphus (Mock orange), which is also highly scented. But the versatile jasmines can be used in any type of garden. They can be grown up and over various kinds of support. Use them to cover walls, fences, trellis screens, pergolas, arches and arbors. They can even be trained up large mature trees. Large mature shrubs might also make good hosts, but then pruning of the jasmines becomes more difficult.

There are many species of jasmine but some are too tender to be grown out of doors in cold climates. These are best grown in a cool conservatory. However, there are still many good species suitable for growing in gardens, including *Jasminum beesianum*, a Chinese twiner that is evergreen in milder gardens but deciduous in colder areas. The flowers, produced in the first half of the summer, are fragrant and red-pink in color. It grows to a height of 15ft so would be suitable for training on a wall of the house.

Jasminum humile "Revolutum" (Yellow jasmine), is of garden origin, but the species is a native of China, Afghanistan and the Himalayas. This semi-evergreen scrambler has bright yellow flowers in late spring and early summer and reaches a height of at least 8ft. This is another suitable species for the walls of the house.

The ever-popular Winter jasmine, *J. nudiflorum*, is a scrambling, deciduous, Chinese shrub that is ideally suited to training to a wall. The green stems and shoots carry bright yellow flowers in winter and into spring. Height 10ft. It can also be used as groundcover to clothe a bank.

Jasminum officinale (Common jasmine), a twining, deciduous climber from China and the Himalayas, can grow up to 40ft in height, but may be kept shorter by pruning. It is an extremely popular species and an essential choice for cottage gardens. Sweetly scented white flowers appear in summer and fall. There are several good cultivars and forms including *J. o. f. affine* whose white flowers are tinted with pink; "Aureum" with yellow-variegated leaves; and "Argenteovariegatum" with white-edged leaves.

CONDITIONS

ASPECT   Ideally jasmines should be grown in full sun, where they flower most freely, but partial shade is acceptable. The Winter jasmine, especially, is suitable for partial shade.

AT A GLANCE	
Scrambling climbers. The species in the main text are hardy to 23°F (zone 9), J. nudiflorum is hardy to 5°F (zone 7).	

		Companion Plants
Jan	flowering	Jasmines look lovely intertwining
Feb	flowering	with climbing or rambler roses.
Mar	planting	Ivy is a good companion for the
Apr	planting	winter jasmine.
May	flowering	
Jun	flowering	
July	flowering	
Aug	flowering	
Sep	flowering	
Oct	/	
Nov	/	
Dec	flowering	

SITE — Jasmines are highly adaptable plants and will grow in any well-drained and reasonably fertile soil. The soil should be capable of retaining moisture during dry weather—so add bulky organic matter before planting.

GROWING METHOD

PROPAGATION — The easiest way to propagate jasmines is to carry out serpentine layering in the spring. Alternatively take semi-ripe cuttings in summer. However, hard-wood cuttings in winter are better for *J. nudiflorum* and *J. officinale*, rooting them in a cold frame or in a cool glasshouse.

WATERING — It is important not to allow jasmines to suffer from extended lack of moisture, try to keep the plants well watered during any prolonged dry spells if necessary.

FEEDING — Apply a slow-release fertilizer annually in the spring just as growth is starting. Blood, fish, and bone is a good organic choice.

PROBLEMS — Jasmines may be attacked by aphids, but these pests are easily controlled by spraying with a suitable insecticide.

FLOWERING/FOLIAGE

FLOWERS — Jasmines are grown primarily for their flowers, which are often highly fragrant.

FOLIAGE — Many jasmines have pinnate foliage. It may be evergreen or deciduous, depending on species and/or climate.

PRUNING

REQUIREMENTS — Jasmines vary in their pruning requirements according to species. *Jasminum humile* "Revolutum" needs thinning out regularly to prevent congested growth. When flowering is over, cut out completely no more than two of the oldest stems. Neglected and overgrown plants can be renovated by cutting them back hard in early spring. *Jasminum nudiflorum* requires annual pruning. This should take place as soon as flowering is over. Carry out spur pruning by cutting back the old flowered shoots to within two or three pairs of buds of the main framework of the plant. For established plants of *J. officinale* and *J. beesianum* thin out congested growth as soon as flowering is over by cutting back the flowered shoots. If necessary neglected plants can be hard pruned by cutting back old stems to within 3ft of the ground in late winter or early spring.

TREASURED FOR THEIR SUBTLE fragrance, the flowers of Jasminum officinale also make a delightful display in summer and fall.

Jubaea chilensis

CHILEAN WINE PALM

FEATURES

A native of the warm temperate coastal regions of Chile, the Wine palm is a truly massive tree that dominates the landscape. It eventually forms a huge, fat gray trunk topped with a crown of light to deep green pinnate fronds that can grow to 15ft in length. The trunk contains a lot of sugar, which the Chileans use to make an alcoholic beverage—thus the name. Mature height up to 80ft with a spread of 28ft. It is slow growing when young but when a trunk has formed it develops more rapidly. When young this is an attractive feathery palm that makes a good houseplant and is ideal too for the cool glasshouse or conservatory. Place it outside for the summer. In favored areas it can be grown permanently out of doors.

CONDITIONS

ASPECT   Outdoors grow in a sheltered position in full sun. Indoors provide bright light but do not subject it to direct sun that may scorch the foliage. Provide low to moderate humidity.

SITE   Outdoors grow in well-drained but moisture-retentive soil. In containers grow in soil-based potting compost.

GROWING METHOD

PROPAGATION Sow seeds as soon as available and germinate them at a temperature of 77°F. Very slow to germinate.

WATERING   In containers, moderate watering in growing season from late spring to late summer, then for the rest of the year water sparingly.

FEEDING   In containers apply a balanced liquid fertilizer monthly during the growing season from late spring to late summer.

PROBLEMS   Under glass may be attacked by scale insects and red spider mites.

FOLIAGE/FLOWERING

FOLIAGE   Being evergreen this palm looks good all year round but is especially attractive in spring and summer.

FLOWERS   Long trusses of small purple and yellow flowers in summer followed by yellow fruits.

GENERAL CARE

REQUIREMENTS Remove dead fronds when necessary by cutting them off close to the trunk.

ALTHOUGH SMALL in its younger years and suitable for indoor settings, J. chilensis eventually grows into a mighty palm.

AT A GLANCE		
A feathery palm when young with pale to dark green leaves. Frost hardy, taking a minimum temperature of 23°F (zone 9).		
Jan /		**Companion Plants**
Feb /		Outdoors combine with colorful
Mar planting		summer bedding plants, or plants in
Apr planting		a sub-tropical scheme. Under glass
May foliage		grow with *Strelitzia reginae* (Bird of
Jun flowering		paradise) or *Musa* (banana) species.
July flowering		
Aug flowering		
Sep /		
Oct /		
Nov /		
Dec /		

K

Kalanchoe blossfeldiana

FLAMING KATY

FEATURES

This is familiar to most people as a potted flowering plant. It has scalloped, fleshy dark green leaves, often edged with red, and the original species has bright scarlet flowers. It has been extensively hybridized and there are now forms with flowers in white, yellow, and various shades of pink. There may be some color change or variation depending on aspect and climatic conditions, especially as flowers start to fade. Some of the bright pinks tend to revert to the species scarlet. A very easy-care pot plant for use indoors or out, this is also a fine summer plant for the garden. In ideal warm conditions in the glasshouse border where there is plenty of space, the stems will sprawl and take root, creating new plants.

CONDITIONS

ASPECT   In the garden, flaming Katy prefers morning sun and afternoon shade or light shade all day. Indoors, these plants should be given plenty of bright light.

SITE   Flaming Katy grows best in a well-drained soil that also contains plenty of decayed organic matter. In the open garden make sure that the soil has plenty of added drainage material so that the roots are not kept too wet for too long.

GROWING METHOD

PROPAGATION Very easily grown from either leaf or stem cuttings, taken during the warmer months. The cuttings should be dried out for a few days before planting.

FEEDING   In spring, apply slow-release fertilizer or a small amount of pelletted poultry manure in the open garden. It does not respond well to soil that is too fertile.

PROBLEMS   Flaming Katy is generally free of pests and disease.

FLOWERING

SEASON   The true flowering time is late winter to spring, but commercial growers now force plants so that they are available in flower almost all year round. In the home yard, in the ground or in pots, they should bloom at the proper time. Flowers will generally give several weeks of bright color. After flowering, trim off spent flower heads.

THREE VARIETIES of flaming Katy, bright pink, yellow, and red, are used here as bedding plants with white alyssum.

AT A GLANCE	
K. blossfeldiana is a superb, reliable pot plant with heads of flowers to brighten up the glasshouse. 50°F min (zone 11).	
Jan /	**Recommended Varieties**
Feb flowering	*K. beharensis*
Mar flowering	*K. eriophylla*
Apr flowering	*K. grandiflora*
May sow	*K. marmorata*
Jun /	*K. pubescens*
July transplant	*K. pumila*
Aug /	"Tessa"
Sept /	*K. tomentosa*
Oct /	"Wendy"
Nov /	
Dec /	

Kerria

KERRIA JAPONICA

FEATURES

Graceful and arching, deciduous Kerria japonica makes a fascinating focus to about 6ft high. From April to May, its radiant orange-yellow blooms clothe a profusion of suckering, cane-like, green stems.

Coveted forms are "Pleniflora," magnificent with its double, golden pompons; "Golden Guinea," with beautiful, single, buttercup-yellow flowers; and smaller "Picta"—just 3ft high—whose single, yellow blossoms complement cream-edged, green leaves.

Very hardy and happy almost anywhere, taller kinds making dense and colorful hedges.

CONDITIONS

ASPECT   This shrub flowers best in full sun and performs passably well in shade.

SITE   Kerria will thrive almost anywhere.

GROWING METHOD

FEEDING   Keep growth vigorous and packed with blossom in spring by applying bone meal in March and October. Water new plants frequently to help them establish quickly.

PROPAGATION   Probably the easiest shrub to multiply, it can be increased from semi-ripe cuttings in midsummer; layered shoots from mid-spring to late summer; hardwood cuttings in late fall; and suckers in early spring.

PROBLEMS   No particular pests or diseases.

PRUNING

Cut out from the base a third of older shoots when blooms fade in early summer. Remove green-leaved stems on variegated bushes.

KERRIA HAS SINGLE or double flowers and leaves that develop radiant yellow tints in fall. A charmingly tangled mass of bright yellow flowers in spring makes kerria an attractive screening plant, even at dusk.

AT A GLANCE	
Deciduous shrub with green stems dotted with single or double, yellow blooms in spring. Hardy to -13°F (zone 5).	
Jan /	**Recommended Varieties**
Feb /	"Albescens"
Mar plant	"Golden Guinea"
Apr flower, plant	"Picta"
May flower, plant	"Pleniflora"
June plant, prune	"Simplex"
July plant	
Aug plant	
Sept plant	
Oct plant	
Nov plant	
Dec /	

Kniphofia
RED HOT POKER

FEATURES

These evergreen perennials, also known as torch lilies, make great feature plants, with their bright flower spikes in cream, orange, red, yellow, and many shadings of these colors. Flower stems stand high above the grassy foliage, which may be anywhere from 24in to 6^1/$_2$ft tall. Even out of flower, the distinctive foliage makes red hot poker a good accent plant. Since clumps should remain undisturbed for many years, plant red hot pokers in their final position.

CONDITIONS

ASPECT Needs full sunlight all day. A valuable plant because it tolerates a wide range of exposed windy or coastal areas.

SITE Needs well-drained soil. Although it tolerates poorer soils, especially sandy ones, you will get better results if the soil is enriched with manure or compost.

GROWING METHOD

PROPAGATION Well-established clumps can be divided in late spring. Foliage on new divisions must be reduced by half to allow successful root regrowth to take place. The smaller-growing forms can be planted at 20in spacings, but the large growers may need up to 30in or more. Needs regular watering to establish in prolonged dry spells, after which it is very drought-tolerant.

FEEDING Grows without supplementary fertilizer, but complete plant food applied in the spring should noticeably increase the quantity and quality of the flowers.

PROBLEMS No specific problems are known.

FLOWERING

SEASON Flowering times can vary slightly with species and cultivar. Generally, red hot pokers flower in late summer and early fall.

CUTTING The flowers last well when cut if the stems are scalded for approximately 10 seconds. They make an invaluable tall, stiff background for a display of smaller, flowery cuttings.

AFTER FLOWERING

REQUIREMENTS Spent flower stalks should be promptly cut off. Any dead leaves should be pulled away to give the clump a clean look. Protect the crown with straw or leaves in cold areas.

AT A GLANCE		
A genus of some 70 species of evergreen and deciduous perennials, grown for their flowering spires. Hardy to 5˚F (zone 7).		
Jan	/	Recommended Varieties
Feb	/	"Bees Sunset"
Mar	sow	"Brimstone"
Apr	divide Agla	"Buttercup"
May	transplant	K. caulescens
Jun	flowering	"Little Maid"
July	flowering	"Royal Standard"
Aug	flowering	"Samuel's Sensation"
Sept	flowering	"Sunningdale Yellow"
Oct	flowering	K. triangularis
Nov	/	
Dec	/	

Kochia
SUMMER CYPRESS

FEATURES

Summer cypress is a bushy half-hardy foliage annual that grows up to 3ft high with soft, light-green feathery foliage forming an upright cone- or dome-shape. "Trichophylla" has narrow leaves and looks similar to a dwarf conifer in summer, turning to a fiery bronze red in fall, hence its other common name of burning bush. Grow in groups of 2–3 or singly as the centerpiece of a bedding scheme.

CONDITIONS

ASPECT | Needs full sun to get the best leaf color.
SITE | Grows on most soils but must be well-drained. Add manure/compost before planting.

GROWING METHOD

SOWING | Sow February/March on the surface of a $3^1/2$in pot of moist multipurpose compost but do not cover. Keep at 61°F in a bright spot, and expect seedlings in 2–3 weeks. When large enough, transplant to $3^1/2$in pots of multipurpose compost and grow on, hardening off in late May and planting outdoors after the last frosts. Space plants at least 2ft apart to allow room for development. They can also be planted in rows as a temporary and unusual summer "hedge."

FEEDING | Water thoroughly in early summer for 2–3 weeks after planting. Extra feeding is not essential to get good results.
PROBLEMS | No particular problems.

FLOWERING

SEASON | Not grown for flowers but leaves.
CUTTING | Unsuitable for cutting.

AFTER FLOWERING

GENERAL | Pull up and compost in fall.

SUMMER CYPRESS is so-called because it resembles a dwarf conifer in color and shape. In early fall plants turn bright red. Kochia makes a bold plant for the focus of a bedding display

AT A GLANCE	
A half-hardy annual grown for its light-green leaves on bushy plants which turn red in fall. Frost hardy to 32°F (zone 10).	
Jan /	**Recommended Varieties**
Feb sow	Kochia scoparia:
Mar sow	"Trichophylla"
Apr grow on	
May harden off/plant	**For all-green leaves**
Jun leaves	"Evergreen"
July leaves	
Aug leaves	
Sept leaves	
Oct leaves	
Nov /	
Dec /	

L

Lachenalia aloides

CAPE COWSLIP

FEATURES

Also known as "soldier boys" because of their upright, neat and orderly habit, this bulb is grown as a house plant to produce its colorful bell-like flowers in midwinter. The rather stiff leaves grow to about 6in high and are dark green, often spotted with purple. The 8–12in spikes of 20 or so tubular flowers stand well above the foliage and remain colorful for several weeks. Individual blooms are yellow or orange-red, marked with red, green, or purple; they are often a deeper color in bud, becoming paler as the flowers open. There are several different varieties with subtly varying shades to the flowers.

CONDITIONS

ASPECT   Needs a very brightly lit spot; will stand direct sun for part of the day.

SITE   Grow on a bright windowsill in a cool room, or in a cool greenhouse or conservatory. Lachenalia does not like dry heat.

GROWING METHOD

PLANTING   Plant bulbs in late summer or early fall, growing six to a 5in pot. Set them just below the surface of the compost.

FEEDING   Apply high potash liquid fertilizer every 14 days or so from when the buds appear. Water regularly while plants are in flower.

PROBLEMS   Overwatering or poorly drained compost will cause the bulbs to rot.

FLOWERING

SEASON   Flowers appear between midwinter and early spring.

CUTTING   Not suitable for cutting.

AFTER FLOWERING

REQUIREMENTS   Cut off spent lachenalia flower stems. Continue to water until early summer, then gradually stop watering and allow the pot to dry out until the following fall, when the bulbs can be shaken out and repotted in fresh compost.

CAPE COWSLIPS need a cool room to grow well. In the right conditions they make excellent winter-flowering house plants.

AT A GLANCE	
A tender bulb grown as a house or greenhouse plant for its spikes of yellow or orange tubular flowers in winter.	
Jan flowering	**Recommended Varieties**
Feb flowering	*Lachenalia aloides*
Mar flowering	"Aurea"
Apr /	"Lutea"
May /	"Nelsonii"
Jun /	"Quadricolor"
July /	*L. bulbifera*
Aug plant	"George"
Sept plant	
Oct /	
Nov /	
Dec /	

Laelia
LAELIA SPECIES

FEATURES

There are many different *Laelia* species, coming mostly from Central and the more northern parts of South America. The showy blooms and relative ease of culture make it popular with beginners. It is a varied genus; the size of the plant can vary from 2in high, up to 28in high, and the flower sizes for these species are similarly different. Colors range from pure white, yellow, lavenders, and pinks to deep purples. They are very closely related to the *Cattleya* family and have been extensively interbred to produce the beautiful Laeliocattleyas. *L. purpurata* is perhaps the most well known, being called the queen of laelias. It is the national flower of Brazil and has more cultivated varieties than any other orchid. The laelias have thick, leathery leaves on the top of usually elongated pseudobulbs. Flowers come from inside a sheath at the apex of the newest pseudobulb.

CONDITIONS

CLIMATE   There are both cool and intermediate growing laelias so check the label. The cooler ones need to drop to 50°F in winter, while others need a slightly warmer temperature of 54°F minimum.

ASPECT   Give good light all year round, this is important to encourage flowering. Avoid direct summer sun, which can scorch leaves.

POTTING MIX   Use a very open, coarse bark mix to make sure the roots are never too wet.

GROWING METHOD

PROPAGATION   Although a little slow growing, some laelias will readily propagate after a few years of growing into a larger sized mature plant. Some will shoot from old back bulbs that can be removed at potting time and grown on in a warm, humid place.

WATERING   Make sure the compost dries out in between waterings. In winter keep dry unless the pseudobulbs start to shrivel.

FEEDING   Only apply a liquid feed and mist foliage when the plant is actually in growth.

PROBLEMS   No specific problems are known if cultural conditions are suitable.

FLOWERING SEASON

Most of the laelias are summer flowering, or produce from new pseudobulb in fall.

AT A GLANCE	
Long-lasting, bright flowers, some fragranced. Plants come in a variety of sizes, from 2–18in.	
Jan rest	**Recommended Varieties**
Feb rest	*L. anceps* (lavender)
Mar rest	*L. fallalis* (lavender)
Apr rest, re-pot	*L. briegeri* (yellow)
May flowering, water and feed	*L. harpophylla* (orange)
Jun flowering, water and feed	*L. pumila* (purple)
July flowering, water and feed	*L. purpurata* (various: white to purple)
Aug flowering, water and feed	
Sept water and feed	
Oct rest	
Nov rest	
Dec rest	

Lamium

DEAD NETTLE

FEATURES

Despite its rather unattractive common name, *Lamium* is quite a pretty, soft-leaved groundcover that spreads by running stems (stolons) which root down as they spread. Some are very vigorous and may be invasive, and although individual plants are generally only 6–18 in high, they can spread to cover 6 ft in warm, humid climates. There are many variegated forms with leaves splashed, speckled, or spotted with silver or cream. Different species or cultivars produce flowers that may be pink, purple, cream or yellow. Dead nettle also makes a good basket plant. In the garden it is easy to grow and maintain, and is long lived.

CONDITIONS

ASPECT   Lamium does best in shade or semi-shade and when sheltered from strong wind.

SITE   Tolerates a wide range of soils but is best in well-drained soils rich in organic matter. The ground should also be fairly moist.

GROWING METHOD

PROPAGATION   Easily grown by dividing rooted plants. Alternatively you can grow from seed sown in the spring or the fall.

FEEDING   Fertilizing is not necessary unless the soil is extremely poor, in which case complete plant food can be applied in early spring. An annual mulch with well-rotted organic matter also helps in this case.

PROBLEMS   There are no known problems.

FLOWERING

SEASON   Flowering spikes appear in the summer months, depending on species.

PRUNING

GENERAL   Pruning of plants is unnecessary but if they become too vigorous you may need to remove whole sections with a spade. If growing *L. galeobdolon*, you may need to insert a barrier into the soil to confine it. Use several thicknesses of builders' waterproofing plastic or metal sheeting, up to 1ft deep.

SOFT PINK FLOWERS and foliage boldly striped in silver make dead nettle a very desirable groundcover for any garden.

AT A GLANCE		
Lamium is a useful groundcover with small pretty leaves, but can be highly invasive. Hardy to 0°F (zone 7).		
Jan	/	**Recommended Varieties**
Feb	/	*Lamium galeobdolon*
Mar	/	"Hermann's Pride"
April	/	*L. garganicum*
May	foliage	"Golden Carpet"
June	flowering	*L. maculatum*
July	flowering	"Aureum"
Aug	flowering	"Beacon Silver"
Sept	foliage	"Cannon's Gold"
Oct	foliage	"White Nancy"
Nov	/	
Dec	/	

Lampranthus
LAMPRANTHUS

FEATURES

This group of plants is native to South Africa and is ideal for low-maintenance gardens in areas with low rainfall. *Lampranthus* is best known as a creeping or trailing plant used as a groundcover, but some species are bushier and more like shrubs. Stems of many species root as they spread, making them ideal for soil binding on banks or simply for stopping blowing sand or soil. The fleshy gray-green leaves are angled or cylindrical, and growing stems may reach 20in or so, but are more often around 12in. Individual plants may spread 12in or more in a growing season. The daisy-like flowers, which only open in sun, are shiny, brilliantly colored, and borne in such profusion that the foliage and stems are all but obscured.

VARIETIES

Species commonly grown include *Lampranthus aurantiacus*, with orange flowers; *L. roseus*, with pink flowers; and *L. spectabilis*, with purple to magenta flowers. Many lampranthus sold in nurseries are cultivars or hybrids bred for garden use.

CONDITIONS

ASPECT   These plants must be grown in full sun or flowers will not open.

SITE   Can be grown in almost any type of soil as long as it is well drained. Try to replicate its natural habitat which is mainly coastal South African near-desert conditions; dry and arid.

GROWING METHOD

PROPAGATION *Lampranthus* are easily grown from stem cuttings taken from spring to fall. Species can be grown from seed sown in spring.

FEEDING   Fertilizing is generally unnecessary as plants grown "hard" usually flower better.

PROBLEMS   Snails sometimes graze on foliage causing damage. Plants will not survive in heavy, poorly drained soil.

FLOWERING

SEASON   Flowers appear through late winter and spring or during summer depending on the conditions and the species grown. Flowers may be orange, red, yellow, purple, cream, and many shades in between. In good conditions they will provide excellent, striking colors, especially the bright orange *L. aurantiacus.*

AT A GLANCE	
Prime ingredients for a dry seaside summer garden, offering big bright clusters of flowers. 5°F min (zone 7).	
Jan /	**Recommended Varieties**
Feb flowering	*Lampranthus aurantiacus*
Mar sow	*L. aureus*
Apr /	*L. brownii*
May /	*L. haworthii*
Jun transplant	*L. spectabilis*
July flowering	*L. s.* "Tresco Brilliant"
Aug flowering	
Sept flowering	
Oct /	
Nov /	
Dec /	

Lathyrus

SWEET PEA

FEATURES

Varieties of *Lathyrus odoratus*, or sweet pea, occupy several pages in seed catalogs, but there are two basic groups—the tall climbers reaching 6–8ft, used as cut flowers and for screening, and dwarf "patio" varieties reaching up to 3ft which are used in bedding, baskets, and containers. Not all sweet peas have good scent, so check before buying seeds, and choose a fragrant mixed variety for a range of flower colors, which can be white, pink, red, mauve, orange, or blue, as well as many with picotee and other patterns. Sweet peas are easily-grown hardy annuals.

CONDITIONS

ASPECT   Grow in full sun.
SITE   Needs well-drained soil packed with organic matter. Add compost or rotted manure the fall before sowing or planting. Climbing varieties need canes, bean netting, fences, or other supports to grow through. Use multipurpose compost for planting up baskets and patio containers.

GROWING METHOD

SOWING   Seeds can be sown individually in $3^1/_2$in pots in February/March and germinated in a coldframe, cold porch, or even outdoors in a spot sheltered from rain. Nick or file the tough seed coat until a pale "spot" appears, then sow 1in-deep in soil-based seed compost. Pinch out the growing tips when plants are 3in tall to encourage sideshoots to grow. Grow outside, then plant out in May, 12in apart for climbers, and 6–12in apart for patio varieties used in baskets and containers.
FEEDING   Plants benefit from a monthly feed with liquid tomato food. Water thoroughly in dry spells.
PROBLEMS   Mice will dig young seedlings up so set traps. Powdery mildew can attack leaves in the summer—use a spray containing sulfur.

FLOWERING

SEASON   Seed can also be sown in October, and plants overwintered for flowers from early summer. Spring-sown plants flower from June.
CUTTING   Cut when the first few flowers on the stalk are opening and stand up to their necks in water.

AFTER FLOWERING

GENERAL   Cut off at ground level in fall so the nitrogen-rich roots rot down in the soil.

AT A GLANCE	
A hardy annual climber producing often strongly-scented flowers which are ideal for cutting. Frost hardy to 5˚F (zone 7).	

		Recommended Varieties
Jan	/	*Lathyrus odoratus*
Feb	/	Tall, fragrant varieties
Mar	sow	"Bouquet Mixed"
Apr	grow on	"Great Expectations"
May	plant	"Old Fashioned Mixed"
Jun	flowering	"Old Spice Mixed"
July	flowering	Dwarf/patio varieties
Aug	flowering	"Explorer"
Sept	flowering	"Fantasia Mixed"
Oct	sow	"Jet-Set Mixed"
Nov	/	"Knee-High"
Dec	/	

Lavandula

LAVENDER

FEATURES

Most lavenders grow into rounded bushes about 3ft high and wide, but some dwarf forms grow only 12–16in high. All lavenders are suitable for hedging as they respond well to regular clipping. The highly aromatic foliage is gray-green and flower spikes may be pale lavender to rich purple. Plant a lavender hedge to define a path or to outline a terrace—these are the places where passers-by will brush against them and release the fragrance. Lavender can also be planted to provide color contrast in a formal garden.

CONDITIONS

ASPECT	Needs full sun for good dense growth. Keep them well away from the shade.
SITE	Needs an open, well-drained soil that need not be rich. Add lime to very acid soil before planting lavender. Heavy wet soil needs to be vigorously broken up with plenty of horticultural sand and grit.

GROWING METHOD

PROPAGATION	Grow from tip cuttings taken from spring until fall, or from lateral cuttings with a heel of older wood in fall or early winter. The success rate is usually quite high.
SPACING	For hedging, plant lavenders at 18–24in intervals, dwarf forms at 12–16in intervals.
FEEDING	Needs little fertilizer. Apply pelleted poultry manure in spring as growth begins.
PROBLEMS	Overwatering or poorly drained soils will induce the rotting of roots. Also beware attacks of honey fungus. The stems die back, and the attack can either be swift and sudden or quite gradual, lasting a number of years. The only solution is to dig up the affected plants entirely, dig over the area, and replant with shrubs that better resist such attacks. They include choisya, pieris, and pittosporum.

FLOWERING

SEASON	The main flowering season is in the height of the summer, adding fresh gray-green foliage and blue flowers to planting schemes.
CUTTING	The flowers make wonderful posies and can also be dried. Regular clipping may reduce the flowering display.

PRUNING

GENERAL	Clip the shrub little and often to maintain dense growth. If necessary, hard prune in late winter, but not into old wood.

AT A GLANCE		
Free-flowering, aromatic shrubs that quickly make impressive hedges; a good alternative to box. Hardy to 23°F (zone 9).		
Jan	foliage	Recommended Varieties
Feb	foliage	*Lavandula angustifolia*
Mar	foliage	*L. a.* "Hidcote"
April	foliage	*L. a.* "Munstead"
May	foliage	*L. a.* "Twickel Purple"
June	flowering	*L. x intermedia*
July	flowering	*L. lanata*
Aug	flowering	*L. latifolia*
Sept	foliage	*L. stoechas*
Oct	foliage	
Nov	foliage	
Dec	foliage	

Lavatera

ANNUAL MALLOW

FEATURES

White, rose, pink, and red flowers with a silky sheen are characteristic of annual mallow. Plants grow between 2–4ft depending on variety, and bloom continuously from mid-June onward. Use them as the centerpiece in summer bedding schemes or grow in large blocks in annual borders. An easily-grown hardy annual that is also useful as a cut flower.

CONDITIONS

ASPECT   Must have full sun all day.

SITE   Lavatera needs good drainage but not rich soil —plants flower better if the ground is hungry, making them good plants for light sandy soils. They do well in seaside gardens.

GROWING METHOD

SOWING   Seed is sown outdoors March–May, and earlier sowings mean earlier flowers. Mark out circles 2ft or more across, then sow seed in short drills $1/2$in deep. When seedlings appear thin them out gradually so they are 1–2ft apart by early summer. Growing this way creates a roughly circular block of color, which can be used as the centerpiece of a bedding scheme using annuals.

FEEDING   Feeding is not necessary. Water thoroughly in early summer during long dry spells.

PROBLEMS   Sometimes killed suddenly by soil fungal diseases–grow in a new spot the next season.

FLOWERING

SEASON   Summer.

CUTTING   Grow a few plants just for cut stems.

AFTER FLOWERING

GENERAL   Leave a few plants to self-seed, then pull up.

SOFT PRETTY PINK flowers are borne over many weeks on the annual Lavatera trimestris. There are many lovely cultivars.

AT A GLANCE	
A hardy annual grown for its large, colorful summer flowers on bushy plants 2–4ft tall. Frost hardy to 5°F (zone 7).	
Jan /	**Recommended Varieties**
Feb /	*Lavatera trimestris*
Mar sow	"Beauty Mixed"
Apr sow/thin out	"Dwarf White Cherub"
May sow/thin out	"Loveliness"
Jun flowering	"Mont Blanc"
July flowering	"Mont Rose"
Aug flowering	"Parade Mixed"
Sept flowering	"Pink Beauty"
Oct /	"Ruby Regis"
Nov /	"Silver Cup"
Dec /	

Lavender

LAVENDULA

FEATURES

Never out of fashion, hardy, evergreen lavender forms a rounded shrub 12–30in high. From July to September, its aromatic, gray-green foliage complements spikes of tightly clustered, pale blue, purple, pink, or white flowers. Interplant it with other shrubs or border perennials or set it to form a fetching divide between open-plan gardens.

Choice varieties are: dwarf, compact and rich purple-blue "Hidcote"; equally neat, lavender-blue "Munstead"; and taller French lavender (*Lavandula stoechas* "Papillon"), the dark purple flowers of which are borne in dense, lozenge-shaped heads. Flowers are used fresh in posies and dried for pot-pourri or cosmetics.

Lavender is an archetypal cottage-garden plant. Its common names of French, English, or Italian lavender apply to different species, but even experts find it hard to agree upon which is which.

CONDITIONS

ASPECT   Lavender needs an open situation in full sun with good air circulation. Do not crowd it with other plantings.

SITE   Thriving on most well-drained soils, it prefers coarse, sandy, or gravelly loam. Lime acid soils before planting.

GROWING METHOD

FEEDING   Boost growth of young plants by topdressing the root area with fish, blood, and bone meal in spring and midsummer. When established, after two years, no regular fertilizing is necessary. Water new plantings copiously to help them recover quickly. When well established, lavender is seldom stressed by droughty spells.

PROPAGATION   Take semi-ripe cuttings from early to mid-fall. Alternatively, work sharp sand into the crown in spring, watering it well, so lower branches are buried. Detach rooted layers in fall and move them to their new positions.

PROBLEMS   Lavender is seldom troubled by pests or diseases but may succumb to root rot in heavy or overwet soils. If crowded, in sheltered gardens, the foliage may die back. Remove dead growth and thin out stems to improve air circulation.

PRUNING

Use shears to trim dead blooms from bushes and hedges after flowering. Rejuvenate older, "tired" plants and help them bloom freely by shortening the previous year's flowered stems to new shoots within 2–4in of the base. Do this from early to mid-spring. Never cut back into older wood, for it seldom regenerates and plants may die.

AT A GLANCE		
Aromatic, grayish-leaved evergreen with scented, lavender, purple, pink, or white flowers in summer. Hardy to 14°F (zone8).		
Jan	/	Recommended Varieties
Feb	/	"Hidcote"
Mar	/	"Loddon Pink"
Apr	plant, prune	"Munstead"
May	plant	"Nana Alba"
June	plant	"Twickel Purple"
July	flower, plant	*L. vera*
Aug	flower, plant	*L. stoechas* "Papillon"
Sept	flower, plant	
Oct	/	
Nov	/	
Dec	/	

Lemon Verbena

ALOYSIA TRIPHYLLA, SYN. LIPPIA CITRIODORA

FEATURES

A large, bushy, deciduous shrub that grows 3–10ft in height, lemon verbena has long, lemony-scented, narrow leaves. Spikes or sprays of small white to mauve flowers appear in the axils of the leaves in summer. The leaves give this plant its herby quality, and their fragrance can be released simply by brushing against them in the garden. It can be grown in containers and in cooler areas brought indoors over winter, although container plants do not reach the same height as garden plants.

CONDITIONS

ASPECT   Requires a sheltered, sunny position with winter protection. Against a sunny wall is ideal.

SITE   Likes rich soils. Needs mulching against frosts.

GROWING METHOD

SOWING   Grow from softwood cuttings in late spring or hardwood cuttings in the fall. Trim a 5in piece from the parent bush, removing a third of the upper leaves and a few of the lower leaves. Place in a sandy potting mix. Moisten the mix and cover the pot with a plastic bag to create a mini-greenhouse. Pot on into good quality potting compost when the cutting has taken root and shows renewed leaf growth. Plant in the garden when the plant is growing strongly.

FEEDING   The plant is tolerant of dry conditions and will rarely require watering except when grown in a pot. Mulch with straw in the fall to protect from frost. Give an application of a balanced general fertilizer in spring.

PROBLEMS   Spider mite and whitefly can be a problem. Hose leaves frequently to remove pests or use organic soap and pyrethrum or recommended chemicals.

PRUNING

Prune each season to contain its straggly growth habit, and cut out frost-damaged shoots in spring. It can be trained into a formal standard.

HARVESTING

PICKING   Sprigs of leaves can be harvested at any time.

STORAGE   Hang the branches in a cool, airy place and strip off the leaves when they are dry. Store dried leaves in airtight jars. Fragrance remains for some years.

FREEZING   Put in a freezer bag and freeze for up to 6 months.

AT A GLANCE		
A deciduous shrub with lemon-scented leaves which are popular ingredients in pot-pourris and sachets. Hardy to 23˚F (zone 9).		
Jan	/	**Parts used**
Feb	/	Leaves
Mar	/	**Uses**
Apr	/	Culinary
May	plant harvest	Medicinal
Jun	harvest	Cosmetic
July	harvest	Craft
Aug	plant harvest	Gardening
Sept	plan tharvest	
Oct	/	
Nov	/	
Dec	/	

USES

CULINARY	Fresh or dried leaves can be used for herbal tea or in cooking where a lemony flavour is required, as with fish, poultry, marinades, salad dressings, and puddings, and to flavour oils and vinegars.
MEDICINAL	Lemon verbena tea has a mild sedative effect and is good for nasal congestion and indigestion. Caution: long-term use may cause stomach irritation.
COSMETIC	The leaves can be used in skin creams and the essential oil is used in perfumery.
CRAFT	The strong long-lasting fragrance makes dried leaves a popular component of pot-pourris and sachet fillings.
GARDENING	Lemon verbena is an attractive border and container plant.

Lepanthopsis

LEPANTHOPSIS SPECIES

FEATURES

This is one of several orchid genera, including *Pleurothallis* and *Dryadella*, that is truly miniature. The plant size reaches only 1¹/₄in at the most and the flower stem is about the same again. The plant produces a tiny spray of these exquisite little flowers, which measure only ¹/₈in across. The flowers are a vivid deep purple and star-shaped, which makes them a little easier to pick out, however you may still need a magnifying glass. The unusual orchid, *L. astrophorea* "Stalky," is just one of a genus of around 25 different species widely found in Central America. This genus was originally classified with the *Pleurothallis* until it was proclaimed to be different enough to be given its own name. It grows well with other members of the "Pleurothallid Alliance" including masdevallias. It can be grown for many years in the same small pot, as it will not outgrow it very easily and will stay almost perpetually in flower.

CONDITIONS

CLIMATE	This orchid is mostly cool growing but will tolerate slightly warmer intermediate conditions if necessary.
ASPECT	Provide good shade for this little plant so it does not dehydrate too much.
POTTING MIX	As it is growing in a tiny pot and has a very fine root system, use a fine grade of bark with a little perlite and sphagnum moss.

GROWING METHOD

PROPAGATION	Will propagate quite easily once you have let the plant grow on for several years to fill the pot. For best results, though, keep

as one plant; it won't take up that much room.

WATERING	Small pots tend to dry out more quickly than large ones so water regularly to keep from drying out. Mist the foliage also.
FEEDING	Give the plant a little weak orchid feed during the summer when it is in its more active growth.
PROBLEMS	No specific problems are known if cultural conditions are suitable.

FLOWERING SEASON

Can be all the year round on a mature plant; generally does not have a strict flowering season. Long lasting for such tiny flowers.

A TRULY MINIATURE ORCHID, Lepanthopsis astrophorea "Stalky," has flowers only a few millimetres across but is seldom out of bloom. Although small in stature, a mature specimen will grow into a larger plant measuring 3–4in across if left undivided for years.

AT A GLANCE	
Miniature, only 1¹/₄in high but small flowers bloom continually. Best in sheltered, controlled environment.	
Jan water	**Recommended Varieties**
Feb water	*L. astrophorea* "Stalky"
Mar water, re-pot	
Apr water, re-pot	
May water	
Jun water and feed	
July water and feed	
Aug water and feed	
Sept water	
Oct water	
Nov water	
Dec water	

Leucanthemum

SHASTA DAISY

FEATURES

Leucanthemum x *superbum* (Shasta daisy) looks wonderful when planted in a mixed border, where the large white flowers mix with more brightly colored flowers. Despite being easy to grow and multiplying rapidly, the daisies do not become a menace. Flower stalks can grow 24–36in tall, while the dark green leaves are only 4–6in high. Shasta daisies make striking cut flowers, livening up any arrangement. There are a number of named cultivars, some, such as "Esther Read," "Wirral Supreme," and "Cobham Gold," with double flowers. (Despite its name, the flowers on "Cobham Gold" are cream, not gold.) "Everest" is probably the largest of the single cultivars, though it is rarely available.

CONDITIONS

ASPECT   Prefers full sunlight all day and wind protection.
SITE   The soil should be well drained, and improved by the addition of decayed compost or manure.

GROWING METHOD

PROPAGATION   Divide the clumps in early spring or late summer, replanting only the younger, vigorous, outer growths, each with its own set of roots and shoots. Plant the divisions approximately 10in apart. Cuttings of young, short shoots can also be taken in early spring.
FEEDING   Apply complete plant food as growth begins in the spring. Liquid fertilizer applied in late spring should help produce better blooms.

PROBLEMS

PROBLEMS   The main problems are aphids, slugs, earwigs, and chrysanthemum eelworm. The first can be tackled with a proprietary spray, and the second and third by traps (saucers filled with beer, and inverted flower pots filled with straw placed on bamboo canes). In the case of eelworm, evident from browning/blackening, drying foliage from the base upward, the whole plant must be destroyed.

FLOWERING

SEASON   Flowering is all summer long.
CUTTING   Cut flowers regularly for indoor decoration, which will also prolong the garden display.

AFTER FLOWERING

REQUIREMENTS   Cut back spent flower stems to the ground.

AT A GLANCE	
L. x superbum is a vigorous, clump-forming perennial with many attractive cultivars, mainly in white. Hardy to 23˚F (zone 9).	
Jan /	Recommended Varieties
Feb /	*Leucanthemum* x *superbum*
Mar divide	"Aglaia"
Apr transplant	"Alaska"
May transplant	"Bishopstone"
Jun flowering	"Cobham Gold"
July flowering	"Horace Read"
Aug flowering	"Phyllis Smith"
Sept flowering	"Snowcap"
Oct divide	
Nov /	
Dec /	

Leucojum
SNOWFLAKE

FEATURES

Easily grown snowflakes have clusters of white, bell-shaped flowers, each petal bearing a bright green spot on its tip. Foliage is a rich, deep green and bulbs multiply readily to form good sized clumps in a few years.

There are three types of snowflake; spring snowflake (*Leucojum vernum*), summer snowflake (*L. aestivum*), and fall snowflake (*L. autumnale*). The spring snowflake flowers in February or March, while the summer snowflake, despite its name, usually flowers in late spring. Spring snowflake reaches a height of about 8in; summer snowflake up to 24in, and fall snowflake 6in, with very fine, narrow foliage. The flowers have a passing resemblance to snowdrops, but are easily distinguished by their rounded, bell shape and taller growth.

CONDITIONS

ASPECT   Grows well in sun but also happy in shade or in dappled sunlight. Fall snowflakes prefer an open, sunny position.

SITE   Low-growing species are excellent for rock gardens or the front of borders; taller summer snowflakes toward the middle of a border. Spring and summer snowflakes prefer a moisture-retentive soil enriched with organic matter: fall snowflake needs light, free-draining soil.

GROWING METHOD

PLANTING   Plant bulbs 3in deep and 4–8in apart in late summer or early fall.

FEEDING   An annual mulching with decayed manure or compost after bulbs have died down should provide adequate nutrients. Keep the soil for spring and summer snowflakes moist throughout the growing season.

PROBLEMS   No specific problems are known.

FLOWERING

SEASON   Spring snowflake flowers between midwinter and early spring; summer snowflake mid to late spring; and fall snowflake in September.

CUTTING   Best enjoyed in the garden.

AFTER FLOWERING

REQUIREMENTS   Remove spent flower stems. Divide crowded clumps when the foliage dies down, and replant immediately.

AT A GLANCE		
Delicate looking plants with white bells tipped with green, appearing in spring or early fall. Hardy.		
		Recommended Varieties
Jan	/	*Leucojum aestivum*
Feb	flowering	"Gravetye Giant"
Mar	flowering	*Leucojum autumnale*
Apr	flowering	"Cobb's Variety"
May	flowering	"Pulchellum"
Jun	/	*Leucojum vernum*
July	/	"Carpathicum"
Aug	/	"Vagneri"
Sept	plant/ flower	
Oct	plant	
Nov	/	
Dec	/	

Lewesia

LEWESIA

FEATURES

The genus has 19 or 20 hardy species, and is exclusively American. The best place to grow them is on a well-drained south-facing slope, in a rock garden or even on a wall. They are low growing, often with bright flowers which are funnel shaped. The color range is mainly on the pink-magenta side, with some that are yellow and white. There are many excellent kinds to choose from, the best being *L. bracyhcalyx* which flowers in late spring and early summer, *L. cotyledon* which flowers from spring to summer in purple-pink, and *L. tweedyi* which flowers at the same time in a peachy-pink color. The best thing about lewesias is that they hybridize easily, and a collection of different plants should soon yield interesting offspring. The excellent Cotyledon Hybrids come in all colors from yellow-orange to magenta.

CONDITIONS

ASPECT   These plants need full sun to thrive and if their position, the base of a wall perhaps, also reduces winter wet, all the better.

SITE   The soil must be fast draining, and to that end you must dig in plenty of horticultural sand or grit to provide the kind of conditions that the plant receives in its native California. Lewesias also enjoy reasonable fertility, with some added compost.

GROWING METHOD

PROPAGATION   Since lewesias freely hybridize, you do not have to do too much propagating. But you can propagate favorite colors by seed (except for the Cotyledon Hybrids) in the fall, or pot up offsets in the summer.

FEEDING   Plants grown outside in the border might benefit from an early-spring application of a standard plant feed. Pot-grown lewesias, perhaps on a show bench in an alpine house, benefit from a mild liquid feed in the early spring.

PROBLEMS   A fatal problem for lewesias is excessive moisture during the winter, otherwise watch out for slugs and snails. Remove them by hand each night to prevent the plants from becoming an instant salad.

FLOWERING

SEASON   Lewesias are highly valued for their smallish tubular flowers, generally about 1inch across. They are most highly visible when the plant is growing in a crack in a wall. In the garden they would be rather lost.

AT A GLANCE		
Marvelous small early season flowers in a wide range of colors. Excellent in small pots. Hardy to 5˚F (zone 7).		
Jan	/	**Recommended Varieties**
Feb	/	*Lewesia brachycalyx*
Mar	repotting	*L. cotyledon*
Apr	/	"Sunset Group"
May	flowering	*L. Cotyledon* Hybrids
Jun	flowering	"De Pauley"
July	/	"George Henley"
Aug	/	"Guido"
Sept	sow	*L. pygmaea*
Oct	/	*L. tweedyi*
Nov	transplant	
Dec	/	

Ligularia

LIGULARIA

FEATURES

Ligularia, with its bright yellow daisies, has four key advantages. It mainly flowers in mid- and late summer, and tolerates dappled shade, making it invaluable for the border. It often has interesting, well-displayed foliage; it can be shaped like a kidney, a five-pointed star, or be oval, held on tallish stems. The fourth advantage is that these are tall plants, adding height to schemes, being from 36in to 6ft tall. They can be used in small groups to punctuate arrangements of smaller plants, or form an impressive massed display. The flowers are yellow or orange. *L. dentata* "Othello" has purple-tinged leaves with a red underside, and "Desdemona" has brownish-green leaves, similarly colored beneath. With room for only one ligularia, "The Rocket" offers height, yellow flowers, black stems, and interesting, big-toothed foliage.

CONDITIONS

ASPECT   Tolerates full sun and some light shade. Also requires shelter from cutting winds.

SITE   The soil must be moist—ligularias grow well beside ponds and streams—for a big performance. If the soil begins to dry out to any degree, the plants quickly show signs of distress by wilting.

GROWING METHOD

PROPAGATION Increase the species by sowing seed or division in the spring or fall. Cultivars can only be raised by division. Make sure that the emerging new growth is well-watered, and never allowed to dry out. Set out from 24in to 4ft apart.

FEEDING   Border plants need plenty of well-rotted manure or compost, and a deep mulch to guard against moisture loss.

PROBLEMS   Slugs and snails can be a major problem, especially as the leaves emerge. Pick off or treat chemically.

FLOWERING

SEASON   Generally from late summer into the fall, but some flower in mid-summer, and *L. stenocephala* in early summer.

CUTTING   It is not advisable to strip the plants of their impressive flowering stems, especially when you only have room for a few plants.

AFTER FLOWERING

REQUIREMENTS Cut back to the ground.

AT A GLANCE		
A genus of 150 species of perennials grown for their tall flower spikes and large, architectural foliage. Hardy to 0°F (zones 6–7).		
Jan	/	Recommended Varieties
Feb	sow	*Ligularia dentata*
Mar	sow	"Desdemona"
Apr	transplant	"Othello"
May	transplant	"Gregynog Gold"
Jun	/	*L. przewalskii*
July	flowering	"The Rocket"
Aug	flowering	*L. wilsoniana*
Sept	/	
Oct	divide	
Nov	/	
Dec	/	

Ligustrum ovalifolium
GOLDEN PRIVET

FEATURES

Many of the 50 species of privet have been grown in the past as hedges. This variety, *Ligustrum ovalifolium* "Aureum," or golden privet, can grow to 12ft but is usually seen hedged to 3–6$\frac{1}{2}$ft. Its foliage may be variegated dark green and gold but is often almost entirely yellow. This is a quick growing, hardy and easy-care plant, able to tolerate a wide range of conditions. It can be grown as a solid dividing hedge, or can be clipped and pruned to give all kinds of different shapes. The form "Argenteum" has leaves with a white margin if the yellow seems a bit too brash.

CONDITIONS

ASPECT | Must have full sun all day for dense growth and to retain the golden color.
SITE | Should be well drained but it does not need to be rich. Giving privet a spring feed of slow-release fertilizer, and/or a spring mulch, helps keep it in good condition.

GROWING METHOD

PROPAGATION | Grow from semi-ripe tip cuttings taken in the summer. Alternatively use hardwood cuttings taken in the winter.
SPACING | Plants can be spaced at 16–20in intervals to achieve a good, thick hedge.

FEEDING

FEEDING | Can be grown without supplementary fertilizer. If the soil is very poor, apply all-purpose plant food in spring.
PROBLEMS | There are no known problems.

FLOWERING

SEASON | Flowers appear in midsummer. Many people find the scent unpleasant and overpowering.

PRUNING

GENERAL | As the growth of this plant is particularly rapid, privet needs to be trimmed frequently. Cut out any growths that you can see are reverting to plain green. As flowers appear, shear or tip prune to avoid fruit setting.

A FAVORITE PLANT for hedging since Victorian times, golden privet needs very little care indeed.

AT A GLANCE		
Excellent, all-purpose, robust hedge with summer flowers that can be shaped and pruned. Hardy to 0˚F (zone 7).		
Jan	foliage	**Recommended Varieties**
Feb	foliage	*Ligustrum japonicum*
Mar	foliage	*L. lucidum*
April	foliage	*L. lucidum*
May	foliage	"Excelsum Superbum"
June	flowering	*L. obtusifolium*
July	foliage	*L. ovalifolium*
Aug	foliage	"Argenteum"
Sept	foliage	*L. ovalifolium*
Oct	foliage	"Aureum"
Nov	foliage	*L. vulgare*
Dec	foliage	

Lilac

SYRINGA

FEATURES

A vast and fragrant, deciduous family from S.E. Europe to E. Asia, its cone or plume-like flowers light up May and June. Most popular are varieties of *Syringa vulgaris*. Enchanting, double-flowered forms are mauve-pink "Belle de Nancy," dark purple "Charles Joly," and violet-red "Paul Hariot". Captivating singles include white "Maud Notcutt" and creamy-yellow "Primrose". All make upright focal points to 8–10ft.

The Canadian Hybrids—rose-hued "Bellicent" and pale lilac "Elinor"—tolerate shade better than *S. vulgaris* and bear plumy blossom. Accommodating dwarf varieties, to 4ft, for small gardens or rockeries, are lilac-pink *S. meyeri* "Palibin" and *S. pubescens* "Superba".

CONDITIONS

ASPECT   Lilac flowers best in full sun but tolerates light shade. Choose an open site, protected from strong, drying winds, where air circulates freely, to reduce risk of leaves becoming mildewed.

SITE   These shrubs need well-drained, organically rich soil. Avoid chalky spots, which may cause lime-induced chlorosis, when leaves turn creamy yellow and die.

GROWING METHOD

FEEDING   Apply a complete plant food, such as Growmore or fish, blood, and bone meal in spring and midsummer.

PROPAGATION   Commercially, varieties are usually budded or grafted on to privet rootstock. Alternatively, take soft-tip cuttings in early summer or semi-ripe cuttings from mid- to late summer.

PROBLEMS   Lilac blight, characterised by angular, brown spots, destroys leaves and buds. There are no chemical controls, so cut back affected shoots to healthy, white tissue and burn prunings.
When mildew strikes, leaves are felted with powdery-white mold. Improve air flow by thinning crowded shoots and spraying with carbendazim, mancozeb, or sulfur when symptoms appear.

PRUNING

Cut out spent flowers when petals fade. Keep bushes youthful and blooming freely by pruning out a quarter of the older shoots each year in winter. Remove basal suckers.

AT A GLANCE		
Perfumed, cone- or plume-shaped blooms in many shades appear in spring. Hardiness rating according to species.		
Jan	/	**Recommended Varieties**
Feb	/	*Syringa pubescens*
Mar	plant	"Miss Kim"
Apr	plant	"Superba"
May	flower, plant	*S. vulgaris*
Jun	flower, plant	"Belle de Nancy"
July	plant	"Charles Joly"
Aug	plant	"Mme Lemoine"
Sept	plant	"Mrs Edward Harding"
Oct	plant	"Primrose"
Nov	plant, prune	*S. x prestoniae*
Dec	prune	"Elinor"

Lilium

LILY

FEATURES

Lilies are tall, stately plants that carry a number of large, trumpet-shaped blooms on each flowering stem. Flowering stems may be anywhere from about 2ft to over 6ft high. There are 80–90 species of lily and many hundreds of cultivars, so it is difficult to outline their requirements concisely. Lily flowers are often fragrant and the main color range includes white, yellow, pink, red, and orange—many have spotted or streaked petals. A quite small range of lily bulbs is usually available in garden centers in fall and these should be planted as soon as possible after their arrival: lily bulbs have no tunic or outer covering and so can dry out unless they are carefully handled. For a greater range of species and hybrids you will need to contact specialist growers and mail order suppliers. Many lily enthusiasts belong to societies devoted to learning more about the enormous range of types available and their cultivation.

TYPES

Some of the more popular species grown are *L. auratum*, golden-rayed lily, which has white petals with gold bands; *L. candidum*, Madonna lily, which is pure white; *L. martagon*, Turk's cap lily, with fully recurved, dark red petals with dark spots; *L. regale*, the regal lily, with white flowers that have purple backs to the petals and a yellow base; *L. speciosum* which has white petals with a deep pink center and reddish spots; and *L. tigrinum*, tiger lily, dark orange with black spots and revurving petals. As well as the species, many hybrid varieties are grown, which are classified into a number

of groups. Among the most popular are the Asiatic hybrids, short to medium height, with upward-facing flowers produced early in the season; and the Oriental hybrids, which are taller and more refined, with nodding, strongly scented blooms. Asiatic hybrids are ideal for pots and are available pot-grown throughout the summer.

CONDITIONS

ASPECT   The ideal situation is a sunny position with a little dappled shade during part of the day. They need protection from strong wind.

SITE   Lilies grow well when mixed with other plants that will shade their roots, in a bed or border, or in containers. Plant them where their perfume can be appreciated. Soil must be well- drained with a high organic content. Dig in copious amounts of well-rotted manure or compost a month or so before planting.

AT A GLANCE	
Stately plants with trumpet-shaped, usually intensely fragrant flowers on tall spikes.	
Jan /	Recommended Varieties
Feb /	"Apollo"
Mar /	"Barcelona"
Apr /	"Casa Blanca"
May /	"Corsage"
Jun flowering	"Enchantment"
July flowering	"Green Dragon"
Aug flowering/plant	"Mrs R. O. Backhouse"
Sept flowering/plant	"Orange Triumph"
Oct plant	"Shuksan"
Nov plant	"Tamara"
Dec /	

GROWING METHOD

PLANTING Plant 4–9in deep and 9–15in or so apart in fall or early spring. Bulbs must not be bruised or allowed to dry out, and they should be planted as soon as possible after purchase. Apply a layer of compost or manure to the soil surface as a mulch after planting. Your stock of lilies can be increased by bulb scales, bulbils or offsets, according to type.

FEEDING If the soil contains plenty of organic matter these plants should not need a lot of feeding. Apply a slow-release granular fertilizer as growth starts and after flowering. Water regularly during dry spells but avoid overwatering which may rot the bulbs.

PROBLEMS Most problems with lilies result from poor cultivation or unsuitable growing conditions. Gray mold (botrytis) can be a problem in cool, humid conditions, especially if plants are overwatered or if air circulation is poor. The small, bright red lily beetle and their larvae can cause a lot of damage in some areas: control them with a contact insecticide and clear away plant debris in which the adults overwinter.

FLOWERING

SEASON Lilies flower some time between early summer and fall with many flowering in middle to late summer. Flowering time depends on the species and, to some extent, the conditions.

CUTTING Lilies make wonderful and very long-lasting cut flowers. Cut them when flowers are just open or all buds are rounded and fully colored. Don't cut right to the bottom of the stem—retain some leaves on the lower part. Change water frequently and cut off spent flowers from the cluster to allow the other buds to develop fully.

AFTER FLOWERING

REQUIREMENTS Remove spent flower stems as they finish blooming. Remove only the flowering stem and leave as much foliage as possible. Don't be in a hurry to cut back yellowing growth too soon: allow the plant to die back naturally and mulch with chipped bark for the winter. Bulbs are best left in the ground for several years. When they are lifted they must be divided and replanted at once, as having no tunic on the bulb means they dry out very quickly. If they can't be planted at once, store them in damp sphagnum moss or peat.

THIS BURNED ORANGE HYBRID shows the characteristic dark spotting in its throat. Lilies make excellent cut flowers.

Limnanthes

POACHED EGG FLOWER

FEATURES

Limnanthes douglasii has cup-shaped white flowers with bright yellow centers, which explains its common name of poached egg flower. Plants grow to 6–9in in height and have a spreading habit. A hardy annual, it self-seeds very easily and keeps on coming. Grow in annual beds, along path edges and among other plants in borders.

CONDITIONS

ASPECT   Prefers full sun and an open situation.
SITE   Needs moisture-retentive soil with rotted organic matter mixed in well ahead of sowing.

GROWING METHOD

SOWING   Spring or fall are the sowing times. Sow from March to May or in September. Either sow seed in short drills 1/2in deep or mark areas of soil, scatter the seed over the surface, and rake in. Seedlings appear after 1–2 weeks and should be thinned out so they are about 3–6in apart, although this is not too critical. If sowing in fall do not thin until spring in case of winter losses.

FEEDING   Feeding is not necessary, but water thoroughly in dry spells during early summer.
PROBLEMS   No special problems.

FLOWERING

SEASON   Overwintered plants flower from late spring depending on the weather, and are very attractive to bees and beneficial garden insects.
CUTTING   Not suitable for cutting.

AFTER FLOWERING

GENERAL   Pull plants up as soon as they are over.

POACHED EGG FLOWER has 1in-wide flowers like tiny eggs in early summer, and attractive, divided, fern-like leaves. The seeds of Limnanthes go everywhere after flowering and seem to enjoy spreading along path edges in particular.

AT A GLANCE		
A hardy annual that quickly self-seeds, producing masses of yellow/white flowers in summer. Frost hardy to 5°F (zone 7).		
Jan	/	Recommended Varieties
Feb	/	*Limnanthes douglasii*
Mar	sow	
Apr	sow/thin	
May	sow/thin	
Jun	flowering	
July	flowering	
Aug	/	
Sept	sow	
Oct	/	
Nov	/	
Dec	/	

Limonium

STATICE

FEATURES

Annual varieties of Limonium sinuatum grow up to 3ft tall and have peculiar winged stems. The actual flowers are small, but statice is grown for its papery bracts of purple, white, pink, apricot, yellow, rose, or blue, which persist all summer, and can be used as a cut and dried flower. A half-hardy annual that is used solely for cutting, or in the case of the short varieties as a bedding/ container plant.

CONDITIONS

ASPECT	Grow in full sun in an open position.
SITE	Must have very well-drained soil, and is quite happy in sandy, light soils that are on the "hungry" side. If growing dwarf varieties for containers use multipurpose compost. Statice does exceedingly well in seaside gardens.

GROWING METHOD

SOWING	Sow seed in February/March in a 3$\frac{1}{2}$in pot of multipurpose compost and keep lat 64°F. Transplant to cell trays, grow on, then harden off in late May and plant after the last frosts 6–18in apart. If growing for cut flowers, seed can be sown outdoors in rows from early May, $\frac{1}{2}$in deep and thinned to similar spacings.
FEEDING	Does not need regular feeding, but water well if dry straight after planting out.

PROBLEMS

PROBLEMS	Plants may rot on heavy, wet soils, and powdery mildew can attack the leaves in late summer, but this is rarely serious.

FLOWERING

SEASON	Long flowering period throughout summer.
CUTTING	Ideal cut flower. Can be used fresh, or cut and dried by hanging bunches upside down in a dry airy place. Cut when the flowerheads are showing maximum color. Dried flowers retain their color well over a long period.

AFTER FLOWERING

GENERAL	Pull plants up and compost when all the flowers have been cut or have gone over.

LONG AFTER the small pale flowers have faded the colorful papery bracts are still going strong, and they keep their color when dried.

AT A GLANCE	
A half-hardy annual grown for its heads of brightly colored bracts used for bedding and drying. Frost hardy to 23°F (zone 9).	

Jan	/	**Recommended Varieties**
Feb	sow	*Limonium sinuatum*
Mar	sow/transplant	**Tall varieties**
Apr	grow on	"Art Shades Mixed"
May	grow on/harden	"Forever Mixed"
Jun	plant/grow	"Forever Moonlight"
July	flowering	"Sunburst Mixed"
Aug	flowers/cutting	"Sunset Mixed"
Sept	flowers/cutting	**Short varieties**
Oct	/	"Biedermeier Mixed"
Nov	/	"Petite Bouquet"
Dec	/	

Limonium latifolium

SEA LAVENDER

FEATURES

Limonium latifolium (sea lavender) is a perennial type of statice often grown for its tall, finely branched stems of tiny white and pale lavender flowers, which are widely used both in fresh and dried floral arrangements. Flower stems may be over 20in high, and the cultivar "Violetta" has deep violet flowers. The plant forms a basal rosette of broad, rounded, slightly fleshy leaves growing around 10in high. Clumps may ultimately spread 18in or more wide. This is a good plant for rockeries because it is quite drought tolerant. Sea lavender is native to parts of south-east and central Europe, thriving in dry summers and cold winters.

CONDITIONS

ASPECT   Prefers full sun all day, and tolerates exposed windy or coastal sites.
SITE   The soil must be very well drained, but need not be rich. In fact, sea lavender tolerates very poor soil.

GROWING METHOD

PROPAGATION   Grows from seed sown as soon as it is ripe, when the flowers have dried and turned brown, or from root cuttings taken in spring. New plantings should be spaced about 10–12in apart. Water regularly to establish new plants, and then give an occasional deep soaking during prolonged dry spring and summer weather.
FEEDING   Does not need feeding, but a little complete plant food may be applied in early spring, giving a decent boost.

PROBLEMS

Heavy, poorly drained soils or overwatering may cause the plant to rot and collapse.

FLOWERING

SEASON   Sea lavender flowers in late summer, when its spikelets of lavender flowers with white calyces begin to appear.
CUTTING   Flowers can be cut for drying when most of the flowers on the stem have fully opened.

AFTER FLOWERING

REQUIREMENTS   Cut off any remaining flower stems when they are past their best.

SEA LAVENDER has broad, slightly fleshy leaves, and flowers for several months. It is equally successful as part of a free-flowing design or, as shown, as a segregated, eye-catching feature.

AT A GLANCE	
L. latifolium is a perennial grown in windy coastal areas for its abundant, late summer flowers. Hardy to 0°F (zones 6–7).	

Month		Companion Plants
Jan	/	Eremurus
Feb	/	Escallonia
Mar	divide	Linum
Apr	transplant	Kniphofia
May	/	Olearia
Jun	/	Perovskia
July	/	Scabiosa
Aug	flowering	
Sept	flowering	
Oct	sow	
Nov	/	
Dec	/	

Linaria

TOADFLAX

FEATURES

Linaria is commonly known as toadflax and has dainty little flowers like tiny snapdragons in a wide color range including white, cream, yellow, red, blue, and pink. Plants grow 9–24in and are good massed in drifts in annual borders, or used as fillers in mixed border plantings. Most annual toadflax are varieties of *Linaria maroccana*. A hardy annual that can be sown direct outdoors.

CONDITIONS

ASPECT   Needs a warm, sunny spot.
SITE   Well-drained soil enriched with manure or compost ahead of planting is essential. Very good plants can be grown on light, sandy soils.

GROWING METHOD

SOWING   Seeds are best sown in short drills ¹/₂in deep March–May. Mark the sowing areas with a ring of light-colored sand and label if sowing more than one annual in the same bed. The seedlings will appear in rows and can be told from nearby weed seedlings quite easily. Thin the seedlings out so they are finally 4–6in apart by early summer. Alternatively, leave them to grow as small clumps of 4–6 plants every 12in or so.

FEEDING   Feeding is rarely needed but water well after the final thinning if the soil is dry.
PROBLEMS   No special problems.

FLOWERING

SEASON   Flowers appear early to mid summer.
CUTTING   Not usually used for cutting.

AFTER FLOWERING

GENERAL   Leave a few plants to die down and self-seed. Others can be pulled up and composted.

WHEN SOWN IN BOLD PATCHES varieties of Linaria maroccana soon knit together to produce a tapestry of color if one of the mixtures such as "Fairy Bouquet" is grown. Clumps can also be carefully lifted and planted into patio pots in late spring and early summer.

AT A GLANCE		
A hardy annual grown for its spikes of pretty flowers like small snapdragons appearing in summer. Frost hardy to 5°F (zone 7).		
Jan	/	**Recommended Varieties**
Feb	/	*Linaria anticaria*
Mar	sow	*Linaria maroccana*
Apr	sow/thin out	"Fairy Bouquet"
May	sow/thin out	"Fantasia Blue"
Jun	thin/flowers	"Fantasia Mixed"
July	flowering	"Fantasia Pink"
Aug	flowering	"Northern Lights"
Sept	flowering	*Linaria reticulata*
Oct	/	"Crown Jewels"
Nov	/	
Dec	/	

Liriope muscari

LILYTURF

FEATURES

This plant, known as lilyturf, is sometimes confused with *Ophiopogon jaburan* which is called white lilyturf. The two are similar but *Ophiopogon* has white flowers. *Liriope* grows in early summer about 12–14in high. The species has dark green leaves, but there are variegated forms as well. A spike of deep violet flowers stands well above the leaves. A tough and useful Far Eastern plant for the garden, especially as it flowers in the fall.

CONDITIONS

ASPECT   Will grow in shade or dappled sunlight, but flowers best in full sun.

SITE   Tolerates most soils but acid is preferred; grows best in well-drained soil enriched with plenty of organic matter.

GROWING METHOD

PROPAGATION   The easiest method of increase is to lift and divide the clumps in the spring. Replant the divisions approximately 3–4in apart. Water young plants regularly during prolonged dry spring and summer weather. Plants tolerate drought but prefer some regular water.

FEEDING   Apply complete plant food in the spring.

PROBLEMS   No specific problems are known.

FLOWERING

SEASON   The flowering begins in the early fall, and continues until the end of the season.

CUTTING   Lasts quite well in water.

AFTER FLOWERING

REQUIREMENTS   Cut off spent flowerheads once the flowers have dropped. As growth dies down toward winter, cut it off cleanly.

STRIKING FLOWER SPIKES in deep violet add to the attraction of this variegated form of liriope. Among its many uses, liriope makes an excellent edging for garden beds. Here it accentuates the circular form

AT A GLANCE		
L. muscari is a stout perennial ideal for difficult places, which also provides good ground cover. Hardy to 0°F (zones 6–7).		
Jan	/	Recommended Varieties
Feb	/	*Liriope muscari*
Mar	sow	"Big Blue"
Apr	divide	"Gold Banded"
May	transplant	"Majestic"
Jun	/	"Monroe White"
July	/	Companion Plants
Aug	/	Dicentra
Sept	flowering	Dryopteris
Oct	flowering	*Euphorbia robbiae*
Nov	flowering	Polypodium
Dec	/	Ribes
		Vinca major and *V. minor*

Lithodora diffusa

LITHOSPERMUM

FEATURES

This small, prostrate groundcover shrub is highly popular because of its brilliant blue flowers which cover the plant in late spring and early summer. It looks well and flourishes if grown in rockeries or on the edges of raised beds where it has perfect drainage. *Lithodora diffusa* can also be grown as a wall plant or between pavers or stepping stones. It does, however, need to be mass planted to get the best effect. There are a couple of cultivars available that have flowers either slightly larger than those of the species or in a different shade of blue, but it is, in fact, hard to beat the straight species for attractiveness.

CONDITIONS

ASPECT Needs full sun exposure. Do not attempt to hide it away in the shade. The consequent damp soil will also be a major problem.

SITE This plant needs an acid soil. If you do not have acid soil in the garden it can be grown in tubs surrounding a feature plant.

GROWING METHOD

PROPAGATION Grows from cuttings taken in late summer or from seed sown in the fall.

FEEDING Apply complete plant food in spring as new growth commences.

PROBLEMS

No pest or disease problems are known, but permanently wet and poorly drained soil will kill these plants.

FLOWERING

SEASON This evergreen shrub has a decent flowering period from late spring to early summer. To make sure that it is well seen, also try growing it on rockeries where it thrives with the excellent drainage. The forms "Grace Ward" and "Heavenly Blue" are the best and easiest to get.

CUTTING Flowers are unsuitable for cutting.

PRUNING

GENERAL Lightly prune these plants after flowering to remove spent stems.

INTENSE ROYAL BLUE FLOWERS are the highlight of this lithospermum planting, which trails over a low retaining wall.

AT A GLANCE		
Lithodora diffusa is a shortish evergreen, 6in high, with good forms making fine cover in acid soil. Hardy to 0°F (zone 7).		
Jan	foliage	**Companion Plants**
Feb	foliage	Azalea
Mar	foliage	Calluna
April	foliage	Erica
May	flowering	Gaultheria
June	flowering	Hydrangea
July	foliage	Kalmia
Aug	foliage	Pieris
Sept	foliage	Vaccinum
Oct	foliage	
Nov	foliage	
Dec	foliage	

Lithops
LIVING STONES

FEATURES

Living stones, stone plants, pebble plants and flowering stone are just a few of the common names assigned to these curious succulents. They are so completely camouflaged that it would be very easy to miss them entirely unless they were in flower. In their native south-west and South Africa, they generally grow buried in sand with only the tips of their leaves exposed. Their bodies are composed of a pair of very swollen, fleshy leaves on top of a fused double column with a gap or fissure along their length. The upper surfaces of the leaves are variously patterned and textured according to species and conditions. These plants are best grown in small pots where their curious shapes and markings can be observed. They make an excellent display.

CONDITIONS

ASPECT   These plants should be grown in a position where there is full sun all day. They are best grown in pots on show benches in a glasshouse. They can cope with extreme heat, and attempts to shade them during the hottest part of the day are quite unnecessary.

SITE   The soil provided for living stones should drain very rapidly and small gravel or pebbles should be used as a mulch. Only use very fine pieces of gravel to set off the plants, though with some varieties it is tempting to camouflage them. It is amusing to let visitors see if they can distinguish between the real stones and the plants.

GROWING METHOD

PROPAGATION   These plants can be grown from divisions of offsets or from seed in spring to early summer. As living stones are not rapid growers, the clumps are best left undivided until they are about 4in across.

FEEDING   Half-strength soluble liquid plant food can be given every 4–6 weeks through the active growth period.

PROBLEMS   Most problems arise from overwatering or a poorly drained growing medium. Look out for aphids when in flower.

FLOWERING

SEASON   Flowers that emerge from the fissure of the living stone are daisy-like and yellow or white.

THIS CLUSTER of intricately patterned Lithops turbiniformis *is livened by a bright yellow flower.*

AT A GLANCE		
Astonishing tiny succulents in a wide range of colors and patterns. Highly collectible. 41˚F min (zone 11).		
Jan	/	**Recommended Varieties**
Feb	/	*Lithops aucampiae*
Mar	sow	*L. dorothea*
Apr	transplant	*L. julii*
May	flowering	*L. mormorata*
Jun	flowering	*L. karasmontana*
July	flowering	*L. salicola*
Aug	flowering	*L. schwantesii*
Sept	flowering	*L. turbiniformis*
Oct	/	
Nov	/	
Dec	/	

Livistona chinensis

CHINESE FAN PALM

FEATURES

The Chinese fan palm is a native of Japan and Taiwan. Of moderate size when mature, the trunk has a distinctive swollen base. The pinnate, shiny, dark green leaves grow up to 6ft in length and are carried on spiny stalks. The eventual height is up to 40ft, with a spread up to 15ft. This palm, suitable as a houseplant when young, is also recommended for a cool glasshouse or conservatory and is happy to be placed out of doors for the summer. It can be grown in a container for many years.

CONDITIONS

ASPECT   Provide bright light but do not subject it to direct sun. Provide moderate humidity. Outdoors place in a sheltered position.
SITE   In containers grow this palm in soil-based potting compost.

GROWING METHOD

PROPAGATION Sow seeds as soon as available and germinate them at a temperature of 73°F.
WATERING   Water well in growing season from late spring to late summer, then for the rest of the year water sparingly.

FEEDING

FEEDING   Apply a balanced liquid fertilizer monthly during the growing season.
PROBLEMS Under glass may be attacked by scale insects and red spider mites.

FOLIAGE/FLOWERING

FOLIAGE   This palm looks good all year round but is especially attractive in spring and summer.
FLOWERS   Trusses of cream-colored flowers are produced in summer followed by grayish or bluish fruits.

GENERAL CARE

REQUIREMENTS Remove dead fronds when necessary by cutting them off close to the trunk.

The moderate-sized Livistona chinensis *(Chinese fan palm) has long stems before the eruption of leaves at the top of the plant. A beautiful peacock's tail of leaves makes it a striking houseplant or conservatory specimen.*

AT A GLANCE	
The trunk has a swollen base and supports dark green leaves. Provide a minimum temperature of 37–41°F (zones 10–11).	
Jan /	Companion Plants
Feb /	Under glass grow with other palms
Mar planting	such as *Jubaea chilensis* and with
Apr planting	other bold foliage plants such as
May foliage	*Musa* species (banana), and *Citrus*
Jun flowering	species. Outdoors combine with
July flowering	colorful summer bedding plants or
Aug flowering	include in a subtropical scheme.
Sep /	
Oct /	
Nov /	
Dec /	

Lobelia

LOBELIA

FEATURES

Choose the bushier "edging" varieties for bedding schemes and the "trailers" for hanging baskets, flower bags, and containers. Flower color ranges from white through pink, mauve and white to blue, and striking two-toned varieties like "Riviera Blue Splash" are also available. Edgers grow 4–6in tall, trailers up to 18in long when well-fed, and plants have a similar spread. Varieties of *Lobelia erinus* are available as single or mixed colors, and modern coated seed makes sowing much easier. A range of varieties are available as young plants by mail order. Half-hardy.

CONDITIONS

ASPECT   Flowers best when grown in full sun.
SITE   Enrich soil with rotted compost or manure before planting. Drainage must be good, but lobelia must also have adequate moisture all through the season. For baskets and containers use multipurpose compost and add slow-release fertilizer granules before planting up.

GROWING METHOD

SOWING   Sow January–March in a 3^{1}/$_{2}$in pot of multipurpose compost. Sow the tiny seeds evenly over the surface but do not cover, and put in a well-lit spot at 64°F. When the seedlings form a green "mat," carefully tease them apart into small clumps of 4–6, and transplant each clump to one unit of a multi-cell tray. Grow on, harden off in late May and plant after frosts.

FEEDING   Feed fortnightly with high-potash liquid feed, and never allow the plants to dry out.
PROBLEMS Trouble-free, but if seedlings keel over in spring water with copper-based fungicide.

FLOWERING

SEASON   Flowers appear from June onward.
CUTTING   Not suitable for cutting.

AFTER FLOWERING

GENERAL   Go over plants with shears when they look untidy and water with liquid feed—this encourages more flowers. Compost in fall.

LOBELIA FLOWERS are tubular with a large lower "lip" divided into three rounded lobes. Dark flowers have pale throats.

AT A GLANCE		
A half-hardy annual used as an edging plant or a trailing plant for baskets, with many small flowers. Frost hardy to 32°F (zone 10).		
Jan	sow	**Recommended Varieties**
Feb	sow/transplant	*Lobelia erinus:*
Mar	sow/transplant	**Edging varieties**
Apr	grow on	"Cambridge Blue"
May	harden off/plant	"Crystal Palace"
Jun	flowering	"Mrs Clibran Improved"
July	flowering	"Riviera Lilac"
Aug	flowering	**Trailing varieties**
Sept	flowering	"Cascade Mixed"
Oct	/	"Fountains Mixed"
Nov	/	"Regatta Mixed"
Dec	/	"String of Pearls Mixed"

Lobelia cardinalis

CARDINAL FLOWER

FEATURES

To most people, lobelia is a small edging plant with bright blue flowers. There are, however, about 400 species of lobelia, many of them perennials. This herbaceous species with bright scarlet flowers is also known as the cardinal flower and grows to about 36in tall. With its dark green leaves and bright flowers, it really stands out—it is sometimes used as a feature plant. It can also be used in a mixed border or mass-planted among shrubs, so long as the ground retains plenty of moisture.

CONDITIONS

ASPECT — Grows in full sunlight or semi-shade.
SITE — Needs rich and moisture-retentive soil, as these plants are not tolerant of drought. A streamside setting is ideal.

GROWING METHOD

PROPAGATION — Plants are usually divided every two or three years, in the spring. Plant the divisions about 12in apart. Lobelia must be kept moist and well watered while it is in active growth, especially during prolonged dry spells in the spring and summer.
FEEDING — Apply a complete plant food, and a mulch of compost or manure in the spring.

PROBLEMS

PROBLEMS — Slugs and snails will attack the flower spikes. Put down slug pellets or beer traps.

FLOWERING

SEASON — There is a long flowering period through the summer and fall period when the brilliant scarlet blooms appear.
CUTTING — Flowers are not suitable for cutting.

AFTER FLOWERING

REQUIREMENTS — Cut off spent flower stems. The dark-leaved hybrids ("Cherry Ripe") are not fully hardy and need a thick, protective winter mulch.

THIS LOBELIA is also known as cardinal flower, an apt description, since the tall spikes of flowers are the same scarlet as a cardinal's robes. In its natural habitat in North America this lobelia grows on wet meadows and river banks. It thrives on plenty of moisture.

AT A GLANCE		
L. cardinalis is a clump-forming, short-lived perennial, grown for its striking, vivid red flowers. Hardy to 5°F (zone 7).		
Jan	/	Recommended Varieties
Feb	/	Lobelia "Cherry Ripe"
Mar	sow	"Dark Crusader"
Apr	divide	"Kompliment Scharlach"
May	transplant	"Queen Victoria"
Jun	/	L. siphilitica
July	flowering	L. tupa
Aug	flowering	
Sept	flowering	
Oct	/	
Nov	/	
Dec	/	

Lobularia

ALYSSUM

FEATURES

Lobularia maritima, alyssum, has masses of tiny flowers in various colors in round heads; white, pink, lavender, and purple. All varieties smell sweetly of honey, although you need to get up close. None grow more than 6in high, making alyssum ideal as an edging plant, but it is also useful for planting in pots, troughs, and hanging baskets.

CONDITIONS

ASPECT   Grow alyssum in a spot receiving full sun.
SITE   Must have well-drained soil and adding rotted organic matter helps retain soil moisture. For baskets and patio containers plant using multipurpose potting compost.

GROWING METHOD

SOWING   Alyssum grown for bedding and containers is best raised in early spring. Sow a whole packet of seeds in February/March in a 3^1/$_2$in pot of multipurpose compost, and just cover. When seedlings are ^{1}/$_2$in tall split up into small clumps of 4–6 seedlings and transplant each to individual units of a multi-cell tray. This is especially useful to get a good spread of different flower colors when growing a mixed variety. Grow on and harden off in late May before planting out. Seeds can also be sown direct into the soil in an annual border during April/May ^{1}/$_2$in deep.

FEEDING   Extra feeding is unnecessary.
PROBLEMS Look out for slugs—they will attack newly-planted alyssum, especially after rain.

FLOWERING

SEASON   Flowers often appear before planting and until late summer—clip them over with shears and water well to encourage a second flush.
CUTTING   Not suitable as a cut flower.

AFTER FLOWERING

GENERAL   Seeds will self-sow very easily, and come up the following spring. Compost when finished.

"CARPET OF SNOW" is used here in a bed to create living lines and patterns around slightly taller plants like these violas.

AT A GLANCE	
A low-growing hardy annual for edging summer bedding schemes, with honey-scented flowers. Frost hardy to 5°F (zone 7).	
Jan /	**Recommended Varieties**
Feb sow	*Lobularia maritima*
Mar sow/transplant	"Aphrodite"
Apr sow/grow on	"Creamery"
May sow/harden off	"Easter Basket Mixed"
Jun flowering	"Easter Bonnet"
July flowering	"Golf Mixed"
Aug flowering	"Golf Rose"
Sept flowering	"Little Dorrit"
Oct /	"Rosie O'Day"
Nov /	"Snow Carpet"
Dec /	"Snow Crystals"

Lonicera

HONEYSUCKLE

FEATURES

Honeysuckles are widely grown climbers, ranking in popularity with clematis and jasmines. Like the latter, many have highly fragrant flowers and are valued for this alone, but the blooms also make a colorful display in the summer. They have a very informal habit of growth, making them ideally suited to cottage and country gardens, where they could be grown with old-fashioned flowers and other plants, such as old roses. Try growing them with climbing roses and let them intertwine for some really stunning effects, although bear in mind that pruning of both may then be more difficult. Owners of more modern gardens should also consider growing honeysuckles as they will not look out of place.

Honeysuckles can be grown up a variety of supports, including walls, fences, pergolas, arbors, arches, obelisks in a shrub border, and large mature trees. They look particularly at home in a woodland garden, as they often grow in woodland conditions in the wild. The Common honeysuckle or Woodbine, *Lonicera periclymenum* and its cultivars, makes good groundcover in shrub borders and woodland gardens. Some species can be grown in tubs and trained as standards, including *L. japonica* "Halliana" (Japanese honeysuckle) and *L. periclymenum* cultivars.

There are many species and cultivars to choose from but the following are probably among the best loved. *Lonicera* x *brownii* "Fuchsioides" (Scarlet trumpet honeysuckle), has clusters of slightly fragrant, tubular, orange-scarlet flowers in summer. A twiner of garden origin, it is deciduous or, in some climates, evergreen, and can attain a height of 12ft.

Lonicera caprifolium, (Italian honeysuckle), a native of Europe and western Asia, is a deciduous twiner producing, in summer, clusters of highly fragrant, tubular, cream or yellow flowers flushed with pink. It can grow to a height of 20ft.

The extremely vigorous *L. japonica* "Halliana" (Japanese honeysuckle), is a semi-evergreen or evergreen twiner with white tubular flowers which turn yellow as they age. The blooms are highly fragrant and the flowering period is from spring to the end of summer. It grows to a height of 30ft. The species is a native of eastern Asia.

The Common honeysuckle, also known as Woodbine, *L. periclymenum*, is a native of Britain where it scrambles over hedgerows. It is a very vigorous twiner that produces fragrant flowers from mid- to late summer. The species is not generally grown in gardens, most gardeners preferring to use its cultivars. *L. p.* "Belgica" is popularly known as the Early Dutch honeysuckle and has white blooms that age to yellow. These are flushed with red on the outside. *L. p.* "Serotina" is the Late Dutch honeysuckle with cream flowers that are flushed with reddish-purple

AT A GLANCE		
Vigorous twiners with tubular flowers in summer. Hardy to temperatures of up to 5°F (zone 7).		
Jan	/	**Companion Plants**
Feb	planting	Honeysuckles look good
Mar	planting	accompanied by climbing or
Apr	planting	rambler roses.
May	flowering	
Jun	flowering	
July	flowering	
Aug	flowering	
Sep	flowering	
Oct	/	
Nov	/	
Dec	/	

on the outside. Both of these decorative cultivars can grow up to 20ft tall.

Hailing from the USA, *Lonicera sempervirens*, known as Trumpet honeysuckle, is an evergreen or deciduous twiner with tubular flowers that are reddish orange on the outside but yellow-orange within. The flowers are produced throughout summer and into fall. It reaches up to 12ft in height.

CONDITIONS

ASPECT	All species and their cultivars will grow in full sun or partial shade.
SITE	Honeysuckles are very adaptable and will grow in any well-drained but moisture-retentive, humus-rich soil of reasonable fertility.

GROWING METHOD

PROPAGATION	The easiest method of propagation is to carry out serpentine layering in the spring. Alternatively take softwood or semi-ripe cuttings in spring and summer. Sow seeds in fall and stratify over winter.
WATERING	Do not let honeysuckles suffer from prolonged lack of moisture. Water the plants thoroughly if the soil starts to dry out during long dry periods in the summer.

FEEDING	Apply a slow-release fertilizer, such as the organic blood, fish and bone, in the spring.
PROBLEMS	Plants may become infested with aphids during the summer.

FLOWERING/FOLIAGE

FLOWERS	Honeysuckles are grown primarily for their flowers, and the scented kinds are most popular.
FOLIAGE	Evergreen or deciduous, the leaves being arranged in opposite pairs.

PRUNING

REQUIREMENTS	The congested growth of *Lonicera japonica* can be thinned out in early spring. Prune back any very long shoots. If renovation is needed, cut back the entire plant to within 3ft of the ground in late winter or early spring. With the species *L. periclymenum*, *L. x brownii*, *L. caprifolium*, and *L. sempervirens*, you can either allow them to grow at will or reduce the flowered shoots by one-third in early spring to restrict the size of the plant. Shears may be used to trim the entire plant. Renovation pruning is the same as for *L. japonica*.

TOLERANT OF partial shade, Lonicera japonica "Halliana" is also fast-growing and makes an ideal cover for pergolas. The fluted blooms of Lonicera sempervirens hang in attractive bunches that add to their visual impact.

Lonicera nitida

HONEYSUCKLE

FEATURES

This small-leaved, dense evergreen plant is sometimes known as box-leaf honeysuckle. It is quick growing but also long lived. While plants can reach almost 8ft in height, they are most often seen hedged at about 20in or even less. Honeysuckle is an ideal shrub for formal hedges around garden beds or, when it is allowed to grow taller, for dividing sections of a garden or accenting a path or drive. It can also be clipped to various shapes for topiary. Honeysuckle bears strongly perfumed cream flowers during the late spring and early summer, although few blooms appear if the plants are kept close clipped.

CONDITIONS

ASPECT   Prefers an open, sunny position but will also tolerate some partial shade.

SITE   The soil should be well drained but need not be rich, although soil that is high in organic content will give more vigorous growth and a better display of white flowers.

GROWING METHOD

PROPAGATION   Can be grown from firm tip cuttings taken in early or midsummer.

SPACING   For a quick effect, honeysuckle can be planted at 10in spacings, but 18in might be more sensible.

FEEDING   Apply complete plant food in early spring.
PROBLEMS   There are no known problems, but keep an eye out for aphid attacks.

FLOWERING

SEASON   Small, perfumed, creamy flowers appear in late spring and early summer. However, if the plants are clipped regularly through the growing season flowers may not develop.

PRUNING

GENERAL   To maintain low, dense growth honeysuckle needs regular clipping throughout the growing season; up to three cuttings in a season is quite typical.

TINY, CLOSE-GROWING leaves make this an ideal choice for hedging where a tight formal shape is wanted.

AT A GLANCE		
Lonicera nitida is a highly valued, quick growing, scented evergreen shrub with blue berries. Hardy to 0°F (zone 7).		
Jan	foliage	Companion Plants
Feb	foliage	Campsis radicans
Mar	foliage	Clematis
April	foliage	Climbing rose
May	flowering	Cobaea scandens
June	flowering	Ipomoea
July	foliage	Jasmine
Aug	foliage	Lonicera similis var. delavayi
Sept	foliage	Tropaeolum
Oct	foliage	
Nov	foliage	
Dec	foliage	

Lunaria

HONESTY

FEATURES

Honesty, *Lunaria annua*, a hardy biennial is also known as the money plant because of its large circular, smooth, silvery seedheads that resemble coins. It grows up to 3ft tall and is a plant that is best left to do its own thing, self-seeding very quickly, and thriving under dry hedges where most plants will not grow, and will seed into mixed borders. Flowers are purple or white and appear in early spring, and variegated varieties are available.

CONDITIONS

ASPECT   Succeeds in sun or the shade cast by hedges and large shrubs.
SITE   Thriving in poor soils, plants grow larger still if they are sown into soil that has been improved with rotted manure or compost, and produce the best seedheads for drying.

GROWING METHOD

SOWING   Mark out patches using sand and sow the large seeds 1in deep in short drills, with 2–3in between each seed in March. Seedlings are quick to appear and can be thinned or left to develop as they are. Next spring look out for seedlings and move them when small to where you want plants to grow.

FEEDING   Needs no extra feeding or watering.

FLOWERING

SEASON   Flowers from early spring to early summer.
CUTTING   Can be cut for flowers but some must be left to set seed if you want the large, silvery heads.

AFTER FLOWERING

GENERAL   Cut when the seedheads are mature and dry, on a warm day, and hang upside-down in a dry, airy place until you can carefully remove the outer skin of the pod. Leave a few plants to die down naturally and self-seed.

THE SEEDHEADS of Lunaria annua *are sought after for dried flower arrangements. Here they are still in the green stages of growth.*

AT A GLANCE		
A hardy biennial grown for its pretty purple/white flowers followed by large silvery seedheads. Frost hardy to 5°F (zone 7).		
Jan	/	**Recommended Varieties**
Feb	/	*Lunaria annua*
Mar	sow/flowers	"Fine Mixed"
Apr	thin/flowers	"Mixed"
May	thin/flowers	**Variegated leaves**
Jun	flowering	"Variegata"
July	/	**White flowers**
Aug	/	"Alba Variegata"
Sept	/	
Oct	/	
Nov	/	
Dec	/	

Lupinus

ANNUAL LUPIN

FEATURES

By growing annual lupins from seed you can enjoy the features of their perennial relatives without giving up too much space in the yard. Annual lupins are smaller, growing between 1–3ft tall, but have very colorful spikes in mixed shades and also striking single colors such as the blue-flowered *Lupinus texensis*. Hardy annuals. Seeds and plants are poisonous if eaten.

CONDITIONS

ASPECT	Needs full sun.
SITE	Well-drained, light soil is best for annual lupins, but mix in rotted manure or compost.

GROWING METHOD

SOWING	The large seeds can go straight into the ground in April, but to ensure germination the tough seed coat must be nicked with a sharp knife or rubbed down with a file until the pale inside just shows. Next, soak the seeds on wet tissue paper and sow when they have swollen up, 3–6in apart and 2in deep, where you want plants to grow. Thin seedlings to 6in apart when well established. To grow in pots do the same, sowing one seed to a 3½in pot, then plant out.

FEEDING

FEEDING	Lupins need no extra feeding.
PROBLEMS	Fat green lupin aphids can kill entire plants, so use a spray containing permethrin.

FLOWERING

SEASON	Flowers appear from midsummer.
CUTTING	Cut when some buds at the base of the flower spike are fully open.

AFTER FLOWERING

GENERAL	Cut off to leave the nitrogen-rich roots to rot in the ground, and compost the tops.

SHORTER AND SQUATTER than their perennial cousins, annual lupins can create a sea of color when sown in large drifts like this. As the flowers fade the spikes should be removed completely with pruning shears to divert energy into new flowers rather than seed pods.

AT A GLANCE		
A hardy annual grown for its spikes of colorful and spicey-scented flowers during summer. Frost hardy to 5°F (zone 7).		
Jan	/	**Recommended Varieties**
Feb	/	*Lupinus hybrids*
Mar	/	"Biancaneve"
Apr	sow	"New White"
May	thin out	"Pink Javelin"
Jun	flowering	"Pixie Delight"
July	flowering	"Sunrise"
Aug	flowering	**Yellow flowers**
Sept	flowering	*Lupinus luteus*
Oct	/	**Blue flowers**
Nov	/	*Lupinus texensis*
Dec	/	*Lupinus varius*

Lupinus polyphyllus

LUPINS

FEATURES

This herbaceous perennial lupin is generally known as the Russell lupin, named after the hybridizer who began developing many fine strains of this plant early this century. It produces tall, densely packed spires of blooms in myriad colors. Growing well over 42in tall, these are plants for a massed display. They flower in early to mid-summer and can look unsightly after flowering; placed at the rear of a border the problem is solved. Although they can be cut for indoor use they give much more value in the yard, with several spikes per plant. The only irritation is that plants can be short-lived, and should therefore be divided regularly.

CONDITIONS

ASPECT	Grows in full sunlight or semi-shade, but it does need wind protection.
SITE	Soil need not be rich—moderate fertility will suffice—but it must be well drained. Light, slightly sandy, acidic soil is ideal.

GROWING METHOD

PROPAGATION	Division of these plants may be difficult. Many strains come true from seed, which should be soaked in warm water before planting in the spring or fall. Cuttings can be taken from new shoots emerging from the crown in early spring. Set plants approximately 12–16in apart. Give ample water to young plants to help them establish.
FEEDING	Needs little fertilizer, as lupins fix nitrogen in nodules on their roots. High potash fertilizer may be applied as buds begin to form.

PROBLEMS

Powdery mildew may be a problem in humid conditions; if necessary, spray with a fungicide. Control lupin aphids with an appropriate spray. Virus may cause stunting and discoloration. Destroy affected plants.

FLOWERING

SEASON	Early and mid-summer.
CUTTING	Flowers may be cut for the vase.

AFTER FLOWERING

REQUIREMENTS	Cut off the spent flower stems before they manage to set seed. This will encourage smaller spikes to follow.

LUPINS ARE traditional favorites for perennial borders, where they provide vertical interest. Here they are growing among oriental poppies, campion, and gray-leaved germander.

AT A GLANCE		
L. polyphyllus is an attractive, summer-flowering perennial with striking vertical spires of purple flowers. Hardy to 5°F (zone 7).		
Jan	/	Recommended Varieties
Feb	/	Band of Noble Series
Mar	sow	"Esmerelder"
Apr	transplant	"Helen Sharman"
May	transplant	"Kayleigh Ann Savage"
Jun	flowering	"Olive Tolley"
July	flowering	"Pope John Paul"
Aug	/	"The Page"
Sept	/	"The Chatelaine"
Oct	sow	
Nov	/	
Dec	/	

Lycaste

LYCASTE SPECIES AND HYBRIDS

FEATURES

This group of mostly epiphytic orchids originate in cloud forests in Central America and northern parts of South America. Most are found in the forks of trees but some grow in pockets of leaf litter on rocks. Lycastes can grow into clumps with large leaves and they need space to show to advantage. They produce robust pseudobulbs from which the leaves emerge in the spring. In fall the leaves will die off. Flowers are borne singly on leafless stems but each pseudobulb may produce several stems. In the most commonly grown species *Lycaste skinneri* (syn. *L. virginalis*) the flowers may vary from pure white to rose pink. There are other species and numerous hybrids with green, yellow, or even deep red flowers. Some beautifully shaded or mottled.

FOR BEGINNERS

A good species to try is *L. deppei* from Mexico and Guatemala. This is a green flower flecked with red and with a red-spotted yellow lip. It is also fragrant.

CONDITIONS

CLIMATE	All are frost sensitive and not ideal for the tropics. Many are happy in a 50–86°F range. Some species may drop lower during their dry rest.
ASPECT	Plants require good shade in summer. Early morning sun with shade for the rest of the day is suitable. Ensure good air circulation.
POTTING MIX	Use a mix of crushed fine to medium bark. Do not overpot. Select a pot large enough to take the root ball with a little extra space.

GROWING METHOD

PROPAGATION	Divide plants after flowering if they are very crowded. Leafless pseudobulbs can be detached from the clump and potted up.
WATERING	Give ample water during hot weather and when in active growth but avoid overhead watering. Keep compost dry when dormant.
FEEDING	Plants respond well to regular fertilizing during the growing season. Use soluble liquids or granular fertilizers. Those formulated for cymbidiums are suitable.
PROBLEMS	No specific problems are known if cultural conditions are suitable.

FLOWERING SEASON

Mainly winter to early spring.

AT A GLANCE		
Relatively easy to grow but best in greenhouse. Deciduous, with flowers in spring with the new growth.		
Jan	rest	**Recommended Varieties**
Feb	rest	*L. aromatica* (yellow)
Mar	flowering, water and feed	*L. cruenta* (yellow)
		L. deppei (green/red)
Apr	flowering, water and feed	*L. skinneri* (white/pink)
May	flowering, water and feed	*L.* "Auburn" (pink)
		L. "Always" (pink/red)
Jun	flowering, water and feed	
July	flowering, water and feed, re-pot	
Aug	water and feed	
Sept	water and feed	
Oct	rest	
Nov	rest	
Dec	rest	

Lychnis coronaria

ROSE CAMPION

FEATURES

Rosettes of soft, silver-gray foliage make *Lychnis coronaria* a very useful plant in the garden, and they contrast with the deep cerise or magenta flowers that appear on stems 12–16in high. There is also a white-flowered form. Easily grown in a sunny, well-drained position, rose campion tends to be short-lived, but it self-seeds prolifically to provide a fresh supply. It can be grown as a border plant or as part of a mixed perennial display. *L. flos-jovis* is another species where silvery foliage effectively combines with purple-red blooms. Another popular species of lychnis is the Maltese cross, *L. chalcedonica*, which has mid-green leaves and produces a rounded head of bright scarlet flowers. Pink and white forms, and a double, "Flore Plena," are also available.

CONDITIONS

ASPECT   Grows best in full sunlight, but it tolerates shade for part of the day.
SITE   Needs very well-drained soil, but the soil need not be especially rich.

GROWING METHOD

PROPAGATION   Tends to self-seed. These plants may show variation from the parent plant. Divide clumps in spring, discard the oldest, lackluster sections, and space the new vigorous ones about 8in apart. There are some beautiful strains to be raised from seed, with mixtures of white, deep violet, carmine, and rose-pink flowers, and a pastel eye.

FEEDING   Needs little fertilizer. A little complete plant food may be given in early spring.
PROBLEMS   No pest or disease problems are known, but overwatering or prolonged summer rain in heavy ground may cause rotting.

FLOWERING

SEASON   Flowers in mid- to late summer, but it is well worth the wait, with a big showy display that maintains interest in the border at a time when many other plants are flagging.
CUTTING   Flowers are unsuitable for cutting.

AFTER FLOWERING

REQUIREMENTS   If you do not want plants to self-seed, dead-head with vigilance as the flowers fade. This should also prolong blooming. Completely spent stems should be cut off as low to the ground as possible.

AT A GLANCE	
L. coronaria is a flowery, short-lived purple-red perennial that gives a prolific late summer display. Hardy to 5°F (zone 7).	

Month		Recommended Varieties
Jan	/	
Feb	/	*Lychnis alpina*
Mar	sow	*L. chalcedonica*
Apr	division	*L. coronaria*
May	transplant	"Alba Group"
Jun	/	*L. c.*
July	flowering	"Atrosanguinea Group"
Aug	flowering	*L. flos-cuculi*
Sept	flowering	*L. viscaria* subsp. "Splendens Plena"
Oct	sow	*L. yunnanensis*
Nov	/	
Dec	/	

Lysimachia nummularia

CREEPING JENNY

FEATURES

Usually seen in its golden-leaved form, "Aurea," this groundcover has small, rounded leaves on stems that spread and root down as they go. The bright yellow leaves seem to light up the area where it is growing and it is often grown as a basket plant. Small, bright yellow flowers are produced in good conditions, and are more common on the plain species. Growth is flat, rarely more than 2in above the ground and one plant will cover 20in or so within a growing season, if conditions are good. *Lysimachia nummularia* can be long lived.

CONDITIONS

ASPECT Grow *L. nummularia* in either sun or semi-shade but always give it some protection from the hottest summer sun. The golden form will lose its bright color unless it gets enough sun or bright light.

SITE Prefers a well-drained but moist soil rich in organic matter. It is well worth forking in plenty of compost before planting so that it gets off to an excellent start.

GROWING METHOD

PROPAGATION This plant is easily grown from division of the rooted sections of the parent plant. However, it also grows well from firm-tip cuttings that are taken during the summer months. They quickly start to root.

FEEDING Complete plant food may be applied in early spring, but unless soil is very poor this will not be necessary.

PROBLEMS

No specific problems are known but these plants will die if they are short of water during the summer months. If one group of plants is going to get watered during a drought, make sure *L. nummularia* is included.

FLOWERING

SEASON Small, yellow flowers are produced right through the summer.

PRUNING

GENERAL No general pruning is necessary but *L. nummularia* may need occasional trimming to confine its growth to the desired area. If the central growth starts to become thin, cut back some of the trailing stems to promote more growth from the center.

AT A GLANCE		
L. nummularia is a reliable ground-hugging spreader with a spread of yellow flowers in summer. Hardy to 0°F (zone 7).		
Jan	/	Recommended Varieties
Feb	/	*Lysimachia atropurpurea*
Mar	/	*L. ciliata*
April	/	*L. clethroides*
May	foliage	*L. minoricensis*
June	flowering	*L. nummularia*
July	flowering	"Aurea"
Aug	foliage	*L. thyrsiflora*
Sept	foliage	*L. vulgaris*
Oct	foliage	
Nov	/	
Dec	/	

Lysimachia punctata

LOOSESTRIFE

FEATURES

Loosestrife, which is widely naturalized in Europe and northeast North America, has stalks of bright yellow flowers in summer. It thrives in damp, boggy ground and can easily become invasive. The flowering stems reach 3ft high, bearing slightly coarse foliage. Other species offer white flowers on stiff, blue-green stems (*L. ephemerum*), while *L. nummularia* "Aurea" is a complete contrast. It grows 2in high, but spreads indefinitely, with evergreen, bright yellow leaves and summer flowers in a matching color. With room for only one, try *L. clethroides*, which has attractive white flowers (36 x 24in). The new variegated form, *L. p.* "Alexander" is a great success.

CONDITIONS

ASPECT   Loosestrife tolerates both full sun and light, dappled shade, but growing in the former gives by far the best results.

SITE   Moist ground is essential. Add plenty of organic matter to border plants, and mulch well to guard against moisture loss.

GROWING METHOD

PROPAGATION Seed can be difficult. The most reliable method is by spring or fall division.

FEEDING   Humus-rich ground produces the best display. Fork plenty of well-rotted manure and compost around the plants in the spring.

PROBLEMS   Colonies of slugs and snails can be a major problem, attacking and disfiguring the new, emerging foliage. Either pick off

by hand or treat chemically. Plants grown in areas cut by strong winds may need to be staked.

FLOWERING

SEASON   Flowers appear in the summer, their timing depending on your chosen variety.

CUTTING   They make unremarkable cut flowers, given the enormous competition in summer, but are nonetheless very useful when bulking out large displays with their flowering spires.

AFTER FLOWERING

REQUIREMENTS Cut back the old, spent flowering stems down to the ground.

A STRONG, MASSED DISPLAY of loosestrife. Individually unremarkable, a clump makes a splendid feature beside a pond or stream.

AT A GLANCE		
L. punctata is an erect, herbaceous perennial grown for its yellow flowers and ability to colonize damp areas. Hardy to 0˚F (zones 6–7).		
Jan	/	Recommended Varieties
Feb	/	*Lysimachia atropurpurea*
Mar	/	*L. ciliata*
Apr	divide	*L. clethroides*
May	/	*L. minoricensis*
Jun	flowering	*L. nummularia*
July	flowering	"Aurea"
Aug	flowering	*L. thyrsiflora*
Sept	/	*L. vulgaris*
Oct	divide	
Nov	/	
Dec	/	

Macleaya cordata

PLUME POPPY

FEATURES

The plume poppy is an essential plant for the rear of the border, tall, graceful, and showy. Growing 8ft tall, it sports long, thin stems with mid- and late summer panicles of pale white flowers. "Flamingo" has pinkish flowers. The large, lobed foliage is equally attractive. With more room in the border, *M. microcarpa* can be grown. It is slightly invasive and has pink flowers, while "Kelway's Coral Plume" produces coral-pink flowers opening from pure pink buds. The plume poppy's natural habitat is Chinese and Japanese meadows, where it makes large impressive colonies, spreading quickly through the damp soil by underground rhizomes and flowering all summer long.

CONDITIONS

ASPECT	Macleaya likes full sun and light shade, although the former produces a longer, better display. Avoid dark areas and open, windy sites; shelter is required.
SITE	Light, well-drained soil is ideal.

GROWING METHOD

PROPAGATION	The quickest, easiest results are either by making spring or fall divisions, or by separating lengths of rhizome when the plant is dormant. Make sure each has its own root system. Water new plants well, and space out at 3ft intervals.
FEEDING	Provide moderate applications of compost and well-rotted manure in the spring as a mulch.

PROBLEMS

Colonies of slugs can be a severe problem, badly attacking the new, vigorous growth. Either pick off by hand or treat accordingly with chemicals.

FLOWERING

SEASON	Flowers appear in mid- and late summer, on long, thin stems, producing an airy display.
CUTTING	Macleaya make very attractive cut flowers, requiring a regular change of water, their airy panicles adding considerably to both formal and flowery arrangements.

AFTER FLOWERING

REQUIREMENTS Cut back old growth to the ground.

THE PLUME POPPY starts inauspiciously, but quickly puts out tall, white summer flowers, making it an indispensable feature plant.

AT A GLANCE		
M. cordata is a rhizomatous perennial with gray-green foliage, grown for its tall flower spikes. Hardy to 0°F (zones 6–7).		
Jan	/	**Companion Plants**
Feb	/	Clematis Gypsophila
Mar	/	Hibiscus
Apr	division	Miscanthus
May	/	Lobelia
Jun	/	Osteospermum
July	flowering	Rose
Aug	flowering	Salvia
Sept	/	
Oct	division	
Nov	/	
Dec	/	

Magnolia

MAGNOLIA

FEATURES

Heralding spring, *Magnolia stellata*, a deciduous, bushy shrub to around 7ft, illuminates borders with a multitude of fragrant, strap-petalled, starry, white flowers from March to April. Also called star magnolia, it is ideal for small gardens. Fetching varieties are pink-budded, white-flowered "Royal Star," white-flowered "Centennial," whose blooms are 5^{1}/$_{2}$in across, and "Waterlily," another handsome, white variety with flared, double chalices that command close attention.

Most other magnolias, such as evergreen *M. grandiflora*, which flowers best if fan-trained on a sunny, sheltered wall, and varieties of *M. soulangeana*, soar to around 15ft.

CONDITIONS

ASPECT   No matter how large or small the variety, magnolias should be sheltered from strong winds. To flower well, they must receive at least half a day's sunshine.

SITE   *M. stellata* and *M. grandiflora* prosper in well-drained, acid, neutral, or alkaline soil. *M. soulangeana* abhors chalk. Dig in plenty of organic matter well ahead of planting.

GROWING METHOD

FEEDING   Encourage bountiful blooms by applying an acidifying fertilizer—brands for azaleas and camellias are ideal—in April and July.

PROPAGATION   Take soft-tip cuttings from late spring to early summer. Increase *M. grandiflora* from semi-ripe cuttings in midsummer. Layering is more reliable but takes longer. Peg down shoots from spring to late summer and detach rooted stems a year later in fall.

PROBLEMS   Soft, unfolding leaves can be scorched by hot, dry, or salty winds, so position plants carefully.

PRUNING

GENERAL   Seldom necessary. If a shrub requires shaping or crowded branches need removing, tackle it when flowers fade in mid-spring. Never prune in winter, as corky tissues are liable to rot.

THE LARGE, cupped white flowers of Magnolia grandiflora *have a heavy texture.*

AT A GLANCE		
White or pink flowers are thickly borne on leafless branches in early spring. *M. stellata* is hardy to -13°F (zone 5).		
Jan	/	**Recommended Varieties**
Feb	/	*M. grandiflora**
Mar	flower, plant	"Heaven Scent"*
Apr	flower, plant	"Little Gem"*
May	flower, prune	"Lennei"
Jun	plant, prune	"Picture"
July	plant, flower*	*M. stellata*
Aug	plant, flower*	"Centennial"
Sept	plant, flower*	"Royal Star"
Oct	/	* summer flowering
Nov	/	
Dec	/	

Mahonia

MAHONIA

FEATURES

Ground-hugging, weed-suppressing, and good for stabilizing steep banks, tall and sculptural, evergreen mahonias have shiny, spiky, holly-like leaves that develop burnished coppery or reddish tints in winter. Flamboyant, citrus-scented heads of yellow or golden-clustered, slender, cone-like flowers appear from November to May. Blooms are followed by decorative, bluish-black berries. From 2ft to 8ft high, depending on the species, taller kinds make fetching focal points, dense screens or dashing background plants.

Varieties of suckering, ground-covering *Mahonia aquifolium*, which thrives in light shade, effectively carpet rooty areas around trees and shrubs. Position orb-shaped and free-flowering *M. x media* "Charity" and more upright "Lionel Fortescue" to light up winter.

CONDITIONS

ASPECT   Thriving in sun or dappled shade, mahonias resist cold winds.

SITE   These shrubs flourish in all but very chalky conditions. Improve poor soils by adding bulky organic matter several weeks before planting.

GROWING METHOD

FEEDING   Boost growth by working fish, blood, and bone meal or Growmore into the root area in mid-spring and midsummer. If they are growing where there is root competition, mulch thickly to help conserve moisture.

PROPAGATION   Raise species from seeds in early to mid-spring, in a garden frame. Take leaf-bud cuttings in mid-fall or mid-spring and root in a heated propagator. Divide *M. aquifolium* into well-rooted portions in mid-spring.

PROBLEMS   Control mahonia rust by spraying with penconazole, mancozeb, or bupirimate with triforine. *M. aquifolium* and *M. bealei* have some resistance to this disease.

PRUNING

M. AQUIFOLIUM. Prevent plants from becoming leggy by removing one stem in three after flowering.
TALL, BUSHY HYBRIDS: Remove flower heads when blooms fade; rejuvenate old, gaunt plants by shortening stems by half their height in May.

TALL, BUSHY MAHONIAS display shuttlecocks of citrus-scented, pale lemon to golden flowers from early winter to early spring. Decorative, blue berries follow in the fall.

AT A GLANCE	
Carpeting or upright evergreens, with holly-like leaves, color borders from November to March. Hardy to -13°F (zone 5).	
Jan flower	**Recommended Varieties**
Feb flower	*M. aquifolium*
Mar flower	"Apollo"
Apr flower, plant	"Atropurpurea"
May prune, flower	"Smaragd"
June plant	*M. japonica*
July feed	*M. lomariifolia*
Aug plant	*M. x media*
Sept plant	"Charity"
Oct plant	"Lionel Fortescue"
Nov flower	"Winter Sun"
Dec flower	

Malcolmia

VIRGINIAN STOCK

FEATURES

Keep a packet of Virginian stock, *Malcolmia maritima* seed to hand at all times and sow a pinch of seeds every two weeks in gaps and under windows—plants will flower just a month later. They grow 6–8in high with small, single, four-petalled, sweetly scented flowers in red, mauve, pink, yellow, and white from June–September. They can also be sown into patio tubs. Hardy annual.

CONDITIONS

ASPECT   Prefers full sun but tolerates some shade.
SITE   Will grow on most soils but needs good drainage to do well.

GROWING METHOD

SOWING   Seed can be scattered in small patches 12in across on the soil where you want flowers, and mixed in using your fingertips, or it is simply scattered along the cracks in paths and driveways, from March onward, and repeated every few weeks all through the summer. Mark sown areas in borders with a label or circle of light-colored sand. Seedlings soon come up and there is no need to bother with thinning. For early flowers the following spring sow in October.

FEEDING

FEEDING   Not necessary.
PROBLEMS   Trouble-free.

FLOWERING

SEASON   Expect flowers all summer long with repeat sowings.
CUTTING   Unsuitable as a cut flower.

AFTER FLOWERING

GENERAL   Pull up as soon as the plants are over, and resow. Self-sown seedlings soon appear.

JUST FOUR WEEKS after sowing plants will be in flower. Malcolmia maritima *thrives in the thin light soils of seaside gardens. Pink is just one of the colors found in Virginian stocks. Expect reds, yellows, and whites from a variety like "Fine Mixed."*

AT A GLANCE	
Hardy annual grown for its pink, red, yellow, or white flowers. Flowers a month after sowing. Frost hardy to 5°F (zone 7).	

		Recommended Varieties
Jan	/	*Malcolmia maritima*
Feb	/	"Fine Mixed"
Mar	sow	"Mixed"
Apr	sow/flowers	
May	sow/flowers	
Jun	sow/flowers	
July	sow/flowers	
Aug	sow/flowers	
Sept	sow/flowers	
Oct	sow	
Nov	/	
Dec	/	

Masdevallia

KITE ORCHID

FEATURES

These unusual flowers are not obviously divided into petals and sepals but appear as solid, sometimes triangular shapes, often with long tails. Flowers may come singly or in small sprays above or within the foliage. The color range includes white, pink, red, yellow, orange, and greenish brown. Some flowers have contrasting venation that looks like stripes. Masdevallias are native to tropical America where they occur from warm lowlands to high altitudes. Plants may be epiphytes, lithophytes, or terrestrial and most are found in high elevations in cloud forests. They lack pseudobulbs, growing from a root system that produces short, upright stems, each with a single fleshy leaf.

CONDITIONS

CLIMATE This orchid is frost sensitive but classed as cool growing; it prefers a range of about 50–75°F.

ASPECT Needs about 70 per cent shade in the summer months; less in winter. Maintain high humidity but keep air moving with fans as good ventilation is needed to grow these little plants well.

POTTING MIX Use a small pot just large enough for the roots. Use a compost of fine-grade bark mixed with charcoal, perlite, and pea gravel.

GROWING METHOD

PROPAGATION This is not easy. Large clumps may be divided after some years. Each division should be made up of at least four stems to make sure they continue to grow well.

WATERING Keep the compost moist at all times, especially in warm weather. Growing in small pots, with fine compost, they tend to dry out easily.

FEEDING Use soluble liquid plant foods, which can be applied during normal watering in the growing season diluted to half strength.

PROBLEMS No specific pest or disease problems are known if the exacting growing conditions are met. If the long flower tails shrivel in warm weather the humidity is too low or the temperature is too high.

FLOWERING SEASON

Flowering depends on species but most flower through spring or summer. When grown to a large plant, masdevallias will provide a lovely show of dainty blooms.

AT A GLANCE	
Miniature orchids, 1$\frac{1}{4}$– 6in high. Best in cool greenhouse. Flowers $\frac{1}{4}$–1$\frac{1}{4}$ in across with long tails.	
Jan rest	Recommended Varieties
Feb rest	M. barlaeana (red)
Mar water and feed,	M. coccinea (varies)
Apr water and feed,	M. tovarensis (white)
re-pot	M. Angel
May water and feed,	"Frost" (yellow)
re-pot	M. Marguerite (orange)
Jun water and feed,	M. Whiskers (orange/
re-pot	purple)
July water and feed	
Aug water and feed	
Sept water and feed	
Oct water and feed,	
rest	
Nov rest	
Dec rest	

Matthiola
BROMPTON STOCK

FEATURES

The sweetly scented flowers of Brompton stocks are held above the gray-green leaves on plants up to 18in tall. There is a full range of pastel colors with some stronger purples, crimson and magenta as well; the flowers are double. Brompton stocks are beautiful in massed spring plantings, giving off a delicious strong fragrance. They are grown as biennials.

CONDITIONS

ASPECT   Need full sun and a sheltered position.
SITE   Must have well-drained soil. Incorporate rotted manure or compost into the soil a few weeks before planting. Tall varieties will need short stakes to prevent their flowers flopping.

GROWING METHOD

SOWING   June/July is the time to sow seed, in a 3^1/$_2$in pot of multipurpose compost. When the seedlings are large enough, transplant one seedling to a 3^1/$_2$in pot of multipurpose compost, water well and grow on. Later, pot on into 5in pots. When the first frosts arrive take the young plants into a coldframe, cold greenhouse or porch, standing them outside during mild spells. Keep on the dry side and only water when they wilt. Plant out from February onward when the soil is workable, or pot on into large pots and grow in a cool conservatory or porch with canes for support.
FEEDING   Do not feed until 2–3 weeks before planting out, then give a liquid feed.

PROBLEMS

PROBLEMS   Cabbage butterflies will lay eggs on young plants in late summer and caterpillars can strip leaves, so use a spray containing permethrin, or pick them off by hand.

FLOWERING

SEASON   Brompton stocks will fill beds and borders with color and scent during April and May, weather permitting. They perform best in calm, mild spells with plenty of sunshine. While most plants will have double flowers, there may be singles that can be put to one side, planted separately, and used for cutting.
CUTTING   A good cut flower. Scald stems after picking and change vase water every couple of days.

AFTER FLOWERING

GENERAL   Dig plants up when the show is over and prepare the ground for summer bedding plants. Add to the compost heap/bin.

AT A GLANCE		
A hardy biennial sown in summer for strongly-scented pink flowers the following spring. Frost hardy to 5°F (zone 7).		
Jan	grow on	**Recommended Varieties**
Feb	plant	*Matthiola incana*
Mar	plant	"Brompton Mixed"
Apr	flowering	"Brompton Dwarf Mixed"
May	flowering	"Spring Flowering Mixed"
Jun	sow	
July	sow/transplant	
Aug	transplant	
Sept	grow on	
Oct	grow on	
Nov	grow on	
Dec	grow on	

Meconopsis
HIMALAYAN BLUE POPPY

FEATURES

Meconopsis betonicifolia is the beautiful blue poppy everyone loves. There is probably no other plant that produces such an intense sky-blue flower. Its natural habitat is very high altitude alpine meadows in China. Plants do not flower the first year, and they die down in winter, growing and blooming in the second year. If meconopsis is prevented from blooming the first time it sets buds, it is more likely to become perennial. Growing to almost 6^1/2ft in its native habitat, in cultivation it is more likely to be 20–28in tall. Looks best when grown as part of a massed display, or threaded through a border.

CONDITIONS

ASPECT Needs partial, dappled shade; also provide some protection from strong, cutting, drying winds.

SITE Needs well-drained soil that is rich in organic matter. In colder regions it grows best in acid soil.

GROWING METHOD

PROPAGATION Grows from fresh ripe seed sown in the fall, or in spring. Give winter seedlings frost protection in a greenhouse, but beware of damping off, and plant out in late spring or early summer. Initially, water well. Do not waterlog or the crowns will rot.

FEEDING Apply a little general fertilizer in the spring.

PROBLEMS Overwet soil, especially during winter, will rot the crown. Downy mildew may be a problem in some seasons. Spray plants with a fungicide at the first sign of an attack.

FLOWERING

SEASON Abundant flowers begin appearing at the start of summer.

CUTTING While they make extremely good cut flowers, they do not last long.

AFTER FLOWERING

REQUIREMENTS Remove spent flower stems, unless you are waiting for seed to ripen. Once growth dies down, cut it off at ground level.

NO OTHER blue flower has quite the same startlingly clear color as the amazing blue poppy, a true delight whenever it can be grown.

AT A GLANCE

M. betonicifolia is a deciduous perennial, making a strong show, with blue or white early summer flowers. Hardy to 0˚F (zones 6–7).

Jan	/	Recommended Varieties
Feb	/	*Meconopsis cambrica*
Mar	sow	*M. betonicifolia*
Apr	transplant	*M. grandis*
May	transplant	*M. napaulensis*
Jun	flowering	*M. quintuplinervia*
July	flowering	*M. x sheldonii*
Aug	flowering	"Slieve Donard"
Sept	flowering	*M. superba*
Oct	sow	
Nov	/	
Dec	/	

Melianthus major

HONEY BUSH

FEATURES

This very striking evergreen plant, with its unusual blue-green foliage, really stands out. It is grown as a feature in a mixed border or as a focal point in an annual or perennial display. In a large yard it could be repeat-planted to tie together various arrangements. Honey bush can grow to 6ft in height, and it spreads by suckers, forming a large clump if left undivided. The dark mahogany-red flowers contain copious quantities of nectar, attractive to bees. Although native to South Africa, and initially tender here, after two years the base becomes woody and it can survive outside if given good frost protection in mild areas. It can also be grown in a large pot.

CONDITIONS

ASPECT   Needs full sun all day (i.e. a south-facing wall).

SITE   Soil must be well drained but it need not be specially rich—in fact over-rich soils will produce good foliage effects but poor flowering. However, the outstanding architectural foliage is the main reason for growing this striking plant.

GROWING METHOD

PROPAGATION   Grows from seed sown in the spring or from division of suckers from an existing plant, also in spring. Plant at least 39in apart. For best growth, give deep watering every week or two in hot, dry spells during the growing season. It will, however, tolerate drought well.

FEEDING   Apply a complete plant food in the spring.

PROBLEMS   Red spider mites may strike. Use an appropriate insecticide.

FLOWERING

SEASON   Dark crimson flowers may appear in late summer or earlier on long stems that survive the winter.

CUTTING   Flowers are probably best left on the plant, as they do not smell particularly pleasant.

AFTER FLOWERING

REQUIREMENTS   Cut off the spent flower stems, unless you are waiting for seed to set and ripen. Protect the base and roots with straw or bracken against frost. The older and woodier the plant, the better its chance of survival.

NECTAR-RICH, these dark red flowers are very attractive to insects. The foliage too is unusual, with its distinctive color and form.

AT A GLANCE		
Melianthus major is a tender, southern African plant with wonderful, architectural foliage. It is damaged below 41°F (zone 11).		
Jan	/	Companion Plants
Feb	/	Canna
Mar	sow	Choisya
Apr	divide	Hosta
May	transplant	"Krossa Regal"
Jun	flowering	Philadelphus
July	flowering	Pinus
Aug	flowering	Pseudopanax
Sept	/	Salvia
Oct	/	
Nov	/	
Dec	/	

Mexican Orange Blossom

CHOISYA TERNATA

FEATURES

A spring prince, evergreen *Choisya ternata*, to 6ft or more high, is regaled with orange-fragrant, starry, white flowers in April and May and again in October. Its glossy, trefoil leaves spill citrus scent when you brush against them.

"Sundance," a smaller, golden-leaved form, is particularly striking in winter when its foliage assumes orange-yellow tints. Intriguingly different—leaves are long and narrow—"Aztec Pearl" bears pink-budded, white blossoms.

CONDITIONS

ASPECT   Full sun or light shade, but "Sundance" needs more light than *C. ternata* or "Aztec Pearl," otherwise its leaves will pale to green and lose their appeal. In northern gardens, position all three kinds against a warm, sunny wall.

SITE   *Choisya* thrives in fertile, acid, neutral, or alkaline soil. Enrich nutrient-starved, quick-draining, sandy loam, or stony patches with bulky organic manure.

GROWING METHOD

FEEDING   Apply a complete plant food, such as Growmore or fish, blood, and bone meal in early spring and midsummer. Water regularly and copiously in long, dry periods.

PROPAGATION   Increase choisya from semi-ripe cuttings from mid- to late summer, or layer stems from early to late summer.

PROBLEMS   No specific pests or diseases but flowering diminishes if shrubs are not pruned regularly and left to become woody.

PRUNING

GENERAL   In cold areas, cut back frost-damaged shoots to healthy, white wood in spring. Keep mature bushes—over five years old—flowering freely by removing from the base a third of the older branches when blooms fade in May or June.

WAFTING CITRUS SCENT on a warm breeze, starry-flowered, evergreen Mexican orange blooms in spring and fall.

AT A GLANCE		
Hardy evergreen shrubs—"Sundance" has yellow leaves—with orange-scented, white flowers in spring. Hardy to 14°F (zone 8).		
Jan	/	**Recommended Varieties**
Feb	/	*C. ternata*
Mar	/	"Aztec Pearl"
Apr	flower, plant	"Sundance"
May	flower, prune	
June	flower, prune	
July	plant	
Aug	plant	
Sept	flower, plant	
Oct	/	
Nov	/	
Dec	/	

Mimulus

MONKEY FLOWER

FEATURES

The genus has 150 species, and while they are classified as annuals, perennials and shrubs of varying degrees of hardiness, from the gardener's viewpoint most are grown as the first. *M. cardinalis*, scarlet monkey flower, however, is an attractive, reliable perennial. It grows 3ft high, producing vertical stems with eye-catching, tubular scarlet flowers in summer. Clumps usually spread 24in. In the wild, from western North America down to Mexico, it is pollinated by hummingbirds. *M. luteus*, monkey musk, has yellow flowers with a red throat, and self-seeds freely through the garden. *M. guttatus* has attractive, funnel-shape yellow flowers.

CONDITIONS

ASPECT   Mimulus thrive in either full sun or light shade.

SITE   Provide rich, moist soil. In their natural habitat many mimulus grow alongside streams and ponds. They are ideal for the bog garden or a running stream. However, *M. cardinalis* will tolerate drier ground.

GROWING METHOD

PROPAGATION   Divide in spring, setting out vigorous new clumps up to 3ft apart. Softwood cuttings can be taken in the early part of summer, while semi-ripe, slightly hardier ones can be taken after mid-summer. Sow seed in spring or fall.

FEEDING   Add plenty of well-rotted manure and compost, and a spring mulch to preserve moisture loss.

PROBLEMS   Slugs and snails can be a major problem, devouring tender new growth. Either pick them off by hand, trap and remove, or treat with a chemical.

FLOWERING

SEASON   The flowers appear from late spring to summer.

CUTTING   Mimulus make good cut flowers, though they do not tend to last long. Regular, fresh supplies will be needed.

AFTER FLOWERING

REQUIREMENTS   Cut back to ground level in late fall, and remove the dead foliage which can prove a haven to slugs and snails.

MONKEY FLOWERS have blooms that are face-like and marked with intricate patterns and spotting. They are good for shaded areas such as along the edges of a path. Monkey flowers will bloom in just nine weeks.

AT A GLANCE	
Mimulus contains many ideal, damp garden plants, creating colonies with bright flowers. Several hardy to 5°F (zone 7).	
Jan /	**Recommended Varieties**
Feb /	*Mimulus aurantiacus*
Mar divide	Calypso hybrids
Apr transplant	*M. cardinalis*
May flowering	"Whitecroft Scarlet"
Jun flowering	"Highland Red"
July flowering	*M. lewisii*
Aug flowering	*M. ringens*
Sept /	
Oct sow	
Nov /	
Dec /	

Miscanthus sinensis

MISCANTHUS

FEATURES

This is a group of large, ornamental, herbaceous perennial grasses. The plain green species is not often grown as the many cultivars with striped or banded foliage are much more decorative. Cultivars range in height from about 32in to 6^1/$_2$ft. Clumps spread from short, thick rhizomes and become very wide after a few years if not divided. Commonly grown cultivars include "Zebrinus" with distinct, horizontal gold banding, and "Variegatus" with long cream or white stripes, while other varieties such as "Silberfeder," "Morning Light" and var. *purpurascens* are worth seeking out. All produce pale, creamy beige feathery plumes of flowers in late summer, and fall, often accompanied by good fall color. The tall growers look good crested with frost.

CONDITIONS

ASPECT   Grows best in full sun, but tolerates shade for part of the day.

SITE   Prefers a soil that has been heavily enriched with organic matter to aid moisture retention. Avoid any damp or boggy ground. Good drainage really is essential for a massed, architectural display.

GROWING METHOD

PROPAGATION   Clumps can be lifted and divided in spring. This can require considerable muscle and effort because the roots are extremely tenacious. Replant the divisions approximately 12in apart, or closer if you want quicker, immediate coverage. Water well until established.

FEEDING   Complete plant food can be applied in the spring, when new growth begins, but it is not essential if the soil contains plenty of manure or compost.

PROBLEMS   No specific pest or disease problems are known to attack this plant.

FLOWERING

SEASON   Flowering plumes appear well above the foliage in the fall.

CUTTING   Plumes can be cut and dried like pampas grass.

AFTER FLOWERING

REQUIREMENTS   Once foliage starts to die off and become unsightly, cut it off at ground level. If the foliage is left uncut to provide winter shapes and outlines, especially when frosted, it must be cut back by early spring.

AT A GLANCE		
M. sinensis is a deciduous, large perennial, growing 6ft x 6ft. Produces blue-green foliage. Hardy to 0°F (zones 6–7).		
Jan	/	Recommended Varieties
Feb	sow	"Ferne Osten"
Mar	sow	"Flamingo"
Apr	transplant	"Gracillimus"
May	divide	"Kleine Fontane"
Jun	/	"Kleine Silberspinne"
July	/	"Morning Light"
Aug	flowering	"Strictus"
Sept	flowering	"Undine"
Oct	flowering	
Nov	/	
Dec	/	

Mock Orange
PHILADELPHUS

FEATURES

Often but erroneously called syringa—the correct name for lilac—its sumptuous, creamy white, single, or double and richly citrus-vanilla-scented blooms fill and brighten the high-summer gap, when the spring display of shrubs is fading and fall contenders have yet to form flower buds. Ranging in height from 2ft to over 10ft, there are candidates for most situations.

Coveted tall varieties, 6–10ft, are: large, single, and pink-centerd "Beauclerk"; semi-double and yellowish-white *Philadelphus coronarius*; and double or semi-double, pure white "Virginal". Couple flowers with striking foliage by planting semi-double, creamy white *P. coronarius* "Aureus," the leaves of which open lemon-yellow and mature to greenish yellow. This plant is perfect for lighting up a sunny or dappled shady border.

Set the smallest member, "Manteau d'Hermine," just 2–3ft high, on a rock garden and enjoy its massed, double, creamy white blossoms. Taller kinds are good for hedging.

CONDITIONS

ASPECT Ideal for windswept, hillside gardens and for tolerating salty breezes, mock orange thrives almost anywhere. All flower best in full sun and lemon-leaved *P. coronarius* "Aureus" keeps its radiant leaf color in light shade.

SITE Thriving in most soils—acid sand, chalk, or heavy clay—it is best to enrich poor patches with bulky organic matter dug in several months before planting.

GROWING METHOD

FEEDING Encourage bounteous blossom on sandy soil by applying annually sulfate of potash in late winter and late summer. Regardless of soil, topdress the root area with a balanced fertilizer in April and July. In a dry spring, water regularly to encourage strong, new shoots, which will flower the following year.

PROPAGATION Strike cuttings of semi-ripe shoots from mid- to late summer. Root them in a cold frame or on a sunny windowsill.

PROBLEMS Blackfly can colonize and cripple soft shoot tips. Control them by spraying with pirimicarb, which does not harm beneficial insects.

PRUNING

When blooms fade, cut back flowered shoots to current-year stems, which will perform the f ollowing year.

AT A GLANCE		
A deciduous shrub whose single or fully double, creamy white flowers appear from June to July. Hardy to -13°F (zone 5).		
Jan	/	Recommended Varieties
Feb	/	Under 1.8m (6ft)
Mar	plant	"Belle Etoile"
Apr	plant	*Coronarius*
May	plant	"Aureus"
June	flower	"Manteau d'Hermine"
July	flower	"Sybille"
Aug	prune	Over 1.8m (6ft)
Sept	/	"Beauclerk"
Oct	plant	*Coronarius*
Nov	plant	"Virginal"
Dec	/	

Moluccella

BELLS OF IRELAND

FEATURES

A half-hardy annual, also known as shell flower, moluccella is very lightly scented, and produces 2–3ft tall spikes in summer. It has small flowers surrounded by the more obvious and showy bell- or shell-like apple-green bracts. You can grow moluccella in flower beds and mixed borders, but its main value is as a cut flower, either fresh or dried. It is long-lasting when dried in late summer, the green spikes gradually fade from green to pale brown through fall and into winter.

CONDITIONS

ASPECT   Needs an open spot in full sun.
SITE   Must have good drainage, and working rotted manure or compost into the ground before sowing or planting helps. Avoid exposed, windy spots or the tall stems may be flattened.

GROWING METHOD

SOWING   Either sow seed in 3¹/₂in pots of multipurpose compost in February/March at 64°F, or sow directly in the soil where they are to grow in late April and May. Gradually thin out so plants are spaced 12–16in apart. Plants raised under cover are hardened off before being planted.
FEEDING   If organic matter has already been added to the soil, extra feeding is not necessary, but keep plants well-watered during long dry spells.

PROBLEMS

PROBLEMS   Seeds can sometimes be slow and difficult to germinate, so put them in the bottom of a refrigerator for two weeks before you sow, to "chill" them, then sow in pots as described above and expect seedlings in 2–3 weeks.

FLOWERING

SEASON   Even after the actual flowers have faded the green bracts go on providing color and interest until they are cut for drying.
CUTTING   Ideal as a cut flower, used fresh or dried. Cut when flowers are well-formed. Leaves can be removed to display the green bracts better. The stems dry to a light brown color.

AFTER FLOWERING

GENERAL   Remove roots when stems have been harvested, but leave a few behind to develop on the plant and finally shed seeds, which will self-sow.

AT A GLANCE	
A half-hardy annual grown for its tall spikes of green bracts that are used for drying. Frost hardy to 32°F (zone 10).	
Jan /	**Recommended Varieties**
Feb sow	*Moluccella laevis*
Mar sow	
Apr transplant/grow	
May plant/sow	
Jun flowering	
July flowering	
Aug flowering	
Sept flowers/cutting	
Oct /	
Nov /	
Dec /	

Monarda didyma

BERGAMOT

FEATURES

This aromatic herbaceous perennial is also known as bee balm and Oswego tea. The name "bee balm" refers to its nectar-rich flowers, which are very attractive to bees, and "Oswego tea" to its use by the Oswego Indians and early colonists of North America as a tea substitute. Growing approximately 36in tall, bergamot flowers from mid- to late summer. The heads of tubular flowers are red, pink, white, or purple, with some outstandingly named cultivars, including "Cambridge Scarlet" and "Croftway Pink." It is easy to grow—being a member of the mint family, its roots spread vigorously. It makes a lively addition to a mixed planting for its bright scarlet or pink flowers.

CONDITIONS

ASPECT   Grows in either full sunlight or semi-shade, but flowering will be best in the open.

SITE   Needs well-drained soil that is made moisture-retentive by the addition of large amounts of decayed organic matter.

GROWING METHOD

PROPAGATION Lift and divide clumps in the spring before new growth begins. Replant the young, vigorous outer growths 8–12in apart. Plants usually need dividing every two or three years. Bergamot may be also be grown from seed sown in the early spring or fall, but this does not develop true to type. It needs regular, deep watering through prolonged dry spells in the heat of summer.

FEEDING

FEEDING   If the soil is well supplied with humus, but a little fertilizer is needed. Apply some complete plant food in the spring.

PROBLEMS   Since snails love to eat the new growth as it appears, take precautions. Mildew can be a problem at times. You may need a fungicide spray or it might become severe. Remove all dead and diseased leaves.

FLOWERING

SEASON   Flowers in mid- and late summer.

CUTTING   Makes a decent cut flower. Use the scented leaves in a pot pourri.

AFTER FLOWERING

REQUIREMENTS Prune off spent flower stems. Cut plants back to ground level once growth begins to die off.

THE HOT-PINK FLOWERS on this bergamot are easy to place in the yard. They combine well with blue or white schemes.

AT A GLANCE	
M. didyma is a clump-forming perennial with lance-shape leaves, and bright, late summer flowers. Hardy to 0˚F (zones 6–7).	
Jan /	**Recommended Varieties**
Feb sow	"Aquarius"
Mar sow	"Beauty of Cobham"
Apr transplant	"Cambridge Scarlet"
May transplant	"Croftway Pink"
Jun /	"Fishes"
July flowering	"Mahogany"
Aug flowering	"Prarienacht"
Sept /	"Sagittarius"
Oct sow	"Scorpion"
Nov /	
Dec /	

Moraea

PEACOCK IRIS, BUTTERFLY IRIS

FEATURES

Of the 120 species of *Moraea*, most come from South Africa with others native to tropical Africa and Madagascar. Few are in cultivation but it is worth seeking out this unusual plant from specialist bulb growers. All grow from corms and some, such as *M. spathulata*, grow only a single leaf, which may be 8–20in high.

Flowers are like those of irises, with three showy outer petals and three smaller, rather insignificant inner ones. The commonest species is *M. spathulata*, with bright yellow, summer flowers on 2ft stems. Moraea aristata has white flowers with a large blue blotch at the base of the outer petals, while *M. villosa* bears flowers in a range of colors with a blue blotch on the petals. Plant peacock iris in groups for the best effect.

CONDITIONS

ASPECT	Moraea needs full sun all day.
SITE	A warm, sunny, and sheltered position is necessary. This corm needs well-drained soil with plenty of decayed organic matter incorporated into it before planting. Moraea also makes an attractive plant for the conservatory or home when grown in containers. Use John Innes or soiless potting compost.

GROWING METHOD

PLANTING	Plant corms 2in deep and 8in apart in spring.
FEEDING	Performance is improved by applying a balanced fertilizer as flower buds appear. Container-grown plants should be liquid-fed every three weeks or so through the growing season. Water in dry conditions, but take care not to make the soil too wet or the corms will be liable to rot.
PROBLEMS	No specific pest or disease problems are known for this plant.

FLOWERING

SEASON	Flowers throughout the summer.
CUTTING	Not suitable for cutting.

AFTER FLOWERING

REQUIREMENTS	Cut off spent flower stems unless you want to obtain seed from them. In fall, lift the corms and store them in a dry place over winter, ready for replanting the following spring.

IT IS EASY to see how this pretty bulb got its common name of peacock iris. Iridescent blue spots are sharply defined against the white petals.

AT A GLANCE		
An uncommon bulb with iris-like flowers, often strikingly marked. Needs a warm, sunny position.		
Jan	/	Recommended Species
Feb	/	*Moraea aristata*
Mar	/	*M. bellendenii*
Apr	plant	*M. gawleri*
May	/	*M. spathulata*
Jun	flowering	
July	flowering	
Aug	flowering	
Sept	/	
Oct	/	
Nov	/	
Dec	/	

Muscari

GRAPE HYACINTH

FEATURES

Vigorous and easy to grow, grape hyacinths have blue flowers of varying intensity. There are several species and named varieties available, including the double "Blue Spike" and the feathery "Plumosum." *Muscari aucheri* (*M. tubergenianum*) is known as "Oxford and Cambridge" because it has pale blue flowers at the top of the spike and is dark blue at the base, reminiscent of the English universities' uniform colors. Grape hyacinths are a great foil for other bright spring-flowering bulbs such as tulips or ranunculus. Flowers are lightly scented and are carried on a stem about 4–8in tall. This plant gives the most impact when planted in drifts: in large yards where there is space it can easily be naturalized in grass or under deciduous trees.

CONDITIONS

ASPECT   Best in full sun or dappled sunlight such as is found under deciduous trees.

SITE   Useful on rockeries, in the front of borders, and for naturalizing under trees, but the plants can be invasive. Muscari needs well-drained soil, preferably with plenty of organic matter incorporated before planting.

GROWING METHOD

PLANTING   Plant the bulbs about 3in deep and 4in apart in late summer or early fall.

FEEDING   Supplementary feeding is not usually necessary, but a light sprinkling of general fertilizer after flowering helps to ensure good growth. Watering is not normally necessary unless the weather is exceptionally dry.

PROBLEMS   No specific problems are known.

FLOWERING

SEASON   Flowers appear in early to mid-spring.

CUTTING   Although not often used as a cut flower, it lasts in water quite well if picked when half the flowers on the stem are open.

AFTER FLOWERING

REQUIREMENTS   Remove spent flower stems if required. Bulbs can be divided every 3–4 years in fall, replanting immediately. The foliage appears in the winter, long before the flowers.

ROYAL BLUE grape hyacinths here border a garden of daffodils and pop up from among the groundcover of snow-in-summer.

AT A GLANCE		
Pretty, easy-to-grow, little bulbs with short spikes of intense blue bells in spring.		
Jan	/	Recommended Varieties
Feb	/	*Muscari armeniacum*
Mar	flowering	"Blue Spike"
Apr	flowering	"Early Giant"
May	flowering	*Muscari azureum*
Jun	/	"Album"
July	/	*Muscari comosum*
Aug	/	"Plumosum"
Sept	plant	
Oct	plant	
Nov	/	
Dec	/	

Myosotis

FORGET-ME-NOT

FEATURES

Forget-me-nots are useful spring bedding plants, producing swathes of pink, blue, or white flowers from April onward. They go well with bulbs like tulips which push up through the myosotis flowers. Grow as a hardy biennial and use shorter varieties such as "Blue Ball," reaching 6in, in winter and spring patio containers. None grow more than 12in tall, and these are the ideal choice for spring bedding displays. Available by mail order in fall as ready-grown young plants.

CONDITIONS

ASPECT	Full or dappled sunlight is suitable.
SITE	Responds well to soil with plenty of rotted compost or manure mixed in that holds plenty of moisture. When planting containers in fall ensure good drainage and use a multipurpose compost.

GROWING METHOD

SOWING	Seed is sown direct into the ground May–July, in drills 1/2in deep. Thin seedlings as they develop so plants are eventually 3–6in apart, keep weed free and water copiously in dry spells. Plant into their flowering positions/containers in October and water to settle in.

FEEDING

FEEDING	Do not feed after planting in fall, but scatter a general granular fertilizer around plants in spring as they show signs of growth.
PROBLEMS	Powdery mildew can affect leaves but this is generally not worth treating.

FLOWERING

SEASON	From late winter to early summer.
CUTTING	Not suitable for cutting.

AFTER FLOWERING

GENERAL	Remove plants to make way for summer bedding, but if you leave a few to die down they will self-sow into the soil.

FORGET-ME-NOTS flower from early spring after growing slowly during the winter months. Flowers often have yellow "eyes."

AT A GLANCE	
A hardy biennial grown for its small flowers which appear in masses from early spring. Frost hardy to 5°F (zone 7).	
Jan /	**Recommended Varieties**
Feb /	*Myosotis sylvatica*
Mar /	"Blue Ball"
Apr flowering	"Carmine King"
May flowers/sow	"Compindi"
Jun sow	"Indigo"
July grow on	"Light Blue"
Aug grow on	"Music"
Sept grow on	"Rosylva"
Oct plant	"Royal Blue"
Nov /	"Spring Symphony Mixed"
Dec /	"Victoria Mixed"

Narcissus

DAFFODIL AND NARCISSUS

FEATURES

Daffodils are probably the best known and most widely grown of all bulbs and to many they are the true indicator of spring. They look wonderful mass-planted in the garden or naturalized in grass, but they also make great pot plants and excellent cut flowers. The best-known color is yellow, but there are also flowers in shades of white, cream, orange, and pink. The trumpet, or cup, is often a different color to the petals and may be bicolored.

There are many species and cultivars and the genus *Narcissus* has been divided into 12 different groups, depending on the form and size of the flowers. The height varies from 3–20in, depending on variety.

GROUPS

TRUMPET | The trumpet (cup) is at least as long as the petals, and there is one flower per stem.

LARGE CUPPED | Cup is shorter than, but at least one-third of, the length of the petals. One flower per stem.

SMALL CUPPED | The cup is less than one-third of the length of the petals; flowers usually carried singly.

DOUBLE | Double or semi-double flowers carried single or in small groups. The whole flower may be double, or just the cup.

TRIANDRUS | Two to six pendant flowers with reflexed petals per stem.

CYCLAMINEUS | Slightly pendant flowers with long trumpets and strongly reflexed petals, usually one per stem.

JONQUILLA | Several flowers per stem, with short cups. Sweetly scented.

TAZETTA | Half hardy. Very fragrant flowers in clusters of 10 or more per stem. Early flowering.

POETICUS | Small red or orange cup and broad white petals, usually one or two per stem. Often strongly fragrant. Late flowering.

WILD | A varied group containing the species and natural varieties found in the wild.

SPLIT CUPPED | The cup is split to varying degrees for at least one-third to half its length.

MISCELLANEOUS | Hybrids that do not fit into any of the other divisions.

CONDITIONS

ASPECT | These bulbs grow best in a sunny spot or under deciduous trees where they will receive sun in the early spring.

SITE | Grow narcissi in beds and borders, on rockeries, or in containers for the patio or in the home. Soil must be well-drained, ideally with some well-rotted organic matter dug in a month or so before planting.

AT A GLANCE		
Well-known spring-flowering bulbs in a wide variety of flower forms and sizes. Most types are very hardy.		
Jan	flowering	**Recommended Varieties**
Feb	flowering	"Carlton"
Mar	flowering	"Cheerfulness"
Apr	flowering	"February Gold"
May	flowering	"Irene Copeland"
Jun	/	"King Alfred"
July	/	"Minnow"
Aug	plant	"Peeping Tom"
Sept	plant	"Pipit"
Oct	plant	"Thalia"
Nov	/	N. bulbocodium
Dec	/	N. canaliculatus

GROWING METHOD

PLANTING   Planting depth will vary greatly according to the size of the bulb. Plant so that the nose is covered to twice the height of the bulb, in September or October. Plant as early as possible for the best results.

FEEDING   Feed with a balanced fertilizer in early spring. Plants can be given a liquid feed after the flowers have faded. Watering may be necessary in very dry spells, particularly once flowering has finished.

PROBLEMS   Basal rot can occur in storage; destroy bulbs with any sign of softening or rot at planting time. Similar symptoms can be caused by stem eelworm; these bulbs should also be destroyed by burning. Narcissus fly lays eggs near the necks of the bulbs; these hatch into larvae that tunnel into the bulb and weaken or destroy it. Bulbs in light shade are less susceptible to attack. Pull soil up round the necks of the bulbs after flowering to discourage egg laying.

FLOWERING

SEASON   Depending on area and variety, flowers may be carried anywhere from midwinter to early summer. Bulbs indoors may be brought into flower for Christmas or earlier; specially treated bulbs are available to ensure early flowering.

CUTTING   This excellent cut flower should last a week with frequent water changes, or with the use of proprietary cut flower additives. For longest vase life pick daffodils when the buds are about to burst open or as soon as they are fully open. Cut, don't pull, the stems as low as possible. Cut off any white section at the base of the stem. Don't mix daffodils with other flowers until they have spent a day in a vase on their own as their slimy sap may reduce the vase life of other blooms.

AFTER FLOWERING

REQUIREMENTS   Spent flowers should be removed before they set seed. Allow foliage to die down naturally; do not tie the leaves in clumps. Where bulbs are naturalised in grass, do not mow the grass until at least six weeks after the flowers have faded. Premature removal of leaves will have a detrimental effect on growth and flowering the following season. If drainage is good, bulbs may be left in the ground and clumps can be divided after flowering every three years or so. Bulbs grown indoors in pots can be planted out in the garden after flowering, where they should recover in a season or two.

THE ESSENCE OF SPRING BEAUTY is captured in this drift of mixed daffodils and delicate white blossom. As the planting has been kept to the edge of the lawn, the grass can be mown while still allowing the bulb foliage to die down naturally.

Nasturtium

TROPAEOLUM MAJUS

FEATURES

A popular trailing garden plant. Compact varieties grow to about 24in while large varieties can spread up to 10ft. The wide leaves are roundish and dark green to variegated in color and have a peppery taste. The funnel-shaped, five-petalled, and spurred flowers appear in late spring and summer and range from creamy white through yellow to salmon, brilliant orange, and red. Some varieties have double flowers and all have a slight perfume. Each bud produces a cluster of seeds. (Double forms do not produce seed.) This plant grows well in containers.

CONDITIONS

ASPECT   Prefers full sun although it will grow in semi-shade. Leaf growth is more pronounced in shady situations and may hide the blooms.

SITE   Nasturtiums do not like an over-rich soil but good drainage is necessary. Too rich a soil will encourage leaves at the expense of flowers.

GROWING METHOD

SOWING   For early flowers sow the large seeds under glass in spring. Plugs or small pots are ideal. Plant out 8in apart when all danger of frost has passed. Seeds can be sown outdoors in May directly where they are to grow, but the plants will not flower until a few weeks later than the early sowings.

FEEDING   Do not water excessively, especially when plants are well established. Nitrogen encourages the growth of leaves. More flowers and seeds will be produced if you hold back on the fertilizer and compost.

PROBLEMS   Sap-sucking blackfly (aphids) love nasturtiums. Vigorously hose the pest off or treat the plant with an appropriate spray. Caterpillars, particularly those of the cabbage white butterfly, can also be a problem.

HARVESTING

PICKING   Pick fresh leaves, buds, and flowers as required. Harvest seeds just before they lose their green color.

STORAGE   Leaves and flowers do not store well and should be used immediately. Buds and seeds can be pickled in vinegar, stored in airtight jars and used at a later date.

FREEZING   Put in a freezer bag; freeze for up to 6 months.

AT A GLANCE		
Attractive trailing annuals with brightly colored flowers, grown for decoration and for the kitchen. Hardy to 23°F (zone 9).		
Jan	/	**Parts used**
Feb	/	Leaves
Mar	plant	Flowers
Apr	plant	Buds
May	plant harvest	Seeds
Jun	plant harvest	**Uses**
July	harvest	Culinary
Aug	harvest	Gardening
Sept	harvest	
Oct	harvest	
Nov	/	
Dec	/	

USES

CULINARY   All parts of this herb are edible and have a spicy, peppery flavour. Fresh leaves and flowers are used in salads or the flowers can be used alone as a garnish. Buds and seeds are used as a substitute for capers. Caution: do not eat large quantities at one time.

GARDENING   Because they are so attractive to aphids, nasturtiums are excellent companion plants for vegetables such as cabbages, broccoli, and other brassicas. The aphids will flock to the nasturtiums and leave the vegetables alone.

Nemesia

NEMESIA

FEATURES

No varieties of *Nemesia strumosa* grow more than 12in high making them ideal for beds and containers. Grown as a half-hardy annual, flowers can be single colors or bright and varied mixtures. Good as edging for troughs and windowboxes. Very easy to grow.

CONDITIONS

ASPECT   Must have full sun to grow successfully.
SITE   In containers use multipurpose compost with slow-release fertilizer mixed well in. Soil with plenty of organic matter dug in well-ahead of planting gives good results, and must be well-drained.

GROWING METHOD

SOWING   Raise plants by sowing in small pots of soil-based seed compost starting in March/April (and repeating every few weeks for a succession of flowers), just covering the seeds. Keep at 60°F in a light place, and transplant to cell trays when seedlings are large enough to handle. Grow on and harden off in late May before planting after the last frosts, 6–12in apart. In containers make sure they are not swamped.

FEEDING   Give a liquid feed to plants grown as bedding every two weeks, with a hand-held feeder. Regular watering in dry spells is vital.
PROBLEMS   Plants may rot off in heavy, wet soils.

FLOWERING

SEASON   For more flowerheads, pinch out growing tips of plants when they are 4in high.
CUTTING   Not suited to cutting.

AFTER FLOWERING

GENERAL   Pull plants up when finished—this is quite often as they have a short flowering period.

THE TWO-LIPPED FLOWERS of nemesias come in an array of colors and they all have patterns deep in the flower's "throat."

AT A GLANCE		
A half-hardy annual grown for its pretty lipped flowers, used for bedding and patio containers. Frost hardy to 32°F (zone 10).		
Jan	/	Recommended Varieties
Feb	/	*Nemesia strumosa*
Mar	sow	**Mixed colors**
Apr	sow/transplant	"Carnival Mixed"
May	harden off/plant	"Pastel Mixed"
Jun	flowering	"Sparklers"
July	flowering	"Tapestry"
Aug	flowering	**Single colors**
Sept	flowering	"Blue Gem"
Oct	/	"Fire King"
Nov	/	"KLM"
Dec	/	"National Ensign"

Nemophila

BABY BLUE EYES

FEATURES

Nemophila is an easy annual sown in fall or spring. Flowers are sky-blue, white, or black/white. Plants grow to 8in high, with feathery leaves and a carpeting habit. Use them in borders, on rockeries, and around the edge of containers and windowboxes.

CONDITIONS

ASPECT | Needs full sun or part shade to succeed.
SITE | Needs well-drained soil, but mix in well-rotted organic matter before sowing to retain moisture. *Nemophila* will thrive in most multipurpose composts used in containers.

GROWING METHOD

SOWING | Sow seeds straight into the soil in fall or spring, in drills $^1/_2$in deep. Seeds sown in fall will produce young plants that survive the winter and flower earlier. Gradually thin plants out so they are 3–6in apart as flowers appear.
FEEDING | On well-prepared soil feeding is unnecessary, although large beds can be fed monthly with a general liquid feed applied through a hand-held feeder. Keep plants watered in dry spells or they may quickly die off.

PROBLEMS | Aphids can attack the soft leaves, so use a spray containing permethrin.

FLOWERING

SEASON | On fall-sown plants flowers appear from early spring to the first frosts, but appear slightly later on spring-sown plants.
CUTTING | Not suitable for use as a cut flower.

AFTER FLOWERING

GENERAL | Leave plants to set seed and die back before removing—nemophila self-seeds and plants will appear on their own each spring.

NEMOPHILA can be grown with other hardy annuals such as limnanthes, the poached egg flower, for a striking color combination.

AT A GLANCE	
A hardy spreading annual grown for its flowers for beds, rockeries and container edges. Frost hardy to 5°F (zone 7).	
Jan /	**Recommended Varieties**
Feb /	*Nemophila menziesii*
Mar /	(Also listed as *N. insignis*)
Apr sow	"Baby Blue Eyes"
May flowers/sow	"Penny Black"
Jun flowering	"Snowstorm"
July flowering	*Nemophila maculata*
Aug flowering	"Five Spot"
Sept flowers/sow	
Oct /	
Nov /	
Dec /	

Neoregelia

NEOREGELIA SPECIES

FEATURES

Often called heart of flame or blushing bromeliads, neoregelias are very popular for their ease of culture and their dazzling variety. In nature they grow as epiphytes on trees or as terrestrials. Species vary from tiny plants not more than 2in wide to those spreading to over $3^{1}/_{4}$ft. They can be grown as houseplants or as epiphytes attached to logs in the conservatory. However, to enjoy them at their best they should be sited low where their beauty can best be appreciated. The group has been widely hybridized, resulting in some truly outstanding cultivars.

FLOWERING

Most varieties produce a startling color change in the center of the plant at flowering time, the color remaining long after flowering has ceased. This color is mostly red, hence the common name "Blushing Bromeliad". This group lacks the tall, showy flowering spikes of other genera as the flowers—purple, blue, or white—form in the center of the leaf rosette.

FOLIAGE

Leaf rosettes are wide and spreading, the foliage shiny with serrated margins. Leaves may be plain green, red, burgundy, or patterned with stripes, bands, or spots, or even marbled.

N. CAROLINAE

Neoregelia carolinae is undoubtedly the most commonly grown and numerous lovely hybrids have originated from this species. The straight species forms a compact rosette with leaves about 10in long. The color of the center at flowering varies through shades of crimson to cerise and the flowers are deep violet. *N .c. tricolor* has foliage that is cream and green striped. This takes on a pinky red flush as flowering begins and the center of the plant turns crimson. Other varieties of this species include those with cream or white margined leaves. *N. carolinae marechalii* is another fine species but without the cream stripes. Leaves are plain olive green but flushed with crimson at the base during flowering.

N. SPECTABILIS

The fingernail plant, *N. spectabilis*, has red-tipped olive green leaves banded gray on the undersides. A hardy species, it is best grown in bright light, where the undersides of the leaves take on a rosy pink color. Place high up on a shelf so that the gray-barred, pink foliage is seen to advantage.

AT A GLANCE	
Varieties vary in size and flowers do not last long. Similar to guzmanias but broader leaves. Keep frost free.	
Jan water	**Recommended Varieties**
Feb water	*N. carolinae*
Mar re-pot if needs it	*N. carolinae marechalii*
Apr remove offset	*N. carolinae tricolor*
May move away from sunlight	*N. spectabilis*
Jun mist and water	
July flowering, water	
Aug buy plant	
Sept reduce water	
Oct water crown	
Nov keep frost free	
Dec keep frost free	

OTHER SPECIES

Another species used in hybridizing is *N. fosteriana* which features burgundy foliage. *N. marmorata* has wide leaves growing about 12in long. They are marbled in red on both sides and have red tips. *N. eleutheropetala* has sharply spined mid-green leaves that turn purple-brown at the center. The inflorescence mixes white flowers and purple-tipped bracts.

CONDITIONS

POSITION These plants must be grown in frost-free conditions with a minimum temperature of 50°F. A cool greenhouse, conservatory, or light room are perfect. Most neoregelias grow well in filtered or dappled sunlight. Where summers are very hot with long hours of sunshine, greenhouse shading may be needed. Indoors these plants will thrive in bright light but not direct sun through a window. For shady spots with no direct sun, the plain green leaved varieties will do best.

POTTING MIX The compost must be free draining and coarse to allow air to the roots. A mix of bark and gravel or coarse sand is suitable, with added charcoal if this is available. Don't overpot as roots may not utilize all the mix and watering becomes a problem. A pot large enough for a year's growth is ideal—stones or large pebbles can be put in the base to prevent the plant toppling over. Keep the leaf bases just above soil level.

GROWING METHOD

PROPAGATION Detach offsets from the parent plant once they are a good size. New roots form more rapidly if the offset is potted into a seed-raising compost mix or a mix of sand and peat or peat substitute, whichever you prefer.

WATERING Water should be kept in the cup at all times. Water about twice a week in summer, with daily misting unless the atmosphere is extremely humid. In winter water only occasionally. When watering, flood the central cup so that stagnant water is changed to avoid problems of rot.

FEEDING In the house, greenhouse or conservatory, plants can be given slow release fertilizer when active growth resumes in mid-spring and again in early to midsummer. Many growers believe plants grown without fertilizer produce more vibrant colors. Feed once a month in summer or when the plant is actively growing.

PROBLEMS There are no specific problems if cultural conditions are suitable. Apart from rots, usually caused by overwatering in cool weather, dying leaf tips are a sign of trouble. This symptom could be caused by cold, by dry, hot conditions, by drought or by frequent overwatering.

FLOWERING SEASON

Flowers are short lived. They do not usually rise above the rim of the cup. Most flower during late spring or summer.

Nepeta x faassenii

CATMINT

FEATURES

The gray-green leaves of Nepeta x faassenii are a lovely foil for other, brighter colors in the garden. Its mauve-blue flowers are produced over a long period too, making this is a useful plant for a sunny spot in the garden. It is quite quick to establish and is fairly long lived. The height is rarely more than 1ft and one plant may cover 18in or so, making roots as it goes. The foliage is aromatic when bruised and can then be attractive to cats. N. x faassenii is sometimes used as a cover planting between roses, especially old roses, as it provides a pleasing contrast in texture and color. It is a great favorite for garden edgings and cottage garden plantings and can be grown in a hanging basket or container. There is a cultivar known as "Six Hills Giant," which has taller growth and larger flowers.

CONDITIONS

ASPECT   This plant grows best in full sun but tolerates shade for part of the day.

SITE   Needs well-drained soil and tolerates poor soils, but growth is best if some organic matter is dug in well ahead of planting time.

GROWING METHOD

PROPAGATION   N. x faassenii is easy to grow from rooted suckers, which are produced freely. It may also be grown from cuttings taken through summer. Alternatively, lift and divide established plants in the spring as active growth begins.

FEEDING   Does not generally need fertilizer, but if the soil is very poor, complete plant food may be applied in early spring. In good conditions extra feeding is not necessary.

PROBLEMS   No specific problems are known but overwatering or heavy, poorly drained soil can eventually kill this plant.

FLOWERING

SEASON   N. x faassenii has a long flowering period from early summer into early fall. The colors are generally on the soft side being pale blue, or lilac-pink. The best display is in early summer, but by cutting it back you promote fresh new growth and another good display.

PRUNING

GENERAL   Cut back old growth in spring to promote young, fresh growth.

AT A GLANCE		
N. x faassenii is a good plant for cottage gardens, with sprays of lavender flowers and grayish leaves. Hardy to 5°F (zone 7).		
Jan	/	Recommended Varieties
Feb	/	Nepeta x faassenii
Mar	/	N. govaniana
April	/	N. grandiflora
May	foliage	N. nervosa
June	flowering	N. racemosa
July	flowering	"Six Hills Giant"
Aug	flowering	
Sept	flowering	
Oct	foliage	
Nov	/	
Dec	/	

Nerine

NERINE, GUERNSEY LILY

FEATURES

Nerine bowdenii brightens the fall garden, producing its heads of bright pink flowers before the leaves appear. It is easy to grow and flowers last well when cut. Bulbs should be planted where they can be left undisturbed for several years; they flower best when crowded and after a dry summer. They can also be grown in containers. Flower stems grow 12–18in high and the deep green, strappy leaves from 8–12in long.

The Guernsey lily (*N. sarniensis*) has bright red flowers, and other species and cultivars of nerines may be red, white, pink or apricot, but only *N. bowdenii* is hardy enough to grow outdoors in this country.

CONDITIONS

ASPECT   Nerines require full sun and a warm, sheltered spot.
SITE   A useful plant for borders, especially under the shelter of a south-facing wall. The soil should be free-draining and moderately fertile. In cold areas and with the more tender species, grow bulbs in pots of John Innes potting compost.

GROWING METHOD

PLANTING   Plant in middle to late summer or in mid-spring, 4in deep and 6in apart. In containers, plant with the neck of the bulb at or just below soil level.

FEEDING   Can be grown successfully without supplementary fertilizer. However, if you wish, you can give weak liquid fertilizer every couple of weeks once flower buds appear until growth slows down. Water regularly while in active growth but keep the bulbs dry during the dormant period.
PROBLEMS   No specific problems are known.

FLOWERING

SEASON   Flowers appear during early fall.
CUTTING   Nerines last well as cut flowers with frequent water changes.

AFTER FLOWERING

REQUIREMENTS Cut off spent flower stems. Outdoors, mulch the planting site for winter protection.

TALL AND ELEGANT, these bright pink nerines appear as the summer garden fades away in fall.

AT A GLANCE	
Heads of funnel-shaped pink flowers appear on leafless stalks in fall. Needs a warm, sheltered position.	
Jan /	**Recommended Varieties**
Feb sow	*Nerine bowdenii alba*
Mar sow	*Nerine bowdenii*
Apr plant	"Mark Fenwick"
May /	"Pink Triumph"
Jun /	"Wellsii"
July /	*N.* "Corusca Major"
Aug plant	*N.* "Fothergillii Major"
Sept flowering	*N. undulata*
Oct flowering	
Nov flowering	
Dec /	

New Zealand Tea tree

LEPTOSPERMUM SCOPARIUM

FEATURES

Bejewelled from May to June with stalkless, disc-like blooms amid small, narrow leaves, twiggy and slender, purplish-stemmed *Leptospermum scoparium* is an evergreen worth caring for. Forming a rounded bush, 6–8ft high, it is usually grown against a sheltered wall. Alternatively, set it among other shrubs that shield it from biting winds.

Trained as a mini-standard, it makes a fetching feature for a sun-soaked patio.

Favoured varieties are double "Red Damask," single, clear pink "Huia," and double, white "Snow Flurry". Be warned: tea trees may be short-lived unless conditions are ideal.

CONDITIONS

ASPECT | *Leptospermum* needs full sun and protection from cold, north or east winds. Ideally fan-train it against a south- or west-facing wall. Make sure air freely circulates to reduce risk of mildew felting and crippling leaves.

SITE | The planting area must be well drained. Improve light, sandy soils by digging in old manure or well-rotted garden compost.

GROWING METHOD

FEEDING | Encourage robust flowering growth by applying an acidifying fertilizer in spring and midsummer. Water young plants regularly in their first year after planting.

Thereafter, soak the root area periodically in dry periods and mulch with shredded bark.

PROPAGATION | Multiply plants from soft-tip cuttings in June or semi-ripe cuttings in late summer.

PROBLEMS | Plants are susceptible to root rot in clay soils. Avoid it by forking in grit or gravel before planting. Webbing caterpillars, such as lackey moth, can cause leaves to drop. Cut off and destroy egg bands or webbed shoots and spray with permethrin, bifenthrin, or fenitrothion.

PRUNING

If leptospermum outgrows its allotted space, remove one shoot in three from the base, when flowers fade in midsummer. Do not cut back into older wood as it seldom re-grows. Remove straggly shoots in spring.

SMOTHERED WITH TINY, disc-like blooms from May to June, Leptospermum "Red Damask" is best fan-trained against a warm, sunny wall in all but very mild areas.

AT A GLANCE	
A slightly frost-tender evergreen, it is studded with tiny, red, pink, or white blooms from May to June. Hardy to 23°F (zone 9).	
Jan /	Recommended Varieties
Feb /	"Huia"
Mar /	"Kiwi"
Apr plant	"Red Damask"
May flower, plant	"Snow Flurry"
June flower, plant	
July plant, prune	
Aug plant	
Sept plant	
Oct /	
Nov /	
Dec /	

Nicotiana

TOBACCO PLANT

FEATURES

Not grown for tobacco but for their tubular flowers. Choose from dwarf modern varieties growing 1ft tall with upward-facing flowers, for bedding and containers, to *Nicotiana sylvestris* at 5ft for large borders—plant it behind other plants and especially against a dark evergreen background so that the large leaves as well as the flowers are shown off to best effect. Some release scent in the evening, so plant near doors and windows, or grow a few in large tubs that can be moved into the house or conservatory on a warm summer evening. Flowers can be pink to lime-green. A half-hardy annual. Widely available as young plants in a good selection of varieties.

CONDITIONS

ASPECT	Full sun or light shade. The flowers stay open longer in sun.
SITE	Grow in well-drained, moisture-retentive soil with rotted manure/compost mixed in. For container growing use multipurpose compost.

GROWING METHOD

SOWING	Use 3$\frac{1}{2}$in diameter pots of multipurpose compost, sow the fine seed on the surface in March, but do not cover, and keep in a light place at 70°F. Tiny seedlings emerge within three weeks. Transplant to cell trays of multipurpose compost or into 3$\frac{1}{2}$in diameter pots when each young plant has developed

3–4 small leaves. Grow on and harden off in late May, then plant after the last frosts in your area, 12–18in apart depending on the variety grown.

FEEDING	Liquid feed weekly outdoors. Add slow-release fertilizer granules to container compost before planting.
PROBLEMS	Use a spray containing pirimicarb for aphids. Destroy plants attacked by virus, showing any puckered and mottled leaves

FLOWERING

SEASON	Flowers all summer. Nip off dead flowers.
CUTTING	Not suitable.

AFTER FLOWERING

GENERAL	Remove plants after first frosts. It is possible to collect seed from Nicotiana sylvestris that can then be sown the following spring.

AT A GLANCE	
A half-hardy annual grown for it colorful and often scented flowers, used in bedding/containers. Frost hardy to 32°F (zone 10).	

		Recommended Varieties
Jan	/	*Nicotiana sanderae*
Feb	/	"Domino Mixed"
Mar	sow	"Domino Salmon Pink"
Apr	transplant/grow on	"Havana Appleblossom"
May	harden off/plant	"Hippy Mixed"
Jun	flowering	"Lime Green"
July	flowering	"Merlin Peach"
Aug	flowering	*Nicotiana langsdorfii*
Sept	flowering	*Nicotiana sylvestris*
Oct	/	
Nov	/	
Dec	/	

Nigella

LOVE-IN-A-MIST

FEATURES

Love-in-a-mist has fine, feathery leaves, with a fringe of foliage surrounding and slightly veiling each of the flowers, hence its common name. When the spiky seed pods appear it is also called devil-in-a-bush. Flowers are blue, pale and deep pink, white, or purple. *Nigella* grows 18in tall and is good for big drifts in beds or for cutting. Hardy annual. The variety "Transformer" has novel seed pods.

CONDITIONS

ASPECT	Give it a sunny spot in an open position.
SITE	Needs good drainage but isn't too fussy about soils—rotted organic matter may be dug in ahead of planting, but this is not essential, and good results can be had on quite thin, poor soils as long as it is grown in full sun.

GROWING METHOD

SOWING	Sow in March or September, in short drills ¹/₂in deep. Thin plants as they grow so there is about 6–8in between them as they begin to produce flower buds. Leave thinning of fall-sown plants until spring in case there are winter losses. Plants can also be raised in cell trays, sowing 2–3 seeds per tray and removing all but the strongest seedling—nigella does not like disturbance.
FEEDING	Does not need extra feeding during summer.
PROBLEMS	Plants are trouble free.

FLOWERING

SEASON	Fall-sown plants flower from late spring, spring-sown from early summer.
CUTTING	Delightful cut flower. Remove foliage from lower part of stalk to prolong flower life.

AFTER FLOWERING

GENERAL	The inflated seed pods that form are useful in dried flower arrangements. Pick stems after pods have dried on the plant and hang upside- down in a warm, airy place. Nigella self-seeds prolifically and will produce masses of seedlings the following spring. Dead plants can be pulled up and composted.

AFTER THE FLOWERS come the curiously attractive seedheads that give the plant its other common name, devil-in-a-bush.

AT A GLANCE		
A hardy annual grown for its flowers and its attractive, inflated seed pods which can be dried. Frost hardy to 5˚F (zone 7).		
Jan	/	**Recommended Varieties**
Feb	/	*Nigella damascena*
Mar	sow	"Dwarf Moody Blue"
Apr	flowers/thin	"Miss Jekyll"
May	flowering	"Miss Jekyll Alba"
Jun	flowering	"Mulberry Rose"
July	flowering	"Oxford Blue"
Aug	flowering	"Persian Jewels"
Sept	flowers/sow	"Shorty Blue"
Oct	/	*Nigella orientalis*
Nov	/	"Transformer"
Dec	/	

Odontoglossum

TIGER ORCHID

FEATURES

This large group of evergreen orchids comes from Central and South America. They are epiphytes or lithophytes and most occur at high altitudes. They grow from pseudobulbs from which one or two leaves emerge. The flower spikes are very variable and may be short or tall, upright or arching in habit, but all originate from the base of the pseudobulb. Some species are grown but it is the hybrids that are widely cultivated. Hybrids occur in almost every color of the rainbow and are marked in an extraordinary range of patterns. The odontoglossums will readily breed with other closely related genera to give an ever increasing range of flower types. This interbreeding can also often make the plants much more tolerant to warmer or cooler conditions. Some examples are crossed with *Oncidium* to make *Odontocidium*, with *Miltonia* to create *Odontonia* and with *Cochlioda* to make *Odontioda*. When a third genus is involved then the names change again—for example *Odontoglossum* x *Oncidium* x *Cochlioda* makes a *Wilsonara*.

CONDITIONS

CLIMATE — Needs a frost-free, but generally not hot, climate and prefers a temperature range from 50–77°F. High humidity is essential for this orchid.

ASPECT — Needs shade, especially in summer when shadecloth of about 70 per cent should be used. Reduce in winter to provide maximum light to encourage flowering.

POTTING MIX — Needs very open and free-draining soil. A suitable mix would contain medium grade bark, charcoal, pea gravel, or very coarse, washed sand. A little chopped sphagnum moss can be added. Do not overpot. Use pots just large enough to confine the roots.

GROWING METHOD

PROPAGATION — Divide plants after flowering but only when the container is overflowing. Plants resent frequent disturbance.

WATERING — Never allow plants to become bone dry but roots should never be sodden. Frequency of watering depends on the mix used and the weather. Mist plants in hot, dry weather.

FEEDING — Use soluble liquid plant foods at half the recommended strength every couple of weeks through the warmer months.

PROBLEMS — No specific pest or disease problems are known for this orchid.

FLOWERING SEASON

The flowering season is very variable, depending on the species or hybrid.

AT A GLANCE		
Popular and easy to grow houseplants. Different varieties with attractive dark green foliage and sprays of flowers.		
Jan	less water	**Recommended Varieties**
Feb	less water	*O. crispum* (white)
Mar	water and feed	*O. cordatum* (yellow/brown)
Apr	water and feed	*O. hallii* (yellow)
May	water and feed	*O. laeve* (brown/white)
Jun	water and feed	Odontocidium Purbeck Gold
July	water and feed	(yellow/brown)
Aug	water and feed	Odontonia Boussole
Sept	water and feed	"Blanche" (white)
Oct	less water	Vuylstekeara Cambria
Nov	less water	"Plush" (red/white)
Dec	less water	

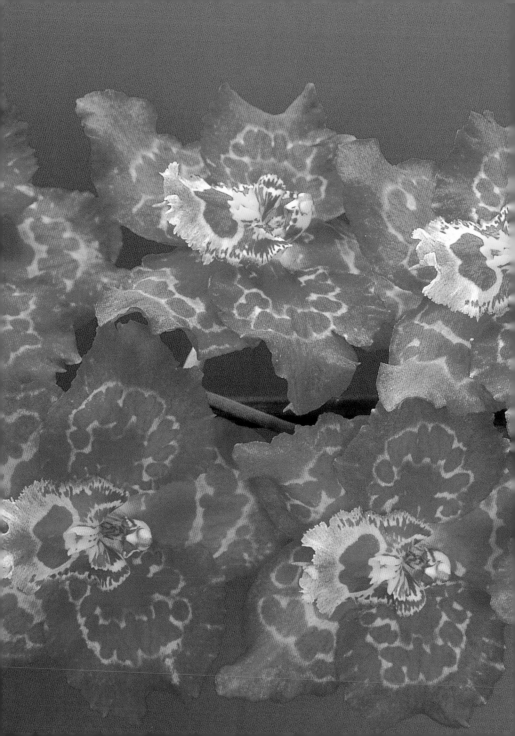

OTHER ODONTOGLOSSUMS TO GROW

O. CRISPUM This species, with pure white flowers, was imported into Britain in large quantities at the beginning of the 20th century, when it commanded enormous prices. Still sought after, it is not found in such abundance as it used to be. Hybrids that have been made with it still retain the beautiful white coloring but tend to be easier to grow, making them good for beginners.

O. CORDATUM A more compact species which is relatively easy to grow and flower for the amateur enthusiast. Star-shaped golden yellow and chestnut brown flowers are approximately $2^{1}/_{2}$in across and between three and six are held on a short arching spray.

O. HALLII Larger growing, the plant height being around 12in with a spray of large yellow flowers, spotted in brown which have the added bonus of being scented and usually summer flowering.

O. LAEVE Although this species has small flowers, colored in dark green and brown with a contrasting white and magenta lip, there are a lot of them held on a very tall, branching flower spike which can be up to $3^{1}/_{4}$ft high. The flowers have a strong, sweet fragrance, which will fill your greenhouse. The plant is strong and vigorous growing which makes it good for ease of culture. There are literally thousands of Odontoglossum hybrids available with new ones being produced all the time; here are some examples to choose from.

VUYLSTEKEARA "Cambria "Plush": This is a complex hybrid between three different genera, which make up part of the "Odontoglossum Alliance" of related genera. It is one of the all time classic hybrids and has been around since the 1930s and is still very popular today. Its ease of culture and free-flowering habit make it an ideal beginners' orchid as well as being very showy with its large bright red flowers, the lip white with red spotting.

ODONTOCIDIUM Purbeck Gold: This is another classic variety, this time in a brilliant golden yellow, the petals and sepals with just a touch of chocolate brown. Flowers are 3in across on a spray reaching 12–20in, depending on the maturity of the plant. These orchids are very easy to grow and flower.

BEALLARA Tahama "Green": The addition of Brassia into the breeding of Glacierthis hybrid gives the flower a stunning, star-shaped appearance. The large blooms can measure up to $2^{1}/_{2}$in across. The translucent green of the flower is contrasted with the dark red in its center. Produces tall sprays with between six and a dozen of these showy, long-lasting flowers. Tolerant of varying temperatures, this orchid will flower well in cool or warm environments. A vigorous grower, it makes an excellent specimen plant in just a few years.

Brilliant colors and intricate patterns are now appearing in many of the newer Odontoglossum hybrids.

Oenothera

EVENING PRIMROSE

FEATURES

Evening primrose is an essential plant for formal and cottage-style yards. While each flower (white, yellow, or pink, depending on the variety) opens and fades fast, barely lasting 24 hours, there is an abundance of new buds developing through the summer and early fall. The plant has two extra advantages. Often fragrant, and often tall, it can make an eye-catching addition to the border. *O. biennis*, the traditional favorite, is actually an annual or biennial. *O. fruticosa*, a biennial or perennial, has two fine forms, "Fyrverkeri" ("Fireworks"), which has red buds opening to yellow flowers and purple-tinged leaves, and subsp. *glauca*, with yellow flowers and purple leaves.

CONDITIONS

ASPECT Grow in an open, sunny position.
SITE Moderately rich soil will suffice, although evening primrose can self-seed and appear in even the stoniest ground.

GROWING METHOD

PROPAGATION Sow seed or divide in early spring, or take cuttings of non-flowering shoots. Keep in a frost-free place in winter, plant out in spring.
FEEDING Not necessary, although moderate quantities of manure will suffice in especially poor soil.

PROBLEMS Slugs tend to be the main problem, attacking tender new growth. Pick off or treat with chemicals. The sturdy kinds of evening primrose are free-standing, but others (*O. macrocarpa*) may require support.

FLOWERING

SEASON Lasts from late spring to late summer, with flowers tending to open in early evening, when they release their scent.
CUTTING Short-lived but attractive flowers.

AFTER FLOWERING

REQUIREMENTS Collect seed when ripe, if required, and then cut spent stems to the ground.

EVENING PRIMROSE earns its name by blooming at dusk. There are perennial species that keep their blooms open all day.

AT A GLANCE	
A genus of mainly annuals and biennials, with excellent perennials. Scented and yellow flowering, they are hardy to 5°F (zone 7).	
Jan /	Recommended Varieties
Feb sow	*Oenothera biennis*
Mar divide	*O. fruticosa*
Apr transplant	"Fyrverkeri"
May flowering	subsp. *glauca*
Jun flowering	*O. macrocarpa*
July flowering	*O. speciosa*
Aug flowering	"Rosea"
Sept /	*O. stricta*
Oct /	"Sulphurea"
Nov /	
Dec /	

Oleander

NERIUM OLEANDER

FEATURES

Frost-tender and principally a conservatory plant, evergreen oleander enjoys a summer airing on a sunny, sheltered patio or terrace. Depending on variety, it makes a handsome shrub, 4–6ft high. Sumptuous heads of white, yellow, pink, apricot, cerise, or scarlet, single or double blooms appear from June to November. Thrusting, upright stems are clad with slender, leathery leaves. Oleanders are long-lived and flower early in life. Choice varieties include: semi-double, light pink "Clare"; single, apricot "Madame Leon Blum"; double, white "Soeur Agnes"; and single, deep red "Hardy's Red." Double, pink-flowered "Variegatum," with cream or yellow-rimmed leaves, is very popular with flower arrangers. The plant is poisonous if eaten.

CONDITIONS

ASPECT   Oleander needs full sun and shelter from cold winds to prosper and flower freely. Only in frost-free gardens can it be grown outdoors all year round. Elsewhere, grow it in a pot indoors—in a lounge or conservatory—and move it outside when frosts finish in late May.

SITE   This shrub thrives in most free-draining soil types but abhors heavy, waterlogged clay. If growing it in a large pot or tub, set it in proprietary tub or hanging basket compost.

GROWING METHOD

FEEDING   Border plants: Encourage large clusters of blossom by sprinkling bone meal over the root area in spring and fall and hoeing it in.

TUB GROWN   (indoors in winter): Insert slow-release fertilizer granules into the compost in spring. Repot root-bound plants in spring. Though oleander tolerates long, dry periods, soak roots occasionally in hot, dry weather.

PROPAGATION   Raise plants from seeds sown in a heated propagator in spring or take semi-ripe cuttings in midsummer.

PROBLEMS   If plants are attacked by limpet-like scale insects, control them by spraying two or three times, fortnightly, with malathion or horticultural soap.

PRUNING

GENERAL   Keep oleander youthful and blooming freely by shortening flowered shoots by half their length when blossoms fade. Ensure plants stay neat and bushy by shortening side shoots to 4in in spring.

AT A GLANCE		
Studded with showy blooms in many colors, frost-tender oleander is usually grown in a conservatory. Hardy to 45°F (zone 11).		
Jan	/	Recommended Varieties
Feb	/	"Clare"
Mar	plant	"Emile"
Apr	plant, prune	"Géant des Batailles"
May	flower, plant	"Luteum Plenum"
June	flower, plant	"Professor Granel"
July	flower, plant	"Soeur Agnes"
Aug	flower, plant	"Soleil Levant"
Sept	flower, plant	"Variegatum"
Oct	flower	
Nov	flower	
Dec	/	

Olearia x haastii

DAISY BUSH

FEATURES

If you need a highly unusual idea for a flowering hedge, this is it. A New Zealand bushy shrub with small, dark green leaves in the spring, and a white felt-like covering beneath. It is grown for its big show of white starry flowers in mid- and late summer, and the scent is a bit like that of hawthorn. The flowers are followed by brown fluffy seedheads. It grows at least 4ft high, and easily as wide, so just five plants would create an impressive summer windbreak hedge. It can be livened up with climbers like clematis and honeysuckle. A nearby purple Buddleja davidii, flowering at the same time, gives a strong contrast of colors. Despite its southern origins, this olearia is perfectly hardy.

CONDITIONS

ASPECT	Full sun gives the best display of flowers. Do not hide theses shrubs away in the shade.
SITE	The more sun the better.

GROWING METHOD

PROPAGATION	The best results are from summer cuttings, which are semi-ripe, in pots of cuttings compost. They should take quite quickly. Give frost-protection the first winter, for planting out the following spring.
SPACING	Set plants from 2–3ft apart.
FEEDING	A spring application of a slow-release fertilizer should suffice. The ground should have been well prepared before planting, with generous quantities of well-rotted organic matter. Make sure there is good drainage.
PROBLEMS	Olearia is virtually trouble-free. An easy grow, low-maintenance shrub.

FLOWERING

SEASON	Olearia x haastii flowers at the height of summer, and makes an incredible sight when, as an enormous hedge, it is in full flower. Contrasting colored climbers can easily be grown through it.

PRUNING

GENERAL	Only needed to keep the plant in shape, or remove frost damage. If cutting to restrict size, prune up to one-third of last year's growth.

THE FLOWERS of O.x haastii develop through the season, before giving way to the fluffy, brown seedheads, providing interesting texture.

AT A GLANCE		
Olearia x haastii is a bushy shrub with a summer show of white flowers. Thrives in coastal areas. Hardy to 5˚F (zone 7).		
Jan	foliage	**Companion Plants**
Feb	foliage	Clematis
Mar	foliage	Cobaea scandens
April	foliage	Ipomoea
May	foliage	Lapageria
June	foliage	Passion flower
July	flowering	Rose
Aug	flowering	Tropaeolum
Sept	foliage	
Oct	foliage	
Nov	foliage	
Dec	foliage	

Opuntia

OPUNTIA

FEATURES

Variously known as prickly pear, Indian fig, and cholla, with many more local common names, this is a very large genus of cactus with a vast geographical range. Opuntia are jointed or segmented cactuses with mainly padded and flattened joints, although sometimes these are cylindrical or rounded. Species occur naturally from southern Canada and throughout the Americas, continuing to Patagonia on the tip of South America. Long grown as living fences in their native areas, many prickly pears were introduced to other countries for this purpose, with disastrous results.

PRICKLY PEAR

O. aurantiaca, *O. stricta*, and *O. vulgaris* and a number of other species have become quite appalling weeds in Australia, Africa, and India. By 1925, there was estimated to be above 10 million acres (25 million hectares) of land infested by prickly pear in Australia. A huge program of biological control was initiated, involving the introduction of the Cactoblastis moth and cochineal insects.

INDIAN FIG

The Indian fig, *O. ficus-indica*, is widely grown in many parts of the world for its fruit. It is a tree-like cactus up to 17ft high and wide.

OTHER TYPES

Although many species of opuntia are too large to place anywhere except in a large desert garden, there are numerous other shapes and sizes, with some that are suitable for pot culture. Bunny ears, *O. microdasys*, has dark green pads dotted with white areoles, and white, yellow, or brown bristles. The brown-bristled form is known as teddy bear ears. These plants rarely grow more than 16–24in high and wide, and suit both containers or the yard. *O. tunicata* is a small, spreading bush about 24in high and up to 3ft wide. Its thick, creamy spines take on a satin sheen in sunlight. Beaver tail, *O. basilaris*, has purple-gray flat pads with few spines and spreads by branching from the base, so is rarely more than 16in high. *O. erinacea* is clump-forming with flattened blue-green pads, but it is the variety ursina with masses of fine hair-like spines—known as grizzly bear cactus— that attracts many growers. In the wild it grows in California and Arizona, has 4in long pinky orange flowers, and grows about 18in high.

FLAT, PADDLE-SHAPED segments and the sizeable growth of the edible Opuntia ficus-indica *make an impact in the landscape.*

AT A GLANCE		
The largest group of cactus with some outstanding plants; excellent shapes and dangerous spines. 41°F min (zone 11).		
Jan	/	Recommended Varieties
Feb	/	*Opuntia basiliaris*
Mar	sow	*O. clavarioides*
Apr	transplant	*O. ficus-indica*
May	flowering	*O. microdasys*
Jun	flowering	*O. imbricata*
July	flowering	*O. tunicata*
Aug	flowering	*O. verschaffeltii*
Sept	flowering	*O. vestica*
Oct	/	
Nov	/	
Dec	/	

CHOLLAS

It is well worth knowing something about this rare group, which are rarely seen outside specialist botanical collections. The chollas (pronounced "choyas") are

enormously variable in their habit of growth. They include the very spiny, almost furry-looking *O. bigelovii*, which grows to about 3–6^1/$_2$ft high, and the more open, tree-like *O. versicolor*, which may reach almost 13ft in height. Most of this group have easily detached segments, in particular the jumping cholla, *O. fulgida*, which hooks on to anything that passes, usually taking root and growing where it falls.

CONDITIONS

ASPECT   Best grown in an open, sunny situation.
SITE   Provide container-grown plants with sharply drained, standard cactus mix. In the garden, they tolerate a wide range of soils as long as they drain well. All opuntias dislike having their roots cramped in a small space. The larger plants should eventually be moved to a border in the glasshouse. If you opt for a regime of constant potting up, note that the spines are vicious.

GROWING METHOD

PROPAGATION   Easily grown from stem segments which should be separated from the parent plant from spring to fall. They can also be grown successfully from seed sown in spring.
FEEDING   In spring and mid-summer, plants in the ground can be given pelletted poultry manure or granular slow-release fertilizer.

Potted plants should have a dose of slow-release fertilizer in the spring or an occasional liquid feed during the growing season.

PROBLEMS   Few problems are encountered if growing conditions are suitable. The two worst offenders to look out for are scale insects and mealybugs. You will invariably need to spray to remove them, since the dangerous spines prevent you from getting in close to carry out treatment with a swab.

FLOWERING

SEASON   The flowers of opuntia are produced sometime during spring or summer, depending on species. The majority of species has yellow flowers, but these may also be orange, purple, or white. For example, the bright yellow flowers of *O. tunicata* appear from spring to summer, while *O. basilaris* bears its bright rose-pink flowers in summer.
FRUITS   Berry-like fruits form after the flowers fade, and in some species these are edible. The Indian fig has bright yellow flowers that are followed by deep red to purple fruit. It is widely cultivated around the world for its fruit. Prepare the fruit for eating by washing and using a brush to remove the spines. Slice off the top and bottom, slit the skin, and peel. Serve in slices with a squeeze of lemon or lime juice. You can also use the pulp to make jam. *O. cochenillifera* is a source of cochineal—although today this dye is mainly synthesized.

Ornamental Cherry

PRUNUS

FEATURES

Deciduous or evergreen shrubs or trees 4–14ft tall, the prunus family embraces a wide range of forms. Flowers are single or double, in white, pink, and red shades. Neat dwarf Russian almond (*Prunus tenella* "Firehill") has semi-double, rosy-crimson flowers, which sleeve 4ft stems in April. Also useful for small gardens is *P. x cistena* "Crimson Dwarf," whose white flowers appear just before coppery-red leaves.

White-flowering and low-growing evergreen kinds— *P.* "Otto Luyken" among them—are excellent for carpeting shady spots. Taller laurel (*P. laurocerasus* "Rotundifolia") makes a dense evergreen hedge to 6ft.

CONDITIONS

ASPECT   Deciduous flowering cherries, needing full sun to perform well, should be sheltered from strong winds. Evergreens thrive in light shade.

SITE   All prunus prosper on any well-drained soil enriched with organic matter. Evergreen varieties also thrive on thin, sandy soils.

GROWING METHOD

FEEDING   Work bone meal into the root area in spring and fall. Water freely in dry spells, especially when flower buds are forming.

PROPAGATION   Increase evergreen, carpeting and hedging varieties from semi-ripe cuttings from mid- to late summer. Flowering cherry trees, however, are normally grafted on to *P. avium* rootstock.

PROBLEMS   Control silver leaf disease by cutting back and burning affected shoots to 6in beyond infected, purple-stained tissue, in midsummer.

PRUNING

EVERGREENS: Shear laurel hedges in spring and late summer.

DECIDUOUS VARIETIES: No regular pruning is necessary. Cut out crowding shoots from mid- to late summer.

HERALDING SPRING and suitable for all sizes of garden, white-, pink-, or red-flowering cherries associate beautifully with magnolias.

AT A GLANCE		
Huge family of spring-flowering cherries and carpeting or hedging evergreens. Hardiness rating, according to species.		
Jan	/	**Recommended Varieties**
Feb	/	Evergreen
Mar	plant, flower	"Otto Luyken"
Apr	prune, flower	*P. laurocerasus*
May	flower, plant	"Rotundifolia"
June	plant, flower	"Zabeliana"
July	plant, prune	**Deciduous**
Aug	plant, prune	"Amanogawa"
Sept	plant	*P. x blireana*
Oct	plant	"Cheal's Weeping"
Nov	plant	*P. mume*
Dec	/	*P. tenella*
		"Firehill"

Ornithogalum

CHINCHERINCHEE, STAR OF BETHLEHEM

FEATURES

There are around 100 species of *Ornithogalum* originating in Africa, Asia and parts of Europe, but the chincherinchee, *O. thyrsoides*, is perhaps the best known, with its imposing spikes of white summer flowers growing up to 18in. The leaves are narrow and sword-shaped. Other commonly grown species are *O. arabicum*, whose scented white flowers have a striking black eye, *O. nutans*, with delicate spikes of dangling white flowers, and *O. umbellatum*, or star of Bethlehem, which forms clumps of grassy foliage studded with pure white, upward-facing white blooms: these are all spring flowering. Chincherinchee and *O. arabicum* are frost tender.

CONDITIONS

ASPECT   Prefers an open position in full sun but will grow in light shade. *O. thyrsoides* can be grown outside in summer though it will not survive the winter; in cold areas it can be grown as a pot plant in the home or greenhouse.

SITE   Good for mixed borders, rockeries or naturalising in grass. The bulbs need well-drained but not very rich soil.

GROWING METHOD

PLANTING   Plant bulbs in spring or fall, 2in deep and about 8–12in apart.

FEEDING   Not usually essential, but an application of balanced or high potash fertilizer given as the plants start into growth may improve flowering. Watering is not necessary unless the season is exceptionally dry; for container-grown plants, keep the compost just moist.

PROBLEMS   This bulb is generally trouble-free.

FLOWERING

SEASON   Flowers will appear spring and early summer.

CUTTING   This is a first class cut flower.

AFTER FLOWERING

REQUIREMENTS Cut spent flower stems at ground level. Non-hardy species should be lifted in fall and stored in a dry, cool place for replanting the following spring. Hardy species can be divided after flowering and replanted immediately.

CHINCHERINCHEE gives a long and pretty floral display, as the flowers open slowly from the bottom up to the top of the cone.

AT A GLANCE		
Half-hardy and hardy bulbs producing attractive white flowers in spring or early summer.		
Jan	/	**Recommended Species**
Feb	/	*Ornithogalum arabicum*
Mar	/	*O. longibracteatum*
Apr	plant/ flower	*O. montanum*
May	flowering	*O. nutans*
Jun	flowering	*O. oligophyllum*
July	flowering	*O. thyrsoides*
Aug	/	*O. umbellatum*
Sept	/	
Oct	plant	
Nov	/	
Dec	/	

Osmanthus

OSMANTHUS

FEATURES

An easy, enchanting, and small, glossy, leathery-leaved evergreen from western China and Japan, osmanthus forms an orb of shoots and colors spring and fall.

Light up April and May with *Osmanthus* x *burkwoodii*. Growing to around 6ft high by 4ft across, its toothed, pointed leaves foil slender stems massed with clusters of small, white, vanilla-fragrant, tubular blooms. Create a riveting feature by grouping it with orange or yellow deciduous azaleas. It also makes a dense, wind-proof hedge.

Closely related *O. delavayi* is another spring-flowering treasure. Arching to 5ft high, it too is smothered with bunches of small, white blooms that spill jasmine perfume on to the air. Small, black fruits follow them.

Later, from September to October, comes taller *O. heterophyllus*, to 10ft high and across, the soft leaves of which deceive you into thinking it is a form of holly. It does a sterling job in coloring the closing year with a profusion of tiny, white blossoms.

Its colored-leaved varieties—purple "Purpureus" and creamy "Aureomarginatus"—are stunning throughout the year.

CONDITIONS

ASPECT All, apart from *O. delavayi* which is best grown again against a sheltering, warm wall in cold districts, thrive in the open.

SITE If possible, set plants in free-draining, humus-rich soil that does not dry out or become waterlogged. Fortify sandy or chalky soils with bulky organic manure.

GROWING METHOD

FEEDING Boost growth by sprinkling Growmore or some other balanced fertilizer over the root area in spring, repeating in midsummer. Water it in if the soil is dry. Foliar feed in droughty spells, when roots have difficulty absorbing plant foods, to speed uptake of nutrients. Water new plants copiously and follow with a mulch of bark, cocoa shell, or well-rotted garden compost.

PROPAGATION Increase varieties by layering flexible shoots from late spring to late summer or take semi-ripe cuttings from mid- to late summer.

PROBLEMS Seldom attacked by pests or diseases.

PRUNING

No regular cutting back is necessary. If awkward shoots need removing, do it in spring when flowers have finished. Shorten stems to just above a joint or to new shoots. Trim a hedge of *O.* x *burkwoodii* when flowers fade in May.

AT A GLANCE		
Spring- or fall-flowering evergreens for sun or light shade, *O.* x *burkwoodii* makes a stocky hedge. Hardy to 23°F (zone 9).		
Jan	/	**Recommended Varieties**
Feb	/	*O.* x *burkwoodii*
Mar		*O. delavayi*
Apr	flower, plant	*O. heterophyllus*
May	flower, plant	"Aureomarginatus"
June	prune	"Purpureus"
July	/	"Variegatus"
Aug	/	
Sept	flower, plant	
Oct	flower	
Nov	/	
Dec	/	

Osteospermum

OSTEOSPERMUM

FEATURES

Many varieties of osteospermum can be bought in spring as young plants, but others can be grown from seed and treated as half-hardy annuals. Growing from seed is a cost-effective way of raising large numbers of plants quickly. Favorite plants can be potted-up in fall and kept in a well-lit frost-free place over winter, then increased by cuttings in spring. In mild areas plants will often survive the winter outdoors and carry on producing a few flowers except in severe spells. In some catalogs it is listed as dimorphotheca. Plants can grow 12–30in tall.

CONDITIONS

ASPECT   Must have full, baking sun for best results.

SITE   Is not fussy about soil but it must be very well-drained. A sheltered spot with the sun beating down all day is ideal. Plants also perform well in containers and these should be sited in full sun facing south if possible. Use multipurpose compost.

GROWING METHOD

SOWING   March/April is the time to sow, sowing seed thinly in 3$\frac{1}{2}$in diameter pots of soil-based seed compost, and just covering. Germinate at 64˚F in a bright spot. Seedlings are transplanted to cell trays or individual 3$\frac{1}{2}$in pots when large enough to handle. Harden off for two weeks and start planting from mid-May onward.

FEEDING   Water well to establish and then water only in long spells of hot, dry weather. Extra feeding is unnecessary, but container-grown plants will benefit from occasional liquid feeds given for the benefit of other plants.

PROBLEMS   Aphids can attack the leaves, flower stalks and buds so choose a spray containing permethrin and wet both sides of the leaves.

FLOWERING

SEASON   Flowers appear from early summer onward with a peak later on when temperatures reach their highest.

CUTTING   Flowers are unsuitable for cutting.

AFTER FLOWERING

GENERAL   After the main flowering give plants an overall clipping to tidy them up and maintain compact growth. Lift and pot favorite plants and keep frost-free over winter.

AT A GLANCE	
A hardy/half-hardy annual grown for its brightly-colored daisy-like flowers that appear all summer. Frost hardy to 23˚F (zone 9).	
Jan /	**Recommended Varieties**
Feb /	*Osteospermum* hybrids
Mar sow	"Gaiety"
Apr sow/transplant	"Giant Mixed"
May harden off/plant	"Glistening White"
Jun flowering	"Ink Spot"
July flowering	"Potpourri"
Aug flowering	"Salmon Queen"
Sept flowering	"Starshine"
Oct flowering	"Tetra Pole Star"
Nov /	
Dec /	

Oxalis

WOOD SORREL

FEATURES

A number of species of oxalis are very invasive, but others are very decorative and well worth growing. Most have clover-like leaves and five-petalled, satiny flowers which are furled in bud. The usual color is pink or white; there are also purple, yellow, orange, or red varieties. Some species need greenhouse cultivation in this country. Height varies from 2–8in.
   O. adenophylla is the most popular species, with grayish leaves and silvery flowers;
   O. enneaphylla has white flowers and attractive, folded, silvery leaves. *O. laciniata* has narrow leaflets and purple, veined flowers. Once known as *O. deppei*, *O. tetraphylla* has brown-marked leaves and pink flowers.

CONDITIONS

ASPECT   Grow in full sun for good flowering and compact leaf growth.
SITE   Grow on a rockery or near the front of a border, preferably in a confined bed where growth can be controlled. The more invasive varieties are best grown in pots. Free-draining soil is preferred.

GROWING METHOD

PLANTING   Plant in early fall, 3in deep and 4in apart. It is usual to plant clumps in growth rather than the tiny tubers or rhizomes.
FEEDING   Supplementary fertilizer is rarely needed.

PROBLEMS   Few problems are usually encountered although some oxalis do suffer from the fungal leaf disease rust. Pick off the worst affected leaves and avoid overhead watering.

FLOWERING

SEASON   Most species flower through early and mid-summer.
CUTTING   Flowers are unsuitable for cutting.

AFTER FLOWERING

REQUIREMENTS   Plants can be divided after flowering in summer. Clear away dead foliage once the leaves have died down; beware of putting plant debris from invasive varieties on the compost heap.

THIS PRETTY PINK OXALIS makes a charming groundcover here on the edge of a paved area.

AT A GLANCE		
A low-growing, clump-forming plant with clover-like leaves and attractive, satiny flowers. Can be invasive.		
Jan	/	Recommended Varieties
Feb	/	"Beatrice Anderson"
Mar	/	"Bowles' White"
Apr	/	"Ione Hecker"
May	/	"Royal Velvet"
Jun	flowering	*O. enneaphylla*
July	flowering	"Alba"
Aug	/	"Minutifolia"
Sept	planting	"Rosea"
Oct	planting	*O. tetraphylla*
Nov	/	"Iron Cross"
Dec	/	

P

Pachysandra terminalis

PACHYSANDRA

FEATURES

Sometimes also known as Japanese spurge, this is an ideal groundcover under trees as it is happy in shade and tolerates dry soil. It has glossy, toothed leaves in a rosette form. Quite fast growing but long lived, it rarely grows more than 8in high. It spreads with runners and makes a dense, weed-suppressing cover once established. Plant at about 1ft intervals for quick cover. *Pachysandra terminalis* produces greenish white flower spikes in spring. There is a cultivar with white variegated leaves known as "Variegata."

CONDITIONS

ASPECT   Although tolerant of sun or shade, this plant is best in shaded and fairly sheltered positions.

SITE   Tolerates damp or dry soil but not heavy, waterlogged clays.

GROWING METHOD

PROPAGATION   Grows from divisions of older clumps lifted in the spring. Make sure that each section looks healthy, and has buds and roots, before replanting it in the garden.

FEEDING   Apply complete plant food in early spring.

PROBLEMS   No specific problems are known.

FLOWERING

SEASON   Greenish white flower spikes are produced in the first part of summer but they are not very showy. Note that there are two other forms but that they do not offer a choice of flowers. "Green Carpet" has finer, smaller leaves, and "Variegata" has foliage with a white edge.

PRUNING

GENERAL   Pruning is not necessary. If growth becomes too dense and congested, it is a simple matter to thin it out—pull up unwanted plants, or lift clumps and replant the younger growths.

A LOVELY SHEEN is a feature of the foliage on this variegated form of pachysandra, while the cream leaf margins brighten the leaves and add interest to what is already a handsome plant. This is a long-term planting and is an ideal groundcover under trees.

AT A GLANCE	
Pachysandra terminalis is an evergreen with shiny dark leaves. White flowers appear in early summer. Hardy to 0˚F (zone 7).	
Jan foliage	**Companion Plants**
Feb foliage	Euonymus
Mar foliage	Hydrangea
April foliage	Mahonia
May foliage	Phillyrea
June flowering	Rubus
July foliage	Sambucus
Aug foliage	Skimmia
Sept foliage	Vaccinium
Oct foliage	Viburnum
Nov foliage	
Dec foliage	

Paeonia

PAEONY SPECIES AND CULTIVARS

FEATURES

Beautiful to look at and fragrant, too, peonies are among the aristocrats of the plant world, and although there are only 33 wild species, there are many hundreds of cultivars. Peonies were prized by the Chinese for many hundreds of years, and by the early 18th century they had developed the garden peonies from which the forms of P. lactiflora (often referred to as Chinese peonies) are generally descended. Peonies were first introduced into Europe at the end of the 18th century. Peonies are divided into two groups: the tree peonies, which are shrubby and derived from P. suffruticosa, and the herbaceous peonies, of which the cultivars of P. lactiflora are most commonly grown. Although the name "tree peony" is used, this is an exaggeration—they rarely grow more than 6¹/₂ft tall. Herbaceous peonies grow about 39in high and wide. Plants are long-lived.

FLOWERS

Flowers may be single or double and come in every shade of pink, red, purple, white, and cream, many with a delicious light perfume. Some flowers have a large central boss of golden stamens, and some have fringed or crimped edges on the petals. Among the categories of flowers recognized are: small, 2–4in across; medium, 4–6in across; large, 6–8in across; and very large, over 8in across. Tree peonies are generally 2–12in. Other categories have been developed in the United States where a great deal of hybridizing is practiced.

CONDITIONS

ASPECT   Needs full sunlight or semi-shade, with protection from strong winds.

SITE   Soil must be well drained, but heavily enriched with manure or compost. Dig it over deeply to allow the free spread of roots.

GROWING METHOD

PROPAGATION   Divide plants in the spring or fall, taking care not to break the brittle roots. Each division must have roots and dormant growth buds. Crowns should be replanted 1in below the surface, and spaced about 20in apart. Plants can be raised from seed but they will take four to five years to reach flowering size, and only the species will be true to type. Peony seeds generally need two periods of chilling with a warm period between, and care should be taken not to disturb the seeds

AT A GLANCE		
Jan	/	Recommended Varieties
Feb	/	P. cambessedesii
Mar	/	"Defender"
Apr	divide	P. lactiflora
May	transplant	"Bowl of Beauty"
Jun	flowering	"Festiva Maxima"
July	/	"Sarah Bernhardt"
Aug	/	P. mlokosewitschii
Sept	/	P. obovata
Oct	sow	
Nov	sow	
Dec	sow	

during this time. Most seeds germinate during the second spring after sowing.

FEEDING Apply a general fertilizer in early spring. At the same time, mulch but avoid the crown.

PROBLEMS Botrytis or gray mold is the main problem with peonies. It can cause rotting of stems and leaf bases. Destroy affected foliage, improve drainage and air circulation, and spray with a fungicide. Replace the top layer of soil carefully around the plants.

FLOWERING

SEASON The flowering period is invariably in early summer. Some peonies bloom for only a short time, but the flowers on other types are much longer lasting.

CUTTING Cut flowers for indoor use when the blooms are opening. Peonies are excellent cut flowers, which will last longer if kept in a cool part of the home and given frequent water changes.

AFTER FLOWERING

REQUIREMENTS Remove spent flower stems, but allow the foliage to die down naturally before trimming it back. Some varieties produce lovely fall color. Do not cut down the flowering stems of varieties such as *P. mlokosewitschii* that produce handsome berries.

HINT

Disturbance Peonies may flower poorly, if at all, in the first year after planting, but this should improve year by year. Generally speaking, peonies are best left undisturbed; even 50-year-old clumps can be seen flowering profusely. It may be wiser to increase your stock by buying young container-grown plants than split a precious specimen.

THIS HALF-OPENED peony flower gives a hint of delights to come, with a touch of white against the bright pink.

Papaver nudicaule

ICELAND POPPY

FEATURES

Varieties of *Papaver nudicaule* are available in a wide range of colors and range from 10–30in tall depending on variety. They can be treated as either half-hardy annuals or hardy biennials sown in summer or fall. Tall varieties are used for cutting. Plants sown early flower from April onward.

CONDITIONS

ASPECT   Can be grown in cool and warm areas.
SITE   Poppies need well-drained but moisture-retentive soil with plenty of rotted organic matter added ahead of planting or sowing.

GROWING METHOD

SOWING   Sow seed outdoors April-June or in September. Scatter the seed thinly along shallow drills $1/2$in deep, and rake over with fine soil. Thin out when seedlings are 2in high, so that the spacing is ultimately at about 6–12in intervals by October. Do not disturb the fine roots when thinning out, and always water when finished to settle plants back in. Thin fall-sown poppies in spring in case of winter losses. For earlier flowers sow in pots at 60°F in February and grow in cell-trays, planting in late May.
FEEDING Extra feeding not needed.

PROBLEMS

PROBLEMS Fall-sown plants may rot off in heavy soils, so sow in cell trays and keep dry in a coldframe over winter, planting out in spring.

FLOWERING

SEASON   Flowers appear during early summer and should be picked off as they fade.
CUTTING Excellent cut flower. Pick when buds are just opening. Singe stem ends before arranging.

AFTER FLOWERING

GENERAL Leave a few plants to self-seed, but otherwise pull up after the flowers are finished.

ICELAND POPPY has petals with the texture of crepe paper and a velvety sheen. The center of the flower is a mass of yellow stamens. Their tall stems mean the flowers of Papaver nudicaule *waft gently in the breeze, and look good like this, massed in bedding.*

AT A GLANCE		
A hardy biennial (or half-hardy annual) grown for its large showy flowers that appear in summer. Frost hardy to 5°F (zone 7).		
Jan	/	**Recommended Varieties**
Feb	/	*Papaver nudicaule*
Mar	/	**Biennials**
Apr	sow	"Large Flowered Special Mixture"
May	flowers/sow	"Meadow Pastels"
Jun	flowers/sow	"Red Sails"
July	flowering	"Wonderland Mixed"
Aug	flowering	**Half-hardy annuals**
Sept	flowers/sow	"Summer Breeze"
Oct	plant	
Nov	/	
Dec	/	

Papaver orientale

ORIENTAL POPPY

FEATURES

The oriental poppy is a clump-forming perennial with a variety of different forms, and colors ranging from soft hues to sharp red. They all bear the hallmarks of the species P. orientalis from northeast Turkey and Iran, which has a large cupped bowl of a flower with paper-thin petals. Growing up to 36in tall, with a similar spread, they self-seed freely, creating attractive colonies. They look the part in both wild or natural gardens, and large mixed borders. "Black and White" is a striking contrast of white petals and a black mark at its base. "Cedric Morris" is soft pink with a black base. "Indian Chief" is reddish-brown.

CONDITIONS

ASPECT   Provide full sunlight, the conditions it receives in its natural habitat.
SITE   Rich soil and good drainage bring out the best in these plants.

GROWING METHOD

PROPAGATION   Since they self-seed freely, propagation may not be necessary. Slicing off sections of root in late fall or early winter will provide abundant new plants. The success rate is invariably high. Alternatively, divide clumps in the spring, or sow seed in pots in the fall in a cold frame. Plant out the following spring, 9in apart.

FEEDING   Add plenty of rich, friable compost in spring to add fertility to poor soils. This also improves the drainage, which needs to be quite good.
PROBLEMS   Fungal wilt and downy mildew can be problems; spray at the first sign.

FLOWERING

SEASON   The flowers appear from late spring to mid-summer.
CUTTING   Poppies do not make good cut flowers.

AFTER FLOWERING

REQUIREMENTS   When the flowers have died down, severely cut back the foliage to the ground. This will produce a second showing of attractive summer leaves.

THIS FRINGED RED FLOWER indicates the wide range of colors within P. orientale. No border should be without one.

AT A GLANCE		
P. orientalis is a perennial with 12in-long leaves, and big, cupped flowers in a range of colors. Hardy to 0°F (zones 6–7).		
Jan	/	Recommended Varieties
Feb	/	*Papaver orientale*
Mar	/	"Allegro"
Apr	division	"Beauty of Livermere"
May	flowering	"Black and White"
Jun	flowering	"Goliath Group"
July	flowering	"Mrs Perry"
Aug	/	"Patty's Plum"
Sept	/	"Perry's White"
Oct	sow	"Picotee"
Nov	/	"Turkish Delight"
Dec	/	

Papaver rhoeas

SHIRLEY POPPY

FEATURES

Shirley poppies, varieties of *Papaver rhoeas*, generally grow to about 2ft high, have a very delicate appearance, and come in a wide range of colors including pastels. There are single or double varieties and they look effective in large drifts, but can also be sown in patches 1–2ft across and used as fillers in mixed borders. Each flower can be 3in across. A hardy annual.

CONDITIONS

ASPECT   Avoid any shade and grow in full sun.
SITE   Must have very well-drained soil. Rotted compost or manure should be added to the soil a few weeks before sowing.

GROWING METHOD

SOWING   The fine seed can either be scattered on the soil and simply raked in, and the area marked with a circle of sand, or it can be sown in short $^1/_2$in deep drills. March–May and September are the sowing times. Gradually thin out the seedlings until they are 12in apart, but avoid transplanting as they dislike disturbance. If sowing in fall leave thinning until the following spring in case of winter losses.

FEEDING   Extra summer feeding is not required, but water thoroughly should plants start to wilt.
PROBLEMS   Trouble-free.

FLOWERING

SEASON   Fall-sown plants flower from late spring onward, while spring-sown flower in summer.
CUTTING   Suitable as a cut flower if stems are scalded before arranging.

AFTER FLOWERING

GENERAL   Leave a few plants to die down and self-seed.

WHEN ALLOWED TO self-seed, poppies will come up among other plants. Unwanted plants are very easily pulled out.

AT A GLANCE		
Shirley poppies are hardy annuals sown in spring or fall and grown for their large flowers. Frost hardy to 5˚F (zone 7).		
Jan	/	**Recommended Varieties**
Feb	/	*Papaver rhoeas*
Mar	sow	"Angels Choir Mixed"
Apr	sow/thin	"Angel Wings Mixed"
May	flowers/sow	"Mother of Pearl"
Jun	flowering	"Selected Single Mixed"
July	flowering	"Shirley Double Mixed"
Aug	flowering	"Shirley Single Mixed"
Sept	flowers/sow	
Oct	/	
Nov	/	
Dec	/	

Parodia

BALL CACTUS

FEATURES

While the species is now known as parodia, you will find that many ball cactuses are still under the old name of notocactus. These superb cactuses are native to Brazil, Paraguay, Uruguay, and Argentina. Mostly rounded in form, although a few are column shaped, they are easy to grow and flower profusely. Many ball cactuses have deeply furrowed surfaces, but the coverage of spines varies greatly; some forms are thickly covered and others have quite sparse spines. *P. concinnus* is a small tubby shape with primrose-yellow flowers, while *P. leninghausii* can form a thick column up to 3ft high and has large yellow flowers. *P. herteri*, prized for its hot pink-purple flowers, is squat-shaped and blooms when it reaches tennis-ball size. *N. uebelmannianus* is another squat grower, with large purple or yellow flowers.

CONDITIONS

ASPECT   Ball cactuses will grow in full sun or in very light shade. When standing pots outdoors in summer, make sure that the plants receive some shade around midday.

SITE   When growing in pots, use a standard well-drained compost. In the ground, ball cactuses like equally well-drained soil with some well-rotted compost that slightly increases fertility.

GROWING METHOD

PROPAGATION   Grow from seed in spring or from offsets taken in summer. None of the species will produce offsets until quite mature. Increase watering in the spring and allow the soil to dry out between waterings during the summer.

FEEDING   Apply slow-release fertilizer in spring, or feed the plants with some low-nitrogen liquid fertilizer every 6–8 weeks throughout the growing season.

PROBLEMS   This is generally a trouble-free type of cactus that is easy to grow.

FLOWERING

SEASON   The flowers appear on the crown of ball cactuses during the spring or summer months. The central stigma of the flower is nearly always a deep reddish-purple to pink color. While the majority of the ball cactuses have yellow flowers, it is possible to obtain other species that have attractive flowers in red, pink, purple, or even orange colors. Contact a cactus nursery which specialises in parodia.

FRUITS   In ideal growing conditions, as in the wild, you may find that after the flowers fade fleshy fruits ripen to red.

AT A GLANCE		
Generally globular or spherical, ribbed spiny cactuses from South America. Funnel-shaped blooms. 45°F min (zone 11).		
Jan	/	**Recommended Varieties**
Feb	/	*Parodia chrysacanthion*
Mar	transplant	*P. concinna*
Apr	flowering	*P. herteri*
May	flowering	*P. horstii*
Jun	flowering	*P. leninghausii*
July	flowering	*P. magnifica*
Aug	sow	*P. mammulosa*
Sept	/	*P. nivosa*
Oct	/	*P. rutilans*
Nov	/	*P. schwebsiana*
Dec	/	

Parsley

PETROSELINUM

FEATURES

Parsley grows from a strong tap root with erect, 12in tall stems bearing divided, feather-like, small leaves which may be flattish or curly depending on variety. Tiny, yellowish-green flower clusters are borne on tall stalks in summer, and produce small, brown, oval and ribbed seeds. Common varieties of this biennial or short-lived perennial plant include curly parsley, P. crispum, plain-leaved or Italian parsley, P. crispum var. neapolitanum, and Hamburg or turnip-rooted parsley, P. crispum var. tuberosum.

CONDITIONS

ASPECT   Grow in full sun or light shade.
SITE   Parsley plants like a rich, deep, well-drained soil.

GROWING METHOD

SOWING   Sow seed under cover in spring in pots or plug trays rather than seed trays as parsley dislikes being transplanted. The seed can be difficult to germinate so help to create optimum conditions by soaking the seeds in warm water for 24 hours and then pouring boiling water over the soil to raise the temperature. Plant the young seedlings out, 6in apart, after they have grown several true leaves. If parsley is grown in containers, the pots should be at least 8in deep, and the longer tap root of Hamburg parsley will require a pot that is even deeper. Once parsley plants are established in the garden, the mature plants can be left to self-sow when they go to seed during the summer months in their second year of growth.

FEEDING   Keep the soil moist and do not let it dry out in dry weather. Occasional feeds of a nitrogen-rich liquid fertilizer will promote more leaf growth.

PROBLEMS Carrot fly and root aphids can be particular problems. Destroy affected plants. Slugs also love young plants.

PRUNING   Parsley can be kept productive by frequent pruning and by nipping out the flower stalks whenever they appear.

HARVESTING

PICKING   New growth comes from the center of the stem, and so always pick parsley from the outside of the plant. Pick this vitamin-rich, nutritious herb as needed. Dig up young roots of Hamburg parsley in fall.

STORAGE   Broad-leaved Italian parsley, with its stronger taste, gives a better result when dried than the other varieties.

AT A GLANCE		
Parsley, with its tasty green leaves, is one of the best known of all the culinary herbs. Frost hardy to 4°F or below (zone 7).		
Jan	/	**Parts used**
Feb	/	Leaves
Mar	plant	Flowers
Apr	plant harvest	Roots
May	plant harvest	**Uses**
Jun	plant harvest	Culinary
July	harvest	Medicinal
Aug	harvest	Cosmetic
Sept	harvest	Gardening
Oct	/	
Nov	/	
Dec	/	

FREEZING   Curly parsley freezes well. Put sprigs in freezer bags and freeze for up to 6 months.

USES

CULINARY   Parsley is used in salads, as a garnish, and in cooking. Hamburg parsley is used as a root vegetable.

COSMETIC   An infusion can be used as a hair rinse. Chew raw parsley to promote a healthy skin.

MEDICINAL   Parsley is very nutritious and it is a strong diuretic. Fresh parsley is a breath freshener, and is recommended for taking away the smell of garlic on the breath. It has been used in poultices and to make an antiseptic dressing for wounds and bites. Caution: Do not use medicinally during pregnancy.

GARDENING   Parsley makes an attractive edging plant.

Passiflora caerulea

BLUE PASSION FLOWER

FEATURES

The Blue passion flower is a fast-growing climber from Brazil and Argentina with evergreen or semi-evergreen foliage. The very complex flowers, basically bowl shaped, come in a striking color combination of white and green, zoned with blue, purple, and white. This species grows to at least 30ft tall. As it is not one of the hardiest climbers available the Blue passion flower is best grown against a warm, sunny, sheltered wall. This makes it an ideal subject for a courtyard garden or any similar enclosed area. Alternatively, it could be grown on the wall of the house. It really flourishes in mild parts of the country, and in colder areas this plant will need adequate protection from cold drying winds.

CONDITIONS

ASPECT   Best in full sun but can also be grown in partial shade. This plant needs to be well sheltered from cold winds.
SITE   Grows in any reasonably fertile, well-drained yet moisture-retentive soil.

GROWING METHOD

PROPAGATION Take softwood or semi-ripe leaf-bud cuttings in spring and summer. Carry out serpentine layering in the spring. Sow seeds in spring, after soaking in hot water for 24 hours. Germinate at 64°F.
WATERING   If the soil starts to dry out in the summer water the plant well.

FEEDING   Apply a slow-release fertilizer in the spring, such as the organic blood, fish, and bone.
PROBLEMS   Passifloras are not usually troubled by pests and diseases out of doors.

FLOWERING/FOLIAGE

FLOWERS   Bowl-shaped flowers over a very long period, followed by egg-shaped light orange fruits.
FOLIAGE   Dark green and deeply lobed.

PRUNING

REQUIREMENTS Train a framework of permanent stems on the support and in spring just before growth starts, carry out spur pruning by cutting back flowered shoots to within two or three buds of this framework.

The flowers of Passiflora *are famous for their intricate petals and stamens. Only P.* caerulea *is hardy enough to be grown outside.*

AT A GLANCE	
A vigorous tendril climber producing exotic-looking flowers followed by orange fruits. Hardy to 23°F (zone 9).	
Jan /	**Recommended Varieties**
Feb /	*P. c.* "Constance Elliot" has white
Mar /	flowers.
Apr planting	
May planting	
Jun flowering	
July flowering	
Aug flowering	
Sep flowering	
Oct flowering	
Nov /	
Dec /	

Pelargonium
BEDDING GERANIUM

FEATURES

Better known as geraniums, seed-raised pelargoniums are available with large bright flowerheads for bedding, and also as trailing "ivy-leaved" types. Seeds are sown January/February and need warmth to succeed, so consider buying them as young plants delivered ready-grown in spring. Varieties for bedding and patio containers grow no more than 1ft, while ivy-leaved types can spread and trail up to 2ft. Flowers may be single colors or mixtures—the new "ripple" varieties are eye-catching. Plant 1–2ft apart. All are half-hardy annuals.

CONDITIONS

ASPECT | Must be grown in full sun.
SITE | Well-prepared soil with rotted compost or manure mixed in gives best results. Soil must be well-drained, and when planting up containers use multipurpose compost with slow-release fertilizer mixed in. Bedding geraniums do well in terracotta containers.

GROWING METHOD

SOWING | Sow January/February in a heated propagator in a guaranteed temperature of 64°F. Seedlings appear in 2–3 weeks and can be transplanted to 3in pots or cell trays of multipurpose compost. Plants must have good light and a temperature of 61–64°F to grow well. Pot on into 4–5in diameter pots, harden off in late May, and plant out after the last frosts.
FEEDING | Liquid feed bedding plants every 2–3 weeks.
PROBLEMS | Heavy wet soils can lead to rotting of the stems, so grow in containers. Snap off faded flowerheads to avoid gray mold.

FLOWERING

SEASON | Flowers appear from early summer onward.
CUTTING | Not suitable.

AFTER FLOWERING

GENERAL | Pull up and compost. Favorite plants can be kept dry and frost-free over winter.

TO ENSURE a continuous display through the warm months, spent flowers should be removed regularly.

AT A GLANCE	
Half-hardy annuals grown for their flowers and also the attractive ivy-like foliage of some varieties. Frost hardy to 32°F (zone 10).	
Jan sow	**Recommended Varieties**
Feb sow	*Pelargonium* hybrids
Mar transplant	**FOR BEDDING**
Apr pot on	"Avanti Mixed"
May harden off/plant	"Raspberry Ripple"
Jun flowering	"Ripple Mixed"
July flowering	"Sensation Mixed"
Aug flowering	"Stardust Mixed"
Sept flowering	"Video Mixed"
Oct /	**Ivy-leaved varieties**
Nov /	"Summertime Lilac"
Dec /	"Summer Showers"

Pelargonium oblongatum

PELARGONIUM

FEATURES

It might sound odd to include a pelargonium in a group of succulents, but about 220 of the 280-odd species are just that. (Do not confuse them with the hardy outdoor geraniums.) *Pelargonium oblongatum* comes from South Africa, in particular the northern region of Namaqualand. It was not actually collected until the early 19th century, making it quite a recent pelargonium since most of the others were collected well before this. It has a 6in long oblong tuber (hence the Latin name), leaves with coarse hairs, and pale yellow flowers delicately feathered with maroon markings. It is definitely a collector's item, and could be the start of a collection with the orange-red *P. boranense* discovered in 1972 in Ethiopia, and *P. carnosum*, also from Namaqualand.

CONDITIONS

ASPECT   The key requirement is bright sun; the more heat the better. In its native landscape it completely avoids any shade.

SITE   It needs to be grown in a pot where it can be properly cared for. Provide an open, free-draining compost. It is surprisingly easy to keep provided it is kept on the dry side while dormant in the summer. Active growth is, as in the southern hemisphere, from fall onward. Leaf drop is in the spring.

GROWING METHOD

PROPAGATION   While it can be raised from seed, as with all pelargoniums stem cuttings give an extremely high success rate. Take them in mid-fall, as new growth begins, and keep warm over winter avoiding a chilly windowsill. When mature, water well in the winter-spring period, with a reduction over summer.

FEEDING   Provide a mild fortnightly liquid feed when in full growth to boost the flowering show in the spring.

PROBLEMS   Keep a check for aphids. They form tight packed clusters on the tasty young stems; spray accordingly. Once they take hold they can become quite a nuisance.

FLOWERING

SEASON   There is a show of star-shaped flowers in the spring. After the bright blowsy colors with sharp reds and lipstick pinks of the more traditional pelargoniums like "Happy Thought" they come as a quieter, interesting surprise.

AT A GLANCE		
P. oblongatum is a pelargonium with a difference. Try this species with delicate pale flowers. 36°F min (zone 10).		
Jan	/	**Recommended Varieties**
Feb	/	*Pelargonium abrotanifolium*
Mar	/	*P. cucullatum*
Apr	repotting	*P. fruticosum*
May	flowering	*P. graveolens*
Jun	flowering	*P. papilionaceum*
July	/	*P. peltatum*
Aug	/	*P. radens*
Sept	sow	*P. tomentosum*
Oct	/	
Nov	transplant	
Dec	/	

Penstemon

BEARD TONGUE

FEATURES

This very large group of perennials consists of 250 species and countless cultivars, all originating in a wide variety of habitats in the southern and western United States. Their tubular or funnel-shaped flowers come in a range of shades of pink, red, purple, lavender, blue, and white, some with a contrasting throat. There is a large range of cultivars in many of these shades. Collections of young rooted cuttings can also be bought. Penstemons have a long flowering period, through the summer to mid-fall, especially if the spent blooms are regularly cut, but many plants can be short-lived. Take cuttings regularly. The various species and hybrids grow anything from 4 to 24in tall.

CONDITIONS

ASPECT   Grows best in full sunlight with some protection from strong, cutting winds. Since most varieties are not fully hardy, warmth and shelter are essential.

SITE   Needs very open and well-drained soil.

GROWING METHOD

PROPAGATION   They grow well from cuttings taken in mid-summer, then overwintered in a greenhouse frame. A wide range of penstemons can be grown from seed, which is widely available. They need a cold period before germination; sow in the fall or refrigerate the seed for three weeks before sowing in the spring.

FEEDING   Apply a general fertilizer as new growth commences in the spring.

PROBLEMS   No specific pest or disease problems, but root rot may occur on sticky clay soil.

FLOWERING

SEASON   Most have a fairly long flowering period, from the summer to mid-fall. However, many can only be seen as true perennials in milder parts of the country, being killed by winter frosts; raise new stock to replace any losses. "Garnet" is the hardiest.

CUTTING   This is not a satisfactory cut flower.

AFTER FLOWERING

REQUIREMENTS   Either cut entirely to the ground, or leave some stems as frost protection. Protect clumps with a mulch of straw or bracken.

MANY MONTHS of fine bloom can be expected from this fine red cultivar—well into the fall, if it is regularly deadheaded.

AT A GLANCE		
A large genus of perennials grown for their late-season flower display. Hardiness varies from the frost-tender to 5℉ (zones 10–7).		
Jan	/	**Recommended Varieties**
Feb	sow	"Alice Hindley"
Mar	sow	"Beech Park"
Apr	transplant	"Chester Scarlet"
May	transplant	"Evelyn"
Jun	flowering	"Garnet"
July	flowering	"Margery Fish"
Aug	flowering	"Osprey"
Sept	flowering	"Pennington Gem"
Oct	flowering	"Rubicundus"
Nov	/	
Dec	/	

Periploca graeca

SILK VINE

FEATURES

This is a vigorous deciduous climber, a native of south-west Europe and south-west Asia. The Silk vine is grown primarily for its attractive-looking star-shaped flowers in the summer. Unfortunately these flowers also have a rather unpleasant fragrance. It is the most commonly grown species, of which there are about 11 altogether in the genus. Growing to a height of 28ft, the Silk vine is suitable for a warm sheltered wall or close-boarded fence where it will be well protected. This plant is also suitable for a pergola or trellis screen, as long as the chosen site is well sheltered from cold and drying winds. It will make an ideal climber for a courtyard garden with its own favorable microclimate.

CONDITIONS

ASPECT   The Silk vine requires a position in full sun that is also warm and sheltered.
SITE   Any soil is suitable provided it is well drained.

GROWING METHOD

PROPAGATION   Sow seeds in the spring and germinate them in a temperature of 61°F. Root semi-ripe cuttings during the summer.
WATERING   Do not let this climber suffer from drought. Water the plant well if the soil starts to dry out excessively.

FEEDING

FEEDING   An annual application, during the spring, of a slow-release fertilizer will keep the plant going. The organic blood, fish and bone is a suitable choice.
PROBLEMS   The Silk vine is not usually troubled by any pests or diseases.

FLOWERING/FOLIAGE

FLOWERS   Star shaped, yellow-green, and purple, followed by long thin seed pods that split open to reveal silky seeds, hence the common name.
FOLIAGE   Deep green shiny leaves make a good background for the flowers.

PRUNING

REQUIREMENTS   In early spring simply trim if necessary to keep the plant within its allotted space. Eventually renovation pruning may be needed by thinning out the oldest stems.

AT A GLANCE		
A vigorous deciduous climber with star-shaped yellow-green and purple flowers in summer. Hardy to 23°F (zone 9).		
Jan	/	**Companion Plants**
Feb	/	Grow with other climbers and wall
Mar	planting	shrubs that need similar conditions,
Apr	planting	such as *Abutilon megapotamicum.*
May	/	
Jun	/	
July	flowering	
Aug	flowering	
Sep	/	
Oct	/	
Nov	/	
Dec	/	

Persicaria affinis

PERSICARIA

FEATURES

Persicaria affinis is a very useful evergreen groundcover plant. It forms an extensive carpet of dark green foliage that turns brown-bronze in the fall. The eyecatching 3in long spikes of bright red flowers are held on stems well clear of the foliage. Individual plants grow about 1ft high, and twice as wide. There are several excellent forms which many consider superior to the species. "Darjeeling Red" has larger, 4in long leaves, some even bigger, and two-tone flowers that start pink and darken to red. "Donald Lowndes" has more pointy leaves, and pale then dark pink flowers. "Superba" is pink tinged red, with bronze leaves in fall.

CONDITIONS

ASPECT It needs either bright sun or light shade. It should perform equally well in both.

SITE Provided the soil is on the moist side and does not dry out, which is the key requirement, it should thrive. An excellent plant for growing near streams where the soil remains quite damp. In the right conditions it forms very good groundcover, and can even be invasive.

GROWING METHOD

PROPAGATION The quickest method involves digging up plants in the spring or fall, and dividing them into strong healthy sections. Make sure each has good roots.

FEEDING This is rarely necessary.

PROBLEMS *P. affinis* and its forms are generally problem free, though slugs can attack fresh new growth. However, the forms which are most prone to slug and snail damage are *P. campanulata* and *P. virginiana*.

FLOWERING

SEASON Given plenty of sun, these plants should have a long flowering season. It begins about the middle of summer and graces the garden well into the fall.

PRUNING

GENERAL Pruning is not necessary.

DENSE PINK SPIKES appear from midsummer, later highlighted against striking red-bronze fall leaves.

AT A GLANCE		
Persicaria affinis is a remarkably reliable evergreen groundcover plant, with a long flowering season. Hardy to 5°F (zone 7).		
Jan	foliage	**Companion Plants**
Feb	foliage	Francoa
Mar	foliage	Geum
April	foliage	Gunnera
May	foliage	Hellebore
June	foliage	Hosta
July	flowering	Iris
Aug	flowering	Lychnis
Sept	flowering	Primula
Oct	flowering	Rheum
Nov	foliage	
Dec	foliage	

Petunia

PETUNIA

FEATURES

Petunias come in a wide range of different types depending on whether they are raised from seed or bought as young plants. Seed-raised varieties fall into the following groups: Millifloras—small flowers 1in across on compact mounds, for containers and hanging baskets; Multifloras—plenty of 2in-wide flowers on bushy plants. For bedding and patio containers, with good weather resistance; Floribundas—intermediate in size between multifloras and grandifloras with 3in flowers; Grandifloras—large trumpet-like 5in flowers that can bruise in heavy rain and are best for containers in a sheltered position. These all grow 9–12in tall and can spread up to 2ft, and are also available as double-flowered varieties. Plant 9–12in apart. Flower color varies from single shades to striped, picotee, and other variations. Many seed-raised varieties are also widely available as young plants. An increasing number of petunias are only available as young plants, setting no seed. These are suited to container growing.

CONDITIONS

ASPECT	Choose a sunny, south-facing situation for petunias in beds and containers.
SITE	Avoid spots exposed to wind. Light, free-draining soil with rotted compost/manure mixed in is best. In containers use multipurpose compost.

GROWING METHOD

SOWING	Sowing can take place January–March where a temperature of 70°F is possible. Sow onto the level surface of a 3$\frac{1}{2}$in pot of multipurpose compost, but do not cover seeds, and keep in the light.

Seedlings will appear inside two weeks, and should be transplanted to cell trays of multipurpose compost when large enough. Pot on into 3$\frac{1}{2}$in diameter pots, grow-on and harden off before planting out in early June.

FEEDING	Give a weekly liquid feed with a high-potash fertilizer to encourage flowers. Mix slow-release fertilizer granules with container compost.
PROBLEMS	Slugs eat leaves in wet weather–use pellets or slug traps. Plants with mottled, crinkled leaves affected by virus should be destroyed.

FLOWERING

SEASON	Flowers appear all summer. Pick off dead flowers regularly.
CUTTING	Not suitable.

AFTER FLOWERING

GENERAL	Remove when flowers end.

AT A GLANCE		
A half-hardy annual grown for all-round use in summer bedding, hanging baskets and containers. Frost hardy to 5°F (zone 7).		

Month		Recommended Varieties
Jan	sow	*Petunia hybrida*
Feb	sow	**Millifloras**
Mar	sow/transplant	"Fantasy Mixed"
Apr	pot on/grow on	**Multifloras**
May	harden off/plant	"Celebrity Bunting"
Jun	flowering	"Summer Morn Mixed"
July	flowering	**Floribundas**
Aug	flowering	"Mirage Mixed"
Sept	flowering	"Niagara Mixture"
Oct	/	**Grandifloras**
Nov	/	"Daddy Mixed"
Dec	/	

Phlox

ANNUAL PHLOX

FEATURES

Annual phlox are versatile plants that can be used for bedding, containers, and as unique cut flowers. They are half-hardy annuals, growing between 4–18in tall depending on the variety—taller are better for cutting. Flower color ranges from the blue of "Bobby Sox" to the varied shades of "Tapestry" which is also scented. Several varieties are now available as young plants by mail order. Flowers are long-lived and plants are easy to care for.

CONDITIONS

ASPECT   Needs full sun.
SITE   Needs well-drained soil with manure or compost mixed in to improve moisture holding. Phlox grow well in multipurpose compost used to fill summer containers.

GROWING METHOD

SOWING   Sow seed in February/March in 3^1/$_2$in pots of multipurpose compost, keep at 64ºF, and expect seedlings in 1–3 weeks. Transplant to cell trays or 3^1/$_2$in pots, pinch out the tips when 3in high, and grow on until late May, then harden off and plant after the last frosts in your area.

FEEDING   Add slow-release fertilizer granules to compost before planting containers, which should be sufficient. Plants in beds can be given a liquid feed every 2–3 weeks in summer.
PROBLEMS   Plants will struggle on heavy soils in a cold spring so delay planting until warmer weather.

FLOWERING

SEASON   Flowers appear all summer until frosts.
CUTTING   Tall varieties are good for cutting and some like "Tapestry" have a strong, sweet scent.

AFTER FLOWERING

GENERAL   Pull up after flowering and compost them.

THE FLOWERS OF annual phlox open at their peak to make rounded heads of color that can completely fill summer containers.

AT A GLANCE	
A half-hardy annual grown for its heads of colorful flowers, for bedding, containers, and for cutting. Frost hardy to 23˚F (zone 9).	
Jan /	**Recommended Varieties**
Feb sow	*Phlox drummondii*
Mar sow/transplant	"African Sunset"
Apr grow on	"Bobby Sox"
May harden off/plant	"Bright Eyes"
Jun flowering	"Brilliant"
July flowering	"Cecily Old & New Shades"
Aug flowering	"Double Chanel"
Sept flowering	"Phlox of Sheep"
Oct /	"Tapestry"
Nov /	"Tutti-Frutti"
Dec /	"Twinkle Mixed"

Phlox paniculata

PERENNIAL PHLOX

FEATURES

Easy to grow and producing a summer-long display of flowers, perennial phlox has a place in any perennial collection. Plants may grow from 16 to 36in tall, and the clumps spread rapidly; position new plantings 12in apart. The large heads of flowers, some with a contrasting eye, come in shades of red, pink, orange, mauve, purple, and white. This plant looks best mass-planted, either in solid blocks of one color or in mixed colors. Also note the highly popular, new variegated cultivars. With mixed plantings, ensure that the taller forms do not obscure the shorter ones.

CONDITIONS

ASPECT	Prefers full sunlight with some protection from strong wind.
SITE	Needs a well-drained soil enriched with organic matter.

GROWING METHOD

PROPAGATION	Divide clumps in the fall every three or four years, making sure that each division has a crown and a good set of roots. Replant only the younger, vigorous outer growths, discarding the rest. Plants propagated from root cuttings will be free of eelworm.

FEEDING	Apply a complete plant food in spring and mulch well with rotted manure or compost, but do not cover the crowns.
PROBLEMS	Powdery mildew can be a problem. Spray with a fungicide. Phlox eelworm causes leaves to shrivel, and shrubs distort. Plants must be destroyed.

FLOWERING

SEASON	From the summer into early fall.
CUTTING	It makes a good cut flower.

AFTER FLOWERING

REQUIREMENTS	Remove spent flower stems as they fade. In late fall, cut off any remaining growth. Give the plants a thorough tidy-up for the winter.

THE ATTRACTIVE, individual flowers on the heads of perennial phlox last right through the season, making it essential in any border.

AT A GLANCE	
P. paniculata is an erect, herbaceous perennial with scented flowers, and many excellent cultivars. Hardy to 5°F (zone 7).	

Jan	/	**Recommended Varieties**
Feb	sow	*Phlox paniculata*
Mar	sow	"Alba Grandiflora"
Apr	transplant	"Blue Ice"
May	transplant	"Bumble's Delight"
Jun	/	"Eventide"
July	flowering	"Le Mahdi"
Aug	flowering	"Prince of Orange"
Sept	flowering	"Prospero"
Oct	divide	"White Admiral"
Nov	/	
Dec	/	

Phlox subulata

ALPINE PHLOX

FEATURES

Phlox subulata grows about 6in high and spreads into a mat about 20in across. In bloom it is a mass of small, flattish flowers in white, pink, rose, mauve or blue. There are many named cultivars available and they can flower for several weeks. *P. subulata* grows ideally in rockeries, trailing over walls or on slightly sloping ground where excellent drainage is assured. Although plants last well over several years, the best blooming comes from younger plants. Start new plants every few years to maintain vigor.

CONDITIONS

ASPECT   Grow this plant in full sun.

SITE   Must have very well-drained soil (if it is at all on the heavy side, make sure that it is well broken up with plenty of horticultural sand and grit), but the soil need not be very rich.

GROWING METHOD

PROPAGATION   Detach rooted sections from the parent plant in early spring, or take tip cuttings during summer and early fall.

FEEDING   Apply complete plant food as new growth begins in the spring.

PROBLEMS   No specific problems are known but poor drainage will rot the plants.

FLOWERING

SEASON   Flowers should be produced from mid-spring to early summer. For a color contrast also grow "Amazing Grace" which has pale pink flowers, "Scarlet Flame" in scarlet, and "Temiskaming" in magenta.

CUTTING   Flowers are not suitable for cutting.

PRUNING

GENERAL   No pruning is needed beyond shearing off the spent flower heads.

THE DAINTY FLOWERS on alpine phlox create a tremendous impact when they are massed in full bloom.

AT A GLANCE		
Phlox subulata makes an evergreen mat of fresh green leaves with bright late spring flowers. Hardy to 5°F (zone 7).		
Jan	foliage	**Recommended Varieties**
Feb	foliage	*Phlox adsurgens*
Mar	foliage	"Chattahoochee"
April	foliage	"Emerald Cushion"
May	flowering	*P.* "Kelly's Eye"
June	flowering	*P.* x *procumbens*
July	foliage	*P. subulata*
Aug	foliage	"Amazing Grace"
Sept	foliage	"G. F. Wilson"
Oct	foliage	"Marjorie"
Nov	foliage	"McDaniel's Cushion"
Dec	foliage	"Scarlet Flame"

Phoenix canariensis

CANARY ISLAND DATE PALM

FEATURES

This well-known and widely grown palm is a native of the Canary Islands. Of medium size, it eventually forms a fat heavy trunk. Wide arching fronds, which are very spiny at the base, grow up to 20ft in length on mature plants, and carry many bright or deep green leaflets. The mature height is up to 50ft with a spread of 40ft. As a young specimen this palm makes an ideal houseplant and it can also be recommended for an intermediate to warm conservatory or glasshouse. Place it out of doors for the summer. This palm will produce flowers and fruits in warm climates.

CONDITIONS

ASPECT   Provide bright light but do not subject it to direct sun. Provide moderate humidity. Outdoors place in a sheltered position.

SITE   In containers grow this palm in soil-based potting compost.

GROWING METHOD

PROPAGATION   Sow seeds as soon as available and germinate them at a temperature of 66–75°F.

WATERING   Water freely in growing season from late spring to late summer, then for the rest of the year water sparingly.

FEEDING   Apply a balanced liquid fertilizer monthly during the growing season from late spring to late summer.

PROBLEMS   Under glass may be attacked by red spider mites and scale insects.

FOLIAGE/FLOWERING

FOLIAGE   Being evergreen this palm looks good all year round but is especially attractive during the spring and summer.

FLOWERS   In summer trusses of yellow or cream flowers are produced, followed by yellow fruits.

GENERAL CARE

REQUIREMENTS Remove dead fronds when necessary by cutting them off close to the trunk.

CLASSIC PALM FRONDS, as produced by Phoenix canariensis. *They are particularly pleasing when they sway in light breezes. Rising majestically above the lower shrubs,* P. canariensis *stocky trunk finishes in a triumphant display of arching fronds.*

AT A GLANCE	
The bright or deep green leaves, consist of many leaflets. Provide a minimum temperature of 50–61°F (zone 11).	
Jan /	**Companion Plants**
Feb /	Under glass grow with other palms
Mar planting	such as *Howea forsteriana*, and with
Apr planting	other foliage plants like *Monstera*
May foliage	*deliciosa*. Outdoors combine with
Jun flowering	brightly colored summer bedding or
July flowering	subtropical plants.
Aug flowering	
Sep /	
Oct /	
Nov /	
Dec /	

Phoenix roebelenii

PYGMY DATE PALM

FEATURES

A native of Laos in south-east Asia, this is a small, slender, elegant-looking palm of feathery appearance that may be multi- or single stemmed. The leaves, which grow up to 4ft in length, have many shiny dark green leaflets which are somewhat spiky, so be careful where you place it. The eventual height is at least 6ft with a spread of 8ft. Widely grown as an indoor plant, it can also be recommended for an intermediate to warm conservatory or glasshouse. It will be happy out of doors for the summer.

CONDITIONS

ASPECT   Provide bright light but do not subject it to direct sun. Provide moderate humidity. Outdoors place in a sheltered position.
SITE   In containers grow this palm in soil-based potting compost.

GROWING METHOD

PROPAGATION Sow seeds as soon as available and germinate them at a temperature of 66–75°F. If produced, remove and pot up rooted offsets.
WATERING   Water freely in growing season from late spring to late summer, then water sparingly.
FEEDING   Balanced liquid fertilizer monthly during the growing period.

PROBLEMS

Under glass may be attacked by red spider mites and scale insects.

FOLIAGE/FLOWERING

FOLIAGE   Looks good all year round but is especially attractive in spring and summer.
FLOWERS   Cream flowers in summer, followed, if male and female plants are grown, by black fruits.

GENERAL CARE

REQUIREMENTS Remove dead fronds when necessary by cutting them off close to the trunk.

THE DELICATE LEAVES of Phoenix roebelenii sprout from equally delicate stems, creating a subtle and elegant palm that can be grown indoors, and outdoors in warm areas. The plant's white flowers are rarely seen in Britain, as it needs warmer conditions for them to set seed.

AT A GLANCE	
An elegant slender palm with long, feathery, dark green shiny leaves. Provide a minimum temperature of 50–61°F (zone 11).	
Jan /	**Companion Plants**
Feb /	Under glass grow with other palms
Mar planting	such as *Howea forsteriana*, and with
Apr planting	other foliage plants like *Monstera*
May foliage	*deliciosa*. Outdoors combine with
Jun flowering	brightly colored summer bedding or
July flowering	subtropical plants.
Aug flowering	
Sep /	
Oct /	
Nov /	
Dec /	

Photinia

PHOTINIA

FEATURES

Evergreen and deciduous photinias, with their dense foliage, are among the most popular of hedging plants. The dark green, slightly leathery foliage is highlighted by bright pinky-red new growth. If the plant is trimmed regularly, this new growth is evident throughout the growing season. In spring and summer clusters of small white flowers appear. If unpruned, most bushes will grow to 10–15ft high but they can be hedged at around 6ft. Photinias do, however, make very fine tall hedges and windbreaks. These plants are moderate growers and will be long lived if grown in suitable conditions.

CONDITIONS

ASPECT   Needs to be grown in full sun. Will also tolerate some degree of partial shade.
SITE   Soil must be well drained and ideally should contain plenty of organic matter.

GROWING METHOD

PROPAGATION Can be grown from semi-ripe cuttings taken during the summer.
SPACING   Plant at about 3ft spacings.
FEEDING   Apply complete plant food during the spring and summer growing season.
PROBLEMS   Photinias have no specific pest problems but will quickly succumb to root rot in heavy, poorly drained soil. It is therfore essential that you do not grow them in cold wet clay.

FLOWERING

SEASON   Clusters of white flowers appear during spring. One of the earliest is *Photinia* x *fraseri*, *P. glabra* flowers inearly summer, and *P. nussia* in mid-summer.
CUTTING   Flowers are not suitable for cutting.

PRUNING

GENERAL   Carry out the main pruning in late winter but lighter pruning can be done at other times of the year. Light summer pruning promotes plenty of attractive young foliage.

FLUFFY, CREAMY-WHITE flowers can be profuse on unpruned photinia. Few, if any, are seen on a formally trained hedge.

AT A GLANCE	
Under-used shrubs giving fresh new growth, often vividly colored, and early season white flowers. Hardy to 5°F (zone 7).	

		Companion Plants
Jan	foliage	Anemone
Feb	foliage	Bluebell
Mar	foliage	Crocus
April	flowering	Daffodil
May	flowering	Erythronium
June	flowering	Fritillaria
July	flowering	Hyacinth
Aug	foliage	Iris
Sept	foliage	Scilla
Oct	foliage	Tulip
Nov	foliage	
Dec	foliage	

Physostegia virginiana

OBEDIENT PLANT

FEATURES

This is an easy-care, fast-growing perennial. Since it spreads by stolons (runners) and seed, large clumps can develop in one season. Excess plants are quite easily removed. The dark green leaves are only 4–6in long, but flowering stems bring the height up to 4ft. The flowers in the species are pinky-mauve, but there are cultivars with flowers in various shades of pink, red, and white. It looks best when planted in large drifts in a border, or among shrubs. The common name refers to the fact that flowers remain fixed the way they are turned. It is also sometimes known as "false dragon's head."

CONDITIONS

ASPECT	Grows well in both full sunlight and semi-shade. However, some form of protection from strong winds is desirable. The taller varieties may need staking.
SITE	Tolerates a wide range of soils, but the best results occur when it's grown in well-drained soil, rich in organic matter.

GROWING METHOD

PROPAGATION	Divide old clumps in the spring, planting new divisions in groups for the best effect. The oldest sections can be discarded. Because of its vigorous habit, you need to divide it every couple of years. *Physostegia* tolerates dry periods well, but you must water young plants regularly until they are established.

FEEDING	Apply a complete plant food in spring. Mulch with decayed organic matter at the same time.
PROBLEMS	No specific problems are known.

FLOWERING

SEASON	Flowers appear from mid- to late summer into the fall.
CUTTING	Frequent cutting of blooms should produce a second flush of flowers. Scald-cut the stems to prolong their vase life.

AFTER FLOWERING

REQUIREMENTS	Remove spent flower stems and tidy up growth as it dies down.

OBEDIENT PLANT looks best in large plantings. It is well worth devoting yard space to it, since the flowers last for several months.

AT A GLANCE		
P. virginiana is a spreading, tall perennial with purple or lilac-tinged flowers lasting into the fall. Hardy to 32°F (zone 10).		
Jan	/	**Recommended Varieties**
Feb	/	*Physostegia virginiana*
Mar	divide	"Alba"
Apr	transplant	"Crown of Snow"
May	transplant	"Red Beauty"
Jun	/	"Summer Snow"
July	flowering	"Vivid"
Aug	flowering	*P. v.* subsp. *speciosa*
Sept	flowering	"Bouquet Rose"
Oct	sow	
Nov	/	
Dec	/	

Pieris

PIERIS

FEATURES

A captivating, evergreen shrub, 16in–9ft high and across, its bell-shaped, white, pink, or red flowers glorify spring. Its other, equally prized asset is its glowing pink or reddish shuttlecocks of new leaves. There are many varieties. Aptly named "Flaming Silver"—2ft high, ideal for a narrow border—has fiery, new leaves which when mature are suffused with silver.

CONDITIONS

ASPECT   Not a candidate for exposed gardens, pieris needs shielding from strong, cold winds and hot, leaf-scorching sunshine.

SITE   Abhorring any degree of lime, this shrub needs deep, rich, well-drained soil. Create a good home for it by digging in generous amounts of organic material well ahead of planting time.

GROWING METHOD

FEEDING   Boost robust growth by applying an acidifying fertilizer in spring and midsummer. Help young plants recover quickly from transplanting by watering regularly in droughty spells and mulching with moisture- conserving organics.

PROPAGATION Multiply plants by pegging down low shoots from mid-spring to late summer or take semi-ripe cuttings from mid- to late summer.

PROBLEMS   New leaves may be damaged by wind frost.

PRUNING

GENERAL   Cut off faded blooms and dead or damaged shoots in early summer. Rejuvenate old bushes by shortening gaunt shoots to half their height in mid-spring. Keep cuts moist in dry spells to encourage rapid regrowth.

YOUNG PIERIS LEAVES open a vivid shade of pink or scarlet before turning yellow and ultimately green.

AT A GLANCE	
New, red, evergreen leaves complement sprays of white, pink, or red, bell-shaped flowers in spring. Hardy to 14°F (zone 8).	

		Recommended Varieties
Jan	/	"Debutante"
Feb	/	"Firecrest"
Mar	flower	"Flaming Silver"
Apr	flower, plant	"Forest Flame"
May	flower, prune	"Mountain Fire"
June	plant, prune	"Pink Delight"
July	plant	"Valley Valentine"
Aug	plant	
Sept	plant	
Oct	/	
Nov	/	
Dec	/	

Pileostegia viburnoides

PILEOSTEGIA

FEATURES

This is a very vigorous, tall-growing evergreen climber that supports itself by means of aerial roots produced from the stems. It is related to schizophragma. *Pileostegia* is a native of China, Taiwan and India. This climber is grown for its flowers, which are produced in summer and fall, and for its dense, good-looking foliage that effectively hides the support. Growing up to 20ft in height, pileostegia is suitable for growing on high walls or up large mature trees but is not a suitable subject for small gardens or where space is restricted. It is also a good shade survivor, which might make it a suitable choice for shaded areas that other climbers cannot endure.

CONDITIONS

ASPECT   *Pileostegia* will endure most light conditions, from full sun to full shade.

SITE   This climber will grow in any reasonably rich soil provided the drainage is good.

GROWING METHOD

PROPAGATION   Take semi-ripe cuttings in summer and ideally root them in a cold frame.

WATERING   Do not let this climber dry out excessively, so water well in prolonged dry spells in summer.

FEEDING   An annual feed, in spring, of slow-release fertilizer, such as the organic blood, fish, and bone, is all that is required.

PROBLEMS   Pileostegia is not troubled by pests or diseases.

FLOWERING/FOLIAGE

FLOWERS   The heads of cream-white flowers are produced late in the summer.

FOLIAGE   The deep green elliptical leaves have a leathery texture.

PRUNING

REQUIREMENTS   Prune in early spring. Minimal pruning needed. Shorten any over-long or badly placed shoots as necessary. This climber produces most flowers at the top so do not prune to reduce height. Hard renovation pruning is acceptable if necessary—simply leave a main framework of stems. Ideally spread this type of pruning over several years to prevent too much loss of flower following pruning.

PILEOSTEGIA VIBURNOIDES shows a fetching contrast between its bold leaves and its lacy puffs of cream-white flowers.

AT A GLANCE		
Vigorous evergreen climber with deep green foliage and cream-white flowers in late summer and fall. Hardy to 23°F (zone 9).		
Jan	/	**Companion Plants**
Feb	/	Due to its vigour, best grown alone,
Mar	planting	but could combine with a vigorous
Apr	planting	rambler rose.
May	/	
Jun	/	
July	/	
Aug	flowering	
Sep	flowering	
Oct	flowering	
Nov	/	
Dec	/	

Pinks

DIANTHUS

FEATURES

Popular garden plants, pinks are very pretty, short-lived, hardy perennials. A wide range of species and varieties is available, which vary in height from about 6in to 24in or more. One of those with the longest herbal tradition is *Dianthus caryophyllus*, the clove carnation. The rich, sweet, clove scent of the flowers has made it popular in perfumery for more than 2000 years. Generally pinks have narrow, gray-green, lance-shaped leaves. The flowers appear in spring or summer, in shades of pink or white, and are usually highly fragrant. Plants can become straggly after a few years, and are best discarded and replaced with young plants that have been grown from cuttings.

CONDITIONS

ASPECT   Pinks prefer a sunny, sheltered site.
SITE   Grow them in a very well-drained soil that is not too rich, and preferably alkaline.

GROWING METHOD

SOWING   Pinks can be grown from seed, but the resulting plants can be very variable. Sow the seed under glass in trays of gritty seed compost in spring or fall. Take care not to overwater and be sure to ventilate well. Plant out in spring, after hardening off, at about 1ft apart. Named forms can be propagated by cuttings, division, or layering. Take cuttings in late summer. Plants can also be layered at this time of year. The plants can also be dug up after they have finished flowering, and any rooted stems can be severed and replanted.

FEEDING   Pinks tolerate relatively dry conditions. Be careful not to overwater. Pinks need little feeding. A light dressing of a balanced general fertilizer may be given in early spring. Do not mulch as this can cause the stems to rot.
PROBLEMS   The main pest is red spider mite. Also virus, leaf spots, and leaf-attacking insects may cause problems.
PRUNING   Remove dead flowerheads to prolong flowering.

HARVESTING

PICKING   Pick flowers when newly open. If the petals are to be used in cooking, remove the white heel from each of the petals as this has a very bitter flavour.
STORAGE   Dry on racks in a cool, airy place. Petals can also be crystallized.
FREEZING   Not suitable for freezing.

DIVINE FLOWERS: The name Dianthus comes from the words "dios," meaning divine, and "anthos," meaning flower.

AT A GLANCE	
Attractive perennials with highly fragrant flowers, which have a long tradition of use in perfumery. Hardy to 4°F (zone 7).	
Jan /	**Parts used**
Feb /	Petals
Mar plant	**Uses**
Apr plant	Culinary
May plant harvest	Medicinal
Jun plant harvest	Craft
July plant harvest	Cosmetic
Aug plant	Gardening
Sept plant	
Oct /	
Nov /	
Dec /	

USES

CULINARY	Fresh petals can be used in salads, and also puddings and savoury dishes. They can also be used to flavour oils, vinegar, syrup, or white wine. Crystallized petals can be used to decorate cakes and puddings.
MEDICINAL	The petals can be used to make a tonic cordial, or can be infused in white wine to make a nerve tonic.
CRAFT	Dried petals can be used to add color and scent to pot-pourri mixes, and used to make scented sachets etc.
COSMETIC	Fresh petals can be used to scent a variety of cosmetic products.
GARDENING	Pinks are amongst the most decorative of all the garden herbs.

Platycodon
BALLOON FLOWER

FEATURES

Also known as Chinese bellflower, this herbaceous perennial grows approximately 20in high, slightly taller in perfect conditions. It has a shortish flowering period in late summer, and the open, bell-shape flowers come in a range of blue shades, but also in white and pale pink. Flowers last well when cut. There are several named cultivars available, including double and semi-double examples. Since clumps are compact and spread slowly, they are best planted where they can remain undisturbed for some years. The new growth appears in late spring; mark its position to avoid hauling it out as a weed.

CONDITIONS

ASPECT Grows in sun or dappled sunlight.
SITE Grows best in a well-drained soil enriched with plenty of organic matter.

GROWING METHOD

PROPAGATION Seed is the best means of propagation; sow in the spring. Young shoots can be taken as cuttings, and the double forms must be grown from cuttings. Also, clumps can be lifted and divided in the spring; replant the divisions approximately 8–10in apart. Give newly bedded plants a regular watering during prolonged dry spells in the spring and summer.

FEEDING Apply a complete plant food when new growth begins to appear in the spring.
PROBLEMS Slugs can be a major problem devouring new growth. Either pick off by hand or treat chemically.

FLOWERING

SEASON A relatively short display, which is more than compensated for by the nature of the exquisite flowers.
CUTTING Flowers can be cut for the vase.

AFTER FLOWERING

REQUIREMENTS Cut all spent flower stems right back to the ground, and then the whole plant as the growth dies off.

THE BUDS of platycodon swell into a balloon shape, hence the common name, then pop open to reveal these beautiful flowers. This well-established clump of balloon flower is supported by stakes guaranteeing height, as well as color.

AT A GLANCE	
P. grandiflorus is a one-specie genus grown for its beautiful purple-blue flowers. Several fine cultivars. Hardy to 5°F (zone 7).	
Jan /	**Companion Plants**
Feb /	Aster
Mar sow	Clematis
Apr divide	Dahlia
May transplant	Fuchsia
Jun /	Osteospermum
July /	Phygelius
Aug flowering	*Rhodochiton atrosanguineus*
Sept flowering	Rose
Oct /	
Nov /	
Dec /	

Pleione

PLEIONE SPECIES AND HYBRIDS

FEATURES

Extremely cold tolerant, these orchids are native to cool areas of northern India, and to southern China and Taiwan where they are usually found in damp woodland. They are deciduous and may be terrestrial, epiphytic, or lithophytic. They die down completely in winter and renew the small pseudobulbs in spring. Plants are rarely more than 6in high and may spread to about 12in. They grow in very shallow pots. Flowers appear before the leaves and are most often white, pink, mauve, purple, or even yellow. The lip may be fringed and spotted. Individual blooms are not long lasting but make a fine display when planted en masse. Each small pseudobulb flowers only once and then produces a folded, elliptical leaf. Pleiones make very easy orchids for beginners and especially for enthusiast children. Their compact habit and ease of culture make them ideal house plants for a very cool windowsill or greenhouse. Some alpine growers even include them in their collections. The pots can be placed out of doors for the summer months.

CONDITIONS

CLIMATE Some are frost hardy, others frost tender but all prefer cool to cold conditions. A minimum temperature in winter of 10˚F is acceptable to these plants as long as they are in their leafless, dormant phase.

ASPECT Needs a sheltered spot in filtered sunlight with shade during the hottest part of the day. Glasshouse-grown plants will need heavy shading and cooling in summer.

POTTING MIX The mix of bark, pea gravel, small pebbles, and chopped sphagnum moss or fibre peat must be perfectly drained.

GROWING METHOD

PROPAGATION Plants need re-potting annually at the end of winter when old pseudobulbs can be discarded. It is then, in the early spring, that the new shoots are just starting to grow, with the flower buds inside. As well as removing last year's dead pseudobulb, trim back the dead roots when re-potting. Some varieties are likely to break double each year so the number of pseudobulbs multiply easily over the years.
Occasionally, small extra pseudobulbs can be formed at the top of the old, shrivelled bulb. These can be removed at potting time and planted in with the larger main bulb. In a few years time, these will be large enough to flower.

AT A GLANCE		
Very easy to grow and ideal for greenhouse. Can reach 6in high and flowers average 2in across.		
Jan	rest	**Recommended Varieties**
Feb	repot, flowering	*P. formosana* (lilac pink)
Mar	flowering, water and feed	*P. formosana* var. alba (white)
Apr	flowering, water and feed	*P. maculata* (white/red)
		P. praecox (pink)
May	water and feed	*P. speciosa* (cerise)
Jun	water and feed	"Eiger" (lavender)
July	water and feed	"Piton" (lilac)
Aug	water and feed	"Shantung" (yellow)
Sept	flowering, rest	"Stromboli" (pink)
Oct	flowering, rest	"Versailles" (pink)
Nov	rest	
Dec	rest	

WATERING Keep soil moist once growth has started in spring. Water regularly during flowering and the development of the pseudobulbs. These orchids make fine root systems which can dry out easily if not regularly watered. When pseudobulbs are fully matured, reduce the frequency of watering. Keep plants dry in winter while dormant and leafless. To avoid resting pseudobulbs from becoming too wet during winter remove from their pots after their leaves have fallen and leave to dry out in an empty tray or pot. You can also see clearly when the new growth starts and can then pot them up again.

FEEDING Give regular, weak liquid fertilizer once growth commences and continue until pseudobulbs are well matured.

PROBLEMS Slugs and snails are a constant problem but there are no other specific pest problems. Plants can die from root rot if they are constantly wet while dormant or if they dry out completely during the growing season when they can dehydrate.

FLOWERING SEASON

Most species flower in spring but some flower in the fall.

OTHER PLEIONES TO GROW

P. FORMOSANA Probably the most popular *Pleione* species to grow, the number of bulbs multiplies up quickly over the years so a superb show can be achieved in quite a short time. Soft lavender pink petals and sepals with dark pink and brown spotting on the white lip.

P. FORMOSANA VAR. ALBA A pure white, albino form of the above which has only a touch of yellow in the center of the lip. The pseudobulbs are also devoid of any purple coloring and are a clear apple green. Grows slightly smaller than the pink variety.

P. SPECIOSA Known for its very vibrant cerise colored flowers which will brighten up the early spring months when it is in flower.

P. MACULATA An unusual species as this one flowers in the fall, one of only two species that does. White blooms, with dark red patterning in the lip, are also unusual in a mostly pink dominated genus.

P. PRAECOX The second fall flowering species, this time in traditional pink. These two grow in just the same conditions as the spring flowering types but are perhaps a little more of a challenge. A few hybrid pleiones have been bred between the species; the following are a few examples which are easy to grow:

P. EIGER One of the first to flower in the spring season, short stem with a pale lavender flower, very pretty and easy to keep.

P. PITON A very large sized flower in comparison to the others, $2^1/2$in across, on a taller stem, 4in high, a lovely subtle purple shade with bold spotting on the lip.

P. SHANTUNG One of the most well known of the hybrid pleiones due to it being a yellow hybrid, the darkest form being *P. Shantung* "Ducat". Grows well but may not multiply as quickly as some of the others. The most commonly seen variety is *P. Shantung* "Ridgeway" AM/RHS, a soft yellow with a pink blush.

Polianthes tuberosa

TUBEROSE

FEATURES

Tuberose is known for its heavily perfumed flowers—tuberose oil is used in perfume production. A double form known as "The Pearl" is the most widely grown. It can be grown in a sunny, sheltered border, but is often more reliable when grown as a conservatory or house plant, especially in cooler areas. The scent can more easily be appreciated under cover. A flower spike 2ft or more high appears from the basal leaves in summer and early fall. The waxy flowers have a heavy texture and are white with a pinkish tinge at the base. Tubers that have bloomed once will not reflower the following season—new tubers must be planted each year.

CONDITIONS

ASPECT   Prefers full sun and shelter from strong wind.
SITE   Grow in a warm, sheltered border, or in containers for the conservatory, house, or greenhouse. Use either John Innes or soil-less potting compost.

GROWING METHOD

PLANTING   Plant 2in deep, or 1in deep in containers.
FEEDING   When growth appears, liquid feed with a balanced fertiliser every 14 days through the growing season. Water sparingly to start with, but keep the plant moist at all times when in growth.

PROBLEMS   No particular problems are known.

FLOWERING

SEASON   Flowers should appear during late summer or in early fall.
CUTTING   Makes an excellent cut flower. Cut spikes for the vase when two or three of the lower blooms are fully open. Removing spent flowers from the spike as they fade will help to prolong the vase life.

AFTER FLOWERING

REQUIREMENTS   Tubers are usually discarded at the end of the season. Offsets are produced, and these may sometimes be grown on to flower in two years or so, but they are often disappointing.

PINK-TINGED BUDS open to the heavy-textured cream flowers, so prized for their characteristic strong perfume.

AT A GLANCE		
Valued for its intensely fragrant, creamy white flowers that are carried on tall spikes in late summer.		
Jan	/	**Recommended Varieties**
Feb	/	*Polianthes tuberosa*
Mar	plant	"The Pearl"
Apr	/	
May	/	
Jun	/	
July	/	
Aug	flowering	
Sept	flowering	
Oct	flowering	
Nov	/	
Dec	/	

Polygonatum

SOLOMON'S SEAL

FEATURES

This lovely herbaceous perennial is ideal for naturalizing in the dappled shade of a yard. The plant has a graceful, arching habit with stems 24–36in long. The finely veined foliage tends to stand up on the stem, while the tubular white bell flowers hang down. It grows from a creeping rhizome and will spread to form a colony of plants, given the correct conditions. If space is no problem, plant several to start your display, letting them form large colonies. A number of other species are grown, some, such as *P. odoratum*, with scented flowers; "Flore Pleno" has double flowers. There are two variegated, eye-catching forms.

CONDITIONS

ASPECT   Needs a sheltered spot in part or full shade.
SITE   The soil should drain well but be heavily enriched with organic matter to retain some moisture at all times. The plants benefit from an early spring mulch.

GROWING METHOD

PROPAGATION   Established clumps can be divided in early spring; new divisions should be positioned 8–10in apart. This plant is best left undisturbed for several years, if possible. Young plants need to be watered regularly during the growing season; do not let them dry out.
FEEDING   Apply complete plant food as new growth commences in the spring.

PROBLEMS

Plants can be severely devastated by attacks of sawfly larvae, which reduce them to skeletons. Either treat with a spray, or pick off the caterpillars.

FLOWERING

SEASON   Flowers appear in late spring.
CUTTING   Flowers can be cut for indoor decoration. They last fairly well and make a good display.

AFTER FLOWERING

REQUIREMENTS   Do not cut down the flower stems or you will end up weakening the plant, and consequently losing the attractive, yellow fall tints.

CLUSTERS OF NARROW, bell-like flowers are suspended from the stems Solomon's seal; it enjoys woodland conditions.

AT A GLANCE	
P. x hybridum (multiflorum) is a rhizomatous perennial with green-tipped white flowers and black fruit. Hardy to 0°F (zones 6–7).	
Jan /	**Recommended Varieties**
Feb /	*P. biflorum*
Mar divide	*P. falcatum*
Apr transplant	"Variegatum"
May flowering	*P. hookeri*
Jun /	*P. odoratum*
July /	"Flore Pleno"
Aug /	*P. verticillatum*
Sept /	
Oct sow	
Nov /	
Dec /	

Pomegranate

PUNICA

FEATURES

Deciduous and bearing carnation-like, single or double, brilliant orange-red flowers for most of the summer, Punica granatum makes a bushy shrub to 7ft high and across. Only single-flowered varieties bear fruits. Grow them as specimen plants in very sheltered borders in frost-free gardens. Elsewhere, treat this shrub as a pot plant and confine it to a conservatory from fall to late spring. Move it on to a sunny patio or terrace when frosts finish in late May or early June.

CONDITIONS

ASPECT   If you are growing pomegranate outdoors, it must be in full sunshine and protected from cold winds.

SITE   To excel, this shrub needs well-drained loam or clay-loam soil enriched with humus-forming organics.

GROWING METHOD

FEEDING   Boost growth and stimulate plenty of blossom-bearing shoots by applying bone meal in spring and the fall. Encourage young plants to establish quickly by watering liberally in the first spring and summer after planting. In September, return potted plants that have decorated a patio for summer to a frost-free conservatory or greenhouse.

PROPAGATION Increase this plant from semi-ripe cuttings taken from mid- to late summer.

PROBLEMS   New shoots on outdoor plants can be damaged by late spring frosts, so site the shrubs carefully.

PRUNING

GENERAL   Remove badly placed shoots from late spring to early summer. Keep wall-trained specimens shapely by shortening flowered shoots to within four leaves of the main framework when blooms fade.

DELICIOUS FRUITS APPEAR on outdoor or patio pot plants after a long, warm summer. Under glass, in a higher temperature, fruits swell to a greater size.

AT A GLANCE	
Deciduous with orange flowers in summer, it can be grown outside only in very sheltered areas. Hardy to 39°F (zone 10).	
Jan /	Recommended Varieties
Feb /	"Flore Pleno Luteo"
Mar /	"Flore Pleno Rubro"
Apr plant, prune	*P. granatum nana*
May plant, prune	"Striata"
June flower, plant	
July flower, plant	
Aug flower, plant	
Sept plant	
Oct /	
Nov /	
Dec /	

Portulaca

SUN PLANT

FEATURES

Commonly known as sun plant, portulaca grows 6in high with a spreading habit and succulent leaves. The 2in flowers open in sun, although modern varieties open even on dull days. It thrives in poor, dry soils and is easily ruined by too much coddling. A half-hardy annual, for beds, pots, and rockeries.

CONDITIONS

ASPECT   A hot, sunny position gives the best plants.

SITE   Unless soil is very well-drained plants are prone to rotting. Otherwise plants grow and flower well even where the soil is quite poor—particularly in seaside gardens—as they are adapted to live on little water. Grow them on their own in patio containers, using soil-based potting compost mixed fifty-fifty with sharp grit. Do not feed, and water only when plants start to wilt. Place pots in blazing sunshine.

GROWING METHOD

SOWING   Sow seeds in March/April in 3½in pots of soil-based seed compost and germinate at 64°F in good light. Keep the seedlings on the dry side and transplant to cell trays of soil-based compost with grit added. Grow on, harden off in late May, and plant after frosts, watering in well, then only when plants wilt.

FEEDING   Feeding portulaca is not necessary.

PROBLEMS   Seedlings will "damp off" if the compost is kept too wet. If they do fall over, water the pots lightly with a copper-based fungicide.

FLOWERING

SEASON   Flowers appear throughout summer and into early fall.

CUTTING   Not suitable.

AFTER FLOWERING

GENERAL   Pull plants up after the first fall frosts and add their fleshy remains to the compost heap.

SUN PLANTS can survive the winter in mild seaside gardens, and thrive in the well-drained soil of rockeries.

AT A GLANCE	
Portulaca is a half-hardy annual grown for summer flowers. Gives good results even on thin soils. Frost hardy to 32°F (zone 10).	
Jan /	Recommended Varieties
Feb /	*Portulaca grandiflora*
Mar sow	"Cloudbeater Mixed"
Apr sow	"Double Mixed"
May harden off/plant	"Kariba Mixed"
Jun flowering	"Patio Gems"
July flowering	"Sundance"
Aug flowering	"Sundial Mango"
Sept flowering	"Sundial Mixed"
Oct /	"Sundial Peppermint"
Nov /	"Swanlake"
Dec /	

Pot marigold
CALENDULA OFFICINALIS

FEATURES

A bushy hardy annual with light green leaves and brightly colored flowers in shades of orange from spring to fall. The traditional cottage garden pot marigolds have single, bright orange flowers, but many more decorative double and semi-double varieties are readily available. However, if these are allowed to self-seed, which they will do freely, the single form will eventually come to dominate again.

CONDITIONS

ASPECT	Pot marigolds grow best in full sun or light shade. They can become leggy if grown in deeper shade.
SITE	Pot marigolds are very tolerant plants, growing in most soils that do not get waterlogged, but they do best in well-drained, not too rich soils.

GROWING METHOD

SOWING	Propagate from seed sown in spring or fall. Plant out 12–18in apart. Pot marigolds will self-sow freely. Do not allow the soil to become waterlogged.
FEEDING	No special feeding required.
PROBLEMS	Slugs may eat the young leaves. Blackfly may be a problem late in the season. Cut out infested areas and spray with horticultural soap. Mildew may also be a problem, but generally this does not occur until flowering is over. Remove and burn affected parts to prevent it from spreading.

PRUNING	No special requirements. Pinch out growing tips to prevent the plant becoming leggy. Deadhead regularly to encourage continuous flowering.

HARVESTING

PICKING	Pick the flowers just as they open for use fresh or dry. Pick leaves when they are young for fresh use.
STORAGE	Dry pot marigold flowers slowly at low temperatures, on a non-metal rack in a cool airy place.
FREEZING	The petals can be frozen in ice cubes and used as required to decorate drinks.

USES

CULINARY	Petals can be used fresh in salads, butters, and cheeses, and also in cooked dishes including omelettes, soups, etc. They can also be used to add color to rice dishes. Young leaves can also be added to salads.

AT A GLANCE	
A popular annual herb with brightly coloured flowers that have a wide range of herbal uses. Hardy to 5°F or below (zone 7).	

Jan	/	**Parts used**
Feb	/	Flowers
Mar	plant	Leaves
Apr	plant	**Uses**
May	plantharvest	Culinary
Jun	harvest	Medicinal
July	harvest	Cosmetic
Aug	harvest	Craft
Sept	plant	Gardening
Oct	/	
Nov	/	
Dec	/	

MEDICINAL	Pot marigold flowers have antiseptic, anti-fungal, and anti-bacterial properties and have traditionally been used medicinally for a wide range of conditions, including the treatment of wounds, burns, stings and bites, chilblains, and varicose veins. An infusion was also used as an eyewash. The sap from the stem is said to remove warts.
COSMETIC	Pot marigold can be used to make a range of cosmetic preparations. For example, infused flowers can be used to make skin and hair care preparations. Used in a skin lotion, they are said to help clear up spots.
CRAFT	The dried petals can be used to add color to pot-pourri. The fresh petals produce a yellow dye.
GARDENING	A traditional and popular cottage garden flower. Being sensitive to temperature, they give an indication of the weather. Open flowers are said to forecast a fine day.

Potentilla

CINQUEFOIL

FEATURES

There are over 500 species of cinquefoil, including annuals, perennials, and small shrubs. All have the characteristic five-lobed leaf, and the single or double flowers may be white or in shades of yellow, red, or pink. Cinquefoil belongs to the rose family, and the foliage can be attractive, even when plants are not in flower. They may be from 2–20in or more high. The short types make good edging plants, while the taller ones can be used successfully in a mixed planting. Since flower stems tend to flop over, they may need light support. Many red cinquefoils are hybrids of *P. atrosanguinea*, while some yellows derive from *P. argyrophylla* and *P. recta*. Some cinquefoils tend to self-seed.

CONDITIONS

ASPECT   While it needs full sunshine, cinquefoil will also tolerate some dappled shade.
SITE   Needs well-drained soil enriched with some organic matter.

GROWING METHOD

PROPAGATION   Species and single-flowered varieties grow from both seed and cuttings. Sow the seed in early to mid-spring. The hybrid doubles must be grown from divisions taken during the spring or fall, or you can use spring cuttings. The plant spacing depends on ultimate size, and may be anywhere from 6 to 16in.

FEEDING   Apply a complete plant food as new growth commences in the spring.
PROBLEMS   Since these plants can easily flower themselves to death, propagate regularly to ensure you always have a good supply.

FLOWERING

SEASON   Flowers may begin in late spring in warm spells, but the main flowering period is during the summer months. Give the plant a light trim in early spring to force plenty of new growth and buds.
CUTTING   Flowers do not last well when cut.

AFTER FLOWERING

REQUIREMENTS   Cut off spent flower stems at ground level, and tidy up the plants as the growth dies off. In milder areas the foliage may hang on.

AT A GLANCE	
A 500-species genus, mainly of herbaceous perennials and shrubs. An excellent color range. Hardy to 0°F (zones 6–7).	

		Recommended Varieties
Jan	/	
Feb	/	*Potentilla cuneata*
Mar	sow	"Gibson's Scarlet"
Apr	transplant	*P. megalantha*
May	transplant	*P. nepalensis*
Jun	flowering	"Miss Willmott"
July	flowering	"William Rollison"
Aug	flowering	
Sept	flowering	
Oct	sow	
Nov	/	
Dec	/	

Potentilla fruticosa

CINQUEFOIL

FEATURES

This is a small, easy-care, informal flowering shrub. It grows about 3ft high and has masses of yellow flowers from late spring right through to mid-fall. It can be grown in one long yellow hedge, but looks best in a sequence of different potentillas. Look for those flowering in contrasting red, pink, white and orange, but make sure that they all grow to, or can be pruned to, the same height. All you need do is give them the gentlest late winter prune all over to stimulate plenty of new growth. The flowers appear on the current season's growth. When buying a potentilla look at the label carefully since some only grow 4in high.

CONDITIONS

ASPECT   The plants generally prefer full sun, but will tolerate partial shade.
SITE   Over-rich soil is not necessary. Potentillas prefer the ground to be slightly on the poor side, with excellent drainage. Clay soil must be well broken up with plenty of added horticultural sand and grit.

GROWING METHOD

PROPAGATION   The quickest methods are either by division in the spring or fall, or taking cuttings in the first part of summer. They strike very quickly.
SPACING   Plant at 2ft intervals, allowing each plant to grow about 4ft wide.

FEEDING

FEEDING   They benefit from a feed in the spring of a slow-release fertilizer.
PROBLEMS   There are no known problems.

FLOWERING

SEASON   An exceptional flowering period, with the yellow flowers in bloom from the spring, through summer, into the fall. The flowers, which resemble small wild roses, have five petals—hence the name cinquefoil.

PRUNING

GENERAL   In the fall, after flowering, prune for shape and to take out any old, dead, or twiggy wood. Give a light late winter prune if necessary.

CATCHING THE LATE afternoon sun, these flowers of Potentilla fruticosa make bright yellow highlights among the dark green foliage.

AT A GLANCE	
Potentilla fruticosa makes the perfect small, informal, flowery hedge. It has many excellent forms. Hardy to 5°F (zone 7).	
Jan /	**Recommended Varieties**
Feb /	*Potentilla fruticosa*
Mar /	"Daydawn"
Apr /	"Friedrichsenii"
May flowering	"Goldfinger"
Jun flowering	"Katherine Dykes"
July flowering	"Maanelys"
Aug flowering	**Companion Plants**
Sep flowering	Box
Oct flowering	Fuchsia
Nov /	Lavender
Dec /	

Pride of Madeira

ECHIUM CANDICANS (FASTUOSUM)

FEATURES

A somewhat sprawling shrub with gray-green leaves, Pride of Madeira is an exciting challenge. Growing to about 5ft high and spreading to 7ft or more, it produces long, fat spikes of sapphire to violet-blue flowers in late spring and early summer. Being frost tender, it is best grown in a pot and consigned to a high conservatory or large greenhouse. Move it to a sheltered, sunny patio or terrace in June and bring it indoors when nights turn chilly in September. It matures in 3–5 years and flowers early in life.

CONDITIONS

ASPECT   Echium needs full sun all day. Under glass, air must freely circulate.

SITE   Set this plant in a large pot of multipurpose compost augmented with a quarter part Perlite to ensure good drainage. Pot it on in early spring when roots fill the container and mat the compost as the need for watering increases.

GROWING METHOD

FEEDING   Boost growth by liquid feeding with a high-potash fertilizer, weekly from spring to late summer. Alternatively, insert aggregates of slow-release fertilizer granules into the compost in spring.

WATERING :   *Echium* tolerates very dry conditions and needs only an occasional soaking in prolonged droughty weather.

PROPAGATION   *Echium* is raised from seed in spring or early summer. Alternatively, take semi-ripe heeled cuttings tugged from older stems, in midsummer. Root cuttings in a propagator heated to around 70°F.

PROBLEMS   No particular pest or disease troubles this plant. If aphids colonize shoot tips, tackle them with pirimicarb or natural pyrethrins.

PRUNING

Remove spent flower heads and shorten shoots outgrowing their allotted space.

AT A GLANCE	
Frost tender, with blue flowers in summer. In chilly areas, it must be overwintered under glass. Hardy to 30°F (zone 9).	
Jan shield from frost	Recommended Varieties
Feb shield from frost	*E. candicans*
Mar shield from frost	
Apr plant	
May plant	
June flower, plant	
July flower, prune	
Aug flower, prune	
Sept flower, plant	
Oct /	
Nov /	
Dec /	

Primula

POLYANTHUS

FEATURES

Polyanthus, a hybrid type of primula, is perfect in patio pots or mass-planted in the garden for a stunning spring display. Its very brightly-colored flowers up to 2in across, on stems 6–12in tall, rise from neat clumps of bright green, crinkled leaves. A hardy perennial, it is grown as a hardy biennial for spring bedding and containers. Widely available as young plants.

CONDITIONS

ASPECT	Grows in full sun or light shade under trees.
SITE	Needs well-drained soil but with plenty of organic matter mixed in to help retain moisture—plants do not like to be bone dry at any stage while growing. For containers use multipurpose compost with gravel or chunks of styrofoam put in the base.

GROWING METHOD

SOWING	*Polyanthus* seed can be tricky to germinate, and the most important rule is not to keep it too warm. Sow in 3½in pots of peat-based seed compost from March–July, barely cover, then stand outside in a covered, shaded spot out of the sun. Seedlings will appear 2–3 weeks later. Transplant to cell trays or 3½in pots of peat-based potting compost, and pot on into 5in pots when roots are well-

developed. Grow during the summer in a shaded spot and do not let them dry out. Plant out in October where flowers are required the following spring, in beds or containers with bulbs and other plants.

FEEDING	Feed fortnightly with liquid feed in summer.
PROBLEMS	Slugs can devour leaves so use slug pellets. Never bury the crowns or plants may rot.

FLOWERING

SEASON	Flowers appear earlier in mild winters and carry on throughout spring.
CUTTING	Charming in spring posies.

AFTER FLOWERING

GENERAL	*Polyanthus* taken from spring displays can be planted in borders where they will form large clumps and flower regularly every spring.

AT A GLANCE	
A hardy biennial grown for its bright spring flowers for use in bedding and containers. Frost hardy to 5°F (zone 7).	

		Recommended Varieties
Jan	/	Primula hybrids
Feb	flowering	"Crescendo Mixed"
Mar	flowers/sow	"Dobies Superb Mixed"
Apr	flowers/sow	"Giant Superb Mixed"
May	flowers/sow	"Gold Lace"
Jun	sow/grow	"Harlequin Mixed"
July	sow/grow	"Heritage Mixed"
Aug	grow	"Large Flowered Mixed"
Sept	grow	"Pacific Giants Mixed"
Oct	plant	"Spring Rainbow Mixed"
Nov	/	"Unwins Superb Mixed"
Dec	/	

Primula vulgaris

PRIMROSE

FEATURES

This is the true primrose of European woodlands. The species generally has soft, pale yellow flowers tucked in among the leaves on very short stalks, although white or pale pink forms are occasionally found. Cultivars come in a huge range of colors, with single or double flowers, some on short stalks, others on quite tall ones. Primroses look their best when mass-planted under deciduous trees, or in drifts at the front of a lightly shaded bed or border. They can also be grown well in pots. Plants grow from about 4 to 6in high, with flowering stems about the same height.

CONDITIONS

ASPECT   Prefers to grow in semi-shade, and must have protection from the summer sun.

SITE   Grows best in a medium-to-heavy moisture-retentive soil, heavily enriched with organic matter. Mulch around the plants in spring.

GROWING METHOD

PROPAGATION   Lift and divide the crowns after flowering, in late fall, and replant about 4–6in apart. Sow your plant's own seed when ripe (from late spring to early fall); sow bought seed in early spring. Do not let young plants dry out.

FEEDING   Little fertilizer is needed if the soil is well enriched with plenty of humus, but a little general fertilizer in early spring gives an extra boost.

PROBLEMS   Generally trouble-free.

FLOWERING

SEASON   Flowering usually lasts for several weeks during the spring. Deadheading prolongs the blooming. Massed displays look best.

CUTTING   Makes a fine small bouquet, mixed with a range of other early spring miniatures.

AFTER FLOWERING

REQUIREMENTS   In suitable conditions, plants may self-seed. Remove dead leaves around the plant base.

AT A GLANCE		
P. vulgaris is an evergreen or semi-evergreen with scented, spring, generally pale yellow flowers. Hardy to 5°F (zone 7).		
Jan	/	Recommended Varieties
Feb	sow	"Ken Dearman"
Mar	flowering	"Miss Indigo"
Apr	flowering	*Primula vulgaris*
May	flowering	"Lilacina Plena"
Jun	/	*P. v.* subsp. *sibthorpii*
July	/	"Wanda"
Aug	/	
Sept	sow	
Oct	divide	
Nov	/	
Dec	/	

Prunus laurocerasus

CHERRY LAUREL

FEATURES

If left unpruned, cherry laurel grows into a tree-like shape, but pruned it makes an imposing hedge for a larger garden, most often to about 10ft, thus providing privacy and a windbreak. The evergreen foliage is dark green and glossy; perfumed white flowers are followed by red, cherry-like fruits. This is a very long-lived plant. There are a number of excellent cultivars available.

CONDITIONS

ASPECT	Grows in sun or partial shade.
SITE	This plant prefers to root into well-drained soil that is heavily enriched with decayed organic matter. Therefore, avoid the two extremes of nutritionless, free-draining chalk soil and a heavy, wet, boggy ground.

GROWING METHOD

PROPAGATION	Grow from semi-ripe tip cuttings that are taken in midsummer. It can also be grown from seed if the ripe berries are picked, cleaned of the pulp and then stored in damp sand or damp sphagnum moss in the refrigerator for about three months before they are sown.
SPACING	It should be planted at about 3ft spacings. Do not be tempted to plant any closer together because crowding them is counter-productive—give them space to grow.

FEEDING	Apply plant food after spring flowering.
PROBLEMS	No specific problems are known.

FLOWERING

SEASON	The small, white, scented flowers appear in spring. However, flowers will not appear if the plant is pruned in late winter.
BERRIES	The flowers are followed by red berries that ripen to black. Birds love them. A good alternative to holly, box, and yew.

PRUNING

GENERAL	If you want flowers, do your main pruning immediately after flowering has finished; otherwise it can be done in late winter. Other trimming can be done throughout the growing season if necessary.

AT A GLANCE	
Prunus laurocerasus can make a 6m (20ft) high tree, but pruned is a fine, sturdy, thick hedge. Hardy to 0°F (zone 7).	
Jan foliage	**Companion Plants**
Feb foliage	Anemone
Mar foliage	Bluebell
Apr flowering	Crocus
May flowering	Daffodil
Jun foliage	Erythronium
July foliage	Fritillaria
Aug foliage	Hyacinth
Sep foliage	Iris
Oct foliage	Scilla
Nov foliage	Tulip
Dec foliage	

Pulmonaria

LUNGWORT

FEATURES

Lungwort is well suited to planting under trees, between shrubs, or at the front of a shady border. The abundant flowers appear before the leaves have fully developed, and are mostly in shades of blue, pink, and white. The foliage is very handsome, often silver-spotted, and if sheared over after flowering, produces a second, fresh mound of leaves. The whole plant is rarely more than 10–12in high, and when established is very decorative, even out of flower. The plant gets its common name from the similarity between a spotted leaf and a diseased lung.

CONDITIONS

ASPECT   Grows best in light shade, or in borders that are shady during the hottest part of the day. The leaves quickly wilt under a hot sun.

SITE   The soil should be heavily enriched with decayed organic matter, but it also needs to drain quite well.

GROWING METHOD

PROPAGATION   Grows from ripe seed, or by division of clumps, either after flowering or in the fall. Replant divisions approximately 6in apart. Better still, let plants freely hybridize. Young and established plants need moist soil during the growing season.

FEEDING   Apply a little complete fertilizer in early spring and mulch well.

PROBLEMS   No specific problems are known.

FLOWERING

SEASON   Lungworts flower in the spring.

CUTTING   Flowers last quite well in a vase.

AFTER FLOWERING

REQUIREMENTS   Spent flowers can be cut off if you do not want seeding to occur. After the flowers have finished, the foliage can be cut back to produce new fresh growth for the summer. Otherwise, little attention is required until the fall, when the foliage can be tidied as it fades.

AT A GLANCE		
A genus of 14 species of deciduous and evergreen perennials. A flowering spreader for damp shade. Hardy to 0°F (zones 6–7).		
Jan	/	**Recommended Varieties**
Feb	/	*Pulmonaria angustifolia*
Mar	flowering	"Munstead Blue"
Apr	flowering	*P. longifolia*
May	flowering	"Bertram Anderson"
Jun	divide	*P. officinalis*
July	/	"Cambridge Blue Group"
Aug	/	"Sissinghurst White"
Sept	/	*P. rubra*
Oct	divide	*P. saccharata*
Nov	/	"Argentea Group"
Dec	/	

Pulsatilla vulgaris

PASQUE FLOWER

FEATURES

The soft purple flowers appear before the leaves on this small, spring-flowering perennial. The whole plant is covered with silky hairs, giving it a delicate appearance that belies its hardy nature. After the petals have fallen, a decorative seedhead forms. The finely divided leaves grow from 4 to 6in long, while the flowers may be on stems 4–12in tall. Pasque flower should be planted in groups or drifts to get the best effect. There are now pink, white, and red forms available. Since the leaves and flowers may cause skin irritation, wear gloves when handling if you have sensitive skin.

CONDITIONS

ASPECT   Prefers full sun but tolerates semi-shade.
SITE   Needs very well-drained, gritty soil, rich in organic matter. They thrive on lime.

GROWING METHOD

PROPAGATION Divide existing clumps after the foliage has died down, and then replant the divisions approximately 6–8in apart. Named varieties must be divided, but the species can also be grown from seed sown as soon as it is ripe in July. Overwinter the seedlings in a greenhouse or frame. Pot up when the new leaves begin to show in the spring.

FEEDING   Apply a little general fertilizer when growth commences in the spring.
PROBLEMS   No specific pest or disease problems are known for this plant.

FLOWERING

SEASON   Flowers appear in the spring and early summer, generally before the leaves. They last well and the display is prolonged by the pretty, silky seedheads.
CUTTING   The flowers are unsuitable for cutting, but the seedheads add to an attractive display.

AFTER FLOWERING

REQUIREMENTS Plants should be left alone until the seedheads have faded or fallen. Cut off spent stems, and trim off the foliage as the plant dies.

AT A GLANCE		
P. vulgaris is an attractive, clump-forming perennial, with bell-like, silky flowers in shades of purple. Hardy to 0°F (zones 6–7).		
Jan	/	Recommended Varieties
Feb	/	*Pulsatilla alpina* subsp. *apiifolia*
Mar	/	*P. halleri*
Apr	flowering	*P. halleri* subsp. *slavica*
May	flowering	*P. vernalis*
Jun	flowering	*P. vulgaris*
July	sow	"Eva Constance"
Aug	sow	*P. v.* var. *rubra*
Sept	/	
Oct	divide	
Nov	/	
Dec	/	

Puya
PUYA SPECIES

FEATURES

This group of terrestrial bromeliads contains the largest species known, *Puya raimondii* from Peru and Bolivia, which is capable of growing to 9–12ft high. This very slow-growing plant takes up to 100 years to produce its first flower spike, which contains thousands of individual flowers. Puyas are mostly terrestrial, although some are rock dwellers, and most come from inhospitable habitats in the Andes. In nature most are pollinated by humming birds or starlings. Some come from cold, damp, windswept regions, others from dry grasslands where intense sunlight, heat, and drought are balanced by heavy winter frosts. Many team well with succulents that require similar conditions.

APPEARANCE

Most are large, from 3^1/4ft upwards, and grow in clumps so that ample space is needed. The heavily spined leaves may be green or gray and silver and are a decorative feature. They form dense rosettes from which tall spikes of flowers appear. Flowers are green, violet, blue, or white, often with colorful contrasting bracts.

SPECIES

P. venusta grows to about 41/4ft, producing eye-catching purple flowers on a tall, rose-pink stem and bracts. *P. berteroniana*, over 3^1/4ft high, has metallic greenish blue flowers.

CONDITIONS

POSITION	Many tolerate cold winters if kept dry. Most endure extremes of climate with very high daytime temperatures and freezing nights. Grows best in the large conservatory or greenhouse border.
POTTING MIX	The growing medium must be coarse and well drained. A mix of coarse sand and crushed rock with added peat or a peat substitute would be suitable.

GROWING METHOD

PROPAGATION	Remove offsets from spring to fall.
WATERING	Water regularly to establish plants but once established they need only occasional deep watering while in active growth.
FEEDING	Little or no fertilizer is needed.
PROBLEMS	Generally trouble-free and easy to grow.

FLOWERING SEASON

Flowering times vary with species and district. Most have long-lasting blooms.

AT A GLANCE		
Varieties vary in size. Flowers any time of year and last for a long time. Can go outside in summer. Keep frost free.		
Jan	keep dry	**Recommended Varieties**
Feb	keep dry	*P. alpestris*
Mar	water	*P. berteroniana*
Apr	remove offsets	*P. chilensis*
May	repot	*P. coerulea*
Jun	water	*P. mirabilis*
July	water, take outside	*P. venusta*
Aug	/	
Sept	bring in	
Oct	reduce water and remove offsets	
Nov	keep dry	
Dec	keep dry	

Pyracantha
FIRETHORN

FEATURES

These evergreen shrubs with thorny stems are often planted as hedges in rural areas, but they are just as much at home in suburban districts. Unpruned, they will be 6^1/$_2$–10ft high but are often pruned to less than that. Firethorns are fairly fast growing but are also long lived. The leaves are glossy and clusters of small, white flowers appear in spring or early summer. These are soon followed by bright red or orange berries (the "fire" of the firethorn) which are very decorative and most attractive to birds. Branches of the bright red or orange berries can be cut for indoor decoration once they are fully colored. Be careful where you plant it though because the sharp pointed spines are dangerous.

CONDITIONS

ASPECT   Needs full sun and tolerates exposure to wind. Will tolerate some partial shade.

SITE   Grows on a wide range of soils, including poor soils, but best growth will be in those enriched with organic matter. For a good show of bright colored berries, rich soil is best.

GROWING METHOD

PROPAGATION   Grow from seed removed from ripe berries and planted fresh. Plants can also be grown from semi-ripe cuttings taken in summer.

SPACING   Plant at intervals of 28in–3ft.

FEEDING   Feeding is not essential, but on poor soils give complete plant food in early spring.

PROBLEMS

They suffer from a range of pests and diseases like caterpillars, scale, canker, and fireblight.

FLOWERING

SEASON   The white flowers appear in the spring (*Pyracantha rogersiana*), early summer (*P.* "Orange Charmer"), and mid-summer (*P. angustifolia*). Although they provide a good show, they are outdone by the brilliant berries.

BERRIES   The flowers are followed by clusters of berries that will ripen to a blazing red, orange, or yellow, depending on the species.

PRUNING

GENERAL   Best pruned in spring. Start training and pruning in the first couple of years of growth.

AT A GLANCE		
High quality berrying plants that make an eye-catching hedge. Beware of the spines though. Hardy to 5°F (zone 7).		
Jan	foliage	Recommended Varieties
Feb	foliage	*Pyracantha coccinea*
Mar	foliage	"Red Column"
Apr	flowering	"Golden Charmer"
May	flowering	"Mohave"
Jun	flowering	"Orange Glow"
July	flowering	*P. rogersiana*
Aug	foliage	*P. rogersiana*
Sep	foliage	"Flava"
Oct	foliage	"Soleil d'Or"
Nov	foliage	"Watereri"
Dec	foliage	

R

Ranunculus

BUTTERCUP

FEATURES

Buttercups basically divide into the invasive and the less-so. Take care which you chose for the border. The genus contains about 400 species of annuals, biennials, and perennials, with a wide range of demands, which vary from free-draining alpine slopes to ponds.

R. ficaria, lesser celandine, is a woodland type with early spring, yellow flowers that can become a weed. There are several cultivars; "Brazen Hussy" has dark brown foliage and yellow flowers, while "Salmon's White" is cream with a blue tint on the reverse.

R. aconitifolius "Flore Pleno," fair maids of France, likes full sun and has white, long-lasting flowers. And *R. flammula*, lesser spearwort, is a marginal aquatic for early summer with yellow flowers.

CONDITIONS

ASPECT
It tolerates a wide range of conditions from medium to dappled shade, to full sun. When buying a ranunculus do carefully check its specific needs.

SITE
This too varies considerably from moist, rich soil, to fertile, free-draining ground, to gritty, fast-draining soil for the alpine types, to ponds and pond margins for the aquatics.

GROWING METHOD

PROPAGATION
Divide in the spring or fall, or sow fresh, ripe seed in the fall.

FEEDING
This depends entirely on the natural habitat and growing needs of the plant. Border perennials need reasonable applications of well-rotted manure in the spring, as new growth appears, while the woodland types need plenty of leafy compost dug in around the clumps.

PROBLEMS
Slugs and snails are a particular nuisance; pick off or use chemical treatment.

FLOWERING

SEASON
From late spring to mid-summer, depending on the chosen variety.

CUTTING
All ranunculus make excellent cut flowers, being especially useful in spring before the main flush of garden flowers.

AFTER FLOWERING

REQUIREMENTS
Cut back all spent stems.

A STRONG, vivid display of ranunculus showing how they can enliven a border. By mixing two or three different varieties you will certainly get extra impact. However, since some types of ranunculus can rapidly multiply and spread, you must take great care when selecting a particular variety.

AT A GLANCE		
A large genus of over 400 species with many annuals, biennials, and perennials, hardy to 5°F (zone 7) for all kinds of garden.		
Jan	/	Recommended Varieties
Feb	/	*Ranunculus aconitifolius*
Mar	sow	"Flore Pleno"
Apr	transplant	*calandrinioides*
May	flowering	*R. ficaria*
Jun	flowering	"Brazen Hussy"
July	flowering	"Picton's Double"
Aug	/	"Salmon's White"
Sept	/	*R. flammula*
Oct	divide	*R. montanus*
Nov	/	"Molten Gold"
Dec	/	*R. gramineus*

Ranunculus asiaticus

RANUNCULUS, PERSIAN BUTTERCUP

FEATURES

One of the brightest and most colorful of all spring-flowering bulbs, ranunculus can be massed in mixed colors or blocks of single color in the yard or in containers. Left in the ground they may give several seasons, although they are often treated as annuals. However, the woody, oddly shaped tubers can be lifted and stored like other bulbs. The many-petalled flowers of ranunculus come in bright yellow, cream, white, reds, and pinks, and stems of some strains may reach 18in in height. Although there are single flowered varieties, double or semi-double types are by far the most popular. They are usually sold as color mixtures, but separate red and yellow forms are sometimes available from specialist suppliers. *Ranunculus* blooms make very good cut flowers, lasting well in the vase.

CONDITIONS

ASPECT   Prefers full sun all day with shelter from very strong wind.
SITE   Ideal for beds, borders, and containers, where they will make a colorful display. The soil should be well-drained, ideally with plenty of compost or manure dug in a month or so before planting.

GROWING METHOD

PLANTING   Plant the woody, tuberous roots 1–2in deep and about 6in apart, with the claws pointing down, in early spring. Soaking the tubers in water for a few hours before planting gets them off to a good start.
FEEDING   Liquid feed with a balanced fertilizer every two weeks from when the flower buds start to appear. Keep the soil moist when the ferny leaves appear, particularly during bud formation and flowering.
PROBLEMS   Usually trouble free, though powdery mildew may occur in hot, dry seasons. Spray with a general fungicide if necessary.

FLOWERING

SEASON   Flowers throughout the summer.
CUTTING   Cut flowers early in the morning and change the water frequently to prolong vase life.

AFTER FLOWERING

REQUIREMENTS Cut off spent flower stems. When the foliage has died down completely, tubers can be lifted, cleaned and stored in dry peat in a frost-free place until the following spring. After three seasons tubers are best replaced.

AT A GLANCE		
Brightly colored, many-petalled, poppy-like flowers are carried above attractive ferny foliage in summer.		
Jan	/	Recommended Varieties
Feb	/	"Accolade"
Mar	planting	"Red form"
Apr	planting	"Yellow form"
May	/	
Jun	flowering	
July	flowering	
Aug	flowering	
Sept	/	
Oct	/	
Nov	/	
Dec	/	

Reseda

MIGNONETTE

FEATURES

Mignonette has greenish, pink, red, yellow, or coppery flowers and grows to 12in. It is not particularly striking but is grown mainly for its strong, fruity fragrance—grow it near doors, windows, in patio pots, and near sitting areas to appreciate the qualities of this easily-grown hardy annual. It makes a good addition to cottage-style borders.

CONDITIONS

ASPECT	Needs full sun.
SITE	Needs well-drained soil—dig in organic matter and add lime to acid soils.

GROWING METHOD

SOWING	Seed is sown directly into the ground in short drills ^{1}/2in deep, 6in apart. Thin seedlings to 6in apart. Sowing can take place in March/April or September/October. Fall-sown plants need protecting with cloches during cold spells, and should not be thinned until spring. For pots, sow a pinch of seeds in each unit of a cell tray and thin to 2–3 seedlings, grow on and plant up when ready—reseda does not like root disturbance.

FEEDING	Extra feeding is not usually necessary
PROBLEMS	Free of troubles.

FLOWERING

SEASON	Flowers appear from late spring on fall-sown plants, later on spring-sown.
CUTTING	Cut when just a few flowers are opening. Dried flowers retain their fragrance.

AFTER FLOWERING

GENERAL	Pull plants up when they are past their best, but leave a few to produce seeds and self-sow.

MIGNONETTE FLOWERS individually are insignificant, but the strong sweet fragrance is striking and well worth the effort of sowing. The flowerheads of Reseda odorata *branch out as they develop. Sow along path edges so the fragrance can be enjoyed.*

AT A GLANCE	
An easily grown hardy annual grown for its highly fragrant spikes of summer flowers. Frost hardy to 5°F (zone 7).	

Month		Recommended Varieties
Jan	/	*Reseda odorata*
Feb	/	"Crown Mixture"
Mar	sow	"Fragrant Beauty"
Apr	sow/thin out	"Machet"
May	thin out	"Sweet Scented"
Jun	flowering	
July	flowering	
Aug	flowering	
Sept	flowers/sow	
Oct	sow	
Nov	/	
Dec	/	

Rhapis excelsa

MINIATURE FAN PALM

FEATURES

A native of southern China, this small palm forms clumps of thin, almost bamboo-like stems. The fan-shaped leaves have long stalks and are divided virtually to their bases, giving the impression of leaflets. This palm was imported to 17th century Japan and became popular among aristocratic circles. A number of cultivars were bred by the Japanese. The leaves of this versatile and undemanding plant are deep green and glossy and can grow up to 12in in length. The eventual height and spread of the plant is 5–15ft, but it is slow growing. Very suitable as a container plant, it makes a good houseplant and is also recommended for the intermediate conservatory or glasshouse. It will also be happy placed out of doors for the summer.

CONDITIONS

ASPECT   Provide bright light but do not subject it to direct sun. Provide moderate humidity. Outdoors place in a sheltered position.
SITE   In containers grow this palm in soil-less potting compost.

GROWING METHOD

PROPAGATION   Sow seeds as soon as available and germinate them at a temperature of 81°F. Alternatively remove and pot rooted offsets in spring, or divide an entire clump.
WATERING   Water freely in growing season from late spring to late summer, then for the rest of the year water moderately.

FEEDING   Apply a balanced liquid fertilizer monthly during the growing season from late spring to late summer.
PROBLEMS   Under glass may be attacked by red spider mites.

FOLIAGE/FLOWERING

FOLIAGE   Being evergreen this palm looks good all year round but is especially attractive in spring and summer.
FLOWERS   Clusters of cream flowers are produced in summer followed by white, waxy fruits if fertilization has taken place.

GENERAL CARE

REQUIREMENTS   Remove dead fronds when necessary by cutting them off close to the trunk.

AT A GLANCE	
Forms clumps of thin stems topped with fan-shaped, glossy leaves. Provide a minimum temperature of 50–55°F (zone 11).	
Jan /	**Companion Plants**
Feb /	Under glass grow with other palms
Mar planting	such as *Phoenix* species and with
Apr planting	other foliage plants like *Monstera*
May foliage	*deliciosa.* Outdoors combine this
Jun flowering	palm with brightly colored summer
July flowering	bedding or subtropical plants.
Aug flowering	
Sep /	
Oct /	
Nov /	
Dec /	

Rhododendron

LODER'S WHITE

FEATURES

Rhododendrons come in all shapes and sizes, from 3ft high to tree-like giants growing 20ft or so. They are traditionally grown as individual eyecatchers, with a big show of flowers anytime from late fall to late summer, though the bulk perform in the spring and early summer. They can also make thick hedges or windbreaks, in the case of *Rhododendron* "Loder's White" about 8ft high and wide. You need a big garden, and one with acid soil. The plants also need dappled shade, and protection from cold winds. With adequate space, grow different colored rhododendrons to make a patchwork effect. It is worth visiting a specialist collection to see the full range now available.

CONDITIONS

ASPECT   Sun with dappled shade is ideal, approaching a light woodland setting. Avoid both full sun and constant shade.

SITE   Acid soil is absolutely essential. Individual plants can be grown in tubs with ericaceous compost. Trying to turn an alkaline garden area acid by adding replacement acid soil might work for one season, but thereafter the surrounding alkaline soil will gradually seep back in, and the rhododendrons will falter.

GROWING METHOD

PROPAGATION Take semi-ripe cuttings from midsummer.

SPACING   *R.* "Loder's White" should be spaced about 4ft apart. Do not try and plant them any closer together. Each shrub needs to be able to show off all its flowers.

FEEDING   Give an annual mulch using leaf mold.

FLOWERING

SEASON   It flowers right in the middle of summer, at the height of the season. After flowering, attempt to deadhead as much as possible to preserve energy for next year's display. Adding other rhododendrons that flower in early and late summer will extend the show.

PRUNING

GENERAL   Leave to realize its full potential. It will automatically thicken up and get quite bushy.

The flowers of the rhododendron are among the most sumptuous to be found. And this rhododendron is no exception to the rule. The frilly petals are set off by delicate stamen to create a delightful texture. The blooms time their appearance to perfection, enjoying the midsummer sun.

AT A GLANCE		
Rhododendron "Loder's White" gives an excellent display packed with scented white flowers. Hardy to 5°F (zone 7).		
Jan	foliage	**Recommended Varieties**
Feb	foliage	*Rhododendron*
Mar	foliage	"Anna Rose Whitney"
Apr	foliage	"Blue Peter"
May	foliage	"Cynthia"
Jun	flowering	"Gomer Waterer"
July	flowering	"Hydon Dawn"
Aug	foliage	"Kilimanjaro"
Sep	foliage	"Loderi King George"
Oct	foliage	"Mrs Furnival"
Nov	foliage	"Razorbill"
Dec	foliage	

Rhodohypoxis baurii

ROSE GRASS

FEATURES

This enchanting little plant, which comes from high altitude areas of South Africa, is ideally suited to growing in a rock garden, on the edge of a border or in pots. The slightly hairy leaves, similar to those of a broad-leaf grass, grow to around 4in high. The flowers, which are white or pink through to deep rosy crimson, are about the same height. As they have become better known several varieties with deeper color or larger flowers have become available. They have six petals with one set of three appearing to be set on top of the other, so the flower has no visible eye. The floral display is long lasting, from late spring through to late summer. If grown in the garden the positions of these plants should be marked in some way as they are completely dormant during winter.

CONDITIONS

ASPECT Grows best in full sun in a sheltered spot.
SITE Suitable for rockeries, scree gardens, or containers. The soil must be well drained but enriched with decayed organic matter. It needs to be lime free, as rose grass is not tolerant of alkaline soils. Good quality potting compost mixed with a little extra sharp sand should be adequate for containers.

GROWING METHOD

PLANTING Tubers should be planted in late spring about 2in deep and 4in apart. Lift and divide offsets in the fall.

FEEDING Mulch garden plants with decayed manure or compost in late winter or early spring. Potted plants that have not been repotted will benefit from slow-release fertilizer in early spring. Water regularly during the growing period in dry spells, but keep dry through winter.

PROBLEMS No specific problems are known.

FLOWERING

SEASON The long flowering period runs from late spring through to late summer.
CUTTING Flowers are unsuitable for picking.

AFTER FLOWERING

REQUIREMENTS Spent blooms can be snipped off or ignored. Protect plants from excess winter rainfall; a sheet of glass supported horizontally over the plants on four wooden stakes should prevent the crowns rotting off in wet weather.

AT A GLANCE		
A tuberous alpine with mounds of attractive pink or white flowers carried for a very long season.		
Jan	/	Recommended Varieties
Feb	/	"Alba"
Mar	plant	"Dulcie"
Apr	plant	"Dawn"
May	flowering	"Douglas"
Jun	flowering	"Eva-Kate"
July	flowering	"Fred Broome"
Aug	flowering	"Garnett"
Sept	flowering	"Harlequin"
Oct	/	"Picta"
Nov	/	"Ruth"
Dec	/	"Stella"

Ricinus

CASTOR OIL PLANT

FEATURES

A striking and memorable plant grown for its large, lobed, exotic-looking leaves, which are used for bedding, borders, and large tubs and containers. The often brightly-colored summer flowers are followed by spiny seed clusters. By nature an evergreen shrub, ricinus is fast growing and plants are raised fresh from seed each year—in long hot summers they can reach 6ft by 3ft tall and wide. Annual flowering climbers like thunbergia or ipomoea will climb its stems, their bright orange/blue flowers contrasting with the often deeply colored ricinus foliage. All parts of the plant are poisonous, especially the seeds. Treat as a half-hardy annual and scrap plants at the end of the summer.

CONDITIONS

ASPECT   Must have full sun. In northern areas choose a sheltered, south-facing spot.

SITE   Soil should be well-drained with plenty of rotted compost or manure dug in. Use loam-based or multipurpose potting compost in containers. In windy spots, stake plants.

GROWING METHOD

SOWING   Soak the hard seeds overnight in warm water, then sow individually in $3^1/2$in diameter pots of soil-based compost, 2in deep in March, and keep at 70°F. Seedlings appear within three weeks. Pot on into 5in diameter pots when 6in tall. In beds plant 3–6ft apart after the last frosts.

FEEDING   Apply liquid feed weekly from early summer, or mix slow-release fertilizer with the potting compost before planting.

PROBLEMS   Red spider mite attacks leaves. Wetting the leaves thoroughly every day can help, or use a spray containing bifenthrin.

FLOWERING

SEASON   The large leaves keep coming all summer long and are joined later by clusters of flowers that rise up above them.

CUTTING   Leaves are useful for flower arranging, but avoid getting the sap on skin.

AFTER FLOWERING

GENERAL   Plants are usually killed by the first frosts of fall. Ripe seeds can be saved for sowing again the following spring.

BY MIDSUMMER the leaves of ricinus will have formed a dense canopy when grown in beds and planted 2–3ft apart.

AT A GLANCE		
A half-hardy annual with large, exotic leaves in a range of colors, and prized as bold bedder. Frost hardy to 32°F (zone 10).		
Jan	/	**Recommended Varieties**
Feb	/	*Ricinus communis*
Mar	sow	"Carmencita"
Apr	pot on	"Carmencita Pink"
May	harden/plant	"Impala"
Jun	leaves	"Gibbsonii"
July	leaves	"Red Spire"
Aug	leaves	"Zanzibarensis"
Sept	leaves	
Oct	/	
Nov	/	
Dec	/	

Rock Rose

CISTUS

FEATURES

A dandyish Mediterranean native, evergreen cistus delights us from June to August with a daily succession of saucer-shaped, crumpled, silky blooms. Bushes range in size from carpeting, white and maroon-blotched *Cistus lusitanicus* "Decumbens," to 2ft high, to white and yellow-centered *C. laurifolius*, an imposing sentinel that rises to 5ft. There are pink-, crimson- and lilac-flowered varieties, too. All varieties perform early in life and taller kinds make stunning, informal flowering hedges. Small, pot or tub-grown species and varieties, such as neat and bushy "Silver Pink" with its grayish-silvery leaves, illuminate a sun-baked patio.

CONDITIONS

ASPECT   Rock roses must have full sun all day to make compact, free-flowering plants. They do not mind exposed sites or salt-laden breezes, but may be damaged by frosty winds. Avoid growing them in areas of high rainfall as blooms are spoilt by prolonged, wet weather.

SITE   Plants make the strongest growth on humus-rich, sandy, or gravelly loam, which drains quickly; they are less spirited on heavy, badly drained soils. In nature, rock roses flourish on porous limestone. If your soil is acid, boost growth by adding lime before planting.

GROWING METHOD

FEEDING   These plants need little or no fertilizer. Apply a light dressing of bone meal in spring and fall. Once plants are growing strongly, water is seldom needed, even during weeks of drought.

PROPAGATION   Take semi-ripe cuttings in summer. Species can be grown from seeds or cuttings. Varieties must be raised from cuttings.

PROBLEMS   No particular pest or disease afflicts cistus, but hard pruning into older wood can inhibit stumps from re-growing.

PRUNING

Encourage newly planted shrubs to branch freely and make dense bushes by pinching out shoot tips several times throughout the first two summers. Cut back frost-damaged stems to healthy growth in spring.

A MEDITERRANEAN drought resister, free-flowering rock roses are also coveted for their aromatic leaves, which distil "honey" on a warm day. A rapid succession of crumpled, silky, often-blotched blooms in white, pink and cerise are your reward for planting cistus.

AT A GLANCE	
Drought-resisting evergreen for light soil, it is smothered with white, pink, or red blooms in summer. Hardy to 23°F (zone 9).	

		Recommended Varieties
Jan	/	**Small—up to 3ft**
Feb	/	
Mar	/	*Cistus* x *corbariensis*
Apr	plant, prune	"Silver Pink"
May	flower, plant	*Cx skanbergii*
June	flower, plant	"Sunset"
July	flower, plant	**Tall—over 3ft**
Aug	plant, prune	"Alan Fradd"
Sept	plant	*C. laurifolius*
Oct	/	*C.* x *purpureus*
Nov	/	
Dec	/	

Rodgersia
RODGERSIA

FEATURES

A six-species genus with particularly interesting foliage, and flowers, ideal for the border or shady woodland garden. The three most commonly grown types are *R. aesculifolia, R. pinnata*, and *R. podophylla* (the last two having handsome, bronze new foliage). All form big, bold clumps in the right conditions. The first has crinkled leaves like those of a horse-chestnut, up to 10in long, with tall panicles of creamy white flowers; height 6^1/$_2$ft. *R. pinnata* "Superba," 4ft, has purple-bronze foliage and white, pink, or red flowers. And *R. podophylla*, 5ft, with creamy green flowers, also has horse-chestnut-type leaves, reddish in the fall.

CONDITIONS

ASPECT   *Rodgersia*, from the mountaineous Far East, like full sun or partial shade. They thrive in both conditions.

SITE   Grow in rich, damp ground; they grow by streams in the wild, and also in woodland settings.

GROWING METHOD

PROPAGATION Either divide, which is the easiest method, or grow from seed in the spring, raising the plants in a cold frame. Water the new young plants well, and do not let them dry out in prolonged, dry spells. They quickly wilt and lose energy, and their performance is badly affected.

FEEDING   Add plenty of well-rotted manure or compost to the soil. The shadier the conditions, the less rich the soil need be.

PROBLEMS   Vine weevil grubs can demolish the roots of container-grown perennials. While slugs rarely attack the new emerging growth, when they do strike they can ruin a potentially impressive display with tall, astilbe-like flowers. Pick off any offenders or treat with a chemical.

FLOWERING

SEASON   Flowers appear in mid- and late summer, and in early summer in the case of *R. sambucifolia*.

CUTTING   *Rodgersia* make good cut flowers, helping create an impressive display.

AFTER FLOWERING

REQUIREMENTS Cut the spent stems to the ground, and promptly remove all debris.

NO GARDEN IS COMPLETE without rodgersia. They can be grown apart from other plants, perhaps surrounded by gravel, highlighting the shapely, distinctive leaves. Or grow them in a mixed border, where they add strength and structure.

AT A GLANCE		
These tall, clump-forming perennials add structure to any dampish garden. Whitish summer flowers; hardy to 0°F (zone 7).		
Jan	/	Recommended Varieties
Feb	/	*Rodgersia aesculifolia*
Mar	sow	*R. pinnata*
Apr	dvide	"Elegans"
May	transplant	"Superba"
Jun	/	*R. podophylla*
July	flowering	*R. sambucifolia*
Aug	flowering	
Sept	/	
Oct	/	
Nov	/	
Dec	/	

Romneya coulteri

CALIFORNIAN TREE POPPY

FEATURES

Also known as the matilija poppy, this lovely perennial is not always easy to accommodate. It is native to the canyons and dry riverbeds in parts of California where there is generally rain only in winter, and where summers are hot and dry. When conditions are suitable, this plant can spread via underground roots. The large, white, summer flowers have beautiful crinkled petals that look like silk. Plants grow from 3 to 6$\frac{1}{2}$ft tall, and the blue-green foliage is deeply cut and attractive. Place these perennials in groups among shrubs or mixed perennials. Most plants available are likely to be hybrids of the standard species and *R. coulteri* var. *trichocalyx*.

CONDITIONS

ASPECT   Romneya needs bright, full sunlight all day.

SITE   Needs well-drained, preferably sandy or gravelly loam; avoid thick, heavy, wet clay. They can be tricky and slow to establish, but thereafter thrive, given the correct conditions.

GROWING METHOD

PROPAGATION   Grows from seed sown in the spring, but it is easiest propagated from root cuttings or suckers growing away from the main plant in spring. Wait until plants are very well established before attempting to disturb the roots—something they do not react well to. Position plants approximately 16in apart. Water regularly in the spring, when the foliage is growing and buds are appearing; thereafter, water occasionally in prolonged, dry spells.

FEEDING   Give a little complete plant food in early spring.

PROBLEMS   Poor drainage can kill Californian tree poppies. Can become invasive.

FLOWERING

SEASON   Right through the summer.

CUTTING   Like all poppies they make lovely cut flowers. Scald or burn the stems before arranging.

AFTER FLOWERING

REQUIREMENTS   Cut off spent flowers. As the plant flowers on new growth, it is best to cut it down to the ground in winter. Protect the crown with straw or bracken in cold areas.

CRIMPED WHITE PETALS around a mass of golden stamens make the matilija poppy as effective in close-up as in a group.

AT A GLANCE	
This is a deciduous sub-shrub with gray-green leaves and highly attractive white summer flowers. Hardy to 0°F (zones 6–7).	
Jan /	**Companion Plants**
Feb /	Ceanothus
Mar sow	Clematis
Apr division	Delphinium
May transplant	Helenium
Jun flowering	Hemerocallis
July flowering	Pelargonium
Aug flowering	Pennisetum
Sept /	Philadelphus
Oct /	
Nov /	
Dec /	

Romulea

ROMULEA

FEATURES

These small plants have grassy leaves and brightly colored, crocus-like flowers. There are 75 species native to parts of Africa, the Mediterranean and Europe, most in cultivation being South African. Growing 3–6in high, depending on species, they are ideal for rock gardens and pots where their neat growth can be admired. The color range includes cream and yellow, many shades of blue and violet, and also pinks and reds: many flowers have a very attractive "eye" of contrasting color in the center of the flower. The most popular type, *R. bulbocodium*, has pale lavender flowers with a yellow throat, and is hardier than some of the other species. Flowers remain closed in dull weather.

CONDITIONS

ASPECT	Needs full sun all day. The flowers will not open in shady conditions.
SITE	Grows best when grown in a sharply draining, rather sandy soil. Good for scree beds, rockeries and containers.

GROWING METHOD

PLANTING	The small corms should be planted some 2in deep and 2–3in apart in the fall.
FEEDING	Fedding is not normally necessary for this plant, but in poor soils some balanced fertilizer may be applied as growth begins. Water freely to keep the soil

moist through the growing season but keep plants dry during the summer, when they die down.

PROBLEMS	No specific pest or disease problems are known for romulea.

FLOWERING

SEASON	Flowers are carried throughout the spring months.
CUTTING	None of the species has flowers that are suitable for cutting.

AFTER FLOWERING

REQUIREMENTS	Protect the crowns with a mulch of peat or similar material for the winter months. Overcrowded clumps can be lifted and divided when the flowers have faded.

PALE LAVENDER PETALS and a recessed deep gold throat make Romulea bulbocodium *worth growing. It tolerates cool conditions.*

AT A GLANCE	
A low-growing plant with crocus-like flowers which open wide in full sun. Needs a protected position.	
Jan /	Recommended Species
Feb /	*Romulea bulbocodium clusiana*
Mar flowering	*R. flava*
Apr flowering	*R. sabulosa*
May flowering	
Jun /	
July /	
Aug /	
Sept plant	
Oct plant	
Nov /	
Dec /	

Rosa

ROSE SPECIES AND HYBRIDS

FEATURES

The climbing roses rank among the most popular of all climbing plants. There are climbing roses suitable for walls and fences of all sizes, and vigorous ramblers and climbers that can be allowed to grow up through large mature trees and evergreen conifers. Many climbers and ramblers are ideal for pergolas, arches, arbors, and obelisks.

Modern hybrid climbers such as "Alchemist" are the most popular. They are recurrent flowering, producing several flushes of flowers in summer, and there is a large range to choose from in a wide selection of colors. Older cultivars may have only one flush of blooms.

Ramblers, both species and cultivars, are generally more vigorous than modern hybrid climbers and need plenty of space. Many have only one main flush of flowers in the summer, such as the popular old "Albertine" and "Wedding Day."

Species roses are also well worth considering, including *Rosa banksiae*, the double white Banksian rose. This climber has double, sweetly scented, white flowers in late spring and is one of the earliest roses to flower. Also recommended is the yellow Banksian rose, *R. b.* "Lutea," with double yellow flowers. The species itself is very tall, up to 40ft, but the yellow cultivar is much shorter, about 20ft. The Banksian roses are hardy to 23°F and are best grown on a warm sunny sheltered wall or fence.

CONDITIONS

ASPECT	Full sun is required for best flowering.
SITE	Roses like a fertile, deep, moisture-retentive, yet well-drained soil. Dig in plenty of bulky organic matter before planting to provide humus, which helps to retain moisture during dry periods. Keep roses well mulched with bulky organic matter.

GROWING METHOD

PROPAGATION	It is not really feasible for home gardeners to propagate many of the climbing roses. Commercially they are propagated by budding onto suitable rootstocks. You could try ramblers and species roses from hardwood cuttings in winter. Root them in a cold frame.
WATERING	Keep roses well watered if the soil dries. They dislike very dry or drought conditions.

AT A GLANCE	
Summer-flowering scramblers, with flowers in a wide range of colors, many being fragrant. Most roses are hardy to 5°F (zone 7).	
Jan planting	**Companion Plants**
Feb planting	Summer-flowering clematis are
Mar planting	particularly good companions. You
Apr planting	can allow the two to intertwine.
May flowering	
Jun flowering	
July flowering	
Aug flowering	
Sep flowering	
Oct planting	
Nov planting	
Dec planting	

FEEDING | You could use a proprietary rose fertilizer. Alternatively apply blood, fish, and bone fertilizer. Apply in the spring as growth is starting, and after the first flush of flowers.

PROBLEMS | Roses have more than their fair share of problems: aphids, rose black spot, rose powdery mildew and rose rust, to name some of the most troublesome. Wherever possible buy disease-resistant roses. Carry out preventative spraying to control diseases, starting as soon as new foliage appears. Use a combined rose spray.

FLOWERING/FOLIAGE

FLOWERS | May be single, semi-double, or fully double, fragrant or without scent. Flowering may be a single flush in the summer, or repeat-flowering throughout summer.

FOLIAGE | The leaves are made up of leaflets in varying shades of green, often shiny, but generally not particularly attractive.

PRUNING

REQUIREMENTS | Roses flower on current or previous year's shoots, so prune annually. Wherever possible train stems horizontally as they then produce better distributed flowers, instead of blooming only at the top. Of course, this method of training is not possible when growing on pergola pillars and obelisks. There are hybrid climbing roses that are suitable for these types of supports, or spiral training could be used to give you blooms all the way up the support. Ramblers flower best on stems produced in the previous year, but will also flower on older ones. Prune after flowering by cutting out some of the oldest flowered stems to ground level. Then space out and tie in the remaining stems. For modern hybrid climbers train a main framework of stems to the support. This produces side shoots that in turn produce flowers. Prune in late winter or early spring by cutting back side shoots to two or three buds from the main stems. Cut back the oldest stems once they start producing fewer flowers.

Rosa gallica
ROSA GALLICA VAR. OFFICINALIS

FEATURES

A prickly shrub that can reach a height of 4ft, the apothecary's rose, *Rosa gallica*, is a dense bush that spreads by suckers, often forming impenetrable thickets. The fragrant, semi-double, deep pink-red flowers appear in summer, followed in fall by dull red hips. Leaves are elliptical in shape and leathery.

CONDITIONS

ASPECT From south-east Europe and western Asia, apothecary's rose is best grown in full sun. An open site with good air movement helps reduce fungal diseases.

SITE Grows in a wide range of soil types but drainage must be good, especially in areas of high summer rainfall. Deep, friable clay-loam with plenty of well-rotted organic matter is best.

GROWING METHOD

SOWING Can be grown from seed collected from ripe hips in fall but sown in spring, or from suckers detached from the parent plant in late winter. Each sucker must have its own roots; replant at once. Take hardwood cuttings about 8in long in late fall; insert them into potting compost or vacant garden beds and keep moist. Rooted cuttings can be potted up or planted into the garden a year later.

FEEDING Established plants can survive on rain alone in areas of regular rainfall but the plant will look and flower better if given an occasional deep soaking during dry spells in summer. Give a balanced general rose fertilizer in spring. Mulch in spring with well-rotted organic matter to improve the soil, feed the plant and conserve moisture.

PROBLEMS Suffers from the usual rose problems: aphids, caterpillars, scale insects, and fungus diseases, especially in humid conditions. Combined insecticide/fungicide, usually sold as "rose spray," controls aphids, caterpillars, and fungus diseases, and may also include a foliar feed.

PRUNING Does not need annual pruning and can be left alone for years. To rejuvenate an old bush, cut stems to the ground in winter.

HARVESTING

PICKING Hips are harvested in fall when fully ripe; flowers can be picked for immediate use as they appear.

STORAGE Both hips and flowers may be stored for a few days in sealed containers in the

AT A GLANCE		
The apothecary's rose is a prickly shrub, grown for its vivid, highly perfumed flowers and its hips. Hardy to 4°F (zone 7).		
Jan	/	**Parts used**
Feb	plant	Flowers
Mar	plant	Hips
Apr	/	**Uses**
May	/	Culinary
Jun	harvest	Medicinal
July	harvest	Craft
Aug	/	Cosmetic
Sept	harvest	Gardening
Oct	plant harvest	
Nov	plant	
Dec	/	

refrigerator. The petals can be dried for use in pot-pourris, herbal sachets, etc.

FREEZING   Rose hips and flowers are best used fresh.

USES

CULINARY   Rosehips are made into jellies, syrups, and liqueurs (all have a very high proportion of vitamin C). Petals are used to flavor vinegar or are crystallized and eaten as a sweet.

MEDICINAL   Infusions made from the hips and/or petals are said to be good for headaches and a range of other common complaints such as diarrhoea, fever, mouth ulcers, and toothache.

CRAFT   Hips and petals are used in crafts. Dried petals are added to pot-pourris. Attar of roses, an essence extracted from the flowers, is a perfuming agent.

COSMETIC   Petals can be used to perfume creams, etc.

GARDENING   This makes a good large-scale groundcover, barrier planting or hedge.

Rosa hybrids

ROSE

FEATURES

Most people think of roses as shrubs, standards or climbers but there are a number of roses that can be used for groundcover. The "Noatraum" rose, with its bright pink blooms, was introduced within the last few years and is deservedly popular for its long flowering period and disease resistance. There is also "Snow Carpet," with masses of small white blooms, while the excellent Japanese "Nozomi" has pink-white flowers. Look at rose catalogs for others that can be used this way.

CONDITIONS

ASPECT   Must have full sun and good air circulation. and plenty of room to spread in all directions.

SITE   Soil should be well drained and well prepared by the addition of large amounts of organic matter. Add lime to acid soils.

GROWING METHOD

PROPAGATION   Many of these roses strike fairly easily from cuttings of dormant wood taken in the fall. Some roses must be budded on to species understocks.

FEEDING   Apply complete plant food in spring and again in midsummer. Spreading an organic matter mulch round the plant in the spring will help to feed the soil.

PROBLEMS   Roses are vulnerable to attack by a number of garden pests and diseases. Aphids clustering on new growth can simply be hosed off or sprayed with pyrethrum. Black spot and powdery mildew can be troublesome in humid weather, you may have to resort to chemical spraying of the plants. Many groundcover roses have good resistance to these diseases.

FLOWERING

SEASON   A succession of blooms appear from summer to fall, depending on the variety.

CUTTING   Usually short stemmed, groundcover roses add to most cut flower displays.

PRUNING

GENERAL   Cut off spent flower stems throughout the season. The main rose pruning is done in early spring. At other times remove any dead, diseased or damaged wood.

AT A GLANCE		
Some roses make excellent flowering groundcover, adding an extra layer of interest. Hardy to 0°F (zone 7).		
Jan	/	**Recommended Varieties**
Feb	/	*Rosa* "Grouse"
Mar	/	"Hertfordshire"
April	foliage	"Magic Carpet"
May	foliage	"Max Graf"
June	flowering	"Nozomi"
July	flowering	"Raubritter"
Aug	foliage	"Snow Carpet"
Sept	foliage	"Suffolk"
Oct	foliage	
Nov	/	
Dec	/	

Rosa rugosa

ROSE

FEATURES

Flowering hedges are making a comeback, and one of the best involves Rosa rugosa. It grows about 7ft high and wide, and makes a good, tough barrier. Extremely hardy, bushy, and tolerant of coastal winds and sandy soils (it dislikes clay instead), this rose scores high marks. It also has a long purple-rose flowering season from early summer, large cherry-red hips, and even fall color. Two excellent forms of this useful species are "Alba," with single white flowers against dark green leaves, and the crimson-wine "Rubra." The cross between *R. rugosa* and *R. wichurana* led to "Max Graf," which is quite different and makes a good weed-obscuring groundcover, about 2ft high. It does not make a hedge. Other crosses involving *R. rugosa* have produced many excellent shrub roses, especially the white "Blanc Double de Coubert," which grows 6ft high.

CONDITIONS

ASPECT   Provide full sun, or at the very least dappled shade. The sunnier the garden, the better.

SITE   Famed for growing in sandy soils, average garden conditions are fine. So too are beds with deep rich soil and plenty of humus, though sound drainage is always required. The plant does not like heavy clay soils, and these will need to be broken up and lightened so that water drains away more freely.

GROWING METHOD

PROPAGATION   In the fall take 8in long hardwood cuttings, and set in trenches with the top quarter showing above soil level. They make roots slowly and will be ready to plant out the following fall.

SPACING   Set *R. rugosa* about 4ft apart.

FEEDING   Feeding twice a summer with a proprietary rose feed will be fine. Also, mulch with well-rotted organic matter.

PROBLEMS   No serious problems that should alarm potential growers.

FLOWERING

SEASON   An excellent extended season, with long, pointed buds. Though the flowers can be short-lived in hot weather, there is no let-up in the development of more buds.

PRUNING

GENERAL   Not necessary beyond giving a light trim in February to promote plenty of fresh new shoots. At the same time remove old, unproductive stems or those that have died.

AT A GLANCE		
Rosa rugosa is an excellent multi-purpose shrub, giving great flowers and scent through summer. Hardy to −18°C (0°F).		
Jan	/	**Companion Plants**
Feb	/	Clematis
Mar	/	Crocus
April	foliage	Cyclamen
May	foliage	Erythronium
June	flowering	Ipomoea
July	flowering	Primrose
Aug	flowering	Winter jasmine
Sept	flowering	
Oct	flowering	
Nov	/	
Dec	/	

Rosemary
ROSMARINUS OFFICINALIS

FEATURES

A perennial, evergreen, woody shrub, rosemary has thin, needle-like leaves, which are glossy green above and are whitish to gray-green and hairy below. They have a fragrance reminiscent of pine needles. In spring, small-lobed flowers appear among the leaves. They are pale blue to pinkish or white, depending on the variety. There are several varieties of rosemary, ranging in habit from the upright (*R. officinalis*) to the dwarf (*R. officinalis* "Nana") and the prostrate (*R. officinalis* "Prostratus"). Among the many very popular varieties are "Miss Jessop's Upright" (which is very good for hedges) and pink rosemary (*R. officinalis* "Roseus"). Rosemary bushes can be between 20in and 6ft 6in in height, depending on variety. This is a good herb to grow in containers, and it also grows well in seaside positions where not much else will grow, as it will withstand salt.

CONDITIONS

ASPECT   Rosemary likes a sunny, sheltered and reasonably dry position. Although hardy in most areas, protection is advised in severe weather and in colder areas, particularly for young plants.

SITE   Rosemary needs to be grown in a well-drained soil in order to lessen the risk of root rot, and the plant is more fragrant when it is grown in alkaline soils.

GROWING METHOD

SOWING   Propagate mainly from cuttings and layering. Seeds are not often used because they have long germination times and tend not to come true to type. Take 4in long cuttings in late spring or early fall, trim off the upper and lower leaves and place the cuttings in small pots containing a moist mixture of two-thirds coarse sand and one-third compost. Cover with a plastic dome and set aside in a semi-shaded position until roots and new leaves form. Or layer by scarifying the underside of a lower branch and firmly securing it to the soil with a wire peg. Cover with sand and keep moist until roots form. Cut off and replant.

FEEDING   Prefers soil to be on the drier side; give average garden watering. Mulch in spring and also give an application of a balanced general fertilizer at this time.

PROBLEMS   No particular problems.

PRUNING   Prune if compact bushes are desired. Trim after flowering to prevent plants becoming straggly. Do not cut back in the fall or when there is a danger of frosts as the plants could be damaged.

AT A GLANCE		
Evergreen shrub with fragrant leaves and flowers, much used in cooking and crafts. Hardiness varies: 4 to 23˚F (zones 7–9).		
Jan	harvest	**Parts used**
Feb	harvest	Leaves
Mar	plant harvest	Flowers
Apr	plant harvest	**Uses**
May	plant harvest	Culinary
Jun	plant harvest	Medicinal
July	plant harvest	Craft
Aug	plant harvest	Cosmetic
Sept	harvest	Gardening
Oct	harvest	
Nov	harvest	
Dec	harvest	

HARVESTING

PICKING
Fresh leaves or sprigs 2–4in long can be picked as required. Pick flowers in spring.

STORAGE
Dry sprigs in a cool, dry place, strip leaves from the stems and store in airtight jars.

FREEZING
Store sprigs in plastic bags and freeze for up to 6 months. To use, crumble before they thaw.

USES

CULINARY
Fresh, dried, or frozen leaves are used in cooking, marinades, and salad dressings. Fresh leaves are used in vinegars, oils, teas, and butters. Fresh flowers are good in salads or as decorations for puddings and desserts.

MEDICINAL
Rosemary has many uses, including treatment for headaches, digestive problems, and poor circulation. It has anti-bacterial and anti-fungal properties, and can also be used as an insect repellant. Caution: do not use in large doses.

CRAFT
It is used in pot-pourris and herb wreaths.

COSMETIC
Rosemary hair rinses help control greasy hair.

Rossioglossum

CLOWN ORCHID

FEATURES

This incredibly showy and fascinating orchid was originally part of the *Odontoglossum* family. Probably the best known of the species is *R. grande*, commonly known as the clown orchid. A little man in a colorful yellow and red outfit can be seen at the top of the lip. A few hybrids have been made between some of the species such as *R. Jakob* Jenny (*grande* x *insleayi*) and *R. Rawdon* Jester (*grande* x *williamsianum*). The pseudobulbs are oval-shaped and a handsome green with a pair of large, broad leaves in the same color. The flowers tend to be very long lasting with quite a waxy texture and reaching an amazing 6in across from petal tip to petal tip.

CONDITIONS

CLIMATE   Traditionally a popular orchid to grow in a cool greenhouse or conservatory, with a minimum temperature of 50°F throughout the year.

ASPECT   The leaves prefer a shady position so protect from bright sun. Dappled shade is preferred; a north facing aspect in summer is ideal and south facing in winter.

POTTING MIX   A fairly open mix is ideal, bark based with some peat or similar mixed in.

GROWING METHOD

PROPAGATION   Rossioglossums are quite slow to grow and take many years to reach an easily dividable plant. Therefore, leave the plant until the pot is full before moving to a larger size and only split when necessary and possible.

WATERING   Likes a well-defined resting period in winter, which goes on well into spring. Water regularly from the point when the new growth starts increasing over the growing season and decrease to a stop in the fall. Allow compost to dry out a little in winter.

FEEDING   Use a half strength general plant food every two or three waterings in the growing season.

PROBLEMS   If a dry rest period is not observed then the plant can suffer from over-watering in the winter which can lead to root rot. Avoid spraying the foliage in winter as this can lead to spotting which can cause fungal infection.

FLOWERING SEASON

R. grande traditionally flowers in fall but some hybrids, such as *R. Rawdon* Jester will bloom easily in late spring and summer.

AT A GLANCE		
Good for beginners in the home or conservatory. Flowers reach 6in across and spike 12in above foliage.		
Jan	rest	Recommended Varieties
Feb	rest	*R. grande*
Mar	rest	*R. insleayi*
Apr	rest	*R. williamsianum*
May	flowering, water and feed	*R. Jakob*
Jun	flowering, water and feed	"Jenny"
July	water and feed	*R. Rawdon*
Aug	water and feed	"Jester"
Sept	flowering, water and feed	(all yellow/brown)
Oct	flowering, rest	
Nov	rest	
Dec	rest	

Rubus henryi

RUBUS

FEATURES

The genus *Rubus* is huge, containing over 250 species, some of which are well-known edible fruits such as blackberries and raspberries. There are also numerous ornamental species and one of the most decorative is *R. henryi* var. *bambusarum*. This handsome evergreen climber from China has long spiny stems with white hairs. It is grown for these attractive stems, as well as for the foliage and summer flowers. It is a vigorous plant, growing 20ft tall, and is a good subject for a shrub border or woodland garden. In these situations it can be grown either as a climber, perhaps over a large shrub, up a mature tree, or on an obelisk or as a groundcover plant.

CONDITIONS

ASPECT   Suitable for sun or partial shade.
SITE   *R. h.* var. *bambusarum* will grow in any soil that is well drained and reasonably fertile.

GROWING METHOD

PROPAGATION   Take semi-ripe cuttings in summer. You can also use semi-ripe leaf-bud cuttings. Layer stems in the spring. Groundcover plants may self-layer.
WATERING   It likes moist conditions so do not allow the plant to dry out during prolonged dry spells in summer.
FEEDING   Apply a slow-release fertilizer in the spring, such as the organic blood, fish, and bone.

PROBLEMS   Not generally troubled by pests or diseases.

FLOWERING/FOLIAGE

FLOWERS   Clusters of small bowl-shaped pink flowers are followed by shiny black berries.
FOLIAGE   The shiny deep green three-lobed leaves with white undersides are very attractive.

PRUNING

REQUIREMENTS   Pruning aims to ensure plenty of new stems, so in late winter or early spring each year cut some of the stems that produced flowers the previous year down to ground level. New shoots will then appear from the base of the plant in the spring.

MANY OF THE DECORATIVE members of the Rubus genus are grown for their glossy and pleasantly-shaped leaves.

AT A GLANCE		
R.h. var. *bambusarum* is a handsome blackberry relation with spiny stems and pink summer flowers. Hardy to 5°F (zone 7).		
Jan	/	**Companion Plants**
Feb	planting	This climber looks good with shrubs,
Mar	planting	particularly woodland-garden kinds.
Apr	planting	
May	/	
Jun	flowering	
July	flowering	
Aug	flowering	
Sep	/	
Oct	/	
Nov	/	
Dec	/	

Rudbeckia

CONEFLOWER

FEATURES

The coneflower rewards a bright, sunny position with a bold display of daisy-like flowers. The genus consists of annuals, biennials, and perennials, with some traditional garden favorites. R. fulgida, Black-eyed Susan, grows 36 x 18in, producing yellow-orange flowers at the end of summer, into the fall. "Goldsturm" has bigger flowers but only grows two-thirds as tall. For a powerful, vigorous display at the back of the border, try *R. lacinata*. It has thin, wiry stems, lemon-yellow flowers, and puts on a mid-summer to mid-fall display that can reach 8ft high, while its spread is relatively contained at just 3ft.

CONDITIONS

ASPECT   A bright, open sunny position is essential. Avoid shady areas. The plant's natural habitat is North American meadows and big, open woods.

SITE   Do not plant in over-dry, Mediterranean-style yards. The soil must remain heavy and lightly damp. In the wild *R. fulgida* grows in marshy valleys.

GROWING METHOD

PROPAGATION   Either divide in the spring or fall, or sow seeds in the spring in a cold frame. Do not let the new, young plants dry out.

FEEDING   Fertility must be quite high. Dig large quantities of well-rotted manure and compost into poor soil.

PROBLEMS   Slugs can be a major problem. Keep watch, and pick them off by hand or treat chemically. A potentially good flowering display can be quickly ruined if they take control.

FLOWERING

SEASON   A long flowering season from the summer to late fall.

CUTTING   Rudbeckia make good cut flowers, adding height and color to any arrangement. They are especially useful, having a dark-colored central disk (black, brown, or green) in the center of the flower.

AFTER FLOWERING

REQUIREMENTS   Cut back to the ground, although some stems can be left to provide interesting shapes over winter, especially when frosted.

THE DAISY-LIKE FLOWER shape of the coneflower, a bright color, and a central dark marking. It looks best in a bold group display.

AT A GLANCE		
A near 20-species genus with annuals, biennials, and perennials, often with striking, yellowish flowers. Hardy to 0°F (zones 6–7).		
Jan	/	Recommended Varieties
Feb	/	"Goldquelle"
Mar	sow	"Herbstonne"
Apr	divide	*Rudbeckia fulgida* var. *deamii*
May	transplant	*R. f.* var. *sullivantii*
Jun	/	"Goldsturm"
July	flowering	*R. laciniata*
Aug	flowering	*R. maxima*
Sept	flowering	
Oct	flowering	
Nov	divide	
Dec	/	

S

Sabal palmetto

BLUE PALMETTO, CABBAGE PALMETTO

FEATURES

A native of southern USA (it is the state tree of both Florida and South Carolina), this large palm has a fat, rough-textured trunk and tends to dominate the landscape in the wild. The feathery, fan-shaped leaves are deep green and deeply divided. They attain a length of 6ft and are carried in a somewhat rounded crown. The mature height of this palm is 100ft, with a spread of up to 22ft. As a young plant it makes a good houseplant and is also recommended for the cool conservatory or glasshouse. It likes to be placed out of doors in a bright spot for the summer.

CONDITIONS

ASPECT   Provide bright light but do not subject it to direct sun. Provide high humidity in summer. Outdoors place in a sheltered position.
SITE   In containers grow this palm in soil-based potting compost.

GROWING METHOD

PROPAGATION   Sow seeds as soon as available and germinate them at a temperature of 66–75°F.
WATERING   Moderate watering in growing season from late spring to late summer, then water sparingly.
FEEDING   Apply a balanced liquid fertilizer monthly during the growing season from late spring to late summer.

PROBLEMS   Under glass may be attacked by scale insects and red spider mites.

FOLIAGE/FLOWERING

FOLIAGE   Being evergreen this palm looks good all year round, but it is especially attractive during the spring and summer.
FLOWERS   Long trusses of cream flowers are produced in summer, followed by small black fruits.

GENERAL CARE

REQUIREMENTS   Remove dead fronds when necessary by cutting them off close to the trunk.

THE DEAD FRONDS of this S. palmetto *have been trimmed to allow neat, healthy growth to appear at the top of the plant.*

AT A GLANCE		
The dark green, deeply divided, fan-shaped leaves are feathery. Provide a minimum temperature of 41–45°F (zone 11).		
Jan	/	**Companion Plants**
Feb	/	Looks good with other cool-
Mar	planting	growing palms and is an ideal
Apr	planting	subject for combining with brightly
May	foliage	colored summer bedding plants
Jun	flowering	outdoors. Under glass could
July	flowering	combine with bougainvillea.
Aug	flowering	
Sep	/	
Oct	/	
Nov	/	
Dec	/	

Sacred Bamboo

NANDINA DOMESTICA

FEATURES

Reminiscent of bamboo, nandina is a slender-stemmed evergreen that slowly spreads by suckers to make a fascinating focal point. Grown for its brightly hued, cream, orange, pink, and red leaves, its "airy" shoots create an impression of "lightness". Nandina, much prized for Japanese-style gardens, may also be sited elsewhere to contrast effectively with darker-toned and heavier-textured plants. Small, white flowers from June to July are followed by attractive, red berries, which linger into fall. Makes a handsome bush to 4ft high by 3ft across.

CONDITIONS

ASPECT   Thriving in full sun or semi-shade, it needs shielding from cold winds, which can blacken leaves. Ideally, plant it at the foot of a south- or west-facing wall.

SOIL   Nandina prefers well-drained and humus rich, sandy loam. Augment chalk or heavy clay soils with bulky organic materials a month or two before planting.

GROWING METHOD

FEEDING   Encourage luxuriant foliage and large clusters of fruit by working bone meal into the root area in spring and the fall. Once established, nandina is fairly drought resistant. Mulch with well-rotted garden compost, manure, shredded bark, or cocoa shell in spring to insulate roots from moisture-extracting sunshine.

PROPAGATION   In the fall, extract seeds from ripe berries, sow in pots and raise in a garden frame. Take semi-ripe cuttings from mid- to late summer. Use a spade to split up large clumps in mid-spring.

PROBLEMS   Severe winter weather may kill shoots to ground level and new growth from roots may be slow in appearing.

PRUNING

GENERAL   No regular cutting back is necessary. Rejuvenate old clumps in May by removing a third of the older stems at ground level.

NANDINA'S FALL BOUNTY of bright red berries follows a summer display of white flowers. Leaves are greenish but tinted cream, pink, orange, and red. Unlike true bamboo, the sacred version is light, airy, and not invasive and is ideal for colonising a restricted space.

AT A GLANCE	
Bamboo-like evergreen whose cream-, orange-, and pink-tinted leaves complement white flowers. Hardy to 14°F (zone 8).	
Jan /	**Recommended Varieties**
Feb /	"Firepower"
Mar	"Nana Purpurea"
Apr plant	"Richmond"
May prune	
June plant, flower	
July plant, flower	
Aug plant, flower	
Sept plant	
Oct /	
Nov /	
Dec /	

Sage
SALVIA

FEATURES

Sage is an evergreen sub-shrub growing to about 30in. The long, oval, gray-green leaves, velvety in texture, have a slightly bitter, camphor-like taste, while the flowers, borne on spikes in spring, are colored from pink to red, purple, blue, or white, depending on variety. There are many varieties of this beautiful herb. The most common hardy edible types are common or garden sage (*S. officinalis*), purple sage (*S. o.* "Purpurascens"), and golden or variegated sage (*S. officinalis* "Icterina"); and the more tender tricolor sage (*S. o.* "Tricolor"), and pineapple sage (*S. elegans*, syn. *S. rutilans*) are also popular. Sage needs to be replaced every four years or so as the plant becomes woody. Many ornamental sages are also grown in gardens.

CONDITIONS

ASPECT — Most varieties prefer a sunny, sheltered, well-drained position.

SITE — Garden beds in which sage is to be grown should have a rich, non-clayish soil. Add lime to acid soils, followed by plenty of organic matter. Good drainage is absolutely essential for sage plants, and so you may find it necessary to raise the beds to at least 8in above the surrounding level.

GROWING METHOD

SOWING — Common sage can be grown from seed. Germination takes 2–3 weeks. Plant out when all danger of frost is passed, spacing plants 18–24in apart. Cuttings 4in long can be taken in spring or fall. Remove the upper and lower leaves and plant the cuttings in small pots containing a mix of two-thirds coarse sand to one-third compost. Water, then cover plants with a plastic bag to create a mini-greenhouse. Plant out when the cutting has developed roots and new leaves. Sage may also be layered; scarify the lower side of a branch and peg it into the soil to take root.

FEEDING — Give a deep soaking once a week in dry spells. Apply a balanced general fertilizer in spring.

PROBLEMS — Spider mites can be a problem and will need to be sprayed with an insecticide. If the plant suddenly flops over for no apparent reason this is probably due to bacterial wilt affecting the vascular system. Remove affected plants. Root rot can be avoided by providing good drainage.

PRUNING — Prune in spring to keep a compact, bushy shape. Cut off flowerheads as the flowers fade to stop plants from setting seed.

AT A GLANCE		
Evergreen shrub with silver-gray leaves used in the kitchen for stuffing, herb teas, etc. Hardiness varies: 4 to 23°F (zones 7–9).		
Jan	/	Parts used
Feb	/	Leaves
Mar	plant harvest	Flowers
Apr	plant harvest	Uses
May	plant harvest	Culinary
Jun	plant harvest	Medicinal
July	harvest	Cosmetic
Aug	harvest	Craft
Sept	plant harvest	Gardening
Oct	harvest	
Nov	/	
Dec	/	

HARVESTING

PICKING   Leaves or flowers can be picked at any time as required. For drying purposes, harvest leaves before flowering begins.

STORAGE   Dry leaves on racks in a cool, airy place and then store them in airtight jars.

FREEZING   Leaves can be chopped, packed in freezer bags and then frozen for up to 6 months.

USES

CULINARY   Fresh or dried leaves are used extensively as a flavoring in stuffings, marinades, and cooking. The individual fruity flavour of pineapple sage complements citrus fruits and the edible flowers look decorative in salads or as a garnish. Sage leaves of many varieties can be used in herbal teas, vinegars, and herb butters.

MEDICINAL   Sage has long been highly regarded for its healing properties. Uses include treating colds, sore throats, and mouth ulcers. Caution: do not take in large quantities or for extended periods.

COSMETIC   Sage hair rinses, used regularly, will darken gray hair.

CRAFT   Dried leaves, especially those of purple sage can be added to pot-pourri.

GARDENING   It is said that sage can be planted with cabbages to deter cabbage white butterflies.

Salpiglossis
SALPIGLOSSIS

FEATURES

Salpiglossis blooms are trumpet-shaped and come in a range of colors, all with patterned veins. They must have shelter and warmth to do well, so for guaranteed success use them in containers on sunny patios or in south-facing beds protected from the wind. Choose mixed colors or try dark brown "Chocolate Pot," striking "Kew Blue" or even the blue/yellow mix Chili Blue." Half-hardy, growing up to 2ft. Available as young plants.

CONDITIONS

ASPECT   Must be in full sun and protected from wind.

SITE   Drainage must be good or plants will rot—prepare soil by digging in plenty of rotted manure or compost well before planting. Use multipurpose compost in containers and make sure there is a 2in layer of gravel in the base to guarantee good drainage. Support plants with twigs or short canes as they get taller and begin to flower.

GROWING METHOD

SOWING   Sow in a $3^1/_2$in pot in February/March and just cover the fine seed. Keep at a temperature of 75°F in a light place, and when seedlings are large enough transplant to cell trays or $3^1/_2$in pots. Grow on and then harden off in late May before planting after frosts in early June. Plants are quite brittle so handle carefully.

FEEDING   Little additional feeding should be needed for plants in bedding displays, but containers can be liquid-fed every two weeks if slow-release fertilizer is not used; otherwise just water well.

PROBLEMS   The flowers are very prone to bruising and damage by wind and heavy rain, so pick off casualties after unsettled spells to avoid an attack by gray mold which can cause rotting.

FLOWERING

SEASON   Flowers appear throughout the summer.

CUTTING   Weak-stemmed as a cut flower.

AFTER FLOWERING

GENERAL   Pull up after fall frosts and compost.

PETAL VEINING in salpiglossis is intricate and gives rise to the common name of painted tongue. Many different colors are available.

AT A GLANCE		
Half-hardy annual grown for its exotic flowers but needing a sheltered spot in the yard. Frost hardy to 32°F (zone 10).		
Jan	/	Recommended Varieties
Feb	sow	*Salpiglossis sinuata*
Mar	transplant/sow	"Batik"
Apr	grow on	"Bolero"
May	harden off/plant	"Carnival"
Jun	flowering	"Casino"
July	flowering	"Chili Blue"
Aug	flowering	"Chocolate Pot"
Sept	flowering	"Chocolate Royale"
Oct	/	"Festival Mixed"
Nov	/	"Flamenco Mixed"
Dec	/	"Kew Blue"
		"Triumph Mixed"

Salvia
SCARLET SAGE

FEATURES

Salvia splendens or scarlet sage is used in bold groups in bedding and is also a useful container plant. Most varieties grow to 1ft with similar spread, but giants like "Rambo" with red flowers reach 2ft. Flowers are long and tubular, in spikes, and colors other than the typical vibrant red include pink, mauve, salmon, pastel shades, and even bicolors such as "Salsa Bicolor Mixed," with white tipped blooms. Choose single colors or mixtures. Grown as a half-hardy annual but is in fact a perennial plant. Several varieties are usually available as young plants by mail order.

CONDITIONS

ASPECT	Plant salvias in a warm spot in full sun.
SITE	Tolerates a wide range of soils but drainage must be very good or plants may rot. Mix in well-rotted compost or manure before planting and use multipurpose compost for filling patio pots and windowboxes. Make sure plastic containers have drainage holes, and drill some if necessary, then put in 2in of gravel.

GROWING METHOD

SOWING	February/March is the time to sow salvias, using 3$^{1}/_{2}$in pots of multipurpose compost. Lightly cover seeds and keep in a bright spot such as a windowsill at 64°F; expect seedlings in 2–3 weeks. Transplant into cell trays or 4in pots, grow on, harden off in late May before planting 6–12in apart.

FEEDING	Liquid feed plants in beds monthly. Mix slow-release fertilizer with compost at planting.
PROBLEMS	Heavy wet soils can cause root rots, and slugs and snails will eat leaves of young plants in damp and wet spells. Use slug pellets.

FLOWERING

SEASON	Cut faded spikes right back and plants will often produce a succession of flowers right into the late summer months.
CUTTING	Not suitable.

AFTER FLOWERING

GENERAL	Dig out when over and compost.

IF BRIGHT RED hurts your eyes, try one of the newer mixed salvia varieties containing more subtle shades of mauve, pink, and salmon.

AT A GLANCE		
A half-hardy annual grown for its often bright flowers which are useful for bedding and pots. Frost hardy to 32°F (zone 10).		
Jan	/	**Recommended Varieties**
Feb	sow	*Salvia splendens*
Mar	sow/transplant	"Blaze of Fire"
Apr	grow on	"Firecracker"
May	harden off/plant	"Orange Zest"
Jun	flowering	"Phoenix Mixed"
July	flowering	"Phoenix Purple"
Aug	flowering	"Rambo"
Sept	flowering	"Red Arrow"
Oct	/	"Scarlet King"
Nov	/	"Scarlet O'Hara"
Dec	/	"Sizzler Burgundy"

Saponaria

SOAPWORT

FEATURES

Saponaria includes plants for the border and wild garden, and for rock gardens. *S. officinalis* is the one for the former, making a brightly colored invader—the form "Rubra Plena" spreads more than most. *S.* "Bressingham" provides good cover for a rock garden. It grows 3in high, spreading 12in wide, and has gorgeous, dark pink flowers. It is sometimes called "Bressingham Hybrid." The common name arises because the leaves of *S. officinalis* can be used as a kind of soap.

CONDITIONS

ASPECT   This plant is exclusively for a place in full sun. Do not try to grow it anywhere else.

SITE   The soil needs to be reasonably fertile, but the main requirement is excellent drainage and plenty of added grit.

GROWING METHOD

PROPAGATION   You can either take cuttings in the first part of summer, or increase your stock and cover by sowing seed in the spring or the fall. Note that each plant has a good spread though. You are unlikely to need many cuttings.

FEEDING   Do not attempt to over-feed, which is counter- productive. Average fertility is fine.

PROBLEMS   The border plants can be shredded in extreme cases by slugs and snails, but because "Bressingham" grows in the rockery, which contains gritty sharp stone in the soil, slugs will keep well away.

FLOWERING

SEASON   A decent summer show of dark pink flowers.

PRUNING

GENERAL   Not necessary.

DELICATE ROCK-GARDEN PLANTS are often grown singly, but S. "Bressingham" is best densely planted as a filler or edging plant.

AT A GLANCE	
S. "Bressingham" gives good cover in the rock garden and produces pink flowers in summer. Hardy to 0°F (zone 7).	
Jan /	**Recommended Varieties**
Feb /	*Saponaria*
Mar /	"Bressingham"
April /	*S. caespitosa*
May foliage	*S. ocymoides*
June flowering	*S. officinalis*
July flowering	"Alba Plena"
Aug foliage	"Rosea Plena"
Sept foliage	"Rubra Plena"
Oct foliage	*S. x olivana*
Nov /	
Dec /	

Savory

SATUREJA

FEATURES

Summer savory (*S. hortensis*) is an annual plant growing to about 1ft and with small, narrow, grayish leaves that turn slightly purple during summer and early fall. The leaves are attached directly to a pinkish stem, and small white flowers appear on the plant in summer. The winter savories, both the upright (*S. montana*) and the prostrate (*S. montana* "Repens") varieties, are perennial forms and have low-growing (they may reach 1ft) or sprawling habits. Glossy, dark green, lanceolate leaves grow from woody stems in summer and white to lilac flowers are grouped in terminal spikes.

CONDITIONS

ASPECT   Both varieties of savory prefer to be grown in full sun. They do not like very cold, wet conditions, and winter savory may require some winter protection.

SITE   Savories like well-drained, alkaline soils. Use a soil testing kit to see how much lime to add to an acid soil. Summer savory prefers a richer soil and is ideal for container growing; winter savory favours a less rich, rather sandy soil.

GROWING METHOD

SOWING   Sow seeds of summer savory directly into their final garden position in spring, after the weather has warmed up. Lightly cover them with soil and keep the soil around them damp. When the seedlings are established, thin them out to 6in apart and give the plants support by mounding soil round the base. Although it can be grown from seed, winter savory is best propagated by cuttings and root division done during either the spring or the fall. Remove the upper and lower leaves of 4–5in long cuttings and insert the trimmed stems into a mixture of two-thirds coarse sand and one-third compost. Water the container and cover it with plastic supported on a wire or bamboo frame to make a mini-greenhouse effect. Plant the seedlings out when new leaves appear and a root structure has developed. Pieces of the divided root of the parent plant can be potted up and grown on and later these can be transplanted into the open garden.

FEEDING   Water these plants regularly although both summer and winter savories are able to tolerate dry conditions. Mulch winter savory in winter and spring and give a dressing of a balanced general fertilizer in spring.

PROBLEMS Savories are not worried by pests or diseases to any great extent with the

AT A GLANCE		
Both summer and winter savory have strong flavors and are used in cooking. Hardy to 4 to14°F (zones 7–8).		
Jan	harvest	**Parts used**
Feb	harvest	Leaves
Mar	plant harvest	**Uses**
Apr	plant harvest	Culinary
May	plant harvest	Medicinal
Jun	harvest	
July	harvest	
Aug	harvest	
Sept	plant harvest	
Oct	harvest	
Nov	harvest	
Dec	harvest	

exception of root rot, which sometimes can affect the winter varieties. Good drainage is essential for these plants.

PRUNING   Winter savory can be pruned in fall after it has finished flowering, but leaving it unpruned will leave top growth to protect the shoots below. It can be pruned in early spring—this will also provide cuttings from which you can grow new plants.

HARVESTING

PICKING   Fresh leaves of both summer and winter varieties can be picked at any time for immediate use or for drying.

STORAGE   Dry leaves in a cool, airy space and then store them in airtight jars.

FREEZING   Pack sprigs in freezer bags and freeze for up to 6 months.

USES

CULINARY   Summer savory has a peppery flavour and is called the "bean herb" as it complements beans and other vegetables. It is also used in herb vinegars and butters. Winter savory is stronger and coarser and has a more piney taste: use it with game meats and terrines. Either summer or winter savory can be used to make savory tea.

MEDICINAL   Summer savory is said to be good for the digestion, for the treatment of stings, and as a stimulant.

Saxifraga x urbium

LONDON PRIDE

FEATURES

Saxifraga x *urbium* is a useful, quick-spreading, attractive plant producing scores of leathery, fresh green leaves. In summer whiteish-pink flowers appear on tall stems. It grows 1ft high and is quite invasive. There are several other first-rate groundcover saxifrages. One is "Bob Hawkins." It forms a carpet of rosettes with variegated leaves, and white flowers tinged green in summer. It grows 8in high, and spreads about 1ft. *S. exarata moschata* makes a cushion with cream or yellow star-like flowers. It is much shorter at 4in, and spreads about 1ft. The form "Cloth of Gold" is even better and has gold colored foliage that stands out.

CONDITIONS

ASPECT — *S.* x *urbium* thrives in the shade, both light and deep. Keep it out of the sun.

SITE — The best soil for *S.* x *urbium* is moist and rich, with plenty of well-rotted organic matter added before planting. An annual spring mulch around the base should boost its performance, with extra rosettes.

GROWING METHOD

PROPAGATION — *S.* x *urbium* can easily be increased by taking off a rosette in the spring, and treating it as a cutting. It will quickly root. You can also sow by seed in the fall.

FEEDING — Given rich, moist soil, this plant should not need extra nutrients. It only requires a boost on poor soil.

PROBLEMS — The biggest problem comes from slugs and snails. Both can devastate the young foliage. Use slug pellets as required, or keep a look out at night by torchlight.

FLOWERING

SEASON — The flowers appear in the summer. They are held high above the foliage.

PRUNING

GENERAL — The only pruning necessary is to slice off unwanted spreading growth to keep London pride in a particular area.

SAXIFRAGA x URBIUM *is an easy plant to grow, and makes a graceful plant to flank a shady pathway through the garden. Leathery leaves with unusual serrated edges contrast beautifully with the airy blooms that are held high above them.*

AT A GLANCE	
Saxifraga x *urbium* is an extremely useful plant growing well in the shade. It is also a prodigious spreader. Hardy to 0°F (zone 7).	
Jan foliage	**Recommended Varieties**
Feb foliage	*Saxifraga*
Mar foliage	"Bob Hawkins"
April foliage	*S. cuneifolia*
May foliage	*S. exarata moschata*
June flowering	*S. marginata*
July flowering	*S. paniculata*
Aug foliage	*S. sempervivum*
Sept foliage	*S.* x *urbium*
Oct foliage	
Nov foliage	
Dec foliage	

Scabiosa

SCABIOUS

FEATURES

Scabious is a vital ingredient of cottage-style, flowery gardens, rock gardens, and mixed borders. From hot, dry, stony sites, mainly in the Mediterranean, it provides pale hues in blue, pink, yellow, or white. The flowers are held above long, thin stems, many attracting bees and butterflies. Heights generally range from 12 to 36in. There are plenty of interesting choices, and top of the list are the dwarf forms "Butterfly Blue" and "Pink Mist," both relatively new and proving extremely popular. On the plus side, they flower for six months; the down side is they are short-lived. Take cuttings to maintain the display.

CONDITIONS

ASPECT   Full sunlight is essential.
SITE   Dryish, free-draining soil is important, so that the roots are not plunged in soaking wet ground over the winter months. The soil must also veer from the neutral toward the slightly alkaline.

GROWING METHOD

PROPAGATION Scabious is not long-lived, and begins to lose its vigor and impact after three years. It is therefore vital to replenish the garden with spring divisions, or to sow fresh, ripe seed in pots in a cold frame to maintain a good supply.
FEEDING   Do not over-feed the soil, which will be counter-productive, producing leaf growth at the expense of flowers. Very poor soils, however, may need some additions of compost in the early spring.
PROBLEMS   Spray at the first sign of powdery mildew.

FLOWERING

SEASON   The flowers appear right through the summer, in some cases not until mid-summer, often into early fall.
CUTTING   Scabious make excellent sprays of cut flowers, and are indispensable for indoor arrangements, either adding to flowery schemes or softening more rigid, structured ones.

AFTER FLOWERING

REQUIREMENTS Cut all spent stems down to the ground.

SCABIOUS ARE VERSATILE PLANTS. They make a wonderful addition to most yards, whether schematic or cottage-style.

AT A GLANCE		
A genus of annuals, biennials, and perennials, providing abundant soft colors. Good for romantic displays. Hardy to 0˚F (zones 6–7).		
Jan	/	**Recommended Varieties**
Feb	/	*Scabiosa caucasica*
Mar	sow	"Chile Black"
Apr	divide	"Clive Greaves"
May	transplant	"Miss Willmott"
Jun	flowering	*S. columbaria* var. *ochroleuca*
July	flowering	*S. lucida*
Aug	flowering	"Pink Mist"
Sept	flowering	
Oct	sow	
Nov	/	
Dec	/	

Schisandra chinensis

SCHISANDRA

FEATURES

The genus contains about two dozen species, some of which are evergreen, others being deciduous. *Schisandra chinensis* is one of the best known and most widely grown. It is a deciduous climber from eastern Asia, specifically India and Burma, and is suitable for growing on shady walls, fences, and trellis screens. It is also an ideal subject for a woodland garden, as the species grows in woodland conditions in the wild. It looks equally at home in a shrub border. This climber can be grown up large mature trees or over large shrubs, but this technique is only recommended for gardens in mild climates. Height 30ft. Female plants produce small red berries, used in Chinese medicine to treat a wide range of ailments.

CONDITIONS

ASPECT   Grows well in either full sun or partial shade.

SITE   Moisture-retentive but well-drained, reasonably fertile soil is recommended.

GROWING METHOD

PROPAGATION   Sow seeds as soon as collected in the fall and germinate them in a cold frame. Take semi-ripe cuttings in summer.

WATERING   Apply water if the soil starts to dry out excessively during the summer.

FEEDING   Apply a slow-release fertilizer, such as the organic blood, fish and bone, in the spring.

PROBLEMS   Schisandra is not troubled by pests or diseases.

FLOWERING/FOLIAGE

FLOWERS   Fragrant cream flowers are carried in clusters. Female plants produce red fruits in pendulous spikes. You will need to grow a male plant close by for fruit production to take place.

FOLIAGE   The elliptical leaves are deep green and shiny.

PRUNING

REQUIREMENTS   No regular pruning needed but cut back any overlong or badly placed shoots to within several buds of the main stems. You can also cut back shoots to keep the plant within its allotted space. Renovation may be needed after some years, cutting the oldest stems down to the ground. This is best done over a few years to prevent too much loss of flower. Pruning is carried out in late winter or early spring.

AT A GLANCE	
A twining climber which has clusters of cream flowers followed by red fruits. Hardy to 5°F (zone 7).	
Jan /	**Companion Plants**
Feb planting	*Schisandra* associates well with
Mar planting	shrubs and woodland-garden plants
Apr planting	
May flowering	
Jun flowering	
July flowering	
Aug flowering	
Sep /	
Oct /	
Nov /	
Dec /	

Schizanthus

POOR MAN'S ORCHID

FEATURES

Also known as butterfly flower, schizanthus is stunning when used in bedding or in large pots and troughs. It has fern-like foliage and brilliantly colored, trumpet-shaped flowers in rich tones of pink, purple, magenta, pastels, or white. The flower throats are intricately patterned. Only the dwarf varieties reaching 8–12in are worth growing outdoors, and they must have shelter from strong winds and the hot midday sun. Schizanthus is a half-hardy annual and very sensitive to even slight frost.

CONDITIONS

ASPECT	Must be sheltered and have full sun.
SITE	Well-drained soil that has been enriched before planting with rotted manure or compost produces strong plants. Peat- or coir-based potting compost guarantees good results when containers are used.

GROWING METHOD

SOWING	Seeds are sown in March at 61˚F in small pots of peat- or coir-based seed compost, and seedlings appear after 1–2 weeks. Transplant to cell trays or 3^{1}/2in pots, grow through spring and plant after hardening off, in early June. Space plants 6–12in apart. Pinch out growing tips when 4in high to make bushy plants.

FEEDING

FEEDING	Liquid feed monthly, and water containers regularly—if slow-release fertilizer is added to the compost extra feeding is not necessary.
PROBLEMS	No special problems.

FLOWERING

SEASON	Flowers reach a peak in mid to late summer and keep coming if faded stems are removed.
CUTTING	Not usually used as a cut flower.

AFTER FLOWERING

GENERAL	The soft leafy plants soon break down when put on the compost heap.

THE EXOTIC APPEAL of schizanthus earns it the common name of poor man's orchid. Each flower has a network of darker veining. The finely divided leaves are the perfect foil for the large heads of flowers.

AT A GLANCE	
A half-hardy annual grown in containers on patios or in south-facing borders for summer flowers. Frost hardy to 32˚F (zone 10).	
Jan /	**Recommended Varieties**
Feb /	*Schizanthus pinnatus*
Mar sow	"Angel Wings Mixed"
Apr transplant	"Disco"
May harden off	"My Lovely"
Jun plant/flowers	"Pierrot"
July flowering	"Star Parade"
Aug flowering	
Sept flowering	
Oct /	
Nov /	
Dec /	

Schizophragma

SCHIZOPHRAGMA

FEATURES

Schizophragma hydrangeoides is a deciduous climber from Japan and Korea. It supports itself by means of aerial roots. It is a lofty climber, growing up to 40ft tall, so it preferably needs a high wall or fence. Alternatively, grow it through a large tree, or use it as groundcover, for example in a woodland garden or shrub border. This climber is grown mainly for its unusual and conspicuous heads of flowers produced in summer, but the foliage is also attractive and covers its support well. There is one other species in the genus, *S. integrifolium*, which is not quite so hardy.

CONDITIONS

ASPECT	A good choice of plant for partial shade but it also grows well in full sun. Must be well sheltered from cold drying winds.
SITE	Well-drained yet moisture-retentive soil that contains plenty of humus.

GROWING METHOD

PROPAGATION	Take semi-ripe cuttings in summer. Sow seeds in fall and stratify over winter.
WATERING	Do not let the plant suffer from lack of moisture, so water well if the soil starts to dry out in summer.
FEEDING	An annual spring application of slow-release fertilizer such as the organic blood, fish, and bone will keep the plant going all season.

PROBLEMS	This climber is not usually troubled by pests or diseases.

FLOWERING/FOLIAGE

FLOWERS	Flat heads of cream flowers with large oval bracts of the same color around the edge.
FOLIAGE	The large, oval, deep green leaves are attractive in season.

PRUNING

REQUIREMENTS	No regular pruning needed. If necessary, after flowering, cut back by about two-thirds any overlong shoots and trim the plant to fit the available space.

SCHIZOPHRAGMA HAS PLENTY to shout about, with rich green leaves in season and ebullient white blooms. In the summer, it is a seething mass of pleasant white flowers, so densely packed that the foliage is hardly visible.

AT A GLANCE	
A self-clinging climber with large flat heads of cream flowers surrounded by conspicuous bracts. Hardy to 5°F (zone 7).	
Jan /	**Recommended Varieties**
Feb /	*Schizophragma*
Mar planting	"Moonlight" has variegated foliage
Apr planting	"Roseum" has rose-tinted bracts
May /	
Jun /	
July flowering	
Aug flowering	
Sep /	
Oct /	
Nov /	
Dec /	

Schizostylis coccinea

KAFFIR LILY

FEATURES

The beautiful, scarlet or pink, gladiolus-like flowers of schizostylis add a very welcome splash of color to fall borders, coming as they do right at the end of the season. The tall, grassy leaves form a clump from which 2–3ft spikes of flowers rise, bearing some 8–10 open, star-shaped blooms. There are several named varieties in a range of pink and red shades: "Major" has large, deep red flowers, "Viscountess Byng" is a delicate pink, and "Tambara" is a rich, rosy pink. "November Cheer" is one of the latest-flowering varieties. Schizostylis is not suitable for cold, exposed yards, but grows and spreads rapidly where conditions suit it.

CONDITIONS

ASPECT   A sheltered spot in full sun or light shade suits this plant.

SITE   Suitable for the middle of the flower border; in cold districts they do well as pot plants in a conservatory or greenhouse. Moisture-retentive, fertile soil is required.

GROWING METHOD

PLANTING   Plant in spring, 2in deep and 12in apart. Pot-grown plants are available for planting in summer and fall. Rhizomes can also be planted in 8in pots of soil-less or John Innes compost in a sheltered position outdoors, being brought into a cool conservatory or greenhouse before the first frosts for flowering inside.

FEEDING   Keep the soil moist at all times. Feed pot-grown plants with high potash liquid fertiliszer every 14 days from early summer until flower buds form.

PROBLEMS   No specific problems are generally experienced.

FLOWERING

SEASON   Flowers from late September into November.

CUTTING   The flower spikes are excellent for cutting, lasting well in water. Pick them when the buds start to show color.

AFTER FLOWERING

REQUIREMENTS Cut down faded flower stems. Protect the crowns with a mulch of chipped bark, straw, or dry leaves over winter. Overcrowded plants can be divided in fall.

AT A GLANCE		
A valuable late fall-flowering plant for the border, with colorful scarlet or pink, gladiolus-like flower spikes.		
Jan	/	**Recommended Varieties**
Feb	/	"Jennifer"
Mar	plant	"Mrs Hegarty"
Apr	plant	"November Cheer"
May	/	"Sunrise"
Jun	/	"Tambara"
July	/	"Viscountess Byng"
Aug	/	
Sept	flowering	
Oct	flowering	
Nov	flowering	
Dec	/	

Schlumbergera

CHRISTMAS CACTUS

FEATURES

This group of easily grown cacti originated from only about six species, and now features almost 200 cultivars of popular flowering pot plants which are more familiar to some as *Zygocactus*. *Schlumbergera* species, or Christmas cacti, are epiphytic and grow on trees or sometimes rocks in their native Brazilian habitat where their flowers are pollinated by humming-birds. Their popularity as pot plants is assured because most of them flower in fall or winter, hence their common name. They have flat, jointed stems arching into small bushes, making them ideal for hanging baskets as well as pots. They come into vigorous growth in summer, and start flowering once the day length is less than 12 hours. Christmas cacti make excellent gifts.

VARIETIES

The silky, irregularly-shaped flowers are mainly in shades of pink or red, but hybrids can be almost pure white to cream, salmon, apricot, cerise, violet, and scarlet. Some display yellow tones that revert to pink as temperatures fall. *S. truncata*, the crab cactus, and *S. x buckleyi*, the Christmas cactus, provide the origins of many of the modern hybrids.

CONDITIONS

ASPECT   Best in partial shade or with morning sun and afternoon shade in a sheltered situation.

SITE   For an established pot plant, John Innes No. 2 with added grit for good drainage is ideal. Repot every three years in the spring. It is too tender to be grown outdoors.

GROWING METHOD

PROPAGATION   These plants are easy to grow from cuttings of stem sections taken in spring or summer.

FEEDING   A light, regular summer feed will promote plenty of new growth and guarantee an excellent display of flowers.

PROBLEMS   Generally easy to grow, these plants will suffer if grown in full sun and may not flower. Overwatering causes root rot and subsequent collapse of stems.

FLOWERING

SEASON   Masses of flowers appear in fall or winter. Once flower buds have formed, do not move the plants until buds begin to open. Flowers in spring if kept at 36–39°F over winter. Gradually increase the temperature in spring.

AT A GLANCE	
High performance pot plants which give a big show of bright color around Christmas. Easily grown. 45°F min (zone 11).	

		Recommended Varieties
Jan	flowering	*Schlumbergera*
Feb	flowering	"Bristol Beauty"
Mar	/	*S. x buckleyi*
Apr	sow	"Gold Charm"
May	flowering	"Joanne"
Jun	transplant	"Lilac Beauty"
July	/	*S. opuntioides*
Aug	/	*S. truncata*
Sept	/	
Oct	/	
Nov	flowering	
Dec	flowering	

Scilla

SQUILL

FEATURES

The most familiar scillas are the dwarf varieties that flower in early spring. They include *Scilla siberica* (Siberian squill), which has clusters of nodding blue bells about 6in high, and *Scilla mischtschenkoana* (*S. tubergeniana*), which has starry, pale blue flowers with a deeper blue stripe on the petals. This species grows only 2–4in high. S. bifolia grows to 2–6in, with a spike of 15 or more star-shaped flowers in blue, pink, or white. Leaves of all these species are elongated and strap shaped. *Scilla peruviana*, the Cuban lily, is quite different—a tall, early summer-flowering bulb with densely packed, conical heads of purple-blue flowers.

CONDITIONS

ASPECT   Tolerates full sun but the flowers will have better, longer lasting color if they are grown in semi-shade.

SITE   Grow in beds and borders, in almost any kind of soil as long as it drains well. Soils enriched with organic matter will give better results.

GROWING METHOD

PLANTING   Plant the bulbs about 2–4in deep and 6–8in apart in late summer or early fall.

FEEDING   Apply a balanced fertiliser after flowering in early summer. Water during dry spells before and during the flowering season.

PROBLEMS   No specific pest or disease problems are known for this plant.

FLOWERING

SEASON   The flower spikes appear during late spring and early summer.

CUTTING   Flowers can be cut successfully for indoor decoration.

AFTER FLOWERING

REQUIREMENTS   Faded flower spikes should be cut off just above ground level. Clumps will usually need to be lifted only every 4–5 years unless they are very congested. Divide crowded clumps in late summer, replanting immediately to avoid drying out of the bulbs.

THE SIBERIAN SQUILL, Scilla siberica, *makes its appearance in early spring. "Atrocoerulea" has particularly rich blue flowers.*

AT A GLANCE		
Mainly dwarf bulbs with starry or bell-shaped blue or white flowers in early spring.		
Jan	/	**Recommended Varieties**
Feb	flowering	*Scilla bifolia*
Mar	flowering	"Rosea"
Apr	flowering	*S. siberica*
May	flowering	"Alba"
Jun	flowering	"Spring Beauty"
July	/	*S. peruviana*
Aug	plant	"Alba"
Sept	plant	*S. peruviana elegans*
Oct	plant	*S. peruviana venusta*
Nov	/	
Dec	/	

Sedum

STONECROP

FEATURES

Most plants in this large and diverse group of succulents are ideal for growing in pots, as well as in the garden where they can be used as edging, in rockeries, or tucked into walls. *Sedum spectabile* is often planted in perennial borders where other succulents may look out of place. *S. sieboldii* has spreading stems and rarely exceeds 6in in height. It has very attractive, almost round, blue-green leaves arranged in threes. It has a variegated green and gold form. *S. spathulifolium* forms a dense, low mat of small rosettes. Its variety "Cape Blanco" has a white bloom on gray-green or purplish rosettes. *S. adolphii* has yellowish green, star-like rosettes with reddish hues at times. Although capable of growing to 1ft, it is more usually 8in in height.

CONDITIONS

ASPECT   Full sun is best for most species, but some will tolerate light shade.

SITE   The soil or potting mix must be very well drained for these plants, and the addition of organic matter for garden plants will give them a decent boost, but only moderate levels are required.

GROWING METHOD

PROPAGATION   Division of plants is best done in the early spring. Cuttings can be taken at any time during the warm summer months.

FEEDING   Slow-release fertilizer or a little pelletted poultry manure given in the spring. In the main, they are best left alone with only a little cutting away of dead stems. Keep a watch at night for attacks by slugs and snails, especially when new spring growth is appearing.

PROBLEMS   These plants are usually trouble-free.

FLOWERING

SEASON   Flowering time depends on species, but many flower in summer to fall. Flowers of several species are attractive to butterflies and bees, such as *S. spectabile* which has large flower heads of mauve-pink, rosy red, or brick red on stems 16–24in high in fall. *S. sieboldii* has starry pink flowers that appear in masses in late summer or fall. *S. adolphii* has starry flowers that are white. "Ruby Glow" is a low-spreader with dark ruby red flowers appearing from mid-summer into the fall, and "Herbstfreude" produces marvellous pink fall flowers that eventually turn copper-red.

AT A GLANCE		
About 400 species, from annuals to shrubs, with a terrific range of shapes and strong colors. Most hardy to 5°F (zone 7).		
Jan	/	**Recommended Varieties**
Feb	/	*Sedum cauticola*
Mar	/	"Herbstfreude"
Apr	transplant	*S. kamtschaticum*
May	/	*S. morganianum*
Jun	/	"Ruby Glow"
July	flowering	*S. rubrotinctum*
Aug	flowering	*S. spectabile*
Sept	flowering	"Brilliant"
Oct	sow	*S. spurium*
Nov	/	"Schorbuser Blut"
Dec	/	"Vera Jameson"

Sedum spectabile

ICE PLANT

FEATURES

One of over 600 species of succulent sedums, spectabile is unusual because it is frequently used in perennial plantings where many succulents look out of place. It has fleshy, soft green leaves on stems that can reach 24in tall. Similar varieties are available with purple and variegated leaves. Since the new growth appears at the base of older stems, dividing plants is easy. The large heads of flowers are a soft mauve-pink in the species, but there are cultivars with colors ranging from bright hot pinks to rosy red, and the brick red of "Herbstfreude" ("Autumn Joy"). The plants flower from late summer into the fall. This is an easy-care plant that accepts a wide range of conditions.

CONDITIONS

ASPECT — Prefers full sun, but tolerates some light shade for part of the day.

SITE — While it can grow in a sandy, well-drained soil, it will tolerate a heavier soil, which gives it an advantage over other sedums.

GROWING METHOD

PROPAGATION — Clumps of plants are easily pulled apart or sliced apart with a spade in the spring or late fall. The divisions are best replanted at approximately 6–8in intervals. Division gives very high success rates. It is also possible to propagate sedum by striking from stem cuttings. Water regularly to establish new young plants.

FEEDING — Slow-release fertilizer can be applied in the spring, as new growth commences.

Avoid overfeeding, because this may result in plenty of sappy leaf growth at the expense of a display of flowers.

PROBLEMS — Plants in containers may rot at the base if overwatered. Vine weevil grubs may devour both bases and roots with devastating effect.

FLOWERING

SEASON — The late, highly rewarding display occurs at the end of summer, running through the fall.

CUTTING — A long-lasting cut flower.

AFTER FLOWERING

REQUIREMENTS — Leave the skeletal flowerheads over winter to provide attractive, burnished tints.

DENSE FLOWERHEADS of Sedum spectabile provide a rich source of nectar, attracting butterflies and other insects.

AT A GLANCE	
S. spectabile is a clump-forming, late season perennial with pink flowers. Many excellent forms. Hardy to 5°F (zone 7).	

		Recommended Varieties
Jan	/	*Sedum alboroseum*
Feb	/	"Mediovariegatum"
Mar	/	*S. cauticola*
Apr	divide	"Herbstfreude" ("Autumn Joy")
May	/	"Ruby Glow"
Jun	/	*S. spectabile*
July	/	"Brilliant"
Aug	flowering	*S. telephium maximum*
Sept	flowering	"Atropurpureum"
Oct	divide	
Nov	sow	
Dec	/	

Selenicereus

SELENICEREUS

FEATURES

There are about 20 species in this group of very long-stemmed climbing epiphytic cactuses. They are native to the forests of the south-western United States, central America, the West Indies, and Colombia, where they live on trees or rocks. *Selenicereus* species have long been cultivated in Mexico for a drug used in the treatment of rheumatism and in Costa Rica for a heart-stimulant drug. They are now being cultivated in Germany and elsewhere for use in medicine, especially in the treatment of heart disorders. These plants have long, angled, or tubular stems bearing small spines on the ribs, but it is their aerial roots that enable them to climb and cling on to their host plants. They will continue to grow upwards and spread as long as they find support.

VARIETIES

S. grandiflorus is the species most often grown. Its flowers have outer petals that are yellow to brown, but the inner flower is pure white. Two other species found in cultivation are *S. pteranthus* and *S. spinulosus*. Both have cream, white, or pale pink flowers. These plants can be grown in the ground, or rooted in large pots set against some strong support.

CONDITIONS

ASPECT   Being epiphytic, these extraordinary cactuses need to be kept out of direct sunlight. They like filtered, dappled light, or as second best, light for half the day, shade for the rest.

SITE   Plants need well-drained compost with added decayed organic matter. An orchid mix would suit them.

GROWING METHOD

PROPAGATION   Plants are easily grown from stem segments taken from spring to early fall. They can also be grown from seed sown in spring.

FEEDING   Apply slow-release fertilizer in spring, or liquid feed occasionally in the growing season.

PROBLEMS   No specific pests or diseases are known, but keep an eye out in the summer for scale insects and mealybugs.

FLOWERING

SEASON   The spectacular, scented flowers do not appear until the plants have become quite mature. They open on summer evenings.

FRUITS   The fleshy fruits are hairy or spiny.

AT A GLANCE	
Strange, thin climbing stems with outstanding scented flowers, from South American forests. 59°F min (zone 11).	
Jan /	Recommended Varieties
Feb /	*Selenicereus grandiflorus*
Mar sow	*S. hamatus*
Apr /	*S. innesii*
May transplant	*S. pteranthus*
Jun flowering	*S. spinulosus*
July flowering	**Companion Plants**
Aug flowering	Epiphyllum
Sept /	Hatiora
Oct sow	Schlumbergera
Nov /	Selenicereus
Dec /	

Senecio
DUSTY MILLER

FEATURES

Grown for its attractive silver-gray foliage, *Senecio cineraria* is often found listed under "cineraria" in seed catalogs. Use in bedding schemes and as a foliage container plant. Plants grow up to 12in tall and wide in summer, but if left outdoors over winter can be twice that if the yellow flowerheads are allowed to develop. Usually grown as a half-hardy annual, senecio is naturally an evergreen, eventually developing a tough woody base.

CONDITIONS

ASPECT	Must have full sun.
SITE	Well-drained soil is needed, but plants do well in light, sandy soils, especially in seaside gardens. Use multipurpose compost in pots.

GROWING METHOD

SOWING	Start plants in February/March at 68°F, by sowing seed in a small pot of compost and just covering. Expect seedlings after 1–2 weeks and keep in good light. Keep compost slightly on the dry side to avoid "damping off." Transplant to cell trays or 3½in pots, grow on, then harden off at the end of April and plant in May, 12in apart.
FEEDING	Planted containers need liquid feed every two weeks, and regular watering. Plants stand dry spells outside but water them if they wilt.

PROBLEMS

If seedlings collapse, give a light watering with a copper-based fungicide.

FLOWERING

SEASON	The silvery leaves are attractive all summer.
CUTTING	Foliage can be used in arrangements.

AFTER FLOWERING

GENERAL	Pull up and compost in fall. In many areas plants will survive the winter if left and produce bigger clumps of leaves and flowers.

A WHITE WOOLLY LAYER covering the otherwise green leaves gives senecio its attractive silvery-gray appearance. Overwintered plants will keep on growing the following season, get larger, and also produce heads of bright yellow flowers.

AT A GLANCE		
Prized for its silver-gray leaves and grown as a foliage bedding plant and for using in containers. Frost hardy to 23°F (zone 9).		
Jan	/	**Recommended Varieties**
Feb	sow	*Senecio cineraria*
Mar	sow	**Fine, divided leaves**
Apr	transplant	"Dwarf Silver"
May	harden off/plant	"Silver Dust"
Jun	leaves	**Rounded leaves**
July	leaves	"Cirrus"
Aug	leaves	
Sept	leaves	
Oct	leaves	
Nov	/	
Dec	/	

Shrubby Bindweed

CONVOLVULUS CNEORUM

FEATURES

A coveted, silvery, silky-leaved evergreen whose pink buds open to flared, white and yellow-eyed, trumpet blooms from June to August, *Convolvulus cneorum* makes a low hummock to 18in high and 2.5ft across and has many uses.

Create a feature all will admire by associating it with *Ceanothus* "Zanzibar," prized for its powder-blue flowers and golden-variegated leaves.

Plant shrubby bindweed to highlight a rock garden or star in a patio pot or deep windowbox.

It is not fully hardy, so consign it to a very sheltered border and cover it in late fall with several layers of bubble plastic draped over an open-topped wigwam of canes. Make sure the plastic does not touch its foliage. If you plant it in a patio pot for summer, move it to a cold greenhouse for winter.

CONDITIONS

ASPECT   Find it a sheltered, sunny spot—it revels against a south- or west-facing wall— where it will not be damaged by chilly winds.

SITE   Not fussy, it thrives in well-drained, acid to neutral soil. If your garden has badly drained clay, work in plenty of grit or sharp sand or set the plant on a raised bed. It is vital that roots are not "treading" water.

GROWING METHOD

FEEDING   Boost growth by working fish, blood, and bone meal or Growmore into the root area in April and July. Add a slow-release fertilizer to patio tub compost. If planting coincides with a droughty spell, foliar feed weekly to help the plant absorb nutrients more quickly. Water copiously after planting to settle soil around the roots. Follow by mulching with a 2 in layer of well-rotted organic material to conserve moisture.

PROPAGATION   Increase shrubby bindweed from semi-ripe "heeled" cuttings of new side shoots from late summer to early fall.

PROBLEMS   If hard frost causes shoot tips to die back, prune them to just above a healthy bud in late spring.

PRUNING

Pruning is unnecessary unless the plant is ageing. Then, in early spring, reduce gaunt and woody stems by half their length, cutting to just above a joint or to new shoots. Keep stumps moist to help them sprout. The best way to do this, apart from sprinkling them with water, is to coat them with a plastic-based anti-transpirant, normally used for helping Christmas trees retain their needles.

AT A GLANCE	
A borderline hardy evergreen with silvery leaves; trumpet-shaped flowers appear from June to August. Hardy to 14°F (zone 8).	
Jan shield from frost	**Recommended Varieties**
Feb shield from frost	(only the species
Mar /	*C. cneorum* is grown)
Apr plant, prune	
May plant	
June flower, plant	
July flower, plant	
Aug plant	
Sept plant	
Oct /	
Nov /	
Dec /	

Shrubby Cinquefoil

POTENTILLA FRUTICOSA

FEATURES

Potentilla fruticosa flowers continuously from late May to September, its small, saucer-shaped blossoms clustering on dense, wiry stems. Carpeting or bushy, to 5ft—taller kinds making colorful hedges—it is hardy and a good choice for cold gardens. Easy, eye-catching varieties are: grayish-green-leaved and white-flowered "Abbotswood"; creamy-yellow "Tilford Cream"; ground-covering "Dart's Golddigger"; chrome-yellow "Goldstar"; salmon-pink "Pretty Polly"; vermilion-flame "Red Ace"; and deep orange to brick-red "Sunset". All are good contenders for patio and terrace tubs and pots or deep, generous windowboxes. Arrange a potted group in several harmonizing colors to flank a doorway or form a focal point at the end of a path.

CONDITIONS

ASPECT   A good choice for borders exposed to cold winds, shrubby cinquefoil flowers profusely in an open, sunny position or very light shade. If possible, plant it facing south or west where trees will not overshadow it.

SITE   A very adaptable plant, it thrives in most soils, from heavy, often waterlogged clay to light, sandy areas that become parched in summer. It does not mind a little lime but on very chalky soils it is liable to become stressed and suffer from chlorosis, when leaves turn creamy or yellowish and die.

GROWING METHOD

FEEDING   Encourage robust flowering shoots by working fish, blood, and bone meal or some other balanced fertilizer into the root area in spring and midsummer. Apply bone meal in the fall to release plant foods in spring. If, in sandy soil, leaf margins turn brown, indicating potash deficiency, rectify by applying sulfate of potash in February and watering it in. Once the plant is established, watering is seldom needed, but soak newly planted shrubs to settle the soil around the roots.

PROPAGATION   Increase plants from cuttings of semi-ripe shoots in midsummer. Root them in a garden frame or on a sunny windowsill.

PROBLEMS   Shoots produce their leaves very late in spring, deceiving us into thinking them dead.

PRUNING

Keep bushes youthful and flowering freely year after year by removing a third of the older shoots in spring. Rejuvenate very old, woody plants at the same time by cutting them back to within 4in of the base. Trim hedges in spring.

AT A GLANCE	
Deciduous, bushy plants, which also make good hedges, they flower from May to September. Hardy to -13°F (zone 5).	

		Recommended Varieties
Jan	/	Carpeting
Feb	/	"Dart's Golddigger"
Mar	plant	"Pretty Polly"
Apr	plant, prune	"Red Ace"
May	plant, flower	"Sunset"
June	plant, flower	Bushy
July	plant, flower	"Goldfinger"
Aug	plant, flower	"Goldstar"
Sept	plant, flower	"Red Robin"
Oct	plant, flower	"Tilford Cream"
Nov	plant	
Dec	/	

Shrubby Veronica

HEBE

FEATURES

An immense and handsome family of small, rounded-leaved or larger, willow-leaved, evergreen New Zealanders, hebes' clustered or cone-shaped spikes of massed, tiny flowers illuminate May to late October. Resisting air pollution, these shrubs are ideal for seaside gardens in mild districts. There are three main, easy and reliable groups:

CARPETERS: Forming a dense mat of weed-suppressing foliage to around 12in high, choice kinds include silvery gray-leaved and white-flowered *Hebe pinguifolia* "Pagei".

BUSHES: Making bushy globes to 4ft, stunning varieties are "Fall Glory," whose violet-blue blossoms color June to November, and "Great Orme," smothered with bright pink flowers from July to October.

TALLER KINDS: Imposing sentinels to 6–10ft, lilac-white *H. salicifolia* is a prince among them.

CONDITIONS

ASPECT   Hebes need an open position in full sun to make robust and free-flowering growth.

SITE   Most well-drained soils suit these plants, but they perform best in humus-rich, sandy loam.

GROWING METHOD

FEEDING   Boost growth by sprinkling fish, blood, and bone meal, Growmore or pelleted chicken manure over the root area in

April and July. Water copiously to establish new plants. Once growing strongly, little water is needed.

PROPAGATION   Take soft-tip cuttings in early summer and semi-ripe cuttings in midsummer.

PROBLEMS   Control leaf spot disease by spraying with carbendazim or mancozeb.

PRUNING

GENERAL   Cut back late-flowering varieties to within 6in of the base, every two years in spring, to encourage bounteous blossom. Remove any reverted, green-leaved stems from variegated varieties as soon as they appear.

SALT-SPRAY RESISTANT, hebes are ideal for brightening coastal gardens in mild districts. They also tolerate air pollution.

AT A GLANCE		
Evergreen carpeters or bushes clothed with cone-shaped flowers in white and many other colors. Hardy to 23°F (zone 9).		
Jan	/	**Recommended Varieties**
Feb	/	"Carl Teschner"
Mar	/	*Hebe* x *franciscana*
Apr	plant, prune	"Blue Gem"
May	flower, prune	"Great Orme"
June	flower, plant	*H. hulkeana*
July	flower, plant	"Midsummer Beauty"
Aug	flower, plant	*H. pinguifolia*
Sept	flower, plant	"Pagei"
Oct	flower	*H. speciosa*
Nov	/	"Gauntlettii"
Dec	/	"Wiri Charm"

Silver Wattle

ACACIA DEALBATA

FEATURES

There are around 900 species of wattle but only *Acacia dealbata* is sufficiently hardy for planting outdoors in mild districts. Rapidly growing to around 12ft, its soft shoots are richly and appealingly clothed with ferny and silvery-sheened, evergreen leaves. In April, year-old shoots are thickly clustered with small, double pompoms of fragrant, bright yellow blossom. Ideally, because several days of temperatures hovering around freezing point may kill shoots, it is best fan-trained against a warm, south-facing wall. Only in relatively frost-free districts can you successfully grow it as a free-standing shrub in the open garden. Elsewhere, set it in a large pot or tub and grow it in a conservatory, moving it outdoors into the open garden only for summer.

CONDITIONS

ASPECT   Choose a warm, sunny site, ideally very sheltered and facing south or south-west, where it will not be exposed to leaf-blackening easterly or northerly winds.

SITE   Any well-drained, lime-free soil suits it. Fortify thin, sandy, or gravelly soils with bulky, humus-enriching manure, or well-rotted garden compost. Aerate heavy clay by working in plenty of grit or shingle. Alternatively, if puddles lie, dig a 18in drainage trench, leading to a soakaway, and fill it with gravel or rubble to within 8in of the soil surface.

GROWING METHOD

FEEDING   Encourage robust growth by annually sprinkling fish, blood, and bone meal, or Growmore over the rooting area in April and July. Water young plants regularly, especially in droughty spells, to help them develop a good, questing root system. Acacia appreciates occasional deep watering.

PROPAGATION   Increase acacia from semi-ripe cuttings in midsummer. Also grow from seed. Speed germination by soaking seeds overnight in hot water to soften the seed coat. Sow directly.

PROBLEMS   Fortunately, it is seldom attacked by sap-sucking pests or caterpillars. If aphids cluster on shoots and cripple them, control them with pirimicarb, horticultural soap, or permethrin.

PRUNING

No regular pruning is necessary. In spring, shorten any stems killed by frost back to healthy side shoots. If acacia outgrows its situation, reduce wayward stems by up to two-thirds in late spring.

AT A GLANCE	
An evergreen, tender tree with silvery, ferny leaves and bobbles of yellow flowers in spring. Hardy to 32°F (zone 10).	
Jan /	Recommended Varieties
Feb flower	*Acacia dealbata*
Mar flower	
Apr plant, flower	
May prune, plant	
June plant	
July plant	
Aug plant	
Sept plant	
Oct /	
Nov /	
Dec /	

Sinningia

GLOXINIA

FEATURES

Gloxinias are tender plants suitable for growing in the home, greenhouse or conservatory, where they will make an impressive, colorful display. The large, showy, brilliantly colored flowers are trumpet shaped, often with speckled throats. Both flowers and leaves have a velvety feel and appearance: the large leaves are mid-green and oval.

Flowers are produced in abundance on well-grown plants, and are available in many colors, from white through pink and red to deepest blue and violet. The edges of the petals may be ruffled, or frilled with a contrasting color; there are several double-flowered varieties.

CONDITIONS

ASPECT   Choose a bright position, but not one which is in direct sun or the foliage will be scorched.
SITE   Gloxinias are house plants requiring average warmth; they dislike hot, dry air and benefit from standing on a dish of moist pebbles for increased humidity. Moisture-retentive soil-less potting compost should be used.

GROWING METHOD

PLANTING   Start the tubers off in moist peat or compost in a frost-free position in spring, potting them up individually once the shoots start to grow. Tubers must be planted with the dished side up, level with the surface of the compost—not buried.

FEEDING   Apply high potash liquid fertilizer every 14 days during the growing season. Keep the compost only just moist until growth has started, then water more freely. Take care to keep water splashes off the leaves and flowers, and never waterlog the compost.
PROBLEMS   Hot, dry air causes the leaves to shrivel and flower buds to fall before opening. Overwatering leads to rotting of the roots.

FLOWERING

SEASON   Flowers throughout the summer.
CUTTING   Not suitable for cutting

AFTER FLOWERING

REQUIREMENTS Gradually reduce watering until the leaves have died back, then store the tubers in dry compost in a cool but frost-free place. Repot in fresh potting compost in spring.

AT A GLANCE		
A showy house plant with colorful, velvety-textured flowers. Minimum temperature 60°F (zone 11).		
Jan	plant	Recommended Varieties
Feb	plant	"Blanche de Meru"
Mar	plant	"Mont Blanc"
Apr	/	"Princess Elizabeth"
May	/	"Gregor Mendel"
Jun	flowering	
July	flowering	
Aug	flowering	
Sept	/	
Oct	/	
Nov	/	
Dec	/	

Sisyrinchium

SISYRINCHIUM

FEATURES

This is a star plant for the border, with spires of pale yellow flowers over summer, 36in high, and iris-like, strap-shaped foliage. The only problem is that it can self-seed too much for the liking of some, although with vigilance the seedlings are easily removed. The genus also offers blue, mauve, and white flowers. *S. idahoense* is a lovely violet-blue, with a yellow throat, growing 12in high, while *S. graminoides* is slightly taller at 20in, with a deeper blue flower, although it self-seeds more prolifically. For a dwarfish, low-growing white, try "Pole Star," good for the rock garden, where it can best be seen and appreciated. It grows to just 1 x 2½in, and is perfectly hardy.

CONDITIONS

ASPECT	Full sun is required, well away from the shade.
SITE	Relatively poor soil is adequate, but free-draining ground is essential. Do not let the plants stand out in damp, wet soil over the winter months.

GROWING METHOD

PROPAGATION	Divide in late summer to guarantee a supply of vigorous plants, since mature ones become quite lackluster after three years. Alternatively, sow seed in the spring. To prevent any established plants from self-seeding, cut off the flowers the moment they begin to fade.

FEEDING	Some enriching with well-rotted manure or compost will provide a boost to poor areas of ground. High levels of fertility, however, are not necessary.
PROBLEMS	Generally trouble-free.

FLOWERING

SEASON	Flowers in early and mid-summer.
CUTTING	They make unusual, striking cut flowers, adding smart verticals to any arrangement, forming a basic structure. Use both flowering stems and foliage.

AFTER FLOWERING

REQUIREMENTS	Cut back the flowering stems to the ground, either promptly to prevent large-scale self-seeding, or later to increase numbers, especially when established plants are past their best.

SISYRINCHIUM IDAHOENSE 'ALBUM' is a clump-forming white flower that is ideal for edging borders.

AT A GLANCE		
S. striatum is an evergreen perennial with spires of pale yellow flowers and long, stiff, pointed leaves. Hardy to 5°F (zone 7).		
Jan	/	Recommended Varieties
Feb	/	*Sisyrinchium angustifolium*
Mar	sow	"Biscutella"
Apr	transplant	"Californian Skies"
May	/	*S. californicum*
Jun	flowering	"E. K. Balls"
July	flowering	*S. idahoense*
Aug	/	*S. macrocarpon*
Sept	divide	"Quaint and Queer"
Oct	/	*S. striatum*
Nov	/	"Aunt May"
Dec	/	

Smoke Bush

COTINUS COGGYGRIA

FEATURES

Remarkably drought-resistant shrub, *Cotinus coggygria*, from central and southern Europe, is appealing twice a year: in June and July when its plumy, 6–8in flowers are reminiscent of pink smoke; and in fall when leaves are suffused with vibrant, fiery, or sunset hues.

Growing slowly to form an obelisk 9ft by 6ft, purple-leaved varieties associate beautifully with lemon-yellow-leaved mock orange (*Philadelphus coronarius* "Aureus"). Purple-leaved kinds also make a fetching host for scrambling Lathyrus grandiflorus, an exuberant, pink-flowered perennial pea. If you do not have sufficient border space for a smoke bush, set it in a large tub of tree and shrub compost and position it to form a statement on your patio or at the end of a path. Plant a pair of shrubs to frame the entrance to a wide driveway.

CONDITIONS

ASPECT	Stalwarts both, green- and purple-leaved varieties are very hardy and unaffected by cold winds.
SITE	The green-leaved family excels in full sun or light shade, but purple-liveried varieties must have bright sunshine or their foliage will pale to insipid green. All prefer humus-rich soil enriched with bulky organic manure or well-rotted garden compost, but they will survive without stress on thin, sandy loam.

GROWING METHOD

FEEDING	Fortify the root area with fish, blood, and bone meal, or Growmore, twice a year: in spring and midsummer. Water it in if the soil is dry.

PROPAGATION	Increase plants from semi-ripe cuttings of new shoots from mid- to late summer. Root them in a lightly shaded garden frame or on a brightly lit windowsill.
PROBLEMS	If shoot tips die after a very hard winter, shorten them to live buds in early spring. Should mildew attack purple-leaved varieties, control it by spraying with fungicide containing carbendazim.

PRUNING

Choose one of three methods:
For a mass of flowers on a large shrub, prune only to remove dead wood.
To achieve a balance of foliage and flowers, take out a third of the oldest shoots each spring.
For dashing foliage, spectacular fall color and no flowers—ideal for purple-leaved varieties—cut back all shoots to 6in from the base in early spring. Keep cuts moist to encourage regrowth.

AT A GLANCE		
Green or purple leaves assume sunset fall tints. "Smoky" flowering plumes make summer special. Hardy to 4°F (zone 7).		
Jan	/	**Recommended Varieties**
Feb	/	"Atropurpurea"
Mar	plant, prune	"Grace"
Apr	plant, prune	"Notcutt's Variety"
May	plant	"Royal Purple"
June	flower, plant	
July	flower, plant	
Aug	plant	
Sept	plant	
Oct	plant	
Nov	plant	
Dec	/	

Solanum

POTATO TREE, POTATO VINE

FEATURES

Two evergreen or partially evergreen species of this genus are generally grown. Both of these are very vigorous, growing to 20ft tall. *Solanum crispum* (Chilean potato tree) from Chile and Peru has fragrant blue flowers in the summer. The cultivar "Glasnevin," with purple-blue flowers, is more widely grown than the species. The Chilean potato tree can be grown on a wall or fence, or used to cover an unsightly outbuilding. *S. jasminoides* (Potato vine) is a half-hardy climber originating from the jungles of Brazil and will need the protection of a cool conservatory in most areas. In the garden it must have a very well sheltered sunny wall. It bears scented, pale blue flower in summer and fall. Both species can be grown as standards.

CONDITIONS

ASPECT	These plants need a warm, very sheltered position in full sun.
SITE	Well-drained yet moisture-retentive, reasonably fertile soil, ideally slightly alkaline.

GROWING METHOD

PROPAGATION	Take semi-ripe cuttings in summer.
WATERING	Water only if the soil starts to dry out excessively in the summer.
FEEDING	An annual application of slow-release fertilizer such as blood, fish, and bone, preferably in the spring, will be sufficient.
PROBLEMS	Plants are prone to attacks from aphids.

FLOWERING/FOLIAGE

FLOWERS	Produces large clusters of potato-like (star-shaped) flowers.
FOLIAGE	The deep green oval leaves of these plants are not particularly attractive.

PRUNING

REQUIREMENTS	Solanums flower on the current year's shoots. Train a permanent framework of stems and spur prune back to this in early spring each year by cutting back lateral shoots to within two or three buds of the main stems. Also prune the plant back to fit the available space. Renovation pruning is not recommended—better to replace overgrown plants. Wear gloves when pruning as the sap can cause an allergic reaction in some people.

AT A GLANCE	
Vigorous climbers with clusters of potato-like flowers. *S. crispum* is hardy to 23°F (zone 9), *S. jasminoides* to 32°F (zone 10).	
Jan /	**Companion Plants**
Feb /	Solanums look lovely with red or
Mar /	pink climbing or rambler roses
Apr planting	
May planting	
Jun flowering	
July flowering	
Aug flowering	
Sep flowering	
Oct /	
Nov /	
Dec /	

Soleirolia soleirolii

BABY'S TEARS

FEATURES

Although native to the western Mediterranean and Italy, this flat, mat-forming, creeping groundcover with tiny leaves flourishes in shady, damp conditions. It is known by many other common names, including mind-your-own-business, Irish moss, Japanese moss, Corsican curse, and Corsican carpet plant. It is often used as a surface cover around the base of potted plants and as a groundcover under shrubs in shady areas. It can become rather weedy as it grows from seeds shed from its inconspicuous flowers, and from small pieces detached from the main growth. In its preferred damp, shady habitat, it is both long lived and persistent.

CONDITIONS

ASPECT   Grows best in shady, damp areas or where it receives dappled sunlight. So do not plant in direct sun as this may cause burning, especially during the height of summer.

SITE   Soleirolia soleirolii will grow in a range of soil types but it prefers well-drained soils that are rich in organic matter. It makes good cover near a stream where the conditions are often ideal, but note that it is a rapid spreader. Check that it will not throttle nearby ornamental plants.

GROWING METHOD

PROPAGATION S. soleirolii will usually propagate itself, sometimes where it is not wanted, but new plants can be started easily from small sections of rooted stems.

FEEDING   Fertilizing is not generally necessary.

PROBLEMS   No specific problems are known.

FLOWERING

SEASON   Flowers can be very tiny and very difficult to see fully without a magnifying glass.

PRUNING

GENERAL   As S. soleirolii is a flat-growing plant, pruning is not necessary. However, you may find that it is necessary to cut back sections of the mat if it becomes too invasive.

THE TINY LEAVES of baby's tears grow very thickly, making it a good weed suppressor. It looks good even in shaded and moist conditions. It will grow over any surface. Although considered a problem by some people, it will flourish where other plants struggle.

AT A GLANCE		
Soleirolia soleirolii is a fantastically invasive spreader with tiny white flowers in summer. Hardy to 5°F (zone 7).		
Jan	foliage	**Recommended Varieties**
Feb	foliage	Soleirolia soleirolii
Mar	foliage	"Aurea"
April	foliage	"Variegata"
May	foliage	**Companion Plants**
June	flowering	Gunnera
July	flowering	Lysichiton
Aug	foliage	Lysimachia
Sept	foliage	Primrose
Oct	foliage	
Nov	foliage	
Dec	foliage	

Solenostemon

COLEUS OR FLAME NETTLE

FEATURES

Look under "coleus" in seed catalogs for a wide range of varieties of this striking foliage plant. A half-hardy annual, solenostemon is a valuable bedding and container plant with large multicolored leaves that add a certain "tropical" and eccentric element to summer gardens. As well as mixtures, dark-leaved varieties like "Black Dragon" can be put to use in color-themed displays. Size range is 8–18in depending on variety, and it is important to remove all flowerheads as they appear or the plant will stop producing leaves. Varieties are available as young plants.

CONDITIONS

ASPECT   Flame nettles need full sun to really thrive and also need shelter from persistent winds.

SITE   Well-drained soil that has had plenty of rotted manure or compost mixed in before planting produces strong plants with good color. Where they are grown in patio containers use multipurpose compost with slow-release fertilizer granules added at planting time.

GROWING METHOD

SOWING   March is the time to sow seed, in $3^1/_2$in pots of multipurpose compost, just scattering the seed on the surface—don't cover. Keep at 75ºF where they get bright light. Seedlings grow slowly but when they are large enough, transplant to $3^1/_2$in pots or large cell trays. Pinch out the growing tip when plants are 3in tall to encourage bushy growth and the maximum number of leaves. Harden off in late May and plant after frosts, 6–12in apart.

FEEDING   Liquid feeding every two weeks during summer maintains vigorous leaf growth. If slow-release fertilizer has been used, feed only monthly with half-strength liquid feed.

PROBLEMS   Slugs and snails attack young plants, so protect with slug pellets or a barrier of sharp grit around each plant.

FLOWERING

SEASON   All flowers should be removed as soon as they appear to encourage maximum leaf growth. Plants generally stay colorful until frosts.

CUTTING   Not suitable.

AFTER FLOWERING

GENERAL   Favorite plants can be lifted and potted up in fall, and kept dry over winter in a frost-free greenhouse or cool room. Take cuttings from these plants in spring.

AT A GLANCE		
A half-hardy annual grown for its brightly-colored leaves which are used in bedding and pots. Frost hardy to 32°F (zone 10).		
Jan	/	Recommended Varieties
Feb	/	*Solenostemon*
Mar	sow	*scutellarioides*
Apr	transplant	"Black Dragon"
May	harden off/plant	"Camelot Mixed"
Jun	leaves	"Dragon Sunset &
July	leaves	Volcano, Mixed"
Aug	leaves	"Fairway"
Sept	leaves	"Flame Dancers"
Oct	/	"Magic Lace"
Nov	/	"Salmon Lace"
Dec	/	"Top Crown"

Solidago

GOLDEN ROD

FEATURES

Golden rod forms large colonies of sometimes quite tall yellow plants, reaching 6ft high. The small flowers in themselves are nothing special, but they appear in such profusion that they make quite an impact. There are plenty of varieties to choose from. The key differences are more to do with height than color. "Crown of Rays" grows to 24in high, and as its name suggests has bright yellow flowers. "Goldenmosa" is almost as bright and grows slightly taller, and has yellow-green foliage. But if you need a golden rod for the rear of the border, especially one where the soil is quite poor, the best choice is "Golden Wings." It can reach 6ft tall, topping smaller plants with its late summer and early fall show. The best choice of golden rod for growing at the front of the border is the 8in-high "Queenie" or *S. virgaurea minuta*.

CONDITIONS

ASPECT   Grow in full sunlight in the border. Avoid borders that are in the shade.

SITE   Free-draining soil, preferably quite sandy or gritty, is ideal.

GROWING METHOD

PROPAGATION   Golden rod self-seeds, but to be sure of getting new plants that are true to type, spring or fall division invariably give successful results.

FEEDING   High soil fertility is not in any way essential. Very poor ground can be improved in the spring, however, by digging in some quantities of well-rotted manure.

PROBLEMS   Powdery mildew can strike quite severely; treat with a fungicide at the first sight of an attack. Repeat sprayings are necessary to control major outbreaks.

FLOWERING

SEASON   Generally mid- to late summer, though sometimes slightly before and after.

CUTTING   Not the best cut flowers—there are better alternatives—but they effectively bulk up any arrangement.

AFTER FLOWERING

REQUIREMENTS Cut back spent flower stems.

THE HIGHLY DISTINCTIVE sight of golden rod: a bright spray of yellow flowers, and long, thin, dark green leaves.

AT A GLANCE		
Varieties of golden rod create mainly big, bold, clumps of bright yellow flowers. Can be invasive. Hardy to 0°F (zones 6–7).		
Jan	/	**Recommended Varieties**
Feb	/	*Solidago cutleri*
Mar	/	*S. flexicaulis*
Apr	divide	"Golden Baby"
May	transplant	"Goldenmosa"
Jun	/	"Queenie"
July	flowering	"Variegata"
Aug	flowering	*S. virgaurea minuta*
Sept	/	
Oct	/	
Nov	/	
Dec	/	

Sparaxis tricolor

HARLEQUIN FLOWER

FEATURES

This showy, easy-care plant has bright flowers of yellow, red, pink, orange, or purple carried on stems that can be anywhere from 6–18in high. Many of the brightly colored flowers have a darker purple or deep red area in the center and a yellow throat. Harlequin flowers hybridise readily, often producing seedlings that have interesting color variations. These are bulbs that thrive in dry, warm areas of the yard. They look their best when mass-planted but can also be grown in containers, where they should be crowded together for best effect. The flowers cut well for indoor decoration. Harlequin flower bulbs increase rapidly by offsets.

CONDITIONS

ASPECT   Needs full sun all day for best results.
SITE   Sparaxis needs a sheltered spot in a reasonably mild area to do well; in cold gardens it is best grown in containers under cover. Soil must be well-drained and moderately fertile.

GROWING METHOD

PLANTING   Corms should be planted 3in deep and 3–4in apart in mid-fall. Mulch the planting area with chipped bark or leafmold for winter protection.
FEEDING   In very poor soil apply a balanced fertiliser in early summer after flowering. Mulch the soil in late winter with well-rotted organic matter. In dry seasons, water when the foliage emerges and as buds and flowers develop if necessary.
PROBLEMS   No specific problems are known.

FLOWERING

SEASON   Flowering should be abundant in late spring and early summer.
CUTTING Sparaxis makes a good cut flower for the home and should last well in water.

AFTER FLOWERING

REQUIREMENTS Allow foliage to die down naturally, then lift the corms and dry them off until it is time to replant in fall. Any cormlets that have formed can be removed when the corms are lifted and replanted separately.

HARLEQUIN FLOWERS come in a veritable kaleidoscope of colors, with the patterned throat revealing yet more colors and patterns. The strong, bright colors are shown to best advantage when they are planted in an open, sunny spot.

AT A GLANCE		
Very brightly colored, star-shaped flowers are carried on slender stems in early summer. Not suitable for cold, exposed yards.		
Jan	/	**Recommended Varieties**
Feb	/	Usually supplied as a color mixture
Mar	/	
Apr	/	
May	flowering	
Jun	flowering	
July	/	
Aug	/	
Sept	/	
Oct	/	
Nov	plant	
Dec	/	

Spiraea

SPIRAEA

FEATURES

An easy and floriferous family of deciduous shrubs, 18in–8ft high, spiraea rewards us with cone- or dome-shaped blooms on upright shoots or on pendulous or arching stems. There are two groups: spring flowering and summer flowering.

The finest early performers, from March to May, are epitomised by the aptly named bridal wreath (*Spiraea arguta*). Its arching stems, to 6ft, are so thickly enveloped with snowy blossom that its leaves are concealed.

Most popular summer-flowering members are forms of *S. japonica.* "Anthony Waterer," aglow with domes of carmine-pink flowers amid pink or cream-tinged leaves; and "Goldflame," prized for its dark pink flowers and radiant golden-orange leaves in spring. Another kind, *S. billiardii* "Triumphans," is ablaze with rose-purple flower cones in July and August.

Plant spiraea to punctuate a border, carpet a rock garden pocket, adorn a patio tub, or screen out an ugly view.

CONDITIONS

ASPECT   Very hardy, these shrubs prefer full sun in which stocky shoots flower well and colored-leaved varieties develop vivid hues.

SITE   They also thrive in a wide range of well-drained soils but dislike dry or very alkaline conditions. Improve sandy patches by digging in plenty of rotted organic matter.

GROWING METHOD

FEEDING   Encourage robust growth by gently working bone meal into the root area in spring and fall. Help new plants recover quickly from transplanting by watering liberally and mulching in dry spells in spring and summer.

PROPAGATION   Take soft-tip cuttings in early summer; semi-ripe cuttings from mid- to late summer; or hardwood cuttings in fall. Some varieties can be divided or increased from suckers in early spring.

PROBLEMS   Control sap-sucking aphids, which colonize soft shoot tips, by spraying with pirimicarb, derris, or horticultural soap.

PRUNING

Spring- and summer-flowering kinds that flower on older shoots: Cut out from the base one older stem in three when blooms fade. Summer-flowering varieties that bloom on the current-year shoots: Shorten all stems to 4in from the base from early to mid-spring. Rejuvenate tall, old, woody varieties making little new growth by cutting all shoots to within 12in of the base in early spring.

AT A GLANCE		
Spring- or summer-flowering shrubs with white, pink, or purple-rose blooms. Some have orange foliage. Hardy to -13°F (zone 8).		
Jan	/	Recommended Varieties
Feb	/	Spring flowering
Mar	plant, flower	*Spiraea arguta*
Apr	plant, flower	*S. thunbergii*
May	flower, prune	"Snowmound"
Jun	flower, prune	Summer flowering
July	flower, prune	"Anthony Waterer"
Aug	flower, prune	*S. x billiardii*
Sept	flower, prune	"Gold Mound"
Oct	plant	"Little Princess"
Nov	plant	"Triumphans"
Dec	/	

Sprekelia formosissima

JACOBEAN LILY

FEATURES

The rich crimson flowers of Jacobean lily are carried singly on stems 12–18in high and the foliage, which is about the same height, appears with or just before the flowers. This plant is sometimes called the Aztec lily and is in fact native to Mexico where it occurs in open, sunny places, often in poor soil. The unusual shape of the flower gives rise to another common name, orchid amaryllis, and the exotic-looking flower could easily be mistaken for an orchid. Unfortunately it is suitable for gardens in mild areas only; in less favored climates it must be grown as a greenhouse or conservatory plant. Formerly much more widely grown than it is today, it deserves to become more popular.

CONDITIONS

ASPECT Grows best in full sun with wind protection. Indoors it likes a bright position.

SITE Suitable for a sheltered border in mild areas, or containers in a greenhouse or conservatory. Outdoors, soil must be well-drained and enriched with compost or manure. Use John Innes potting compost for containers.

GROWING METHOD

PLANTING Plant bulbs in spring, 2in deep and 8in apart. In containers, plant with the neck of the bulb just above the compost surface.

FEEDING Give a high potash liquid feed every two or three weeks throughout the growing season. Water container plants regularly until the foliage starts to die down.

PROBLEMS No specific problems are known.

FLOWERING

SEASON The showy flowers appear in early summer.

CUTTING Can be cut for the vase but usually better enjoyed on the plant.

AFTER FLOWERING

REQUIREMENTS When the leaves die down, lift outdoor bulbs and keep them in a cool, dry place. For container-grown plants, allow the compost to dry out when the leaves die down, then keep the bulb dry in its pot until spring when watering will start it into growth again.

THE SCULPTURED LINES of Jacobean lilies need to be appreciated at close quarters. Growing them in containers is a perfect solution.

AT A GLANCE		
An exotic-looking, rather tender plant that needs greenhouse conditions in cooler areas. Minimum temperature 45°F (zone 11).		
Jan	/	Recommended Varieties
Feb	/	Only the straight species is
Mar	/	grown—no cultivars or varieties
Apr	plant	of this plant are available.
May	/	
Jun	flowering	
July	/	
Aug	/	
Sept	/	
Oct	/	
Nov	/	
Dec	/	

Spurge
EUPHORBIA SPECIES

FEATURES

Pleasing us with a spring to early summer display of yellowish-green, bottlebrush blooms on stems clad with whorls of evergreen leaves, *Euphorbia characias wulfenii* is architecturally magnificent. Forming a dense bush to 4ft, it is ideal for interplanting and tempering vibrant orange, yellow, and red-flowered border perennials. This euphorbia lives for around ten or more years and matures within 2–3 years. Use it in a shrub border or as a background for annuals and perennials.

A related sculptural gem, for sheltered gardens only, is Madeiran honey spurge (*E. mellifera*). Seducing us with large and exotic, lance-shaped leaves, its honey-scented, brownish flower clusters form on shoot tips in spring.

CONDITIONS

ASPECT — Hardy *E. characias* needs full sun; more tender *E. mellifera* requires a sheltered spot.

SITE — These sub-shrubs thrive almost anywhere, even in heavy soils, provided drainage is good. Boost growth in light, sandy soil by incorporating bulky organic manure.

GROWING METHOD

FEEDING — Feeding is not essential but apply fish, blood, and bone meal, Growmore, or pelleted chicken manure in spring.

PROPAGATION — Take soft-tip cuttings from mid-spring to early summer.

PROBLEMS — When crowded, euphorbia may become infected with gray mold, a disease that coats leaves and stems with furry, brownish-gray mould. Control it by cutting infected shoots back to healthy tissue and spraying with carbendazim.

PRUNING

Wear gloves and safety glasses to cut back flowered stems to ground level in early summer. Strong, new shoots replace them and bloom the following year.

THE SHOWIEST PART of a euphorbia "flower" is a pair of lime-green bracts (modified leaves). The true flower is a small, yellow "button." Bearing distinctive, greenish, bottlebrush blooms from early spring to early summer, Euphorbia characias wulfenii is sculpturally appealing. Plant it to form a focal point in a wide border or flank a path or drive.

AT A GLANCE		
Evergreen shrub, *E. characias wulfenii* produces huge, bottlebrush blooms from spring to early summer. Hardy to 10°F (zone 7).		
Jan	/	Recommended Varieties
Feb	/	*E. characias*
Mar	/	"John Tomlinson"
Apr	flower, plant	*E. characias*
May	flower, plant	"Lambrook Gold"
June	flower, prune	*E. characias*
July	prune, plant	"Margery Fish Group"
Aug	plant	*E. characias*
Sept	plant	"Purple and Gold"
Oct	/	*E. characias wulfenii*
Nov	/	*E. mellifera*
Dec	/	

Stachys byzantina

LAMB'S EARS

FEATURES

Stachys byzantina is a low-growing, evergreen perennial often used as an edging plant. It is good in rose beds, but wherever it is planted it must have excellent drainage and full sun. The leaves are densely covered with hairs, giving them a white or pale gray woolly appearance, hence its common name. It produces pink-purple flowers on spikes that stand above the foliage, but they are not especially attractive; it is usually grown for its foliage, and not the flowers. The exceptions are *Stachys macrantha* "Robusta" and *S. officinalis.* "Cotton Ball" has woolly flowers good for dried arrangements. Plants grow 6–8in high, but spread a good distance.

CONDITIONS

ASPECT   Full sun is essential all day for the plants to thrive and perform well.

SITE   Needs very fast-draining soil. It grows well in poor sandy or gravelly soil. Avoid thick, wet, heavy clay at all costs.

GROWING METHOD

PROPAGATION *S. byzantina* grows readily from cuttings that are taken in the spring or fall. The new divisions must be planted out about 8in apart. Water new plants regularly. Once they are established, they need to be watered very occasionally.

FEEDING   Grows without supplementary fertilizer, but a little complete plant food can be applied in the early spring.

PROBLEMS   There are no specific problems but container plants will quickly fail if they are over-watered, and border plants will rot if they become waterlogged.

FLOWERING

SEASON   The flowers are produced in the summer, sometimes into fall. But the tactile gray foliage is by far the chief attraction.

PRUNING

GENERAL   Pruning is rarely necessary. If any cutting back is needed do it in early spring.

SINCE LAMB'S EARS, or lamb's tails, needs good drainage, grow it in an attractive container if your soil is relentlessly heavy and damp. More traditional is this planting, where lamb's ears edge a garden bed. The plants will multiply rapidly, given the right situation.

AT A GLANCE	
Stachys byzantina is a silver-leaved plant that is well worth growing in every garden. Hardy to 0°F (zone 7).	

		Recommended Varieties
Jan	/	*Stachys byzantina*
Feb	/	"Cotton Ball"
Mar	/	"Primrose Heron"
April	foliage	*S. coccinea*
May	foliage	*S. macrantha*
June	flowering	"Robusta"
July	flowering	*S. officinalis*
Aug	flowering	
Sept	foliage	
Oct	foliage	
Nov	/	
Dec	/	

Stanhopea
STANHOPEA SPECIES AND HYBRIDS

FEATURES

Sometimes known as upside-down orchids, stanhopeas must be grown in hanging containers as the flowers emerge from the base of the pseudobulbs and will otherwise be squashed. They push straight through the bottom of the basket and hang down below the foliage. Stanhopeas are evergreen epiphytes from Central and South America. They grow from a fairly large, ribbed pseudobulb and produce large, solitary, dark green leaves. The strange-looking flowers are large, heavy and strongly perfumed. Not everyone finds the perfume pleasant. Flowers are not long lasting but appear in succession. Plants grow rapidly and are very easy to grow into large specimens.

SPECIES

Stanhopea tigrina, with its fleshy yellow flowers blotched dark maroon-red, is the species most often cultivated, although S. wardii is also seen. It also has yellow flowers but with plum to purple spots.

CONDITIONS

CLIMATE   Prefers a cool, humid climate with a minimum of 50°F and tolerates warmer temperatures in summer with shade and high humidity.

ASPECT   Grows in dappled sunlight in a well-ventilated glasshouse.

POTTING MIX   Line the container with soft coconut fiber or other material so that the stems can push through easily. The mix of coarse bark, alone or with charcoal, must be free draining.

GROWING METHOD

PROPAGATION   Divide the pseudobulbs after flowering, but not until the container is full to overflowing. Large specimens are the most rewarding, producing many spikes.

WATERING   Water freely during warm weather and mist plants if humidity drops. Water only occasionally in winter.

FEEDING   During the growing season apply weak liquid fertilizer every two weeks.

PROBLEMS   Can be prone to red-spider-mite or scale insect if not enough humidity is provided. Mist foliage regularly to prevent this.

FLOWERING SEASON

Summer or fall, depending on species. Remove spent flowers once they have faded.

AT A GLANCE		
Easy to grow but can reach 16in high. Flowers are large and strongly scented but short lived.		
Jan	occasional water	Recommended Varieties
Feb	water and feed	*Stanhopea graveolans*
Mar	flowering, water and feed	(yellow)
		S. oculata (cream)
Apr	flowering, water and feed	S. tigrina
		S. wardii
May	flowering, water and feed	S. Assidensis
		(yellow and red)
Jun	flowering, water and feed	
July	flowering, water and feed	
Aug	flowering, water and feed	
Sept	water and feed	
Oct	water and feed	
Nov	occasional water	
Dec	occasional water	

Stauntonia hexaphylla

STAUNTONIA

FEATURES

This is a vigorous, evergreen climber from Japan and south Korea, where it is largely found growing in woodland conditions. It is related and similar to *Holboellia latifolia*. Stauntonias are grown for their attractive bell-shaped flowers, which are produced in spring, and for their lush foliage that serves to cover their support well. Grow this climber on a sheltered wall or fence, or allow it to scramble through a large mature shrub or up a tree. Although this plant is frost hardy it will not survive severe cold spells. In areas that suffer from hard frosts it is best to grow it in a cool conservatory. The eventual height of this plant is 30ft.

CONDITIONS

ASPECT	Full sun or partial shade, warm and well sheltered from cold winds.
SITE	Stauntonia will get by in any well-drained soil that is reasonably fertile.

GROWING METHOD

PROPAGATION	Semi-ripe cuttings taken in summer. Sow seeds in spring and germinate in a temperature of 61°F.
WATERING	Water the plant well if the soil starts to dry out excessively in the summer.
FEEDING	Feed annually in the spring. The slow-release organic fertilizer, blood, fish, and bone can be recommended.
PROBLEMS	There are no problems from pests or diseases.

FLOWERING/FOLIAGE

FLOWERS	Pendulous clusters of scented, white, bell-shaped flowers, tinted with violet may be followed by edible, purple fruits (a male and female plant are necessary to obtain fruits).
FOLIAGE	Deep green, shiny, leathery, hand-shaped leaves make a good background for the flowers.

PRUNING

REQUIREMENTS	Spur pruning. To keep growth under control, shorten lateral shoots to six buds in summer, and then in early spring cut them back again, to within two or three buds of the main stems.

ALTHOUGH IT DOES PRODUCE attractive flowers, S. hexaphylla is also grown for its pleasant, lush, evergreen foliage.

AT A GLANCE	
A vigorous twiner with white, violet-flushed, bell-shaped flowers in spring. Hardy to 23°F (zone 9).	
Jan /	**Companion Plants**
Feb /	Try growing this climber with
Mar /	spring-flowering clematis.
Apr planting	
May flowering	
Jun /	
July /	
Aug /	
Sep /	
Oct /	
Nov /	
Dec /	

Sternbergia lutea
FALL DAFFODIL, LILY-OF-THE-FIELD

FEATURES

Clear, bright yellow flowers, rather like crocuses, appear on 6in stems from their surround of shorter, dark green, strappy leaves. The foliage persists until spring when it dies down to remain dormant until the following fall. Ideal for the rock garden, these plants also show to advantage when planted in the yard in good-sized groups where they can be left to multiply. This is a bulb that could be naturalized in turf but the area would have to be well-marked to avoid cutting off the emerging growth in fall, and the grass could not be mown for several months. Lily-of-the-field can be grown in containers but they are more successful in the open ground.

CONDITIONS

ASPECT Prefers full sun: a summer baking of the dormant bulbs is necessary for good flowering in the fall.

SITE Suitable for a rockery, raised bed, or a sunny, reasonably sheltered border. Very well-drained soil is essential for this plant. Well-rotted organic matter can be dug into the bed ahead of planting.

GROWING METHOD

PLANTING Plant bulbs in summer about 5in deep and the same distance apart.

FEEDING Supplementary fertiliser is generally not needed.

PROBLEMS

PROBLEMS The main problem encountered is rotting of bulbs due to heavy or poorly drained soil. Improve drainage by incorporating sharp sand into the planting area.

FLOWERING

SEASON The small, bright golden flowers appear in fall.

CUTTING These flowers are not suitable for cutting.

AFTER FLOWERING

REQUIREMENTS Ensure the plants are allowed to remain dry once the foliage has died down in early summer. The site may need protection from excessive summer rain with a cloche or similar. Do not disturb established plants unless it is essential.

MOST SCHOLARS today believe Sternbergia lutea *is the plant referred to in the Bible as "the lily of the field." Short in stature but big on impact, it is one of the most delightful of bulbs, especially as it blooms in fall.*

AT A GLANCE		
A crocus-like bulb with flowers appearing in late summer and fall. Needs very well-drained soil to thrive.		
Jan	/	**Recommended Varieties**
Feb	/	*Sternbergia lutea*
Mar	/	Angustifolia Group
Apr	/	*S. clusiana*
May	/	*S. sicula*
Jun	/	
July	plant	
Aug	plant	
Sept	flowering	
Oct	flowering	
Nov	/	
Dec	/	

Stokesia laevis

STOKES' ASTER

FEATURES

Stokes' aster is an easily grown plant that provides great decorative value throughout its long flowering period from mid-summer to early fall. It makes excellent cut flowers, too. Flower stems 12–20in tall rise from a cluster of dark green basal leaves. Although this plant is completely herbaceous in cold areas, the basal growth remains evergreen in mild winters. Its flowers are reminiscent of large cornflowers or asters, and come in shades of blue, white, and mauve. This plant can look outstanding in mass plantings, but is equally at home in a mixed border, or when grown in wooden tubs or pots.

CONDITIONS

ASPECT	While Stokes' aster prefers full sunlight, it barely tolerates dappled shade. Provide a shelter to protect from strong winds.
SITE	Needs well-drained soil enriched with compost or manure.

GROWING METHOD

PROPAGATION	Divide established clumps in the spring or fall, replanting divisions approximately 10in apart. The plant can also be grown from root cuttings taken in the early spring, and from fall seed. It tolerates dry periods, but looks best if given an occasional deep watering during prolonged, dry spells. Provide young plants with twiggy support.

FEEDING	Apply some complete plant food in the spring.
PROBLEMS	Poorly drained, heavy soils induce root or crown rot, which kills plants.

FLOWERING

SEASON	The long flowering period is from late summer into the fall.
CUTTING	Cut flowers regularly for the vase. This both gives a good ornamental display and prolongs the garden show, inducing plenty of new flower buds.

AFTER FLOWERING

REQUIREMENTS	Prune all spent flower stems. As the growth dies back, promptly clear away all of the dead foliage.

THE FLOWERING HEADS of Stokes' aster are quite complex, made up from many "petals" (more properly bracts or ray florets). It is hard to understand why it should go out of fashion, but it is certainly grown less often than before.

AT A GLANCE		
S. laevis is an evergreen, perennial, sprawling plant with large, purple, flat, late summer flowers. Hardy to 5°F (zone 7).		
Jan	/	Companion Plants
Feb	sow	Aster
Mar	divide	Box
Apr	transplant	Dahlia
May	transplant	Fuchsia
Jun	/	Miscanthus
July	/	Penstemon
Aug	flowering	Potentilla
Sept	flowering	Stipa
Oct	flowering	
Nov	divide	
Dec	/	

Sun Rose

HELIANTHEMUM

FEATURES

Varieties of evergreen *Helianthemem nummularium*, commonly called rock or sun rose, make a spreading 4–12in mound to 36in across. From May to July, a network of wiry stems clothed with small, oval leaves are almost hidden beneath a daily succession of single or double flowers in glowing shades of yellow, pink, red, orange, white, or terracotta. Sun roses are perfect for draping rock garden pockets, cascading from retaining walls and aproning roses and other bushes flanking a path. They are not long-lived but easily raised from cuttings of maturing, current-year shoots.

CONDITIONS

ASPECT   Sun rose performs best in an open, brightly lit and airy position where it has room to spread and is not crowded by other plants. Avoid even a hint of shade in which growth is looser, less comely and flowering is inhibited.

SITE   This shrub needs well-drained and slightly alkaline conditions. Add garden lime to raise the pH of acid soil.

GROWING METHOD

FEEDING   Boost lustrous foliage and a wealth of blossom by applying a high-potash rose fertilizer in spring and the middle of summer. Water newly planted shrubs regularly and copiously to help them recover quickly and make good root growth in their first year. Thereafter, they will need watering only in droughty weather. Mulch plants generously with spent mushroom compost.

PROPAGATION   Take semi-ripe heeled cuttings in midsummer. These should make flowering-sized plants by the following spring.

PROBLEMS   Poor drainage or overwatering may kill plants. Powdery mildew can be a problem in crowded borders where air circulates sluggishly. Control this disease by thinning growth and spraying with carbendazim or bupirimate with triforine.

PRUNING

From early to midsummer, when blooms fade, shear back shoots to two-thirds their length. This not only keeps bushes trim and flowering well in spring, but often results in a second, smaller, flush of blossom in fall.

DEEP RED and yellow-eyed blooms and silvery leaves make "Supreme" a prized variety.

AT A GLANCE		
A carpeting evergreen so thickly clothed with flowers from May to July that leaves are concealed by them. Hardy to 14°F (zone 8).		
Jan	/	**Recommended Varieties**
Feb	/	"Golden Queen"
Mar	/	"Henfield Brilliant"
Apr	plant	"Raspberry Ripple"
May	flower, plant	"Red Orient"
Jun	flower, plant	"Supreme"
July	flower, plant	"The Bride"
Aug	plant, prune	"Wisley Pink"
Sept	plant	"Wisley Primrose"
Oct	/	
Nov	/	
Dec	/	

Symphytum officinale

COMFREY

FEATURES

Symphytum officinale is one of the best groundcovering plants. In the right conditions, just one plant can spread 6ft, even climbing over low walls. *S. officinale* has a mass of violet, pink or yellow flowers. Experts prefer other forms like *S. x uplandicum* "Variegatum," which has superb gray-green leaves with a creamy-white edge. The flowers are lilac-pink. The only problem is that it can revert to a dark green leaf, especially in the wrong conditions. It is much less invasive than *S. officinale*, with one plant spreading 2ft. "Goldsmith" also has attractive foliage, dark green leaves with cream markings around the outside, but spreads about half as much as "Variegatum," which has leaves edged in white.

CONDITIONS

ASPECT | This plant thrives in either full sun or partial, dappled shade, such as woodland areas.

SITE | The soil needs to be on the damp side and quite fertile. Clay soil that has been reasonably broken up and lightened is ideal. S. officinale should spread quite quickly.

GROWING METHOD

PROPAGATION | With a fast spreader like *S. officinale*, there is no need to propagate. But when you need more plants to colonize another area, divide plants in the spring. They quickly settle. Close planting gives more immediate cover but just a few plants will give good cover over 8ft or so.

FEEDING | Assuming that the plant is growing in clay soil which is perfectly fertile, additional feeding is not necessary. Otherwise, give a little slow-release fertilizer in spring.

PROBLEMS | *S. officinale* is a remarkably tough and resourceful plant, which is easy to grow and attracts very few problems.

FLOWERING

SEASON | The flowers appear in the spring and early summer. The species which produces the most distinctive colored flowers is *S. caucasicum*, which has bright blue blooms.

PRUNING | Only prune if it is necessary to confine the plant's growth. Slice off any unwanted growth with a spade. Otherwise, let the plant spread wherever it wants.

AT A GLANCE		
Symphytum officinale is a free-spreading, spring-flowering perennial. The leaves are tough. Hardy to 0°F (zone 7).		
Jan	/	**Recommended Varieties**
Feb	/	*Symphytum caucasicum*
Mar	/	"Goldsmith"
April	/	"Hidcote Blue"
May	flowering	*S. ibericum*
June	flowering	*S. officinale*
July	foliage	*S. tuberosum*
Aug	foliage	*S. x uplandicum*
Sept	foliage	"Variegatum"
Oct	foliage	
Nov	foliage	
Dec	foliage	

T

Tagetes
MARIGOLD

FEATURES

The marigold "family" is made up of African and French types, and tagetes. All are easily grown half-hardy annuals and their flowers are among some of the loudest available—bright oranges, reds, yellows, and bronzes that set borders and containers alight. Plant size varies from 6in dwarfs to 3ft giants, and there are unusual flower colors such as "Vanilla" and even bright stripey-petalled varieties such as "Mr Majestic." Use them for bold bedding or as reliable patio container plants. Flowers can be single, semi or fully double and up to 3in across. Many varieties are also available as young plants.

CONDITIONS

ASPECT	Must have a sunny position.
SITE	Marigolds are not too fussy about soils, but mixing in rotted compost before planting helps keep soil moist. For container growing use multipurpose compost with slow-release fertilizer granules mixed well in. Tall varieties of African marigold need shelter from wind.

GROWING METHOD

SOWING	All marigolds can be sown February–April, but a May sowing on a windowsill will also be successful as they are fast growers and soon catch up. Just cover the large seeds with compost and keep at 70°F. Seedlings will appear in a week and can be transplanted to cell trays. Grow on,

harden off in late May and plant after frosts. Nip off any flower buds that appear before and two weeks after planting.

FEEDING	Fortnightly liquid feeding keeps plants in beds going strong. Keep containers well watered.
PROBLEMS	Slugs and snails can strip plants overnight so protect with slug pellets in wet/warm spells.

FLOWERING

SEASON	Early sowings produce earlier flowers and vice-versa. Late sowings provide handy color in late summer and if grown in pots, plants can be used to revive flagging summer containers.
CUTTING	African marigolds are useful for cutting.

AFTER FLOWERING

GENERAL	Pull plants up when finished and compost.

AT A GLANCE		
A half-hardy annual grown for its bright flowers which are ideal for bedding and patio pots/troughs. Frost hardy to 32°F (zone 10).		
Jan	/	Recommended Varieties
Feb	sow	African marigolds
Mar	sow	"Inca Mixed"
Apr	sow/transplant	"Shaggy Maggy"
May	harden off/plant	"Vanilla"
Jun	flowering	French marigolds
July	flowering	"Boy O'Boy Mixed"
Aug	flowering	"Mischief Mixed"
Sept	flowering	"Mr Majestic"
Oct	/	Tagetes tenuifolia
Nov	/	"Lemon Gem"
Dec	/	"Red Gem"

Taxus baccata

YEW

FEATURES

The English yew is extremely long lived and fairly slow growing, but it makes a dense hedge that can be closely clipped. It is also widely used in topiary, and there are specimens that have been clipped for several hundred years. In Britain and Europe yew hedges have been traditionally used to shelter herbaceous borders or as a background for statuary and garden ornaments. Foliage is dark and evergreen, and it produces a red fleshy fruit that is quite poisonous. Unpruned trees may grow to 50ft or more but yew is generally hedged at about 8ft. There are a number of cultivars of yew, providing many variations in form and foliage color.

CONDITIONS

ASPECT   Prefers an open, sunny position. This plant is tolerant of windy sites.

SITE   Soil should be well drained and enriched with organic matter. Mulch around plants with decayed manure or compost. It is tempting to plant yew and then completely forget about it, but good care yields fine, dense growth.

GROWING METHOD

PROPAGATION Take firm cuttings with a heel of older wood in fall. These may not be well rooted until the following summer. Use a hormone rooting gel or powder to increase the strike rate.

SPACING   Yew can be planted at 20in–3ft spacings, depending on the density required.

FEEDING   Apply complete plant food or slow-release fertilizer in spring.

PROBLEMS There are no specific problems. Yew is an easy-care, reliable shrub or small tree.

FLOWERING

PRODUCTS Yew is a conifer, not a flowering plant. It produces very small cones in season as well as bright red, poisonous fruits.

PRUNING

GENERAL   To create your hedge, prune little and often. However, yew can be cut back severely and still regenerate well.

YEW IS THE IDEAL hedging plant for cool climates. Formal shapes can be achieved and maintained over a long time. Mature yew plants have somber, dark green foliage but new spring growth is much brighter.

AT A GLANCE		
Taxus baccata provides a traditional, formal hedge that can be topiarized to give geometric shapes. Hardy to 0°F (zone 7).		
Jan	foliage	**Recommended Varieties**
Feb	foliage	*Taxus baccata*
Mar	foliage	"Adpressa"
April	flowering	"Fastigiata"
May	flowering	"Fastigiata Aurea"
June	foliage	"Fastigiata Aureomarginata"
July	foliage	*T.* x *media*
Aug	foliage	"Brownii"
Sept	foliage	
Oct	foliage	
Nov	foliage	
Dec	foliage	

Thalictrum

MEADOW RUE

FEATURES

Thalictrum aquilegiifolium is easy and quick to grow, a herbaceous perennial reaching about 42in tall. The rather fern-like, blue-green foliage is attractively lobed, and the flowers are mauve-pink in dense, fluffy heads. While the floral display does not last long, the foliage adds months of charm. Meadow rue can be planted in mixed borders or in light shade under trees. There are a number of cultivars, including a white form and one with violet blooms. Also try *T. delavayi* (syn. *T. dipterocarpum*) and its cultivars "Album" and "Hewitt's Double." This has finer foliage and the pink-mauve flowers are star shaped.

CONDITIONS

ASPECT | Grow in either light shade, or in a border with morning sun followed by plenty of afternoon shade.

SOIL | Likes well-drained soil that has been enriched with organic matter.

GROWING METHOD

PROPAGATION | Grows from seed sown in the spring or fall, or by divisions of a clump made in spring. Plant the new divisions approximately 10–12in apart. Do not let the young plants dry out—give regular, deep waterings through dry springs and summers.

FEEDING | As growth begins in the spring, apply complete plant food and mulch around the plants with well-decayed manure or compost.

PROBLEMS | No specific pest or disease problems are known to attack this plant. Generally trouble-free. Note that growth begins late in spring, so avoid damaging new growth while weeding.

FLOWERING

SEASON | Flowers appear during early summer, depending on temperatures.

CUTTING | Both the foliage and flowers can be cut for the vase.

AFTER FLOWERING

REQUIREMENTS | Cut off any spent flower stems, unless you want to save seed. When the plants die down in the fall, cut off the foliage at ground level.

THE FLUFFY PINK FLOWERS of meadow rue do not last long, but the pretty foliage persists well until the fall.

AT A GLANCE	
T. aquilegiifolium is a clump-forming, rhizomatous perennial with gorgeous sprays of purple flowers. Hardy to 5°F (zone 7).	
Jan /	Recommended Varieties
Feb /	*Thalictrum aquilegiifolium* var. *album*
Mar divide	"Thundercloud"
Apr transplant	*T. delavayi*
May /	*T. flavum* subsp. *glaucum*
Jun flowering	*T. kiusianum*
July flowering	*T. minus*
Aug /	*T. rochebruneanum*
Sept /	
Oct sow	
Nov /	
Dec /	

Thunbergia

BLACK-EYED SUSAN

FEATURES

The flowers of thunbergia can be orange, yellow, or white, and sometimes the black eye is missing altogether. Grow as a half-hardy annual for indoors and out. Outdoors, grow up wigwams of 5ft canes, either in borders, or large tubs for a moveable display of color. In hanging baskets thunbergia soon entwines the chains, making an effective camouflage. In patio tubs train plants up through other tall annuals like ricinus and sunflowers, or plant them around the base of outdoor plants in early summer. In colder areas grow plants in the conservatory or porch to guarantee a good show of flowers. Seed pods tend to set very easily which reduces the ability of the plant to keep flowering, so nip these off regularly.

CONDITIONS

ASPECT   A south-facing spot in full sun is essential. In conservatories direct hot sun should be avoided or the leaves may be scorched.

SITE   In containers use multipurpose compost with slow-release fertilizer added. Well-drained, moisture retentive soil, with rotted manure or compost is needed outdoors.

GROWING METHOD

SOWING   Soak seeds overnight then sow three to a 3½in diameter pot in March. Germinate at 64°F. Germination is erratic and seedlings may take a month to emerge. A small wigwam of canes will support the shoots. Grow several plants on in large pots during May, then harden off and plant after the last frosts. They dislike root disturbance.

FEEDING   Liquid feed once a week in summer.

PROBLEMS   Red spider mite attacks leaves. Wet the leaves daily or use a spray containing pirimiphos-methyl. Indoors use the predator phytoseiulus. Whitefly will feed on the leaves and cause sticky "honeydew." Use a spray containing permethrin or the natural encarsia indoors.

FLOWERING

SEASON   Flowers appear all summer and the flowering period is extended when plants are grown under some form of protection.

CUTTING   Not suitable.

AFTER FLOWERING

GENERAL   Nip off faded flowers. Remove outdoor plants after frosts and add to the compost heap.

AT A GLANCE		
A half-hardy annual climber flowering in summer for patio containers, baskets, and bedding. Frost hardy to 32°F (zone 10).		
Jan	/	Recommended Varieties
Feb	/	*Thunbergia alata*
Mar	sow	"Susie Mixed"
Apr	pot on/grow on	
May	harden/plant out	
Jun	flowers	
July	flowers	
Aug	flowers	
Sept	flowers	
Oct	/	
Nov	/	
Dec	/	

Thyme
THYMUS

FEATURES

Thyme is one of the most common of garden herbs, and very many varieties are grown. Most thymes are low, creeping plants although some will grow to 10–12in. The shape of the bush and the color and aroma of the leaves depends on the variety. The leaves are evergreen in shades of green, silver, and gold, and small pink or sometimes white flowers are produced in early summer. Not all thymes are used in cooking, the most commonly used varieties including lemon-scented thyme (*T.* x *citriodorus*), caraway thyme (*T. herba-barona*), common garden thyme (*T. vulgaris*), orange thyme (*T. vulgaris* "Fragrantissimus"), and silver posie thyme (*T. vulgaris* "Silver Posie"). Thyme plants are perennials but usually need replacing every two or three years.

CONDITIONS

ASPECT   Prefers full sun or partial shade.
SITE   Prefers a light, well-drained, not too rich soil, ideally neutral or slightly alkaline, and kept on the dry side. Adding compost will help keep the soil friable. The soil should not be too acid, if necessary add lime.

GROWING METHOD

SOWING   Thymes can be propagated from seed, but this tends to give inferior plants, and named varieties should be propagated by cuttings, division, or layering. If seed is used, sow in spring and take care not to overwater as the seedlings are prone to damping off. Dividing mature plants is the most successful method of propagation. During spring or summer, gently lift the parent plant, cut it into two or three sections, each with good roots, and replant elsewhere in the garden. Cuttings taken in spring or summer and layering are also satisfactory methods of propagation.

FEEDING   Do not overwater. Thymes prefer a dryish soil. Water adequately in dry spells. No fertilizer needed.

PROBLEMS   Spider mites or aphids can affect this herb. Treat with a recommended insecticidal spray. Root rot will set in if the soil is waterlogged.

PRUNING   Prune or clip to prevent woodiness. Trim after flowering to prevent plants becoming straggly.

HARVESTING

PICKING   Fresh leaves and flowers can be picked as required or the whole plant can be cut back to within 2in of the ground in summer.

AT A GLANCE		
Common garden herbs, thymes are popular not only for cooking but also as garden plants. Hardy to 4°F or below (zone 7).		
Jan	harvest	**Parts used**
Feb	harvest	Leaves
Mar	plant harvest	Flowers
Apr	plant harvest	Sprigs
May	plant harvest	**Uses**
Jun	plant harvest	Culinary
July	harvest	Medicinal
Aug	harvest	Craft
Sept	plant harvest	Gardening
Oct	harvest	
Nov	harvest	
Dec	harvest	

| STORAGE | Leaves are dried on the stem by hanging branches in a warm, airy place. Branches are then stripped and stored in airtight jars. |
| FREEZING | Pack in small airtight containers or freezer bags; can be frozen for up to 6 months. |

USES

CULINARY	Thyme is a classic component of the French bouquet garni. Varieties of thyme add special, individual flavors to many dishes. Both leaves and flowers can be eaten fresh in salads or used as garnishes or as a flavoring to honey, vinegars, stuffings, butters, or teas.
MEDICINAL	Thyme has strong antiseptic properties and is used to treat sore throats and as a mouthwash. Caution: avoid during pregnancy.
CRAFT	Can be added to pot-pourris and herb sachets.
GARDENING	Thymes can be grown for their decorative effect as their low, matting habit makes them excellent edging or rockery plants.

Tiarella
FOAM FLOWER

FEATURES

Tiarella trifoliata is a North American clump-forming rhizomatous perennial, making excellent groundcover in light shade. From late spring to mid-summer it produces light airy sprays of white flowers, on 12in-long panicles, held above the foliage. A more invasive plant is *T. cordifolia*, foam flower, from east North America, where it grows in mountainside woods, forming extensive colonies, remorselessly spreading by underground stolons. T. wherryi, also from North America, is more compact and less invasive—the better choice for a smaller, shady area. Its natural habitat is shady ravines and rocky woods. The white flowers are tinged pink. "Bronze Beauty" is a popular choice, benefiting from contrasting white flowers and bronze-red foliage.

CONDITIONS

ASPECT	Thrives in both dappled and darkish shade, which is its natural habitat.
SITE	It tolerates a wide range of soils, but naturally prefers rich, fertile ground, damp but definitely not boggy.

GROWING METHOD

PROPAGATION	Division is the simplest method, although ripe seed can also be sown. Sow in pots in the fall in a cold frame, and keep young plants well watered. Do not let them dry out.
FEEDING	The ground needs to be quite rich. Fork in leaf mold and compost in the early spring, and again in the fall, between plants.

PROBLEMS

Slugs can strike, but given the situation, out of the way in the shade, and the plant's vigor, it is rarely a major problem. Treat with slug pellets if matters get out of hand.

HARVESTING

SEASON	A profusion of white flowers appear from late spring to mid-summer.
CUTTING	There are better choices for airy white sprays in the summer, but nonetheless they make good cut flowers.

AFTER FLOWERING

REQUIREMENTS Cut back to the ground.

THE FOAM FLOWER produces both a fine early summer bloom display, and often burnt-red-colored fall foliage. Given a free run, it will produce a large, spreading clump with wonderful spires of white flowers.

AT A GLANCE		
T. trifoliata is a North American white perennial, ideal for spreading quickly through shady sites. Hardy to 5°F (zone 7).		
Jan	/	**Recommended Varieties**
Feb	/	*Tiarella cordifolia*
Mar	sow	"Elizabeth Oliver"
Apr	divide	*T. polyphylla*
May	flowering	"pink"
Jun	flowering	*T. wherryi*
July	flowering	"Bronze Beauty"
Aug	/	
Sept	sow	
Oct	/	
Nov	/	
Dec	/	

Tiarella wherryi

FOAM FLOWER

FEATURES

Tiarella wherryi is an American clump-forming perennial, ideal for small, shady areas. Its natural habitat is shady ravines and rocky woods. The white flowers are tinged pink. The form "Bronze Beauty" is a popular choice, with contrasting white flowers and bronze-red foliage. Good alternatives are *T. trifoliata* which makes excellent groundcover in light shade. From late spring to early summer it produces light, airy sprays of white flowers on 1ft long panicles, held above the foliage. More invasive still is *T. cordifolia* which spreads by underground stolons.

CONDITIONS

ASPECT Thrives in both dappled and darkish shade, which is its natural habitat.

SITE It tolerates a wide range of soils but naturally prefers rich, fertile ground, damp but definitely not boggy.

GROWING METHOD

PROPAGATION Division is the simplest method, though ripe seed can also be sown. Sow in pots in the fall in a cold frame. And keep young plants well watered. Do not let them dry out.

FEEDING The ground needs to be quite rich. Fork in leafmold and well-rotted organic matter in the early spring, and again in the fall.

PROBLEMS Slugs can strike, and where this becomes a major problem treat with slug pellets. Alternatively keep patrol at night, picking them off by hand. Discard as you will.

FLOWERING

SEASON The flowers appear in late spring, and at the beginning of the summer.

PRUNING

GENERAL Not necessary, but with more invasive kinds prune in the growing season when growth threatens to get out of control.

DELICATE TIARELLA WHERRYI *thrives here in a woodland setting. Its compact growth pattern also makes it ideal edging for a rock garden. Frothy sprays of white flowers give its its pretty common name. It make a charming addition to the garden in spring.*

AT A GLANCE	
Tiarella wherryi is a North American perennial for moist, shady areas. Good show of early season flowers. Hardy to 5°F (zone 7).	
Jan /	**Recommended Varieties**
Feb /	*Tiarella cordifolia*
Mar /	"Mint Chocolate"
April /	"Ninja"
May flowering	"Elizabeth Oliver"
June flowering	*T. polyphylla*
July foliage	"Tiger Stripe"
Aug foliage	*T. wherryi*
Sept foliage	"Bronze Beauty"
Oct foliage	
Nov /	
Dec /	

Tigridia pavonia

TIGER FLOWER, PEACOCK FLOWER

FEATURES

Although each flower of the tiger or peacock flower lasts only a day, there is a succession of spectacular blooms over a long period. Flowers have six petals; the outer petals are large and broad, the inner ones smaller and thinner, usually spotted with a contrasting color. The species is red with a spotted yellow and purple center but there is a large range of colors available, in combinations of white, cream, yellow, orange, pink, mauve, and red, with contrasting spotting around the center of each flower. The tiger flower is also called jockey's cap lily in some parts of the world. Plants usually grow to around 18in. They are often included in mixed borders of summer-flowering shrubs and perennials.

CONDITIONS

ASPECT   Prefers full sun with some wind protection. Grows best in warm, sheltered gardens.

SITE   Grow the plants towards the front of beds and borders, where their flamoyant flowers can be appreciated close at hand. They need well-drained but not particularly rich soil.

GROWING METHOD

PLANTING   Plant in mid to late spring 4in deep and about 6–8in apart.

FEEDING   Growth is usually improved by the application of a balanced fertilizer in spring. Occasional liquid feeds of a high potash fertilizer can be given through the growing season. Water during spring and summer in dry spells.

PROBLEMS   No specific problems are usually experienced with this plant.

FLOWERING

SEASON   Blooms appear from middle to late summer into the early fall.

CUTTING   Flowers are not suitable for cutting.

AFTER FLOWERING

REQUIREMENTS Remove spent flower stems. In sheltered, mild areas and in free-draining soil the bulbs can be left in the ground over winter, but more reliable results are obtained by lifting before the first frosts, and storing bulbs in a frost-free place until the following spring.

THE SHOWY FLOWERS of Tigridia pavonia *often have colorful spotting in the center, making it worth studying them closely.*

AT A GLANCE	
Spectacularly colorful but short-lived flowers are produced in succession from mid to late summer. Best in warmer areas.	
Jan /	**Recommended Varieties**
Feb /	Generally available only as color
Mar /	mixtures.
Apr plant	
May plant	
Jun /	
July /	
Aug flowering	
Sept flowering	
Oct /	
Nov /	
Dec /	

Tillandsia

TILLANDSIA SPECIES

FEATURES

Tillandsias are mostly epiphytes with very poorly developed root systems, and some absorb water and nutrients through their foliage. Habitats vary from sea level to high altitudes and even the desert. One of the best known is Spanish moss, *Tillandsia usneoides*, with thread-like leaves on long silvery stems. Most species form rosettes of green, gray, or reddish foliage, and those from arid regions have silver scales. Soft green-leaved species are generally native to humid forests and adapt well to pot culture, while many from arid regions are more easily grown on bromeliad "trees" or moss pads. Flowers are tubular and may be violet, white, pink, red, yellow, blue, or green.

CONDITIONS

POSITION
Most species need frost-free conditions—a cool greenhouse or conservatory is ideal. Green-leaved species need filtered sunlight year round while the gray- or silver-leaved varieties can be grown in full or partial sun. With a mixed collection it may be advisable to provide filtered sunlight, especially if the humidity is low.

POTTING MIX
The mix must be very open and well drained. Use fairly coarse composted bark or a special orchid mix, sold at garden centers or nurseries. Driftwood, logs, or cork slabs are ideal for mounting plants.

GROWING METHOD

PROPAGATION
Grows from offsets produced sometime during spring to fall. (A few species produce offsets between the leaf axils: these may be difficult to remove without damage.) When they have been cut from the parent plant, allow the bases to dry for a few days before fixing them in their permanent positions with a little PVA glue.

WATERING
Water or mist plants daily during hot weather. Mounted specimens can suffer if not moistened daily. In cool weather mist several mornings a week.

FEEDING
Not necessary although a very weak liquid feed during the warmest months of the year may encourage better growth.

PROBLEMS
No specific problems are known.

FLOWERING SEASON

Flower form and color are variable. Most flower in late spring or summer.

AT A GLANCE		
Easy to look after; grow on a log. Flowers are varied and can appear in almost any month of the year.		
Jan	mist twice weekly	
Feb	mist twice weekly	**Recommended Varieties**
Mar	mist twice weekly,	*T. abdita*
	remove offsets	*T. argentea*
Apr	keep at 61°F;	*T. bulbosa*
	mist twice daily	*T. butzii*
May	flowering, mist	*T. cyanea*
Jun	flowering, mist	*T. usneoides*
July	flowering, mist	
Aug	flowering, mist	
Sept	mist	
Oct	mist twice weekly,	
	remove offsets	
Nov	mist twice weekly	
Dec	mist twice weekly	

Tithonia

MEXICAN SUNFLOWER

FEATURES

Tithonia, as its common name suggests, comes from warmer areas, so does well when there is plenty of sun. Grow as a half-hardy annual. "Fiesta del Sol" is just 1ft tall, while "Torch" can reach 4ft. Flowers are large, exotic-looking and dahlia-like, red-orange, and have a distinct swollen "neck."

CONDITIONS

ASPECT — Must have full sun or plants will suffer.
SITE — Not fussy about soil, but needs good drainage. Plant in a fairly sheltered spot away from cold driving winds. Tithonia has a tendency to go pale and yellow when growing conditions are poor. Grow plants in containers if the soil is heavy, using multipurpose compost.

GROWING METHOD

SOWING — Sow seeds February to April in $3^{1}/_{2}$in pots of multipurpose compost, just covering them, and germinate at 64˚F in a warm place or heated propagator. Transplant to individual $3^{1}/_{2}$in pots or large cell trays and grow on. Harden off for 2–3 weeks and plant in early summer when the soil warms up. If seedlings or young plants turn yellow they are being kept too cold. Can also be sown outdoors in early June where plants are to flower.

FEEDING — Feed container-grown plants twice a month with liquid feed.
PROBLEMS — Slugs may attack the leaves after early summer rains so protect with slug pellets.

FLOWERING

SEASON — Flowers appear from midsummer and later sowings continue to give color into fall.
CUTTING — Suitable for use as a cut flower.

AFTER FLOWERING

GENERAL — Pull up after flowering. May self-seed.

THE DAHLIA-LIKE FLOWERS of tithonia have an "exotic" feel to them and each one can be up to 3in across, on strong stems. The heart-shaped leaves are an added bonus, and each flower also has a distinct swollen "neck."

AT A GLANCE		
A half-hardy annual grown for its large orange flowers on strong stems. Use in bedding and pots. Frost hardy to 32˚F (zone 10).		
Jan	/	**Recommended Varieties**
Feb	sow	*Tithonia rotundifolia*
Mar	sow	**Tall varieties**
Apr	sow/transplant	"Goldfinger"
May	harden off/plant	"Torch"
Jun	flowering	**Short varieties**
July	flowering	"Fiesta del Sol"
Aug	flowering	
Sept	flowering	
Oct	/	
Nov	/	
Dec	/	

Torenia

WISHBONE FLOWER

FEATURES

Wishbone flower needs to be in the "front row" of a summer bedding scheme, or used around the edge of pots and troughs. The variety "Susie Wong" has bright yellow flowers with black throats, and a spreading habit making it ideal for baskets. Half-hardy annuals, torenias grow no more than 1ft in height.

CONDITIONS

ASPECT Choose a sheltered spot with sun.
SITE   Dig in rotted manure or compost a few
        weeks ahead of planting out, or use
        multipurpose compost for container
        growing. Soil and compost used must
        be free-draining. Avoid planting where
        winds are persistent.

GROWING METHOD

SOWING Sow the very small seeds in pots or
        trays in March/April, barely cover and
        keep at 64°F in a well-lit place. When
        large enough the seedlings can be
        transplanted to cell trays and grown on
        until late May, then hardened off and
        planted well after the last frosts, 6in apart,
        or in groups in patio pots. Plant five
        plants to a 16in diameter hanging basket,
        four around the sides and one in the
        center. "Susie Wong" will creep in and
        out of other plants.

FEEDING   Feed regularly every 2–3 weeks with
          a balanced liquid plant food.
PROBLEMS Trouble free.

FLOWERING

SEASON   Throughout summer.
CUTTING Not used as a cut flower.

AFTER FLOWERING

GENERAL Pull or dig out the plants when flowering
         has stopped. They will sometimes self-
         seed, and they will then produce
         seedlings in the following year.

WISHBONE FLOWER gets its common name from the dark markings found on the lower lip of the flowers of some varieties. Shelter is essential for success with torenia, which can also be potted up and grown on as a flowering plant for indoors.

AT A GLANCE		
A low growing half-hardy annual grown for its colorful flowers, for edging in beds and pots. Frost hardy to 32°F (zone 10).		
Jan	/	**Recommended Varieties**
Feb	/	*Torenia fournieri*
Mar	sow	"Clown Mixed"
Apr	sow/transplant	"Susie Wong"
May	grow/harden off	
Jun	plant/flowers	
July	flowering	
Aug	flowering	
Sept	flowering	
Oct	/	
Nov	/	
Dec	/	

Trachelospermum

STAR JASMINE

FEATURES

Trachelospermum jasminoides is a handsome, evergreen, twining climber from China, Japan and Korea. It is valued for its pleasing foliage and for its clusters of strongly perfumed white flowers, which appear in mid- to late summer and age to cream through the flowering season. The blooms are reminiscent of the true jasmine. It is an ideal subject for growing on walls, fences, trellis screens, pergolas, arches and arbours. Star jasmine can also be grown as ground cover, for example in a shrub border, or used for covering a bank. Once established it grows quite quickly, and in maturity it reaches a height of 28ft. In areas subject to very hard winters this climber should be grown in a cool conservatory or glasshouse.

CONDITIONS

ASPECT	Must be very well sheltered and warm. Full sun or partial shade are acceptable.
SITE	This climber likes a good, reasonably rich soil that is well drained.

GROWING METHOD

PROPAGATION	Take semi-ripe cuttings in the summer and then provide them with bottom heat—about 68°F. Carry out serpentine layering in the spring.
WATERING	Do not let the star jasmine suffer from lack of moisture. Water well in summer if the soil starts to become excessively dry.
FEEDING	Give an annual spring application of slow-release fertilizer, such as blood, fish, and bone.

PROBLEMS	There are no problems from pests or diseases.

FLOWERING/FOLIAGE

FLOWERS	Clusters of white, star-shaped, highly fragrant flowers reminiscent of jasmine.
FOLIAGE	Deep green, shiny, oval leaves.

PRUNING

REQUIREMENTS	Needs little pruning. In early spring thin out some of the oldest stems if necessary. Bear in mind that this climber is naturally very dense in habit so do not attempt to thin it out too much. Prune back the plant as necessary to keep it within its allotted space, but avoid hard pruning. It is best to replace very old neglected plants rather than renovate them.

THE WHITE FLOWERS of star jasmine are enjoyed for their appearance as well as their strong perfume.

AT A GLANCE		
A jasmine-like climber with very dense growth and sweetly fragrant white flowers. Hardy to 23°F (zone 9).		
Jan	/	**Companion Plants**
Feb	/	A good companion for red or pink
Mar	planting	climbing roses.
Apr	planting	
May	planting	
Jun	/	
July	flowering	
Aug	flowering	
Sep	/	
Oct	/	
Nov	/	
Dec	/	

Trachycarpus fortunei

CHUSAN PALM

FEATURES

It is not known for certain where this palm originates from but it is probably a native of Burma and China. It gets its common name from the island of Chusan on the east coast of China, where it grows abundantly. It forms a single fibrous trunk topped with fan-shaped, deeply lobed, deep green fronds, which grow up to 30in in length. The eventual height is 70ft, with a spread of 8ft. The Chusan palm has a reputation as one of the hardiest of all palms, and survives snowy winters. It is therefore hardy enough to be grown out of doors, but in regions subject to very hard winters grow the plant in a tub in a cool conservatory or glasshouse and place it outside for the summer.

CONDITIONS

ASPECT   Outdoors grow in a sheltered position in full sun or light dappled shade. Indoors provide bright light but do not subject it to direct sun. Provide low humidity.

SITE   Outdoors grow in deep, well-drained but moisture-retentive soil. In containers grow in soil-based potting compost.

GROWING METHOD

PROPAGATION   Sow seeds as soon as available and germinate them at a temperature of 75°F.

WATERING   In containers, moderate watering in growing season from late spring to late summer, then for the rest of the year water sparingly.

FEEDING   In containers apply a balanced liquid fertilizer monthly during the growing season.

PROBLEMS   Under glass may be attacked by red spider mites and scale insects.

FOLIAGE/FLOWERING

FOLIAGE   Being evergreen this palm looks good all year round but is especially attractive during the spring and summer months.

FLOWERS   Dangling clusters of small yellow flowers are produced in summer, followed, on female plants, by blue-black fruits.

GENERAL CARE

REQUIREMENTS Remove dead fronds when necessary by cutting them off close to the trunk.

MATURE EXAMPLES of T. fortunei, with their characteristic covering of dark fibres, here flank a young one.

AT A GLANCE		
Forms a tall fibrous trunk topped with fan-shaped leaves. Frost-hardy, taking a minimum temperature of 23°F (zone 9).		
Jan	/	**Companion Plants**
Feb	/	Generally grown as a specimen tree
Mar	planting	in gardens. Looks good with formal
Apr	planting	beds of roses as well as brightly
May	foliage	colored summer bedding plants.
Jun	flowering	
July	flowering	
Aug	flowering	
Sep	/	
Oct	/	
Nov	/	
Dec	/	

Tradescantia

TRADESCANTIA / SPIDERWORT

FEATURES

This North American herbaceous perennial is a spreading plant with tapering, strap-like leaves and showy, triangular flowers in rich purple, rose-pink, or white. The flowers generally last only one day but they appear in succession over a long period. There are several named cultivars available. Spiderwort grows from 12 to 24in high, and is multi-stemmed. It is easy to grow in the correct conditions and can make a tall groundcover in filtered sunlight under trees. In a mild winter it may not die down completely.

CONDITIONS

ASPECT	It requires full sunlight or partial shade.
SITE	It grows best in soil that is well drained, but is also heavily enriched with plenty of decayed, organic matter.

GROWING METHOD

PROPAGATION	Clumps can be lifted and divided in the spring and fall. The species can be grown from seed sown in the fall. It is occasionally self-sown. New plantings should be approximately 12–18in apart, depending on how rapidly you need cover. Needs regular watering during a prolonged, dry growing period.
FEEDING	Apply a complete plant food when growth starts in the spring.
PROBLEMS	No specific problems are known.

FLOWERING

SEASON	The long succession of flowers starts in early summer and continues through to mid-fall.
CUTTING	The buds continue to open when cut.

AFTER FLOWERING

REQUIREMENTS	Growth starts to yellow and die back after flowering. Clean away dead foliage, and tidy up for the winter.

SPIDERWORT FLOWERS look like small purple irises but each lasts only a day. The surrounding buds are waiting their turn to open. Dense plantings of spiderwort produce plenty of flowers that thrive in filtered sunlight, ideal for a mixed or herbaceous border.

AT A GLANCE	
T. virginiana is a purple, repeat-flowerer in a genus of largely tender indoor plants. Ideal for the border. Hardy to 5°F (zone 7).	

		Recommended Varieties
Jan	/	
Feb	/	*Tradescantia* x *andersoniana*
Mar	divide	"Bilberry Ice"
Apr	/	"Isis"
May	/	"Osprey"
Jun	flowering	"Purple Dome"
July	flowering	"Red Cloud"
Aug	flowering	"Zwanenburg Blue"
Sept	flowering	
Oct	divide	
Nov	divide	
Dec	/	

Trillium

WAKE ROBIN

FEATURES

Trilliums are deciduous perennials that make excellent groundcover in partial or full shade, with spring and early summer flowers. The color range includes white, maroon, pink, yellow, bronze-green, and red-purple. *T. grandiflorum*, the North American wake robin, has 3in-long white flowers and veined petals. It is long-lived and easy to grow, requiring little attention. *T. sessile* "Rubrum" has claret petals and attractively mottled foliage. Several clones bear this name and there is little to choose between them. At the front of a shady, slightly acidic border, try *T. rivale*. It grows 6in tall and wide, has pointed ovate petals, white or pale pink, with purple speckling toward the base. *T. luteum* has scented yellowish flowers and mottled, pale and dark leaves. It grows 16in tall, spreading by almost the same amount.

CONDITIONS

ASPECT   Mottled or deep shade is required. Avoid open areas with full sunlight.
SITE   The soil should be the acid side of neutral, although some trilliums will tolerate low levels of alkalinity.

GROWING METHOD

PROPAGATION Preferably divide the rhizomes when dormant, ensuring each section has one strong growing point. Note that they are slow to establish. It is quite possible to sow ripe, late summer seed in a cold frame, but the 5–7 years to flower is prohibitively long.

FEEDING   The soil needs to be rich, with plenty of well-rotted leaf mold and compost, being damp and free-draining. Where necessary, provide a thick mulch every spring and fall.
PROBLEMS   Both slugs and snails feed on the tender new foliage. Pick off by hand when this becomes a problem, or use a chemical treatment.

FLOWERING

SEASON   The flowers appear in spring and summer.
CUTTING   They make attractive cut flowers, especially *T. grandiflorum*, with its near diamond-shaped white flowers.

AFTER FLOWERING

REQUIREMENTS Cut spent stems to the ground.

AT A GLANCE		
A 30-species strong genus with rhizomatous perennials, excellent for flowering ground cover in shade. Hardy to 5°F (zone 7).		
Jan	/	**Recommended Varieties**
Feb	/	*Trillium cernuum*
Mar	/	*T. chloropetalum*
Apr	transplant	*T. cuneatum*
May	flowering	*T. erectum*
Jun	flowering	*T. grandiflorum*
July	/	"flore-pleno"
Aug	/	*T. luteum*
Sept	sow	*T. rivale*
Oct	divide	*T. viride*
Nov	/	
Dec	/	

Triteleia

SYN. BRODIAEA LAXA

FEATURES

These pretty bulbous plants are native to Oregon and California. There is some confusion over their correct name; they are often listed as brodiaea, with some species as dichelostemma. *T. laxa* is the most popular form. Flower stems may be 18–24in or so high with the strappy leaves growing to about 12in. The starry flowers are carried in loose clusters and are pale or violet blue with the most popular cultivar, "Queen Fabiola," producing deeper violet-blue blooms with a pale center. The foliage dies back in spring while the plant is in bloom, and the corm remains dormant from midsummer until winter.

CONDITIONS

ASPECT	An open, sunny but sheltered site is necessary.
SITE	Grow this plant in the flower border or in containers. The soil must be light and very well-drained; triteleia cannot stand waterlogging. It can be grown in containers of sandy potting compost where the garden soil is heavy.

GROWING METHOD

PLANTING	Plant corms 3–4in deep and 4–6in apart in fall.
FEEDING	A balanced or high potash fertiliser can be given when the flower buds appear, but normally no feeding is necessary. Plants in containers can be liquid-fed every two weeks. Watering is not normally necessary; the soil should be allowed to dry out while the corm is dormant during the summer.
PROBLEMS	There are no specific pest or disease problems known for this plant.

FLOWERING

SEASON	Flowers appear from early to mid-summer.
CUTTING	Blooms last particularly well as a cut flower.

AFTER FLOWERING

REQUIREMENTS	Flowering stems can be cut off when they are past their peak, or left to set seed. Plants resent disturbance, so should be left alone once planted.

BLUE FLOWERS are always a favorite, and the violet-blue, starry flowers of these triteleias fill a sheltered pocket in the garden.

AT A GLANCE		
Dainty clusters of tubular blue blooms are carried on slender stems in midsummer. Well-drained soil is essential.		
Jan	/	**Recommended Varieties**
Feb	/	*Triteleia hyacinthina*
Mar	/	*T. ixioides*
Apr	/	*T. laxa*
May	flowering	"Queen Fabiola"
Jun	flowering	*T. peduncularis*
July	flowering	
Aug	/	
Sept	plant	
Oct	/	
Nov	/	
Dec	/	

Tritonia

TRITONIA

FEATURES

This is a most undemanding little plant that will give great value in containers or as a cut flower. Tritonias are not fully hardy and in colder areas need to be grown indoors, but in sheltered gardens in milder parts of the country they can be grown outside successfully as long as they have full sun and a well-drained soil. Most species flower from middle to late spring or in early summer on spikes that are around 12in high. *T. crocata* usually has bright orange flowers with darker markings in the throat but there are other forms with bright pink, salmon, or scarlet flowers. *T. disticha rubrolucens* has rose pink flowers and is hardier; it is often listed as *T. rosea*.

CONDITIONS

ASPECT   Grows best in full sun, preferably with shelter from strong wind.
SITE   In mild areas, tritonias do well in pockets of a rockery or planted in generous clumps in a garden bed. Soil must be well drained but it need not be very rich. In cold gardens, grow the corms in pots of John Innes or soil-less potting compost.

GROWING METHOD

PLANTING Plant the corms about 2in deep and 4–6in apart in autumn. Five corms can be grown in a 6in pot.
FEEDING   A light application of balanced fertilizer can be given as growth starts. In containers, liquid feed every 14–21 days. Begin watering container plants when the leaves appear but allow the compost to dry out once the leaves start to turn yellow.
PROBLEMS No specific problems are known.

FLOWERING

SEASON   Flowers are carried from mid-spring to early summer.
CUTTING   Flowers will last in the vase for up to a week.

AFTER FLOWERING

REQUIREMENTS Cut off spent flower stems. Mulch plants growing outdoors for winter protection: allow container plants to remain dry in their pots until planting time.

THIS RICH SALMON TRITONIA (Tritonia crocata*) is planted beside a path where it revels in the reflected heat and somewhat dry conditions. Like most tritonias, it will increase rapidly if it is happy with the growing conditions.*

AT A GLANCE		
Colorful, freesia-like flowers in late spring and early summer. Not suitable for growing outdoors in colder areas.		
Jan	/	**Recommended Varieties**
Feb	/	Usually available only as color
Mar	/	mixtures.
Apr	/	
May	flowering	
Jun	flowering	
July	/	
Aug	/	
Sept	plant	
Oct	/	
Nov	/	
Dec	/	

Tropaeolum

NASTURTIUM

FEATURES

With big seeds and quick growth, tropaeolum, better known as nasturtium, is one of the easiest of all hardy annuals to grow. Plants just 9in tall are perfect for bedding and patio planters, while others will scramble up throughout a dull hedge. The color range is huge, and single and mixed colors are available. For pretty leaves too, grow "Alaska Mixed," which is speckled with white.

CONDITIONS

ASPECT	Needs full sun.
SITE	Poor, thin soil gives excellent results when grown under hedges or in bedding displays.

GROWING METHOD

SOWING	Simply push the large seeds 1–2in into the soil in April, in groups of 3–5 where plants are to flower. Fleshy seedlings appear 2–3 weeks later and they can all be left to develop and form a large clump. If needed for containers, sow three seeds to a $3^1/_2$in pot at the same time and keep warm until seedlings appear, then keep outdoors.
FEEDING	Feeding encourages leaves at the expense of flowers, although if other plants are growing in a container or basket, some extra feeding is unavoidable. Don't feed plants growing in soil.
PROBLEMS	Aphids and caterpillars feed under the leaves, so check regularly and squash if seen.

FLOWERING

SEASON	Flowering is all summer long.
CUTTING	Not used cut, but flowers and the peppery leaves can be used raw in summer salads.

AFTER FLOWERING

GENERAL	Pull up and compost. Self-seeds very easily.

"MOONLIGHT" IS A CLIMBING variety of nasturtium reaching 6ft with soft yellow flowers against light green leaves.

AT A GLANCE		
A hardy annual grown for its colorful flowers and variegated leaves. For beds and containers. Frost hardy to 32°F (zone 10).		
Jan	/	**Recommended Varieties**
Feb	sow	*Tropaeolum majus*
Mar	sow	**Tall climbers**
Apr	transplant	"Climbing Mixed"
May	transplant	"Jewel of Africa"
Jun	flowering	**Short, mixed colors**
July	flowering	"Alaska Mixed"
Aug	flowering	"Gleam Mixed"
Sept	flowering	"Tip Top Mixed"
Oct	/	**Single colors**
Nov	/	"Empress of India"
Dec	/	"Gleaming Mahogany"
		"Moonlight"

Tulbaghia violacea
WILD GARLIC

FEATURES

This is another plant which needs warm, sheltered gardens to do well when left outdoors, though it can be grown as a container plant very successfully in cooler areas. The strappy leaves grow to about 12in with the flowering stems standing 4in or more above the foliage. The individual rosy-violet flowers form a rounded head of bloom. Society garlic flowers through the summer, and stems can be cut for the vase. *Tulbaghia natalensis* grows to 6in high and has fragrant white flowers with a yellow center that gives them a narcissus-like appearance. This is a hardier species which is usually more successful in colder gardens, though it is not as common as *T. violacea.*

CONDITIONS

ASPECT Prefers a position in full sun.
SITE Tulbaghia is a good plant for seaside gardens, and can be included in a mixed border of annuals and perennials or grown in containers. Soil should be well drained and contain plenty of well-rotted organic matter.

GROWING METHOD

PLANTING Plant in spring about 1in deep and 8in or so apart. Congested clumps can be lifted and divided in spring.
FEEDING If the organic content of the soil is high little extra feeding is needed. However, a light dressing of balanced fertilizer may be given as growth becomes active.

Keep the soil moist during the growing season, watering in dry spells as necessary.
PROBLEMS No specific problems are known.

FLOWERING

SEASON Flowers are carried all through summer.
CUTTING Flowers are very decorative when cut for the vase, although the smell of the foliage may discourage some people.

AFTER FLOWERING

REQUIREMENTS Tidy up the foliage and apply a mulch of chipped bark, leafmould or dry leaves for winter protection. Container plants should be allowed to dry out and moved under cover for the winter.

THE PALE PURPLE flowers of wild garlic are pleasantly fragrant, though the crushed foliage has a distinctive onion smell. The flowers appear throughout the summer above the clumps of vigorous, gray-green foliage.

AT A GLANCE		
A slightly tender plant with mounds of grassy foliage and heads of pretty pink summer flowers.		
Jan	/	**Recommended Varieties**
Feb	/	*Tulbaghia violacea pallida*
Mar	/	"Silver Lace"
Apr	plant	
May	/	
Jun	flowering	
July	flowering	
Aug	flowering	
Sept	/	
Oct	/	
Nov	/	
Dec	/	

Tulipa

TULIP

FEATURES

There are over 100 species of tulips and many hundreds of hybrids. Most modern garden tulips are the result of extensive breeding programmes that began in the late sixteenth century in Europe and are continuing to this day. Tulips were all the rage at that time as more and more species were introduced to Europe from Turkey, Iran, and central Asia. Tulip species range in height from about 6–24in but the greatest number of hybrids are probably in the range of 12–16in. Tulips look their best in mass plantings of one color but they can, of course, be mixed. They make very good container plants and are delightful cut flowers. Some of the most charming are the dwarf types which do particularly well in rock gardens and are also very suitable for containers.

Tulip bulbs are widely available in garden centers in late summer and early fall, but to get a wider choice it is often best to obtain catalogues from specialist bulb growers who run mail-order businesses. Many of the species tulips are only available from specialist growers. With careful selection it is possible to have a tulip in flower from early to very late spring. Like daffodils, tulips are split into a number of divisions according to their flower form and time of flowering.

TYPES

SINGLE EARLY Cup-shaped single flowers, up to 16in in early to mid-spring.

DOUBLE EARLY Fully double flowers up to 16in in early to mid-spring.

TRIUMPH Conical then rounded, single flowers up to 20in in mid to late spring.

DARWIN HYBRID Large, single flowers of varying shape, up to 24in in mid to late spring.

SINGLE LATE Single, blocky or square shaped flowers up to 30in in late spring and early summer.

LILY-FLOWERED Single, waisted flowers with pointed petals, up to 24in in late spring.

FRINGED Single flowers with very finely cut petal edges, up to 24in in late spring.

VIRIDIFLORA Single flowers with green bands or streaks on the outside, up to 20in in late spring.

REMBRANDT Single flowers with a broken pattern of feathering or streaking caused by a virus. Up to 30in in late spring.

PARROT Single flowers with very strongly frilled and curled petals, up to 24in in late spring.

DOUBLE LATE Large, fully double flowers up to 24in in late spring.

AT A GLANCE		
Well-known flowers in a very wide range of colors, sizes, and forms, flowering between late winter and late spring.		
Jan	/	Recommended Varieties
Feb	flowering	"Peach Blossom"
Mar	flowering	"Apeldoorn"
Apr	flowering	"Clara Butt"
May	flowering	"China Pink"
Jun	/	"Burgundy Lace"
July	/	"Spring Green"
Aug	/	"Texas Gold"
Sept	/	"Angelique"
Oct	/	"Ancilla"
Nov	plant	T. fosteriana
Dec	plant	T. greigii
		T. tarda

KAUFMANNIANA Single, often bi-colored flowers of a waterlily shape, up to 10in in late spring. Leaves may be mottled.

FOSTERIANA Large, single, wide-opening flowers up to 20in in early to mid-spring.

GREIGII Large, single flowers up to 14in in mid to late spring. Leaves streaked and mottled.

MISCELLANEOUS Any other species, varieties, and hybrids.

CONDITIONS

ASPECT Tulips need full sun for at least half the day, with some wind protection.

SITE Grow tulips in beds and borders, on rockeries or in containers. Soil should be well drained with a high organic content. Add lime to acid soils.

GROWING METHOD

PLANTING Bulbs should be planted in late fall. Planting depth varies according to the size of the bulbs; usually 6−8in for the larger types and 4in for the smaller species. Space them 4−8in apart.

FEEDING Apply liquid fertilizer as soon as buds appear and again after flowers have faded. Water regularly in dry spells, especially once the buds have appeared.

PROBLEMS Tulip breaking virus, causing streaking of the flowers, is carried by aphids. Remove affected plants and keep aphids under control. Tulip fire disease is a type of botrytis or gray mould. It causes small brown spots on flowers and leaves; stems may rot and gray furry growth may develop on the damaged areas. Destroy plants infected with this disease and avoid planting tulips in the same spot for a couple of years. Spraying with a general fungicide may control early infection.

FLOWERING

SEASON Tulips flower somewhere between late winter and late spring, depending on variety.

CUTTING If cutting blooms for the house, choose those that are not fully open and cut them early in the morning. Change vase water frequently.

AFTER FLOWERING

REQUIREMENTS Remove spent flower stems and dead foliage. Tulips may be left in the ground for two or three years, or the bulbs can be lifted once the foliage has died down, cleaned and stored in a cool, dry, airy place. Dwarf tulips tend to be left in the ground, but other varieties usually perform better if they are lifted and replanted every year. If you do not want to lift them annually, make sure the bulbs are planted deeply.

Valerian

VALERIANA OFFICINALIS

FEATURES

Valerian is a tall, spreading hardy perennial, growing to about 3–5ft in height. It is native to Europe and Asia where it is found in grassland and damp meadows, close to streams. It has finely divided mid-green leaves and heads of small white or pale pink flowers that are produced in early summer. Both cats and rats are said to find the smell of valerian attractive, and it is said that the Pied Piper of Hamelin carried the root in order to charm the rats away!

CONDITIONS

ASPECT	Valerian will grow in full sun or deep shade, as long as the roots are cool. The plants may need to be staked if they are grown in exposed positions.
SITE	Valerian is tolerant of most soils, but prefers moist conditions.

GROWING METHOD

SOWING	Valerian can be propagated by division in spring or fall, replanting the divisions immediately into well prepared ground. The seed can be sown in spring, directly where it is to grow. But for more reliable results sow the seed under glass in trays of seed compost. Do not cover the seeds as this will delay germination. When the young plants are large enough to handle they should be planted out in the garden approximately 2–3ft apart. When grown in good conditions, valerian will self-seed.
FEEDING	Keep well watered as valerian prefers moist conditions. Mulch lightly in spring and also apply a dressing of a balanced general fertilizer in spring.
PROBLEMS	Generally free from pests and diseases.
PRUNING	Cut valerian back after flowering to prevent self-seeding. The top growth can be cut down in fall.

HARVESTING

PICKING	Dig up the roots in late fall, when the plants are in their second or third year of growth.
STORAGE	To dry, cut the roots into thin slices and dry in an oven at 120–40°F, turning frequently.
FREEZING	Not suitable for freezing

USES

MEDICINAL	Valerian has been used for many centuries for its healing properties. Traditionally, the root has been used for its sedative and anti-spasmodic effects, and for the treatment of a wide range of

AT A GLANCE		
A tall but undistinguished, strong-smelling herb, with powerful healing properties. Fully hardy to 4°F or below (zone 7).		
Jan	/	**Parts used**
Feb	/	Roots
Mar	plant	**Uses**
Apr	plant	Medicinal
May	plant	Cosmetic
Jun	/	Gardening
July	/	
Aug	/	
Sept	plant harvest	
Oct	plant harvest	
Nov	/	
Dec	/	

conditions, including nervous conditions, insomnia, headaches, and exhaustion. Caution: Do not take valerian in large doses or for extended periods of time. This herb is best taken only under expert supervision.

COSMETIC Despite its rather unpleasant aroma, valerian has been used in perfumery.

GARDENING Nowadays, valerian is used more in the garden than for its medicinal properties. Although not the most decorative of herbs, it is useful to add height at the back of the border. It is also said to be a good companion plant, encouraging the growth of nearby vegetables and other plants by stimulating earthworm activity and increasing phosphorus availability.

Verbascum

MULLEIN

FEATURES

Not all mulleins are reliably perennial—some are best treated as biennials and replaced after two years. However, most are easy to raise. They are grown for their large rosettes of foliage, often silver or gray, from which emerges a tall, striking spike of flowers up to 6ft high. They make eye-catching accent plants in any sunny part of the yard. The various species and their cultivars have flowers in a range of colors, including white and gentler shades of yellow, pink, and purple. The common mullein, *V. thapsus*, also known as Aaron's rod, freely self-seeds. Mullein has a long folk history, first as a candle, then as a medical treatment.

CONDITIONS

ASPECT   Grows best in full sunlight all day.
SITE   Grows in any kind of well-drained soil, even poor and alkaline ones.

GROWING METHOD

PROPAGATION   Grows from seed sown as soon as it is ripe, or from root cuttings taken in late fall or winter. The seed forms on the spike after the flowers have fallen, and is ripe when it has changed color, becoming brown or black. Sow in pots in a cold frame in either the spring or fall. Plants of the larger mullein species need to be planted out approximately 39in apart.

FEEDING   Apply a complete plant food in early spring, when new growth commences.
PROBLEMS   No specific problems are known.

FLOWERING

SEASON   Mullein produces flowers right through the summer, but its amazing spire of a stem remains a big architectural feature long after the flowers have finished.
CUTTING   A nipped-off section of the flowering spire considerably adds to a formal, architectural display.

AFTER FLOWERING

REQUIREMENTS   Cut off the spent flower spike, unless you want seed to set.

MULLEINS HAVE few equals as accent plants, since they are tough and adaptable, capable of tolerating many climates and conditions.

AT A GLANCE	
A 360-species genus, famed for its dramatic, colored spires in summer. Heights 12in–6ft. Hardy to 5˚F (zone 7).	
Jan /	Recommended Varieties
Feb /	*Verbascum bombyciferum*
Mar /	*V. chaixii*
Apr sow	"Album"
May transplant	"Cotswold Beauty"
Jun flowering	"Gainsborough"
July flowering	*V. dumulosum*
Aug flowering	"Golden Wings"
Sept sow	"Helen Johnson"
Oct /	"Letitia"
Nov /	*V. phoeniceum*
Dec /	

Verbena

VERBENA

FEATURES

Most verbenas grow 6–12in tall and are prized for their heads of bright flowers. Mixtures or single shades like "Peaches & Cream" are used for planting containers or for bedding. Raise from seed—although this is tricky—or grow them from mail order plants. Most trailing verbenas are not seed raised but bought as ready-grown plants from garden centers and mail order catalogs in spring.

CONDITIONS

ASPECT   Needs full sun for best results.
SITE   Use multipurpose compost in containers, and mix rotted compost with soil outdoors.

GROWING METHOD

SOWING   To succeed with verbena seed, sow on the surface of peat-based seed compost in March and cover the seeds with a thin layer of fine vermiculite. Water and keep at 70°F. Seedlings appear 2–3 weeks later, and should be kept slightly on the dry side. When large enough, transplant seedlings to cell trays or individual 3in pots, and grow on. Plant after hardening off in late spring/early summer.

FEEDING / PROBLEMS

FEEDING   Feed monthly with balanced liquid feed.
PROBLEMS   Powdery mildew can attack leaves—use a spray containing sulfur at the first signs.

FLOWERING

SEASON   Flowers appear all summer.
CUTTING   Not used for cutting.

AFTER FLOWERING

GENERAL   Pull up when finished and use for compost.

"PEACHES & CREAM" has a unique color that makes it a real winner, at 8in, for patio containers and hanging baskets. It is one of the prettiest of the new cultivars of the annual Verbena x hybrida.

AT A GLANCE	
A half-hardy annual used in bedding and containers. Masses of flowers appear during summer. Frost hardy to 32°F (zone 10).	
Jan /	Recommended Varieties
Feb /	*Verbena hybrida*
Mar sow	Mixed colors
Apr transplant	"Crown Jewels"
May grow/	"Novalis Mixed"
harden off	"Raspberry Crush"
Jun flowering	"Romance Pastels"
July flowering	Single colors
Aug flowering	"Adonis Blue"
Sept flowering	"Apple Blossom"
Oct /	"Peaches & Cream"
Nov /	Spreading/trailing
Dec /	"Misty"

Veronica
SPEEDWELL

FEATURES

Veronicas are sun-loving plants, and include annuals, perennials and sub-shrubs. Veronica gentianoides comes from the Caucasus and is a mat-forming perennial with shiny leaves and spires of pale blue flowers that open in early summer. Growing 18in high and wide, it is good in a border. "Variegata" has creamier leaves than the species, *V. spicata* "Icicle" has white flowers and *V. peduncularis* "Georgia Blue" dark blue flowers. If you need a low-growing plant that spreads well, try *V. prostrata*. It grows 6in high, and has a spread of 16in.

CONDITIONS

ASPECT Only grow in full sunlight. *V. gentianoides* needs wall-to-wall sun and will not tolerate anything less than this.

SITE The key to success is very good drainage. The soil need not be that fertile, and in fact can be quite poor. South-facing banks or slopes often make a very good site.

GROWING METHOD

PROPAGATION Since veronica does not provide the fastest kind of groundcover, it is well worth propagating several more plants. Either divide them in the spring or in the fall, or sow plenty of seed in the fall.

FEEDING

FEEDING Not necessary, but in poor, unpampered soil add a slow-release fertilizer in the spring.

PROBLEMS The main problem is usually downy mildew, which is best tackled by quickly removing all affected leaves, thus providing better air circulation around the plant. Powdery mildew needs to be tackled with a chemical spray.

FLOWERING

SEASON *V. gentianoides* gives a good but brief show of flowers in early summer.

PRUNING

GENERAL Pruning is not necessary.

GENEROUS VERONICAS bear masses of rather stately spires in summer, making them invaluable plants for the front of a border.

AT A GLANCE		
Veronica gentianoides provides a fine array of pale blue flowers in early summer. Hardy to 5°F (zone 7).		
Jan	/	Recommended Varieties
Feb	/	Veronica austriaca
Mar	/	"Shirley Blue"
April	foliage	V. cinerea
May	foliage	V. gentianoides
June	flowering	"Variegata"
July	foliage	V. peduncularis
Aug	foliage	"Georgia Blue"
Sept	foliage	V. prostrata
Oct	foliage	V. spicata
Nov	/	"Icicle"
Dec	/	"Rotfuchs"
		"Wendy"

Viburnum

VIBURNUM

FEATURES

Coveted for their blossom, berries, foliage and architectural habit, deciduous and evergreen viburnums have year-round appeal. Flowers—clusters, globes, and sprays—in pink or white, thickly clothe shoots. Most varieties are sweetly perfumed. Growing 30in–10ft or more, most species and varieties bloom within three years of planting. All make fetching statements: such as evergreen Viburnum tinus, which also makes a dense, winter-flowering hedge; carpeting *V. davidii*, whose female plants are studded with turquoise-blue berries; *V. carlesii*, studded with vanilla-scented, whitish-pink orbs in spring; and *V.* x *bodnantense* "Dawn," clustered with rose-pink flowers from October to March.

CONDITIONS

ASPECT   Viburnums need at least half a day's full sunshine to prosper. Shield large-flowering varieties from cold wind.

SITE   These shrubs prefer well-drained soil enriched with well-rotted organic matter several weeks before planting. In light soils that parch quickly, mulch in spring with moisture-conserving, bulky organics to keep roots cool and active.

GROWING METHOD

FEEDING   Nourish growth by applying a balanced fertilizer, such as Growmore, chicken pellets, or fish, blood, and bone meal, in spring and midsummer. In a cold spring, boost growth of young plants by foliar feeding fortnightly with a high-potash fertilizer. Water frequently newly planted viburnums in warm, dry weather.

PROPAGATION   Take soft-tip cuttings in spring; semi-ripe cuttings from mid- to late summer; and hardwood cuttings in late fall. Layer shoots from mid-spring to late summer.

PROBLEMS   Tackle viburnum beetle, which shreds leaves in summer, by spraying in late spring with permethrin, bifenthrin, or pyrethrum.

PRUNING

V. TINUS. Trim shoots lightly in early spring.
DECIDUOUS: winter-flowering species: Remove one stem in three every 2–3 years in spring.
EVERGREENS: Cut out one stem in three, in midsummer, every four years.

VIBURNUM x BODNANTENSE *'Dawn' bears its rose pink flowers in mid winter. Use it as the centerpiece of a winter garden with skimmias, winter heathers and snowdrops.*

AT A GLANCE		
Light up winter to summer with showy flowers and fall with spectacular, scarlet berries. Hardiness according to species.		
Jan	flower	**Recommended Varieties**
Feb	flower	Winter flowering
Mar	plant, flower	"Dawn"
Apr	flower, prune	"Deben"
May	flower, plant	*V.* x *bodnantense*
Jun	flower, plant	Spring flowering
July	plant, prune	*V. carlesii*
Aug	plant	"Aurora"
Sept	plant	*V.* x *carlcephalum*
Oct	plant	*V.* x *opulus*
Nov	plant	"Roseum"
Dec	/	Fall berrying
		V. betulifolium
		V. davidii

Vinca minor

PERIWINKLE

FEATURES

Vinca minor comes in a plain green-leaved form and several variegated forms, including "Argenteovariegata," although the blue flowers are, as a rule, more profuse on the plain form. They appear during the spring. The plant has a creeping growth habit, rooting down at the nodes, and one plant will eventually cover 6ft. *V. minor* is an excellent carpeting plant for shaded areas under trees, on banks or in large rockeries. Its growth can be rather vigorous, even invasive in warm climates, but it is not as invasive as its close relative *V. major*, which can also be grown in gardens. *V. minor* is very easy to care for and will withstand poor conditions, although growth will be more attractive if it is given some care.

CONDITIONS

ASPECT   *V. minor* grows best in shade, in filtered sunlight or with morning sun and afternoon shade. However, the greater the amount of sunshine received, the more the plant will flower over a longer period.

SITE   Tolerates any kind of soil but prefers a well-drained soil enriched with organic matter.

GROWING METHOD

PROPAGATION   Layering is the easiest way to produce more plants. Rooted sections can also be dug up, or semi-ripe cuttings can be taken in the summer. Given the rate at which it produces, you are unlikely to need to propagate more plants once the earmarked site has been well planted with *V. minor*.

FEEDING   Apply complete plant food once new growth begins in spring.

PROBLEMS   No specific problems are known.

FLOWERING

SEASON   The mauve-blue flowers of *V. minor* appear in spring. Note that there are also many different forms which have plum or purple, pale blue and white flowers.

CUTTING   Flowers are not suitable for cutting.

PRUNING

GENERAL   May need occasional pruning to control its shape and spread. If it gets out of hand you can be as ruthless as you like.

NEATLY EDGED IN CREAM, the foliage of this variegated periwinkle is very decorative. The plant has a dense growth habit.

AT A GLANCE		
V. minor never fails. Masses of groundcover and a long season of blue flowers. Other colors are available. Hardy to 0°F (zone 7).		
Jan	foliage	**Recommended Varieties**
Feb	foliage	*Vinca major*
Mar	foliage	"Maculata"
April	foliage	"Variegata"
May	flowering	*V. minor*
June	flowering	"Argenteovariegata"
July	flowering	"Azurea Flore Pleno"
Aug	flowering	"Gertrude Jekyll"
Sept	flowering	"Le Grave"
Oct	foliage	
Nov	foliage	
Dec	foliage	

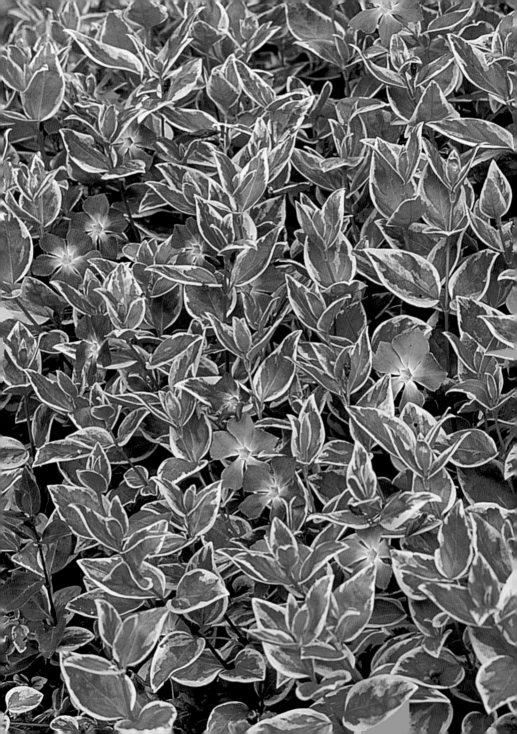

Viola cornuta

VIOLA

FEATURES

Violas are smaller than pansies but they are no less prolific, and what they lack in size they make up for in sheer character. Most are varieties of *Viola cornuta*, and all are quite hardy, being sown in spring or summer. Grow single colors, mixtures like "Bambini," or trailing yellow "Sunbeam" for hanging baskets. Violas grow to around 6in, making bushy little plants for bedding or containers. Try planting them in cottage style wicker baskets. Available as young plants.

CONDITIONS

ASPECT	Grows well in sun or dappled, light shade.
SITE	Soil does not need to be over prepared, but must be well-drained. For container growing use multipurpose compost.

GROWING METHOD

SOWING	Sow from February under cover for flowers the same summer, or outside May–July for flowers the following spring. Either way, sow in a 3^1/$_2$in pot of multi-purpose compost and barely cover seeds. In early spring keep at 60°F and transplant seedlings when large enough to cell trays, grow, harden off, and plant in late May. When summer sowing, stand the pot outside in shade to germinate then treat seedlings the same, planting out in October where you want the plants to flower.
FEEDING	Extra feeding is not usually necessary.
PROBLEMS	Use slug pellets if the leaves are attacked.

FLOWERING

SEASON	Spring-sown plants flower during summer, summer-sown the following spring/summer.
CUTTING	The delicate cut stems of "Queen Charlotte" are sometimes used for making scented posies.

AFTER FLOWERING

GENERAL	Plants often carry on as short-lived perennials, and also self-seed freely.

AT A GLANCE	
A hardy annual grown for its pretty little pansy flowers which appear on branching plants. Frost hardy to 5°F (zone 7).	
Jan /	Recommended Varieties
Feb sow	Viola hybrids
Mar sow	"Bambini Mixed"
Apr sow/flower	"Blackjack"
May sow/flower	"Blue Moon"
Jun sow/flower	"Cuty"
July sow/flower	"Juliette Mixed"
Aug grow on/flowers	"Midnight Runner"
Sept grow on/flowers	"Princess Mixed"
Oct plant	"Sorbet Yesterday, Today & Tomorrow"
Nov /	"Sunbeam"
Dec /	

Viola hederacea

IVY-LEAVED VIOLET

FEATURES

Viola hederacea is an excellent groundcover plant that is suitable for shaded and semi-shaded positions. It is easy to maintain, but can be rather invasive where the conditions are suitable. *V. hederacea* is best kept out of rockeries as it can be almost impossible to confine it to its allotted space. The small, rounded leaves grow from 2–4in high, and the pretty white and mauve violets are carried on stems above the foliage. New plantings should be spaced about 1ft apart. This well-loved plant makes a good groundcover under trees where grass will not grow, as it will tolerate occasional foot traffic. *V. hederacea* also makes a very attractive plant for troughs and hanging baskets.

CONDITIONS

ASPECT Dappled sunlight or shade is suitable but the flowering is better if grown in some sun.

SITE Tolerates a wide range of soils, but try to avoid any extremes, either of a damp or dry kind.

GROWING METHOD

PROPAGATION Can be readily increased from runners or by division of clumps. This is best carried out in either the spring or the fall. Replant each section, making sure that it has got a good root system.

FEEDING Feeding is generally not necessary. If the soil is extremely poor, give a light dressing of blood and bone in early spring.

PROBLEMS

PROBLEMS On the whole, *V. hederacea* is unlikely to suffer from major problems, but keep a close look out for marauding snails and slugs.

FLOWERING

SEASON The main flowering period is late summer. The flowers come in a wide color range, and are either violet (light to dark) or creamy-white. If you get very close you might just be able to detect some scent.

CUTTING The flowers can be cut for a miniature posy.

PRUNING

GENERAL Actual pruning is not necessary but sections may need to be pulled up or cut out if the plant is spreading where it is not wanted.

AT A GLANCE		
Viola hederacea is an evergreen ground covering violet, providing late summer flowers. Hardy to 0°F (zone 7).		
Jan	foliage	**Recommended Varieties**
Feb	foliage	*Viola cornuta*
Mar	foliage	*V. gracilis*
April	foliage	*V. hederacea*
May	foliage	"Huntercombe Purple"
June	foliage	*V. obliqua*
July	foliage	*V. odorata*
Aug	flowering	*V. sororia*
Sept	flowering	*V.* x *wittrockiana* cultivars
Oct	foliage	
Nov	foliage	
Dec	foliage	

Viola odorata

ENGLISH VIOLET

FEATURES

Violets have been in cultivation since ancient times, and were highly valued by the ancient Greeks. In Victorian period an enormous number of varieties was grown, including a wide range of the double Parma violets. The violet's sweet fragrance and elegant flowers make them big favorites with gardeners and florists alike. The plants have a creeping habit, spreading up to 12in, and are rarely more than 6–8in tall. There are cultivars with single or double flowers in purple, pink, white, or bicolors, but the deep purple is probably the best loved. There are other violet species to grow in the garden, from the summer-flowering *V. cornuta*, fine under hybrid tea roses, to the spring/summer *V. sororia* and its form, "Freckles."

CONDITIONS

ASPECT   It needs either shade, or light dappled sunshine.

SITE   For the best results it needs well-drained, moisture-retentive soil, heavily enriched with organic matter.

GROWING METHOD

PROPAGATION   Clumps can be lifted and divided, or runners can be dug up and replanted every couple of years, in the spring or fall. Set out at 8in spacings, with the plant crowns kept just above soil level. Violets self-seed, too. Keep young plants well watered during the first growing season.

FEEDING   Apply complete plant food in spring after flowering ceases.

PROBLEMS   Slugs and snails can be a major nuisance, devouring tasty new growth. Pick off by hand, or treat chemically.

FLOWERING

SEASON   Violets flower from late winter into early spring.

CUTTING   Scalding the stems of cut violets before arranging them will certainly increase their vase life.

AFTER FLOWERING

REQUIREMENTS   No special treatment is needed, but excess runners can be removed during the growing season if they are invasive. This has the added benefit of channeling vigor back to the main crown.

AT A GLANCE		
V. odorata is a rhizomatous, semi-evergreen perennial with blue or white flowers. A good self-seeder. Hardy to 0°F (zone 6–7).		
Jan	/	**Recommended Varieties**
Feb	/	*Viola cornuta*
Mar	flowering	"Alba Group"
Apr	flowering	"Lilacina Group"
May	flowering	"Minor"
Jun	/	*V. odorata*
July	/	"Alba"
Aug	/	"Rosea"
Sept	divide	*V. sororia*
Oct	/	"Freckles"
Nov	/	"Priceana"
Dec	/	

Viola tricolor
WILD PANSY

FEATURES

Viola tricolor is the wild pansy, also known commonly as heartsease or Johnny-jump-up. It is usually grown as a hardy annual but can also be treated as a biennial. Much daintier than its relatives the pansies, these plants are at home in cottage-style beds and as pot edging. A few single colored varieties are available, such as the unusual "Bowles' Black," having black flowers with a small central yellow "eye".

CONDITIONS

ASPECT	Grows well in sun or dappled, light shade.
SITE	Soil does not need to be over prepared, but must be well-drained. Multipurpose compost is best for growing *Viola tricolor* in containers.

GROWING METHOD

SOWING	Sow from February under cover for flowers the same summer, or outside May–July for flowers the following spring. Either way, sow in a 3¹/₂in pot of multipurpose compost and barely cover seeds. In early spring keep at 60°F and transplant seedlings when large enough to cell trays, grow, harden off, and plant in late May. When summer sowing, stand the pot outside in shade to germinate, treat seedlings the same, and plant in October.
FEEDING	Extra feeding is not usually necessary.
PROBLEMS	Use slug pellets if the leaves are attacked.

FLOWERING

SEASON	Spring-sown plants flower during summer, summer-sown the following spring/summer.
CUTTING	Not suitable for cutting.

AFTER FLOWERING

GENERAL	Pull plants up and compost, or leave a few to shed seeds. They will sometimes grow as perennials and last for several years.

EACH FLOWER of wild pansy is like a tiny whiskered "face" and individual plants all vary from each other very slightly. One plant left in the ground to mature through the summer will shed hundreds of seeds which will germinate the next spring.

AT A GLANCE		
A hardy annual grown for its pretty little pansy flowers which appear on branching plants. Frost hardy to 5°F. (zone 7)		
Jan	/	**Recommended Varieties**
Feb	sow	*Viola tricolor*
Mar	sow	Single colors
Apr	sow/flower	Blue
May	sow/flower	"Prince Henry"
Jun	sow/flower	Yellow
July	sow/flower	"Prince John"
Aug	grow on/ flowers	
Sept	grow on/ flowers	
Oct	plant	
Nov	/	
Dec	/	

Viola wittrockiana

PANSY

FEATURES

Pansies are hardy and will flower almost all year around. There are two groups, summer flowering, and fall/winter flowering. None grow more than 8in tall. Flowers are like large flat "faces" up to 3in across. Colors vary enormously from single, pastel shades to striking bicolors, and are available in mixtures or as single colors. Many varieties are available as young plants by mail order. Most are varieties of *Viola wittrockiana*.

CONDITIONS

ASPECT   Fall/winter pansies need full sun. Summer flowering varieties like dappled shade.

SITE   Add plenty of manure to the soil. Winter pansies need excellent drainage. Use multipurpose compost for containers.

GROWING METHOD

SOWING   Sow from February under cover for flowers the same summer, or outside May–July for flowers the following spring. Either way, sow in a $3^{1}/_{2}$in pot of multipurpose compost and barely cover seeds. In early spring keep at 60˚F and transplant seedlings when large enough to cell trays, grow, harden off, and plant in late May. When summer-sowing, stand the pot outside in shade to germinate then treat seedlings the same, planting out in October where you want the plants to flower.

FEEDING   Liquid feed summer plants every two weeks.

PROBLEMS   Spray with permethrin if aphids attack.

FLOWERING

SEASON   Spring-sown plants flower in summer, fall-sown from October onward.

CUTTING   Pansies last a few days in water.

AFTER FLOWERING

GENERAL   Pull up and compost when finished.

PANSY FLOWERS have "faces" that tend to face the sun, especially in early spring. Use them in patio pots with bulbs like tulips.

AT A GLANCE		
Hardy and grown either as an annual or a biennial for flowers in summer and fall/winter. Frost hardy to 5˚F (zone 7).		
Jan	/	**Recommended Varieties**
Feb	sow	*Viola wittrockiana*
Mar	sow	**Summer flowers**
Apr	sow/flower	"Antique Shades"
May	sow/flower	"Padparadja"
Jun	sow/flower	"Romeo & Juliet"
July	sow/flower	"Watercolors"
Aug	grow on/ flowers	**Fall/winter flowers** "Homefires"
Sept	grow on/ flowers	"Ultima Pastel Mixed" "Universal Mixed"
Oct	plant	"Velour Mixed"
Nov	/	
Dec	/	

Violet

VIOLA ODORATA

FEATURES

Viola odorata, the sweet violet, is a low-growing perennial just 6in tall with a wider spread. The dark green leaves are roundish or kidney-shaped with scalloped edges. Small, very sweetly fragrant flowers appear on short stalks in late winter and early spring. They are usually violet in color but there are also mauve, blue, and white forms. Violets spread rapidly by creeping roots.

CONDITIONS

ASPECT   Sun in winter and bright dappled shade in summer are ideal. Flowering is disappointing in too much shade.

SITE   Violets tolerate most soils but do best in deep soil rich in well-rotted organic matter, preferably from composted fallen leaves. Soil must drain freely but it must also remain moist between showers or watering.

GROWING METHOD

SOWING   Violets are easily established by division. Lift immediately after flowering and separate the cylindrical runners. Each division should have its own roots but roots usually form later if they are absent. Plant so that the runners are firmly in contact with the soil but not buried. Scatter seed, collected from ripe but unopened seed pods, where it is to grow or, for better germination, onto trays of seed compost. Cover lightly, keep moist, and place trays in a bright but shady and cool place. The seedlings can be transplanted when they are big enough to handle.

FEEDING   Once established, violets can usually get by on rain where it falls regularly, as long as the soil conditions suit them. If they never go dry for long periods, violets will flourish. Place a mulch of well-rotted manure around plants, but not over the root crown, each spring (this can be hard to do in a densely planted area), or sprinkle a ration of a balanced general fertilizer over the plants in spring. Once or twice during summer, water over the plants with a liquid, organic fertilizer or seaweed-based soil conditioner.

PROBLEMS   Lay bait for slugs and snails, which chew holes in the leaves and destroy flowers. Spider mites and aphids can also damage plants by sucking sap. Spider mites should be treated with an insecticide as soon as they are seen. Aphids are easily controlled with low toxicity pyrethrum, garlic, or fatty acid sprays. If the plants fail to flower, the

AT A GLANCE		
Pretty, low-growing perennial with very sweetly fragrant flowers in late winter. Hardy to 4°F or below (zone 7).		
Jan	/	**Parts used**
Feb	harvest	Flowers
Mar	harvest	Leaves
Apr	plant harvest	**Uses**
May	plant harvest	Culinary
Jun	harvest	Medicinal
July	harvest	Craft
Aug	harvest	Gardening
Sept	plant	
Oct	/	
Nov	/	
Dec	/	

cause may be too much or too
heavy shade or too much high nitrogen
fertilizer.

PRUNING   No pruning is necessary, but if flowers
fail to form cut all the leaves off in early
winter to encourage spring bloom.

HARVESTING

PICKING   Pick flowers as they open and leaves
as needed.

STORAGE   Flowers may be crystallized for
later use.

FREEZING   Not suitable for freezing.

USES

CULINARY   Crystallized flowers are used to decorate
cakes or eaten as a sweet treat. A sweet
syrup and a honey can be made with
fresh flowers.

MEDICINAL   An infusion of the leaves and flowers
can be taken to relieve the symptoms
of colds, etc.

CRAFT   Flowers are used in pot-pourris, floral
waters.

GARDENING   Violets are a very desirable groundcover
in partly shaded areas. Posies of cut
flowers will fill a room with fragrance.

Vitis

VINE, GRAPE VINE

FEATURES

Apart from the well-known edible grape vine, cultivars of *Vitis vinifera*, there are several ornamental vines that are valued for their fall leaf color. *Vitis coignetiae* is a very vigorous species from Japan and Korea and is also one of the largest leaved. In fall the leaves turn brilliant red. It reaches 50ft in height. *V. vinifera* "Purpurea" has purple leaves in summer that become darker in fall, and reaches 22ft. These vines, whose summer foliage is also attractive, are ideal for pergolas, arches and arbours; also trellis screens, walls and fences. They can be used for groundcover, and *V. vinifera* "Purpurea" makes a good standard for the patio.

CONDITIONS

ASPECT   Full sun or partial shade.
SITE   Any well-drained soil, but alkaline or neutral conditions preferred. Soil should also contain plenty of humus.

GROWING METHOD

PROPAGATION   Take hardwood cuttings in late fall or winter, rooting them in a bottom-heat temperature of 70°F. Carry out serpentine layering in spring.
WATERING   Vines will tolerate fairly dry conditions but it is best to water them well if the soil starts to dry out excessively.

FEEDING   Apply a slow-release organic fertilizer in the spring, such as blood, fish and bone.
PROBLEMS   Leaves may be affected by powdery mildew.

FLOWERING/FOLIAGE

FLOWERS   Trusses of tiny green flowers followed by purple or black grapes which, in the ornamental vines, are not palatable.
FOLIAGE   Handsome, large lobed leaves.

PRUNING

REQUIREMENTS   Build up a permanent framework of stems and spur prune annually in mid-winter. Cut back side shoots to within two or three buds of their base. During the summer any very long shoots can be shortened if desired.

THE SCARLET FALL LEAVES of Vitis coignetiae *are brilliant against this pale stone wall.*

AT A GLANCE	
Tendril climbers valued for their large lobed leaves. Hardy to temperatures of 5°F (zone 7).	
Jan /	**Companion Plants**
Feb /	These vines look good with
Mar planting	large-leaved ivies such as *Hedera*
Apr planting	*colchica* and *H. canariensis.*
May foliage	
Jun foliage	
July foliage	
Aug foliage	
Sep foliage	
Oct foliage	
Nov /	
Dec /	

Vriesea

VRIESEA SPECIES

FEATURES

Vrieseas are very adaptable, tolerating conditions in the home, conservatory, or greenhouse. Most are epiphytes growing on trees in forests but some larger species are terrestrials. Few of these larger terrestrials are grown outside specialist collections. Leaves are spineless and may be plain glossy green or attractively banded, spotted or variegated. They form neat rosettes. Many species have striking bracts. The true flowers are usually yellow, green, or white but the bracts may be red or purple, yellow or green. Plants may be 6–8in high or reach over 13ft. Some are very wide spreading.

CONDITIONS

CLIMATE   Copes with very high temperatures if not direct sun; does best in humid conditions. Many species tolerate low, frost-free temperatures. Most prefer bright, filtered light and good air circulation, again similar to the conditions favoured by orchids. A group of these plants will create a more humid microclimate.

POTTING MIX   Need good drainage and aeration. Use coarse bark, sand, gravel, and charcoal as the base, with leaf mold, well-decayed compost, or even polystyrene granules added.

GROWING METHOD

PROPAGATION   Grow from offsets produced at the base of the plant during spring to fall. In spreading species they will be under the foliage: once they are sufficiently advanced remove them before they distort the foliage.

WATERING   Keep the cup in the center of the rosette filled. In summer, water two or three times a week, spray misting on the other days or if humidity is low. In the conservatory or greenhouse, damp down the floor on hot days. In winter, water only every couple of weeks but maintain atmospheric humidity.

FEEDING   Apply slow release granular fertilizer in spring and midsummer, or use soluble liquid foods monthly at half the recommended strength. Ensure fertilizer does not touch foliage. Feed only in the warmer months.

PROBLEM   No specific problems are encountered.

FLOWERING SEASON

Species flower at different times of the year. Most have long-lasting flowers.

AT A GLANCE	
Ideal for mounting or in a pot inside. The scented flowers are long lasting and appear any time of year.	
Jan keep air moist	Recommended Varieties
Feb water center of plant	V. hieroglyphica
	V. carinata
Mar feed	V. x poelmanii
Apr remove offsets, repot	V. x polonia
	V. saundersii
May water and mist	
Jun mist; keep humid	
July mist, needs high temperatures	
Aug mist, water center of plant	
Sept mist	
Oct remove offsets	
Nov keep frost free and water center of plant	
Dec /	

Washingtonia

COTTON PALM

FEATURES

The two species of *Washingtonia* are native to the south-western USA and northern Mexico. They form a single trunk topped with large, fan-shaped, deeply lobed fronds. *Washingtonia filifera* (Desert fan palm, Northern washingtonia), has 6–10ft long gray-green leaves with cotton-like threads and an eventual height of 50–70ft, with a spread up to 20ft. *W. robusta* (Thread palm, Southern washingtonia) has a tapered trunk topped with 3ft long bright green fronds. Its eventual height is 80ft, and its spread reaches 15ft. Young specimens make good houseplants, or grow them in an intermediate glasshouse or conservatory. Place outside for the summer.

CONDITIONS

ASPECT	Provide bright light but do not subject to direct sun. Provide moderate humidity. Outdoors place in a sheltered position.
SITE	In containers grow in soil-based potting compost with some leafmold and coarse sand added to the mixture.

GROWING METHOD

PROPAGATION	Sow seeds as soon as available and germinate them at a temperature of 75°F.
WATERING	Moderate watering in growing season from late spring to late summer, then for the rest of the year water sparingly. In winter, keep the soil almost dry.

FEEDING	Apply a balanced liquid fertilizer monthly during the growing season.
PROBLEMS	Under glass may be attacked by scale insects and red spider mites.

FOLIAGE/FLOWERING

FOLIAGE	Being evergreen these palms look good all year round but are especially attractive in spring and summer.
FLOWERS	Long arching trusses of cream-white flowers are produced in summer, followed by purple or brown fruits.

GENERAL CARE

REQUIREMENTS Remove dead fronds when necessary by cutting them off close to the trunk.

LIVING UP TO ITS NAME of 'skyduster', this particular Wahingtonia robusta *is about 80 yars old.*

AT A GLANCE		
Single-stemmed palms noted for their large fan-shaped, lobed leaves. Provide a minimum temperature of 45–50°F (zone 11).		
Jan	/	**Companion Plants**
Feb	/	Good specimen plants for use
Mar	planting	with summer bedding. Under
Apr	planting	glass grow with bougainvilleas
May	foliage	and Citrus species.
Jun	flowering	
July	flowering	
Aug	flowering	
Sep	/	
Oct	/	
Nov	/	
Dec	/	

Watsonia

WATSONIA

FEATURES

Although there are many species of watsonias in the wild, they are not commonly cultivated plants. The stiff, sword-shaped leaves are similar to those of a gladiolus: the flower spike, growing to over 39in carries tubular flowers in various shades of pink and red, violet, magenta and orange. *Watsonia* is ideally placed towards the back of a mixed border. In all but very warm districts the corms should be lifted in fall and stored in a dry place until it is time to replant them the following spring. The usual species offered is *W. pillansii* (also known as *W. beatricis*), which has orange-red flowers. The slightly more tender *W. borbonica* (*W. pyrimidata*) has rich pink blooms.

CONDITIONS

ASPECT   *Watsonia* needs full sun and a warm, sheltered position.

SITE   These tall plants are good for the back of a border. They can also be grown in pots in a greenhouse. Any well-drained soil is acceptable, but growth will be better if well-rotted organic matter is dug in before planting.

GROWING METHOD

PLANTING   Plant corms in mid to late spring, 4in deep and 12in apart. In warm, sheltered areas, corms can be planted in fall 6in deep and mulched with chipped bark or dry leaves.

FEEDING   Apply a long-acting fertilizer such as general fertilizer in early summer. Watering is necessary only in prolonged dry spells.

PROBLEMS   Generally free from pest or disease problems when grown in an open, sunny position.

FLOWERING

SEASON   Watsonias flower in mid-summer.

CUTTING   Stems can be cut for the vase. They should last well with frequent water changes.

AFTER FLOWERING

REQUIREMENTS   Except in very warm areas, lift the corms after flowering, when the foliage starts to die down. Clean them, allow them to dry, and store in a cool, airy place until the following spring.

THE VIVID PINK FLOWERS of watsonia make it a most desirable plant, but it is not commonly grown in gardens.

AT A GLANCE		
An unusual bulb with tall, stately spikes of pink or red flowers, good for the back of the border.		
Jan	/	**Recommended Varieties**
Feb	/	"Stanford Scarlet"
Mar	/	"Tresco Dwarf Pink"
Apr	plant	*Watsonia borbonica*
May	plant	*ardernei*
Jun	flowering	
July	flowering	
Aug	flowering	
Sept	plant (warm areas)	
Oct	/	
Nov	/	
Dec	/	

Weigela
WEIGELA

FEATURES

Flowering unstintingly from May to June, weigela is a reliable, hardy, deciduous shrub. Growing 4–6ft high and across, there are two main divisions: varieties of *Weigela florida* and a range of hybrids. Two of the showiest forms of *W. florida* are dark purple-leaved and rose-pink-flowered "Foliis Purpureis" and widely grown "Variegata," whose green-and-yellow foliage complements pale pink blooms. Appealing hybrids include "Briant Rubidor," where golden-yellow to green leaves combine pleasingly with a wealth of vibrant, ruby-red flowers. Very different is *W.* "Looymansii Aurea," which must be grown in light shade or its leaves, bright gold in spring, will scorch.

CONDITIONS

ASPECT
Most varieties flower best if planted in full sun. Shield them from strong wind, too, which can damage flowers and "burn" soft, new leaves.

SITE
Encourage vigorous growth by setting plants in well-drained soil, including chalk, enriched with plenty of well-decayed manure.

GROWING METHOD

FEEDING
Boost sturdy shoots sleeved with blossom by topdressing the root area with bone meal in spring and fall and mulching in spring.

PROPAGATION
Take soft-tip cuttings in early summer; semi-ripe cuttings from mid- to late summer; and hardwood cuttings in the fall.

PROBLEMS
Pale green capsid bugs, about $1/4$in long, suck sap from shoot tips and secrete a toxin that kills cells. When leaves unfold, damaged areas become ragged holes. Control by spraying with pirimiphos-methyl or fenitrothion when symptoms seen.

PRUNING

Keep bushes young and packed with blossom by removing from the base one in three of the oldest flowering stems when blooms turn fade.

WEIGELA FLORIDA *brightens late spring with a generous confection of pinkish blossom on year-old shoots.*

AT A GLANCE	
Bushy shrubs bearing trumpet-shaped, white, pink, red, or purple-red blooms from May to June. Hardy to -13°F (zone 5).	

		Recommended Varieties
Jan	/	"Abel Carriere"
Feb	/	"Briant Rubidor"
Mar	plant	"Carnival"
Apr	plant	"Foliis Purpureis"
May	flower, plant	*W. middendorffiana*
Jun	flower, plant	"Newport Red"
July	prune, plant	"Rumba"
Aug	plant	"Variegata"
Sept	plant	
Oct	plant	
Nov	plant	
Dec	/	

Wisteria

WISTERIA

FEATURES

These very vigorous, fast-growing, long-lived deciduous climbers are desired by most garden owners for their spectacular spring display of pendulous, often fragrant flowers that generally appear just before or with the new leaves. The plants eventually develop thick stems and therefore are very weighty, needing strong supports. They are very amenable to training and can be formed into virtually any shape desired. Wisterias are often used to cover large pergolas, when the flowers "drip" down inside in a very dramatic fashion. They can also be trained vertically along veranda railings or low walls. These climbers are often seen on house walls. Wisterias are ideal, too, for growing up large mature trees. If you do not have the wall space or other suitable support for one of these magnificent climbers, then consider growing one in a tub and training it into a standard to decorate the patio. Bear in mind that young wisteria plants can take up to seven years, or even longer, to start flowering, so patience is needed after planting. In the meantime, simply enjoy the foliage, which looks particularly lush when newly opened in the spring.

Probably the most popular wisteria is *W. floribunda* "Multijuga," a cultivar of the Japanese wisteria. The fragrant lilac-blue flowers are carried in pendulous trusses up to 4ft in length. If this cultivar is grown on a pergola it is a truly magnificent sight when in full flower and the trusses are dangling down inside. It grows to a height of at least 28ft. There are many other cultivars of *W. floribunda*. These include *W. f.* "Kuchi-beni" ("Peaches and Cream") with its pink and white flowers, and *W. f.* 'Alba' with white flowers.

Also widely grown is *W. sinensis* (Chinese wisteria), with scented, lilac-blue flowers in trusses up to 12in in length. It is a fast-growing and vigorous climber with dense trusses of flowers, growing to the same height as *W. floribunda* 'Multijuga'. Again there are numerous cultivars.

CONDITIONS

ASPECT Wisterias ideally need a warm sheltered site in full sun. Good growth and flowering are also possible in partial shade.

SITE There is every chance that young wisterias start flowering sooner in poorish or moderately fertile soil. If the soil is too rich they will tend to produce a huge amount of leaf and stem growth instead of focusing their energy on flowers. The site should also be well-drained yet at the same time moisture-retentive.

AT A GLANCE	
Vigorous, deciduous twiner with long trusses of pea-like flowers in spring and early summer. Hardy to 5°F (zone 7).	

		Recommended Varieties
Jan	/	*W. floribunda* cultivars
Feb	/	
Mar	planting	"Alba" (white)
Apr	planting	"Kuchi-beni" (pink and white)
May	flowering	"Rosea" (pink)
Jun	flowering	"Royal Purple" (purple-violet)
July	/	"Violacea Plena" (double, violet-blue)
Aug	/	*W. sinensis* cultivars
Sep	/	"Alba" (white)
Oct	/	"Amethyst" (light rose-purple)
Nov	/	"Prolific" (lilac-blue)
Dec	/	

GROWING METHOD

PROPAGATION   The easiest and most reliable method of propagation for the home gardener is to carry out serpentine layering in the spring. The stems, which are pegged down in a number of places along their length, should be well rooted after a year. Hardwood cuttings of dormant wood may be taken in winter, but these may prove a little slow to root. Once established, wisterias can go on to live for hundreds of years.

WATERING   Keep young plants well watered. Water established plants only if the soil starts to become excessively dry in summer.

FEEDING   Avoid fertilizers that are very high in nitrogen as they result in vegetative growth at the expense of flowers. Instead opt for a balanced slow-release organic fertilizer such as blood, fish, and bone. One application per year, made in the spring just as growth is about to start, will be sufficient. Plants in tubs may need a further feed in the summer as plant foods are quickly leached out of containers.

PROBLEMS   There are a few pests that may trouble wisterias, particularly aphids and scale insects. Also, a fungal leaf spot may appear but it is not considered to be serious. It shows itself as dark brown spots on the foliage.

FLOWERING/FOLIAGE

FLOWERS   The flowers are similar in shape to those of garden peas, and in fact the two plants are related. Unlike peas, though, the flowers are carried in long, pendulous trusses. Blooms are generally fragrant. They appear in late spring and early summer.

FOLIAGE   Large, pinnate, mid- to deep green leaves are attractive in spring and summer.

PRUNING

REQUIREMENTS   Train a permanent framework of stems to the shape desired, then spur prune to this. Wisterias can be trained to virtually any shape, but on walls the espalier is a good shape as it has many horizontal branches. These flower much more freely than branches that are trained vertically. This shape also provides a stable base for heavy wisterias. The espalier is completely flat and consists of a single, upright stem with horizontal branches evenly spaced out on each side. Routine pruning of established wisterias is carried out twice a year to keep new growth under control. In mid-summer cut back the new lateral shoots to within five or six buds of the main framework. Then in mid-winter prune them back further, to within two or three buds of the framework. If renovation pruning ever becomes necessary, spread the task over several years, thinning out one of the oldest stems each year. Otherwise the flower display will be reduced considerably. The heads of standard wisterias are also spur pruned, in the same way as those grown as climbers.

The delicate shade of this Wisteria sinensis *and the abundance of its blooms, make it a favorite in gardens.*

Witch Hazel

HAMAMELIS

FEATURES

Shining like a beacon on a winter's day, witch hazel's twisted, spidery perfumed flowers thickly clothe bare, spreading branches. Hardy and bushy, 8–10ft high and across, this deciduous shrub is a slow but worthwhile grower that rewards patience. Ideally, set it in a lawn with snowdrops and daffodils.

Choice kinds among several undemanding species and varieties are large, golden-flowered Chinese witch hazel (*Hamamelis mollis*), which blooms from December to March. *H. x intermedia* is a hybrid that flowers from February to March and has given us upright and primrose-hued "Westerstede," sulfur-yellow "Pallida," orange and yellow "Diane," and coppery orange "Jelena."

The large, soft-hairy leaves of *H. mollis* turn butter-yellow in the fall. The foliage of "Diane" and "Jelena" is suffused with orange-red before falling. Equally fascinating is the less fragrant Japanese witch hazel (*H. japonica* "Zuccariniana"), which from January to March produces a multitude of pale lemon "spiders."

CONDITIONS

ASPECT   *Hamamelis* flowers more freely in full sun and makes a shapelier, more compact bush than in light shade, in which branches are thinner and further apart and leaves larger. Position coppery red-flowered varieties where the sun shines at an angle through their petals and renders them fetchingly translucent.

SITE   Preferring well-drained, fertile, neutral to acid soil, hamamelis dislikes alkaline, chalky conditions, which causes leaves to become chlorotic. Enrich sandy soils with old manure.

GROWING METHOD

FEEDING   Water freely after planting to encourage rapid recovery. Each spring, mulch with crumbly manure, bark or well-rotted garden compost to keep roots cool and active. In April, topdress the root area with fish, blood and bone meal or Growmore, repeating in July.

PROPAGATION   Layer shoots from mid-spring to late summer. Alternatively, take soft-tip cuttings in late spring and root them in a mist propagating unit in a temperature of 70°F.

PROBLEMS   When buying plants, opt for those more than four years old, which, unlike younger ones, have a greater chance of succeeding.

PRUNING

Not necessary, but if badly placed stems need removing or shortening, to improve symmetry, use sharp secateurs or loppers when flowers fade, in early spring.

AT A GLANCE		
Deciduous and forming a chalice of branches, yellow or orange blooms sleeve stems in winter. Hardy to -13°F (zone 5).		
Jan	flower	**Recommended Varieties**
Feb	flower	*H. japonica*
Mar	plant, prune	"Zuccariniana"
Apr	plant	*H. x intermedia*
May	plant	"Diane"
Jun	plant	*H. x intermedia*
July	plant	"Jelena"
Aug	plant	*H. x intermedia*
Sept	plant	"Pallida"
Oct	plant	*H. x intermedia*
Nov	plant	"Westerstede"
Dec	flower	*H. mollis*

Wormwood

ARTEMISIA

FEATURES

There are many species of artemisia, all with aromatic foliage and pleasant, but not particularly showy, yellow flowers. Wormwood, *A. absinthium*, is an extremely bitter plant with finely divided leaves. The related *A. abrotanum*, is also known as southernwood, or lad's love. There are many ornamental garden artemisias. Sizes and habits, however, vary enormously between species, some being ground-huggers, others being medium-sized, upright shrubs. Leaf shape and color varies, too, and combinations of different artemisias can make very attractive plantings with a silver and gray theme.

CONDITIONS

ASPECT   Full sun is essential, as is an open position to ensure good air movement around the plant.

SITE   Grows best in moderately fertile, very well-drained soil that contains a small proportion of well-rotted organic matter.

GROWING METHOD

SOWING   Wormwood can be started from cuttings taken in late spring and rooted in small pots of moist, sandy potting mix kept in a bright but not fully sunny spot. It may also be grown from seed sown in spring just beneath the surface, either where plants are to grow or in pots or trays of seed compost.

FEEDING   Very little water is needed except in very dry summers. A mulch of well-rotted manure or compost laid under and beyond the plant's foliage canopy (but not right up against the trunk) is usually all the feeding required. Otherwise, sprinkle a handful of general fertilizer under the outer edge of the foliage canopy in early spring.

PROBLEMS   Artemisias may sometimes suffer from blackfly. This can be treated with a liquid horticultural soap.

PRUNING   Cut herbaceous species of artemisia back to ground level in middle to late fall or after frosts have started. Shrubby types may be sheared all over in early spring to make them more compact. Cut back hard in spring if the shrub has become too big and/or untidy.

HARVESTING

PICKING   Leaves are harvested by picking whole stems on a hot, dry morning in summer.

STORAGE   Tie stems together and hang them upside down in a dim, airy place to dry. Dried leaves may be stored in airtight jars.

FREEZING   Not suitable for freezing.

AT A GLANCE	
Perennial herb with decorative, finely divided silvery foliage, traditionally used to flavour absinthe. Hardy to 4°F (zone 7).	
Jan /	**Parts used**
Feb /	Leaves
Mar /	**Uses**
Apr plant	(Culinary)
May plant	(Medicinal)
Jun plant harvest	Craft
July harvest	Gardening
Aug plant harvest	
Sept plant	
Oct /	
Nov /	
Dec /	

USES

CULINARY   Although it is extremely bitter, wormwood was traditionally used to flavor wines and aperitifs such as absinthe and vermouth.

MEDICINAL   Caution: different parts of different types of artemisia have various medicinal uses but do not take any of these herbs without the supervision of a trained herbalist.

CRAFT   Wormwood has insect repellent properties and it can be used to make "moth-repellent" sachets.

GARDENING   Wormwood, as all artemisias, has beautiful foliage and a pleasant aroma. A strong infusion of the leaves sprayed onto vegetables or ornamental plants repels caterpillars and snails; just having the plants nearby will drive some pests away.

Yarrow

ACHILLEA MILLEFOLIUM

FEATURES

Yarrow is a low, mat-forming perennial that has dense, dark green, fern-like foliage. Flat heads of small flowers appear on top of tall, mostly leafless stems during the later summer months and in fall. They may be white, pink, or yellow. This vigorous grower is well suited to growing in rockeries or on banks. Depending on the soil and situation in which it grows it can vary in height from 2in to 24in.

CONDITIONS

ASPECT   Grow in full sun or light shade.
SITE   Well-drained, not-too-rich soil is ideal. Plants grow lax, flower poorly and die young in over-rich soil. They will rot if soil stays wet for long periods after rain or watering.

GROWING METHOD

SOWING   Establish yarrow in new areas by dividing the roots of mature plants in early spring or fall. It may also be started from seed sown in spring in trays of moist seed compost. Just cover the seed and place the containers in a warm, bright but shaded spot until germination is complete. Gradually expose containers to more and more sun, and then transplant seedlings into their final site when they are big enough.
FEEDING   Water deeply but only occasionally. Yarrow does not require constant moisture as it has deep roots that will find water at lower levels in the soil. No feeding is necessary.

PROBLEMS   No particular problems.
PRUNING   Cut plants to the ground in middle to late fall or after frosts have started. New growth will appear in spring.

HARVESTING

PICKING   Harvest leafy stems and flowers on a dry morning when plants are in the early stages of full bloom. Tie them together and hang them upside down in a dry, dim, airy place. If they are to be used to make dried arrangements, hang each flower stem separately.
STORAGE   When the stems are dry, remove the flowers and leaves and break the leaves and stems into small pieces. Store these in airtight jars.
FREEZING   Not suitable for freezing.

USES

CULINARY   Young, small leaves have a slightly bitter flavor. Add a few chopped young

AT A GLANCE	
Although considered a weed by many, yarrow is an excellent companion plant and herbal tonic. Hardy to 4˚F or below (zone 7).	
Jan /	**Parts used**
Feb /	Leaves
Mar plant	Stems
Apr plant	Flowers
May plant harvest	**Uses**
Jun harvest	Culinary
July harvest	Medicinal
Aug harvest	Cosmetic
Sept plant	Craft
Oct /	Gardening
Nov /	
Dec /	

leaves to salads or sandwiches for a piquant taste.

MEDICINAL Herbal tea made from the dried stems, leaves, and flowers is a good general pick-me-up, blood cleanser, tonic for the kidneys, fever treatment and, reputedly, a slimming aid. Also used externally as wound healer.

COSMETIC An infusion can be used as a herbal skin cleanser.

CRAFT Flowers can be used in dried floral arrangements.

GARDENING Although considered a weed in lawns, yarrow is an excellent companion plant, increasing the disease resistance of nearby plants and increasing their flavour and fragrance. It has been called the "plant doctor." Add it to the compost heap to speed rotting.

Zantedeschia

ARUM LILY, CALLA LILY

FEATURES

Arum lilies are greatly prized for their beautiful waxy flowers, pure white with a golden central spadix. The arrow-shaped leaves are deep green, and the whole plant can grow up to 39in high. Several species are suitable for growing only in a greenhouse or conservatory, but *Z. aethiopica* can be grown outside in reasonably sheltered gardens. It likes moist, boggy conditions, and often grows best beside a pond or water feature: it can be grown as a marginal plant in up to 12in of water. *Z. elliottiana*, the golden arum, and *Z. rehmannii*, the pink arum, are good greenhouse or conservatory plants.

CONDITIONS

ASPECT   Can be grown in full sun or light shade. It should be sheltered from strong wind.

SITE   *Z. aethiopica* can be grown on the fringe of a pool or in a border in moist, humus-rich soil. Other arum species need rich but free-draining soil and are grown in a greenhouse or conservatory in containers.

GROWING METHOD

PLANTING   Plant rhizomes 6in deep and 18in apart in spring.

FEEDING   Apply liquid fertilizer as buds appear and continue to feed every 14–21 days while plants are in bloom. Keep the soil moist at all times while the plants are in active growth during spring and summer.

PROBLEMS   Leaf spot can cause dark blotches on all parts of the plant and may cause premature leaf drop. It often occurs where conditions are too cool and damp. Destroy affected parts and spray with a suitable fungicide.

FLOWERING

SEASON   Flowers in early summer.

CUTTING   Flowers are excellent for cutting.

AFTER FLOWERING

REQUIREMENTS Remove flower stems as they fade. Mulch outdoor plants with dry leaves for winter.

ARUM LILIES have long been favorites with flower arrangers for their texture and sculptural shape which adds form to an arrangement.

AT A GLANCE		
A rhizomatous plant grown for its beautiful waxy white flower spathes. Needs greenhouse conditions in some areas.		
Jan	/	**Recommended Varieties**
Feb	/	*Zantedeschia* aethiopica
Mar	/	"Crowborough"
Apr	plant	"Green Goddess"
May	/	
Jun	flowering	
July	flowering	
Aug	/	
Sept	/	
Oct	/	
Nov	/	
Dec	/	

Zephyranthes

ZEPHYR LILY, RAINFLOWER

FEATURES

With its starry white flowers and shiny green, grass-like foliage, zephyr lily is a bulb for mass planting in sheltered gardens. It is quite easy to grow and can remain undisturbed for years where conditions suit it. It can be planted in borders or on a rockery, and it can also be grown very successfully in containers. The crocus-like flowers are carried in late summer or fall, especially after showers of rain, which accounts for its common name of rainflower.

Zephyranthes candida is the species suitable for growing outdoors in Britain; it generally reaches a height of 8–10in. Z. *grandiflora* (also called *Z. rosea*) has lovely rosy pink flowers but is only suitable for cultivation in a greenhouse or conservatory, as is the yellow flowered Z. *citrina*.

CONDITIONS

ASPECT	Grows best in full sun.
SITE	Grow in beds or borders or in pockets in a rockery. Needs a well-drained but moisture-retentive soil. Growth will be improved if soils contain some humus.

GROWING METHOD

PLANTING	Plant in spring, 2in deep and 4in apart. For greenhouse cultivation, plant 5 bulbs in a 5in pot in loam-based potting compost.
FEEDING	Supplementary fertilizer is generally not needed. Spread a mulch of well-decayed manure or compost around the bulbs in spring. Water in dry spells during spring, but stop watering when the foliage starts to die down.
PROBLEMS	No specific problems are usually experienced with this plant.

FLOWERING

SEASON	Flowers appear from late summer into fall, or in mid-summer in the greenhouse.
CUTTING	Flowers are not suitable for cutting.

AFTER FLOWERING

REQUIREMENTS	Spent flower stems may be cut off but this is not essential. No special treatment is needed as the bulbs are best left undisturbed for several years. If you wish to lift and divide a clump this is best done in spring. Greenhouse plants should be allowed to dry out when the leaves die down, and started into growth again by plentiful watering the following spring.

AT A GLANCE		
An attractive, low-growing plant with crocus-like flowers in the fall.		
Jan	/	**Recommended Species**
Feb	/	*Zephyranthes candida*
Mar	/	Z. *citrina*
Apr	plant	Z. *flavissima*
May	/	Z. *grandiflora*
Jun	flowering	
July	flowering	
Aug	/	
Sept	flowering	
Oct	flowering	
Nov	/	
Dec	/	

Zinnia

ZINNIA

FEATURES

There is a zinnia for every garden. Dwarf varieties at 6in tall are suited to beds and containers, while "Dahlia-Flowered Mixed" has big heads on stems 2ft high, and is useful for mixed borders. Modern varieties have fully double flowers, and some like "Zebra Mixed" are stripey. "Starbright Mixed" is an unusual variety with masses of small orange and gold flowers. Red, yellow, pink, scarlet, orange, lavender, purple, white, and even green are typical flower colors. Half-hardy annual.

CONDITIONS

ASPECT   Zinnias enjoy heat and need sun and shelter.

SITE   Must have well-drained soil, previously improved with rotted organic matter. For containers use multipurpose compost.

GROWING METHOD

SOWING   Although half-hardy, zinnias grow best when sown direct where they are to flower, in short drills 1/2in deep. Do this in May and cover seedlings with a piece of garden fleece on frosty nights. Thin out seedlings so the young plants are eventually 6–24in apart, depending on their final size. To grow dwarf varieties in containers sow 2–3 seeds to a 3in pot at the same time, leave just the strongest, grow on, and plant when ready, not disturbing the roots.

FEEDING   Extra feeding is usually not necessary.
PROBLEMS   Powdery mildew can be a problem, so avoid planting too close—sulfur sprays can help. Stem rots cause plants to collapse suddenly.

FLOWERING

SEASON   Flowers appear from midsummer onward.

CUTTING   Very good cut flower. "Envy Double" is a striking plant with double green flowers.

AFTER FLOWERING

GENERAL   Pull up in fall and compost.

ZINNIA FLOWERS tend to come as doubles but plants sometimes appear that are single. If pinched when young zinnias make bushy, branching plants that fill gaps in mixed borders quickly. Take dead flowers off.

AT A GLANCE	
A half-hardy annual grown for its bright flowers in a wide range of colors, for bedding and cutting. Frost hardy to 32°F (zone 10).	
Jan /	**Recommended Varieties**
Feb /	Zinnia hybrids
Mar /	Tall varieties
Apr /	"Allsorts"
May sow	"Dahlia-Flowered Mixed"
Jun thin out	"Zebra Mixed"
July flowering	**Short varieties**
Aug flowering	"Belvedere"
Sept flowering	"Fairyland"
Oct flowering	"Persian Carpet Mixed"
Nov /	"Starbright Mixed"
Dec /	"Thumbelina"

INDEX

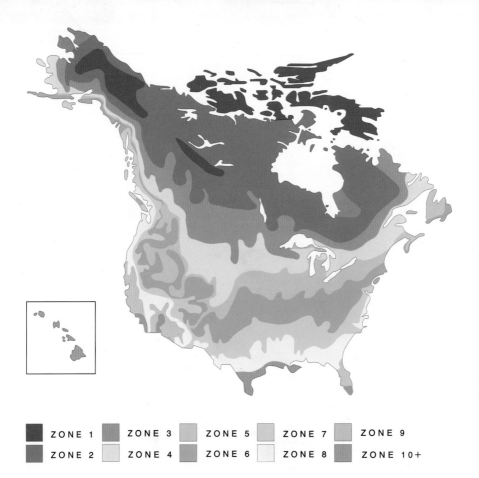

ZONE 1 ZONE 3 ZONE 5 ZONE 7 ZONE 9

ZONE 2 ZONE 4 ZONE 6 ZONE 8 ZONE 10+

Published by Bay Books, an imprint of
Murdoch Books Pty Limited.

Murdoch Books Pty Limited Australia
Pier 8/9
23 Hickson Road
Millers Point NSW 2000
Phone: + 61 (0) 2 8220 2000
Fax: + 61 (0) 2 8220 2558

Murdoch Books UK Limited
Erico House
6th Floor North
93-99 Upper Richmond Road
Putney, London SW15 2TG
Phone: + 44 (0) 20 8785 5995
Fax: + 44 (0) 20 8785 5985

Printed by Sing Cheong Printing Company Limited.
Printed in China

© Text, design and photography Murdoch Books Pty
Limited 2005